OXFORD **READERS**

Racism

Edited by Martin Bulmer *and* John Solomos

OXFORD
UNIVERSITY PRESS

OXFORD
UNIVERSITY PRESS

Great Clarendon Street, Oxford OX2 6DP

Oxford University Press is a department of the University of Oxford.
It furthers the University's objective of excellence in research, scholarship,
and education by publishing worldwide in

Oxford New York

Athens Auckland Bangkok Bogotá Buenos Aires Calcutta
Cape Town Chennai Dar es Salaam Delhi Florence Hong Kong Istanbul
Karachi Kuala Lumpur Madrid Melbourne Mexico City Mumbai
Nairobi Paris São Paulo Singapore Taipei Tokyo Toronto Warsaw

with associated companies in Berlin Ibadan

Oxford is a registered trade mark of Oxford University Press
in the UK and in certain other countries

Published in the United States
by Oxford University Press Inc., New York

Introductions, selection, and editorial matter © Martin Bulmer and John Solomos 1999

The moral rights of the authors have been asserted

Database right Oxford University Press (maker)

First published as an Oxford Reader 1999

British Library Cataloguing in Publication Data

Data available

Library of Congress Cataloging in Publication Data

Racism / edited by Martin Bulmer and John Solomos.
(Oxford readers)
Includes bibliographical references.
1. Racism. I. Bulmer, Martin. II. Solomos, John. III. Series.
HT1521.R3417 1999 305.8—dc21 99–21004
ISBN 0–19–289300–9

10 9 8 7 6 5 4 3 2 1

Typeset in Dante
by Cambrian Typesetters, Frimley, Surrey

Printed in Great Britain
on acid-free paper by
Biddles Ltd
Guildford and King's Lynn

Racism

Martin Bulmer is Foundation Fund Professor of Sociology at the University of Surrey and Academic Director of the Question Bank in the ESRC Centre for Applied Social Surveys, London. Previously he taught at the University of Southampton, the London School of Economics, and the University of Durham and has been a visiting professor at the University of Chicago, as well as briefly a member of the Government Statistical Service. Since 1992 he has been editor of the journal *Ethnic and Racial Studies*. His recent works include *Directory of Social Research Organisations*, second edition (with Sykes and Moorhouse, 1998) and *Citizenship Today: The Contemporary Relevance of T. H. Marshall* (editor with T. Rees, 1996).

John Solomos is Professor of Sociology in the Faculty of Humanities and Social Science at South Bank University. Before that he was Professor of Sociology and Social Policy at the University of Southampton, and he has previously worked at the Centre for Research in Ethnic Relations, University of Warwick, and Birkbeck College, University of London. Among his publications are *Black Youth, Racism and the State* (1988), *Race and Racism in Britain* (1993), *Race, Politics and Social Change* (with Les Back, 1995), and *Racism and Society* (with Les Back, 1996).

OXFORD **READERS**

The Oxford Readers series represents a unique resource which brings together extracts of texts from a wide variety of sources, primary and secondary, on a wide range of inderdisciplinary topics.

Available

Aesthetics
Edited by Patrick Maynard and
Susan Feagin

Class
Edited by Patrick Joyce

Classical Philosophy
Edited by Terence Irwin

Ethics
Edited by Peter Singer

Ethnicity
Edited by John Hutchinson and
Anthony D. Smith

Evolution
Edited by Mark Ridley

Faith and Reason
Edited by Paul Helm

Fascism
Edited by Roger Griffin

Feminisms
Edited by Sandra Kemp and
Judith Squires

The Mind
Edited by Daniel Robinson

Nationalism
Edited by John Hutchinson and
Anthony D. Smith

Political Thought
Edited by Michael Rosen and
Jonathan Wolff

Racism
Edited by Martin Bulmer and John
Solomos

Sexuality
Edited by Robert A. Nye

War
Edited by Lawrence Freedman

Forthcoming

Anti-Semitism
Edited by Paul Lawrence Rose

The British Empire
Edited by Jane Samson

Consciousness
Edited by Geoffrey Underwood

Nazism
Edited by Neil Gregor

Revolution
Edited by Jack Goldstone

Slavery
Edited by Stanley Engermann,
Seymour Drescher, and Robert
Paquette

*To Michael and Georgina
and Nikolas and Daniel*

Preface

In putting together a major volume such as this one we have inevitably accumulated a series of debts that we are pleased to acknowledge. We are particularly grateful to George Miller at Oxford University Press for encouraging us to produce this Reader and for keeping a kindly eye on our progress, including being very understanding when the pressures of academic life delayed the project at certain stages. The process of producing this volume was made much more feasible by the efficiency with which OUP handled the complex task of getting all the necessary permissions for the various extracts used. The Libraries at the London School of Economics, the University of Warwick, and the University of Southampton were helpful in allowing us to track down some of the more obscure sources. We have also been helped in putting this volume together by the support of our respective universities and departments, and by Guida Crowley, Managing Editor of *Ethnic and Racial Studies*. We are also grateful for the help, advice, and encouragement one or other of us received at various stages of the project from colleagues across the globe, including Les Back, Chetan Bhatt, Clive Harris, Michael Keith, John Rex, Liza Schuster, John Stone, and Howard Winant, and the stimulation provided by editing together the journal *Ethnic and Racial Studies*. Finally, we are grateful to Shelley Cox at OUP for seeing the book through production, and to Edwin Pritchard for his meticulous copy-editing.

Martin Bulmer, University of Surrey
John Solomos, South Bank University

Contents

IV. Racist Movements

V. Anti-Racism

VI. Racism and the State

VII. Theories of Racism

VIII. The Future of Racism

Racism

White Comedy

I waz whitemailed
By a white witch,
Wid white magic
An white lies,
Branded a white sheep
I slaved as a whitesmith
Near a white spot
Where I suffered whitewater fever.
Whitelisted as a white leg
I waz in de white book
As a master of de white art,
It waz like white death.

People called me white jack
Some hailed me as white wog,
So I joined de white watch
Trained as a white guard
Lived off de white economy.
Caught an beaten by de whiteshirts
I waz condemned to a white mass.

Don't worry,
I shall be writing to de Black house.

Benjamin Zephaniah

General Introduction

The photographic image on the cover of this book and the verbal images contained in Benjamin Zephaniah's poem 'White Comedy' express in different ways the extent to which racial domination can permeate a society and the social distance which can separate black people and white people. Almost always the white person or white group has been in a position of superiority, and the black person or group in a situation of inferiority, lesser power or influence, and having to justify themselves. W. E. B. Du Bois wrote movingly of the resulting sense of duality for black people:

Why did God make me an outcast and a stranger in mine own house? . . . the Negro is a sort of seventh son, born with a veil, and gifted with second-sight in this American world,—a world which yields him no true self-consciousness, but only lets him see himself through the revelation of the other world. It is a peculiar sensation, this double-consciousness, this sense of always looking at one's self through the eyes of others, of measuring one's soul by the tape of a world that looks on in amused contempt and pity. One ever feels his twoness,—an American, a Negro; two souls, two thoughts, two unreconciled strivings; two warring ideals in one dark body, whose dogged strength alone keeps it from being torn asunder. (Du Bois 1989 [1903]: 5)

Such manifestations of racism are a depressing reminder of the continuing importance of racism as a social and political issue in the contemporary global environment. The regrettable need for a book such as this is evident from the fact that in recent times racism is very much a vibrant influence on current social and political movements and in some cases on state policies (Solomos and Back 1996; Cornell and Hartmann 1998). Whatever the expectations of social theorists in the earlier part of this century may have been, the need for a book treating the phenomenon of racism analytically remains evident. Questions about race, racism, and ethnicity have become important preoccupations of debate in the social sciences and humanities at the end of one millennium and the beginning of another, to a considerable degree displacing preoccupation with class and other forms of social inequality (Goldberg 1990; Bulmer and Solomos 1999). W. E. B. Du Bois prophetically observed in 1903 that 'the problem of the twentieth century is the problem of the colour line—the relation of the darker to the lighter races of men in Asia and Africa, in America and in the islands of the sea' (1989 [1903]: Forethought). At the turn of the twenty-first century, the 'colour line' remains important in various ways. Socially structured racial inequality and disadvantage persist. Developments in a number of countries have highlighted the power of racial ideas in forging movements and political parties, often with murderous consequences. The outcome of these mobilizations have become clear in some situations, while in others they remain to be seen.

But as we reach the eve of the next century hardly anybody needs to be reminded of the virulence of racism as a social phenomenon, or indeed of the importance of understanding the origins and contemporary role of racial ideas and societies structured along racial lines.

Seeking to understand these phenomena means being clear about what is subsumed under the term 'racism' and its associated concept 'race'. How has the category of race come to play such an important role in shaping contemporary social relations? This is a question that is at the heart of much of the growing body of literature in this field, and it is the one that we have kept at the forefront of our own thinking about how best to organize this volume. This is not to say that there is agreement about how best to answer this question. On the contrary, scholars and researchers show little sign of agreeing about what we mean when we use notions such as *race, racism, ethnicity,* and related social categories. *Ethnicity* is a somewhat different, though related, concept to that of race and racism, and we are not concerned with ethnicity as such, which has a separate volume in this series (Hutchinson and Smith 1996). Cornell and Hartmann highlight some of the conceptual dilemmas when they argue:

What about race? Are races ethnic groups? Consider Black Americans. Certainly many people consider them a race or at least a part of one. How so? If they are a race, are they not an ethnic group? Could they be both?

Before we can answer these questions, we have to wrestle with the definition of race. As with ethnicity, it is common in contemporary society to talk about races, race relations, and racial conflict as if we had a clear idea what constitutes a race and where the boundary falls between one race and another. Race, however, is as slippery a concept as ethnic group, and its slipperiness has a long history. (1998: 21)

Cornell and Hartmann are by no means the only scholars to raise questions about the very status of categories such as race and racism (Miles 1989; Goldberg 1993). Many of the questions raised amount to the following: Is race a suitable social category? What do we mean when we talk of racism as shaping the structure of particular societies? What role have race and racism played in different historical contexts? Is it possible to speak of racism in the singular or racisms in the plural? These questions are at the heart of many of the theoretical and conceptual debates that dominate current debates, and yet what is interesting about much of the literature about race and racism is the absence of commonly agreed conceptual tools or even agreement about the general parameters of race and racism as fields of study.

A working definition of racism to be used as a starting point here is that racism is an ideology of racial domination based on (i) beliefs that a designated racial group is either biologically or culturally inferior and (ii) the use of such beliefs to rationalize or prescribe the racial group's treatment in society, as well as to explain its social position and accomplishment (Wilson 1973).

Although *race* and *ethnicity* are terms often used in conjunction or in parallel, to refer to social groups which differ in terms of physical attributes accorded social significance in the case of race or in terms of language, culture, place of origin, or common membership of a descent group without distinguishing physical characteristics in the case of ethnicity, there is no equivalent term to *racism* in relation to ethnicity. Perhaps *ethnic conflict* is analogous, but this is more of a descriptive term of certain consequences of the existence of different ethnic groups which may or may not occur. *Racism* as a concept is much more closely tied to the concept of race, and is a reminder that where members of society make distinctions between different racial groups, at least some members of that society are likely to behave in ways which give rise to *racism* as a behavioural and ideational consequence of making racial distinctions in the first place. Unfortunately the opposite does not hold. A society which denied or did not formally acknowledge the existence of different racial groups would not necessarily thus rid itself of *racism*. Indeed the recent literature on racial and ethnic classification in censuses, surveys, and administrative records shows that the identification of members of a society in terms of the racial, ethnic, or national origin may be a prerequisite to taking action to counteract *racism* (Peterson 1995; Petersen 1997; Bulmer 1996).

The recent explosion of scholarship and research has, if anything, not only highlighted a certain lack of consensus but has led to intense debate about the very language that we use in talking about race and racism. In this environment it may be seen as a foolhardy enterprise to attempt to put together in one volume a selection of texts, both historical and contemporary, that lays out the broad contours of racism as a field of scholarship. Yet this is precisely what we have sought to do in putting together a reader on *Racism*. We have sought, more specifically, and in line with the concern of this series as a whole, to produce a volume that allows students and general readers alike to reflect both on the history of racism and on current trends and future developments. Our key concern throughout has been to give voice to a range of scholars from a variety of disciplines, theoretical perspectives, and geographical locations. It is difficult to do justice to the richness of a field of scholarship and research in one volume, but our concern has been to allow readers an opportunity to think through the key dimensions of racism and provide a guide to important arguments and debates.

In selecting the readings that make up this volume we have exercised our judgement about two things. First, what are the main themes that need to be covered both in terms of past and current research agendas? Second, we have selected the authors and the particular texts that we believe have helped to shape this field of study. We have borne in mind the need to balance including as wide a range of authors as possible with including extracts substantive enough to allow readers to get a feel for the arguments developed by particular authors. We have included extracts that, while perhaps not always representative of the whole corpus of an author's *œuvre*, provide a particular insight into the issues and debates that concern us in this volume.

We have organized the Reader into six interlinked parts for the purposes of analytical clarity. Section I includes a range of selections that explore the origins and evolution of racist ideas. The aim here is to illustrate the complex range of ideas that have shaped the evolution of racist thinking and show how scholars have interpreted the process of evolution and change. Section II moves on to look at the institutionalized forms of social relationships and the role of particular social and economic institutions in the reproduction of racism. It has a particularly strong historical orientation. Key formative processes covered here include the institution of slavery, particularly the Atlantic slave trade, the expansion of Europeans overseas, western imperialism and colonialism, and the movement of ethnic groups within the imperial system. Drawing on these broader historical narratives Section III moves on to look at a range of manifestations of racism in the twentieth century. These range from the oppression of black people in the United States, the persecution of Jews in Nazi Germany, racial divisions under apartheid in South Africa, to wider manifestations of institutionalized racism. Section IV focuses specifically on racist movements and mobilizations. The selections look at a range of forms of racist political movements and organizations and the complex sets of ideas that shape their actions. Section V links up with the concerns of the previous part by exploring a range of responses to racism that attempt to develop an anti-racist perspective. The selections included here range from various forms of black political mobilization to broader forms of anti-racist mobilization. Section VI takes up a theme that has been at the heart of much of the debate about racism, namely the role of state institutions. The various selections in this part explore the role that state and political institutions have played in specific historical and contemporary contexts. The final two parts of the Reader return to some of the wider conceptual agendas touched upon at the beginning. Section VII includes a range of theoretical perspectives that have sought to explain racism as a social phenomenon. The various extracts explore the role played by class, gender, and other social relations in shaping ideas about racial and ethnic groups. Finally, Section VIII brings together selections that reflect in one way or another on the vexed question of the future of racism.

Each of these parts functions in such a way as to provide an overview of trends and debates within the sub-field. That is why we have been careful to include scholars from a variety of perspectives in each part of the book. But we see all parts as linked up to our over-arching concern to allow readers to gain an insight into the history and development of racism as a social category. We shall return to some of these linkages later on in the volume, but first we would like to take the opportunity offered to us as editors to reflect on at least some of the main themes that arise from the various selections that follow. We do this partly to link up some of the threads of arguments that are dispersed through the volume as a whole, but also because we want to highlight some issues for reflection and contemplation.

Ideas about Race

Let us take, first of all, the issue of the origins and evolution of ideas about race. One of the themes that runs throughout this volume is that the very notion of *race* has no fixed and unchanging meaning. From a historical view it is clear from research on the usages of the notion of race over the past two centuries that it has taken on various forms in different national contexts (Goldberg 1993; Gossett 1997; Montagu 1997). Although the notion of *racism* is of more recent vintage it is also clear that its usage has varied enormously throughout most of this century (Miles 1989). Indeed it is no exaggeration to say that both race and racism remain essentially contested concepts, whether it be in the academic or the political spheres.

As we attempt to illustrate in this volume, however, the history and contemporary forms of racial ideologies have been the subject of a vast amount of scholarship and debate in recent times. As the various extracts in Sections I and II seek to show the history of ideas about race can be traced as far back as ancient times. But most scholars have focused their attention on the rise of racism in the aftermath of European expansion into other parts of the globe. A number of writers have located the rise of modern racism within the processes of intellectual and social transformation that characterized European societies in the period of the late eighteenth and nineteenth centuries. Historians generally agree that the idea of *race* came into common usage in the period from the mid- to the late eighteenth century. This period is commonly seen as the high point of the Enlightenment, and yet it is also during this era that doctrines about race came to be articulated in a consistent manner. A clear statement of this periodization is provided by George Mosse:

Racism has its foundations both in the Enlightenment and in the religious revival of the eighteenth century. It was a product of the preoccupation with a rational universe, nature, and aesthetics, as well as with the emphasis upon the eternal force of religious emotion and man's soul. It was part, too, of the drive to define man's place in nature and of the hope for an ordered, healthy, and happy world. (Mosse 1985: 3)

It is certainly from the eighteenth century that we can trace the flowering in a number of European societies of writings about race, and the emergence of what we now call racism. The idea that races existed involved the affirmation in popular, scientific, and political discourses that humanity could be divided into distinct groupings whose members possessed common physical characteristics. In addition to this basic idea, however, the belief in the existence of races of humankind involved both the attribution of different origins to human groupings and the attribution of cultural and social significance to racial boundaries.

Michael Banton, among others, has shown in some detail how the usage of the term 'race' has changed over time, particularly in the context of British and European society (Banton 1977, 1987; Banton and Harwood 1975). He agrees with the periodization of the usage of the idea of race which locates the late eighteenth century as the key period. But he also seeks to locate the growth in the usage of race within a broader social context:

Physical differences between peoples have been observed throughout human history; all over the world people have developed words for delineating them. 'Race' is a concept rooted in a particular culture and a particular period of history which brings with it suggestions about how these differences are to be explained. (Banton 1980: 39)

Banton's account provides valuable insights into the variety of usages of race over the past 200 years or so. He shows how writers from Britain, France, and Germany began to use the notion of race to refer to the existence of racial types. If we accept the above argument it follows that we have to go beyond the notion that race and racism are fixed transhistorical categories.

In summary, it seems clear that the usage of the category of race to classify various types of human being is relatively recent, and indeed that the widespread usage of the language of race is a phenomenon of the post-Enlightenment period. Whatever the longer-term history of images of the 'other' in various societies and historical periods it does seem clear that only in the late eighteenth century and early nineteenth century does the term 'race' come to refer to supposedly discrete categories of people defined according to their physical characteristics. In short, the concept as we understand it today came into being relatively late in the development of modern capitalist societies. Although usages of the term 'race' have been traced somewhat earlier in a number of European languages, the development of racial doctrines and ideologies begins to take shape in the late eighteenth century, and reached its high point during the nineteenth and early twentieth centuries. This is, of course, not to say that the category of race was not used in earlier times. But it is clear that from towards the end of the eighteenth century the meanings attached to the notion of race began to change quite significantly. Michael Biddiss notes that:

Before 1800 it [race] was used generally as a rough synonym for 'lineage'. But over the first half of the nineteenth century 'race' (and its equivalents in a number of other European languages) assumed an additional sense that seemed, initially, tighter and more scientific. This usage was evident, at its simplest, in the growing conviction that there were a finite number of basic human types, each embodying a package of fixed physical and mental traits whose permanence could only be eroded by mixture with other stocks. (Biddiss 1979: 11)

The attempt to classify humanity according to the idea that 'races' embodied 'a package of fixed physical and mental traits' was to become a key concept in the social and political debates of the nineteenth and twentieth centuries. Such ideas became part of popular cultural images about racial groups, but they also became an integral element of thinking in science and medicine and in embryonic social sciences such as anthropology and sociology. Ideas about the specific attributes of 'races' became common currency among both dominant and subordinate groups.

The continuing debates about the origins, evolution, and consequ⌐ ideas about race show no sign of disappearing. On the contrary, a new w⌐ scholarship has started to explore the same broad terrain as earlier generati⌐ of scholars, albeit within new terms of discourse (Kohn 1995). We have tried t⌐ reflect some key aspects of these debates in Sections VII and VIII, which bring together a range of views and perspectives about the theorization of race and racism in the present political environment.

Slavery, Imperialism, Colonialism

As will be clear from the way we have organized this volume we do not think it possible to understand the full social significance of racism without a detailed analysis of institutionalized forms of social relationships and the role of partic- ular social and economic institutions in the reproduction of racism. It is not our intention here to reduce the contemporary situation to historical factors and processes alone. But at the same time we want to warn against the dangers, all too common in much of the recent social science literature in this field, of ig- noring the history of racism and seeing contemporary forms in almost com- plete isolation from the past. This collection does not devote a great deal of attention to migration as a separate process, but there is no doubt that the en- slavement of tens of millions of people of African origin and their transporta- tion to the Americas constitutes one of the most important historical roots of contemporary racism in a country like the United States.

We hope that by looking at some central features of the historical back- ground we shall be able to uncover the range of factors and processes that have gone into the making of specific racist discourses, practices, and effects. This will allow readers to explore in more detail the complex ways in which ideas about race have been shaped by historically specific sets of social relations, e.g. by slavery in its various forms, relations of domination in colonial and imperial settings, by class, by gender, and other sets of power relations.

In Section II, and elsewhere, we have included extracts that explore the role of particular social and economic institutions in the reproduction of racism. While there is a danger of drifting into a reductive mode of analysis, we have in- cluded these extracts in order to emphasize the impact of processes of Euro- pean exploration, expansion, slavery, colonization, and imperial domination on ideas about race. The interest in these processes is that they are seen as being at the root of the emergence of racial ideas and values, e.g. in relation to the sup- posed 'inferiority' of black Africans. For example, in much of the contemporary literature on race relations in the United States and Britain, the development of racism is seen as related in one way or another to the historical experience of slavery, colonialism, and other institutions of 'white supremacy' (Fredrickson 1981).

This point, however, touches upon another theme which we have only hinted at so far: namely, the intertwining between the emergence of the language of race and the processes of economic expansion and capitalist development which were going on at the same time (Curtin 1964; Jordan 1968; Todorov 1993). How do ideas about the categorization of human beings into 'races' link up to the development of new patterns of economic and social exploitation? In what sense can we see racial ideas as either the outcome or as integral elements of wider economic and social transformations?

Thus, with the decline and eventual disappearance of the European slave trade from Africa in the first half of the nineteenth century, and the slower and more gradual disappearance of slavery itself in the Americas, the ownership of black slaves by white masters was succeeded by other forms of unfree labour such as indentures, share cropping, and debt bondage. Hugh Tinker's (1974) monograph on the export of Indian labourers within the British Empire is entitled *A New System of Slavery*, and chronicles the ways in which the migrants were kept subordinated and dependent upon those for whom they worked. Yet this system had the most profound consequences in the long term. Just as persons of African descent in the Americas are in great measure descendants of slaves, Indian minorities in countries as various as Fiji, Mauritius, Trinidad, and Guyana are in part descendants of indentured labourers brought to work on colonial plantations in the nineteenth century.

A recurrent theme in debates about the history of slavery is the issue of the relationship between processes of capitalist economic expansion and exploitation and the emergence of racism and racial ideologies. Arguments have waged fiercely between economic determinists such as Eric Williams's book on *Capitalism and Slavery*, originally published in 1944, which sought to locate slavery as essentially an economic phenomenon which arose because of the need to exploit labour through coercion. For Williams racism was a consequence, not the cause, of slavery: the product of the need to justify the institution of slavery and the means of coercion on which it relied (Solow and Engerman 1987; Blackburn 1988).

Williams's approach can be contrasted to arguments that slavery, particularly in the Americas, was essentially racial in origin, and based on beliefs about racial inferiority. In this approach, racial difference rather than economic exploitation is the key process, linked to the power held by the white dominant group, and their ability to enforce their wishes upon the slave population. Chief among the criticisms have been two fundamental points: (i) first, it has been argued that it is far too simple to see slavery as an economic phenomenon; (ii) second, economic determinist approaches have been criticized for viewing the development of racist ideologies in purely functionalist terms, i.e. as serving simply as a justification for the exploitation of labour power. These criticisms have been backed up by historical research which tends to question the usefulness of viewing either slavery or racist ideologies from a purely economic perspective. Interestingly enough this research has been produced by writers influenced by

Marxism as well as by non-Marxist historians. The argument about the relationship between slavery and the process of capitalist development is a continuing one (see for example Engerman and Genovese 1975) and has been carried on both in sociology and history.

The debate may be followed by comparing Oliver Cox's *Caste, Class and Race* (1948), written from a Marxist perspective, with the approach of David Brion Davis and George Fredrickson in this collection. Cox located the origins of 'race prejudice' from the period of European expansion at the end of the fifteenth and beginning of the sixteenth centuries. He argued that racism arose from the need to exploit labour in the form of slave labour. 'Race prejudice' constituted a justification for the exploitation of the labour power of certain groups of workers, and was 'a social attitude propagated among the public by an exploiting class for the purpose of stigmatizing some group as inferior in that the exploitation of either the group itself or its resources or both may be justified' (1970 [1948]: 393). Other scholars such as George Fredrickson accord much more independent importance to racial difference, and a more differentiated Weberian theoretical standpoint which distinguishes between the subordination of black people as individuals and 'societal racism' in which an entire colonial society enforced subordinate status over black slaves. He accords independent importance to the role of ideas, and the importance of selfishness, greed, and the pursuit of privilege in sustaining the institution.

What seems clear from these debates is that any rounded account of the origins and transformation of racism needs to be contextualized within a broader historical analysis. A number of recent studies have highlighted the complex role that race and ethnicity played in the process of European expansion and domination. A good example of this mode of analysis is Eric Wolf's *Europe and the People without History* (1982). This is one of the most challenging attempts to look at the extent to which the histories of Europe, Africa, the Americas, and Asia were shaped from 1400 onwards by the experience of European expansion and the economic, social, and political transformations that resulted. These processes of transformation inevitably involved complex constructions of the 'other' that went hand in hand with the changing patterns of economic, social, and political interchange. These can be set alongside accounts such as Victor Kiernan's analysis of European attitudes in *The Lords of Human Kind* (1969) and J. S. Furnivall's classic account of the so-called 'plural society' as it developed in South-East Asia in the early twentieth century, with three 'pillarized' racial groups, the white European rulers and merchants, the Chinese middlemen engaged in commerce, and the indigenous population. Plural society theorists such as M. G. Smith (1969) and John Rex (1970) have argued about whether such societies were held together by the polity or the economy—Furnivall argued that members of such societies met only in the market place—but this has led to fruitful debates about the relative roles of economic exploitation and political control in certain types of late colonial societies.

A more specific account of the role of race in the process of European expansion is provided by Winthrop Jordan's classic study *White over Black* (1968).
Jordan's account is particularly interesting because of the way he manages to
capture in some detail the changing representations of Africans from the sixteenth to the nineteenth centuries within the context of America. Rejecting the
view that there has been a uniform and unchanging view of Africans ever since
the sixteenth century, Jordan provides a systematic and richly detailed account
of the representations of Africans' skin colour, religions, relation to other
human groups, and sexuality. His account shows in some detail that the first impressions articulated by Europeans of Africans in the sixteenth century were
transformed quite fundamentally by the experience of slavery and economic
domination, by changing political and ideological environments, and by cultural changes.

Slavery in its various historical forms, and specifically the Atlantic slave trade,
did not have a purely economic rationale and its impact was as much on social
and power relations as on economic institutions (Patterson 1982). In relation to
the Atlantic slave trade there is a wealth of historical evidence about the impact
that the institution of slavery had on European images of Africans (Manning
1990; Lovejoy 1983). As Jordan and others have persuasively argued these images
did not remain fixed and unchanging across time and space. It seems quite clear
that during the seventeenth and eighteenth centuries the development of the
slave trade was an important part of the wider process leading to the development of European images of Africans and other peoples.

In the crucible of these transformations, ideas about 'national identity'
began to take a firm hold in European societies. In the case of Britain, for example, the idea of a unified national identity was very much an invention of the
period from the mid-eighteenth to the early nineteenth century (Colley 1992).
Indeed it is important to note that ideas about 'Englishness' or 'Britishness'
were never fixed and unchanging, and that they had to be reworked and fashioned around new values throughout the past two centuries (Samuel 1989: volumes ii and iii).

Contemporary Trends and Developments

We have, so far, emphasized two related themes. First, that ideas about race
emerged in specific social and political environments. Second, that the development of racism needs to be situated within a historical perspective that takes account of time and place. What we have tried to show is that in order to place the
role of racism in the contemporary social context, we need to situate the divergent historical processes that have shaped the understandings of race and racism
that are current in our societies. There is, as we are fully aware, a much broader
and deeper historical sociology of racism. As the work of a number of scholars
has shown, there have been a variety of both national and supra-national

processes at work in influencing the development of racist ideas and movements, and these cannot easily be subsumed under a monolithic category of racism. This key theme links up to some of the central problems which have arisen in recent attempts to contextualize racism within a historical perspective. Whatever the merits of the account we have given of specific processes it seems clear that it is important not to lose sight of the historical moments and the wider context within which ideas about race emerge, develop, and take on social significance.

A number of interesting attempts have been made to provide a comparative historical sociology of the workings of racism. The work of writers such as George Fredrickson provides an interesting and valuable model of this type of work (Fredrickson 1981, 1988). Fredrickson's account in his classic study *White Supremacy: A Comparative Study in American and South African History* (1981) seeks to capture both the differences and similarities between these two societies through a richly contextualized analysis of the role of patterns of settlement, images of the 'natives', racial slavery, race mixture and the colour line, and the changing social relationships of race in the twentieth century. He illustrates the value of contextualizing the historical development of racial ideas and racialized social relations not only in specific contexts, but the need to challenge some common assumptions about the social history of both America and South Africa. Additionally, his account provides a useful reminder of the role of state institutions in shaping the constantly changing contours of the 'colour line'. In addition to Fredrickson a number of other researchers have illustrated the importance of historically situated accounts of how ideas about race emerged and took shape in particular societies.

There is by now a rich body of historical work which has analysed the ways in which ideas about race have linked up with specific patterns of economic, social, and political transformation. But much of the contemporary social science literature on race and racism remains largely uninformed by historical research or by more contemporary studies of the wider processes that have shaped racial institutions (Poliakov 1982). This has resulted in a lack of historical reflexivity about the historical background to the emergence of modern racism and a failure to come to terms with the transformations of racial ideologies and practices over time and space. Yet what is also clear is that without an understanding of the historical context it is unlikely that we shall be able to come fully to terms with the question of how racial ideas have emerged out of and become an integral part of specific societies.

Part of the complexity of analysing the historical impact of racism is that it is often intertwined with other social phenomena, and indeed it can only be fully understood if we are able to see how it works in specific social settings. Additionally, it is clear that racism is increasingly not an ideology which can be easily reduced to biological arguments as such. Contemporary racial thought invokes a range of markers of 'difference' in order to construct the stereotypes and images on which racism relies. On one level one can agree with Goldberg when he argues that 'Racists are those who explicitly or implicitly ascribe racial characteristics of others that they take to differ from their own and those they take to be like them. These characteristics may be biological or social' (Goldberg 1990: 296). But even this definition seems to be a bit narrow when we look at the changing terms of racial discourses in contemporary societies. For what has become clear through comparative research is that only through a deeply contextualized account of the sources of racial ideas can we really grasp the variety of racisms that have emerged in specific historical environments.

Racism and Anti-Racism

Much of the focus of this volume is on delineating the ideological and institutional forms of racism. But it is undoubtedly the case, as Paul Gilroy notes in his contribution to this volume, that both racism and anti-racism have also played an important role in mobilizing racial categories in many societies. This is why we devote a significant part of the volume to exploring key facets of the ideas, values, and mobilizations of racist movements, anti-racist organizations, and minority political identities. Precisely because racial categories are not fixed and unchanging they have been the subject of continual contestation and reworking. It is also the case that ideas about race have been shaped by different historical and social processes and in a complex variety of ways, including important regional, religious, cultural, and political differentiations.

In this context it is important to remember that identities based on race and ethnicity are not simply imposed, since they are also often the outcome of resistance and political struggle in which racialized minorities play an important and active role. For this reason some argue that it is more accurate to speak of a racialized group rather than a racial group, since race can be a product of racism as well as vice versa. As well as being in some cases institutionalized structurally, racism can be an ideological defence of specific social and political relations of domination, subordination, and privilege. Racism operates as other ideologies do, by constituting new historical and ideological subjects. Race, and also ethnicity, can be viewed in terms of the representation of difference.

This is why in this volume we have chosen to focus on the dynamics of the political mobilization of race and social change. The advantage of this approach is that it allows us to go beyond abstract speculation and examine in some detail the political institutions, mobilizations, and policies in a variety of nation states that have helped to bring the present situation about. Many contemporary theorists of race have largely been concerned with global and somewhat abstracted analyses of racial and ethnic relations. Our focus is rather different: it is on the dynamics of racialized processes in the context of particular situations. This approach also stands in marked contrast to the deep-seated tendency to view race as a fixed and unchanging category. Such a tendency is evident in the arguments of both radical researchers who work from a monolithic conception of contemporary forms of racism and in the bulk of the mainstream research on the politics of race, which takes as its starting point a narrow definition of political institutions and forms of participation and mobilization.

It is important to remember that there is no single monolithic racism which structures ideas and values in all societies, or which shapes social relations in all specific environments. Rather there are quite distinct racisms that are constructed and reconstructed through time and space by social action. This helps to explain the complex forms which the racisms that we see around us today take, both in terms of their theoretical justifications and the political mobilizations associated with them. It is only by understanding the full implications of this rather simple point that we can begin to develop a better and relevant approach to the question of how it is that we can counter the dangers of contemporary racisms and construct alternative models of democracy that can allow for the representation of difference.

Racism and the State

In the present socio-political environment it is perhaps more clear than it has ever been that the analysis of racism and related phenomena, such as ethnic nationalism, cannot ignore the need for systematic comparative research on the role of the state and political institutions in shaping race and ethnic relations in different societies. The importance of state institutions and political processes in structuring racial and ethnic issues has been clear throughout most of the twentieth century. As Michael Burleigh and Wolfgang Wippermann illustrate in their magisterial analysis of the Nazi 'racial state', state power played an important role in perhaps the most concerted attempt to implement a programme of constructing a 'racially pure' society (see Section VI). More importantly, however, it is also clear that attempts to use state power to enhance the interests on one or other racial or ethnic grouping have been at the heart of racial movements and ideologies throughout the past century. As Mosse has shown the holocaust was very much the product of the combination of strong state regulation and modern technology: 'The holocaust could not have taken place without the application of modern technology, without the modern centralised state with its card files and communication systems, and without the brutalisation of men's minds by the experience of the First World War' (Mosse 1985: 232). This is of course not to say that the holocaust or other attempts at genocide were the inevitable product of modernity and of modern state power. But it is important to recognize that the events in the former Yugoslavia and Rwanda during the 1990s need to be situated very much in relation to the state and political mobilization and not constructed as some timeless expression of ethnic and religious hatred.

There are other important examples of the use of state power to reinforce relations of domination. Perhaps the most important one is the history of the apartheid system in South Africa, which involved a concerted attempt to use state institutions as a basis for institutionalizing by force and by regulation a system of racial segregation. Deborah Posel's detailed study of the making of the apartheid state from the 1940s to the 1960s is a good example of the kind of detailed scholarly research that has helped to delineate the particular forms of the relationship between the state and racial institutions (Posel 1991). Desmond King (1995) has shown how in the USA the federal government prior to the Civil Rights era participated in the maintenance of segregated race relations throughout the country, not just in the South.

Beyond Racism?

Underlying much of the academic and public discussion about race and racism at the present time there is a concern with an issue that has not received as much attention as it deserves, namely: Is there a way in which we can think of a world beyond racism? Whether this question is treated implicitly or expounded on explicitly it is at the heart of many of the political and moral dilemmas that confront scholars in this field. It may be, of course, that Patricia Williams is right when she points in her contribution to the lack of an imagination of what a world beyond racism could look like. But as she goes on to argue this is not an inevitable situation and there are possibilities for us to debate and envision ways in which we can move beyond racism. The question that remains to be fully addressed is exactly how and why this process may or may not happen.

While we have not attempted to give a prescriptive feel to this volume, in the concluding section of this Reader we look to the future. We include the views of a number of scholars who have attempted to explore the social, cultural, and political processes that may shape the future of racism and its institutional forms.

As we look towards the next century and millennium, one of the main questions that has to be faced is the issue of how to deal with the challenges presented by the growth and pervasiveness of racism. Within both popular and academic discourse there is growing evidence of concern about how questions about race and ethnicity need to be reconceptualized in the mainstream of social thought. This has been achieved more successfully in the case of gender than it has in societies where members of racial minorities are demographically in a minority. The concept of the multicultural societies (Wieviorka 1998) has been used increasingly; indeed in contemporary European societies this can be seen as in some sense the main question which governments of various kinds are trying to come to terms with. Important elements of this debate include the issue of the political rights of minorities, the status of minority religious and cultural rights, and the changing boundaries of national identity. Underlying all of these concerns is the much more thorny issue of what, if anything, can be done to protect the rights of minorities and develop more inclusive notions of citizenship and democracy that bring in those minorities that are excluded on racial, ethnic, or nationality criteria.

There are clearly quite divergent perspectives in the present social and political environment about how best to deal with all of these concerns. There is, for example, a wealth of discussion about what kind of measures are necessary to tackle the inequalities and exclusions which confront minority groups. At the same time there is clear evidence that existing initiatives are severely limited in their impact, given the socially entrenched character of much racist behaviour. A number of commentators have pointed to the limitations of legislation and public policy interventions in bringing about a major improvement in the socio-political position of minorities. And racism remains theoretically challenging, a phenomenon demanding that we continue to hone our analytical tools as social scientists to try to comprehend its continuing influence:

Because racism changes and develops, because it is simultaneously a vast phenomenon framed by epochal historical developments, and a moment-to-moment historical reality, we can never expect to fully capture it theoretically. Nor can we expect that it will ever be fully overcome. That does not mean, however, that we are free to desist from trying. (Winant 1998: 765)

We hope that in reading the texts included in this volume readers will be able to situate the study of race and racism within its historical as well as contemporary context. While these extracts are merely a sample of the research and scholarship on these issues, we also hope that they will encourage both students and general readers to immerse themselves more fully in the wealth of new scholarship about racism, some of which is reflected in the suggestions for further reading at the end. We are of course aware that some of the extracts included in this volume put forward assumptions or claims that are antithetical to the arguments developed in other extracts or in this Introduction. But it is precisely such a diversity of views and perspectives that we wanted to reflect.

Section I

Racist Ideas

INTRODUCTION

Given recent developments across the globe few would disagree that one of the key social and political issues faced by many societies is the question of racism and the social and political conflicts associated with its presence. Whether one looks at Western Europe, Eastern Europe, North America, or Africa the salience of race and racism as social issues is evident in a multiplicity of ways. What is often less clear in the context of contemporary debates in both the popular media and in academic discourses is the question of whether racism is a relatively new phenomenon or the product of ideas and processes with a much longer historical provenance. In other words, how do we begin to make sense of the relationship between contemporary trends and historical context. This key concern in turn generates a number of questions: about the changing nature of ideas about race; about the meaning attached to racism in historical and contemporary terms; and the interplay between racial ideas and wider economic, social, and cultural processes.

It is with these questions that we begin this Reader, as the various extracts included in this section are all concerned in one way or another with how we can best begin to locate the history of ideas about race within a broadly historical perspective. It is of course impossible to give a fully rounded picture of the changing role of ideas about race across time and space, but we have sought to bring together a series of extracts that help to locate racial ideas within specific historical processes and at the same time provide a point of entry into debates about the origins of racism and forms of racial domination. Frank Snowden's opening piece can be seen as an attempt to situate the meanings and impact of ideas about racial differentiation in the 'ancient world'. This has proved to be an important arena of intellectual debate, particularly on the issue of the difference between modern and ancient views about race and its social significance. Snowden's account provides an interesting overview of the central elements of ancient views about blacks and it helps to illustrate that ideas about differences on the basis of colour and phenotypical features were to be found in ancient societies, though they cannot by any means be compared to our modern notions about what is now called 'race'. What Snowden's account does illustrate, however, is that the attribution of social significance to colour and ethnic differences took on a variety of forms, not all of which are related to modern ideas.

Snowden's analysis provides an interesting contrast with the analysis to be found in the extracts by Philip Curtin and Michael Banton, which focus more specifically on the changing ideas about race in the period of European capitalist expansion and conquest. Curtin's account focuses on the linkages between the emergence of the language of race and the processes of economic expansion and capitalist development which were going on at the same time. While Curtin eschews a narrow economic analysis of the origin of modern racial thinking his account helpfully illustrates the linkages between patterns of European expansion and the articulation of ideas about the attributes of Africans and other 'races'. His account is a pertinent reminder of the important role that European expansion and trade played in influencing ideas about 'other' races within societies such as Britain, and provides an interesting insight into both the generation and the dissemination of racial ideas and images. Banton's analysis takes as its starting point the need to place the 'racialisation of the world' against the background of the important transformations in social, economic and cultural relations that have shaped societies over the past three centuries or more. Insisting on the need not to lose sight of the variety of usages of race over this period he shows how in societies as diverse as Britain, France, and Germany the notion of race came to be used in both popular and scholarly discourses to refer to the existence of distinct racial types. Banton is particularly concerned to highlight the complex and often contradictory ideas that went into the making of racial ideas and doctrines in the eighteenth and nineteenth centuries.

The next four extracts are all taken up in one way or another with the question of the evolution and transformation of racist ideas and their impact on the construction of ideologies of racial domination and exclusion. George Mosse's account of the origins of European racism seeks to argue for the centrality of the eighteenth century as an important turning point in the development of racial thinking. Mosse's account links up with a theme that has preoccupied a number of more recent commentators on the history of racial ideas, namely the linkages between Enlightenment thought and the articulation of ideas about the origins of racial diversity and the differences between the cultural and intellectual attributes of different groups. Reginald Horsman's argument focuses specifically on the development of ideas about 'superior' and 'inferior' races. Focusing on intellectual trends and ideas in America and Europe he attempts to show that the attribution of 'superiority' to some racial groups was a crucial element in the development of racial thinking in the nineteenth century.

The final two extracts focus specifically on the ideas of the author who is often seen as the 'father of modern racism', namely Comte Arthur de Gobineau. Michael Biddiss's paper attempts to situate Gobineau in the context of intellectual and social changes that were shaping France and other European societies. Biddiss is in particular interested in the ways in which Gobineau's ideas linked up to wider trends within European thought, as well as on the ways in which his ideas were taken up by other racial thinkers. Biddiss provides a valuable insight into Gobineau's preoccupation with racial degeneration through miscegenation, and his view of the origin of differences between different 'races'. Such ideas were to prove an integral element of later racial thinking in a number of countries, including France and Germany. Leon Poliakov continues this analysis through an assessment of the ways in which Gobineau conceptualized the role of different 'races' in the development of human history. Poliakov's account highlights the ways in which such themes as racial superiority, anti-Semitism, and the linking of civilization to particular racial types were an important thread in the thinking of Gobineau and his contemporaries.

The themes touched upon in this first part of the Reader are ones that we shall return to in a number of the other parts, since they provide a backdrop against which we can view key analytical questions that follow. In particular we shall take up some of the central issues about the historical development of racism from the nineteenth to the twentieth century in Sections II and III.

1 Images and Attitudes

The Image of Ethiopians in the Greco-Roman World

In their observations on Ethiopia and Ethiopians, classical writers provided a much more detailed and variegated picture of Nubians than any other Mediterranean peoples. Not limiting their interest primarily to military coverage, the Greeks and Romans in their accounts of the Ethiopians touched on a broad range of subjects, including anthropology, sociology, history, mythology, and religion.

From Homer to the fifth century

Ethiopians appear for the first time in Greek literature in the Homeric poems, where they are remote peoples, the most distant of men, sundered in twain, dwelling by the streams of Ocean, some where the sun rises, some where it sets. Their only earthly visitor was Menelaus, who said that he came to their country after wanderings in Cyprus, Phoenicia, and Egypt. Homer's Olympian gods were fond of visiting the 'blameless' Ethiopians: Zeus, followed by all the other gods, feasted for twelve days with them; Poseidon and Iris shared their sacrifices. Epaphus, according to Hesiod, was the child of the almighty son of Kronos, and from him sprang the black Libyans and high-souled Ethiopians. These early Ethiopians are shadowy individuals; their ethnic identity and precise location, uncertain. By the time of Xenophanes, however, word had reached the Greeks that Ethiopians were black-faced and flat-nosed and, by the fifth century, that they lived in Africa south of Egypt.

The first writer to enlarge upon Homer's blameless and Xenophanes' flat-nosed Ethiopians was Herodotus. African Ethiopians, according to Herodotus, differed from the Ethiopians of the east only in speech and hair, the former being the most woolly-haired people on earth and the latter having straight hair. The capital of African Ethiopia was Meroë, a 'great city' whose inhabitants greatly honored the gods Zeus (Amun) and Dionysus (Osiris). Ethiopia, according to Herodotus, had been ruled by only one Egyptian king, though it had contributed eighteen kings as rulers of Egypt. One of these was Sabacos, who invaded Egypt with a great army of Ethiopians and ruled Egypt for fifty years. As king of Egypt, Sabacos never put wrongdoers to death but instead required them, according to the severity of their offense, to contribute to civic improvement by raising the embankments of their cities. Uneasy lest he commit sacrilege, Sabacos voluntarily retired from Egypt after he had been terrified by a dream that he would assemble Egyptian priests and put them to death.

Like Sabacos, the king of the Macrobian Ethiopians, called the tallest and most handsome men on earth, had a high regard for justice. Having discerned the deception of the spies whom the Persian king Cambyses (ca. 530–522 B.C.) had sent when planning an Ethiopian expedition, the perspicacious Macrobian king remarked that the Persian king was unjust, for no just man would covet a land not his own. And, with a dramatic display of his dexterity in handling a huge bow, he instructed Cambyses' spies to inform the king that 'when the Persians can draw a bow of this greatness as easily as I do, then to bring overwhelming odds to attack the Macrobian Ethiopians; but till then, to thank the gods who put it not in the minds of the sons of the Ethiopians to win more territory than they have.' Herodotus continues that Cambyses, receiving this response, became angry and, acting like a mad man, embarked without adequate preparation upon an Ethiopian campaign, which he was forced to abandon because of a shortage of supplies and cannibalism among his troops. Further, Cambyses imposed no tribute on either the Ethiopians bordering Egypt whom he had subdued on his ill-fated march to the Macrobians or on those living near Nysa. These Ethiopians, according to Herodotus, brought gifts to the Persians every other year—about two quarts of gold, two hundred blocks of ebony, five boys, and twenty large elephant tusks. A striking confirmation of this statement appears in a scene on a relief of the Audience Hall at Persepolis begun by Darius: among the gifts brought by a diplomatic delegation from Kush were an elephant tusk, an okapi, and a vessel with a lid, perhaps containing gold.

The comparison between Ethiopian and Egyptian practices was a matter of interest to Herodotus. Discussing two figures of Sesostris that the Egyptian king had engraved on rocks to Ionia to celebrate a triumph, the historian noted that the equipment and dress were both Egyptian and Ethiopian. He was not certain whether the Egyptians adopted the very ancient custom of circumcision from the Ethiopians or vice versa. In commenting on the Egyptian soldiers who had settled in Ethiopia in the reign of Psamtik I, Herodotus observed that Ethiopians learned Egyptian customs and became milder-mannered by intermixture with Egyptians.

The Athenian dramatists of the fifth century B.C. played to an interest in a distant people brought closer to home by recent experiences: Ethiopian contingents in Xerxes' army and their bows of palm-wood strips, four cubits long, were a reality for some Greeks. Although the Greeks had encountered Ethiopians as enemies in the Persian Wars, there was no specifically anti-black sentiment in Greek drama. In the *Suppliant Maidens* of Aeschylus, the color of the Danaids was not an issue to King Pelasgus and his Argives when they were confronted with a decision on a question that they realized involved the possibility of war. Most un-Greek in appearance, 'black and smitten by the sun,' the Danaids, descendants of Io, received asylum in Argos. Exploiting a curiosity about a 'far-off country of a black race who lived by the fountains of the sun,' the dramatists turned to legends with African settings. The Memnon story was treated in the *Memnon* and *Psychostasia* of Aeschylus and in the *Aithiopes* of Sophocles. Both Sophocles and Euripides wrote an *Andromeda*;

the Busiris legend inspired comedies by Epicharmus, Ephippus, and Mnesi-machus and a satyr play by Euripides. The titles and extant fragments of these plays, all of which apparently included Ethiopians, reveal little about the precise treatment of the myths. The vase painters, however, with whom these 'Ethiopian' legends were also popular, provided some details as to setting and costumes and, most important in developing the fifth-century concept of an Ethiopian, left no doubt about the physical characteristics of Ethiopians: some were pronouncedly Negroid; others were mulattoes.

In view of the interest in dramatic festivals and the size of the audiences, it is not unlikely that the plays of Aeschylus, Sophocles, and Euripides stimulated more widespread discussion of Ethiopians in Greece than at any earlier period, except perhaps when reports had first come back from Greek mercenaries and settlers in Egypt. Following performances of plays on Ethiopian themes, the-atregoers may well have concerned themselves with related questions such as the significance of 'Ethiopian phialai' mentioned among offerings to Athena or the reason for the appearance of Ethiopians on the phiale that the statue of Nemesis at Rhamnus (not far from Marathon) held in its right hand. Were these Ethiopians related in any way to Homer's blameless Ethiopians? Or what was the identity of the Negro whose image was struck on the coins of Athens and Delphi? Was he Delphos, the son of the Black Woman, and did his features re-semble those of the Ethiopians in Xerxes' army? These and similar questions would not have escaped the attention of curious Greeks.

The Ptolemaic period

After the fifth century very little new was added to the Greek image of the Ethiopian until the Ptolemaic era. An indication of the kind of information cir-culated after the activity of the Ptolemies in Ethiopia is found in extracts from *On the Erythraean Sea*, a treatise by the second-century B.C. geographer and his-torian Agatharchides, whose sources included accounts of merchants and eye-witnesses as well as the royal archives in Alexandria. Excerpts from Agatharchides, surviving in Diodorus and Photius, provided new anthropolog-ical details: one group of Ethiopians was called Simi, because of their markedly flat noses; the Acridophagi (Locust Eaters) were described as exceedingly black. Inland Ethiopian tribes, whom Agatharchides located imprecisely in the south, were divided into four major categories: river tribes who planted sesame and millet, lake dwellers who garnered reed and soft wood, nomads who lived on meat and milk, and shore dwellers who fished. Basic Ethiopian diet was also sometimes reflected in the nomenclature of tribes such as the Struthophagi (Ostrich Eaters), the Spermatophagi, who ate nuts and fruits of trees, and the Elephantophagi (Elephant Eaters). In his account of the Ichthyophagi (Fish Eaters) Agatharchides introduced certain elements of idealization, absent in Herodotus' earlier record of Ethiopians. Autochthonous people who wore no clothes and had wives in common, the Ichthyophagi led a utopian existence, free from want, greed, and envy, which elicited from Agatharchides moralistic conclusions about their way of life. Unlike Greeks, the Ichthyophagi were not concerned with superfluities but, rejecting useless things, strove for a divine way of life. With no desire for power, Agatharchides continues, they were not distressed by strife; nor did they imperil their lives by sailing the sea for the sake of gain. Needing little, they suffered little; gaining possession of what was sufficient, they sought no more. And they were not governed by laws, for those who are able to live uprightly without the sanction of written law need no ordinances.

Agatharchides also mentions other Ethiopians, closer to the everyday reality of the Hellenistic world and a source of concern to the Ptolemies. In preparation for an Ethiopian campaign an unnamed Ptolemy, perhaps Epiphanes (205–180 B.C.), has included among his mercenaries five hundred horsemen from Greece. It was no doubt the threat of Ethiopian warriors, skilled in the use of their huge bows and deadly poisonous arrows, that induced an experienced regent to offer this advice against undertaking an expedition into Ethiopia: 'Why futilely announce an impossible task and pay attention to invisible hopes rather than to manifest dangers?'

The early empire

For a fuller image of the Ethiopian in Ptolemaic times. Diodorus, a historian of the late first century B.C., who used Agatharchides as one of his sources, is a useful supplement for our understanding of the Ptolemaic image of Ethiopians. Some of the 'primitive' Ethiopians of Diodorus wore no clothes at all, some covered only their loins, and others their bodies up to the waist. Some were filthy and kept their nails long like beasts, and a few did not believe in any gods at all. In general, says Diodorus, these Ethiopians cultivated none of the practices of civilized life found among the rest of mankind and their customs were in striking contrast to Greco-Roman practices—differences that Diodorus explains in terms of environment. After describing the effects of the excessive cold of the north on Scythia and its inhabitants, and of the torrid heat on the regions beyond Egypt and the Trogodyte country, Diodorus concludes that it was not surprising that 'both the fare and the manner of life and the bodies of the inhabitants should differ very much from such as are found among us.'

The fourth-century B.C. historian Ephorus had said that some write only about the savage Scythians because they know that the terrible and marvelous are startling, but had insisted that the opposite facts should also be noted. Diodorus noted that some of his sources on both Egypt and Ethiopia had accepted false reports or invented tales to please their readers. Refusing to accept such an approach, in the spirit of Ephorus, Diodorus was not blind to the achievements of other Ethiopians whose reputation for wisdom was great, and whose religious practices made them a kind of chosen people in the eyes of the gods. The peoples who inhabited the island of Meroë and the region adjoining

Egypt, according to Diodorus' sources, were considered to be the first of all men and the first to honor the gods whose favor they enjoyed. It was largely because of Ethiopian piety, Diodorus continues, that the gods doomed to failure the attempts of foreign rulers such as Cambyses to invade and occupy their country. These Ethiopians were not only pioneers in religion but also originated many Egyptian customs. From these Ethiopians, in Diodorus' account, the Egyptians, who were colonists sent out by the Ethiopians, derived their beliefs concerning their burial practices and the role of priests, shapes of statues, and forms of writing.

In the early Roman Empire lesser-known regions of both the distant south and the far north were reported to be inhabited by imaginary creatures, perhaps invented by writers such as those whom Diodorus rejected. Included among the inhabitants of inner Africa, according to Pliny the Elder, were the Trogodytae, who had no voices but made squeaking noises; the Blemmyae, who had no heads and their mouths and eyes attached to their chests; the Himantopodes (Strapfoots) with feet resembling leather thongs, who crawled instead of walking; and noseless and mouthless tribes who through a single orifice breathed, ate, and drank by means of oat straws. Pliny acknowledges in another description of inner Africa that he was dealing with unreality by his prefatory statement that he was coming to purely imaginary regions—the land of the Nigroi, whose king was said to have only one eye, the Pamphagi, who ate everything; and the Anthropophagi, who ate human flesh. Similarly, Pliny is apparently expressing his doubt about fabulous creatures of this type when he explains that coastal Ethiopians, the Nisicathae and Nisitae, names meaning three- and four-eyed men, were so designated not because they were physically bizarre but because they were unusually accurate in the use of bow and arrow.

Like other writers in the early empire, however, Pliny also followed Ephorus' caveat on inaccurate reporting and continued the old tradition of writing about the more familiar Ethiopians, whose wisdom and 'priority' of institutions came to be important elements in the image of Ethiopians current in the empire. Ethiopian wisdom, according to Pliny, was to be attributed to the mobility of the southern climate in the same manner as the fierceness of northerners was to their harsh environment. Lucian informs us that Ethiopians first gave the doctrine of astrology to men and, 'being in all else wiser than other men,' transmitted their discoveries about the heavens to the Egyptians. In the *Aethiopica* of Heliodorus, a high priest of Isis states that during a visit to the Ethiopian court he had enriched his Egyptian knowledge with Ethiopian wisdom.

Echoes of the glory of the Twenty-fifth Dynasty were still heard in the early empire and were reported with apparent admiration. Strabo included Tearco (Taharqa) the Ethiopian among the world's great conquerors, with Sesostris, Psamtik, and the Persians from Cyrus to Xerxes, and cites Megasthenes as his source for the statement that Taharqa advanced as far as Europe. The Sabacos of Diodorus resembles very closely that of Herodotus with one exception:

Diodorus adds that in piety and uprightness Sabacos far surpassed his predecessors, and contrasts Ethiopian justice with the harshness, injustice, and arrogance of the Egyptian Amasis. Freedom-loving Ethiopians, according to Seneca, who had talked with centurions after their return from the Ethiopian mission under Nero's auspices, rejected Cambyses' threat of slavery and, instead of accepting servitude with outstretched arms, sent envoys and replied in words befitting the free and insulting to kings.

The importance, if only propagandistic, that Augustus attached to Petronius' Ethiopian campaigns is perhaps suggested by the inclusion of his Ethiopian victories in the official record of his administration and achievements known as the *Res Gestae Divi Augusti* (Deeds of the Deified Augustus). Copies of this document, originally engraved on bronze tablets outside the emperor's mausoleum in Rome, and set up in some if not all the provinces, were constant reminders to the Roman world of the Meroïtic threat to Egypt's southern boundary. The many terracotta figurines of Negro warriors from the Roman period found in Egypt provide vivid illustrations of Rome's Ethiopian adversaries mentioned by authors of the early Roman Empire. In spite of Augustus' difficulties with African blacks, Vergil did not hesitate to pay tribute to the assistance that Ethiopians had given to Rome's ancestors in the Trojan War. Aeneas, as he gazed with deep emotion at scenes depicted on the outer walls of Dido's temple at Carthage, recognized himself and the armor of his black ally, Memnon. In his account of Augustus' Ethiopian campaign, Pliny pointed out that Ethiopia had not been made a desert by the armies of Rome, but that the region, a powerful and famous country down to the Trojan War, once ruler of Syria and the Mediterranean coasts, had been exhausted by a series of wars with Egypt.

Another important source for the image of Ethiopians projected during the early empire was Josephus, whose *Jewish Antiquities* included several episodes highlighting Ethiopia's prominence as an independent state of considerable military power. Enlarging upon the reference to Moses' Kushite wife in the Old Testament, Josephus added a story of the love of an Ethiopian princess for her father's enemy in time of war. The Ethiopians, according to Josephus, invaded Egypt, repulsed an Egyptian counterattack, and marched as far north as Memphis and the sea, conquering as they went. Only after the Egyptians, in response to word from God, appointed Moses as their general were the Ethiopians driven back to their capital and forced to abandon hope of subduing Egypt. As Moses was besieging the Ethiopian capital, Josephus continues, Tharbis, daughter of the Ethiopian king, fell madly in love with Moses and sent him a proposal of marriage, which he accepted upon condition that she surrender the city. Moses fulfilled his promise to marry the princess once the city was captured, celebrated the nuptials, and led the victorious army back to Egypt.

With slight variations, Josephus describes several other martial events involving Ethiopians mentioned in the Old Testament. Among these are two

Ethiopian campaigns in Palestine: the sack of Jerusalem by Isokos (Shishak), with many tens of thousands of troops and 400,000 infantrymen, most of whom were Libyans and Ethiopians; and the invasion by Zaraios (Zerah), king of the Ethiopians, at the head of an army of 900,000 foot soldiers, 100,000 horsemen, and 300 chariots, and his defeat by Asa. Sennacherib, the Assyrian king, failed in Egypt, according to Josephus, because as he was about to attack Pelusium he received word that Tharsikes (Taharqa), king of the Ethiopians, was coming to aid the Egyptians, and he decided to withdraw.

Other 'scriptural Ethiopians' appear in *Jewish Antiquities*. The Queen of Sheba becomes the Queen of Egypt and Ethiopia, 'thoroughly trained in wisdom and admirable in other things,' and an Ethiopian servant of Zedekiah is responsible for saving Jeremiah by convincing the king whose favor he enjoyed that the prophet had been wronged. Josephus retold Ethiopian history at a time when blacks were well-known anthropological types and brought to the attention of the early empire some themes that Christian exegetes were to use frequently in interpreting the mystery of the Church—the marriage of Moses to the Ethiopian woman; Ebed-melech, the rescuer of the prophet Jeremiah; and the visit of the Queen of Sheba to Solomon. At the same time, *Jewish Antiquities* reinforced the recurrent image of black warriors and their widely respected kingdom, and may have reminded the historian's contemporaries of events closer to their own era: the Ethiopian attack on the Romans in Egypt at the time of Augustus had been foreshadowed by the ancient Ethiopian invasion of Egypt; and the wise Queen of Sheba had a later counterpart in the Ethiopian queen, whose ambassadors were diplomatically so skillful as to gain from Augustus all their requests.

Late impressions of Ethiopians

One of the last works in classical literature to treat at some length an Ethiopian theme is the *Aethiopica* of Heliodorus. Hydaspes, the king of the Ethiopians in the third- or fourth-century romance, is a model of wisdom and justice; he prefers not to put men to death; in the tradition of Piye, he instructs his warriors to refrain from slaughter and to take the enemy alive. When his foe pleads for survival, Hydaspes grants mercy. In the same charitable spirit he proclaims, as he glances at the bleeding Oroondates, the viceroy of the king of Persia: 'A noble thing it is to surpass an enemy in battle when he is standing, but in generosity when he has fallen'—a sentiment Vergilian in spirit and reminiscent of Anchises' words, 'Spare the humble and subdue the proud.' In gratitude for the Ethiopian's decision to allow him to return to his province, Oroondates renders obeisance to Hydaspes, an honor that Persians reserved for their king, and calls the Ethiopian ruler the most just of mortals for having granted him life and freedom instead of death or slavery. Like the Macrobian king who did not covet the land of others, Hydaspes is content with the natural boundaries of the Cataracts and, having accomplished his mission, returns to Ethiopia. Though on the point of following a tradition of sacrificing foreign prisoners to the gods, Hydaspes, convinced by the chief of his advisers (called Gymnosophists) of the inappropriateness of such a practice, persuades his people to renounce human sacrifice.

In the fourth century, the epic poet Quintus of Smyrna revived the glorious exploits of Memnon and his black soldiers. The arrival of a countless host of Ethiopians brings joy to the beleaguered Trojans, who flock to the streets to see them; hope is rekindled that the Ethiopians might burn the Greek ships. The Ethiopians of Quintus are foremost in battle, killing many a warrior. Nor are they forgotten by heaven after Memnon's death because a god speeds them off from the battlefield, and as they mourn the death of their king, Dawn changes them into birds, afterwards called 'the Memnons,' who continue to utter wailing cries as they fly about Memnon's tomb.

The classical image of blacks in retrospect

Certain lines of the Greek and Roman profile of Ethiopians remained basically unchanged from Homer to the end of classical literature—and the image was essentially favorable. Following Ptolemaic exploration of Nubia, reports reached the Greeks about hitherto lesser-known Ethiopians, far to the south of Egypt. The extant excerpts of Agatharchides, the first to describe these southern tribes in detail, show that there was no tendency, even upon first discovery, to barbarize these Ethiopians. On the contrary, Agatharchides idealized some of them in a kind of philosophical treatise on 'primitives.' Diodorus, whose picture of Ethiopians was one of the most comprehensive in classical literature, adopted a balanced method of reporting, without generalizing about nudity or community of wives and without giving undue emphasis to the exceptional. While not omitting practices of 'primitive' Ethiopians that were strikingly unusual from the Greco-Roman point of view, Diodorus also included an account of those Ethiopians whom his sources regarded as the *first of all men* and as the originators of divine rituals most pleasing to the gods. Even after the Greeks and Romans had encountered Ethiopians as enemies, classical writers continued to treat without rancor ancient 'Ethiopian' themes—military power, love of freedom and justice, piety, and wisdom.

Throughout the history of classical literature, elements of idealization and unreality appear in some descriptions of distant peoples, especially those in the far north and south. The distant regions of Scythia and Ethiopia, for example, were at times the homes of fabulous creatures or wild and ferocious tribes; at other times the inhabitants were characterized as paragons of justice. But the view that most of the Ethiopians of classical literature were unrelated to reality needs reconsideration. Even Homer's blameless Ethiopians may have stemmed from reports of Ethiopian piety, and the poet's black, woolly-haired Eurybates may have reflected an awareness of a black power on the southern edge of the Greek universe. Nubia, as far south as Meroë, was a region often as well known in the Greco-Roman world as it had been to the Egyptians. In fact, Africanists have found many observations of classical writers of considerable value in the reconstruction of the Napatan-Meroïtic Kingdom of Kush.

From the time of Herodotus onward, classical authors, despite some unreliable reporting and occasional fanciful creations, were often dealing with African realities and were much more knowledgeable than has been realized. Herodotus was the first of several writers to reflect an awareness of the Ethiopian Dynasty. The historian's account of Sabacos' piety is reminiscent of the Napatan's victorious Piye and is corroborated to some extent by Shabaka's interest in restoring religious texts of the Old Kingdom, attested by inscriptional evidence. Herodotus' mention of Ethiopians in the population of Cyprus may have been based on knowledge of an Ethiopian presence dating back at least to Amasis' conquest of the island in the Twenty-sixth Dynasty. In his description of Cambyses' plans for an Ethiopian campaign, Herodotus describes a 'table of the sun,' said to have been a meadow outside the city where boiled meat was placed by magistrates for whoever wanted to partake of it. The historian in this passage, according to specialists on Meroë, has provided an apt description of the site of the Sun Temple, located outside the city of Meroë in an area that can be described appropriately as a meadow because vegetation still grows there more readily than in the surrounding plain. Herodotus' account of Macrobian expertise in archery and his description of the bows of Xerxes' Ethiopian auxiliaries—like Heliodorus' later description of the Ethiopians' unerring skill in hitting their target, their adversaries' eyes—point to an ancient military tradition in the south: the bow had been the typical weapon of the Nubians since the days of the black archers at Gebelein and Assiut, and as late as the seventh century A.D. Nubian bowmen, known to the Arab invaders as 'pupil smiters,' were respected for their skill in blinding their opponents.

Lucian's statement that Ethiopians invented astrology may have stemmed in part from the reports of travelers who had visited Meroë. Astronomical equipment and graffiti representing actual sketches of astronomical calculations, dating from the second century B.C., have been found at Meroë. Remains of Meroïtic temples show that astronomical orientation was an important factor in the layout of these structures. It is tempting to suggest that Greek and Roman visitors to Meroë, impressed by their 'discoveries' at the southern periphery of the world, circulated the belief that astrology was an Ethiopian gift to mankind and gave rise to further speculation that a number of Egyptian institutions had an Ethiopian origin.

Much of what has sometimes been classified as an 'idealization' of Ethiopians, when not actually a reflection of facts, may have been based on reports of what Herodotus heard at Elephantine or of informants such as the Ethiopian ambassadors with whom Diodorus spoke. Ethiopian partisans would certainly have emphasized the justice of the southerners' cause and their efforts to protect their country from foreign exploitation. Sympathetic references to

Ethiopian justice and resistance to foreign aggression such as those of Herodotus, Diodorus, and Seneca, therefore, should perhaps be regarded as a tribute to the objectivity of classical writers in recording the Ethiopian point of view rather than as the idealization of an unknown, distant people. Finally, the Greco-Roman image of blacks, even if at times idealized or not always based on historical fact, must have had an enormous impact on the day-to-day attitudes toward blacks. What is significant is not the objective truth of ancient reports, but the frame of mind that made them possible. Perceptions are often influential in shaping social attitudes and are important factors to be considered in assessing the Mediterranean view of blacks.

Nubia was perceived by its contemporaries as an independent country, rich in coveted resources, inhabited to a large extent by dark-skinned and Negroid peoples, who from time to time played a significant role in the international politics of the day. Nubia as a military power on the periphery of the Mediterranean world was by far the most prominent feature of the ancient profile of blacks. The ability of Nubia, a nation of skilled archers, to defend itself from foreign exploitation gained the respect of its enemies, even of Egyptians and Assyrians in spite of the often exaggerated and contemptuous claims of their 'official' accounts. The services of Ethiopian warriors undoubtedly won the gratitude of others for whose causes they fought in various parts of the Mediterranean world. The Twenty-fifth Dynasty was not only known among contemporaries, but its accomplishments were considered worthy of note and admiration by later chroniclers. The requests of Baal of Tyre and Hezekiah of Judah for Napatan assistance illustrate Asiatic awareness of the dynasty's influence. The Book of Nahum recalled the glory of the Napatan kingdom long after its fall at the hands of Assyrians. That Taharqa was still regarded as a great military leader six hundred years after his death is evident from Strabo's list of famed world conquerors.

It is important to emphasize that the overall, but especially the more detailed Greco-Roman, view of blacks was highly positive. Initial, favorable impressions were not altered, in spite of later accounts of wild tribes in the far south and even after encounters with blacks had become more frequent. There was clear-cut respect among Mediterranean peoples for Ethiopians and their way of life. And, above all, the ancients did not stereotype all blacks as primitives defective in religion and culture.

[From *Before Color Prejudice: The Ancient View of Blacks* (Cambridge, Mass.: Harvard University Press, 1983), 46–59.]

2 The Africans' 'Place in Nature'

In its early stages, with little background in conscious or rationalized theory, British consideration of African race and African culture was highly dispersed. It was not a central problem discussed as such, but a peripheral question that had to be taken into account by several groups of writers. 'The Negro's place in nature' naturally had a role in whatever reporting came from Africa or the West Indies. It was discussed from another point of view by biologists, who were just then concerned with the problem of explaining human varieties. In quite another context, men of letters used the convention of the 'noble savage' for their own purposes. Finally, the anti-slavery writers of a dominantly Christian and humanitarian turn of mind were forced into a discussion of race by their efforts to reform imperial policy.

Of these four groups, only the travel writers had adequate access to empirical data. Their information, therefore, had to serve the others as a store from which they could draw as it suited their needs and interests. Travel reports contained something for everyone, with accounts varying from the most bitter condemnation of Africans and their way of life to an equally broad-minded tolerance. If there was a principal thread running through the whole body of information, it was one of moderate xenophobia. Slave traders, officials, and planters were all men sent out to live in dangerous tropical conditions. They were there to do a job, and one that necessarily brought them into contact with alien peoples whose culture they did not understand. Their resentments were those of foreign visitors in any country. In Africa they often thought they were cheated, and they disliked the strangeness of African customs. In America they took the slaves to be obstinate, rebellious, thievish, and lazy—which they probably were: these are the expected attributes of slaves in any society.

But for all their xenophobia, the travellers were unusually free of racial antagonism. Most men connected with the slave trade, and even the West Indian planters (to say nothing of the enlightened travellers with their ethnographic and humane interests), were less inclined to emphasize racial factors than those who stayed in England. This was especially true of their accounts of day-to-day dealings with the Africans. In 1789, for example, sixteen recent visitors to West Africa reported to a Privy Council Committee on the African trade. While most of them had been concerned in one way or another with the slave trade, none mentioned an assumed African racial inferiority as a bar to future development. They had little respect for the African way of life, but those who belonged to the Company of Merchants Trading to Africa had in Philip Quaque, their official Chaplain at Cape Coast, an African who was later the most highly paid man on their staff, except the Governor himself.

The travellers often condemned individual Africans as bad men—or all Africans as savage men—but they left the clear impression that Africans *were* men. The African way of doing things might be curious or unpleasant, but individual Africans were shown with abilities, faults, and virtues in much the same proportion as Europeans. Merchants on the African coast (in contrast to planters in the West Indies) dealt with Africans as partners in trade—not, perhaps, equal partners, or the partners an Englishman might choose, but nevertheless men of substance whose views could not safely be ignored. Thus the image of Africans in America was radically different from the stereotype of the servile Africans of the Americas.

Moderate xenophobia, with emphasis on the fact of moderation, was reproduced in the popular attitude toward Africans in England, especially among those in day-to-day contact. Negro servants who came to England from the colonies were popular with their masters and were often valued by the aristocracy in preference to white servants. They were also popular with their European fellow-servants, and with members of the English working class who came to know them. Some racial tension was present, but it came from the normal distrust of strangers, from sexual competition or the belief that Negroes took away employment from Englishmen. However wrong-headed these attitudes might be, either on the Coast or in England, they arose from the practical concerns of one people dealing with another. As such, they were in touch with social reality. Race as such was a *mark* identifying the group—not a *cause* of the group's other characteristics.

A different kind of attitude emerged when the travellers abstracted from qualities of individuals and began to talk about the group—not individual men but the collective 'Negro.' Reporting of this kind became increasingly common in the 1780's, as the Africa interest felt itself threatened by the rise of the anti-slave-trade movement. Several writers began to project a double image, relatively friendly to individual Africans but unfriendly to the collective African. Individuals in Norris' *Memoirs of the Reign of Bossa Ahadee*, for example, are clearly living portraits of men not especially different from men elsewhere, while 'the African' in his collective image is an inhuman savage.

As the element of political purpose made its appearance, so did a certain degree of circularity between the works of travellers to Africa and those of theorists in Britain. Lt. John Matthews, the pro-slavery author of an account of the Coast in 1785–1787, wrote from what were ostensibly his own observations. Some parts of his works were in the matter-of-fact tradition of earlier reports, but some were clearly derived from Edward Long, an early 'scientific' racist resident in Jamaica, who had never visited Africa. Long's low assessment of 'the Negro's place in nature' thus found its way into Matthew's book, where it could later be picked up as a piece of first-hand evidence from Africa.[1]

The tendency to write about the abstract and collective 'Negro' was strongest among biological writers, whose business it was to deal with abstractions of this kind. Where the travellers set out to report what they saw, without the necessity of building their evidence into a system, the eighteenth-century biologists began with a system and used empiricism to make it as accurate as they could. Their principal aim was to examine, classify, and arrange the whole order of nature in a rational pattern.

This emphasis on the creation of a large-scale system tended to distract attention from the systematic study of man. The first concern of naturalists like Linnaeus and Banks was the world-wide collection of specimens to build up a picture of botany and the zoology of the 'lower animals,' which made up the largest part of the whole order of nature. No individual or group of scholars was concerned with anthropology, defined a century later as 'that science which deals with all phenomena exhibited by collective man, and by him alone, which is capable of being reduced to law.'[2] The physical structure of man belonged institutionally to anatomical studies, as a branch of medicine. Data about human culture and society outside of Europe was collected by whatever travellers happened to have the interest to write down what they saw. Analysis of these data was mainly left to a rather vague and still-undifferentiated social science, most often under the rubric of 'moral philosophy.' The scientific study of human varieties therefore fell by default to the biologists, as a kind of appendix to their general systems of nature.

The major eighteenth-century classifications of nature began with Linnaeus' *Systema Naturae*, first published in 1735, and later revised with additions. This work and its successors formed the basic framework of modern biological classification, and they were decidedly set in the eighteenth-century modes of thought. One of the important items of intellectual lumber common to educated men was the ancient belief that God (or Nature, according to taste) had so organized the world that all creation was arranged in a 'Great Chain of Being'— that all living things could be classified and fitted into a hierarchy extending 'from man down to the smallest reptile, whose existence can be discovered only by the microscope.'[3]

Since man had a place as the highest term on the scale, the varieties of mankind had also to be taken into account, and the biologists assumed from the beginning that they too could be arranged in hierarchic order. Linnaeus himself included a racial classification, which changed slightly in different editions of his work. Initially it was a simple system based on skin color, with a white, red, yellow, and black race, each of them placed on one of the four major continents. In 1758 he divided *genus homo* into two species to make room for orang-outangs and certain rumored wild men without speech. This later division seemed to be called for by another assumption implicit in the Great Chain of Being: since God in His perfection must have created a perfect hierarchy of living things, the gap between any two creatures was not expected to be very great—not, certainly, so great as that between man and the higher apes.

Other authorities used a four-fold classification like that of Linnaeus, or else dropped back to the ancient and familiar Biblical distinction between the descendents of Ham, Shem, and Japhet, and thus to a three-fold division. Or, the three-fold division could be extended to five by introducing mixed races. J. F. Blumenbach of Göttingen worked with three primary races, the Caucasian, Ethiopian, and Mongolian. American Indians were taken to be a mixture of Caucasian and Mongolian, and a Malay race was supposedly a mixture of Mongolian and Ethiopian. Blumenbach's term 'Caucasian' for the European variety lasted into the twentieth century, but later authorities using the five-fold system adopted their own variants. Thus, John Hunter in England took the European, American, and African to be three primary varieties, with two other mixed races to fill out the scheme. By any of these systems of classification, the African variety was always considered a primary stock, if only because of its skin color, so strikingly different from that of Europeans.

Whatever the number of races, the second problem was to arrange them in order of quality. Since there is no strictly scientific or biological justification for stating that one race is 'higher' than another, the criteria of ranking had to come from non-scientific assumptions. All of the biologists gave some order of classification, but few of them stated their basis for doing so. Their unstated assumptions, however, were clear enough, even when they were not explicit. All of them began by putting the European variety at the top of the scale. This was natural enough, if only as an unthinking reflection of cultural chauvinism. It could be held to follow from their assessment of European achievements in art and science, or even from the 'fact' that God had given the One True Religion to the whites. It was taken for granted that historical achievement was intimately connected with physical form—in short, that race and culture were closely related.

[From *The Image of Africa: British Ideas and Action 1780–1850* (London: Macmillan, 1965), 34–9.]

MICHAEL BANTON

3 The Racializing of the World

A great many writers in France, Germany, Britain, and the United States, theologians, anatomists, physiologists, ethnologists, poets, and travellers contributed to the vigorous and confused debate about race and the historical examination of it is still far from complete. Because 'race' meant different things to different writers, and was the source of much of the confusion, it is more helpful to use the concept of 'type' as a clue that leads through the maze. In the sense that is relevant here, the concept of type originates with Cuvier in the early years of the nineteenth century. It comes into English through one of the major figures in the study of race, James Cowles Prichard, and quickly spreads, especially in the United States where it is built into the new doctrine systematized in Nott and Gliddon's book *Types of Mankind*, published in 1854. Whether Gobineau should be seen as an expositor of this doctrine is less straightforward. In his *Essai sur l'Inégalité des Races humaines* he made some use of the doctrine of type, and in many books his essay on the inequality of races is interpreted from this standpoint; but his essay has also been interpreted as extending the romantic conception of the complementarity of race in the course of expounding a pessimistic political philosophy.

The notion of type was a convenient one because it was not tied to any particular classificatory level in zoology, so that it was easy to refer to the physical types characteristic of particular nations, to 'types of cranial conformation', or to say that a skull 'approximates to the Negro type' without having to establish just what that type was. This was appreciated at the time, for W. F. Edwards in his important essay of 1829 observed

In identifying a combination of well defined characters as a type—a word which has the same sense in ordinary speech and in natural history—I avoid all discussion about the rank which a group so characterized will occupy in a general classification, since it suits equally well the distinctions between variety, race, family, species, genus, and other categories yet more general. (1829: 125)

As the evidence about the diversity of human forms accumulated, more and more writers tended to refer to various kinds of type, and, indeed, the construction of typologies of various kinds became a characteristic of nineteenth-century scholarship. The conception of racial types is more central to the debate about race than is the attempt to classify the peoples of varying regions. It contrasts sharply with the conceptual apparatus that Darwin made necessary, and it remains at the core of a now discredited ideology of racial determinism which looks like retaining some political significance for the remainder of the twentieth century.

At the beginning of the controversy the word 'race' does not appear at all. In the eighteenth century there had been a strong tendency to rank all the things in the world—mineral objects, vegetables, and animals from the lowest to the highest—as constituting a 'great chain of being'. It was argued that each form shaded imperceptibly into the next one so that it was arbitrary and misleading to separate them into distinctive categories. The Swedish botanist Linnaeus, however, produced a classification which won very general acceptance. Plants and birds were identified first as members of classes, then orders, then genera, and finally species (though there might be varieties within species). Linnaeus introduced the practice of naming species by two words of which the first is the name of the genus. Each genus and each species has only one correct name. Many scientists of his day thought that a more systematic understanding of God's creation took them one step nearer to the Creator. Knowledge was growing rapidly and there was a desire for synthesis that reached its height in the middle of the nineteenth

century. Medical studies of the anatomy and physiology of Europeans were becoming more systematic. Better reports were coming in about the physical character and the culture of men in distant parts of the world, and scientists were
beginning to make sense of the previously confusing evidence about the higher
apes and the reputedly lower varieties of *Homo sapiens*. [. . .]

Where did the theory of racial types come from? Evidence has been presented to suggest that the principal source lay in the complex of ideas about the
prehistory of the world and the origin of species, but it was influenced by the
current state of very partial knowledge about peoples living outside Europe, by
the contemporary feeling almost of intoxication about the rate of material
progress in Europe and the context of racial contacts overseas in which most of
the 'authorities' had made their observations of non-European peoples. There
are grounds for believing that the criticism of the slave trade stimulated West
Indian planters to develop doctrines of the racial inferiority of blacks in the clos-
ing years of the eighteenth century. The works of the egregious Edward Long
are regularly quoted in support of such an interpretation. But the evidence is
still far from satisfactory and it appears as if the theory of racial typology may
well have been more important to the spread of beliefs about natural inferiority.
James Cowles Prichard, who was a very sober observer indeed, commented in
1826 that in England black men from the West Indies were able to find English
wives 'which is a proof, not only of their own good taste in this respect, but also
that our countrywomen, the lower orders of them at least have no invincible repugnance to the negro race'. Yet it is more interesting to note that when he went
on to ask 'whether the faculties of the mind . . . are less perfect in the Negro' he
should have written

as far as I have had opportunities of collecting information on the subject, from the
most judicious observers, the result has been a most decided assurance that Negroes are
not by any means inferior in intellect to Europeans; at least that, in the sphere of action
in which they are placed, no such inferiority is displayed. This has been the almost uniform testimony of many intelligent planters and medical practitioners from the West
Indies, with whom I have conversed. Among the former, though this class of men has
often been accused of a sinister bias, their prejudices and interest leading them, as it is
said, to undervalue the Africans, I have not met with an individual out of a great number, who has not given a most positive testimony as to the natural equality of the
African Negro and the European. (Prichard, 1826: 129, 177–78)

It would seem, therefore, that controversies about the slave trade may have had
only a limited effect upon the growth of racial doctrines in England and that the
more powerful developments came later in the nineteenth century.

The theory of racial typology which gathered together some of the speculations of the earlier part of that century contained what can now be seen as
rather obvious mistakes. The mistaken theories in the field of embryology
were fairly quickly rectified, as was the doctrine of the permanence of types in
its biological context and certain of the theories about hybridity. But theories

claiming that Negroes had a more limited brain capacity than whites, and that the progress of civilizations was determined by underlying racial types, have lasted longer and cause many readers to ask: who were these scholars? Was there anything in their personal backgrounds which has a place in an explanation of their errors?

The personal background to the theory of Joseph Arthur de Gobineau (1816–1882) is certainly relevant. He was born into a bourgeois family with aristocratic pretensions that had been devoted to the Bourbon dynasty and completely opposed to the aspirations of the French Revolution. His experiences of family life, with both his mother and his wife, included much that was unhappy. Gobineau attracted attention in a Parisian salon and earned a living from journalism until the Revolution of 1848, after which he obtained a succession of diplomatic appointments up to 1877. The writer who has most carefully examined his racial theory, Michael Biddiss, believes that the dominant theme in his work is that of pessimism. The human world was degenerating and its decline could no longer be halted. The events of 1848 were compelling evidence of the lengths to which the process had gone. The blood of the creative races had lost its purity and therefore its power. Colonial expansion would only hasten the self-destruction. Personal relations with non-Europeans seem not to have played an important part in the theme of the *Essay* which he wrote without ever having left Europe. In 1855, when he first came in contact with a black people, he wrote home about the Somalis saying that never before had he seen 'creatures so beautiful and perfect'. Gobineau's own philosophy implied the negation of meaningful political action and during his lifetime it was without influence. The reader who takes up Gobineau's four volumes expecting to find there a doctrine suited to the claims of either the aristocracy or the bourgeoisie of his generation must be struck by its utter uselessness for such purposes.

Robert Knox (1791–1862) was the son of an Edinburgh school teacher who for some years pursued a promising medical career. He served as an army surgeon in Belgium and for three years in South Africa, afterwards establishing himself as a very successful lecturer on anatomy in Edinburgh. His ideas about race may well have been formed during the early 1820s but in 1828 there was a mishap which cast a blight upon the remainder of his life. Medical teachers had to obtain cadavers from some disreputable sources. Two men, Burke and Hare, who were convicted of murder, had sold the body of one of the deceased to an agent acting on behalf of Dr Knox and though he was formally cleared of liability his position in Edinburgh became untenable. Thereafter he held only occasional medical appointments and maintained himself for some periods by writing and lecturing. The unhappiness he must have experienced may well explain the disjointed and dogmatic nature of his pronunciations upon race when they appeared in book form. Though the opposite of a romantic, Knox was politically a radical who implies that had the revolutionaries of 1848–9 possessed his insight, they could have moulded these events to their greater advantage. But his book is muddled and certainly expounds no philosophy of political action. He warns his readers that the future is not theirs to control 'ask yourselves what climatic changes destroyed the mammoth, the ane-plotherium, the dinotherium, the sivatherium? the fishes of the ancient world? the sourians? Man destroyed them not; yet their race is run. Why dies out, al-most before our eyes, the apteryx? . . . The destroying angel walks abroad un-seen, striking even at the races of men.' He pours scorn on the delusions that beset races when formed into powerful nations, in which hubris is so promi-nent, sarcastically quoting a London sermon as evidence that Condorcet's the-ory of the advance of mankind towards perfection must be inapplicable to the English since they are already perfect (1860: 467, 574). The only sensible policy it seems, in Knox's eyes, was for each race to keep to itself within its natural borders. [. . .]

Nor were racial theories used only to disparage coloured peoples. In India the Aryan theory pointed to common ties between the British and the native popu-lation rather than to a division between them, yet neither the British nor the In-dians responded to it in any uniform manner. When Max Muller, the Oxford professor of Sanskrit, used the Aryan theory to praise the culture of ancient India and to emphasize the common descent of Englishman and Bengali, this probably evoked no hesitations in Chelsea drawing rooms, for it seemed to prove the providential nature of British rule in India. Englishmen in India were less attracted to it, though Sir Henry Maine, who was at one time Law Member of the Government of India (and himself a scholar who made little use of racial ideas), remarked 'I myself believe that the government of India by the English has been rendered appreciably easier by the discoveries which have brought home to the educated of both races the common Aryan parentage of English-man and Hindoo'.

The message that the Englishman was an elder brother who had been sepa-rated from some other members of his family and had now returned to help them learn the skills he had acquired in his more extensive travels, was wel-comed by some Indians, but the Brahmins had reason to fear its implications for the claims to privilege within Hindu culture. Many Indian nationalists stressed the superior political organization and spirituality of the Aryans. They used the expression 'Aryan' in a moral rather than a geographical sense, and without much historical content. Some employed it as a rallying cry. In such ways its sig-nificance was diluted, probably on account of its unacceptable presuppositions. The Aryan theory would have denied equality to Indian non-Aryans, including out-caste Dravidians, tribal people, Muslims and Jews. Though some national-ists were not averse from this, the reformers may have been more impressed by the desirability of claiming equal rights for all Asians and have opposed the Aryan theory because it distracted attention from the true obstacles to unity. Nor did the British find that the racial aspect of the theory suited their political ends very closely. To insist on the primacy of racial heredity was to imply that

British attempts at reform in India would be useless unless the racial character of the population was changed. The myth of the Aryan past was more serviceable, for it fitted with the mid-Victorian belief in progress and could represent the British as the most progressive branch of the most progressive race. That same myth also validated the claim that British rule in India was merely a family reunion, justifying it to Hindu audiences. But it is just as important to note that, for one reason or another, British officialdom made almost no use of the Aryan theory with respect to India in the period 1850–70 and that thereafter it attracted relatively little official attention.

The study of the processes by which racial categories were developed and applied should also comprehend the intellectual response of black people which is early evident in works such as James Africanus Beale Horton's *West African Peoples and Countries* of 1868. In this volume by an Edinburgh-trained doctor from Sierra Leone, one chapter is devoted to the 'false theories of modern anthropologists'. It presents evidence in conflict with the theories of Knox, Vogt, and contemporary typologists. Soon afterwards a West Indian-born scholar who entered the diplomatic service of Liberia, Edward Wilmot Blyden, brought together some of his essays in *Christianity, Islam and the Negro Race* (1887), an impressive volume expounding arguments which can best be seen as reactions to racial typology. Blyden wrote: 'each of the races of mankind has a specific character and a specific work. The science of Sociology is the science of race.' Nations were forming along racial lines, and Negroes, though equal to whites, would never resemble them (1887: 94, 122, 277). Across the Atlantic a similar response can be seen in *Froudacity*, the book in which a black Trinidadian, J. J. Thomas, attacked J. A. Froude's account of the English in the West Indies. He asked: 'What is it in the nature of things that will oust the African race from the right to participate, in times to come, in the high destinies that have been assigned in times past to so many races that have not been in anywise superior to us in the qualifications, physical, moral and intellectual, that mark out a race for prominence amongst other races?' (1889: 180–81).

Replies such as these did not challenge the assumption that every man possessed racial attributes. They accepted it, but maintained that Europeans had been in error in their application of the theory. Nor did they draw upon the ideas that went into racial theories in order to build a political programme. In Sierra Leone and Trinidad this was scarcely necessary, for political change could easily take place within the structures fashioned under colonialism. Africans could respond to their political subordination by creating movements that brought together into nations congeries of peoples which might previously have been distant but were already conscious of their separately belonging together as peoples. As nationalism was so respectable an ideology in European political philosophy, there was rarely anything to be gained by appealing to race. In the United States the picture was more complex; but from the 1880s the theme of 'race pride' was increasingly stressed by black leaders and the belief that Negroes like every other race, had distinctive but complementary qualities was voiced by them and by some of their white sympathizers.

[From *The Idea of Race* (London: Tavistock, 1977), 27–9, 54–7, 60–2.]

GEORGE MOSSE

4   Eighteenth-Century Foundations

Eighteenth-century Europe was the cradle of modern racism. The major cultural trends of that century vitally affected the foundations of racist thought. This was the age of Enlightenment, during which an intellectual élite attempted to substitute an emphasis upon man's inherent reason and virtue for the 'ancient superstitions of the past.' The Enlightenment was a revolution in aesthetic and intellectual tastes and conventions, but it found a specific focus in the revolt against Christianity. Christianity was regarded as synonymous with 'ancient superstitions,' and Voltaire's cry, 'Écrasons l'infâme,' was echoed by many other writers. The 'enlightened' turned to the classics for inspiration and support in their revolt. But while they sharpened their critical minds on Greek and Roman models, Christianity proved to be alive and well for the mass of the population.

The eighteenth century was also a time of religious fervor and revival. Pietism on the continent of Europe and evangelism in England spanned the eighteenth century, running parallel to the Enlightenment. These movements stressed the need for an emotional Christian commitment, and displayed the yearning for true community in the notion of fellowship and a 'religion of the heart.' The tension between the Enlightenment and this underlying Christianity characterized much of the century during which modern racism was born and nurtured. European racism was fed by both trends, despite their conflict. The Enlightenment and the Pietistic and moralistic atmosphere would impress their stamp equally on racist thought.

The Enlightenment was also characterized by a radical attempt to define man's place in nature. Nature and the classics were thought vital for a new understanding of man's position in God's universe and were therefore taken as setting new standards of virtue and beauty. Thus from the outset of this sweeping inquiry into the nature of man and the universe, natural science and the moral and aesthetic ideals of the ancients joined hands. Indeed, these two crucial components were so bound together that it is impossible to separate the inquiries of the Enlightenment *philosophes* into nature from their examination of morality and human character.

Science and aesthetics influenced one another reciprocally. In large measure, the scientific endeavor was directed toward a classification of the human races according to their place in nature and the effect of the environment. The beginning of the new science of anthropology during the second half of the century was based upon the attempt to determine man's exact place in nature through observation, measurements, and comparisons between groups of men and animals. Moreover, the quest for unity and harmony in the affairs of man and the cosmos led to belief in the unity of body and mind. This, in turn, was supposed to express itself in a tangible, physical way, which could be measured and observed. Both phrenology (reading the skull) and physiognomy (reading the face) had their origins in the last decade of the century.

But these observations, measurements, and comparisons that were basic to the new eighteenth-century sciences were combined with value judgments following aesthetic criteria derived from ancient Greece. The Enlightenment passion for the new sciences and the reliance upon the classics as authority were fused in this manner. Whatever the physical measurements or comparisons made, in the last resort the resemblance to ancient beauty and proportions determined the value of man. This continuous transition from science to aesthetics is a cardinal feature of modern racism. Human nature came to be defined in aesthetic terms, with significant stress on the outward physical signs of inner rationality and harmony. Scientific classification was based upon the subjective ideals of the Enlightenment.

As it grew up, racism would also make contact with evangelism and pietism, which combined to form the second fundamental trend of the century. Here the need for an authentic and significant experience of God found an outlet in a Christianity marked by the call to give oneself to Christ. This was also bound up with the ideal of living a Christian life of love for one's neighbor as part of a renewed sense of community. Through printed tracts and preaching, an emotive atmosphere was created, very different from the rationalist Enlightenment of the intellectuals. From our point of view, this meant an emphasis upon the instincts, upon intuition, and upon the emotional life of the 'inner man' which would eventually lead to racial judgments about man's soul. A longing for coherence, for community, and for an ideal in the face of a changing world was always to the forefront.

In short, racism had its foundations both in the Enlightenment and in the religious revival of the eighteenth century. It was a product of the preoccupation with a rational universe, nature, and aesthetics, as well as with the emphasis upon the eternal force of religious emotion and man's soul. It was part, too, of the drive to define man's place in nature and of the hope for an ordered, healthy, and happy world. Eventually, the racist outlook fused man's outward appearance with his place in nature and the proper functioning of his soul. Thus, religious emotion became integrated in racism as part of the 'racial soul.' Nevertheless, at first the Enlightenment concept of God and of the unity of human nature played a dominant role in the emergence of racism. We must therefore undertake a deeper examination of the Enlightenment before returning to the Pietistic contributions. [. . .]

The foundations of racism were strengthened by two additional factors—the growing contact between white and black, and the introduction into Europe of the Jews as a newly emancipated minority. As a result of travel, knowledge about Africa and the West Indies had increased; moreover, a number of blacks had lived in England for some time. Jews, of course, had always lived in Europe, but since the sixteenth century they had been herded into ghettos and separated from the rest of the population. Indeed, the Jewish 'nation' (as it was commonly and revealingly called, with its different dress, customs, religion, and language, was the only sizable group of a foreign people in Christian Europe. But toward the turn of the nineteenth century, thanks to the Enlightenment and the French Revolution, many ghetto walls fell and Jews entered into European life, while at the same time the contact with blacks became more frequent.

The growing intensity of contact with other peoples was what mattered. Those strangers who were rare in Europe and whose home was barely known were regarded with benign curiosity. Thus, a Chinese partook of the character of a sage—an image popularized by the Jesuits. Chinese in Europe were a novelty, much honored wherever they went. Moreover, they benefitted from the Chinese vogue in the mid-eighteenth century: Chinese gardens, Chinese porcelain, even mock Chinese villages. The Chinese seemed to complement and extend the roccoco and baroque world of illusion. The 'noble savage' had also for a period fulfilled this function, but familiarity and greater contact bred contempt and fear of ever present Negroes and Jews. Eventually, the Chinese too were drawn into the racist picture. Comte Joseph Arthur de Gobineau, one of the most famous racial theoreticians of the mid-nineteenth century, was to set the tone for a hostile view of the yellow races, but by that time there had been a vastly extended contact between Europe and the Orient. Thus, it is untrue that sentiments about black inferiority could have existed without contact with blacks, or that anti-Jewish feelings could have persisted even where there was no knowledge of Jews. The reverse was actually the case. People needed to see the frightening stranger, so supposedly different from themselves, with their own eyes.

There was, for example, a direct connection between the ways Englishmen regarded their blacks at home and abroad in the Empire. The number of blacks in London increased during the eighteenth century, and the fears about intermarriage and violence at home reflected the vision of blacks in Africa or the West Indies. They were regarded less as exotic than as objects for education and discipline. Attempts were made to inculcate in them the proper morality and to imbue them with the gospel of work. If, at times, the English at home reduced the black to the level of an ignorant beast and even held some as slaves, the view of the slave as a chattel in Africa or the West Indies was modified by efforts at their conversion to Christianity. Nevertheless, there were clear signs of a crystalization of racial feeling, and the fear that English blood might be tainted through intermarriage became increasingly widespread.

Similar views of the Negro prevailed among anthropologists conversant with travel reports. Thus Blumenbach, writing from Germany, accused Negroes of extremism, lack of a sense of proportion, and lack of culture. But he still believed that the Negro, like everyone else, was created in the image of God and therefore should not be treated brutally.[1] Christian missionaries shared such compassion. The racial attitude toward the black was not yet clear-cut, though he consistently ranked low whenever men were classified.

The Jews were either ignored by anthropologists during most of the eighteenth century or considered part of the Caucasian race, and still believed capable of assimilation into European life. Even a champion of their emancipation such as Wilhelm Christian Dohm thought that Jews were Asiatic by origin. But in 1781 Dohm declared that Jews were capable of enlightenment and should be assimilated. Ideas of cosmopolitanism, equality, and toleration operated for the Jew as they could not for the Negro; after all, the Jew was white. Typically for the age, Johann Kaspar Lavater, in classifying human faces toward the end of the eighteenth century, gave the Jews aquiline noses and pointed chins; even so, he admitted that he did not know how to classify them properly, and in the end gave up.[2] Indeed, only after the mid-nineteenth century was racism applied to Jews with any consistency.

No one seemed to feel such ambiguity toward blacks. Blacks, unlike Jews, had a fixed lowly position in the 'great chain of being.' No longer were they the noble savages 'with virtue fraught.' More often they were considered close to the animal world. It was thought no coincidence that the gorilla had its home in Africa side by side with the black; travelers had popularized the notion that there must be a close relationship between apes and blacks. Anthropologists chimed in, especially when aesthetic judgments came to the fore. Peter Camper, writing in 1792, was not the only anthropologist to compare the skulls of apes and Negroes. But here the 'great chain of being' also intruded: was the black the 'missing link' between animal and man? The chain must be kept complete. If there was a gap, lower creatures must be promoted one step in order to fill the void. Thus, for example, apes might become the lowest type of man, so providing the 'missing link': 'Inferior orders in succession rise to fill the void below.'

The English anthropologist Edward Tyson had posited the Pygmies as this link in 1699. He criticized the ancients for seeing Pygmies as human when in fact they were more akin to animals. Significantly Tyson, a physician and a fellow of the Royal Society, based his arguments on classical mythology.[3] The concept of the man-beast had never vanished from Europe. It was widely believed that apes were, in fact, not a totally different species but a lower species of man, who refused to speak in order not to become slaves. For Tyson, Pygmies were apes because of their flat noses and their small stature. This latter point was repeated by others as proof of the animal nature of these blacks, even when such scholars as Camper and Buffon attempted to demonstrate that apes were a different species from man. But in spite of basic differences between man and ape,

Camper still believed the Negro to be closer to monkeys than the rest of the human race. He cited as his reason the Negro's appearance, as well as skull measurements, but in reality the aesthetic criterion was paramount, as it was for Tyson. Most anthropologists equated small stature with racial inferiority: 'Size is the characteristic of Caucasian nobility,' wrote Christian Meiners.[4] Nose shape was also a determinant for the black, whose flat nose was taken, once again, as proving closeness to the animal world, while the so-called hooked Jewish nose likewise became an outward sign of the absence of inward grace.

The reconstruction of the 'chain of being' was an exercise in which many eighteenth-century anthropologists joined. Thus, Meiners posited a hierarchy from the lowliest creatures, through apes, through the legendary 'Negro of the forest,' to 'Hottentots,' 'Bush-Negroes,' and aborigines, and further to the yellow races and Slavs, until he arrived at the white race which was the master of the world. That he believed in the inevitable decline of the superior race through miscegenation makes him, in fact, a forerunner of Gobineau. Always the outward beauty of form was adduced as one of the most important ways of classifying the species within the hierarchy of the universe.

Characteristically, as these examples show, diverse notions were combined in such classifications: the natural order, ancient mythology, travelers' tales, and aesthetic prejudice. At the same time, the cosmopolitanism of the Enlightenment and its pull toward environmental theories of human behavior tended to counteract idealist and Romantic prejudice. Man was a part of nature, and the laws of nature themselves must produce the observable differences between groups of men. If, as Locke thought, all ideas were acquired and not inherited, racial differences were chance variations. Because nature, man, and indeed all the world are formed in the image of God, and are pregnant with possibilities, the Negro could not be doomed or regarded as inferior. Blumenbach was not the only early anthropologist who stated such a belief, for Lamarck and Buffon also lent their weight to this view.

Despite the ambivalence of these scientists, and because of the equally strong pull toward subjective judgments of permanent superiority and inferiority, for a time science and aesthetic presuppositions existed side by side. The world of ideal-types, of myth and symbol, was given its dynamic through concepts basically opposed to the Enlightenment: pietism, evangelism, and pre-romanticism. The link between the Enlightenment and such a world view was forged by anthropologists who in their racial classifications would pass from science to art.

[From *Toward the Final Solution: A History of European Racism* (Madison: University of Wisconsin Press, 1985), 1–3, 12–16.]

5 Superior and Inferior Races

Although American intellectuals in 1815 generally accepted the environmental view of racial differences which they had inherited from the European Enlightenment, there were already signs that informed American opinion was ready to provide a scientific rationale for what was believed by many of those in direct contact with blacks and Indians. In providing this rationale American scientists were clearly participating in a general interest in racial differences that dominated western thought by the 1850s; but they were also responding to needs within American society itself. By the 1840s the American theorists on race were providing a mass of material defending innate differences between races; these ideas were sweeping all before them in America and were being used in Europe by those who were challenging the long-established views on the unity of the human race.

As early as 1808 Dr John Augustine Smith attacked Samuel Stanhope Smith's environmentalism in college lectures in New York city, but the first well-publicized onslaught was that of Dr Charles Caldwell. Caldwell was an opinionated and argumentative physician, who from 1811 to the middle of the century consistently and loudly defended the cause of innate racial differences. He published a great deal on a variety of subjects and lectured extensively throughout the country. A North Carolinian who had received his medical education at the University of Pennsylvania, Caldwell was professor of natural history at that university before moving to Kentucky in 1819. There he became a prominent member of the medical profession, first at Transylvania University and from 1837 on at a new medical school he founded in Louisville.

Caldwell first attacked Smith's views in 1811 and was unrelenting in his onslaught on environmentalism. He later called Smith's *Essay* 'one of the most fallacious productions I have ever perused.' The crux of Caldwell's objection was that races could not be altered by environment, and he quickly found himself the center of controversy as the religious orthodox claimed he was attacking the idea of the original unity of the human race, which meant, of course, a challenge to Genesis. In later articles Caldwell denied attacking religion, simply stating that climate could not account for the distinction between races; divine involvement had been needed. During the next forty years most American scientists who argued for innate, irreversible differences between races tried to avoid a direct attack on the Bible. Often they argued that because God had originally created Adam and Eve he could also have interposed at a later date to create racial diversity. This usually did not satisfy the religious orthodox, who correctly surmised that any attack on the unity of the human race would ultimately bring a direct challenge to Genesis. Many of Samuel Stanhope Smith's friends and supporters never forgave Caldwell for his attack on the environmental theory, for they connected Smith's death in 1819 with his distress at the attack. [. . .]

The most influential American scientific writing defending innate racial differences was not to appear until after 1839, but public assertions of the existence of superior and inferior races increased rapidly in the 1830s. At first the main scientific evidence was advanced by those interested in phrenology, which in the 1830s had an intellectual as well as popular vogue in the United States. When Spurzheim traveled to the United States in 1832, he was received enthusiastically by many of the eastern intellectual elite, and when the visit ended in his unexpected death, his Boston funeral was a major public occasion. The intellectual interest continued until the extensive American lecture tour of George Combe at the end of the decade. Only in the 1840s did scholarly opinion begin to move away from phrenology as the 'practical phrenologists' emphasized the commercial and fortune-telling aspects of the readings of heads and 'bumps.'

Like their European contemporaries, the American phrenologists were optimistic about the possibilities of improvement for those who had a sound basic structure of the brain; but they also argued that nonwhite races had structures that were fundamentally deficient, and that they could not be developed to the level of the white brain. Most phrenologists ignored the problem of the original unity or multiplicity of races and simply asserted that physical comparison of the head or skull of the different races revealed basic differences. In the 1820s and 1830s the phrenologists were in the vanguard of those who perceived innate physical differences between the races, and although their specific analysis of the brain was eventually rejected by American scientists, they at first exerted considerable influence by their supposed empirical comparison of physical structure. Until the 1840s many Americans of impeccable scientific reputation thought that phrenology was a valid approach to the physical comparison of individuals and races.

One of the first general American works of phrenology was that of George Calvert in 1832. Calvert carefully listed thirty-five faculties, represented in different parts of the brain, that controlled a variety of human thoughts, desires, and emotions. He emphasized that the general phrenological doctrine was that a small brain could not manifest a powerful mind; the mind could be developed by education, but its effects were limited by the original organization: 'No skill or education or control of outward circumstances could ever enlarge to excellence the intellectual capacity of an individual with a brain like that of the New Hollander; nor depress to inferiority that of an individual with one like Göthe.'[1] The accusation of inferior basic 'organization' was typical of the analyses of the phrenologists and affected writings that were not specifically phrenological in type. In a general work on the connection between religion and health, Amariah Brigham pointed out in 1835 that 'the dark colored races' (he included the American Indian) had been unreceptive to the missionaries because their

'physical organization' was unsuitable. A basic element in this deficient organization was 'the organ of the mind.' In the dark races of man, the anterior and superior portions of the head were depressed. Accordingly, although
improvement, and even great improvement, was possible, this would take generations and even centuries.[2] It was neither circumstances nor environment but
specific, inherent physical differences that accounted for the failure of the non-
Caucasian races to achieve Christianity and civilization. Phrenologists helped
convince many other scientists as well as laymen that there were specific differences between races.

The intellectual defense of innate racial differences received a further boost
in the 1830s by the widespread southern defense of slavery. Southern apologists
of the institution developed an array of arguments to demonstrate specific and
permanent Negro inferiority. The tacit assumptions of Negro 'difference' and
inferiority which had permeated the colonial period now for the first time were
shaped into a coherent racial theory. It is a commonplace to point out that the
catalyst for this southern defense of its institution was the launching of a northern abolitionist attack in the 1830s, and this certainly stimulated vigorous southern rebuttals; but in a larger sense the Southerners were sharing in, and taking
advantage of, the general shift toward racialist thinking in Europe and the
United States. This racialist thinking was used to justify far more than the southern institution of slavery. It served to defend the subordination or even extermination of non-European peoples throughout the world and was believed by
Europeans to explain the ever-increasing gulf in power and progress that separated them from the peoples they were overrunning. The overt intellectual argument for innate black inferiority was being developed in America before the
full surge of abolitionism, it was not restricted to the South in the 1830s and
1840s, and it was not peculiar to those who wished to defend slavery. [. . .]

As Southerners in the 1830s became increasingly sensitive on the subject of
slavery, they were able to take comfort in the variety of writings in both Europe
and the United States that were challenging the belief in innate human equality.
When in 1833 Richard H. Colfax put out a pamphlet to combat the views of the
abolitionists, he went to a number of European authorities—including Lord
Kames, Voltaire, and Sir William Lawrence—who had emphasized the sharp
differences among the races of mankind, and he expressed his disagreement
with both Blumenbach and Dr Samuel Stanhope Smith. The essence of Colfax's argument was that as the Negroes were of a distinct species no change in
their circumstances could make them equal to the whites. 'There never existed
a tribe of whites,' he wrote, 'who were characterized by as much grossness of
intellect, listless apathy, sluggishness, and want of national and personal pride,
as even the most refined Africans.'[3] European racial arguments attracted considerable interest in the South, and in 1837 J. H. Guenebault to South Carolina
selected those portions of J. J. Virey's *Histoire naturelle* that related to blacks and
reissued them as the *Natural History of the Negro Race*. [. . .]

By the late 1840s the racial question was at the heart of scholarly discussion in the United States, and a variety of writers tried their hand at reconciling racial diversity and religion. The concept of racial inequality had clearly carried the day, but some scholars and many clergymen and laymen were still anxious that the new theories should somehow be reconciled with the account in Genesis. The most general disagreement with Nott and Morton was not that they had divided the world into superior and inferior races, but that in adopting polygenesis as the original reason for racial differences, they had challenged the Mosaic account of Creation. When Charleston minister and naturalist John Bachman presented a comprehensive defense of the unity of the human species in the early 1850s, he had no intention of arguing for Negro equality; he simply maintained that the obvious differences between the races had been brought about by a process of variation that had become permanent.[4]

Bachman turned verbal somersaults to reconcile Genesis, racial variation, fixity of species, and Negro inferiority, but he was a scholar and a fine naturalist. Others who took sides in the scientific racial argument were simply amateurs, yet they were often given as much weight as those who claimed to be engaged in empirical research. New York lawyer William Frederick Van Amringe, in a long, diffuse book published in 1848, argued that while all men sprang from Adam and Eve, God had made four distinct species soon after the flood. In reaching his conclusions Van Amringe depended on instinct and observation, not on scientific measurement. Distinct races had existed for nearly four thousand years, and only among the 'Shemetic' species (essentially Caucasian) did the elements of civilization exist. By 'the special favor of the Creator', said Van Amringe, this Shemetic species 'is more highly favoured in constitution than others.' While other species were not as well endowed, it was the duty of the Shemetic species to help them as much as possible: 'it must go on conquering and to conquer, until every species of man shall have been brought to the highest degree of perfection of which the nature of each is susceptible.' Van Amringe did not even suggest that he was trying to base his work on any empirical research, but he was taken seriously and his views disseminated widely through the politically influential *Democratic Review*.[5]

When in 1852 Dr S. Kneeland wrote an introduction to the American edition of an English work on race, he commented that the English author supported the position of diversity of races which had been maintained by Agassiz, Van Amringe, and Morton. Kneeland saw nothing strange in lumping together the conclusions of two of the most eminent men of science in America with the amateur meanderings of a lawyer. Kneeland said the key question was not whether a race could be improved, but whether all had the same capacity for being improved. 'History need not be very deeply consulted,' he wrote, 'to convince one that the white races, without an exception, have attained a considerable degree of civilization and refinement; and that the dark races have always stopped at a considerably lower level. There must have been a time when the

Caucasian was as ignorant and uncivilized as the American [Indian] or the African; all were once simple children of Nature . . . the former have advanced, the latter have degenerated from the original type of their species.' All the evidence, wrote Kneeland, led to the conclusion 'that the dark races are inferiorly organized, and cannot, to the same extent as the white races, understand the laws of Nature.'[6]

By the early 1850s the inherent inequality of races was simply accepted as a scientific fact in America, and most of the discussion now concerned either the religious problem of accepting polygenesis as an explanation of racial differences or the problem of exactly defining the different races. The general tendency was for greater and greater refinement of racial divisions, both among the white and the colored races, but some, in their zeal to debase the nonwhites, were willing to accept the Caucasians as a unified group. In an extremely popular work on Negroes and slavery published in 1853, New York physician John H. Van Evrie erased all racial, national, and class distinctions among Caucasians in order utterly to condemn the blacks. Van Evrie said of the Caucasian that 'the flowing beard, projecting forehead, oval features, erect posture and lordly presence, stamp him the master man wherever found.' The colored races, he argued, were capable of only limited development, and he suggested that perhaps Confucius, and many other ancient Chinese, were Caucasian.[7]

[From *Race and Manifest Destiny: The Origins of American Anglo-Saxonism* (Cambridge, Mass.: Harvard University Press, 1981), 116–17, 120–2, 123–4, 133–5.]

MICHAEL BIDDISS

6 Gobineau and the Origins of European Racism

Gobineau's racism originates with his revulsion against a society which had rejected the virtues of nobility. His social pessimism is a matter of class-consciousness. The writers of French history had for long made such a connection between race and class. The racial interpretation of French history might be traced back to Caesar and Tacitus, but a more conventional origin is to be found in the sixteenth century theory of François Hotman. He described a league between the Gauls and Germans in defence of their common liberty against Roman tyranny. Successors, such as Adrien de Valois, made a distinction between the Gallo-Romans and the Franks. The classic exposition was that of Henri de Boulainviller. He believed that the Franks had conquered the Romans, who were themselves the earlier conquerors of the Gauls. The Franks henceforth formed the French nobility, claiming their position and property by right of conquest. But, like Gobineau, Boulainviller was disturbed by the encroachments of the lower classes since the golden age of Charlemagne. These elements were permutated again by the Abbé Dubos, who described such conquest as illusory and suggested that the Franks came to Gaul as the allies of Rome. Montesquieu and Mably tried to play down the divisive issue of conquest. But at the Revolution the Abbé Sieyès was happy to reverse the idea and justify the supremacy of the Gallic people over the Frankish nobles by the triumph of the third-estate. Not even the national feeling encouraged by the Revolutionary and Napoleonic Wars could silence the argument over race and class in France. Though such writers as Montlosier, Chateaubriand and Augustin Thierry emphasised harmony among the racial elements, the historical fact of conquest remained unshaken and was at hand for the use of a latter-day Boulainviller. Thus for centuries the elements of the French nation and their rivalries had been used to support contemporary polemics. It was not unnatural that Gobineau, with his class assailed by society, should find inspiration in this source of racial historiography.

But the broadening horizons of the nineteenth century revealed material more extensive than that of France alone. Gobineau, like many in the romantic age, was attracted by the renaissance of interest in the Orient. India, in particular, offered the western world the picture of a civilisation which was not only different, but also alive. Inca culture, for instance, had been but a museumpiece. Hindu mysticism and society revealed a past that lived on in the present. The eighteen thirties was the decade when oriental studies most captured the imagination of intelligent youth, and it was then that Gobineau was assiduously reading works on the East, and gaining some linguistic knowledge. The failed seminarists of that decade—and those like Renan in the next—were frequently men who had been led by their Hebrew studies to yet more exotic interests. When Michelet pondered on India he was confirmed in his conviction of the identity of all mankind. Gobineau was to reach opposite conclusions: but they stemmed from the same interests. [. . .]

Gobineau goes a step further and even claims that the permanence of present racial types is itself the result of the vast amount of climatic energy possessed by the earth when this racial revolution occurred! Original man is equally distinct from each of the new groups. The only signs of common origin among men are a vague resemblance of shape and the facility of hybridisation. Of primal man we have no scientific knowledge: for practical purposes we may ignore him. Thus, having paid lip-service to monogenist theory, Gobineau is now free to work out the consequences of his instinctive leaning towards the opposite argument.

The end-product of this cosmic chaos is the production of the White, Black and Yellow races, each permanent in its characteristics and affected only by hybridisation. Gobineau claims that the terms are not strictly related to skincolouring, but suggests that the latter is a criterion adequate for his purpose. Using the vocabulary of his age, by Whites he means the Caucasian, Semitic and Japhetic races; by Blacks the Hamites; by Yellows the Altaic, Mongol, Finnish and Tartar branches.

The man of Black race is the lowest, marked by animality and limited intellect, but possessing great energy, desire and will. His wild sensuality is the mark of inferiority. He is denoted also by the variability of his moods which make him unaware of the distinctions between vice and virtue. He has little concern for the preservation of his own life, or for that of others, and shows an horrific impassiveness towards suffering.

The Yellow is superior to the negroid and is his antithesis. He tends towards apathy and lacks physical strength. He exhibits none of the moral excesses of the Black, having weak desires and a will which is obstinate rather than extreme. Mediocrity in all things and material enjoyment are favoured by him. He loves utility, respects law, and appreciates moderate liberty. The Yellows prefer theory to practice:

Their desires are limited to living as quietly and as comfortably as they can . . . It is a populace and a bourgeoisie which any founder of civilisation would desire to choose as the basis of his society. Yet it lacks the wherewithal to create that society and give it beauty, energy, and action.[1]

The White is marked by reflective energy or energetic intelligence. He possesses a sense of utility less narrow and more elevated than that of the Yellow. He perseveres in the face of obstacles and has great physical power. His extraordinary instinct for order is a result not of his desire for repose but of his wish for self-preservation. A singular love of life and liberty characterise him. But honour is placed even above life. Though less sensual than the other races, the Whites have superior intelligence. The race is composed of Chamites, Semites, and Japhetides. The true Aryans belong only to the last branch and, having spread from the central Asian plateau, they have formed the Hindu, Iranian, Hellenic, Celtic, Slavonic, and Germanic peoples.

The three races are marked by these permanent intellectual and physiological inequalities, and the White race in particular is possessed of an innate idea of its superiority. All men combine the instincts of moral and material satisfaction and in the most elevated race we come nearest to the happy harmonisation of the two. Each race has conflicting feelings of repulsion and attraction for the others. Race-mixture is brought about by the prevailing influence of the latter. Though such mixture is the vehicle of degeneration it is a necessary evil. For Gobineau stresses that civilisation can only be created by the mixture of the White race with an element of alien blood. Unlike the theories of the later 'gobinists' this is not a racism of absolute blood-purity. Gobineau the pessimist invents a subtler theory whereby the hybridisation which is the creator of civilisation is also the agent of its decadence, for it is in practice impossible to restrain the alien blood within the bounds where it remains fruitful rather than destructive. Civilisation moves to its inevitable degeneration through a stage of extreme activity, to morbid torpor, and on to death. There is little compensation to be found in the fact that mixture frequently improves the lower race. Gobineau's view of art also shows his ambivalent attitude to blood-mixture. The passion of the artistic temperament is a negroid characteristic. The creation of great art needs the combination of reflection and emotion, and is therefore the result of blending the White and the Black. [. . .]

The subsequent treatment of Gobineau's theory was far from what he intended, and he became the inventor of twentieth century racism rather by accident. Gobineau was a theorist of Aryanism rather than of Germanism, and propounded a great mother-race-idea to which Anglo-Saxonism, Teutonism, and even Celticism were all indebted. But, historically speaking, he was most available for German use. Wagner fêted him at Bayreuth, and from the composer, via Schemann, Nietzsche, H.S. Chamberlain, Spengler and Rosenberg, to Hitler there is a chain of intellectual and personal links. Those relationships are another story, but here is a preview of its climax in the pages of *Mein Kampf*:

History shows, with a startling clarity, that whenever Aryans have mingled their blood with that of an inferior race the result has been the downfall of the people who were the standard-bearers of a higher culture . . . Every manifestation of human culture, every product of art, science and technical skill, which we see before our eyes today is almost exclusively the product of the Aryan creative power . . . The Aryan neglected to maintain his own racial stock unmixed and therewith lost the right to live in the paradise which he himself had created . . . That is how cultures and empires decline and yield their places to new formations.

Such words could almost be Gobineau's own. But, whereas the Frenchman had despaired of the world and had withdrawn from it while degeneration triumphed, the German continued to hope. Like Wagner and unlike Gobineau, Hitler trusted in regeneration—and erupted into world politics to achieve it. Never was hope more harmful. From much the same 'facts' about race Gobineau and Hitler drew very different conclusions. But, then, the facts were unimportant; it was the symbol that was the same.

[From 'Gobineau and the Origins of European Racism', *Race*, 7/3 (1966), 256–7, 262–3, 269.]

LEON POLIAKOV

7   **Gobineau and His Contemporaries**

Historical and literary studies about Gobineau since the end of the last century have often speculated about his sources. One curious hypothesis put forward by a German author in 1926 suggested that Gobineau was initiated into the mysteries of race by Disraeli during meetings which might have taken place between them in Paris. A more solidly based attribution was proposed by Jean Boissel, who showed that some of the key ideas of the *Essai sur l'inégalité des races humaines* were derived from Courtet de l'Isle. But however they were transmitted, Gobineau merely systematized in a very personal way ideas which were already deeply rooted in his time. His own contribution consisted mainly in his pessimistic conclusions, which sounded like the death knell of civilization. With a pretence of science, he gave vent to bitterness and disappointment of every kind. He himself admitted that science was for him 'only a means to assuage a hatred of democracy and of the Revolution'. He expressed his message even more clearly in the following phrase in a letter which he sent in 1856 (just after his book was published) to Tocqueville: 'I do not say to people: *you are to be forgiven or condemned*, I say to them: *you are dying*.' [. . .]

The range of Gobineau's reading was vast and he enlisted all the anthropological literature of his time as well as the writings of the leading 'physiologists' in support of his thesis. But, as far as the historical sources of his inspiration are concerned, the Bible must take first place. He followed the Biblical chronology (the human species, if not the universe itself, was five or six thousand years old); he borrowed his essential ideas about mankind from the Book of Genesis. According to him, this dealt only with the white race, which held 'the monopoly of beauty, intelligence and strength'. This race, which had been guided by Providence from the start, had emerged from northern Asia and had divided into three branches, those of Ham, Shem and Japheth (the future Aryans). All three were equally endowed with talents and virtues but, according to Gobineau, the white race was blessed from infancy with 'the two main elements of all civilization: a religion and a history'.

As to the origin of the inferior or 'secondary' coloured races, Gobineau, not wishing either to contradict the old tradition of the Church or to affiliate them to the chosen white race, sought refuge in inconsistency. He admitted, without attaching much importance to it, the existence of 'a man of a first creation called Adam', but he preferred to leave this mysterious personage 'out of the controversy'. In his eyes, an abyss divided this 'Adam' from the black and yellow races which he thought were indigenous to Africa and America respectively. In a word, he was a monogenist in theory and a polygenist in practice.

On the other hand, Gobineau assumed the existence, in all branches of the human species, of a 'racial instinct' which was opposed to cross-breeding ('the law of repulsion'). But the very qualities of the white race, its civilizing urge towards social intercourse and its expansion through conquests, ended up by creating an opposite tendency ('the law of attraction'). It followed that the white race, and therefore civilization itself, were fragile and ephemeral, since these 'alloys' or infusions of inferior blood soon produced devastating effects. The laws of 'historical chemistry' decreed that the mixed 'ternary' or 'quaternary' sub-races must be degenerate. Thus the Hamites were the first to 'saturate themselves in black blood', as a result of expansion and conquest, and became thoroughly degraded. Such was also the destiny of the Semites, though to a lesser degree. Only the sons of Japheth, the Aryans, remained more or less completely pure, at least until the beginnings of the Christian era. Thereafter they too embarked, in the course of their expansion, on the same downhill course.

However, it would be a mistake to think that Gobineau regarded coloured people as objects of contempt or as mere brutes. On the contrary, his judgement of them is surprisingly moderate. He insisted on the gulf which separated them from the great apes, and he reproached the anthropologists of his period for their exaggerations. 'Most scientific observers up to now have displayed a marked tendency to debase the lowest types of humanity more than the facts warrant. Almost all the early information about a tribe of savages portrays it in falsely repellent colours.' He attributed to the Blacks in particular 'a universal force of imagination' which the civilizing Whites did not have and which he saw as the source of all the arts.

The black element is certainly indispensable for developing artistic genius in a race, for we have seen what outbursts of fire, flames, sparks, vivacity and spontaneity are intrinsic to its soul and how much the imagination, that mirror of sensuality, and all cravings for material things prepare it to receive those impressions which are produced by the arts.

As for the Jews, to whom Gobineau attributed relatively unadulterated Semitic blood, his description of them might easily have been inspired by Disraeli. It ends with what is almost a panegyric of the Chosen Race:

The Jews were encircled by groups which, speaking dialects of a language related to their own, also had for the most part quite a close blood-relationship with them. Yet they outstripped all these groups. They appeared as warriors, agriculturalists and merchants. Under a singularly complicated form of government, which reconciled not only monarchy and theocracy but also the patriarchal power of the heads of families and the democratic power of the people as represented in the assemblies and by the prophets, they could be observed moving across the centuries in prosperity and glory and overcoming, by one of the most intelligent systems of emigration, the obstacles to their expansion imposed by the narrow limits of their domain. And of what did this domain consist? Modern travellers are able to assess at what a cost of enlightened effort the cultivators of Israel maintained its artificial productivity. For since this chosen race ceased to inhabit these mountains and plains, the well where Jacob watered his flocks has filled with sand, Naboth's vineyard has been overrun by the desert, and the site of Ahab's palace covered by brambles. What figure did the Jews cut in this miserable corner of the earth? I repeat, they were a clever people in all their undertakings; a strong, a free, an intelligent people who before losing, in courageous combat, the title of an independent nation, had provided the world with almost as many scholars as merchants.

The fact was, as Gobineau informs us later on in his work, that the 'Hebrew, in the alloyage to which his race was subjected, had a greater share in the essence of the Whites' than his neighbours. Indeed throughout his book Gobineau indulged in endless operations of racial blood-counts which were supposed to explain the course of man's history at all times and in all places. Thus the miracle of Greece, with its flowering of art and philosophy, but also its final decline, were due to a mixture of:

1. Hellenes—Aryans modified by yellow elements but with a great preponderance of the white essence and some Semitic affinities;
2. Aborigines—Slavo-Celtic peoples saturated with yellow elements;
3. Thracians—Aryans mixed with Celts and Slavs;
4. Phoenicians—Black Hamites;
5. Arabs and Hebrews—very mixed Semites;
6. Philistines—Semites perhaps of purer stock;
7. Libyans—almost black Hamites;
8. Cretans and other islanders—Semites more or less resembling the Philistines.

Clearly, cross-breeding of the kind described above, when carried on for centuries, could only cause a deterioration of stock; and, if at the beginning of our era the Germanic invasions produced a temporary respite, the Aryan blood which they introduced was soon to be diluted with the old Roman, Hellenistic or Semitic compounds. It comes as a surprise to find in Gobineau's work no analysis of the blood compound which led to the French Revolution. For him all the bloodstreams of the European nations were equally and inextricably mixed. The final chapters of his book are dedicated to a description of the bastardization of the Aryans; nor is any exception made (as is generally thought) in favour of the Germans, who were also contaminated by residual European blood-types as well as by 'Finnish blood'. Still more tragic were the prospects in the New World, whose inhabitants 'are the products of the detritus of all the ages, of Irishmen and Germans thoroughly cross-bred, of some French who are no less so and of Italians who are more so than all the others'. Furthermore, to this mixture would be added before long the blood of Blacks and Indians from which there could only result the 'juxtaposition of the most degraded beings'.

The same fate was in store for the whole world, and the *Essai* concludes with the following peroration:

The white species will disappear henceforth from the face of the earth. After passing through the age of the gods when it was absolutely pure; the age of heroes, in which the mixtures were moderate in strength and number; the age of the nobility, where human faculties remained considerable though they could not be renewed from dried-up sources, it has descended, more or less swiftly according to the environment, to a final confusion of all the elements. . . . The portion of Aryan blood, already subdivided so frequently, which still exists in our countries and which alone sustains the edifice of our society, advances daily towards the last frontier before total absorption. When this result is achieved the age of unity will have been reached . . . this state of fusion, far from being a consequence of the direct marriage of the three great archetypes in their pure state, will be no more than the *caput mortuum* of an infinite series of mixtures and, consequently, of attenuations. It will be the last stage of mediocrity in all its aspects; mediocrity in physical strength, mediocrity in beauty, mediocrity in intellectual aptitudes, one might almost say annihilation.

Gobineau believed that he could assess the duration of this final stage. Since the flowering of civilization had lasted five or six thousand years, its decline, which had begun several centuries ago, would probably continue for a similar period. Three or four millennia should therefore 'precede the final spasm of our species, when the lifeless earth will continue, without us, to describe its apathetic orbits in space'.

One finds the same lugubrious poetry in Gobineau's letters, as for instance in the passage quoted above: 'I do not say to people: *you are to be forgiven or condemned* (and he added: "I am no more a murderer than the doctor who says that the end is near"); I say to them: *you are dying* (and he added: "Winter is coming and you have no sons").' Such visionaries as Saint-Simon and August Comte— and Ernest Renan with reservations—hoped that a worldwide racial fusion would open up an era of harmonious happiness, an undefined form of eternal life for the human race, thus secularizing the ancient Christian hope of the *parousia*. With Gobineau, who thought himself a good Catholic, any hope of a second coming of the Christ-Messiah had definitely disappeared and the human race had no other prospect than complete annihilation. In this sense his disciples have not misinterpreted him. He was indeed the great herald of biological racism, a man in whom regressiveness seemed to be inspired by the desire to lead humanity back to its point of departure. [. . .]

[From *The Aryan Myth: A History of Racist and Nationalist Ideas in Europe* (London: Chatto, Heinemann for Sussex University Press, 1974), 233–8.]

Section II

Institutional Forms of Racism: Slavery, Imperialism, and Colonialism

INTRODUCTION

The phenomenon of racism on a global scale has deep historical roots. Ever since the earliest migrations brought different ethnic groups into contact with each other, relations of power, domination, exploitation, conflict, and war have existed between them. The outcomes have been very different in different eras and in different parts of the world, but a common consequence has been institutionalized forms of racism in relations between different racial and ethnic groups. For example, the treatment of Indian Americans on the North American continent, or Aboriginal people in Australia, has been characterized by assumptions of racial superiority on the part of white settlers, and behaviour toward the indigenous population which treated this group as inferior and expendable. Slavery in the Western hemisphere and European colonization of other parts of the world outside Europe have created forms of racism which are at the heart of the phenomenon in history. This section provides only a sketch of this long historical background, but it highlights some salient points. Understanding this long historical past is essential for grasping racism in the contemporary world.

Nowhere is this more so than in relation to the institution of slavery. Slavery was not universally a product of racism, in the sense that the institution existed in ancient Greece and Rome, where its basis was not primarily racial at all. The first extract, from David Brion Davis, is a reminder that slavery was also a feature of relations between Muslim Arab nations in what is now the Middle East, and Africans on the east coast of that continent. Arab slavery in East Africa preceded the European slave trade across the Atlantic. In the medieval period, the Muslim world acknowledged the qualities of the civilizations of India and China, but regarded black Africans living to the south as inferior savages. To them, the blackness of Africans suggested sin, damnation, and the devil. The biblical curse of Canaan was constantly invoked to explain why black people could be degraded to the status of slaves as punishment for their ancestor's sin. As Davis suggests, there was a good deal in common between these early Muslim views of Africans, and the Christian justifications for the enslavement which underpinned the much more substantial Atlantic slave trade in black Africans which flourished between the sixteenth and the early nineteenth centuries.

Winthrop Jordan's extract deals with English ideas about Africans in the Elizabethan period, before the importation of black slaves into Britain's American colonies had become strongly established. He points to the association of blackness with negative characteristics, 'the handmaid and symbol of baseness and evil, a sign of danger and repulsion'. This may partly explain why black Africans, in contrast to English indentured servants or native Americans already living there when colonists arrived, were thought particularly suited to being enslaved, and how justifications for the slave trade were often couched in this way, often with a Christian theological gloss. There is no extract dealing with the slave trade as such, but the experience of those captured in Africa epitomized the human degradation involved in being sold into slavery. The notorious 'middle passage' involved domination, disease, and death for many, under inhuman conditions. The change in status emphasized to those enslaved that they were to be treated as less than human from now on.

In the following piece, George Fredrickson emphasizes the inadequacy of ideas alone in explaining the character of black American slavery, and focusing upon the American colonies and the United States, suggests that America was from an early period a genuinely racist society, with a rigid racial stratification buttressed and strengthened by a racist ideology. This contrasts with a Latin American colony such as Brazil (see extract 11 by Genovese and extract 41 in Section VI), where the colour line was not completely rigid, and innate racial differences were not the overriding consideration in all social situations. Fredrickson tackles the very important chicken-and-egg issue of which came first: slavery or racism. Did the institution of slavery lead to racism, or did racism in turn lead to the enslavement of a particular group, black Africans? This has been much debated by historians; due weight is given here to the hypothesis that transported African people became the object of virulent prejudice because they alone of all the minorities in colonies such as Virginia had been enslaved.

In this early period in the American colonies, there were variations and inconsistencies in social practices, so much so that it was only in the eighteenth century that full-fledged societal racism emerged, followed later by a full-fledged ideological justification. Many eighteenth-century explanations for supposed black inferiority were environmentalist, positing climate or social factors in support of the conclusion. Only in the early nineteenth century, according to Fredrickson, did proponents of slavery develop an explicit theory according biological inferiority to slaves, to counter growing humanitarian sympathy with slaves' conditions, and the beginnings of Abolitionism.

In the political economy of racism, social scientists have argued extensively about the relative importance of race and class as underpinning the exploitation of black slaves. The chapter by Eugene Genovese contrasts North American and Latin American slavery, in the light of the historical theses of a substantial difference between them put forward by Frank Tannenbaum and Stanley

Elkins. The original thesis stressed the different colonial history in countries like Brazil, and the influence of Catholicism compared to Protestantism. Genovese puts the emphasis upon the character of the ruling class, seigneurial in Brazil, more bourgeois in the southern states of the United States. The triumph of racism, he argues, was more complete in the American South than in any other part of the New World.

Orlando Patterson's piece is more theoretical. Drawn from a comparative study of the institution of slavery everywhere, including the ancient world, he argues for viewing slavery as an extreme form of domination and exploitation, characterized by a parasitic relationship between slave owners and slaves, and more generally between the dominant whites and the enslaved blacks. This is a two-way relationship of dependence, even though one party holds power of life or death over the other. He places less emphasis in the last resort on the political economy of slavery, and more on the power relations upon which the institution of slavery rested.

The slave trade was declared illegal by the major colonial powers during the first half of the nineteenth century, and American slaves were freed at the end of the American Civil War in 1865. The gradual disappearance of slavery as such, however, did not bring to an end forms of unfree labour which retained many of the features of a parasitic relationship between proprietors and landless workers, and strongly reinforced societal racism. In the American South, for example, various forms of share cropping and debt peonage tied freed slaves to rural agriculture. A monograph on the export of Indian indentured labourers overseas throughout the British Empire in the period from 1820 to 1920 has the title *A New System of Slavery* (Tinker 1974). The legal ending of the institution of slavery by no means meant the end of racism, indeed in some respects it may have led to its accentuation, since its legal protection was less secure.

Racism in the colonial empires of the European powers from the seventeenth to the twentieth centuries was less clear cut, but was ever present, and its historical legacy is a key to understanding more recent relations between white, brown, and black ethnic groups in the contemporary world. Moreover it took different institutional forms under different conditions, so that the relations between colonizer and colonized were established differently in countries such as South Africa, Nigeria, or British India. The brief extract from Victor Kiernan's *The Lords of Human Kind: European Attitudes toward the Outside World in the Imperial Age* touches on European attitudes towards the peoples of the areas from which Atlantic slaves were drawn. The book itself ranges much more widely over India, China, the Far East, the South Seas, Africa, and Latin America, all areas in which European dominion or influence was felt in the Imperial age.

Philip Mason goes further in the next piece; he offers a typology of forms of domination in the colonial world, in relation to the type of colonial regime and size of the European minority in the society. This is offered as part of a debate with sociologists Michael Banton and Pierre van den Berghe about how to characterize colonial societies in terms of domination, paternalism, or competition. Although this is a very compressed discussion of a wide range of historical situations, it conveys how non-European peoples were subordinated to Europeans, to a greater or less extent, and how racism was both a means of maintaining that dominance and a product of the dominance in reinforcing the European sense of superiority and control over their subject peoples.

One particular form of society which appeared in certain colonial societies was the 'plural society', to use the term invented by the scholar of Burma J. S. Furnivall. The plural society was stratified less horizontally than vertically, with the racial groups (whites, commercial middleman minority, indigenous people) forming vertical pillars with separate powers and rights (the indigenous people having least), economic and political differentiation between the pillars, and lack of social and institutional integration between the three pillars. Such plural societies were characteristic of the West Indies and Guyana, parts of South-East Asia (especially Malaya and the Dutch East Indies), Fiji, Mauritius, Kenya, Uganda, Natal, and certain other cases. M. G. Smith, in his extract, highlights features of Caribbean society around the time of its gaining independence. Contrary to Furnivall, who saw plural societies being integrated only in the market place, Smith saw integration taking place only under the political authority of the colonial power or the newly independent country, and it was only power which held the disparate parts together. The relevance of this theoretical discussion about a particular type of society to racism is indirect but crucial. In such a fragmented structure, does it make sense to speak of a single society? Do the members share a common sense of belonging? What holds the society together? A vivid example of the effects of racism occurred in post-independence Uganda, when General Idi Amin expelled the entire Indian middleman commercial minority from the country, in pursuit of Africanization and racial antipathy to this relatively privileged predominantly middle-class ethnic group. Race hatred dissolved the society, and spread the former Asian Ugandans to many parts of the English-speaking world.

The final voice in this historical section is that of a French-speaking West-Indian who worked in Algeria, Frantz Fanon, analysing the situation of the colonized. The colonial world he portrays is divided into the colonizer and the colonized, them and us, and he perceptively analyses the movement toward decolonization which spread through the Third World in the quarter-century after the end of the Second World War in 1945. The paragraph on p. 118 beginning 'The town belonging to the colonised people, the Negro village, the medina, the reservation, is a place of ill fame …' evokes the condition of what he terms 'the wretched of the earth' in that polarized society, and states some of the aspirations of the colonized to be free of their colonial rulers. Logically, this extract might more properly be placed in the next section, on Racism in the Twentieth Century, but it provides a fitting closure to the discussion of the roots of racism in the colonial world created by the European powers.

8 The Expansion of Islam and the Symbolism of Race

In some ancient languages the word for 'slave' simply connoted labor or service. In other languages, however, the word referred at first to the foreign origin of captives, even if it later extended, as in the Third Dynasty of Ur (2345–2308 B.C.), to in-group debt slaves and children who had been sold by their parents. In ancient India the word *dasa* originally referred to the dark-skinned Dravidian people conquered by Aryan invaders. It later came to mean 'slave,' even though fewer Dravidians seem to have ended up in slavery than in the lowest rungs of the caste system or, worst of all, in the ritually unclean category of untouchables. By the Buddhist period slavery had lost its ethnic connotations and a *dasa* could well be light-skinned.[1]

The origin of the European variants of 'slave' presents a somewhat different transition from ethnic reference to a generalized category of 'enslavable barbarian.' During the late Middle Ages, the Latin *servus* and other ethnically neutral terms gradually gave way to *sclavus*, the root of *schiavo, esclavo, esclave, sclau, Sklave,* and 'slave,' all meaning a person of 'Slavic' origin. According to Charles Verlinden, *sclavus* had as early as the tenth century become legally synonymous with 'slave' in the parts of Germany through which pagan Slavic captives were transported to Muslim Spain. But this usage virtually disappeared with the decline of the Umayyad dynasty and the eclipse of the overland trade in slaves to the west. Italian merchants continued to buy large numbers of genuinely Slavic prisoners along the Dalmatian coast, but only in the thirteenth century did they begin to tap one of the most continuously productive sources of slaves in human history—the peoples from Caucasia to the eastern Balkans who were repeatedly subjugated by invaders from Central Asia. Representing a multitude of languages and cultures, these captive Armenians, Circassians, Georgians, Abkhazians, Mingrelians, Russians, Tatars, Albanians, and Bulgarians were no more a distinct people than were the 'Negroes' who later ended up as American slaves. By the early thirteenth century, however, these 'Slaves,' who were highly prized in Egypt, Syria, Cyprus, Sicily, Catalonia, and other Mediterranean markets, had begun to transform the European words for chattel slaves, as distinct from native serfs. Italian notaries applied the label *sclavus* not only to non-Slavic peoples from the Black Sea but also to Muslim captives from such reconquered regions as Majorca and Spain. In 1239 a Corsican notary used *sclava* in recording what Verlinden interprets as the sale of 'une négresse captive.' The rapid extension of *sclavus* to people of non-Slavic origin suggests a growing assumption that true slavery was appropriate only for pagans and infidels who shared the supposed characteristics of 'Slavs,' which were almost identical with the later 'sambo' stereotype of North American blacks. Since Portugal remained on the periphery of the Slavic slave trade but became increasingly involved in religious warfare with Muslim North Africa, the word *escravo* had to compete with such terms as *mouoro*, *guineu*, and *negro*. Later on, the French *noir* and English 'black' became virtual synonyms for 'slave.' Much earlier, the Arabic word for slave, *'abd*, had come to mean only a black slave and, in some regions, to refer to any black whether slave or free.[2]

In antiquity, however, bondage had nothing to do with physiognomy or skin color. It is true that various Greek writers insisted that slavery should be reserved for 'barbarians,' but they considered Ethiopians no more barbarous than the fair Scythians of the north. Skin color and other somatic traits they attributed to the effects of climate and environment. Although it would appear that the ancients put no premium on racial purity and were unconcerned with degrees of racial mixture, we still have much to learn about the changing origins and status of black slaves. The first difficulty arises from the vagueness of such ancient designations as 'Ethiopian' and 'Kushite' as well as the more modern label 'Negro.' As a result of nineteenth-century racist theories, scholars have long contrasted the supposedly superior craniology of 'Nilotic types' with the prognathism and facial angle of 'pure Negroes.' Such a 'mismeasure of man,' to use Stephen Jay Gould's phrase, is not only arbitrary but generally assumes that cultural differences are determined or can be explained by physical traits.[3] Of all the myths surrounding slavery and human progress, none has been more insidious and enduring than the image of sub-Saharan Africans as a single, benighted race condemned to a perpetual coma of savagery except when infused, on the northern fringes of the Dark Continent, with the blood or inspiring example of Eurasian peoples.

We now know that the peoples of prehistoric Africa, like those of other continents, migrated over immense geographic regions, created rich and highly diverse cultures, and developed trading networks that spanned much of the continent. The desiccation of the vast Sahara region had, by the third millennium B.C., increasingly isolated the central and western Sudan from the early civilizations of the Mideast. But African farmers south of the Sahara were the first to domesticate the sorghums and millets that later became valued crops in the Mideast. The southward diffusion of agriculture and cattle husbandry, to say nothing of the rapid spread of metallurgy, especially ironworking, throughout West Africa, provide ample evidence of adaptive and intercommunicating cultures. For the Egyptians, Phoenicians, Greeks, and Romans, however, sub-Saharan Africa remained a land of legend and fantasy, sharply differentiated from the familiar North African states and colonies from the Nile to the Maghrib.

It is of considerable importance that the Nile offered the only corridor between the Mediterranean and the African tropics, providing continuous contact with blacks who had long interacted with the urban civilizations of Egypt and the Mideast. Judging by the surviving iconography, blacks exhibiting a diversity of physical traits were numerous in Egypt after the fifteenth century B.C. Many of these blacks were portrayed as enemy warriors or captive slaves.

But dark-skinned Nubians ruled Egypt during the Twenty-fifth, or 'Ethiopian,' Dynasty and later built temples and pyramids at their capital city, Meroë, above the fifth cataract of the Nile. As the crossroads of African, Asian, and Mediterranean cultures, the Nile valley clearly hastened ethnic and genetic intermixture; but only in racially conscious modern times would it seem important to insist that Nubians, Kushites, or even Ethiopians were not 'true Negroes.' If some classical writers looked upon blacks as primitive people who lived in a torrid land inhabited by crocodiles, giraffes, and leopards, they saw nothing incongruous about armies of disciplined black warriors or such black pharaohs as Taharqa, whose features later generations would identify as unmistakably 'Negroid.' The crucial point, which was transmitted to medieval Europe, was the association of blacks with ancient Egypt.

In Egyptian and especially Hellenistic sculptures, murals, mosaics, plaquettes, masks, phials, vases, and jewelry, one encounters a complete spectrum of 'Negro' types. They include musicians, dancers, acrobats, boxers, jugglers, grooms, gladiators, charioteers, household servants, and soldiers. Insofar as these images depicted actual models and were not mere variants on artistic conventions, most of the models may well have been slaves. If so, the dignity and expressive individuality with which they were usually portrayed stand in marked contrast to the racist stereotypes of later slave societies. Such iconographic evidence does not prove that the ancient world was free from racial prejudice. It does suggest, however, that there was no conventional equation between blackness, slavery, and limited human capability. Throughout antiquity, of course, black slaves were an exotic rarity amid massive populations of Asian and European captives.

The eventual diaspora of African slaves depended on innovations in transport, such as the Arab dhows and Iberian caravels and three-masted carracks that opened the East and West African coasts to long-distance seaborne trade. Although the evidence is fragmentary, the initial innovation may well have been the westward spread of the camel and North Arabian saddle. Camels had been domesticated in southern Arabia and Somalia as early as the third millennium B.C., but, according to Richard W. Bulliet, it was sometime between 500 and 100 B.C. that the invention of the North Arabian saddle provided riders with a secure mount above the camel's hump, bracing them for combat with swords or spears. Though horses were superior for warfare, camels could traverse deserts where horses might perish; for carrying heavy loads camels also proved to be cheaper and more efficient than horse-drawn carts. Throughout the Mideast camels gradually replaced wheeled vehicles as the ordinary means of transport, and camel-breeding nomads gained control of commercial networks that stimulated the growth of such caravan cities as Mecca. During the first centuries of the Christian era, this camel-breeding nomadism appears to have spread westward from the Upper Nile along the southern tier of the Sahara to Darfur, Borku, Tibesti, and on to Mauretania. In Roman North Africa camels were sometimes used for plowing or for hauling carts, but the trans-Saharan caravan trade was developed by Bedouins, Berbers, and other camel-riding nomads who transported gold, ivory, and exotic African commodities from the Sudan to Egypt, from the Fezzan to Tripoli, and from the upper Niger to Morocco, to name only three of the shifting commercial routes. Despite the paucity of direct evidence, it is probable that well before Islam these desert caravans included black slaves who travelled mainly on foot but who were dependent on food and water carried by camel-riding merchants. The camel (often combined with horse cavalry) gave nomads a military advantage over the sedentary peoples of the Sahel and the upper savanna, and also provided the means for long-distance travel across deserts that had blocked the various Mediterranean invaders of North Africa.

Religions of Mideastern origin tended to spread along the southern and western routes of trade. For example, merchants in search of aromatic gums carried Judaism and Christianity into Ethiopia; much later, Islam advanced southward in Africa mainly as a traders' religion. Although all three faiths helped to justify the enslavement of nonbelievers, as distinct from foreigners, neither the Talmud and rabbinic Mishnah, nor the Christian patristic literature, nor the Qur'an and Muslim holy law suggested that blacks were inferior beings suited by nature for bondage. Indeed, rabbinic sources distinguished the cursed descendants of Canaan from the black descendants of his brother Cush, who had supposedly established prosperous kingdoms south of Egypt. Ephraim Isaac notes that 'in some Jewish sources both the children of Shem (including the Israelites) and the children of Ham [the father of Cush, Mizraim, Put, and Canaan] were described as black; the first as "black and beautiful", the latter as "black like the raven." ' Rabbis spoke of the beauty of Moses' Kushite (or Ethiopian) wife, of the black Queen of Sheba, and of Solomon's Kushite scribes. The famous passage in the Song of Songs 'I am black but beautiful, O ye daughters of Jerusalem,' appears to have read, in the Hebrew and earliest Greek versions, 'I am black *and* beautiful.' According to Jean Marie Courtès, Origen established the framework for later Christian exegesis when he interpreted this black 'bride' as the Church of the Gentiles, prefigured by Moses' marriage to an Ethiopian wife, a symbolic 'union of the spiritual Law with the Gentile nations, which in turn foreshadowed the universal Church.' The rabbis were no less inclined to associate the conversion of Ethiopia with the glorious Day of Judgment. Commenting on the passage in Psalms 'Gifts shall come out of Egypt; and Ethiopia shall soon stretch out her hands ["or offerings"] unto God,' they imagined Ethiopians asking, in Ephraim Isaac's translation, 'If the Messiah received gifts from the Egyptians who enslaved [the Israelites] how much more will he not receive from us who have never subjected them to slavery? In reaction to this, other nations will follow the Ethiopians in bringing our gifts and paying homage to the Messiah.'⁴

For early Christians, Ethiopia represented the most remote and dramatically 'other' nation of the known world. In the New Testament the first baptism of a non-Jew occurs when Philip the deacon, traveling south through the Gaza desert, encounters an Ethiopian eunuch riding in a chariot. The eunuch, who held 'great authority' under Ethiopia's Queen Candace and was in charge of her treasure, had been to Jerusalem to worship at the Temple. Philip's conversion and baptism of the Ethiopian became an enduring symbol for Christianizing the world. The theme appeared in Christian iconography from the third century on and was especially popular in northwestern Europe in the sixteenth and seventeenth centuries. The mixture of races in early Christian Egypt probably reinforced the appeal of universal evangelism. For example, Saint Menas, the patron saint of Alexandria, was sometimes depicted with 'Negroid' features on the ampullae sold to pilgrims; in the Nubian states, which became Christianized during the seventh and eighth centuries, Menas appeared for a time as a black warrior-protector, similar to Saint George. By the end of the fourth century, Ethiopian Christians were making pilgrimages to the Holy Land. Ethiopian Christians also captured infidel white slaves in the Arabian Peninsula and supplied black slaves to the labor markets of the Lower Nile. By the seventh century, when Islam began expanding beyond Arabia, the presence of numerous black slaves in Egypt and the Mideast by no means suggested that bondage was becoming a racial institution. And for Muhammad and his early Arab followers, some of whom referred to themselves as 'black,' all human beings were potential converts and brethren; skin color could not signify either a sinful or a pious soul.

It is probable that color symbolism derived in part from astrology, alchemy, Gnosticism, or various forms of Manichaeism influenced Christian and Muslim attitudes toward black people. Until far more research has been done on this subject, one must be extremely cautious in relating black demonology to any changes in the actual enslavement or treatment of Africans. It is clear that patristic writers equated 'Ethiopians' with the cosmic forces of sin and darkness and hence with the human struggle for redemption and salvation. Origen, the head of the catechetical school in Alexandria in the early third century, introduced into patristic literature the allegorical themes of Egyptian blackness and spiritual light. Didymus the Blind, who in the fourth century held the same position in Alexandria that Origen had previously occupied, asserted that 'those who fall beneath the stroke of God's sword are the Ethiopians, because they all share in the malice and sin of the Devil, from whose blackness they take their name.' He also spoke of the necessity of 'wounding' the Ethiopians for their own good and pictured their loss of 'sonship with the Devil' as a cleansing and washing that would make them 'whiter than snow.' Jean Marie Courtès and Jean Devisse have documented the prevalence in early Christian symbolism of Ethiopian demons and tempters, often described as ugly and evil smelling, who represented the spirit of vanity, idolatry, or fornication. The fact that Nubian and Ethiopian Christians adhered to the Monophysite doctrine that Christ has a

single nature strengthened the image of heresy in Byzantine and Roman eyes, an image later confirmed by Africa's association with Islam. As Devisse puts it: 'The linking together of the four ideas—black, other, sinner, dangerous—runs throughout all the manifestations of medieval Western Christian thought. The Saracen, the 'enemy' in the epic poems, and the bird that distracts the saint at prayer are black.' Gernot Rotter has also shown that Arab writers, sometimes drawing on astrological theories, depicted terrifying demons with 'Negroid' traits and described gigantic Africans 'as black as Satan.⁵

But the association of blackness with death, danger, evil, and grief has been common to many cultures, and it is simplistic to assume that such symbolism accounts for the growing Muslim and Christian conviction that black Africans were in some way 'made' to be slaves. The first objection, as we have already seen, is that 'Slavs' and other light-skinned peoples were said to have all the slavish characteristics later attributed to black Africans. The second objection is that color symbolism is usually abstract, ambiguous, and reversible. The black devils and demons of early Christian iconography were usually pure fantasies, as devoid of ethnic traits as the medieval Black Madonnas; yet in medieval Europe, which Islam had largely sealed off from Africa, specifically 'Negroid' blacks were depicted among the resurrected saints on the Day of Judgment and as camel drivers or attendants in scenes of the Adoration. [. . .]

Color symbolism, like the garbled interpretations of the biblical curse of Canaan, provided additional justification for new patterns of enslavement shaped by the Islamization of the trans-Saharan caravan trade. For devout Muslims the crucial and troublesome question was who could legally be enslaved. Apart from Christian enemies who might be ransomed by their brethren, the answer increasingly focused on pagan Africans or on blacks of presumably pagan origin. Ironically, by enslaving or converting so many blacks and by imposing a barrier to Europe's direct knowledge of sub-Saharan Africa. Muslims contributed to Christian ignorance, mythology, and the tendency to identify blacks with Christianity's mortal and 'infidel' enemy.

[From *Slavery and Human Progress* (New York: Oxford University Press, 1984), 32–9.]

WINTHROP D. JORDAN

9 First Impressions: Initial English Confrontation with Africans

When the Atlantic nations of Europe began expanding overseas in the sixteenth century, Portugal led the way to Africa and to the east while Spain founded a great empire in America. It was not until the reign of Queen Elizabeth that Englishmen came to realize that overseas exploration and plantations could bring home wealth, power, glory, and fascinating information. By the early years of the seventeenth century Englishmen had developed a taste for empire and for tales of adventure and discovery. More than is usual in human affairs, one man, the great chronicler Richard Hakluyt, had roused enthusiasm for western planting and had stirred the nation with his monumental compilation, *The Principal Navigations, Voyages, Traffiques and Discoveries of the English Nation*. Here was a work to widen a people's horizons. Its exhilarating accounts of voyages to all quarters of the globe constituted a national hymn, a scientific treatise, a sermon, and an adventure story.

English voyagers did not touch upon the shores of West Africa until after 1550, nearly a century after Prince Henry the Navigator had mounted the sustained Portuguese thrust southward for a water passage to the Orient. Usually Englishmen came to Africa to trade goods *with* the natives. The earliest English descriptions of West Africa were written by adventurous traders, men who had no special interest in converting the natives or, except for the famous Hawkins voyages in the 1560's, in otherwise laying hands on them. Extensive English participation in the slave trade did not develop until well into the seventeenth century. Initially English contact with Africans did not take place primarily in a context which prejudged the Negro as a slave, at least not as a slave of Englishmen. Rather, Englishmen met Africans merely as another sort of men.

Englishmen found the peoples of Africa very different from themselves. 'Negroes' looked different to Englishmen; their religion was un-Christian; their manner of living was anything but English; they seemed to be a particularly libidinous sort of people. All these clusters of perceptions were related to each other, though they may be spread apart for inspection, and they were related also to the circumstances of contact in Africa, to previously accumulated traditions concerning that strange and distant continent, and to certain special qualities of English society on the eve of its expansion into the New World.

The Blackness Without

For Englishmen, the most arresting characteristic of the newly discovered African was his color. Travelers rarely failed to comment upon it; indeed when describing Africans they frequently began with complexion and then moved on to dress (or, as they saw, lack of it) and manners. At Cape Verde, 'These people are all blacke, and are called Negroes, without any apparell, saving before their privities.' Robert Baker's narrative poem recounting his two voyages to the West African coast in 1562 and 1563 introduced the people he saw with these engaging lines:

> And entering in [a river], we see
>   a number of blacke soules,
> Whose likelinesse seem'd men to be,
>   but all as blacke as coles.
> Their Captain comes to me
>   as naked as my naile,
> Not having witte or honestie
>   to cover once his taile.

Englishmen actually described Negroes as *black*—an exaggerated term which in itself suggests that the Negro's complexion had powerful impact upon their perceptions. Even the peoples of northern Africa seemed so dark that Englishmen tended to call them 'black' and let further refinements go by the board. In Shakespeare's day, the Moors, including Othello, were commonly portrayed as pitchy black and the terms *Moor* and *Negro* were used almost interchangeably. With curious inconsistency, however, Englishmen recognized that Africans south of the Sahara were not at all the same people as the much more familiar Moors. Sometimes they referred to West Africans as 'black Moors' to distinguish them from the peoples of North Africa.

The powerful impact which the Negro's color made upon Englishmen must have been partly owing to suddenness of contact. Though the Bible as well as the arts and literature of antiquity and the Middle Ages offered some slight introduction to the 'Ethiope,' England's immediate acquaintance with 'black'-skinned peoples came with relative rapidity. People much darker than Englishmen were not entirely unfamiliar, but really 'black' men were virtually unknown except as vaguely referred to in the hazy literature about the sub-Sahara which filtered down from antiquity. Native West Africans probably first appeared in London in 1554; in that year five 'Negroes,' as one trader reported, were taken to England, 'kept till they could speake the language,' and then brought back again 'to be a helpe to Englishmen' who were engaged in trade with Africans on the coast. Hakluyt's later discussion of these Africans suggests that these 'blacke Moores' were a novelty to Englishmen. In this respect the English experience was markedly different from that of the Spanish and Portuguese who for centuries had been in close contact with North Africa and had actually been invaded and subjected by people both darker and more 'highly civilized' than themselves. The impact of the Negro's colour was the more powerful upon Englishmen, moreover, because England's principal contact with Africans came in West Africa and the Congo, which meant that one of the lightest-skinned of the earth's peoples suddenly came face to face with one of the darkest.

In England perhaps more than in southern Europe, the concept of blackness was loaded with intense meaning. Long before they found that some men were black, Englishmen found in the idea of blackness a way of expressing some of their most ingrained values. No other color except white conveyed so much emotional impact. As described by the *Oxford English Dictionary*, the meaning of *black* before the sixteenth century included, 'Deeply stained with dirt; soiled, dirty, foul. . . . Having dark or deadly purposes, malignant; pertaining to or involving death, deadly; baneful, disastrous, sinister. ... Foul, iniquitous, atrocious, horrible, wicked. ... Indicating disgrace, censure, liability to punishment, etc.' Black was an emotionally partisan color, the handmaid and symbol of baseness and evil, a sign of danger and repulsion.

Embedded in the concept of blackness was its direct opposite—whiteness.

No other colors so clearly implied opposition, 'beinge coloures utterlye contrary':

> Every white will have its blacke,
> And everye sweete its sowre.

White and black connnoted purity and filthiness, virginity and sin, virtue and baseness, beauty and ugliness, beneficence and evil, God and the devil. Whiteness, moreover, carried a special significance for Elizabethan Englishmen: it was, particularly when complemented by red, the color of perfect human beauty, especially *female* beauty. This ideal was already centuries old in Elizabeth's time, and their fair Queen was its very embodiment: her cheeks were 'roses in a bed of lillies.' (Elizabeth was naturally pale but like many ladies then and since she freshened her 'lillies' at the cosmetic table.) An adoring nation knew precisely what a beautiful Queen looked like.

> Her cheeke, her chinne, her neck, her nose,
> This was a lillye, that was a rose;
> Her bosome, sleeke as Paris plaster,
> Held upp twoo bowles of Alabaster.

By contrast, the Negro was ugly, by reason of his color and also his 'horrid Curles' and 'disfigured' lips and nose. A century later blackness still required apology: one of the earliest attempts to delineate the West African as a heroic character, the popular story *Oroonoko* (1688), presented Negroes as capable of blushing and turning pale. It was important, if incalculably so, that English discovery of black Africans came at a time when the accepted English standard of ideal beauty was a fair complexion of rose and white. Negroes seemed the very picture of perverse negation.

From the first, however, many English observers displayed a certain sophistication about the Negro's color. Despite an ethnocentric tendency to find blackness repulsive, many writers were fully aware that Africans themselves might have different tastes. As early as 1621 one writer told of the 'Jetty coloured' Negroes, 'Who in their native beauty most delight, / And in contempt doe paint the Divell white'; this assertion became almost a commonplace. Many accounts of Africa reported explicitly that the Negro's preference in colors was inverse to the European's. Even the Negro's features were conceded to be appealing to Negroes.

[From *The White Man's Burden: Historical Origins of Racism in the United States* (New York: Oxford University Press, 1974), 3–7.]

10 Social Origins of American Racism

The term *racism* has become a source of considerable confusion. In its limited, precise, and original sense, racism is 'the doctrine that a man's behavior is determined by stable inherited characters deriving from separate racial stocks and usually considered to stand to one another in relations of superiority and inferiority.' Racism, according to this definition, is a matter of conscious belief and ideology and can be distinguished from prejudice, which is a matter of attitude or feeling, and discrimination, which is a description of behavior. In recent popular discussion, however, racism has tended to lose this original meaning and to become synonymous with patterns of action that serve to create or preserve unequal relationships between racial groups. This, for example, is the sense in which the expression *white racism* is now commonly used. One way to bridge the gap between the academic and the popular meanings of the term *racism* is to distinguish between the explicit and rationalized racism that can be discerned in nineteenth- and early twentieth-century thought and ideology and the implicit or societal racism that can be *inferred* from actual social relationships. If one racial group acts as if another is inherently inferior, this is racism in the second sense, even if the group may not have developed or preserved a conscious and consistent rationale for its behavior. As will be plain from the historical survey to follow, implicit racism can exist without explicit racism; indeed, events in the twentieth century suggest that societal racism can continue to thrive long after ideological racism has been discredited in the educated circles of a dominant group. Nevertheless, explicit or ideological racism is of some historical importance and merits attention. By giving legitimacy to pre-existing patterns of racial subordination, it strengthens a system and enables it to counter serious ideological challenges, such as those which emanated from the democratic revolutions of the eighteenth century and from the rise of bourgeois democracy.

This dual definition of racism is broad, but not so broad as to make it impossible to distinguish between genuinely racist societies and other inegalitarian societies that may be manifestations of racial prejudice and discrimination but that nevertheless cannot be described as racist in their basic character. Most members of one racial group in a certain kind of biracial or multiracial society may be in a de facto subordinate situation, even in slavery, and unfavorable stereotypes about this group may be part of the dominant race's mythology. Yet such a society is not racist in the full sense of the word if the resulting status differences can readily be justified on nonracial grounds—as part of a generalized belief in social hierarchy, for example—and if the discrimination for reasons of color is not consistently and universally applied to individual members of what is, in a statistical sense, the socially inferior group. If some members of this group can, despite their physical characteristics, achieve high status because of such attributes as wealth, education, and aristocratic culture, there is evidence of the overriding importance of nonracial status criteria. In such a situation, race becomes only one factor in determining status, an attribute which can be outweighed or neutralized by other factors. Students of comparative race relations will readily recognize that the pattern just described is one many observers have found to be characteristic of the biracial or multiracial societies of Latin America. The Brazilian phrase 'money whitens' sums up the values of a society for which race is far from irrelevant as a basis of social classification but which nevertheless does not draw a rigid color line or sanction behavior that could be justified *only* on the grounds that blacks or mulattoes are innately inferior to whites.

Unlike Brazil and other Latin American countries, the United States has been a genuinely racist society. On the whole it has treated blacks as if they were inherently inferior, and for at least a century of its history this pattern of rigid racial stratification was buttressed and strengthened by a widely accepted racist ideology. Although few would deny that explicit or ideological racism—the formal doctrine of inherent biological inferiority—became popular at a relatively late date in American history, recent historians have tended to see implicit or societal racism as having sprung up very early, partly because of certain preexisting European attitudes toward blacks which gave a special character to the natural antipathy of English settlers toward any people who were obviously strange and different. In this essay, I examine this proposition critically with an eye to shedding some light on the following question: To what extent was America really born racist as a result of pre-existing attitudes and to what extent did it become so as a result of social, economic, and political developments that took place well after the colonists' initial contacts with Africans?

It is clear that among Englishmen there was indeed a vague prejudice against blacks even before the first colonists set foot in North America. As a result of early contacts with Africa, Englishmen tended to associate blackness with savagery, heathenism, and general failure to conform to European standards of civilization and propriety. Contributing to this predisposition to look upon Negroes with disfavor were the conscious and unconscious connotations of the color black. The association of black with evil was of course deeply rooted in Western and Christian mythology; it was natural to think of Satan as the Prince of Darkness and of witchcraft as black magic. On the unconscious level, twentieth-century psychoanalysts have suggested, blackness or darkness can be associated with suppressed libidinous impulses. Carl Gustav Jung has even argued that the Negro became for European whites a symbol of the unconscious itself—of what he calls 'the shadow'—the whole suppressed or rejected side of the human psyche. The rudiments of such a complex may have manifested themselves in Elizabethan England. A tendency to project upon blacks the kind of libidinous sexuality that whites tried to suppress in themselves would certainly have been helped along by a hazy and inaccurate knowledge of African sexual practices and by a smirking consideration of what was implied by the fact that many Africans went around completely or virtually naked. In Shakespeare's *Othello*, Iago pursues his vicious campaign against the Moor by skillfully playing on associations of blackness with bestial sexuality, as well as on a sense of the unnaturalness of interracial union. He tells Desdemona's father, for example, that 'an old black ram / Is tupping your white ewe' and that his daughter is 'covered with a Barbary horse.'

There is no question, then, that sixteenth- and seventeenth-century Englishmen were predisposed to accept an unfavourable stereotype of the black character. But how significant is this as an explanation for the development of societal racism in the colonies? Recent sociological investigations suggest that there is no simple cause-and-effect relationship between stereotyped opinions about a given group and discriminatory actions or policies. It is quite possible for individuals to have a generalized notion about members of another race or nationality that bears almost no relation to how they actually behave when confronted with them.[2] To provide a contemporary example, many Americans who lived through World War II developed an extremely unfavourable set of stereotyped opinions about Germans and Japanese, and as long as the war lasted, these opinions were salient and action oriented. These stereotypes did not dissipate immediately at the end of the war, but they ceased almost immediately to be a reliable index of behavior. Individual Germans and Japanese could now be encountered without great tension or embarrassment, and support could readily be aroused for ties with Germany and Japan that seemed to benefit the United States. What had changed was that Americans had ceased to feel threatened by Germans and Japanese.

If a reduction of fear leads to greater tolerance, its increase promotes hostility. Phillip Mason, the British authority on race relations who first discerned the racial implications of *Othello*, has contended that 'fear may . . . act as a catalytic agent' in the creation of racial feeling, 'changing the nature of factors previously not actively malignant, such as the association of the metaphor of the ideas of white and black with good and evil.'[3] It seems likely that the stereotypes about blacks and blackness held by some Englishmen on the eve of colonization were opinions casually held—beliefs that were 'not actively malignant' and that would not, under all circumstances, have led directly to societal racism. Good evidence that this was indeed the case comes from a study of domestic servitude in Great Britain in the eighteenth century. Although servants from the continent were the object of widespread hostility, blacks were popular with the British lower classes and benefited from an 'almost complete lack of racial bias.'[4] The most obvious explanation for this state of affairs would seem to be that there was no sense of a threat from the blacks, whereas the continental servants were associated with countries of origin that were international rivals of Great Britain.

The story of white–black relations in seventeenth-century America is the story of an evolution toward societal racism. This development was not simply the consequence of a priori attitudes or stereotypes, for here as elsewhere a catalytic agent was required, and as usual the catalyst was fear, a fear that can be described in social terms.

In order to comprehend what occurred, it is necessary to confront the vexed question of the relationship between slavery and racism and to take account of the chicken-and-egg debate among historians over which came first in the southern colonies, slavery or racial prejudice. The basic facts, as near as they can be determined, would seem to be these: between 1619 and the 1640s, a small number of blacks were introduced into Virginia as 'servants.' Some, and perhaps most, of these early arrivals were freed after a limited term of service, somewhat in the manner of indentured servants (indigent white immigrants who were bound to service for a limited period in payment for their passage to the New World). By the 1640s, two trends had become evident: *some* blacks, but no whites, were in fact being held in servitude for life; and fragmentary evidence suggests that discriminatory practices seemed to set black servants off from whites of similar status—for example, Negro women, unlike white women, were apparently used for field work, and a Virginia statute of 1640 enjoined masters to provide arms for all their servants except Negroes. By the 1660s, the status of slavery for some blacks was recognized in law and the first legislation was passed bearing on the subject of interracial marriage and sex relations.

It is extremely difficult to say which came first, whether slavery preceded rudimentary forms of racial discrimination in Virginia or vice versa. Winthrop Jordan has probably drawn the safest conclusion that can readily be deduced from such data by arguing that slavery and race prejudice 'may have been equally cause and effect, continuously reacting upon each other, dynamically joining hands to hustle the Negro down the road to complete degradation.'[5] But perhaps the entire debate, in which Jordan provides what is clearly the last word, is based on dubious premises. It has been assumed that the early development of black slavery among English colonists in Virginia requires special explanation because slavery in a strict sense no longer existed in Great Britain at the time of settlement. But a comparison with other early seventeenth-century British colonies suggests that the remarkable thing about Virginia was that all immigrants were *not* regarded as slaves from the beginning. It seems likely that the ten blacks who arrived in Barbados with the first shipload of white settlers in 1627 were enslaved. In any case, the governor and the council of the island proclaimed in 1636, when there were still only a relatively small number of blacks, that all Negroes would serve for life unless they had specific contracts of indenture. Similarly, the first blacks to arrive in the Massachusetts Bay Colony in 1638 seem to have been regarded as slaves, although at that time, as we have seen, there was still some ambiguity about the status of blacks in Virginia.

How can we explain this tendency of other colonies to assume from the beginning that Negroes were slaves, despite the lack of positive law affirming such a condition? First of all, it must be recognized that although slavery was not sanctioned in the domestic law of Great Britain and did not in fact exist as a social condition, neither was it expressly prohibited. As late as 1547 a law had been passed in England enslaving vagabonds. It had proved unworkable and was repealed purely on economic grounds, because other forms of labor were cheaper. There is no reason to assume that if slavery, even white slavery, had appeared profitable in seventeenth-century England, it would not have been introduced. It actually took a series of judicial decisions in the changed ideological context of the eighteenth century to establish that slavery was contrary to English common law. Before that time, there was no general bias against slavery as a condition; it was widely assumed that, by one means or another, most men must be compelled to work, and that coercion was the mainspring of any economic system. Furthermore, international law in the seventeenth century regarded slavery as licit and as a proper condition for those who could be defined as captives of war, particularly if they happened to be heathens. This was the 'legal' basis of the participation of countries like Great Britain and the Netherlands in the international slave trade, which was justified as a legitimate commerce in those captured in African wars. It is no mystery, then, that when blacks arrived in most colonies, even those of countries that no longer had slavery at home, they were readily seen as enslavable because of their origin in the international trade in heathen captives. To explain what happened, we do not, therefore, have to assume that whites were driven by intense racial prejudice. That blacks were physically vulnerable to enslavement, that there was no deep-seated bias against the institution, and that there was an actual or anticipated need for labor could be explanation enough for the development of black slavery in the colonies of European nations such as Britain, the Netherlands, and France, each of which, unlike Spain and Portugal, no longer practiced slavery at home.

Hence there would seem to be no obvious reason why the first blacks who arrived in Virginia were not automatically and universally regarded as slaves and held lifetime servitude. They were products of the international slave trade and, unlike most white immigrants, had neither a 'free' background nor contracts of indenture. Possible explanations for the fact that many were freed after a limited term of service might include simple ignorance of their international status or the lack as yet of any plans for general dependence on unfree black labor. Conversion to Christianity may have been the path to freedom for some Africans, since it was not definitely determined until later that converts could be enslaved. In any case, it would appear that what really needs to be explained is not that some blacks, of those who arrived before 1640, were held to lifetime servitude, but that some acquired free status despite their background and the presence of selfish economic motives tempting white masters to take advantage of their de facto vulnerability.

It would, of course, be absurd to argue that ethnic prejudice played no role in the gradual degradation of blacks that took place in Virginia. Ethnocentrism— the tendency to discriminate against the stranger, the alien, the physically different—is a virtually universal phenomenon in group contacts, and it is not surprising that there were some early examples of this in Virginia. But Marvin Harris is probably close to the mark when he contends that 'the Negroes were not enslaved because the British colonists specifically despised dark-skinned peoples and regarded them alone as properly suited to slavery; the Negroes came to be the object of virulent prejudices because they alone could be enslaved.'[6] In seventeenth-century Virginia, the vulnerability of blacks, as well as international precedent, probably made them seem the logical candidates for enslavement, even before there was any large-scale dependence on their labor (Virginia did not in fact become a slave plantation society until the end of the century). And a case can still be made for the thesis that 'virulent prejudices,' as compared to milder forms of ethnocentrism and stereotyping, followed in the wake of enslavement and probably did not take full possession of the white mind until slavery had become fully established as the basis of the economic and social order. Earlier examples of what some historians have taken as indications of virulent prejudice are in fact ambiguous. Although Virginia passed a law in 1662 imposing a special fine for interracial fornication, it did not get around to banning interracial marriages until 1691. In Maryland, where slavery and discrimination developed along nearly the same lines as Virginia, a law was passed in 1664 that Winthrop Jordan has described as having 'banned interracial marriages.'[7] Actually it only banned marriages between 'Negro slaves' and 'freeborne English women.' It said nothing about marriages between whites and free blacks, and it was explicitly motivated by a desire to prevent the offspring of unions between indentured servant women and male slaves from following the condition of the mother, as prescribed by law, and eventually becoming free.

Indeed most evidence of 'full-throated indignation against miscegenation' before the 1690s can be explained in large part as a manifestation of the traditional desire to prevent intermarriage between people of different social stations, something that could be very inconvenient to masters of slaves and servants. The resulting legislation was also a clear indication that marriage with Negroes, even Negro slaves, was not deeply repugnant to 'freeborne English women.' If it had been, no law against it would have been necessary. Actually, the tangled and complex history of Maryland's efforts to regulate interracial marriage from 1664 to 1715 provides some strong indications that a deep-seated repugnance to intermarriage on grounds of race alone was slow to develop. The act of 1664 sought to prevent the marriage of white women and Negro slaves because of the legal complications developing from such unions, but the law did not clearly state that such marriages could not take place; it merely prescribed that the women involved, and their children, should henceforth be slaves themselves. Far from preventing interracial liaisons, the law actually encouraged them, because it now became advantageous to masters to use their influence to bring about such unions. 'Hence,' reports a historian of the Negro in Maryland, 'the terms of [white] servant women were brought up and the women themselves were married to slaves apparently with a view to invoking on them the penalties just recited.'[8] Here then were southern slaveowners who were willing for their own economic advantage to connive for the marriage of white women and black men and, what was more, for the reducing of 'freeborne' whites to slavery in a way that was incompatible with the notion that slavery was based strictly on race. In 1681 another law was passed, designed not so much to prevent interracial marriages as to save white servant women from being reduced to slavery. This law merely exempted such women from the prescribed penalty for marrying a Negro slave when it could be demonstrated that the marriage had been contracted at the instigation of the master. But interracial marriages between white servant women and black slaves apparently continued to occur in Maryland until the early eighteenth century.

Another kind of evidence for the delayed development of societal racism in the Chesapeake colonies can be deduced from what we know about the status of free blacks. If free blacks and mulattoes are treated in a way that is not flagrantly discriminatory, then it is clear that actual status and not race per se is the basic determinant of social position. Such appears to have been generally the case in seventeenth-century America. As might be expected, the most unequivocal evidence of such a state of affairs can be found in northern colonies that were not evolving toward a slave-based economy. One study of the Negro in seventeenth-century Massachusetts indicates that free blacks were accorded the same basic rights as whites and were the victims of no significant, discernible social or economic discrimination. Even slaves enjoyed a semblance of equal rights before the law.[9] For Virginia the picture is less clear, because late in the century the status of free blacks was already undergoing a change that would eventuate in the quasi-freedom or lower-caste status characteristic of free blacks in the eighteenth and nineteenth centuries. Although we cannot determine with any accuracy how many free blacks there were in Virginia in the late seventeenth century, they may have comprised a larger portion of the total black population than they would at any subsequent time during the slave era. The origins of this class were diverse. Some became free after serving a definite term or were the descendants of beneficiaries of the early tendency to regard black servitude as similar to white indentured servitude. Others were 'manumitted' after slavery had become a recognized institution (it is significant that private manumission was common until the 1690s, when the first efforts were made to discourage it). Still others, as in Maryland, were the mulatto children of white mothers, who were free at birth.

Before the eighteenth century, free blacks in Virginia apparently had little difficulty in acquiring property or exercising an equal right to vote; some even took legal action against whites or held minor public offices. In short, they seem, for most purposes at least, to have been recognized members of the community. A few became substantial landowners and had slaves of their own. Free blacks were even permitted to own white servants before 1670; indeed, the law passed in that year prohibiting the practice was perhaps the first significant piece of legislation that infringed on their rights. A historian of the free Negro in Virginia had concluded that during the seventeenth century free blacks had 'social privileges about equal to those accorded to freed white servants. A few were prosperous owners of personal and real property, respected by white persons, dealt with by white men in business relations, and permitted to participate in elections. . . . At that time the theory that the Negro was fit for nothing but slavery or some servile capacity had not been so carefully elaborated nor so generally applied as it was in the eighteenth or nineteenth century.'[10] In fact, there would seem to be grounds for arguing that Virginia before the 1690s was not a consistently racist society, despite the presence of black servitude; its racial pattern may have resembled the Latin American model as much as it did the rigidly hierarchical biracialism that later developed.

In the 1690s, however, the situation began to change dramatically. Intermarriage was outlawed, and the first restrictions were placed upon private manumission of slaves. In the eighteenth century, and particularly after an act passed in 1723, free blacks were formally deprived of many of their rights, including the right to vote. This transformation of the free Negro group from a participating element of the community into a pariah class obviously paralleled the transformation of Virginia into a slave plantation economy. Before the 1680s, white indentured servants had provided most of the colony's labor. After that time the shift to a slave-based economy took place very rapidly, largely as a result of the expansion of British slave-trade activity, which meant that slaves were offered in larger numbers and at better prices than previously. Although there was undoubtedly a prior trend toward the degradation of all blacks because of the enslavement of most of them, the final decision to relegate all free blacks to lower-caste status was probably stimulated principally by the growing fears and anxieties of what was now a slaveholding society. Certainly one of the main justifications presented for discrimination against free blacks and for the effort to prevent growth of this class by restricting manumission was the belief that Negroes who were not slaves would provide an unfortunate example for those in servitude and would use their freedom of action to encourage insurrections. As the slave population grew rapidly after 1700, such fears became more intense and led not only to further efforts to limit and control the free black population but also to the elaboration of the severe slave code that served to distinguish North American slavery from its Latin American counterpart.

Comparison with Latin America, however, suggests the need for a further explanation for the growth of societal racism in the slave-based colonies of British North America. In Brazil, for example, a slave plantation economy developed without such intense efforts to prevent manumission and to degrade free people of color. Marvin Harris has attempted to explain this difference by reference to demographic factors. Unlike Brazil, Virginia had from the beginning a relatively large nonslaveholding white population. This population was able to provide necessary services for the slaveholders that in Brazil could only be performed by free blacks and mulattoes. The nonslaveholding whites of the South were available for putting down insurrections, catching runaways, and patrolling plantation areas; for employment as overseers; and for auxiliary economic activities such as raising and herding livestock. In Brazil, according to Harris, such functions were generally performed by free men of color. In short, the free blacks of the colonial and antebellum South had no role to play that would contribute in any way to the security and profitability of the plantation system.[11] Such an interpretation is very persuasive and obviously possesses considerable validity. But Harris's tendency to find the origins of racism almost exclusively in the conscious efforts of the master class to manipulate the nonslaveholders does not fully explain the depth and the apparent spontaneity of the racial feeling that developed.

The different lines of development in Latin America and British North America might be explained by the contrasting social structures within which plantation slavery was accommodated. Spain and Portugal were still fundamentally feudal societies when they established their American colonies. Those who emigrated and became colonial slaveholders were imbued with the conviction that society was an elaborate but clearly defined hierarchy of mutually dependent corporate groups or estates. To their way of thinking, slaves were simply the lowest-ranking group in the hierarchy. If a man ceased to be a slave, it did not mean that he became equal to those at the top, only that he moved up to the next highest rank. The complex system of social differentiation that evolved in Latin America can be seen as an adaptation of medieval concepts of social order and hierarchy to a multiracial situation. In plantation societies, the system meant that those at the bottom were mostly or exclusively black, while those at the top were at least defined as white; in the middle ranks was a range of mixed-blood categories. But an individual could in fact belong to a social class that was predominantly of another physical type if he had the necessary social and cultural characteristics.

The British settlers in North America came from a society undergoing a transition from a traditional medieval social structure with a hierarchy of corporate groups to a capitalist society with an emphasis on competing individuals and a tendency to divide society into two principal classes: a hard-working and productive middle class—'the industrious sort of people'—and a mass of unworthy poor, the dregs of the emerging social system. One spokesman for the rising social and political values of early seventeenth-century England described the poor as 'rogues, beggars, vagabonds,' members of a 'cursed generation' who should be punished and forced to work.[12] The precise attitudes of the earliest

Virginia masters toward their white servants—who were often drawn from the lowest levels of British society—cannot be determined, but they probably partook to some extent of the increasingly virulent contempt of propertied Englishmen for the lower classes. If so, it would have been difficult for them to see black slaves as much lower on the scale of humanity. But it seems probable that the ability of white servants to gain their freedom in the New World and, because of the plenitude of land, to become freeholders rapidly tended to undercut the sense of a huge social chasm between whites, especially in the period before a plantation aristocracy emerged. This leveling process and the gradual decline in the importance of white servitude eventually made the blacks the only conspicuous local examples of a despised lower class that allegedly had to be coerced into working. The existence of universal male suffrage in Virginia before 1670, when property restrictions were imposed by the Crown, was perhaps indicative of the rough sense of equality that developed in the early period. By the end of the century, however, discernible class divisions were developing among free whites, not so much because of the impoverishment of the lower class, which remained by and large an independent yeomanry, but because of the ability of a small number of families to engross land and slaves and take on some of the trappings of an aristocracy. But free whites who had once thought of themselves as equal to anyone in the colony were probably unwilling, to say the least, to accept the notion that they had a clearly defined inferior status.

If this was in fact the situation, we have the ingredients of full-fledged societal racism. From the point of view of the 'aristocracy' there was a functional need to incorporate nonslaveholding whites into the social order on some basis other than that of an acknowledged hierarchy of corporate groups with differing privileges, for such a social ideal was inapplicable to the relatively egalitarian American setting. From the vantage point of nonslaveholders there was a natural tendency to project upon the blacks their own suppressed sense of inferiority as a way of gaining or retaining a sense of status. If this analysis is valid, it would help explain the ostentatious effort to relegate the highest black to a status below that of the lowest member of the dominant race; it would also account for the origins of the persistent emphasis in the South on race as the foundation of a kind of pseudo-equality among whites. Here indeed might be found the basis of the powerful mythology that would later serve to guarantee a consensus in favor of slavery and racial subordination.

Although societal racism—the treatment of blacks as if they were inherently inferior for reasons of race—dates from the late seventeenth and early eighteenth centuries, a rationalized racist ideology did not develop until the nineteenth century. This gap of more than a hundred years between practice and theory can be explained in various ways. First of all, full-fledged racist thought required a change in the conception of man and his relation to the natural world. It took the eighteenth-century Enlightenment to replace the traditional view of man as a child of God who stood above the rest of creation with an image of man as a physical being who was part of the natural world. The new emphasis on the physical side of human nature led to the first systematic efforts to classify the races and to provide scientific explanations of the differences among them. Nevertheless, the dominant eighteenth-century view was that racial characteristics were not innate but were rather the result of environmental factors, such as climate and social habits. The environmentalist theory of human differences, combined with the natural-rights philosophy, led during the era of the American Revolution to an intellectual assault on the institution of slavery, an assault that contributed to the triumph of gradual emancipation in the North and provoked some soul-searching in the South. But the new biological concept of man, with its emphasis on the importance of physical characteristics, could also be used to support the idea that blacks were inherently inferior, a different order of beings from whites and therefore not entitled to the same rights. The view that blacks were created permanently unequal was enunciated by a minority of theorists in the eighteenth century, including the Englishmen Lord Kames and Charles White and the Negrophobic Jamaican planter Edward Long. But despite the fact that Jefferson speculated in the 1780s about the possibility that blacks were inherently inferior in some respects to whites, no one in the United States actually defended institutionalized inequality on the basis of racial theory until well into the nineteenth century.

Societal racism did not require an ideology to sustain it so long as it was taken for granted. Until the revolutionary era no one had seriously challenged slavery and black subordination in the southern colonies. During and after the Revolution there was a challenge of sorts, but the most recent historical studies suggest that it was half-hearted and ineffectual. Even those, like Jefferson, who talked about the abolition of slavery as desirable or even necessary could do so only on the assumption that somehow the southern black population would be removed after being freed, because it was unthinkable that large numbers of the two races could live together in the same territory in a state of mutual freedom. In the absence of a serious political and intellectual challenge to the implicit assumptions of southern biracialism, slaveholders found that they could protect their interests merely by encouraging the belief that emancipation was impractical or, if pushed, by standing firm on their 'rights' as owners of slave property. After all, a basic natural right for which the Revolution had been fought was the right of property.

Obviously, however, the egalitarian philosophy that had been made part of the American creed by the language of the Declaration of Independence carried a long-range threat to slavery and racial caste, a threat that had only briefly surfaced during the revolutionary era before being temporarily put to rest by the Constitution's provisions recognizing the existence of slavery and providing for its protection. In the 1830s, the application of the concept of equal rights to blacks was made with a new evangelical immediacy by the northern abolitionists who, unlike their colonizationist predecessors, not only argued that slavery was an evil but also demanded that blacks be freed immediately and granted full legal equality. This assault, from William Lloyd Garrison and his followers, on the foundations of societal racism forced proslavery southerners and their northern sympathizers to develop and promulgate a racist theory that accorded with their practice.

In a pamphlet entitled *The South Vindicated from the Treason and Fanaticism of the Northern Abolitionists* (1836), William Drayton of South Carolina presented a concise statement of the newly articulated proslavery doctrine: 'Personal observation must convince every candid man, that the Negro is constitutionally indolent and prone to vice; that his mind is heavy, dull, and unambitious; and that the doom that has made the African in all ages and countries, a slave—is the natural consequence of the inferiority of his character.'

As long as the traditional order, societal racism, was not challenged by a radical ideology calling for revolutionary change, it was not necessary to bring ideological consciousness to social assumptions. Before the abolitionists forcefully demanded consistency in the application of egalitarian ideals, it was even possible to subscribe in a general way to an egalitarian philosophy without confronting directly the contradiction between such a creed and the acceptance of slavery and racial discrimination. Once the abolitionists had thrown down the gauntlet, however, proslavery apologists had two choices: They could either reject egalitarianism entirely, as did George Fitzhugh and other theorists of southern paternalism, or they could define blacks as members of another, subhuman species and retain the entire egalitarian, natural-rights philosophy as a white prerogative. The latter view achieved the greater popularity because of its obvious appeal to the nonslaveholding classes of the South and because it could win converts in the North as well. In 1860 William Yancey, the militant Alabama secessionist and fire-eater, told a northern audience, 'Your fathers and my fathers built this government on two ideas: The first is that the white is the citizen and the master race, and the white man is the equal of every other white man. The second idea is that the Negro is the inferior race.'[13] That northerners had discriminated increasingly against their own free blacks during the prewar period of rising white democracy was probably the basis of Yancey's expectation that his doctrine would find favor above the Mason-Dixon line. Northern Democrats of that era even vied with southern proslavery politicians to see who could give the greatest boost to the white ego by repeating ad nauseam that blacks were inherently and unalterably inferior to 'the master race' and were therefore suited only for slavery.

Explicit racism, a public ideology based on the doctrinaire conception of the black man as a natural underling, developed therefore directly out of the need to defend slavery against nineteenth-century humanitarianism. The appeal of this doctrine in the North and the degree to which it eventually contaminated even some of the opponents of slavery are complex subjects that can only be touched on here. In a period when the sweeping egalitarianism associated with the age of Jackson was underlining most social and political distinctions, frightened northern conservatives were led to emphasize racial distinctions as one remaining barrier that could be defended, and they were often aided and abetted by insecure lower-class whites who longed for some assurance of their own status, a sense that they were superior to someone, if only by virtue of the color of their skin. When, by the 1850s, an expansive southern 'slavocracy' was seen as a threat to the northern way of life, the tentacles of racist thought and feeling had gained such a stranglehold that many northern opponents of the extension of slavery carefully disassociated themselves from the abolitionists and their ideal of racial fraternity and argued that theirs was exclusively a white man's cause. That northerners could oppose slavery without a commitment to racial equality helps explain why the Civil War resulted in the emancipation of the Negro from slavery but not from caste discrimination and the ravages of racism.

Racist thought did not reach its crescendo until the end of the nineteenth century, when it latched on to Darwinism—a more convincing scientific support than the earlier theory that blacks had been created separately by God before Adam and Eve had begotten 'the superior white species.' But pseudoscientific Darwinian racism did not differ from the pre-Civil War variety in its basic assumptions about the differences between blacks and whites. What gave the reformulated doctrine its new virulence was its association with an aggressive southern campaign for the legal segregation and disfranchisement of the blacks who three decades earlier had been freed from slavery.

In the modern era a campaign mounted against ideological racism, it has had considerable success. Societal racism, however, has retained much of its strength, and its persistence has prevented the full achievement of racial equality.

In short, it can be said that the long story of the development of American racism, first as a way of life and then as a system of thought, suggests that social forces have played a key role. Subliminal and deeply rooted psychological factors were undoubtedly present, but they can hardly explain the extent to which racial feeling and ideology have been developing and changing, subject to situational variations in intensity and character. America, I would conclude, was not born racist; it became so gradually as the result of a series of crimes against black humanity that stemmed primarily from selfishness, greed, and the pursuit of privilege.

[From *The Arrogance of Race: Historical Perspectives on Slavery, Racism, and Social Inequality* (Hanover, NH: Wesleyan University Press, 1988), 189–205.]

11 Class and Race

I

Modern slavery and the white-black confrontation form part of a single historical process, but it does not follow that slavery can best be understood as a race question. No major problem in the socioeconomic transformation of Western society, apart from the pattern of race relations itself, could possibly be resolved on such grounds. Even the War for Southern Independence, the one major problem that historians have tried to interpret from the point of view of the race question, cannot be satisfactorily dealt with in this way, if for no other reason than that racial hegemony did not require slavery, as many contemporaries clearly understood. To affirm the priority of a class interpretation need not lead us to underestimate the force of racism, much less to expect the automatic or even rapid disappearance of racism in the event of a radical alteration in the class nature of society. As Pierre van den Berghe writes: 'Race is only a special case of more general social facts, [and] it follows that there can be no general theory of race and that race relations must be placed within the total institutional and cultural context of the society studied.'[1] We have been proceeding in agreement with this line of argument but have also been viewing class formation, confrontation, and struggle as the essential dynamic of that historical context.

The work of David Brion Davis and Winthrop D. Jordan demonstrates that Western European prejudice against black people predated and facilitated African slavery, although neither of these scholars would try to establish a causal link. As Jordan writes:

It was the case with English confrontation with Negroes, then, that a society in a state of rapid flux, undergoing important changes in religious values, and comprised of men who were energetically on the make and acutely and often uncomfortably self-conscious of being so, came upon a people less technologically advanced, markedly different in appearance and culture. From the first, Englishmen tended to set Negroes over against themselves, to stress what they conceived to be radically contrasting qualities of color, religion, and style of life, as well as animality and a peculiarly potent sexuality. What Englishmen did not at first realize was that Negroes were potentially subjects for a special kind of obedience and subordination which was to arise as adventurous Englishmen sought to possess for themselves and their children one of the most bountiful dominions of the earth. When they came to plant themselves in the New World, they were able to find that they had not entirely left behind the spirit of avarice and insubordination. Nor does it appear, in light of attitudes which developed during their first two centuries in America, that they left behind all the impressions initially gathered of the *Negro* before he became pre-eminently the *slave*.

He adds:

The concept of Negro slavery there [in Virginia and Maryland] was neither borrowed from foreigners, nor extracted from books, nor invented out of whole cloth, nor extrapolated from servitude, nor generated by English reaction to Negroes as such, nor necessitated by the exigencies of the New World. Not any one of these made the Negro a slave, but all.[2]

Jordan, in his own terms, locates the origins of English racism in the transitional character of society. In our terms, he is locating it within the position of the bourgeoisie, which provided the historical conjuncture for the prevailing social ethos, myths and prejudices, and unfolding economic opportunity.

Once slavery came into being, ethnocentricity and color prejudice passed quickly, although perhaps not immediately, into racism. At that, it required the division of the world among the great Caucasian powers and the attendant vogue of Social Darwinism during the second half of the nineteenth century for a fully developed racist ideology to emerge and conquer the Western world. If scholars like Eric Williams, Marvin Harris, and Herbert Aptheker err in making racism a direct product of slavery, they err less than those who would simply invert the relationship. Previous ideological conditioning made possible a racially based slavery, and the growth of that kind of slavery transformed the conditioning from a loose body of prejudices and superstitions into a virulent moral disorder. Boxer puts it well: 'Modern Portuguese writers who claim that their compatriots never had any feelings of colour prejudice or of discrimination against the African Negro, unaccountably ignore the obvious fact that one race cannot systematically enslave members of another for over three centuries without acquiring a conscious or unconscious feeling of racial superiority.'[3]

The historical bond which held together the second serfdom in Eastern Europe, the quasi-enserfment of the Amerindians, and the enslavement of the blacks manifested itself culturally, as most clearly illustrated by the passion for the French language and for a cosmopolitan culture among the lords of Eastern Europe, who tried in every way possible to put maximum distance between themselves and the despised lower classes. The social function of racism stands out no matter what kind of causal link one tries to establish between economic exploitation and ideology. In Caio Prado's words:

Racial differences, particularly when manifested in such clear somatic traits as color, will, if not create—an opinion open to well-founded doubts, and in my view one which had been incontestably controverted—at least accentuate a discrimination already made on the social level. . . . Racial features give an unmistakeable stamp to existing social differences. They label the individual, helping to raise and strengthen the barriers that separate different classes. Any approach or blending of the classes thus becomes much more difficult, and the domination of one over the other is accentuated.[4]

One might, like Harmannus Hoetink, read the record differently and argue for the centrality of somatic-norm images—for the importance of the aesthetic dimension, as determined by the relative degree of pigmentation in different European peoples.[5] For a class interpretation of the history of slavery, such a reading could be assimilated with one qualification: prejudice, even if seen as deriving from biological and aesthetic factors, would have to be linked to discrimination and the genesis of racist ideology by some such mechanism as Prado describes.

The specific patterns of race relations in the former slaveholding societies of the New World represent the totality of each particular historical and ecological experience. During the slave period three main patterns emerged: that of the Southern United States, that of the Anglo-French Caribbean, and that of Brazil (see chart below). These differences in pattern, presented here schematically and with deliberate simplification in order to dramatize a few main points, can only be accounted for by a combination of historical and ecological influences. Only hopeless romantics think that Brazil is or has ever been free of racial discrimination, but it does present a striking contrast to the United States. Some

Southern United States	Anglo-French Caribbean	Brazil
Caste system		
Two-caste system of whites and Negroes, the latter defined as anyone with some (amounts varied) Negro blood.*	Three-caste system of whites, blacks, and coloreds (those of mixed blood).	Fluid racial system: so many categories of mixture among three races that only the 'pure' were clearly delineated.
Class structure		
Negro = slave. Free Negroes generally a pariah people with limited social functions.	Roughly, coloreds formed a free middle class of traders, artisans, small farmers, etc. In fact, some were slaves and many others planters, bourgeois, and professionals who were divided from whites by caste, not class; others shared class position of poorer whites.	Small producers, artisans, tradesmen, overseers, etc., generally drawn from a wide range of mixed bloods.
Race relations		
Virulent racism, probably weaker among slaveholders than other sections of the whites.	Strong race prejudice, softened by distinction made by whites between colored and blacks.	Prowhite bias but minimum race prejudice. Acceptance, with qualifications, of blacks and various coloreds according to class position: 'Money whitens the skin.'

* I use the term 'blood,' of course, only as a conventional device.

recent scholars, most forcefully Harris,[6] have pointed out that the position of the Brazilian whites as a small portion of the population forced them to build up a colored middle stratum in society to fill roles that, in the Southern United States, could be filled by nonslaveholding whites. This important insight does not suffice to explain the range of responses, for the same might be said of the Anglo-French Caribbean, in which rigid lines were drawn on a three-caste rather than a two-caste basis. The religious, ideological, institutional, and psychological inheritance, stressed excessively by Tannenbaum, Freyre, and Elkins, makes strong claims at this point. This inheritance included Roman Catholic universalism and institutional prerogatives, long contact with Africa and Moorish occupation, and a living slaveholding tradition in law and custom.

The conjunction of historical and immediate socioeconomic factors in the determination of the Brazilian pattern is summed up by Roger Bastide:

Present-day Brazil offers the world a classic example of racial democracy; but, to understand it, the roots of that democracy must be sought in Brazil's past history as a slavestate. The affective relationships which have grown up between whites and Negroes are the outcome of: (a) the ethos of the Portuguese colonists, who belonged to a population which had already intermingled with the Moors in the home-country, and who came, at least at the outset, without white women . . .; (b) the colony's social and economic system (rural patriarchy, latifundia and single-crop agriculture) which brought about the dispersal of the whites over vast stretches of territory and, by obliging them to live among slaves, tended to create a certain solidarity, at least between the master and his negro nurse, his servants in the Casa Grande, and his coloured mistresses. These two factors, taken together with Portuguese Catholicism . . . provide all the material needed for an understanding of Brazil's racial democracy. But this paternalistic rural solidarity began to change in the second half of the eighteenth century when the masters moved to the coastal towns. These towns, instead of bringing the races together, set them further apart. . . . However, miscegenation had already gone too far, and the influence of Catholicism had become too strong, for the vertical mobility of the mulatto to be ended. . . .[7]

We might file a number of objections immediately. The significance of the Portuguese ethos must be evaluated in the light of the impressive evidence of brutality toward blacks in Angola and Mozambique, and the significance of the role of the Church must be evaluated against the undeniable power of the senhores de engenho over the local clergy. Wherever we find slaveholding classes with bourgeois rather than seigneurial origins, we generally find a tendency toward more intense racism. It is a happy coincidence for Hoetink's thesis that Protestantism and capitalism first emerged in the Anglo-Saxon countries, in which the somatic-norm image has been furthest removed from black. Coincidence or no, we need not deny some validity to the assertion of a biological-aesthetic dimension to racism to insist on the greater force of other factors. Even in Brazil a correlation appears between greater race prejudice and capitalist development: the patriarchal Northeast generally displayed greater racial integration than the South. During the abolition crisis of the 1880s, the proslavery party, rooted in the coffee-growing South, unleashed an unprecedented barrage of racist propaganda and appeals to color prejudice. As capitalist industrialization and urbanization advance in Brazil, more evidence of racial discrimination appears. Perhaps the uncovering of evidence increases, rather than the discrimination, but there is enough evidence of deterioration to cause worry.[8]

We therefore find ourselves buffeted between two views. The first stresses the historical background and institutional-moral inheritance and interprets Brazilian discrimination as essentially the result of class rather than racial bias; the other stresses the economic and demographic setting and considers discrimination simultaneously and inextricably a matter of class and race. Undoubtedly, much work needs to be done, but it ought to be apparent already that both historical and immediate factors had to be filtered through the institutions appropriate to specific ruling classes if they were to have force. Color prejudice, blood pride, and other forms of ethnocentricity preceded slavery and prepared the way for racism, understood as an ideology of oppression and subordination. The transition from the former to the latter occurred by means of such institutionalized mechanisms of discrimination as the slave codes, the plantation regime, and the organized caste restrictions against freedmen. But whereas in some societies these discriminations lost some or much of their force after general abolition, in the United States abolition reinforced them. All slave societies displayed racist tendencies, the specific strength of which varied in response to both historical and ecological influences. The strength of the Tannenbaum interpretation, relative to that of Harris, lies in its flexibility, for the former can absorb the latter, whereas the latter rejects historical influences on principle. The extent and depth of racism under slavery depended primarily on the degree to which the slaveholding class acquired a pure or seigneurial character, in contradistinction to a bourgeois character. This character, in turn, grew out of both historical and immediate conditions. The Portuguese background, for example, had its role, but it developed one way in the patriarchal Brazilian Northeast, where it had room to expand, and quite another way in Angola, where a system of capitalist exploitation distorted and limited it from an early date.

During the slave period in all countries intensification of racial antipathy followed commercialization and the ascendancy of bourgeois slaveholding classes. Hubert H. S. Aimes refers to 'the time honored policy of Spain which had for its end the assimilation of blacks into the white race,'[9] and we can accept this formulation despite the many qualifications that ought to be introduced. For much of the early colonial period the Crown tried to maintain racial segregation, but largely for reasons of political and social control. This attempted use of segregation ran afoul of religious sentiments and long-standing ethnic attitudes and could never be enforced with a rigor adequate to its purpose. The appearance of anything akin to Anglo-Saxon racism followed commercialization and bourgeois development, notably in Cuba, where it reached epidemic proportions during the sugar boom of the nineteenth century.

The United States made the worst of both possible worlds. At the very beginning the slave South imported a Protestant, bourgeois, Anglo-Saxon tradition with strong racist overtones. The high level of commercialization during the colonial period reinforced the practices associated with the tradition. From this point on we might have expected a sharp clash between this virulent racism and the paternalistic plantation ethos, and in fact one did develop. Tocqueville pointed out that racial antipathies were deeper in those parts of the country where slavery had been abolished than in those where it had been retained, and recently Eugene H. Berwanger, in his study of the Western frontier during the secession crisis, has made a strong case for the contention that they were deepest in those parts where slavery had never existed.[10] In the South it was a common observation that the planters had much less aversion to Negroes than did the nonslaveholders. When Fitzhugh denounced the abolitionists as enemies of the blacks and insisted that slavery was not essentially a race question, he expressed the logic of that side of the Southern background with which he identified. The softening force of the plantation ethos, which was inherently racist but much less so than its bourgeois counterpart, did not prevail owing to the unique combination of three forces: the historical legacy, the continued pressure of the world market, and the exigencies of social control over a population the majority of which was white. The grim result of this combination was the sterilization of the countertendencies inherent in the plantation system and the triumph of a racism more insidious than any other in the New World. At that, one question will always remain open: What would have happened had the Southern slaveholders survived as a ruling class, for it is possible that the subsequent orgy of extreme racism would have been avoided. The fall of the slaveocracy opened the way to new men in the postbellum era and brought to the top exactly those elements most infected with the racism radiating from slavery as a system permeating all of society and least influenced by the countertendencies inherent in the master–slave relation within the plantation community itself. The remnants of the old aristocracy professed to deplore the demagogy and gangsterism of the Tillmans and Vardamans, but they quietly capitulated and sometimes set the pace for racist vituperation. That capitulation is a long and bitter story in itself; for our immediate purposes it is enough that it occurred after a headlong fall from power and reflected defeat, despair, and a frantic attempt to survive in a new and dangerous world. In this sense, too, the triumph of the bourgeoisie in a society that had been originally shaped by slavery spelled the triumph of racist extremism.

II

By focusing on the nature of the ruling class of each slaveholding regime, we can treat adequately the major problems inherent in comparative historical analysis. We have largely limited ourselves to the question of abolition, as posed by Tannenbaum and Elkins, as a test of the usefulness of a class analysis, but have at least noticed its wider applications. Such an analysis brings us into direct confrontation with the essential duality of the history of slavery in the modern world. The colonization of the New World re-created archaic regimes shaped by the patriarchal plantation, the dominant tendency of which was paternalism. All slave regimes exhibited this tendency, for it was inherent in the master–slave relationship. The strength of this tendency depended primarily on the nature of its particular slaveholding class, which grew up on the spot but was also deeply influenced by its own historic past and relationship to a seigneurial or bourgeois society abroad. Each such class therefore simultaneously displayed general characteristics and yet was unique. Side by side with this process of internal archaic development there continued the far more powerful and ultimately triumphant process of world capitalist expansion—a process that absorbed the independent, internal process within itself and distorted it in decisive ways. The great revolt of the slaveholders of the Old South represented, in this sense, a dramatic reactionary movement to reverse the fundamental thrust of world history. The study of the slave systems of the New World contributes an essential feature to the social and economic history of the wider European world and must progress in a way that renders the subject a coherent whole.

If each slaveholding class was in fact the unique product of a long history on both sides of the ocean, then the strength of Tannenbaum's general argument relative to that of the economic determinists should be obvious. If all slaveholding classes shared other certain fundamental tendencies, arising from their relationship to labor, then the central importance of the mode of production should also be obvious. Yet slavery in the Americas had a racial basis and therefore must be understood, not simply as a class question, but as a class question with a profound racial dimension, which can only be understood as the particular product of each slaveholding regime. A class analysis, in short, is not enough and can only serve as the basis for a much more complex analysis. But then, no one has ever seriously suggested that it could do more.

[From *The World the Slaveholders Made: Two Essays in Interpretation* (London: Allen Lane, 1970), 103–13.]

ORLANDO PATTERSON

12 Slavery as Human Parasitism

I have spoken of masters and slaves, and I have called slavery a relation of domination. But language is more than simply a mode of expression; it also fashions thought. My analysis has attempted to penetrate the dictates of thought inherent in the language and other symbols used by the subjects I have studied. I have therefore devoted a great deal of attention to the symbolic aspects of slavery.

For cultural systems, as anthropologists have long taught us, are at bottom only silent languages.

Interpreting slavery as a relation of domination rather than as a category of legal thought has been an important departure. But now, as a concluding reflection, it is vital to ask whether this conception of the social process we call slavery has disposed of all the hidden conceptual accretions of language. Consider the term 'master.' According to the Oxford dictionary, the word has twenty-nine shades of meanings grouped under four basic headings: 'A man having control or authority,' as the captain of a merchant vessel; 'a teacher or one qualified to teach,' such as a great artist; a 'title of rank or compliment,' such as a college head; and attributive uses and combinations in the sense of 'superior,' for example 'the mastermind.' Who after reading the Oxford dictionary would not want to be a master? And is it any wonder that for generations the dominant school of historical scholarship on slavery in America led by U. B. Phillips, one of the country's distinguished historians, had thoroughly persuaded itself and its audience that the great achievement of American slavery was the civilizing of the black race, its tutorship and elevation from savagery to civilization. The saddest aspect of this bizarre historiography is its sincerity. It was not only insensitivity to the descendants of black slaves that led to such obtuse conclusions, but insensitivity to the cognitive imperatives of language. The ease with which it is possible to shift from the meaning of 'master' as 'a man having control or authority' to that of 'a teacher or one qualified to teach' reflects the ease with which it is possible to shift from conception of the slave plantation as a brutal system of exploitation and human degradation to a pastoral college for the edification of poor savages eager to lean the superior arts of the civilized 'master.'

My conception of slavery as a relation of domination avoids many of these pitfalls. Nevertheless, there remain problems with the term 'domination,' which according to the dictionary means 'ascendancy, sway, control,' not to mention 'angelic powers of the fourth rank.' Domination and its companion exploitation—those two most potent weapons in the logocracy of the left—focus upon the dominator or exploiter as the active agent in the relationship and place upon the exploited the further burden of passivity. Interpreting the relation from the perspective of the dominated, as I have done in this work, goes some way toward redressing the balance—but at the expense of struggling with language.

Is there a better way of rephrasing this conception, what I have called the 're-lation of domination'? The conceptual apparatus of social biologists provides the answer. One of their major classes of social behavior is symbiosis, and within it one of the most significant subclasses is parasitism. Where I speak of a relation of domination, social biologists refer to a relation of parasitism. My feeling on this is not that we learn from social biologists through parallels, but that the way they conceptualize what they study can inform us. Furthermore, we need use the social biologist's approach only as a first step toward an understanding of the more complex dialectics of human parasitism.

Conceiving of slavery as a relation of parasitism has many advantages. Parasitism emphasizes the asymmetry of all such unequal relations: the degree to which the parasite depends on the host is not necessarily a direct measure of the extent to which the host is exploited in supporting the parasite. A parasite may be only partially dependent on its host, but this partial dependence may entail the destruction of the host. Or the host may be totally dependent on the parasite, but the parasitism may only partially influence the host—or may have no effects beyond being a minor nuisance, in which case the relation approaches what biologists call commensalism.

The crucial advantage of this approach is that it offers a useful way of conceptualizing the complexities of dependence. It took the arcane philosophical language of Hegel to uncover what quickly becomes apparent when the conceptual framework of parasitism is used: the dominator, in the process of dominating and making another individual dependent, also makes himself (the dominator) dependent.

At the same time, the paradox of domination can be expressed without taking the argument to its limits. Parasitism suggests a continuum ranging from minor dependence or exploitation to major 'Hegelian' dependence on the part of the dominator and grave survival risks for the dominated. The various combinations of parasitic-dependent and parasitized-exploited may be graded on a continuum ranging from a point just prior to true mutualism to one just this side of total parasitism.

We move closer to the uniquely human aspects of parasitism when we begin to consider the personal satisfaction that the parties experience in their interaction. A significant step in this direction has been provided by the sociologist Anatol Rapoport, who in a fascinating theoretical analysis of human parasitism has shown that while the behavior of the parasitized party is what common sense suggests—he recognizes that the situation is harmful for him under any circumstances and that it is always in his best interest to get out of it—the behavior of the parasite is not so easily understood.[1]

Rapoport derives two important conclusions from his model. His principal deduction is that parasitism is a function of the terms of exchange and that it is always the outcome of an unstable situation. Stable transactions occur only where individuals keep more than they give of whatever they produce and exchange. Wherever individuals are obliged to give more than they keep, there are unstable terms of trade inevitably culminating in parasitism, the condition in which one party produces nothing and consumes a part of the other's product. The inherent instability of the slave relation has been one of the major findings of this work. Where Rapoport, using the language of theoretical economics, speaks of imbalance and disequilibrium, I have spoken of tension and conflict and of dialectical structure.

A second implication of Rapoport's model is that it is incorrect to assume, in commonsense terms, that 'it pays to be a parasite if you are sufficiently lazy.' Parasitism is most rewarding for the parasite when both he and the parasitized party minimize laziness. Indeed, if maximizing leisure or laziness is the parasite's major objective, he is often better off cooperating with the other party in the attainment of the social optimum (the optimal joint utilities of himself and the other person)—in other words, to give up extreme parasitism and move toward mutualism. Effective parasitism is hard work! The southern U.S. slaveholders were basically right in always insisting on this in their defense of the system of slavery, though they did not, of course, express their views in these terms.[2] Where they were completely wrong was in their equally vehement claim that their hardworking parasitism was in the best interest of their parasitized slaves and of all nonslaveholding freemen.[3] The empirical evidence lends further support to Rapoport's deductions in that it is precisely those societies in which slaveholders sought to maximize leisure—for example, the Toradjas of the central Celebes, some of the Fulani slave systems of West Africa, and all of the northwest coast Indians who kept slaves—that we find the relation moving closer to, though never of course reaching, cooperation and mutualism between holder/parasite and slave/host.

On the macrosociological level the parasitism framework is also valuable as a heuristic device. Instead of individual holders and slaves constituting the units in the relationship, the institution of slavery is conceived of as a single process that operates on the total social system. The systemic parasitization of the slaveholder's culture and society naturally reinforces the direct personal parasitism of the slaveholder on his slave. In this sense the slave may be said to suffer both personal and institutional parasitism.

Slavery began as the violent and permanent overpowering of one person by another. Distinctive in its character and dialectics, it originated as a substitute for certain death and was maintained by brutality. Depending on the number of slaves involved and the kind of society in which the slaveholder lived, a variety of means of acquisition and enslavement were utilized by the slaveholder and his associates in recruiting persons to be parasitized. The slave was natally alienated and condemned as a socially dead person, his existence having no legitimacy whatever. The slave's natal alienation and genealogical isolation made him or her the ideal human tool, an *instrumentum vocal*—perfectly flexible, unattached, and deracinated. To all members of the community the slave existed only through the parasite holder, who was called the master. On this intersubjective level the slaveholder fed on the slave to gain the very direct satisfactions of power over another, honor enhancement, and authority. The slave, losing in the process all claim to autonomous power, was degraded and reduced to a state of liminality.

The slaveholder camouflaged his dependence, his parasitism, by various ideological strategies. Paradoxically, he defined the slave as dependent. This is consistent with the distinctively human technique of camouflaging a relation by defining it as the opposite of what it really is. The slave resisted his desocial-ization and forced service in countless ways, only one of which, rebellion, was not subtle. Against all odds he strove for some measure of regularity and pre-dictability in his social life. Because his kin relations were illegitimate, they were all the more cherished. Because he was considered degraded, he was all the more infused with the yearning for dignity. Because of his formal isolation and liminality, he was acutely sensitive to the realities of community. The fierce love of the slave mother for her child is attested in every slaveholding so-ciety; everywhere the slave's zest for life and fellowship confounded the slave-holder class; and in all slaveholding societies the existential dignity of the slave belied the slaveholder's denial of its existence.

The slaveholder retaliated ideologically by stereotyping the slave as a lying, cowardly, lazy buffoon devoid of courage and manliness: the slave became, in his holder's mind, the 'Graeculus' of ancient Rome, the 'Zandj' of medieval Iraq, the 'Quashee' of eighteenth-century Jamaica, the 'Sambo' of the U.S. South, and the 'Diimaajo' ('he who does not give birth') of the Fulani. The slave retaliated not only existentially, by refusing to be among his fellow slaves the de-graded creature he was made out to be, but also directly on the battlefront of the political psychology of his relation with the slaveholder. He fed the para-site's timocratic character with the pretense that he was what he was supposed to be. Still, in his very pretense there was a kind of victory. He served while con-cealing his soul and fooling the parasite. As the Jamaican slaves put it in their fa-vorite proverb, 'Play fool, to catch wise.'

Jamaican slaves were not alone in seeing through the slaveholder's ideologi-cal inversion of reality, yet behaving as if they did not. All slaves, like oppressed peoples everywhere, wore masks in their relations with those who had para-sitized them. It is in their statements to one another, whether via folk sayings or—infrequently—in folk literature, that they revealed what they knew and what they were. Occasionally a slave, feeling he had nothing to lose, would re-move the mask and make it clear to the slaveholder that he understood perfectly the parasitic nature of their interaction. Never was this more forthrightly stated that in the response of an old eighteenth-century Canadian slave to his un-scrupulous master's disingenuous offer to set him free. 'Master,' the withered slave demurred, 'you eated me when I was meat, and now you must pick me when I am bone.'

The ideological inversion of reality was the creation of the slaveholder class, so it is not surprising that few of them expressed reservations about its verac-ity; almost all masters, in fact, genuinely believed that they cared and provided for their slaves and that it was the slaves who, in the words of one southern ex-slave owner, had 'been raised to depend on others.'[4] Even among southerners, though, reality sometimes broke through ideological self-deception. This was most marked during the crisis engendered by the Civil War, and the ensuing discussions of how to solve 'the Negro Problem.'[5] As Lawrence J. Friedman has skillfully shown, southerners forced to examine the realities of their dependence on slaves—and its ideological underpinnings—simply turned away from the truth and ended up with hopelessly contradictory positions. The nearest to the truth that the southerner was prepared to accept was that the relationship was one of mutual dependence. It was a Presbyterian minister, John B. Adger, who articulated this proximity to reality when he stated:

They [the Negroes] belong to us. We also belong to them. They are divided among us and mingled up with us, eating from the same storehouses, drinking from the same fountain, dwelling in the same enclosures, forming parts of the same families . . . See them all around you, in these streets, in all these dwellings; a race distinct from us, yet closely united to us; brought in God's mysterious providence from a foreign land, and placed under our care, and made members of our state and society; they are not more truly ours than we are truly theirs.[6]

Adger's position, itself only a half-truth, was stoutly rejected by nearly all slaveholders. They refused to see their slaves as anything but hopeless parasites and dependents who could only survive in a slave relation under the 'superior mind' of the master, who would 'direct the labor' and ensure his slaves' happiness.[7]

Southern slaveholders were hardly exceptional in their ideological self-deception. The same inversion of reality was to be found among slaveholders everywhere, from the most primitive to the most advanced of slaveholding societies. Ancient Roman slaveholders were generally no different, although enlightened Romans were more given to pragmatism and aristocratic candor than the elite members of other advanced societies. It is not surprising, then, that among this class of slaveholders are the rare cases of open acknowledgment of the reality behind the ideology. To cite Seneca's celebrated observation; 'As many slaves, so many enemies.' But it was another Roman of the first century A.D., Pliny the Elder, who in one of his few inspired moments made himself unique among the slaveholders of all time by laying bare the parasite nature of the relation between slaveholders and slaves:

We use other people's feet when we go out, we use other people's eyes to recognize things, we use another person's memory to greet people, we use someone else's help to stay alive—the only things we keep for ourselves are our pleasures.[8]

However firm their belief in their ideological definition of the slave relation, slaveholders simply could not deny the stark fact that their slaves served under duress: a combination of punishments and rewards was essential. While it was true that the whip struck not just the body of the slave but his soul, slaveholders everywhere knew that incentives were better than punishments to promote efficient service. Treating the slave well was one kind of inducement, though it also supported the slaveholder in a variety of ways. The well-looked-after slave redounded to the generosity and honor of his holder, emphasized the slave's apparent 'dependence,' and gave credence to the paternalism that the parasite craved. For precisely these reasons the slave, even while accepting and allowing himself to be spurred by these incentives, also resented them. Both masters and slaves knew implicitly what the Eskimos have stated explicitly in one of their pithiest sayings: 'Gifts make slaves, as whips make dogs.'

One invaluable weapon emerged in all slaveholding groups: no matter how much the slave struggled, he remained illegitimate. Indeed, the struggle itself forced upon him a need that no other human beings have felt so acutely: the need for disenslavement, for disalienation, for negation of social death, for recognition of his inherent dignity.

And so it was that freedom came into the world. Before slavery people simply could not have conceived of the thing we call freedom. Men and women in premodern, nonslaveholding societies did not, could not, value the removal of restraint as an ideal. Individuals yearned only for the security of being positively anchored in a network of power and authority. Happiness was membership; being was belonging; leadership was the ultimate demonstration of these two qualities. It is an abuse of language to refer to membership and belonging as a kind of freedom; freedom is not a faculty or a power to do something. Remember the paradox that what the manumitted slave gained was never the same thing as what the master gave. The same conclusion has been arrived at, a priori, by philosophers. As Maurice Cranston lucidly argues:

It is a tautology that a man cannot do a thing if he cannot do it. But a man does not say he is free to do a thing simply because he possesses the power or faculty to do so. When he says he can do something, he may mean he has a skill ('I can play Canasta'); or he may mean he has an opportunity ('I can send you some eggs'). He says he is free to do it *only when he wants to refer to the absence of the impediments in the way of doing it* (emphasis added).[9]

Slaves were the first persons to find themselves in a situation where it was vital to refer to what they wanted in this way. And slaveholders, quick to recognize this new value, were the first class of parasitic oppressors to exploit it. In the vast majority of slaveholding societies they regularly took advantage of the slave's discovery of freedom. Only under special circumstances in a few kin-based societies, and a minority of the most advanced modern ones, did slaveholders deem it outside their best interests to exploit their slave's yearning for freedom as a preferred form of incentive. In these rare exceptions the masters resorted to either compensatory emphasis on material incentives or brutal employment of the whip or both.

In all but a small minority of slaveholding societies, then, manumission became an intrinsic part of the process of slavery. In analyzing its meaning and dialectical relation to slavery, I have not only explored how the tension inherent in the relationship was resolved, but have moved, of necessity, from its purely intersubjective to its institutional aspects. Slavery, we have seen, was an institutional process moving through three phases: enslavement, institutionalized liminality, and disenslavement.

Regarding enslavement, we have seen that demand and supply factors reinforced each other in all slaveholding societies. Similarly, while we normally think of manumission as being the result of the negation of slavery, it is also true that manumission, by providing one of the major incentives for slaves, reinforced the master–slave relationship. In material terms, no slaveholding class ever lost in the process of disenslavement or manumission: either the material compensation more than made up for the replacement cost of the slaves or, more frequently, the slave was made over into another, even more loyal and efficient retainer—or the master gained in both instances. There was also a direct two-way link between enslavement and manumission. The rate of the latter was frequently dependent on the volume and elasticity of the former; at the same time, on the demand side, the volume of manumission partly determined the number of persons to be enslaved.

Nor did the slaveholder lose ideologically. Indeed, in institutional terms the entire process was represented as an elaborate cycle of gift exchange, in which the slaveholders found it necessary to draw upon the social and cultural resources of their community. Thus as direct, personal parasitism on the slave was secured and legitimized, the slave relation was transformed into an institutional process in parasitic involvement with the socioeconomic and cultural components of the total social system.

An examination of the nature of the parasitism on the systemic level is outside the scope of this work. I can only hint at its range and complexity. Social and cultural systems always paid a price for becoming involved with slavery, but that price could range from the insignificant to the totally destructive. Up to a certain point it was possible for slavery to flourish without marked social or cultural consequences; this was the case, for example, in tenth- and early eleventh-century England and Han China. Beyond that point, however, no social system could survive without major changes.

The particular configuration of socioeconomic and cultural parasitism determined the kind of slave society that emerged. There was no simple, uniform process. This is not to say, however, that there were no patterns beneath these seemingly random configurations, or that we cannot explain why given slaveholding societies developed specific systemic patterns. Understanding what they were and how they came to be is a goal for future research, in which the nature and dynamics of slave societies will be explored on a broader scale than the interpersonal level I have examined here.

It has been my objective in this book to come to a definitive statement of the fundamental processes of slavery, to grasp its internal structure and the institutional patterns that support it. Throughout this work, however, the ghost of another concept has haunted my analysis, and in this final chapter I have tried to exorcise it. That is the problem of freedom. Beyond the sociohistorical findings is the unsettling discovery that an ideal cherished in the West beyond all others emerged as a necessary consequence of the degradation of slavery and the effort to negate it. The first men and women to struggle for freedom, the first to think of themselves as free in the only meaningful sense of the term, were freedmen. And without slavery there would have been no freedmen.

We arrive then at a strange and bewildering enigma: are we to esteem slavery for what it has wrought, or must we challenge our conception of freedom and the value we place upon it?

[From *Slavery and Social Death: A Comparative Study* (Cambridge, Mass.: Harvard University Press, 1982), 335–42.]

VICTOR KIERNAN
....

13 Africa

The Slave Trade and its Suppression

The Negroes whose toil laid the foundations of the New World came mostly from two regions of western Africa, the Portuguese settlement of Angola and the 'Slave Coast' or southern rim of the great westerly bulge. Along this coast Europeans, without being in occupation of it, could easily come by all the slaves they required on a basis of fair exchange, rum and gunpowder for men and women. African simplicity was not that of a garden of Eden: many of its inhabitants were as willing to sell one another for a bottle as ancient Britons or Russians once were. War-captives, or offenders condemned for crime or witchcraft, were brought down to the coast and disposed of by the chiefs there to the foreign dealers. It is a question worth asking whether this turmoil of man-hunting was the result of the foreign demand, or whether the prime cause was overpopulation, supply stimulating demand. In either case the merchant from Liverpool or Glasgow was no robber, not always even a receiver of stolen goods, and had a clear conscience. It was left to low Spanish, Portuguese, or half-caste slavers to go about catching their wares themselves. Reputable dealers were often on excellent terms with the coastal chiefs, arranged for their sons to go to school in England, and accepted temporary wives from them.

Behind this cordiality the true reaction of Europe and Africa to each other was different. 'The Natives are cheated . . . in every possible way,' wrote the former slave-trader John Newton after his religious conversion, and the more contact they had with the white man the more 'jealous, insidious and revengeful' they grew. Each race looked on the other as 'consummate villains', and a Negro taxed with dishonesty would sometimes retort: 'What! do you think I am a White Man?'[1] Baron Munchausen, some of whose most surprising adventures befell him in Africa—that 'prodigious field of discovery'[2]—once met a party of Negroes who had seized European shipping and started a trade in white slaves for work on plantations in cold latitudes. They had contracted 'a barbarous prejudice . . . that the white people have no souls!'[3]

That black people had only second-rate souls, and that they were better off as slaves, even in Turkey, than in their own land, was a conviction that faded very slowly from the European mind. Albert Smith strolling about the slave-market at Constantinople felt it must be a blessing to these poor degraded creatures to be provided with a master and regular work.[4] He himself might have blinked and gibbered after being marched for a month in an Arab slave-gang. Thackeray was shocked here, less so at Cairo where he fell back on the comforting stereotype of Africans as happy, carefree creatures, shackled in body but spared the heavy load of thought and doubt,[5] the real white-man's-burden as it felt to those who suffered from it and envied the artless classes or races that had never eaten of the tree of knowledge. He was heartened by a holiday festivity in the swarming black suburb of Alexandria. 'Every one of these jolly faces was on the broad grin.'[6]

But officially England, and emotionally many Englishmen, were committed to regarding the slave trade as the world's deepest abomination, which England's duty was not merely to renounce but to persuade or compel others to renounce. Burton stood in the slave-market at Mecca and silently vowed to strike the death-blow at the traffic in eastern Africa.[7] To Ruskin the greatest painting of the greatest artist of the age was Turner's *Slave Ship*, exhibited in 1840. It showed an enormous Atlantic swell at the end of a storm, littered with bodies thrown overboard, and lurid sunset colours falling 'like the shadow of death upon the guilty ship . . . its thin masts written upon the sky in lines of blood'.[8]

Pressure of humanitarian opinion was important here too. There was no reason of pure economics why slavery should not continue, hitched on to capitalism. The US gave up the slave trade only a year after Britain, but John Bull's European competitors, who never believed him to be quite so transparently honest as he liked to be thought, suspected that his aim was to deprive them of an advantage which he himself no longer needed. Through most of the nineteenth century British diplomacy was entangled in vexatious disputes arising out of its attempts to make effective the pledges to abandon slave-trading obtained at the end of the Napoleonic wars. Anti-slavery societies in England kept on prodding the Foreign Office, which would have liked to forget about the matter, to prod the worst backsliders, Spain and Portugal.

Britain, France and the US worked out measures for patrolling the western coasts of Africa, and British tax-payers plumed themselves on the part played by their ships; the navy's popularity owed much to this. Kingston's midshipmen threw themselves with enthusiasm into the work, and held in horror the degenerate Spanish or Portuguese traffickers. 'To an Englishman no class of men are more hateful.'[9] All this could make for self-righteousness, and a belief, not quite extinct today, in Britannia's right to 'police the seas' anywhere. It gave John Bull a sort of treasury of merit, which he felt able to draw on whenever assailed by qualms about items like opium or misgivings about his moral supereminence.

As late as 1888 *The Times* alleged that slave-running still flourished along eastern Africa and across the Indian Ocean, under French as well as Arab auspices.

All round Africa the hunt for the slaver led to closer acquaintance with the continent; it also paved the way for occupation of parts of it. Formerly the argument in defence of the trade, that removal from Africa was the Negro's only chance of redemption, had been repeated by men as prominent as Nelson: now that he was no longer to be carried off to civilization, it might be right that civilization should be carried to him. Sympathy, which he now received, seldom implied respect. Progress was Europe's watchword, and Africa far more even than Asia appeared incapable of it. Its stagnation at a low material level was a fact, which can be tentatively explained in terms of a slow drift of population from north to south, away from the Mediterranean and its culture, over an unwelcoming land-mass where it was too thinly spread to develop a technology equal to some of its arts.[10] These arts found few to appreciate them among Europeans in Africa, one of whom spoke for nearly all when he dismissed its music as 'those unearthly noises which in Africa pass current for song'.[11] Only late in the nineteenth century did artistic Europe begin to discover Africa, its sculpture first and foremost.

Meanwhile African backwardness was accounted for in sundry ways. One was to think of the black man as descended from Ham, the black son of Noah; Europeans were still reading their Old Testaments, and deriving from that ancient oriental source notions as bizarre as any they met with in Dahomey or Swaziland. Missionaries were often advocates of annexation. They were sometimes mixed up with trade; but what weighed more was the desire to see the weak protected against the strong, above all against the slave-raider. They showed best when denouncing the evil done by lawless European enterprise. Once European government was established, and with it a more orderly exploitation, they usually felt obliged as in India to acquiesce in whatever its policies might be.

[From *The Lords of Human Kind: European Attitudes towards the Outside World in the Imperial Age* (Harmondsworth: Penguin, 1972), 210–13.]

M. G. SMITH

14 Ethnic and Cultural Pluralism in the British Caribbean

The British Caribbean consists of Jamaica, the Leeward Islands (St Kitts, Nevis, Antigua, Montserrat, and the British Virgin Islands), the Windward Islands (St Vincent, St Lucia, Dominica, Grenada), Barbados, Trinidad, and Tobago, British Honduras in North America and British Guiana in South America. Except for these last two colonies, the remaining British Caribbean possessions are islands of the Antillean archipelago. Jamaica is over a thousand miles from Trinidad, and more than 500 miles east of British Honduras; British Guiana is larger in area than all the remaining units put together. Jamaica, with a population of one-and-a-half million, accounts for about 47 per cent of the total British

Caribbean population. Despite such differences and distances, these colonies have much in common, historically and at present. They also differ among themselves in various ways.

The islands are overpopulated, while the two mainland territories contain large unsettled areas. All these territories depend on agriculture, and their urban ratios are relatively low. Industrialization is just beginning in Jamaica and Trinidad, nationalism has been slow to develop, and separatism is as pronounced within the colonies as between them. These territories are all depressingly poor, and despite their long histories of capital investment, they are still typical underdeveloped countries.

These societies are all multiracial. Except in the mainland territories, they contain no significant indigenous elements. Their present populations are descended from immigrants from the Old World: Europeans, Africans, Chinese, Indians, Lebanese, and others. Most of Caribbean history consists in the development of these areas by competing European nations through the exploitation of African labor, initially imported as slaves. Negro-white associations have produced a large hybrid group which is culturally, as well as biologically, mixed. The approximate racial compositions of the various colonial populations in 1946 are given in table 1.

These percentages are based on the West Indian census of 1946 and reveal some of the ambiguities inherent in racial classification. Seventy-four per cent of the Dominican population, 37 per cent of the St Lucian population, and 31 per cent of the British Hondurian population are classified as 'coloured.' The

Table 1
Approximate Racial Compositions of Various Colonial Populations, 1946
(Unit = per cent)

Territory	White	Black	Colored	East-Indian	Amer-indian	Chinese	Other
Jamaica	1	78	17.5	2	—	1	0.5
Barbados	5	77	18	—	—	—	—
Br. Guiana	3	38.1	10	43.5	4.3	1	—
Br. Honduras	3.9	38	31.8	2.3	17	—	7*
Antigua	2	85	13	—	—	—	—
Montserrat	0.5	93	6.4	—	—	—	—
St Kitts	2	86.5	11	—	—	—	—
Virgin Is.	0.5	87.2	12.3	—	—	—	—
Trinidad	2.7	46.8	14.1	35.1	—	1	—
Dominica	0.3	24.9	74.6	—	—	—	—
Grenada	0.9	73.6	20.4	4.8	—	—	—
St Lucia	0.5	58.1	37.6	3.8	—	—	—
St Vincent	3.1	73.1	20.5	3	—	—	—

* Black Caribs.

reported racial composition of these colonies differs from that in the remaining territories; but to the best of our knowledge such figures do not connote genuine differences in the composition of these populations.

On the other hand, the East Indian ratios set out above do reflect genuine and very significant differences. It is commonly believed that East Indians now form about 50 per cent of the British Guianese population, and that they are rapidly approaching numerical parity with the Negroid groups of Trinidad. Some people see the recent political split between Dr Cheddi Jagan and Mr L. F. Burnham of British Guiana as essentially racial in character; both men were ministers in the short-lived government of the People's Progressive Party, the first government to be returned in British Guiana on a basis of universal suffrage. Jagan's strength lies with his East Indians, Burnham's with the black and colored groups. In Trinidad also, the East Indian population tends to have its own political organization, but the religious split between Hindus and Muslims has deprived it of unanimity. The refusal of British Guiana to join the British Caribbean Federation, and past hesitancy of Trinidad on this issue, together with the restrictions on immigration to Trinidad from the other colonies, have both been interpreted in other colonies as being due to East Indian political pressure. The division between East Indians and Negro-colored elements in the populations of British Guiana and Trinidad is deeper and sharper than divisions between the Negro, white, and colored populations elsewhere. This may in part be associated with the lack of Indian-Negro miscegenation and the absence of any interstitial group.

The heavy concentration of East Indians in British Guiana and Trinidad is an effect of the large-scale importations of indentured Indian labor to these colonies after the abolition of slavery in 1838. This in turn reflected the labor shortage suffered by planters in Trinidad and British Guiana at that time. In its turn, this labor shortage was an effect of the prohibition of the Atlantic slave trade and of intra-Caribbean slave movements by Britain shortly after she had acquired these fertile territories with their great sugar-producing capacities. Older colonies with played-out land, less profitable sugar production, and larger populations, neither needed nor were able to afford such large-scale labor imports as British Guiana and Trinidad; but as an effect of their differing historical situations, the contemporary social structures of the British West Indian colonies differ significantly as regards their East Indian components. Indian-organized schools now receive government aid in Trinidad, and the Hindu and Mohammedan religions are being increasingly recognized, for example, in matters of marriage. Little research has yet been done on these substantial East Indian populations, but it is known that Hindustani is spoken among them, and that the majority of these East Indians remain loyal to Indian culture and Indian nationalism. These loyalties are related to the slow growth of a Caribbean national sentiment.

The colonial ruling classes and traditions are also diverse. Trinidad, St Lucia,

Grenada, and Dominica have Catholic affiliations as evidence of past associa-tion with France and Spain. In these four colonies a French dialect, known as *pa-tois*, is commonly used among the folk. In areas of continuous British rule, the dialect is based on English. The Roman-Dutch law of British Guiana is a relic of that country's old Dutch connection; in Trinidad, the European cultural section contains Spanish, French, and British elements, and the dominant white culture is a composite of these three traditions. Where Protestantism has been histori-cally dominant, as in Jamaica, Barbados, St Kitts, St Vincent, and Antigua, aes-thetically rich religious syncretisms such as Shango are absent; and Revivalism or Shakerism (Shouting Baptists) is the characteristic folk ritual form.

Small groups of Chinese, Portuguese, Syrians, and Jews are to be found in several of these territories, where they act as specialized occupational groups. Generally, they compete with one another for different sections of the retail and wholesale trade, and in Jamaica, Jews have long been prominent in the legal pro-fession. Where East Indians are found in small numbers, they are assimilated to the black lower class and do not form a separate ethnic group. The Amerindians of British Guiana, British Honduras, and Dominica are not yet significant parts of these colonial populations, but are mainly administered on reservations.

In Trinidad and British Guiana, the East Indian segment is clearly differen-tiated from the remaining population. In the remaining colonies the whites, Negroes, and colored form a standard combination. This association of white, Negro, and colored groups is the historically primary and structurally dominant grouping in the British Caribbean. Despite the racial and cultural polarities within this Negro-white amalgam, miscegenation, acculturation, and assimilation have established a single continuum in racial, cultural, and social terms. The work of Professor Melville Herskovits and his colleagues in the study of Afro-American acculturation provides ample evidence of this cultural continuity; the racial distributions reported by the 1946 West Indian census indicate the extent of racial mixture; and the absence of any race or caste regulations indicates the permissive local attitude toward assimilation.

Nonetheless, there are significant cultural and social differences within this Negro-white combination. Jurors tend to be drawn from the propertied groups, and these tend to be of lighter pigmentation. Primary schools cater to the laboring classes, and these in turn tend to be mainly black. Family forms and mating patterns of the lower class differ remarkably from those of the white or colored elites, and so do lower-class religion, property forms, material culture, occupations, and economic organization.

People born within the West Indies are called 'Creoles'; but East Indians are usually excluded from this reference. Thus Creoles are really persons of Negro, white, or mixed Negro-white ancestry who are natives of the Caribbean. Per-sons of Indian descent are described as 'East Indian' (*sic*) or 'coolies.' Minorities such as the Chinese, that maintain their exclusive identity, are likewise distin-guished from the Creole group, and are referred to in national terms.

It is possible to interpret the historical association between Africans and Europeans in the West Indies as an instance of symbiosis, but between West Indians of African or mixed stock and those of Indian ancestry, competition rather than symbiosis has hitherto prevailed.

To recapitulate, all these British Caribbean territories have a common Negro-white racial and cultural basis. In Trinidad and British Guiana an Indian segment is also present, and in some of the colonies there are also minorities of Jews, Syrians, or Chinese. Comparative treatment of these different social and cultural amalgams directs attention to the differences between ethnic and cultural pluralism. Ethnicity has a number of overlapping but different references, namely, racial origin, nationality, language, and culture. These references invest the idea of ethnic pluralism with an initial ambiguity. In contrast, the idea of cultural pluralism is quite clear. I shall therefore discuss the idea of cultural plurality before returning to the concept of ethnicity as such.

By cultural plurality I understand a condition in which two or more different cultural traditions characterize the population of a given society. To discover whether or not this heterogeneity obtains, we must make a detailed study of the institutions of the population in which we are interested to discover their form, variety, and distribution. In a culturally homogeneous society, such institutions as marriage, the family, religion, property, and the like, are common to the total population. Where cultural plurality obtains, different sections of the total population practice different forms of these common institutions; and, because institutions involve patterned activities, social relations, and idea-systems, in a condition of cultural plurality, the culturally differentiated sections will differ in their internal social organization, their institutional activities, and their system of belief and value. Where this condition of cultural plurality is found, the societies are plural societies. Where cultural homogeneity obtains, the societies are homogeneous units.

By virtue of their cultural and social constitution, plural societies are only units in a political sense. Each is a political unit simply because it has a single government. But the task of government can only be discharged consistently within culturally diverse populations if one or other of these sections dominates the political structure, or if some form of federalism is adopted. In either case, the political structure of plural societies consists largely of the relations between their component cultural sections, and changes in this system of intersectional relations occur together with changes in the political constitution of the unit as a whole. Democratic governmental forms appropriate to plural societies are usually federal. Autocratic governmental forms reserve the ultimate political functions for one or other of the constituent cultural sections, even where some sections are separated territorially—for instance on reservations—and are allowed some internal autonomy. But some uniformity of laws and government is essential if the society is to remain a political unit at all. Excluding government and law, the institutional differences that indicate cultural plurality relate to marriage, family, education, property, religion, economic institutions, language, and folklore. In all these particulars, there are differences within the Negro-white Caribbean community which indicate a condition of cultural plurality. Between the East Indian and Negro-white Creole segment, the cultural difference is still greater.

The idea of ethnic difference is less precise than that of cultural plurality. In some usages of the term, ethnicity refers to race, in others to culture, and in yet others to nationality. The first thing to note is that persons or groups of different races may share a common culture, as in the Mohammedan Hausa-Fulani societies of Northern Nigeria. Conversely, people of the same race may practice different cultures, as in the London of Disraeli, Dickens, and Mayhew, or in the many villages of India. Another important point is that as a rule, the social definition of race differs from the biological definition; moreover different societies may define the same racial groups differently. Thus the population of Guatemala distinguishes between its Spanish, mixed (Ladino), and Indian elements; but to some students these Ladino and Indian groups are racially similar. Similarly, the elite of Haiti reserve the term *Negre* for the subordinate population; but to the Americans, Haitians are Negro by race.

In the United States for instance, ethnicity connotes cultural differences that are quite compatible with the inclusive social order, either because they are differences within a common idiom or a permitted range, or because the groups which practice these variant cultures are numerically weak, and are dependent portions of the larger society. Insofar as nationality is the criterion of ethnicity, some cultural or linguistic difference is often implicit; but once again these differences may be minor variations on general cultural patterns, as for instance family organization, marriage rituals, language, and food habits among the Irish or Italians of New York. Bilingualism and acculturation of these groups is indicated by such terms as Irish-American, Italian-American, and the like. These cultural variations are thus neither inconsistent with one another nor with the wider American society and culture.

If compatibility of institutional norms characterizes ethnic pluralism, their incompatibility may be taken to distinguish cultural pluralism.

Societies depend for integration primarily on the consistency and interdependence of their institutional systems. Hence special problems face a society that contains groups with incompatible institutional allegiances. These problems are most acute when a small ruling group has one cultural tradition and the mass of the population has another. This is the type-situation of British Caribbean history.

In discussing population composition I think race and nationality are appropriate terms. In discussing the cultural homogeneity or plurality of a given population, I think culture is the appropriate term. Where linguistic differences are under study, we can speak of linguistic groups. By isolating these variables and by referring to them directly, we avoid the need for ambiguous concepts, such as ethnicity, and can study the processes and forms of acculturation and assimilation as they occur.

In societies such as those of the British Caribbean which have long histories of acculturation, assimilation, and miscegenation, the concept of ethnicity has doubtful utility, even with regard to such minorities as Jews, Syrians, Portuguese, or Chinese. These are national minorities, and their further classification in terms of race or culture depends unambiguously on our definition of these terms. In analyzing the Negro-white Creole amalgam, we must deal directly with race, culture, and social relations, and seek to determine their covariation or independence. Relations between the East Indian and Creole segments of Trinidad and British Guiana can also be analyzed in these terms. Essentially we are concerned to understand the cultural character and social structure of multiracial populations, which may or may not contain national minorities also. It is difficult to conduct precise studies of these problems with such ambiguous concepts as ethnicity.

Government and the economic system are the two principal sources of social order in the Caribbean. Government acts to limit the chances of conflict, and to limit, maintain, or increase the opportunities for acculturation; the economic system embraces the entire population, although in different degrees and ways. In the first place, the peasantry practices a mixed economy of subsistence and exchange; the townsfolk are mainly involved in the exchange system. In the second place there is division of labor by race and cultural group. By and large East Indians form the bulk of the field-labor force on sugar plantations in Trinidad and British Guiana, Negroes in other colonies. Colored people are heavily represented in clerical occupations, whites in management and executive roles. The professions and the higher ranks of the local civil service now contain members of all racial groups. In occupational distributions, it is the fact of cultural performance and skill that is decisive rather than racial status; and the historic and continuing inequality of opportunities primarily attaches to cultural sections rather than to racial groups as such. Although most field hands are black, many are brown, and some are white. Although most executives are white, many are brown, and some are pure Negro. For analytic purposes the ratios of different racial groups in the same or different occupations do not tell the whole story, since none of these racial segments is culturally homogeneous.

One major preoccupation of plural societies is the choice between eliminating or maintaining their internal differences; and the social and cultural integration of such units is often mooted in terms of this choice. In the history of the British Caribbean possessions, drastic attempts to solve this riddle of integration have been made on three occasions.

In 1838 the abolition of slavery 'freed a race, but failed to create a society.' The numerically minute but politically dominant white planter class which then opposed Abolition, despite its experience that slave production of sugar was no longer economic, feared that social chaos would follow emancipation. With the aid of restrictive property franchises, this white cultural section retained control of the colonial governments for another thirty years, until the sense of their own weakness influenced them to surrender the reins of authority to the Crown and its officers. In Jamaica, this abrogation of the ancient representative constitution took place in 1865, and was openly heralded as the only alternative to a breakdown in the social structure.

Since 1945 this system of Crown Colony rule has been replaced by responsible government based on adult suffrage and operating through ministerial systems. Political parties and trade unions are now recognized institutions, and have flourished under the new regime. At the same time, the idea of a British Caribbean Federation has been actively publicized, and, with the exception of British Guiana, British Honduras, and the British Virgin Islands, these colonies have committed themselves to federation. Yet the chances are that such a federal structure will slow down the rate of change within each of its constituent territories, rather than accelerate it.

[From *The Plural Society in the British West Indies* (Berkeley and Los Angeles: University of California Press, 1965), 10–17.]

PHILIP MASON

 15 **Patterns of Dominance**

A First Attempt at Classification: Numerical Proportion

We are thinking of situations in which there is contact between two groups of people who regard each other as different. We shall not expect to find a smooth chain of types of situation between which one can trace an uninterrupted curve, leading from the barest kind of marginal contact to the extremely complex relationships of modern cities. Nature seldom presents such regularity. Nor shall we expect to find a similar progress in time, a regular succession of certain types of relationship invariably developing in the same order. Various 'cycles' of race relations have, it is true, been described with authority and they have some degree of validity but always, I believe, within a limited field. That is to say, one could, on the basis of such theories, predict what would be the probable sequence of events and relationships if a new minority was introduced into California, provided it was of not more than a certain size and not more than usually exotic in behaviour and appearance. But that cycle or sequence of relationships will not cover past events in other parts of the world.

One cycle which has most illustrious backing[1] predicts that 'contact' will be followed by 'competition', and there will then be two more phases, 'accommodation' and 'assimilation'. This is not, of course, really a cycle, because no one suggests that the whole process would then start again with contact following assimilation. It is an expected sequence of events. But apart from this verbal point, it does not seem illuminating to apply such a scheme to South Africa, where the succession was contact—war—domination; still less to Tasmania, where it was even simpler—contact followed by extermination. Even in the United States, for which the 'cycle' was designed, it is doubtful whether the Negro American is more assimilated than he was twenty years ago. The concept assumes smooth unbroken progress towards harmony but to-day the world-wide revolt against hierarchy and fixed status is everywhere producing movements in the reverse direction.

Much more detailed sequences have been devised, but the more complex and detailed they are, the more closely they fit one pattern, usually American. So we shall be suspicious of any idea that 'cycles' can be universal, though we shall recognize that the sequence of events in one situation may tell us something about the probable sequence of events in a similar situation. There may be a sequence of relationships—though not a cycle which repeats itself—which is frequent in colonial situations; there may also be a sequence of relationships affecting immigrants to an industrial society.

This suggests that there is an overriding difference between situations where the dominant group is indigenous or already established and another set of situations where the indigenous are subordinate. But again there is a complication. The British in India in the seventeenth century were by no means dominant; they were suppliants at the Court of the Moghal Emperors. But by the nineteenth century they were a dominant minority. The same change took place in the case of the Tutsi in Ruanda and the Fulani in Nigeria. And the historical dimension adds a relationship to world thought and to world events. Immigrants to England will behave differently in the twentieth century from immigrants in the eighteenth; there may be similarities in the reactions of the indigenous English but the pattern of world thought is different.

What we shall try to establish is a series of certain broad types of relationship which throw some light on as many situations as possible. But there will be borderline cases which will not fit very neatly into these categories, and, even within one category, events will not always succeed each other in the same order in the same kind of way in every situation. And a situation will move from one category to another in the course of history. It is exactly the difference between two situations that resemble each other within the same category that is illuminating. We shall group these broad categories together and compare them and distinguish and note how one melts into another.

Take for instance 'the plural societies of South-East Asia'—Chinese, Malays, and Indians in Malaysia, as one example. At one time, these lived side by side with little communication except that they were part of the same economic framework, and held together (as a rule) within a common but alien political rule. But, with modern forms of education, inequality began to develop and the process was made more acute when the imperial power withdrew. This is quite a different history from the patterns of conquest and diplomatic triumph which established dominance elsewhere and forms a third grouping of categories, the first two being the subordinate immigrant grouping and the dominant colonial grouping.

There is no end to the complexities. There is a criss-crossing pattern; certain factors are present in varying degrees in every situation and they run right across any grouping of situations into broad categories. But again, they do not behave tidily. One factor is numerical proportion, but we shall not find, for example, that the smaller the dominant minority the more harshly it behaves, nor the reverse. Nor shall we find that there is a critical proportion—when for example a minority increases from 5 per cent to 10 per cent—at which there is invariably a change in political or social behaviour. Still looking at that one factor of numbers or proportion, we may, however, be able to establish certain limits and certain correspondences within which it is possible for a certain kind of situation to develop. But these correspondences are difficult to represent in the form of a chart or graph.

We need not spend long on considering forms of contact which are so peripheral that they really do not much affect the culture of either people. The classical example is 'silent trade'; Herodotus reports silent trade between Carthaginians and natives of the West Coast of Africa; the Carthaginians would leave a pile of goods on the beach, retire to their ships, and send up smoke, when the natives would emerge from hiding and put down a pile of gold which they offered in exchange. They would then go inland and the Carthaginians would take the gold if they thought it enough, but leave both piles and go back to the ships if they did not. The same kind of practice is reported from other parts of the world; it argues a considerable degree of commercial confidence, in spite of personal distrust, and it is not easy to see how the parties first arrive at the bargaining convention. But though the economy of the natives would clearly be influenced by this kind of contract, it is not the kind of relationship we are thinking of, in which two peoples live in the same territory, or compete for parts of it. It may perhaps have been on these lines that Chinese and Indian ships first traded with the East Coast of Africa; all we know is that beads and fragments of pottery are found buried beneath the dry-stone fortresses of Rhodesia and that there was a minimum of cultural influence from these ancient civilizations on the empire of the Monomotapa.

Professor Banton[2] has written of peoples who live side by side in what is described as symbiosis, neither despising the other nor acting aggressively. One fully described example is that of the Mbuti pygmies in the Congo and neighbouring Negro groups. The pygmies live in the forest as hunters and food-gatherers, but periodically decide to come to the agricultural, village world of the Negroes, perhaps for a change of diet or because the hunting is not good. They leave behind their whole set of values, particularly their ideas of what is sacred, and behave as the Negroes wish them to, but go back eventually to the forest and resume their old ways and beliefs. This is certainly one step beyond silent trade, but it does not sound like an *equal* relationship; the Negroes do not reverse the practice and accept the gods of the pygmies. It is perhaps intermediate between parasitism and symbiosis. If the Negro population grew and began to extend cultivation into the forest, the pygmies would find themselves threatened and might eventually be forced into the position of the Twa in Ruanda.

Other examples quoted by Professor Banton are between Eskimo Tungus and Cossacks in North-Western Manchuria, between Lapps and Scandinavian peasants, and between Ladinos and Indians in Guatemala. There is some evidence that neither of the latter two relationships are as free from tension as has been suggested; the Tungus are a group of 'about one hundred and fifty nomadic reindeer herders occupying some seven thousand square miles of territory', while the Cossacks, who speak Great Russian, are literate and agriculturalists, are only one hundred and fifty persons, and live outside the Tungu territory; it seems obvious that these are conditions in which there is no great pressure on resources, and no great need for hostility. It is hardly typical.

I believe that we need not be concerned with these marginal cases and that the term 'symbiosis' is better used of such people as the Parsis in India and the Syrians in West Africa, perhaps of Indians and Burmese under British rule in Burma, or of Malays and Chinese in Malaysia. This is more in accord with the word's original botanical application to organisms which not merely live together and use complementary elements from the soil but actively help each other or even depend on each other, because one performs functions which the other cannot. These peaceful minorities do throw light on our subject; their position may change abruptly—indeed usually *has* changed abruptly.

Professor Banton does not spend long on the Tungus and their reindeer but goes on to draw up a scheme of typical situations between races. Having excluded 'silent trade' on the same grounds as I do, he goes on to suggest six 'orders' of race relations. He distinguishes in the first place between peripheral contact, in which cultural influence is negligible, and *institutionalized contact*, in which there is a group who are specialized intermediaries between two societies. This is his first 'order'. I can supply first-hand evidence of exactly such a group of intermediaries—though again a marginal one—the Marchchas of Garhwal in the Central Himalayas. These people had their headquarters in villages in passes between India and Tibet, at heights of 8,000 to 11,000 feet; here they would sow a crop of barley and a special short quick-growing millet as soon as the snow melted in May or June. In August they would move over the passes, usually about 17,000 feet above sea level, into Tibet, where they would trade sugar and iron for salt, borax, skins, and wool; they came back to their villages in September, cut their barley, and a few weeks later left their villages, which would soon be buried deep in snow, and moved with their flocks to the plains to complete their trade cycle. They were regarded by the Hindu peasantry of the foothills as untouchable, because they were reputed to eat yak-meat in Tibet—and a yak is a kind of cow—and further as an economic threat, because as they moved down in winter they encroached on the grazing and cut wood for fuel; both grass and wood were increasingly scarce as one moved towards the plains. But they did to some extent combine the Hindu and Tibetan cultures. This was possible because the relationship between the two governments was relaxed. Neither wanted the territory or goods of the other; on the other hand, there were no illusions as to which was the more powerful.

But surely we should disregard fascinations of this kind. In Professor Banton's scheme, *institutionalized contact* means a situation in which the overlapping is only limited and exchange between the two cultures is approximately equal. His next order is *acculturation*, in which one of the cultures is so much stronger that it replaces the weaker; since the weaker group adopt the culture of the stronger, they cease to be distinguishable and this will normally lead to the fifth order which is *integration*. But in Banton's scheme institutionalized contact more often leads either to complete *domination* by one group over the other or to *paternalism*. These two are alternatives. Domination is likely to lead to pluralism of an unequal kind, while paternalism is likely to lead to integration. He displays his system in a diagram of which the following is a simplification:

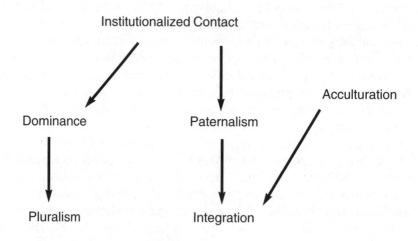

Simplification of Banton's Scheme of Typical Situations between Races

I am not sure that I perfectly follow this division into orders. The test comes when one tries to fit in examples and consider the sequences. Muslim rule in India was, I suppose, domination merging into pluralism, but what about British rule in India? This was, first, institutionalized contact—with the servants of the East India Company acting as specialized go-betweens; later, it was paternalism—perhaps the most perfect example of paternalism there has ever been. But it ended not in integration but in withdrawal. Again, in Rhodesia, in the Cape Colony, Mexico, and Peru, there was first some control by the home government and I think Banton would regard these as coming in the paternalist 'order'; but independence from the home government meant a situation much nearer domination. In South Africa and Rhodesia it has surely become complete domination. In Mexico, the relationship between Spanish and Indian in the early nineteenth century was surely what Banton would regard as 'dominance'. To-day, in most of Mexico, peasants of predominantly Amerindian physical type speak only Spanish and are presumably to be regarded as 'integrated'—though as this is the triumph of one culture over another, it is hard to see how it differs from acculturation. It seems to me that the definitions break down as soon as one begins to trace a progress from one to another.

It might, I suppose, be argued that the arrival of West Indians, Pakistanis, and Indians in Britain produced a situation in which acculturation was taking place, with some doubt as to whether it would turn to integration or unequal pluralism. And there are the Maoris, the North American Indians, and the Australian aborigines; the Australians were almost exterminated, but there have been several changes in policy towards them. It was once hoped to assimilate the American Indian; now the policy is a tolerant pluralism alternating with integration and perhaps with a seventh order—neglect. The changing factors have been world opinion, the conscience of the dominant group and their confidence about their own culture. The tides, it seems to me, flow in a much more shifting and intricate pattern than Banton suggests. But any schematic arrangement faces this kind of difficulty; the examples will not quite fit the pigeon-holes and the sequences are far more fluid, delicate, and shifting than any diagram can represent. All the same, every conscientious attempt to classify these types of situation does illuminate them. Banton's is for me a valuable starting-point, but it needs elaboration.

A rather different approach by Professor P. L. van den Berghe[3] suggests that a situation can be usefully placed in a scale between two extremes. It is confusing that van den Berghe uses the label 'paternalistic' for the system Banton calls 'domination'; but, whatever it is labelled, both would include under this head the plantation system of the Deep South or the countryside in the Transvaal, where race is the overriding sign of social position, where there is little chance of escape from fixed status, where elaborate codes of behaviour govern any contact between the dominant and subordinate groups and where the consequences of belonging to a racial group are defined by law.

At the other extreme of van den Berghe's scale is a more fluid situation, which he calls competitive, in which there is probably an industrial economy and much more opportunity of movement in the social scale. In this type of situation there is some degree of overlapping, in that the best off in the subordinate group may be higher in the scale of profession and earnings than the lowest of those in the dominant group; manners are more fluid and there is ostensibly democratic government involving some conflict of values about the whole system. Perhaps New Zealand would be at this end of the scale, but, in spite of van den Berghe's insistence on the importance of wide comparisons, his schematic outline looks very like the Old Deep South at one end of the scale and the modern North of the United States at the other. Brazil, Mexico, and South Africa, as well as the U.S.A., are examples which van den Berghe has studied thoroughly; of each, he provides a brilliant and perceptive account which is of great value. It is only his model that I find unsatisfactory. All have presented, in the past, a kind of paternalist model not too different from the Deep South, all have, in some respects, moved to something more like his competitive model. He does not, it must be said, suggest that there must necessarily be movement in time from one end of this scale towards the other. If he did, he would clearly exclude South Africa, which in many respects has moved backward. He ignores the distinction, which seems to me real, between dominant and paternalist; it seems to me that South Africa, at least in the Cape Province, once showed signs of paternalism but has clearly moved to dominance with competitive elements. Van den Berghe does specifically limit the application of his model to the four examples, United States, Brazil, Mexico, and South Africa. But he does sometimes write as though it could be used with a wider application, to place a given society at a given moment and also to throw light on its historical development. And this seems a little unreal in the case of societies that never had anything like the agricultural slave society which he puts at one end of his scale.

But there is, it seems to me, a more fundamental objection. Van den Berghe's two models are opposed in respect of a number of variable factors, which he lists. Thus the 'paternalistic' type of situation is agricultural in its economy, while the competitive type is more likely to be manufacturing; the former will have an 'integrated value system' and the latter an ideological conflict. All this—indeed, with one exception, his whole list of variables—seems to me valid as between the Deep South and the North. But the usefulness of this as a model for other societies is limited by the fact—which van den Berghe acknowledges—that his variable factors operate independently.

Take, for example, three of his variable factors: numerical proportion, degree of industrialization, and social stratification. Of numerical proportion, he says that in the paternalistic type the dominant group is a small minority, while in the competitive type the dominant group is a majority. But as soon as one tries to put a society into place in this scale, anomalies appear. If South Africa is contrasted with Colonial West Africa, the South African Republic is surely far more advanced in the organization of labour and in industrial complexity yet far more rigid, and therefore according to the model more backward, in social structure. And the numerical proportions are the reverse of what the scale suggests. The white group in colonial Nigeria was in a much smaller minority.

In fact, the numerical variable really does not work at all in the way suggested;

the British in India were numerically the extreme example of a dominant minority but the social structures of British and Indian were divided by almost vertical lines and great deference was paid by British officials to Maharajas. If we contrast colonial Kenya and Rhodesia, we find Rhodesia more advanced industrially and with a higher proportion of whites, but more rigid socially. Neither in Brazil nor the Deep South was the dominant group 'a small minority'. Perhaps van den Berghe was thinking of the local situation on the plantation, not the general national or regional situation, when he made this point. We shall come back to this question of numbers and look at it in more detail.

In short, as soon as a wider range of examples is set against this model, it becomes apparent that it would be quite mistaken to think of an advanced and a backward society, between which any given society will find a ranking in the scale which will hold good in respect of every factor. One society will develop industrially but may recede socially, as has happened in South Africa. And indeed, all the factors are more complex than this scheme allows. For example, in the 'paternalistic' type of race relations, there is said to be: 'Accommodation: everyone in his place; everyone knows his place: paternalism: benevolent despotism', while on the other side of the scale, opposed to this in the competitive type of society, there is 'antagonism; suspicion, hatred; competitiveness'. But the antithesis is nothing like so simple. Despotism in the Deep South was not uniformly benevolent nor is antagonism a monopoly of the industrial North. Again, the 'stereotype of the lower caste' in the paternalistic type is: 'Childish, immature, exuberant, uninhibited, lazy, impulsive, fun-loving, good-humoured; inferior but lovable'. This is a picture which the Southern American tried to persuade the Northerner, and perhaps himself, that he held of the Negro: but was it really his picture at any period? In Rhodesia and South Africa (of which I know more), there was never a stage at which such words as 'dangerous, treacherous, and unaccountable' should not have been added to the list. I suspect this or something like it was present in Southern minds too. And the Peruvian owner of a hacienda did not usually think of his peons as 'exuberant' or 'fun-loving'.

To revert to numerical proportion, the operation of this important factor is complicated by a number of subsidiary aspects of the situation. It depends on habit and custom; on a sense of permanence in the social system; on outside threat or the possibility of outside help for either party. For example, the South African whites had in most of the nineteenth century to think of a formidable body of warlike tribesmen as well as their African or coloured servants and labourers; on the other hand, there was the possibility of hostility in some circumstances, and help in others, from Great Britain. This was a more complicated set of possibilities than those which confronted the Virginian, who by the mind-nineteenth century had only the slaves and the Northerners to consider. Texas again was more complex, with Indians and Mexicans added to the equation. Quite obviously, the numerical proportion becomes a factor of vital importance in certain societies once the idea of change is introduced. The British in India, as soon as 'Reforms' began in 1919, were in a completely different relationship from before.

Finally—in my list of objections—there are variables which affect the social structure but do not proceed from it. One of the points we shall have to consider is the difference in social structure between Mexico and Peru; one factor, surely, was climate and terrain. In Mexico, the Spaniards centred their rule on the old capital; there was continuity, no abrupt break. But in Peru, they did not want to live at a height of 13,000 feet and started a new capital on the coast. This must be taken into account in any explanation of the harsher division in Peru between the Spanish and the traditional cultures. There were similar factors at work in Africa.

Considering these attempts at classification, I find myself, in general, preferring scales with extreme examples at either end to any system of 'orders' into which actual situations have to be fitted. But we need, I think, a complex set of scales in respect of various factors and a set of groupings, against which to display them. It will sometimes help to group our various situations in broad categories from a particular point of view, but not permanently. Let us take, for example, three categories, two of Banton's orders, domination and paternalism, adding as a third van den Berghe's competitive society. Let us, under these three columns, jot down, almost at random, certain situations. Some of these will be described in more detail later, but they are sufficiently familiar to illustrate the meaning of the categories, which we will not at this stage try to define. Then let us consider one factor, numerical proportion, and note the approximate numerical proportion of dominant to subordinate against each situation. It will be seen that a suggestive hypothesis emerges from this arrangement.

It looks rather as though there was a broad range of proportions within which each of the three categories of subordination can occur. There is no overlapping. Paternalism in my sense is limited to ruling minorities which are very small. The three East African territories (in colonial times) are particularly interesting; an American observer[4] classes them very definitely in the order: Uganda, Tanganyika, Kenya: in respect of the characteristics I regard as 'paternal' rather than 'dominant'—that is, concern for the well-being and development of the subordinate group and a greater degree of social respect for them. And this is the order which the numerical proportions would lead us to expect. But the technical resources of the dominant and their readiness to use them ruthlessly will come into the calculation; also, as we have said, the local attitude to change and world habits of thought.

This sample chart is simplified and deals only with a limited number of categories and situations. We have not included, for instance, Algeria or Senegal. They do not fit exactly into the scheme but do bear out the general trend; proportions total approximately one European to nine Muslims in Algeria in 1960; in Senegal in 1960 one European to eighty Africans. Algeria is thus on the

Table 1
Numerical Proportion of Dominent to Subordinate

Category	Domination	Paternalism	Competition
Situations:	South Africa (1960)	British India	Britain (1968)
	1–4	1–3,000	50–1
	U.S. South (1960)	Nigeria (1952)	U.S. North (1960)
	4–1	1–2,000	15–1
	Rhodesia (1960)	Nyasaland	New Zealand
	1–16	1–1,000 (1945)	13–1
		1–570 (1966)	
	Ruanda	Colonial Kenya	
	(before 1960)	1–100	
	1–6		
	Brahman village in	Tanganyika	
	South India before	1 : 450	
	1919 (three-tier)		
	1: 2: 1		
	Sparta	Uganda	
	1: 1: 2	1: 650	

borders of the dominant and Senegal of the paternalist categories. The list could be considerably extended. But of all factors, numerical example is the easiest to arrange in a scale. We put the British in India at one end with a proportion of about one to three thousand, and we can move through the French as a colonial power in Asia and West Africa, through the French in Algeria to the Tutsi with their one to six, through the South African whites to the Deep South, where the proportion is reversed and the dominant group is a majority of four to one.

It is a more difficult model to follow with other variables, because these are in themselves more complex and it is not easy to rank them numerically. Some obstinately resist enumeration and indeed so change their nature, at different periods and from one region to another, that comparison in any system of ranking is misleading. But an attempt on these lines will, I believe, present fewer anomalies than either of the others we have looked at. [. . .]

There can be many varied approaches to this problem. To me it seems helpful as a preliminary to add more of the historical dimension. We shall therefore look at some forms of contact and some forms of dominance in the pre-industrial age and the problems which a dominant group faces. I shall then look at the patterns which emerge in the industrial age and consider the variable factors which make them different. These seem to fall into three groups, those from the side of the dominant group, those from the side of the subordinate group, and those arising from climate and terrain. The aims with which the dominant group begin are, of course, soon modified by the circumstances of

the territory and by the reactions of the subordinate group and these consequences of contact form another subject.

[From *Patterns of Dominance* (London: Oxford University Press, 1970), 54–65.]

FRANTZ FANON

16 The Wretched of the Earth

National liberation, national renaissance, the restoration of nationhood to the
people, commonwealth: whatever may be the headings used or the new for-
mulas introduced, decolonisation is always a violent phenomenon. At whatever
level we study it—relationships between individuals, new names for sports
clubs, the human admixture at cocktail parties, in the police, on the directing
boards of national or private banks—decolonisation is quite simply the replacing of a certain 'species' of men by another 'species' of men. Without any
period of transition, there is a total, complete and absolute substitution. It is
true that we could equally well stress the rise of a new nation, the setting up of
a new State, its diplomatic relations, and its economic and political trends. But
we have precisely chosen to speak of that kind of *tabula rasa* which characterises
at the outset all decolonisation. Its unusual importance is that it constitutes,
from the very first day, the minimum demands of the colonised. To tell the
truth, the proof of success lies in a whole social structure being changed from
the bottom up. The extraordinary importance of this change is that it is willed,
called for, demanded. The need for this change exists in its crude state, impetu-
ous and compelling, in the consciousness and the lives of the men and women
who are colonised. But the possibility of this change is equally experienced in
the form of a terrifying future in the consciousness of another 'species' of men
and women: the colonisers.

Decolonisation, which sets out to change the order of the world, is, obviously, a programme of complete disorder. But it cannot come as a result of
magical practices, nor of a natural shock, nor of a friendly understanding. Decolonisation, as we know, is a historical process: that is to say that it cannot be
understood, it cannot become intelligible nor clear to itself except in the exact
measure that we can discern the movements which give it historical form and
content. Decolonisation is the meeting of two forces, opposed to each other
by their very nature, which in fact owe their originality to that sort of sub-
stantification which results from and is nourished by the situation in the
colonies. Their first encounter was marked by violence and their existence together—that is to say the exploitation of the native by the settler—was carried
on by dint of a great array of bayonets and cannon. The settler and the native
are old acquaintances. In fact, the settler is right when he speaks of knowing
'them' well. For it is the settler who has brought the native into existence and

who perpetuates his existence. The settler owes the fact of his very existence, that is to say his property, to the colonial system.

Decolonisation never takes place un-noticed, for it influences individuals and modifies them fundamentally. It transforms spectators crushed with their inessentiality into privileged actors, with the grandiose glare of history's flood-lights upon them. It brings a natural rhythm into existence, introduced by new men, and with it a new language and a new humanity. Decolonisation is the ver-itable creation of new men. But this creation owes nothing of its legitimacy to any supernatural power; the 'thing' which has been colonised becomes man during the same process by which it frees itself.

In decolonisation, there is therefore the need of a complete calling in ques-tion of the colonial situation. If we wish to describe it precisely, we might find it in the well-known words: 'The last shall be first and the first last'. Decolonisa-tion is the putting into practice of this sentence. That is why, if we try to de-scribe it, all decolonisation is successful.

The naked truth of decolonisation evokes for us the searing bullets and bloodstained knives which emanate from it. For if the last shall be first, this will only came to pass after a murderous and decisive struggle between the two pro-tagonists. That affirmed intention to place the last at the head of things, and to make them climb at a pace (too quickly, some say) the well-known steps which characterise an organised society, can only triumph if we use all means to turn the scale, including, of course, that of violence.

You do not turn any society, however primitive it may be, upside-down with such a programme if you are not decided from the very beginning, that is to say from the actual formulation of that programme, to overcome all the ob-stacles that you will come across in so doing. The native who decides to put the programme into practice, and to become its moving force, is ready for violence at all times. From birth it is clear to him that this narrow world, strewn with prohibitions, can only be called in question by absolute violence.

The colonial world is a world divided into compartments. It is probably un-necessary to recall the existence of native quarters and European quarters, of schools for natives and schools for Europeans; in the same way we need not re-call Apartheid in South Africa. Yet, if we examine closely this system of com-partments, we will at least be able to reveal the lines of force it implies. This approach to the colonial world, its ordering and its geographical lay-out will allow us to mark out the lines on which a decolonised society will be reorgan-ised.

The colonial world is a world cut in two. The dividing line, the frontiers are shown by barracks and police stations. In the colonies it is the policeman and the soldier who are the official, instituted go-betweens, the spokesmen of the settler and his rule of oppression. In capitalist societies the educational system, whether lay or clerical, the structure of moral reflexes handed down from fa-ther to son, the exemplary honesty of workers who are given a medal after fifty years of good and loyal service, and the affection which springs from harmonious relations and good behaviour—all these esthetic expressions of respect for the established order serve to create around the exploited person an atmosphere of submission and of inhibition which lightens the task of policing considerably. In the capitalist countries a multitude of moral teachers, counsellors and 'bewilderers' separate the exploited from those in power. In the colonial countries, on the contrary, the policeman and the soldier, by their immediate presence and their frequent and direct action maintain contact with the native and advise him by means of rifle-butts and napalm not to budge. It is obvious here that the agents of government speak the language of pure force. The intermediary does not lighten the oppression, nor seek to hide the domination; he shows them up and puts them into practice with the clear conscience of an upholder of the peace; yet he is the bringer of violence into the home and into the mind of the native.

The zone where the natives live is not complementary to the zone inhabited by the settlers. The two zones are opposed, but not in the service of a higher unity. Obedient to the rules of pure Aristotelian logic, they both follow the principle of reciprocal exclusivity. No conciliation is possible, for of the two terms, one is superfluous. The settlers' town is a strongly-built town, all made of stone and steel. It is a brightly-lit town; the streets are covered with asphalt, and the garbage-cans swallow all the leavings, unseen, unknown and hardly thought about. The settler's feet are never visible, except perhaps in the sea; but there you're never close enough to see them. His feet are protected by strong shoes although the streets of his town are clean and even, with no holes or stones. The settler's town is a well-fed town, an easy-going town; its belly is always full of good things. The settler's town is a town of white people, of foreigners.

The town belonging to the colonised people, or at least the native town, the negro village, the medina, the reservation, is a place of ill fame, peopled by men of evil repute. They are born there, it matters little where or how; they die there, it matters not where, nor how. It is a world without spaciousness; men live there on top of each other, and their huts are built one on top of the other. The native town is a hungry town, starved of bread, of meat, of shoes, of coal, of light. The native town is a crouching village, a town on its knees, a town wallowing in the mire. It is a town of niggers and dirty arabs. The look that the native turns on the settler's town is a look of lust, a look of envy; it expresses his dreams of possession—all manner of possession: to sit at the settler's table, to sleep in the settler's bed, with his wife if possible. The colonised man is an envious man. And this the settler knows very well; when their glances meet he ascertains bitterly, always on the defensive 'They want to take our place'. It is true, for there is no native who does not dream at least once a day of setting himself up in the settler's place.

This world divided into compartments, this world cut in two is inhabited by two different species. The originality of the colonial context is that economic reality, inequality and the immense difference of ways of life never come to mask the human realities. When you examine at close quarters the colonial context, it is evident that what parcels out the world is to begin with the fact of belonging to or not belonging to a given race, a given species. In the colonies the economic substructure is also a superstructure. The cause is the consequence; you are rich because you are white, you are white because you are rich. This is why Marxist analysis should always be slightly stretched every time we have to do with the colonial problem.

Everything up to and including the very nature of pre-capitalist society, so well explained by Marx, must here be thought out again. The serf is in essence different from the knight, but a reference to divine right is necessary to legitimise this statutory difference. In the colonies, the foreigner coming from another country imposed his rule by means of guns and machines. In defiance of his successful transplantation, in spite of his appropriation, the settler still remains a foreigner. It is neither the act of owning factories, nor estates, nor a bank balance which distinguishes the governing classes. The governing race is first and foremost those who come from elsewhere, those who are unlike the original inhabitants, 'the others'.

The violence which has ruled over the ordering of the colonial world, which has ceaselessly drummed the rhythm for the destruction of native social forms and broken up without reserve the systems of reference of the economy, the customs of dress and external life, that same violence will be claimed and taken over by the native at the moment when, deciding to embody history in his own person, he surges into the forbidden quarters. To wreck the colonial world is henceforward a mental picture of action which is very clear, very easy to understand and which may be assumed by each one of the individuals which constitute the colonised people. To break up the colonial world does not mean that after the frontiers have been abolished lines of communication will be set up between the two zones. The destruction of the colonial world is no more and no less that the abolition of one zone, its burial in the depths of the earth or its expulsion from the country.

The natives' challenge to the colonial world is not a rational confrontation of points of view. It is not a treatise on the universal, but the untidy affirmation of an original idea propounded as an absolute. The colonial world is a Manichean world. It is not enough for the settler to delimit physically, that is to say with the help of the army and the police force, the place of the native. As if to show the totalitarian character of colonial exploitation the settler paints the native as a sort of quintessence of evil. Native society is not simply described as a society lacking in values. It is not enough for the colonist to affirm that those values have disappeared from, or still better never existed in, the colonial world. The native is declared insensible to ethics; he represents not only the absence of values, but also the negation of values. He is, let us dare to admit, the enemy of values, and in this sense he is the absolute evil. He is the corrosive element, destroying all that comes near him; he is the deforming element, disfiguring all that has to do with beauty or morality; he is the depository of maleficent powers, the unconscious and irretrievable instrument of blind forces. Monsieur Meyer could thus state seriously in the French National Assembly that the Republic must not be prostituted by allowing the Algerian people to become part of it. All values, in fact are irrevocably poisoned and diseased as soon as they are allowed in contact with the colonised race. The customs of the colonised people, their traditions, their myths—above all, their myths—are the very sign of that poverty of spirit and of their constitutional depravity. That is why we must put the DDT which destroys parasites, the bearers of disease, on the same level as the Christian religion which wages war on embryonic heresies and instincts, and on evil as yet unborn. The recession of yellow fever and the advance of evangelisation form part of the same balance-sheet. But the triumphant *communiqués* from the missions are in fact a source of information concerning the implantation of foreign influences in the ore of the colonised people. I speak of the Christian religion, and no one need be astonished. The Church in the colonies is the white people's Church, the foreigner's Church. She does not call the native to God's ways but to the ways of the white man, of the master, of the oppressor. And as we know, in this matter many are called but few chosen.

At times this Manicheism goes to its logical conclusion and dehumanises the native, or to speak plainly it turns him into an animal. In fact, the terms the settler uses when he mentions the native are zoological terms. He speaks of the yellow man's reptilian motions, of the stink of the native quarter, of breeding swarms, of foulness, of spawn, of gesticulations. When the settler seeks to describe the native fully in exact terms he constantly refers to the bestiary. The European rarely hits on a picturesque style; but the native, who knows what is in the mind of the settler, guesses at once what he is thinking of. Those hordes of vital statistics, those hysterical masses, those faces bereft of all humanity, those distended bodies which are like nothing on earth, that mob without beginning or end, those children who seem to belong to nobody, that laziness stretched out in the sun, that vegetative rhythm of life—all this forms part of the colonial vocabulary. General de Gaulle speaks of 'the yellow multitudes' and François Mauriac of the black, brown and yellow masses which soon will be unleashed. The native knows all this, and laughs to himself every time he spots an allusion to the animal world in the other's words. For he knows that he is not an animal; and it is precisely at the moment he realises his humanity that he begins to sharpen the weapons with which he will secure its victory.

[From *The Wretched of the Earth* (London: MacGibbon & Kee, 1965), 29–35.]

Section III

Racism in the Twentieth Century

INTRODUCTION

Slavery, imperialism, and colonialism provide a backdrop to a consideration of a variety of aspects of contemporary racism in the next four sections. In this section, the discussion is brought into the twentieth century and various features of racism exemplified. In the colonial world, the framework of the society had racial domination built into it, and this was worked out in a myriad of ways at the individual level, through racial apartheid in many areas of life such as education, politics, and religion, bars on advancement upon members of non-white races, in many colonial societies proscription of intermarriage, maintaining the races as separate caste-like groups, and so on. With the abolition of slavery and in due course the process of decolonization, some of the structural barriers became less overt, and in the metropolitan societies of the European powers, as well as the northern states of the United States, an ostensibly more open society existed in which racial distinctions were somewhat attenuated. But only somewhat. The structural supports of racism were less visible, but no less real, and the individual experience somewhat more varied than under the monolithic codes of the colonial powers, but nevertheless pervasive and showing elements of continuity.

This is clear in the first and last extracts in this section. W. E. B. Du Bois was the foremost black intellectual in the United States in the first forty years of the twentieth century. Born and brought up in Massachusetts, he was the first black student to gain a Ph.D. at Harvard (in history, in 1896) and until 1910 led an academic career in black colleges and universities in a completely segregated higher education system. 'The Souls of Black Folk' conveys the duality with which black people have to live, what it means to come to terms with being treated as a problem. Du Bois illustrates this vividly with an anecdote about his schooldays, when racial consciousness became overt in exchanges with fellow pupils, and he became aware not only that he was different but that the difference mattered. Ninety years later, reporting on research in English primary schools, Barry Troyna and Richard Hatcher suggest that racism is still a significant factor in children's lives, and that racial name calling in school is sometimes accompanied by harassment on racial grounds out of school. At a personal level, there are continuities in experience despite a general reduction in institutionalized inequalities and some forms of overdiscrimination on racial lines.

Du Bois's essay with its impressive clarion call and his formulation of 'the veil' have had an enduring influence. He himself pursued an academic career for fifteen years, carrying out historical and sociological studies of the conditions of black Americans until, largely ignored by his white academic peers because he was black, he abandoned his academic post and became the editor of the *Crisis*, the magazine of the National Association for the Advancement of Colored People, founded in 1909. For twenty-five years, Du Bois as editor analysed and excoriated American racism, ranging from lynchings and race riots to the maltreatment of black troops in the American army during the First World War. He was also prominent from an early age in anti-colonialist movements on a world scale, and ended his life in his nineties living in the newly independent Ghana at the invitation of its president, Kwame Nkrumah. Black Americans made some legal gains as a result of NAACP activity, but the society remained deeply racist.

Mass migration of non-white peoples from the Third World to the industrial societies of the first world is a phenomenon of the twentieth century. Several extracts deal with the consequences of this migration and the manifestations of racism to which it gave rise. Slavery was of course the great exception, but until the twentieth century, the great cities of the metropolitan countries did not attract large-scale black migration. Large-scale migration of white Europeans to the USA and the Dominions took place in the nineteenth century, and one of these waves, of East European and Russian Jews in the late nineteenth century, created a racist response in Britain in the early years of the twentieth century. Paul Foot's short narrative provides an account of the beginnings of immigration control in Britain. Nowadays immigration control, immigration quotas, granting of right to residence, and the paraphernalia of international movement are taken for granted, but until the Aliens Act of 1905 there was a right of free entry to Britain. This legislation was provoked by the arrival of large numbers of Jewish migrants from the east, some of whom settled in Britain and others of whom moved on to the United States. Racial antagonism was a prime motive, as it has remained in debates on the subject in Britain.

The following extract, by James Grossman, maintains the theme of migration looking at the American situation. After emancipation, former slaves remained resident in the South, and mainly in rural areas. There was some movement into southern cities, but it was only with the cutting off of European migration during the First World War that substantial black migration to northern cities such as Chicago began. Grossman writes of this, the expectations of black migrants escaping the rigid interracial etiquette and climate of fear in the South, and the distancing techniques employed by white Chicagoans. *De facto* segregation in employment and residential segregation rigidly enforced by a variety of devices, legal and otherwise, were balanced by some relaxation in public transport, street cars and railway carriages being generally integrated from quite an early date. The failure of progressive reformers and social workers to address the issue of urban racialism is noted. It was only rare occasions, such as the Chicago Commission studying the race riot of 1919, that social conditions and interracial relations were examined in any depth. The colour line was softened, but racial distinction was an integral part of urban society. Subsequent studies in a variety of countries have shown that patterns of racial discrimination and disadvantage persist for black migrant groups in industrial cities, whether black southerners in New York, black West Indians and their children in London, or North Africans in Paris.

To be sure, northern US cities were not segregated to the extent that the American South still was, or South Africa became during the twentieth century and particularly after 1948 with the election of Afrikaner Nationalists to power. No extract treats the South African case in this section, but see extract 34 by Adam and Moodley in Section V. These two cases surpassed the industrial heartlands of the industrial metropolises, but a careful analysis of racism in the latter reveals that it manifested itself in many institutional and interpersonal ways.

Indigenous peoples, as has already been pointed out, constitute a somewhat different case, and one of the most studied cases of the interaction between settlers and an indigenous people is the case of native Americans. (Aboriginal people in Australia are treated in extract 40 in Section VI by Castles and Vasta.) Stephen Cornell emphasizes, in his analysis of tribalization of native Americans following their concentration in reservations by the federal government from the later nineteenth century, that relations between races, and the forms taken by racism, are conditioned by the response of the weaker group as well as by the wishes of the dominant. The social world is not only structurally determined but to some extent at least constructed by the participants. The monograph from which this extract is taken contains a much fuller analysis of native American–white relations, and the sources of the militant political activism which native Americans demonstrated in the 1960s and 1970s.

The sketch in this section of manifestations of racism in the twentieth century is incomplete. The extract by Paul Foot treats anti-Semitism in British politics, but there is no extract in this section relating to anti-Semitism in Nazi Germany and the Holocaust. The reader is referred to extract 37 by Burleigh and Wippermann in Section VI, as well as to the companion Oxford Readers on *Fascism* and *Anti-Semitism*. Nazi policy, as outlined by Burleigh and Wippermann, should be set alongside the cases outlined in this section, and other cases of genocide internationally in the twentieth century.

A more unusual case of the phenomenon of 'racism' is Frank Dikötter's discussion of the emergence of the idea of race in modern China. He points out that too much discussion of racism assumes that it concerns relations between white and non-white races, and largely ignores non-Western countries such as China or Japan. He analyses the relationship between racism and ethnocentrism in the Chinese context, and the emergence of the idea of a racially exclusive in-group by the early twentieth century. In the contemporary world,

Dikötter is right that there are many cases of racism in relations between groups neither of which is white, and more attention needs to be paid to such situations. The Japanese case can also be instructive in this respect.

Robert C. Smith's discussion of racism in the post-civil rights era in the USA, and Barry Troyna and Richard Hatcher's study of racism in the primary school are both cases of the study of institutionalized racism. Both indicate the ways in which institutionalized racism and individual racism are interwoven with each other in particular settings such as dealing with the police, housing, and education. Smith starts with comments on the relationship between attitudes and behaviour in the field of race, and together these two extracts constitute an effective comment upon claims that because a person or an institution thinks itself to be free from racialist attitudes, the absence of racism is therefore guaranteed.

17 **Of Our Spiritual Strivings**

Between me and the other world there is ever an unasked question: unasked by some through feelings of delicacy; by others through the difficulty of rightly framing it. All, nevertheless, flutter round it. They approach me in a half-hesitant sort of way, eye me curiously or compassionately, and then, instead of saying directly, How does it feel to be a problem? they say, I know an excellent colored man in my town; or, I fought at Mechanicsville; or, Do not these Southern outrages make your blood boil? At these I smile, or am interested, or reduce the boiling to a simmer, as the occasion may require. To the real question, How does it feel to be a problem? I answer seldom a word.

And yet, being a problem is a strange experience,—peculiar even for one who has never been anything else, save perhaps in babyhood and in Europe. It is in the early days of rollicking boyhood that the revelation first bursts upon one, all in a day, as it were. I remember well when the shadow swept across me. I was a little thing, away up in the hills of New England, where the dark Housatonic winds between Hoosac and Taghkanic to the sea. In a wee wooden schoolhouse, something put it into the boys' and girls' heads to buy gorgeous visiting-cards—ten cents a package—and exchange. The exchange was merry, till one girl, a tall newcomer, refused my card,—refused it peremptorily, with a glance. Then it dawned upon with a certain suddenness that I was different from the others; or like, mayhap, in heart and life and longing, but shut out from their world by a vast veil. I had thereafter no desire to tear down that veil, to creep through; I held all beyond it in common contempt, and lived about it in a region of blue sky and great wandering shadows. That sky was bluest when I could beat my mates at examination-time, or beat them at a foot-race, or even beat their stringy heads. Alas, with the years all this fine contempt began to fade; for the worlds I longed for, and all their dazzling opportunities, were theirs, not mine. But they should not keep these prizes, I said; some, all, I would wrest from them. Just how I would do it I could never decide: by reading law, by healing the sick, by telling the wonderful tales that swam in my head,—some way. With other black boys the strife was not so fiercely sunny: their youth shrunk into tasteless sycophancy, or into silent hatred of the pale world about them and mocking distrust of everything white; or wasted itself in a bitter cry, Why did God make me an outcast and a stranger in mine own house? The shades of the prison-house closed round about us all: walls strait and stubborn to the whitest, but relentlessly narrow, tall, and unscalable to sons of night who must plod darkly on in resignation, or beat unavailing palms against the stone, or steadily, half hopelessly, watch the streak of blue above.

After the Egyptian and Indian, the Greek and Roman, the Teuton and

Mongolian, the Negro is a sort of seventh son, born with a veil, and gifted with second-sight in this American world,—a world which yields him no true self-consciousness, but only lets him see himself through the revelation of the other world. It is a peculiar sensation, this double-consciousness, this sense of always looking at one's self through the eyes of others, of measuring one's soul by the tape of a world that looks on in amused contempt and pity. One ever feels his twoness,—an American, a Negro; two souls, two thoughts, two unreconciled strivings; two warring ideals in one dark body, whose dogged strength alone keeps it from being torn asunder.

The history of the American Negro is the history of this strife—this longing to attain self-conscious manhood, to merge his double self into a better and truer self. In this merging he wishes neither of the older selves to be lost. He would not Africanize America, for America has too much to teach the world and Africa. He would not bleach his Negro soul in a flood of white Americanism, for he knows that Negro blood has a message for the world. He simply wishes to make it possible for a man to be both a Negro and an American, without being cursed and spit upon by his fellows, without having the doors of Opportunity closed roughly in his face.

This, then, is the end of his striving: to be a co-worker in the kingdom of culture, to escape both death and isolation, to husband and use his best powers and his latent genius. These powers of body and mind have in the past been strangely wasted, dispersed, or forgotten. The shadow of a mighty Negro past flits through the tale of Ethiopia the Shadowy and of Egypt the Sphinx. Throughout history, the powers of single black men flash here and there like falling stars, and die sometimes before the world has rightly gauged their brightness. Here in America, in the few days since Emancipation, the black man's turning hither and thither in hesitant and doubtful striving has often made his very strength to lose effectiveness, to seem like absence of power, like weakness. And yet it is not weakness,—it is the contradiction of double aims. The double-aimed struggle of the black artisan—on the one hand to escape white contempt for a nation of mere hewers of wood and drawers of water, and on the other hand to plough and nail and dig for a poverty-stricken horde—could only result in making him a poor craftsman, for he had but half a heart in either cause. By the poverty and ignorance of his people, the Negro minister or doctor was tempted toward quackery and demogogy; and by the criticism of the other world, toward ideals that made him ashamed of his lowly tasks. The would-be black *savant* was confronted by the paradox that the knowledge his people needed was a twice-told tale to his white neighbors, while the knowledge which would teach the white world was Greek to his own flesh and blood. The innate love of harmony and beauty that set the ruder souls of his people a-dancing and a-singing raised but confusion and doubt in the soul of the black artist; for the beauty revealed to him was the soul-beauty of a race which his larger audience despised, and he could not articulate the message of another people. This waste of double aims, this seeking to satisfy two unreconciled ideals, has wrought sad havoc with the courage and faith and deeds of ten thousand thousand people,—has sent them often wooing false gods and invoking false means of salvation, and at times has even seemed about to make them ashamed of themselves.

Away back in the days of bondage they thought to see in one divine event the end of all doubt and disappointment; few men ever worshipped Freedom with half such unquestioning faith as did the American Negro for two centuries. To him, so far as he thought and dreamed, slavery was indeed the sum of all villainies, the cause of all sorrow, the root of all prejudice; Emancipation was the key to a promised land of sweeter beauty than ever stretched before the eyes of wearied Israelites. In song and exhortation swelled one refrain—Liberty; in his tears and curses the God he implored had Freedom in his right hand. At last it came,—suddenly, fearfully, like a dream. With one wild carnival of blood and passion came the message in his own plaintive cadences:—

> 'Shout, O children!
> Shout, you're free!
> For God has bought your liberty!'

Years have passed away since then,—ten, twenty, forty; forty years of national life, forty years of renewal and development, and yet the swarthy spectre sits in its accustomed seat at the Nation's feast. In vain do we cry to this our vastest social problem:—

> 'Take any shape but that, and my firm nerves
> Shall never tremble!'

The Nation has not yet found peace from its sins; the freedman has not yet found in freedom his promised land. Whatever of good may have come in these years of change, the shadow of a deep disappointment rests upon the Negro people,—a disappointment all the more bitter because the unattained ideal was unbounded save by the simple ignorance of a lowly people.

The first decade was merely a prolongation of the vain search for freedom, the boon that seemed ever barely to elude their grasp,—like a tantalizing will-o'-the wisp, maddening and misleading the headless host. The holocaust of war, the terrors of the Ku-Klux Klan, the lies of carpet-baggers, the disorganization of industry, and the contradictory advice of friends and foes, left the bewildered serf with no new watch-word beyond the old cry for freedom. As the time flew, however, he began to grasp a new idea. The ideal of liberty demanded for its attainment powerful means, and these the Fifteenth Amendment gave him. The ballot, which before he had looked upon as a visible sign of freedom, he now regarded as the chief means of gaining and perfecting the liberty with which war had partially endowed him. And why not? Had not votes made war and emancipated millions? Had not votes enfranchised the freedmen? Was anything impossible to a power that had done all this? A million black men started with renewed zeal to vote themselves into the kingdom. So the decade flew away, the revolution of 1876 came, and left the half-free serf weary, wondering, but still inspired. Slowly but steadily, in the following years, a new vision began gradually to replace the dream of political power,—a powerful movement, the rise of another ideal to guide the unguided, another pillar of fire by night after a clouded day. It was the ideal of 'book-learning'; the curiosity, born of compulsory ignorance, to know and test the power of the cabalistic letters of the white man, the longing to know. Here at last seemed to have been discovered the mountain path to Canaan; longer than the highway of Emancipation and law, steep and rugged, but straight, leading to heights high enough to overlook life.

Up the new path the advance guard toiled, slowly, heavily, doggedly; only those who have watched and guided the faltering feet, the misty minds, the dull understandings, of the dark pupils of these schools know how faithfully, how piteously, this people strove to learn. It was weary work. The cold statistician wrote down the inches of progress here and there, noted also where here and there a foot had slipped or some one had fallen. To the tired climbers, the horizon was ever dark, the mists were often cold, the Canaan was always dim and far away. If, however, the vistas disclosed as yet no goal, no resting-place, little but flattery and criticism, the journey at least gave leisure for reflection and self-examination; it changed the child of Emancipation to the youth with dawning self-consciousness, self-realization, self-respect. In those sombre forests of his striving his own soul rose before him, and he saw himself,—darkly as through a veil; and yet he saw in himself some faint revelation of his power, of his mission. He began to have a dim feeling that, to attain his place in the world, he must be himself, and not another. For the first time he sought to analyze the burden he bore upon his back, that dead-weight of social degradation partially masked behind a half-named Negro problem. He felt his poverty; without a cent, without a home, without land, tools, or savings, he had entered into competition with rich, landed, skilled neighbors. To be a poor man is hard, but to be a poor race in a land of dollars is the very bottom of hardships. He felt the weight of his ignorance,—not simply of letters, but of life, of business, of the humanities; the accumulated sloth and shirking and awkwardness of decades and centuries shackled his hands and feet. Nor was his burden all poverty and ignorance. The red stain of bastardy, which two centuries of systematic legal defilement of Negro women had stamped upon his race, meant not only the loss of ancient African chastity, but also the hereditary weight of a mass of corruption from white adulterers, threatening almost the obliteration of the Negro home.

A people thus handicapped ought not to be asked to race with the world, but rather allowed to give all its time and thought to its own social problems. But alas! while sociologists gleefully count his bastards and his prostitutes, the very soul of the toiling, sweating black man is darkened by the shadow of a vast despair. Men call the shadow prejudice, and learnedly explain it as the natural defence of culture against barbarism, learning against ignorance, purity against crime, the 'higher' against the 'lower' races. To which the Negro cries Amen! and swears that to so much of this strange prejudice as is founded on just homage to civilization, culture righteousness, and progress, he humbly bows and meekly does obeisance. But before that nameless prejudice that leaps beyond all this he stands helpless, dismayed, and well-nigh speechless; before that personal disrespect and mockery, the ridicule and systematic humiliation, the distortion of fact and wanton license of fancy, the cynical ignoring of the better and the boisterous welcoming of the worse, the all-pervading desire to inculcate disdain for everything black, from Toussaint to the devil,—before this there rises a sickening despair that would disarm and discourage any nation save that black host to whom 'discouragement' is an unwritten word.

But the facing of so vast a prejudice could not but bring the inevitable self-questioning, self-disparagement, and lowering of ideals which ever accompany repression and breed in an atmosphere of contempt and hate. Whisperings and portents came borne upon the four winds: Lo! we are diseased and dying, cried the dark hosts; we cannot write, our voting is vain; what need of education, since we must always cook and serve? And the Nation echoed and enforced this self-criticism, saying: Be content to be servants, and nothing more; what need of higher culture for half-men? Away with the black man's ballot, by force or fraud,—and behold the suicide of a race! Nevertheless, out of the evil came something of good,—the more careful adjustment of education to real life, the clearer perception of the Negroes' social responsibilities, and the sobering realization of the meaning of progress.

So dawned the time of *Sturm und Drang*: storm and stress to-day rocks our little boat on the mad waters of the world-sea; there is within and without the sound of conflict, the burning of body and rending of soul; inspiration strives with doubt, and faith with vain questionings. The bright ideals of the past,—physical freedom, political power, the training of brains and the training of hands,—all these in turn have waxed and waned, until even the last grows dim and overcast. Are they all wrong,—all false? No, not that, but each alone was oversimple and incomplete,—the dreams of a credulous race-childhood, or the fond imaginings of the other world which does not know and does not want to know our power. To be really true, all these ideals must be melted and welded into one. The training of the schools we need to-day more than ever,—the training of deft hands, quick eyes and ears, and above all the broader, deeper, higher culture of gifted minds and pure hearts. The power of the ballot we need in sheer self-defence,—else what shall save us from a second slavery? Freedom, too, the long-sought, we still seek,—the freedom of life and limb, the freedom to work and think, the freedom to love and aspire. Work, culture, liberty,—all these we need, not singly but together, not successively but together, each growing and aiding each, and all striving toward that vaster ideal that swims before the Negro people, the ideal of human brotherhood, gained through the

unifying ideal of Race; the ideal of fostering and developing the traits and talents of the Negro, not in opposition to or contempt for other races, but rather
in large conformity to the greater ideals of the American Republic, in order that
some day on American soil two world-races may give each to each those characteristics both so sadly lack. We the darker ones come even now not altogether
empty-handed: there are to-day no truer exponents of the pure human spirit of
the Declaration of Independence than the American Negroes; there is no true
American music but the wild sweet melodies of the Negro slave; the American
fairy tales and folklore are Indian and African; and, all in all, we black men seem
the sole oasis of simple faith and reverence in a dusty desert of dollars and
smartness. Will America be poorer if she replace her brutal dyspeptic blunder-
ing with light-hearted but determined Negro humility? or her coarse and cruel
wit with loving jovial good-humor? or her vulgar music with the soul of the Sorrow Songs?

Merely a concrete test of the underlying principles of the great republic is the
Negro Problem, and the spiritual striving of the freedmen's sons is the travail of
souls whose burden is almost beyond the measure of their strength, but who
bear it in the name of an historic race, in the name of this the land of their fathers' fathers, and in the name of human opportunity.

[From *The Souls of Black Folk* (New York: Penguin, 1989; 1st pub. 1903), 3–12.]

PAUL FOOT
....
18 **Politics and the Alien**

It is a familiar belief that Britain is not a country of immigration. Yet it is true
only in the negative sense that emigration from industrial Britain since the beginning of the last century has been much greater than immigration. From 1871
to 1931, for instance, Britain lost a net outflow through migration, mostly to her
Empire, of well over 3,000,000 people.[1]

What is wrong is the implication that the inhabitants of the British Isles have
through the centuries avoided the influx of people from other countries. The
history of Britain is a long story of immigration—the immigration of Angles,
Saxons, Normans, Danes, Dutchmen, Belgians and many other people from different parts of the world. In 1540, for instance, as a result of immigration from
the Low Countries, a third of all those who paid subsidy in London to the king
were aliens, and in the St Martin's-Le-Grand Ward there were six Englishmen to
207 foreigners among the taxpayers. Indeed London became so overcrowded
with Protestant refugees that an Order in Council was passed dispatching them
to surrounding towns. Canterbury, Colchester, Norwich and Yarmouth were inundated with waves of immigrants, and by 1569, for instance, there were 3,993
resident Walloons in Norwich alone. This deliberate dispersion of immigrants,

incidentally, is the only example in British history of Government action to avoid 'clotting' in special areas.

In 1685, Louis XIV revoked the Edict of Nantes, so removing from the French Huguenots the last vestige of protection from political and religious persecution. Some 80,000 of these Huguenots came to Britain, again under the friendly auspices of the English Government. Later, in the reign of Anne, some 10,000 Palatines were admitted to Britain from the Continent.

The nineteenth century saw the largest yet flow of immigration into Britain consisting almost entirely of Irishmen. Hundreds of thousands of Irish crossed the sea from their homeland to serve as factory-fodder for an expanding capitalism, with the numbers increasing spectacularly after the Irish potato famine in 1851.

Through all these waves of immigration which profoundly affected the pattern of life in Britain, there were two sharply different attitudes within the host community. First, there was considerable hostility towards the immigrants among the people who had to deal with them. The Huguenots, Palatines and Walloons, whose praises were sung so vociferously by Protestant champions, arrived destitute. They were foreign in their ways and their language. They were not, as later panegyrics attempted to describe them, hardy well-dressed artisans who commended themselves immediately to their new hosts. On the contrary. Among the people with whom they had to deal on entry, they encountered resentment and bitterness.

This was even more true of the Irish. In Scotland and in the West of England, the Irish met with a hostility more vicious than anything met by any immigrant wave before or since. In Scotland particularly, where the bulk of Irish immigrants first settled, racial and religious riots between Scots and Irish were a common feature in the ironworks of the Clyde valley or the mining villages of Lanarkshire. In Glasgow, the local population staged an annual demonstration against the Irish immigrant—which ended with a charming game called 'Hunting the Barney': an Irishman would be hunted out in the narrow closes of the Trongate, and near-murdered for sport.

Much of the resentment against the Irish was religious, but the terms in which the religious bigots rationalized their resentment were as familiar as those which racial bigots use in the 1960s. The Irish were all diseased, ran the propaganda; they were nearly all criminals, and they were certainly all lazy. A continual stream of pamphlets and speeches, often from the worthiest of doctors, ministers and lawyers, spread lies to nourish this religious discord. [. . .]

In the eighty years from 1825 to 1905 not a single immigrant of any nationality was deported by order of the central political authorities. Moreover, despite the considerable feeling within the host community against immigrants—particularly the Irish—this feeling never in all that time translated itself into a coherent political demand for control of immigration, in Parliament or anywhere else.

Indeed even before 1825, immigration control into Britain was rare and slack. Apart from a Royal Prerogative to expel any aliens who did not please the monarch, there were few Acts of Parliament giving powers to keep out or deport the foreigner. [. . .] [T]he Aliens Act of 1826, and the Aliens Registration Act of 1836, which provided, not for control over entry, or for deportation, but simply for registration. Even these registration provisions were very soon abandoned. [. . .]

British politicians of both parties, particularly the Liberals, regarded themselves with some pleasure as champions of the right of political asylum. Persecuted foreigners could come to Britain without hindrance. Such was the slogan of men like Gladstone, who could then justify his grandiloquent speeches about 'the savage, as we call him' having a right to live as much as anyone. Such idealism was bred partly from the fact that British politicians regarded themselves with every justification as leaders of world revolution against feudalism and reaction. Their friends, therefore, were men like Mazzini and Garibaldi who were fighting the same struggle in other countries. Such men were welcomed with open arms.

But the unchallenged supremacy of the British ruling class could not last forever. New industrial nations, some conceived by British emigrants, quickly rose to challenge Britain in the world markets, and the politicians tasted real economic crisis for the first time in their country's industrial history. People started to talk about 'protection' as the solution to the rising status of Britain's competitors. Moreover, the political struggles in these countries, as well as in Britain, were no longer clearly defined as between revolutionaries and feudalists. In many industrial centres throughout Europe and North America, a new class of revolutionary was emerging—not confined this time to saving his country from the evils of Popish feudalism, but concerned to attack all capitalist authority everywhere. [. . .]

The second more vulnerable target was the Jew. The Jews had been emigrating in small numbers from Europe and Russia for decades. By the beginning of the 1880s the latent anti-Semitism in Russia and Rumania had turned into systematic persecution. The Russian May Laws of 1888 and the subsequent pogroms drove the Russian Jews back into their already overcrowded and under-employed Pale. All the considerable resources of Tzarist despotism were deployed against the defenceless and impoverished Jew. Small wonder that the victims turned desperately to emigration and streamed across the boundaries, almost all headed for America.

Throughout the 1890s this stream of emigration remained steady and relatively controlled at source. The tidy mind of the Jew, even when persecuted, organized emigration so that the flow at no stage grew unmanageable. Until the end of the 1890s, each year about 2,500 Jews, on the way to America, decided to stay in Britain. Then the hysterical outburst of anti-Semitism at the turn of the century turned the orderly exodus into a rout. The Rumanian exodus (1900), the series of intensified pogroms, the vicious chauvinism of the Russo-Japanese War (1904) threw the emigration into total confusion. Between 1899 and 1902 figures for immigration into Britain trebled. In all, between the years 1875 and 1914 some 120,000 Jews came to Britain, and almost all of them settled automatically in the hovels of East London.

In 1889 a Select Committee of the House of Commons investigated the immigration question. The Committee concluded that the number of aliens was 'not large enough to cause alarm', that their health was good but that they were clotted in specific areas which had unreasonably to deal with too large a problem, and that they disobeyed the sanitation by-laws. The Committee was not prepared to recommend control legislation, but added that it 'contemplated the possibility of such legislation becoming necessary in the future'.

The sober arguments of the Committee did not halt the mounting campaign against the foreigners, being well received in High Tory circles. In 1892, the Conservatives declared their intention of bringing in control legislation, but were defeated before they could do anything about it. The incoming Liberal Government found no trace of any research work on control in the Home Office. The Marquess of Salisbury, in fact, introduced a Bill in the Lords in 1894 to control immigration, and was somewhat embarrassed when, four years later, under his Premiership, Lord Hardwicke re-introduced almost the same bill and asked for the Prime Minister's support. Lord Hardwicke reinforced his argument with a dose of lukewarm racism:

It would be a very serious matter if the type of population which is now to be found in many districts of the East End, where there is a strong alien element, were to become at all a common type in the poorer districts of our large cities. It would mean, my Lords, that these classes would become to a great extent non-English in character, and that, both in physique and in moral and social customs, they had fallen below our present by no means elevated standard. 23 May, 1898 [. . .]

The Bill was, however, the signal for the formation of a powerful and dedicated anti-alien lobby in the House of Commons which made it its aim to push similar legislation through the House of Commons in the shortest possible time. [. . .]

[A decade later, following the deliberations of a Royal Commission on the subject, the call for further restrictions on alien immigration was renewed. The Liberal opposition found itself split, faced with an aliens Bill, those who represented areas of high immigration being particularly cautious. *Editor*].

In the East End outbursts of violence against the Jews became the norm rather than the exception. The campaign instigated by Sir Howard Vincent, and taken up by Balfour, excited what before had been no real racial problem in the East End of London. On the morning of the Second Reading debate, one of the more unscrupulous of the daily newspapers announced in its leader column: 'It is hoped that every London newspaper under British control will publish a list of the traitors in Parliament who vote against this measure.' Another proclaimed: 'The small-pox epidemic was attributed to the scum washed on our shores from dirty water coming from foreign drain-pipes.'

In this atmosphere Sir Charles Dilke rose in the House to move his amendment. Dilke was still one of the finest speakers in the House, and in this speech he combined his attachment to the labour movement and the working class with the logic and attention to detail which had marked him out for so many years. He started his speech by warning the Tories 'that they have raised a devil which they will find it difficult to lay'. He proceeded coolly to shatter the core of the Conservative argument—showing that immigration in 1902 had in fact decreased from the 1901 figure, and quoting from the House of Lords Committee on Sweating in 1888 which had found that 'undue stress has been laid on foreign immigration, inasmuch as we find that the evils complained of obtained in trades not affected by immigration'. He declared that the cheap labour of women and girls was a far more serious matter for the trade unions than was the influx of immigrant labour.

Dilke dwelt at length on the past history of immigration into Britain pointing out that each wave had initially met with hostility, yet after a generation or two had become accepted and even praised. 'Honourable Members,' he said, 'are always inclined to give away the past. They are always inclined to say that alien immigration was a benefit in its day.'

Dilke ended his extraordinary speech with a peroration which visibly shook the Tory benches, and flung his own backbenchers who supported the Bill into considerable confusion.

I am afraid that in this country, though not in this House, there has been an agitation kindled and fanned and that an anti-Jewish feeling has been aroused. Those who read the newspapers which support this Bill cannot help seeing what their tone is. The faults which are set down against the Jews are caused by persecution in the past—the historical growth of the persecution of that race.

The principle of the right of asylum, strong as it is, in the case of Jews ought to apply with double strength to every one holding Christian principles, as a proper exchange for the hateful and shameful system of persecution. Before you change those principles in this matter an overwhelming case ought to be made out. I have examined the figures, numbers and proportion alleged by the Hon. and gallant Member (Evans Gordon) and I ask the house to say whether any overwhelming necessity has been established for this Bill.

Dilke was followed immediately by a young liberal—Charles Trevelyan—who made up in enthusiasm what he lacked in Dilke's experience and eloquence. Yet the House had to wait until the end of the debate for the most powerful attack of all. It came from John Burns, the old socialist from Battersea who had turned Liberal in 1900. Something about the Tory case for the Bill must have stirred the dying embers of Burns's class consciousness. [. . .]

The combination of Dilke, Trevelyan and Burns had two immediate effects. It reduced the Conservative case to shreds, and the Home Secretary, Mr Aretas Ackers-Douglas, unhappy in any event about his party's collapse before Vincent, flannelled his way through a miserable speech. Even Vincent was not at his best, despite his personal triumph. But the second main effect was more important. The speeches galvanized the vast majority of Liberal Members into outright and vigorous opposition to the measure. The Tory majority at the Second Reading was 124—only slightly less than the overall majority at the 1900 election. But the Liberals opposed the Bill with all the fierceness at their command. A decision to 'send the Bill upstairs' (to Committee) was carried by a majority of only ninety, and in the first six days of the Standing Committee the Government got through three lines of the Bill. On 11 July the Prime Minister was forced to tell the House that the Bill had 'received treatment which would make it impossible to carry the Bill into law in the present session'. The Bill was immediately withdrawn, which led Winston Churchill to conclude that, 'The Government did not desire to pass the Bill', and that it was simply a measure to waste parliamentary time and keep the Conservative Party's extremists happy. [. . .]

On 14 February 1905, the King's Speech promised another Bill to deal with alien immigration, one which, when published, was seen to be a considerably watered-down version of the 1904 Bill; it proclaimed the perennial right of asylum and applied controls only to 'undesirable aliens' who came into Britain on 'immigrant ships' carrying more than twenty third-class passengers.

Three factors distinguished political reaction to this measure from the year before. First, the Liberals could not make up their minds. Although Dilke and Trevelyan divided the House on 2 May, they could muster only fifty-nine votes to 211 for the Tories. Asquith and Campbell Bannerman abstained. Yet as the parliamentary battle developed, so Liberal opposition strengthened.

There were almost 150 amendments to the Bill, and some fifty divisions. Crucial clauses were carried in committee by majorities of only 20 to 30, and at the Third Reading, when Asquith and Campbell Bannerman voted against the Bill, the Government's Second Reading majority was halved.

Furthermore the Tory cause had degenerated still further. Typical of the speeches from the Government side of the House was that of Mr W. Hayes Fisher, the Member for Fulham:

Just as one river could carry a certain amount of sewage, but not the sewage of the whole Kingdom, so one portion of London cannot carry the whole of the pauper and diseased alien immigrants who come into the country.

For the first time in the controversy, Joseph Chamberlain, Member for Birmingham West, came out into the open. Chamberlain had already had some experience in controlling immigration into the colonies. As Colonial Secretary, for instance, he had helped to formulate the Australian Immigration Restriction

Act of 1901. In the spirit of his own Fair Wages Resolution, Chamberlain addressed himself to the working classes:

'It is on the unskilled labourer that this immigrant produces the greatest mischief.' So strong was Chamberlain's commitment to the Bill, that the Prime Minister himself was forced to sum up in the important debates.

The attitude of the more genuine representatives of the working class, the Labour Party, showed the third important change since 1904. In that year, no Labour Member had spoken on the issue, and only three of the Labour Members had voted against the Bill (the others abstained). Yet now, goaded possibly by Chamberlain's hypocrisy, they rallied in stern opposition. Their leader, James Keir Hardie, said that he supported the deportation of criminals and diseased but regarded the Aliens Bill as 'fraudulent, deceitful and dishonourable'. He rounded on Chamberlain, perhaps the worst enemy of the Labour movement at the time, and asked what possible relevance Birmingham had to the alien problem. He pointed out that in 1902 Birmingham suffered from the 'plight' of 121 aliens in the city, while by 1904 the figure had gone *down* to eighty-nine. He said that this miserable legislation should have been replaced by an Unemployed Workmen's Bill, and alleged that 'there is no demand for this Bill from the working classes'.

Nevertheless by the end of August the Bill had become law. Major Evans Gordon was knighted. But the Tories only had six months to administer the Bill before they went to the country in January 1906 and were given the biggest trouncing in British political history. There is some evidence that their anti-alien campaign had won a few votes. Evans Gordon and Vincent retained their seats, and Mr Claude Hay, a prominent campaigner for control, considerably increased his majority in Shoreditch, right against the national 'swing'. Yet many other prominent members of the anti-alien lobby lost their seats, and a Jew, Mr Straus, retained the London East End seat of Mile End. Not all Jews, incidentally were in favour of the unrestricted entry of their fellows. Sir Bernard Cohen, Jewish Tory M.P. for Islington, had voted for the Aliens Act and had been awarded a baronetcy soon afterwards.

[From *Immigration and Race in British Politics* (Harmondsworth: Penguin, 1965), 80–7, 94–9.]

JAMES R. GROSSMAN

19 'Don't Have to Look up to the White Man'

Migrants' expectations of northern race relations varied widely, partly according to the level and sources of information at their disposal. Images rooted in the days of the underground railroad and fertilized by continuing sectional debate and interregional communication led many black southerners to expect that northern whites would not share the racist attitudes that dominated the white South. According to one rumor that spread into southern Mississippi, 'northern people had said that southern people were not treating colored folks right and wanted to move them all North.' One family from Texas expected to encounter 'no discrimination' in Chicago. Negroes, they had heard, 'could go where they pleased without the embarrassment of being hindered because of their color.'

Hopeful but less naive migrants tempered such optimism with the wisdom of experience. Few black southerners interpreted their own experience or their region's history in a manner that would lead them to trust white people. Nor did they necessarily want as much contact with whites as many white Chicagoans feared. There is little evidence that black southerners coming to Chicago were especially interested in integration per se; most were more concerned about legal protection, political rights, and access to the paths to security or mobility. Because segregation implied inequality, racial integration could both guarantee and symbolize full participation in American society. In some aspects of everyday life, many newcomers looked forward to freedom from whites; they evinced little desire to attend integrated churches or spend leisure time with white people.

Optimism and caution coexisted within the context of an image of white Chicago that was often cloudy, and probably inaccurate when it was clear. Coming from a region whose population was largely of either African or British descent, black southerners had been exposed to little information likely to inspire a mental construction of Chicago's ethnic mosaic. Roughly one-third of the city's white residents had emigrated from Europe, and three-fourths had at least one parent who had been born abroad. From Germany, the ethnically diverse Austro-Hungarian and Russian empires, Ireland, Scandinavia, and Italy, immigrants had settled in Chicago and reshaped the city's cultural landscape. Even within the borders of the Second Ward, home to half of the city's black population in 1920 and the most accessible source of housing for newcomers, the white minority included a representative melange. The 15,031 whites included 5,771 immigrants and 6,893 of foreign or mixed parentage, with Jews, Irish, Scandinavians, Italians, and Germans most numerous among the foreign-born, followed by Canadians, Greeks, and Poles.

If most migrants arrived prepared to adapt familiar categories of race to their new environment, most white Chicagoans were disposed to evaluate the potential impact of migration within the context of similar broad preconceptions. Such expectations depended heavily on perceptions about race and the dynamic of migration. Despite considerable variation according to class, neighborhood, ethnicity, and political affiliation, white reactions to the influx generally reflected widely shared assumptions about the passive role of blacks in the migration process in particular and in economic and political processes in general.

A small group of employers, Republican politicians, and blockbusting real-tors encouraged the movement precisely because of these assumptions. These individuals, who had little contact with blacks, had something to gain and per-ceived little potential impact on their everyday lives. Realtors active on the fringes of the ghetto eyed the substantial income opportunities offered by blockbusting. A group of Republican politicians, whose black lieutenants in the ghetto presided over a sophisticated vote-getting apparatus, regarded the new-comers as a large and manipulable bloc of voters. Employers recognized that the migration could solve their acute labor shortage. If blacks proved to be good workers and fit into the stereotypical anti-union mold, they also would help solve the more chronic problem of union agitation. Few other white Chicagoans, however, looked upon the migration so optimistically.

Chicago's major white newspapers, which both reflected and shaped public opinion, pitied black southerners but viewed with pessimism and fear the on-rush of ignorant, degraded, and helpless refugees, objects of the overwhelming social and economic forces emphasized by contemporary observers as causes of the Great Migration. This perspective logically induced an analytic framework dominated by a 'Negro problem,' or the need for black newcomers—like the white immigrants before them—to 'adjust.' Adaptation on the part of the city's institutions or its white population did not seem to be an issue. Characteristics of the migrants as either individuals (the most liberal perspective) or as south-ern Negroes, rather than the limitations structured by class relations and racism, defined the problem. Racial oppression was considered a southern dis-ease, and the Chicago *Tribune* had no difficulty ridiculing blacks and referring to them as a threat to the city's health and morals, while repeatedly decrying southern racism and calling for reform south of the Mason-Dixon line. Com-placency about race relations in Chicago combined with a view of the migrants as hapless but degraded victims to leave many whites at once sympathetic to blacks in general and threatened by the implications of black migration to Chicago in particular.

Even the minority of whites who transcended this perspective were likely to view the influx with trepidation. Recognizing that prevailing racial attitudes in Chicago would shape the Great Migration's threat to civic order, the *Jewish Daily Courier* feared that whites would react violently. It is not unlikely that its self-image as a spokesman for a group that was neither black nor white, but rather stood 'between them,' permitted the Jewish newspaper to extend its cri-tique of southern racial violence to a recognition of the implications of north-ern racism. Until the 1919 race riot, however, few other white Chicagoans expressed such concerns. Whites disagreed about how to meet the threat posed by the influx of blacks, but whatever the proposed solution—violent con-frontation, prophylactic reform, or pressure on newcomers to return South—it was the migrants who were dangerous.

Condemnation of southern racial policies, juxtaposed with a condescending hostility towards the debased victims of those policies and an ambivalence towards them as migrants, had firm roots in Chicago's past. Chicago's vociferous abolitionists, abetted by judges who openly flouted the 1850 fugitive-slave law, had given Chicago a reputation in southern Illinois as a 'nigger-loving town' before the Civil War. Yet the city's white residents had seen no need to let their opposition to slavery interfere with their equal distaste for black people. Like their counterparts elsewhere in the North, antebellum black Chicagoans were segregated, disfranchised, and restricted to a narrow range of occupations. During the quarter-century following the Civil War, state laws removed most of the legal barriers to full citizenship for blacks, permitting them to vote (three years after blacks had secured that right in the reconstructed southern states), serve on juries, and testify against whites. The Illinois legislature also banned school segregation (1874) and segregation in public accommodations (1885; tightened by amendment in 1897). These laws, however, were seldom enforced, and convictions—when obtained—usually resulted in token fines. Like most other white Americans, Chicago's white residents had already imbibed racist values and beliefs which transcended legal niceties as influences on patterns of race relations. Longtime black residents would later nostalgically recall the nineteenth century as a period of interracial amicability, but a shifting color line had always defined a series of boundaries.

The legend of a golden age of race relations in nineteenth-century Chicago cannot be discounted. A few black professionals and servants in wealthy white homes enjoyed cordial relationships with whites, in some ways analogous to what a historian of black Louisville has called 'polite racism.' Although less circumscribed than their contemporaries in that border city and more inclined to agitate for integration and equality, Chicago's black elite could realistically recall paternalistic relationships with whites from this period, as well as romanticize what were usually patronizing friendships. Overt racial conflict seldom flared. On the whole, blacks were essentially invisible to most of white Chicago, constituting only 1.3 percent of the city's population in 1890. Racial hostility began to escalate along with black migration in the 1890s, as the black population more than doubled to 30,150 (1.9 percent of the total population). Like other northern cities, Chicago in the early twentieth century experienced what Ray Stannard Baker described in 1908 as a rapid increase in 'race feeling and discrimination.' This does not, however, imply a change in direction so much as a consolidation of previously less coherent tendencies.

By the time of the Great Migration, Chicago was a divided city, characterized by Richard Robert Wright a decade earlier as more segregated than any other northern metropolis. Wright's evaluation—even if exaggerated—appropriately directs attention to the countless barriers separating black Chicago from the rest of the city, even if it discounted the significant ethnic divisions crucial to an understanding of Chicago's social terrain. Recurrent nativist editorials in the *Defender* and similar complaints by black spokesmen angry about the relative treatment accorded blacks and 'foreigners' indicate that black Chicagoans were well aware of the presence of immigrants and their role in the city's economy. But blacks generally ignored more specific implications of ethnicity in their perceptions of 'white Chicago.' Sources generated from the black community suggest little cognizance of seething hostilities pitting Irish against Italian, Norwegian against Irish, or Pole against Lithuanian, German, or Jew.

Of most immediate significance to the lives of black residents were the fault lines that separated them from others in the city and divided their own community. Class distinctions and hostilities set off most blacks from a significant portion of the white population, culturally, socially, and economically, while also dividing the black community itself. At the same time, popular ideas about racial differences influenced patterns of interaction (or lack thereof) characterizing work, play, prayer, learning, charity, habitation, and other aspects of everyday life. Where whites perceived racial distinctions to be most significant or most threatening, they sought separation or exclusion. Where differences mattered less, or in the case of certain forms of night life made association with blacks perversely desirable, contact was more likely. The Great Migration changed the configuration of these patterns only slightly. But its numerical impact magnified and multiplied them, while exacerbating previously less salient spatial, political, and occupational conflicts.

Largely unaware of the specifics of Chicago race relations, migrants tended to place what they did know within a context shaped by their experience in the South. They knew little of the city's ethnic diversity and even less of the tensions dividing various white ethnic groups, tensions exacerbated during the Great Migration by the conflict across the Atlantic. Black southerners preparing to go North thought about 'the difference between north and south,' as one explained, and their expectations were inextricable from such comparisons. A young man who had 'never ben in the north no further than Texas,' had heard 'how much better the colard people are treated up there than they are down here.' On the whole, therefore, expectations were likely to be fulfilled at some level, given both the qualitative and quantitative differences between North and South. Even after race riots revealed the force of racial hostility in Chicago and other northern cities, migrants who had sought relief 'from the Lynchman's noose and torchman's fire,' felt only a limited sense of disillusion. In addition, many migrants had from the beginning tempered images of greater freedom with traditional wariness of whites, to fashion expectations that were at once naively optimistic and realistically modest.

Much of what they found in Chicago confirmed whatever optimism migrants might have had about the meaning of race in the northern metropolis. The mounting racial conflict that finally culminated in a riot in 1919 cannot obscure certain aspects of Chicago race relations central to the initial perceptions of black southerners arriving during and immediately after World War I. Levels of agitation, however much they varied during the half-century preceding the

Great Migration, reflected a degree of fluidity or at least a certain lack of definition. Moreover, most white Chicagoans cared as little about Negroes as they cared for them, a distinct improvement from the perspective of people accustomed to the southern obsession with racial control. Chicagoans might have been equally committed to white supremacy, but without the threat of a significant black population 'the preoccupation with the issue of race' so essential to southern culture in the early twentieth century was unnecessary, if not irrelevant, in Chicago. At the same time, however, limitations and imperatives structured by ideas about the meaning of race at least indirectly affected nearly all aspects of black life. Black newcomers encountered a city 'free from the outward signs of "segregation,"' as one perceptive white reformer observed in 1913, but also a city where racial labels interacted with the class structure to limit options and define patterns of social interaction.

The 'outward signs of segregation' mattered much to migrants from a region where such signs delineated a caste system defined and legitimized by legal institutions. The absence of Jim Crow laws—indeed, the statutory prohibition of racial discrimination in most aspects of public life—suggested that Chicago at the very least lacked a public ideology of racial dominance. Although discrimination circumscribed black life in Chicago and interacted with the material circumstances of most migrants to relegate them to the worst housing and least desirable employment in the city, the color line was not ubiquitous. Nor did it reflect the public values embodied in the laws of the state and city.

On the streetcars and occasionally elsewhere, the differences transcended the symbolic, as blacks and whites were accorded roughly equal treatment and not segregated. One of the few arenas of frequent and involuntary public interaction across lines of both race and class, the streetcars tested some of the implications of integration: longtime black residents feared that ill-mannered newcomers would cause the race to 'fail,' and migrants marveled at the seeming unconcern of white riders. The stereotypical anonymity of the urban environment, symbolized to Richard Wright by the white man on the streetcar whose 'mind fastened upon some inward thought,' apparently unconcerned about the black rider sharing his seat, could seem liberating to newcomers from the South. Given conventional racial attitudes in Chicago, most whites probably found it distasteful to sit next to a black person. Rather than publicly insulting a black seat-mate however, a white rider would silently bear the discomfort and perhaps complain later to other whites. It was, after all, within that black individual's rights (even if some whites wished to abolish those rights) to take that seat, and objection promised a commotion unlikely to resolve the issue. If some white Chicagoans avoided streetcar lines popular among blacks or stood rather than take an empty seat next to a black rider, the tacit nature of the insult required neither response nor acceptance and therefore differed qualitatively from southern protocols. Despite frequent racial incidents in Chicago during the 1910s, there is little evidence of confrontation on the streetcars during that period.

Interactions in such public arenas as streetcars epitomized meaningful differences between northern and southern race relations. Even if white Chicagoans shared the racial prejudices of white southerners, and most probably did, they seldom aggressively displayed those attitudes in impersonal contacts with blacks. Asked why he felt greater freedom in Chicago, one newcomer commented that blacks were not 'compelled to say "yes ma'am" or "yes sir" to white people, whether you desired to or not.' Whatever their racial attitudes, northern whites did not—and could not—constantly try to strip blacks of their self-respect, dignity, and pride. A black person 'was not counted in the south,' observed one migrant, drawing a contrast with Chicago. Another described the ability to 'go anywhere you want to go . . . don't have to look up to the white man, get off the street for him, and go to the buzzard roost at shows.' The symbols of racial caste which permeated everyday life in the South were harder to find in Chicago: 'a man could feel more like a man.'

Black southerners also could leave behind much of the fear that had so permeated their lives in the South. 'We collord people are almost afraid to walke the streets after night,' explained a Palatine, Texas, man ready to head north. If, as one historian has recently argued, a black 'woman or girl in the South found herself in danger of being attacked whenever she walked down a country road,' and had even greater trepidations about the intentions of male employers, Chicago at least did not so readily accept the inherent legitimacy of 'white men's persistent violation of black women.' Black southerners who had been North remarked on the significance of the 'fear of mob violence' as a distinctive aspect of southern black life, and newcomers to Chicago noticed the difference. Bert Jones, who arrived in 1917, later recalled that a Negro did not have to be afraid to 'rub against a white person or something. . . . You didn't have to be afraid to sit down beside one, or you didn't have to stay in a position of being on your P's and Q's.' Recalling southern communities prepared to lynch a black man for accidentally brushing against a white woman while running to catch a train, migrants could easily appreciate the contrast.

But if black southerners enjoyed 'greater freedom and independence' in Chicago, as nearly all affirmed to interviewers from the Chicago Commission on Race Relations, it was not because whites had rolled out the red carpet—or any carpet at all. The *Daily News* noted in 1916 that 'every year Chicago welcomes, by the thousand, her old southern friends who "summer" by the lake,' but the welcome was clearly reserved for those southerners who were white. Black southerners were greeted with headlines blaring 'NEGROES ARRIVE BY THOUSANDS—PERIL TO HEALTH' and 'HALF A MILLION DARKIES FROM DIXIE SWARM TO THE NORTH TO BETTER THEMSELVES.' During 1916 and 1917, Chicago's three major daily newspapers (the *Tribune*, *Daily News*, and *Herald Examiner*) published forty-five articles on the exodus from the South. Most of the reports dramatically overstated the volume of migration; many, especially in the *Herald-Examiner* and *Tribune*, evoked images of hordes of blacks inundating the city, bringing their disease, vice and low standards of living. According to the Chicago Commission on Race Relations, half of all articles on 'racial matters' printed by these newspapers during 1916–17 either ridiculed blacks or focused on violence, black criminals, or vice. The *New World* generally ignored blacks, although a 1913 reference to 'pickaninnies' was unlikely to foster positive images among its readers. Only the *Daily News* was inclined to portray blacks favorably, even winning praise from the *Defender* on one occasion. Had they paused at the railroad station to pick up a local daily newspaper, black newcomers might have found their exuberance slightly chilled by what they read.

Despite considerable variation, this exaggeration, fear, and disdain defined the general tone of white response to the Great Migration, except for the many Chicagoans who simply paid no attention because they neither lived nor worked near blacks. Chicago's white population shared many—if not all—of the attitudes found among southern whites. Public opinion surveys taken in 1921 indicate that white Chicagoans considered blacks minimally educable, emotional, 'unmoral' (as opposed to immoral; apparently they lacked moral standards), sexual, prone to sex crimes, larcenous, and malodorous. Newspaper articles, even when presented without explicit editorial comment, reinforced such images. Whether focusing disproportionately on vice or issuing well-intended pleas for official attention to problems of disease in the Black Belt, white journalists clearly characterized the black newcomers in terms familiar to white readers. References, however innocent, to 'QUEER SCENES' at train stations, 'pickaninnies,' and rural habits that the *Defender* criticized but white newspapers ridiculed, provided additional conformation to whites certain about the nature of civilized culture and its accoutrements. A streetcar line which served a district once inhabited by whites but now overwhelmingly black became known to white Chicagoans as the 'African Central,' and it is not likely that the term 'African' connoted anything except an image of primitive or savage culture. [. . .]

Until the Great Migration, Chicago's renowned social service institutions had paid little attention to blacks or the impact of racial discrimination. Excluded from most private agencies and often provided inferior service by public institutions, black Chicagoans did not have access to the range or quantity of social services available to white immigrants. Most of what was available had to be provided by financially marginal black institutions. Black neighborhoods contained few, if any, orphanages, day nurseries, old-age homes, clinics, public baths and relief stations. Even some institutions located in or near the ghetto refused to accept black clients. These policies rested on a combination of hostility towards blacks, fear of immigrant reluctance to use interracial facilities, and priorities. Reformers interested in Americanization were unlikely to think about serving the black newcomer who, as the *Defender* and other black spokesmen liked to remind whites more sympathetic to European immigrants than blacks, 'needs no Americanization.' Indeed, for many white reformers this was part of the problem, given uncertainty about the desirability of black entry into the mainstream.

Despite widely shared assumptions about the existence and usefulness of racial categories, however, Chicago's white reformers differed in their attitudes towards blacks. An especially sympathetic and pluralistic minority, dominated by the women associated with Hull House and the University of Chicago Settlement, shared Edith Abbott's opposition to segregated facilities and insistence on enforcing laws requiring public institutions to accept blacks. Jane Addams, proud of her abolitionist heritage, was among the founders of the NAACP and wrote of the 'chains' of racism, forged not only by southern racism but by northern indifference as well. Louise De-Koven Bowen recognized that even if blacks and white immigrants faced many similar problems, racial discrimination distinguished the black experience, with the 'children of the negro' limited in ways unknown to the children of white newcomers. Sophonisba Breckinridge even went so far as to advocate 'welcoming' black newcomers from the South. But these women, and the few men who shared their recognition of the significance of black poverty and racial discrimination, generally remained involved in activities oriented towards white immigrants, even after continued black migration and the expansion of black neighborhoods placed Hull House and other settlements within walking distance for many blacks. While Abbot, Addams, Bowen, Breckinridge, Mary McDowell, and a handful of others served on committees concerned with racial issues, wrote about the black ghetto, and criticized discrimination (usually privately), they tended to accept conventional assumptions about black cultural inferiority and the dangers of racial integration. Bowen's apparent ignorance of the significance of her failure to capitalize 'Negro' symbolized a more general unawareness of black perspective. Their compassion and interest, however exceptional for its time and place, had little impact on the black community, race relations, or the lives of black newcomers.

Most white reformers in Chicago were neither hostile to nor especially interested in black people. If the social gospel that underpinned much of the progressive social impulse grasped what one historian has called 'the tenet that not only individuals but entire communities committed sin or won salvation,' few reformers included racism among the social or individual sins of modern American society. Industrialization and urbanization occupied the conceptual focus of the social gospel's analysis of social problems, relegating racism to a background distorted by a dominant view of black inferiority. Social workers, slightly more sensitive than most other progressives, perceived a problem, but until the Great Migration defined it as rural, southern, and a matter for agricultural reformers. Race relations, black poverty, and related issues, W. E. B. Du Bois told Chicago's exclusive, white City Club, had 'to do with some one on the outside . . . there is always that feeling of remoteness, the feeling that it is not their problem.'

[From *Land of Hope: Chicago, Black Southerners, and the Great Migration* (Chicago: University of Chicago Press, 1989), 161–9, 170–2.]

20 | The Transformations of the Tribe

'Our power is gone and we are dying, for the power is not in us anymore.' Thus said Black Elk, the Oglala medicine man, to John Neihardt in 1931. And perhaps it was so. Black Elk had seen the dead and dying at Wounded Knee and had fought briefly there. He had witnessed in his own life the passage of the Sioux nations from freedom to dependency. In his youth the spirits of the Lakota had given him a magnificent vision, calling him to give aid and leadership to his people, and he felt he had failed in his appointed task. Yet his words of despair came at what, in retrospect, appears to have been a critical time, the start of a decade that would see some crucial developments in an extended Native American renaissance.

It is a recurrent irony of history that renaissance and ruin are so closely intertwined. The new Indian politics owes its particular character to diverse influences, but not least to the patterned ruins of the Indian past. The forces that led to nineteenth-century political collapse laid much of the foundation of twentieth-century political resurgence. They did so in a variety of ways, but most prominently in their impact on the organization and identity of Native American peoples.

Incorporative processes are inherently transformative of the peoples they embrace. They not only reorganize relations among groups and between groups and larger societal systems, and thereby reorganize political opportunities; they also transform the groups themselves. This is as true for Indians as for others. The spread of Euro-American civilization over the North American continent placed intense pressures on the indigenous inhabitants to reorganize and reconceptualize themselves. Some of those pressures were intentional, directed ultimately toward the assimilation of Native Americans into the larger population. Others were by-products of economic and political forces indifferent to the peoples they swept before them. But whatever their genesis, their effects were momentous: the reshaping of social life as well as of the bases on which social life was organized and experienced. Some groups were changed more than others, but few escaped unscathed.

This is not merely a historical curiosity. It is crucial to an understanding of Indian political resurgence. The subjects of history are likewise its objects. The agents of collective action are not given to the world; they are made by it. Through the unfolding of incorporative processes such as those involving Native Americans, groups of people come to occupy common positions within a particular social order and to share distinctive interests or historical experience. As an outcome of that process, and of the clash of ideas attendant upon it, they also come to see themselves and their world in particular ways and, consequently, to act on specific bases: as the poor, the working class, Blacks, women, farmers, even as individuals without attachment to larger, solidary wholes. Group formation, in other words, lies at the heart of collective action, squarely between the impersonal forces of historical change and the concrete, collective responses of human beings.

Two such formative processes have powerfully shaped the pattern of Indian political resurgence. These might be termed, inelegantly, Indianization and tribalization. The first refers to the growth of a supratribal consciousness and constituency, to the eventual emergence of 'American Indians' as a politically self-conscious population. The second refers to the process by which tribes came to be what they are today as political organisms and as focal points of Indian identities.[1]

Both processes began, to a large degree, in the European mind and only later came to be realized in the self-concepts and actions of Native Americans. It is this realization, however, that is important here. Indianization is largely a phenomenon of the twentieth century and will receive its share of attention later. Tribalization, on the other hand, has been a more lengthy and complicated affair. The consolidation and politicization of the tribe as the dominant category of Indian group organization and self-concept is a process with roots reaching back to the early stages of incorporation. While it has continued to the present day, by the reservation years its fundamental shape was already apparent. [...]

Of course tribalization could have advantages for Indians. They, too, had political agendas; they also were in pursuit of peace, secure borders, access to resources available only from their adversaries. Centralized political structures, often including new leadership positions, had advantages in dealings with European and American governments and their representatives. As such dealings came to play a larger role in Indian life, specialized political organization became increasingly advantageous. It also offered opportunities to ambitious individuals or factions seeking to expand their influence or power.

Thus conflict and negotiation fostered—even if they did not always produce—tribal political organization. They put the group in a position where it needed to act, and was expected by non-Indians to act, as a single political unit, encouraging the emergence of tribe as primary functional and conceptual unit in Indian–White relations. But the end of conflict and negotiation brought no end to tribalization. The extension of U.S. hegemony over Native American peoples brought new forces to bear upon them, but with comparable effects. The circumstances changed, but in the crucible of the reservations, the process went on.

Inadvertent Tribalization: The Reservation Years

Of course the goal of federal Indian policy was precisely the opposite—the destruction of the tribal edifice—and at no time more so than during the reservation years. The federal objective was to dismantle kinship and other communal structures and to substitute in their place individualistic political and economic philosophy and organization. The allotment policy inaugurated with the Dawes Act in 1887 was both cornerstone and exemplar of the federal design. By distributing tribal lands to individual tribal members, granting U.S. citizenship to allottees, and making the United States the trustee not, in many cases, of tribal lands but of individually held allotments, the Dawes Act set out to destroy the tribe as a territorial, economic, and political entity.

The campaign was only partially successful, although the costs to Indians were enormous and by no means limited to land. Allotment, the prohibition of certain ceremonies, the forced dismantling of indigenous authority structures, and other policies of the period in many cases precipitated political collapse. Collective decision-making processes atrophied as meaningful decisions were taken out of Indian hands, while much of the substance of decision making under conditions of freedom—hunt organization, camp moves, interband and intertribal relations—was no longer relevant. The institutional substance of tribal life was dissolving under the impact of imposed sociocultural change.

Even so, much survived. The community organization of a few groups was relatively less affected by U.S. control, particularly in the Southwest. The village organization of the Pueblos remained largely intact, while the Navajos and Papagos, comparatively isolated on vast expanses of land, for the most part were spared rigorous controls on their internal affairs until the 1920s. Neither of the latter two, however, had anything like tribal political organization until well into the period of U.S. domination; what survived were more or less traditional systems of local autonomy. Not all southwestern groups were so lucky. The political organization of both the Pimas and the Apaches, for example, were either dominated or transformed by missionary and BIA controls.

Other factors mitigated the impact of these decades. In some cases, as with the Pueblos, traditional structures of religious and political authority—the two were virtually indistinguishable—survived in some fashion by going underground, hidden away from government officials and religious reformers. Allotment itself was only incompletely instituted, and some tribal lands were not affected at all. Finally, as the whole history of Indian–White relations demonstrates, Indian group identities, while scarcely impervious to the assaults of policy, were not solely dependent on economic, political, or territorial continuities, nor on the retention of material ways of living in the world. More important to their survival were other social and cultural continuities: patterns of kinship relations, modes of thought and action, systems of meaning and interpretation. Thus rooted, Indian identities have proven to be complex, resilient, and adaptable; despite substantial changes in the outward manifestations of culture, much survived, including distinctive self-concepts and world views. Surviving with them, though often greatly changed in numbers, lifestyles, and activities, were Indian peoples.

At the same time, tribal survivals were not products solely of Indian isolation or secrecy, the intrinsic durabilities of Indian identities, or even equivocation in government administration. However inadvertently, federal policy circumstantially sustained the tribalizing process. The reservation system both reinforced already existing tribal identities and created new ones, at the same time making the tribe increasingly the focus of political relations between Indians and Whites. The reservation became both setting and instrument of a new phase of tribalization in a context of non-Indian control.

Whether or not individual tribes had their own reservations was of little inherent interest to the federal government, which preferred to concentrate Indians as much as possible in a single area, such as the Indian Territory. But few tribes had readily agreed to leave their homelands, and many had negotiated from a position of strength. By the time the power of these tribes had been reduced, the logistical and political problems of moving them had become substantial. What's more, there was evidence that such transfers could be catastrophic for tribes from very different physical environments.

The result was that many groups ended up on their own reservations. Barring massive and permanent out- or in-migration, survival of these reservations assured survival of the tribal unit. It also meant that the reservation and, by virtue of coextension, the tribe became the principal units of Indian administration, continuing a pattern established by the treaty process.

More important, the reservation system, coupled with government desire for close supervision of Indian life, continued the geographical process of consolidation initiated earlier by conflict. On reservations wholly or largely occupied by a single tribe, bands that had once been territorially discrete often were forced to settle side by side or together on the same spot. Villages were moved and consolidated; widely dispersed rancherias, their lands ceded to or taken by Whites, found themselves concentrated within sharply circumscribed areas. On the San Carlos Reservation in Arizona, traditional Apache band organization was ignored as new patterns of settlement and a unitary administrative system were imposed on the groups gathered there, gradually undermining traditional sociopolitical boundaries. In Minnesota, following the Sioux uprising of 1862, the Santees were removed to the Crow Creek Reservation in South Dakota and eventually to Nebraska. Under the stress of removal, concentration in new territory, and the hands of White administrators, the traditional band organization collapsed and was replaced by more comprehensive political arrangements.

A similar process followed Comanche confinement on a reservation in the Indian Territory. Within a few years, reports William Hagan, 'the original band lines were blurring and Indian spokesmen were emerging more and more as Comanches rather than as Quahadas or Yamparikas [band identities.]' In the Northwest during the contact period, the Nez Perce Indians comprised four informal and loosely organized groups, each in turn made up of more or less autonomous bands. In the 1860s and 1870s, through treaty negotiations and subsequent conflict, Nez Perce lands were drastically reduced. In the process two of these regional groupings, along with their constituent villages and bands, lost their lands and essentially disappeared as identifiable groups. Over time and largely as a result of outside forces, more and more inclusive political structures steadily displaced indigenous Nez Perce sociopolitical organization.

Similar changes occurred among more sedentary agricultural groups. The Papago Indians of Arizona were originally a loose collection of distinct village groups or tribes. The formation of the Papago Reservation in 1917 encouraged the Papagos to think of themselves as a distinct people. 'Their growth to tribal self-consciousness,' writes Henry Dobyns, 'was the direct result of the enforced geographic segregation of the reservation policy.'[2]

In these and other cases, not only did subtribal political organization deteriorate, but subtribal identities did as well. Those tied to particular bands, villages, clans, and the like did not necessarily disappear, but, as Hagan suggests for the Comanches, they gradually gave way to more inclusive, tribal ones.

Not all reservations, of course, were occupied exclusively by one people. In order to maximize land availability, minimize administrative structures, and ease the White Man's Burden, distinct—sometimes even hostile—groups often had to share a restricted land base. In the 1850s, for example, treaty commissioners on the Northwest Coast 'were directed to combine little tribes into big tribes and locate as many as possible on single reservations.'[3] While groups combined in this manner often retained distinct identities, for administrative purposes the reservation population came to be treated as a single unit, in many cases taking on a tribal designation that might be at odds with the subjective Indian reality but encouraged the emergence of a concomitant identity.

This development was characteristic of the Northwest, where some treaties created tribal 'confederations.' The Yakima Indians—today the Confederated Tribes and Bands of the Yakima Nation—are in fact descendants of fourteen separate tribes and bands, including the Yakimas, sharing neither political nor conceptual unity, who were placed on a single reservation created in south-central Washington by the Yakima Treaty of 1855. In the same year the Warm Springs Reservation in north-central Oregon was established by treaty with several bands from two distinct peoples, the Wy-um-pum and the Wasco Indians. Following military campaigns in 1866–68, a small band of Paiutes from southeastern Oregon was moved to the reservation as well. These three groups eventually came to be known collectively as the Warm Springs Indians.

The Flathead Reservation in western Montana, also established by an 1855 treaty, became the home of Flathead, Salish, Kootenai, Pend d'Oreille, Spokane, and other Indians, taking its name from the most famous of these groups. Among them they spoke several different languages, but administratively they were treated as a single tribe. When allotment came to the reservation, for example, the population was listed on a single tribal roll. The Indians also found that in defense of their reservation lands they needed to act together; in 1916 an informally constituted tribal council was formed. In the course of a controversy over dam construction on the reservation, the Indians were referred to both by themselves and others as the Flathead Indians, although the Flatheads proper were outnumbered by other groups. 'The reservation,' writes Ronald Trosper, 'had become a source of identity.'⁴

There were other outcomes as well. Consolidation was not everywhere the case, and for some groups the processes of conflict and confinement led to disintegration. The Mississippi Choctaws and the Eastern Cherokees in North Carolina are remnant bands of the Choctaws and Cherokees who were forced to move to the Indian Territory in the 1830s. When the Great Sioux Reservation was broken up into five parts in 1889, the various Teton groups were mixed and scattered to varying degrees among the new reserves. By the mid-nineteenth century the Potawatomis, driven from most of their western Great Lakes homelands, were dispersed in locations from Ontario to Oklahoma, while the Senecas of the League of the Iroquois were divided ultimately into five parts, three in New York—two of them functioning today under a single government—a Canadian group, and a segment removed to the Indian Territory.

Despite this diversity, however, the trend overall was toward increasingly inclusive political organization and tribal identities. The reservation gave physical reality to tribal boundaries once primarily culturally defined or helped create such boundaries where they had not previously existed. These boundaries now separated not so much Indian from Indian as Indian from White, but did so on the basis of the tribal unit. Federal administration paid little attention to subtribal divisions except where they could be exploited for purposes of control. What rights Indians retained were attached to them now through treaties usually made on a tribal basis; their legal standing was derived from tribal identifications or more generally from Indianness. Relations with the rest of the world, once largely the concern of bands, villages, or lineages, were now tribally defined. Those relations went on largely outside Native American control; nonetheless, to the extent that they left any room at all for expressions of group sentiment or group action, they encouraged tribalism. Administratively treated as tribes, Indians found it made sense to respond the same way.

Thus tribal identification received circumstantial support from the external framework of relations within which the tribe was situated, even as the internal supports of tribal community and consciousness came under attack. Of course the atomistic thrust of Indian policy in the late nineteenth and early twentieth centuries threatened even such remnant communalism as the reservations managed to preserve, particularly as the Indian land base was eaten away through allotment, sale, and fraud, and as a destitute dependency replaced native maintenance activities. The tribe was surviving as an administrative unit, but, however slowly, the community or communities it embraced were being broken down.

Moreover, while tribalization was sustained by administrative practice, this very fact testified to its impotence. Tribal identifications were reinforced, but the tribe remained powerless, both victim and by-product of the structure of subordination.

[From *The Return of the Native: American Indian Political Resurgence* (New York: Oxford University Press, 1989), 71–2, 79–84.]

FRANK DIKÖTTER

21 Group Definition and the Idea of 'Race' in Modern China (1793–1949)

Introduction

Much historical research has been produced in the past three or four decades on the problem of racial prejudice. Two main observations emerge from this corpus of studies.

Firstly, it appears that prevailing opinion views racial prejudice as the cause, rather than the consequence of intergroup competition. Slavery, to take an example that has been most abundantly researched, is readily associated with the African trade of 1450 to 1880. It is apparently less appreciated that slavery is a human phenomenon that has been observed from the most ancient times and still exists today in dozens of nations. Moreover, the large majority of slave movements in history were primarily of an endo-ethnic nature, with slavers and slaves belonging to the same ethnic group.

Secondly, it appears that the stress on the causal nature of racial prejudice in interethnic conflicts has led to the overemphasis of Western-related facts. It is too often assumed that racial prejudice can only be a 'white' phenomenon under which other people, lumped together under the heading 'coloured', had to suffer. The narrow focus of such historical research, which can be partially explained by a vivid sense of guilt of post-colonial Western society and by a still dominant feeling of Euro-centrism, has distorted our comprehension of racial matters in non-Western countries.

Precious little attention has been paid in Western historiography to racial ideas in non-western countries. In the Chinese case, the idea of 'race' (*zhong*, 'seed', 'species', 'race') started to dominate the intellectual scene at the end of the nineteenth century and continued to be considered a vital problem by many intellectuals until the end of the 1940s. The emergence of a social cosmology guided by a racial interpretation of foreign people represented a radical departure from the cultural universalism which characterized traditional China. This article examines the transition from cultural exclusiveness to racial exclusiveness in modern China. The transition started in the middle of the last century and was completed in the 1920s. Even a cursory survey of this historical development is of more than academic interest, as it contributes to a better understanding of how a quarter of mankind came to formulate its vision of the world.

The Emergence of a Racial Consciousness (1793–1895)

Thought in ancient China was oriented towards the world, or *tianxia*, 'all under heaven'. The world was perceived as one homogeneous unity named 'great community' (*datong*). The Middle Kingdom, dominated by the assumption of its cultural superiority, measured outgroups according to a yardstick by which those who did not follow the 'Chinese ways' were considered 'barbarians'. A theory of 'using the Chinese ways to transform the barbarian' (*yong xia bian yi*) was strongly advocated. It was believed that the barbarian could be culturally assimilated (*laihua*, 'come and be transformed', or *hanhua*, 'become Chinese'). In the Age of Great Peace, the barbarians would flow in and be transformed: the world would be one.

Western incursions from the end of the eighteenth century onwards blatantly contradicted this traditional conceptual framework: Westerners were unwilling to pay homage to the Chinese court (the Macartney mission of 1793): they rejected the tribute system which had traditionally regulated contracts with barbarians; they refused to be culturally assimilated; and, mysteriously, they failed to turn into Chinese.

The most dramatic consequence of this new historical development was that the sheer physical presence of Westerners in the beginning of the nineteenth century demonstrated the relativity of China's own world-view. Chinese literati increasingly discovered that the well-established symbolic universe in which they operated was neither total nor absolute.

The Westerner was often negated by being perceived as a devil, a ghost, an evil and unreal goblin hovering on the border of humanity. Many texts of the first half of the nineteenth century referred to the English as 'foreign devils' (*yangguizi*), 'devil slaves' (*guinu*), 'barbarian devils' (*fangui*), 'island barbarians' (*daoyi*), 'blue-eyed barbarian slaves' (*biyan yinu*), or 'red-haired barbarians' (*hongmaofan*).

Racial stereotypes, grafted upon the barbarian imagery that the Chinese had developed since the incipient stage of their civilization, contributed to the cultural defence of the menaced symbolic universe. The traditional social perception of skin colour was central to this process of stereotyping: 'The Chinese call the barbarians "devils", and differentiate them according to their skin colour', wrote Xu Shidong (1814–1873). 'The white ones are cold and dull as the ashes of frogs, the black ones are ugly and dirty as coal', explained Jin He (1819–1885). The hairy appearance of the foreigner was frequently underlined. For one observer, 'the white ones are really ghosts; the sounds of their speech are similar to birds, their shins and chest are covered with hair, their green eyes suffer when they look in the distance'.

The repulsive physical features of the foreigner were interpreted as the outward manifestation of an innate inadequacy. In the absence of anatomical knowledge, speculations about the inner physical organization of the barbarian's body could confirm his non-humanity. Yu Zhengxie (1775–1840), a major scholar remembered for his strong interest in research and his liberal ideas, believed that foreigners had only four chambers in the heart, whereas the Chinese had seven. He also thought that Westerners had four testicles.

Absence of familiarity with physically dissimilar people contributed to the gradual appearance of a racial consciousness in China after the middle of the last century. Racial consciousness often first appears among those who have extended contact with a phenotypically different outgroup. The Canton area in particular and the coastal regions generally first developed a sense of racial identity that was to spread gradually to most of the country. Familiarity with outgroups led both to an increased relativization of the ingroup's cosmological position and to an increased specification of the ingroup's identity.

Intellectuals directly exposed to foreigners were vital in the activation of a racial consciousness. After the 1840s, scholar-officials involved in foreign affairs became increasingly aware of the need for a less Sino-centric perspective. Officials like Lin Zexu (1785–1850), Xu Jiyu (1795–1873) on Wei Yuan (1794–1856) compiled world geographies concerned with more practical valuations of the outside world. By a process of positive differentiation between themselves and other non-Western people, they enhanced their own identity. Xu Jiyu's influential account presented Africa as a desperately chaotic continent, inhabited by retrograde black barbarians. 'It is scorching, miasmatic, and pestilential. Its climate and its people are the worst of the four continents'. Others compared Africa to the *hundun*, or Chaos, the primeval state of the Universe according to Chinese folklore. It was precisely those who attempted to make China adopt a more practical vision who were the most eager to denigrate coloured people. The relativization of the ingroup commanded the conceptual debasement of specific outgroups. Africans functioned as a negative identity for those who attempted to depart from the culturalistic assumptions of the traditional Chinese universe. Stereotypes and misperceptions largely facilitated the emergence of a racial identity, which was vital in the process of relativization and adaptation.

The Reformers and the Idea of Race (1895–1902)

The decisive phase in the process of gradual erosion of China's Sinocentric view of the world was its defeat in the Sino-Japanese war of 1894. The Japanese victory led to an outpouring of patriotic agitation in the country. In a general atmosphere of intellectual ferment, study societies created by the scholar class to discuss political issues sprang up in most parts of the country. Journals and newspapers published by concerned scholar-literati spread ideas of reform. The main concern was the survival of China as a racial unit and as a sovereign state in the face of foreign aggression.

Yan Fu (1853–1921) was perhaps the most outspoken and influential proponent of a new world-view based on racial differences:

There are four main races on the earth: the yellow, the white, the brown and the black. The yellow race's territory is contiguous with the north of Siberia, extending to the

South China Sea, bordered by the Pacific and up to the Kunlun mountains in the west. They have prominent cheek-bones, a shallow nose, long eyes and straight hair. The white race dwells west of the salted lakes of the Ural, on the territory conquered by ancient Rome. They have blue eyes and curly hair, a prominent forehead and deep-set sockets. On the many islands south of Vietnam, west of Luzon and east of India is the brown race. The black race is the lowest. They live in Africa and in the territories around the tropics. They are the so-called black slaves.

Yan Fu's vision was articulated on the notion of race: it drew a dividing line between the western barbarians and the traditional barbarians. He undertook a transfer of China's sense of identity from a cultural unity, traditionally opposed to various barbarians that can eventually be annihilated through a process of absorption, to a racial unity, faced with aggressive alien races in an international context of struggle for survival. In the context of racial struggle, Yan warned against the Western sway over the yellow breed or, worse, the weeding out of the entire yellow race: 'They will enslave us and hinder the development of our spirit and body . . . The brown and black races constantly waver between life and death, why not the four hundred million of yellows'.

Yan Fu's racial bias was clear in his brief presentation of Darwin, which focused exclusively on the theory of struggle for survival. Instead of conveying the individualistic approach of Darwin, Yan pictured evolution as a process of constant struggle between races. Group cohesion, Yan Fu believed, was the principle by which 'the race is strong and the group can stand'.

The inauspicious spectre of interracial war, along with the threat of racial extinction, overshadowing China's future, conveyed a heightened sense of urgency to the intellectuals' discussions of the country's shortcomings in its confrontation with the West. The problem of the survival of the Chinese as a racial unit was the paramount concern shared by the majority of writers of that decade. Liang Qichao (1873–1929), whose writings exerted a lasting influence on two generations of intellectuals, borrowed Yan Fu's ideas of racial identity and racial struggle, but added the American Indians to his classification of races. He divided mankind into five main races: the white, the yellow, the red, the brown and the black races.

This association, which prevailed until 1949, was the pure product of the Chinese inclination for well-ordered symmetrical patterns. Chinese literati preferred to view the world in well-defined colours corresponding to clear-cut continents, similar to the ancient custom of associating the barbarians of the four quarters with different colours: the red or black Di, the white or black Man, the pitch-dark Lang, all surrounding the Imperial Centre, symbolized by the colour yellow.

Ethnocentric reactions of the reformers were mainly directed against the Westerners. Though the coloured people were evidently absent from the social unit with which China was physically confronted, they too were continuously approached in the intellectuals' writings. Ranking appears to be the key phenomenon underlying the Chinese interest in darker people. By downgrading the coloured races, collective self-esteem was enhanced. The Chinese negative perception of Africans was largely a phenomenon of compensation.

In the universe of the reformers, the dominating white and yellow races were opposed to the darker races, doomed to racial extinction by hereditary inadequacy. Liang Qichao perpetuated traditional Confucian ideas about hierarchy by continuously dividing his five races into dichotomous couples like 'noble' (*guizhong*) and 'low' (*jianzhong*), 'superior' (*youzhong*) and 'inferior' (*liezhong*), 'historical' and 'ahistorical'. Tang Caichang (1867–1900) opposed 'fine' (*liangzhong*) to 'mean' (*jianzhong*) races, projecting the social hierarchy that characterized traditional China upon the outside world: in the hierarchy of the Qing dynasty, citizens were divided into 'common people' (*liangmin*) and 'mean people' (*jianmin*). Tang constructed antithetical couplets with the four races that Yan Fu's essays had introduced: 'Yellow and white are wise, red and black are stupid; yellow and white are rulers, red and black are slaves; yellow and white are united, red and black are scattered'. He particularly loathed Australian aborigines, who 'are pitch black, have emaciated limbs, resemble macaques and are more repulsive than the oran-utang one can see in Malaysia'.

Liang Qichao persistently denied any sense of equality to the coloured peoples. India did not flourish 'because of the limitations of her race. All the black, red, and brown races, by the microbes in their blood vessels and their cerebral angle, are inferior to the whites. Only the yellows are not very dissimilar to the whites'. For Liang, blacks and browns were simply lazy and stupid. The reformer Kang Youwei (1858–1927), perhaps the most acclaimed Chinese philosopher of the last hundred years, expounded a utopian vision of the world in a work called *Datongshu*, or 'One World'. Kang wanted to eliminate the darker races in order to achieve universal harmony. Darker races were inferior and should be eradicated. He proposed to whiten the darker races by dietary change, intermarriage, and migration; those who resisted should be eliminated by sterilization.

Racial identity remained the prerogative of reform-minded scholars until the beginning of this century. From the conservatives' point of view, discussions on racial matters were taboo, and they implied a degree of relativization that undermined the bases of their Sino-centric universe. This point is best illustrated by a document entitled the 'Scholars' Covenant', drawn up in 1898 by a group of scholars critical of the reformers. The sixth point of the covenant lambasted the vitiated language of the reformers, and denounced the use of terms like 'yellow race' (*huangzhong*) or 'white race' (*baizhong*). The concept of race introduced a comparative perspective that constituted a menace to the Confucian distinction between civilized Chinese and foreign barbarians.

The general image that emerges from the reformers' writings is that of a yellow race engaged in a merciless war for world supremacy with the white race. This outlook was mainly dictated by China's traditional dichotomous view of a world divided between Chinese and barbarians. The lack of any pluralistic world-view predisposed China to perceive mankind in antithetical terms of dominating and dominated races.

Race, however, was only one form of group definition that the reformers embraced. Group definition is a notion that can only exist in a relational context with other groups. The complexity of this network of relations can persuade a group to adopt more than one self-definition, and some of these may have a certain degree of overlap. These definitions possess a high degree of flexibility, and may vary considerably as a result of the changes in the perceptions and the valuations that the ingroup has about outgroups. In the case of the reformers of the last decade of the nineteenth century, Confucianism still exerted a lasting influence as a religio-moral faith. Kang Youwei's movement for the 'preservation of the faith', for instance, tried to promote Confucianism as a national religion by giving it an institutional legitimation. Despite the many attacks of the reformers on the traditional culturalist world-view, Confucianism remained a powerful form of ethico-spiritual identity.

The Revolutionaries and the Nation-Race (1902–1915)

Race was only consecrated as the ultimate form of group definition by the generation of revolutionaries at the beginning of this century. Whereas the reformers perceived race as a biological extension of the lineage (zu), encompassing all people dwelling on the soil of the Yellow Emperor, the revolutionaries excluded the minorities from their definition of race, which was narrowed down to the Han, the country's main ethnic group. Nationalism was perceived as a key to racial survival (baozhong) for the radical Chinese students studying in Japan during the first decade of this century. The concept of nationalism was couched in terms borrowed from the Japanese. Minzuzhuyi, from the Japanese minzokushugi, exerted the most lasting influence upon the political terminology of the Chinese students. The term literally meant 'racism', and expressed a nationalist vision based on a common race. The overlap of meaning of the term minzu, signifying both race and nation, contributed to the emergence of a concept of nationalism characterized by a vivid racial consciousness. The constant juxtaposition of guo, 'country', to zhong, 'race', in set phrases like 'love the race love the country' (aizhongaiguo), or 'national boundaries and racial boundaries' (guojiezhongjie) also contributed to the infusion of racialist ideas into the Chinese nationalist vision.

The myth of blood was realized by elevating the figure of the Yellow Emperor to a national symbol. Hailed as the first ancestor (shizu) of the Han race, his portrait served as the frontispiece in many nationalist publications. From the middle of 1903 onwards, the radical journals established by students studying in Japan started using dates based on the supposed birthday of the Yellow Emperor, initiator of the Chinese race. Liu Shipei (1884–1919) advocated a calendar in which the foundation year corresponded to the birth of the Yellow Emperor:

'The reformers see the preservation of the religion as a handle, so they use the birth of Confucius as the starting date of the calendar; the purpose of our generation is the preservation of the race, so we use the birth of the Yellow Emperor as a founding date'.

The Yellow Emperor remained a powerful figure for many decades. Despite the historian Gu Jiegang's criticism of the mythical foundations of the figure of the Yellow Emperor in the 1920s, he was still officially revered in 1941 as the founder of the nation and the initiator of the race.

The main feature of Chinese intellectual thought since the 1890s was the preoccupation with the idea of group. The revolutionary nationalists completed the transition from group to race. Zhang Binglin (1869–1936), like many other nationalists, expanded the racial basis of Yan Fu's writings and explicitly associated the principle of *qun* ('group', 'flock') with racial strength. In his article 'On bacteria' (1899), he explained how racial power was proportional to the ability to group (*hequn*): the inferior black, brown, and red races prostrated before the yellow race because they had failed to group. On the other hand, the yellow race was dominated by the white race. The whites had vanquished the yellows because of their greater ability to group.

Traditional values reinforced the concept of racial grouping. Confucian values of filial piety and ancestor worship paved the way for the cult of the Yellow Emperor. Racial loyalty came to be perceived as an extension of family loyalty. The family, often corresponding to the clan in China, was seen as the unit by which the race was composed. The revolutionary Chen Tianhua (1875–1905) actively integrated traditional values into a pattern of racial solidarity in his influential writings:

As the saying goes, a man is not close to people of another family [*xing*, surname]. When two families fight each other, one surely assists one's own family, one definitely does not help the foreign [*wai*, 'exterior'] family. Common families all descend from one original family: the Han race is one big family. The Yellow Emperor is a great ancestor, all those who are not of the Han race are not the descendants of the Yellow Emperor, they are exterior families. One should definitely not assist them; if one assists them, one lacks a sense of ancestry'.

Kin terms were infused into a racial rhetoric that called for the emotional dispositions usually reserved for close relatives: 'The racial feeling comes from the birth onwards. For the members of one's own race, there is surely mutual intimacy and love; for the members of a foreign race, there is surely mutual savagery and killing'. Kin terms fostered the much needed bonds of association and group loyalty.

Contrary to the reformers, who had expressed their ideas of sociopolitical renewal in a frame still dominated by a reference to the past, the nationalists successfully broke away from the culturalist tradition. They elaborated a new sense of identity that narrowly focused on the Han race, pictured as a perennial biological unit descended from a mythological ancestor. Until 1915, however, the nationalist vision of blood and soil remained chiefly confined to the political arena. The idea of race would only reach a much wider audience with the New Culture Movement.

Race after the New Culture Movement (1915–1949)
The New Culture Movement started in 1915 and lasted for several years. It was characterized by a totalistic and iconoclastic attack on the traditional cultural heritage. Many new scholars, often educated in either Japan or the West, were determined to integrate foreign science and culture into the intellectual revolution of their country. They invited the youth to part with the stagnant elements of traditional culture and to accept foreign democracy, science and culture as the founding elements of a new order.

Spurred by this intellectual revolution, the idea of race made rapid progress, infiltrating most domains of intellectual activity. The successive attacks unleashed against the traditional heritage since the middle of the nineteenth century had dramatically undermined the bases of a well-established collective identity and had led to the artificial separation of race and culture. Racial exclusiveness was the warrant for successful cultural iconoclasm. With the New Culture Movement, Western social sciences became an instrument to debunk the traditional culture and to boost racial identity. Science and age-old stereotypes constantly intermingled to accommodate ethnocentric feelings of biological exclusiveness.

The concept of the evolution of species led to the idea of original purity. Visions of a pure and vibrant race were projected into an idealized past to compensate for the nation's degraded position in the new world order created by the West. Science and myth wove a fabric on which the frustrated mind could visualize its fantasies. Wei Juxian, to take but one example, published an article inquiring into the origins of the Han race that was entirely based on mythology. Wei saw the Xia as the genuine descendants of the Yellow Emperor. The Yin, the author believed, descended from the Emperor Yan and had intermarried with the Xia to generate the actual Han race. Wei situated the Xia's place of origin on the Caucasus: they were a pure and white race. The Yin, however, were merely red-skinned barbarians from a part of China now known as Sichuan province. White and red had given birth to the yellow Hans. Wei Juxian maintained the myth of purity by locating the source of pollution in an alien group.

Archaeology was in search for evidence of human beginnings in China. Lin Yan, for instance, carefully examined all the theories that traced the origins of the 'Chinese race' down to alien migrations, but rejected them for lack of scientific proof. Like many of his contemporaries, he cited the Peking Man discovered at Zhoukoudian to prove that the 'Chinese race' had existed on the soil of the Middle Kingdom since the very beginning. He concluded that the country had been inhabited by 'the most ancient original mankind' on earth. Modern archaeology had to corroborate China's traditional ethnocentric theories.

Science was infused in age-old myths to revitalize Sino-centric beliefs that could provide a sense of biological continuity so essential in an age of anxiety.

The transition from cultural universalism to racial nationalism took place in an age dominated by Western racial theories. The tension accumulated by the superiority-inferiority complex of the Chinese *vis-à-vis* Western racial arrogance was often released in depreciative descriptions of the coloured people. In physical anthropology, Africans were simply referred to as the 'black slave race' until the end of the 1920s. Gu Shoubai, perhaps the most popular writer on physical anthropology in the 1920s, divided blacks into a 'little black slave race' (*xiao heinu zhongzu*) and a 'standard black slave race' (*zhun heinu zhongzu*). Gong Tingzhang, another influential pseudo-scientist, reproduced a picture of a black in suit and tie; the caption read: 'Black slave from Africa'. Gong believed that blacks and Australians had small brains and had only attained the level of civilization of Chinese 'stupid peasants' (*yunong*), a remark that reveals how easily native prejudice was projected on newly discovered peoples. Professor Chen Yinghuang believed that the purpose of anthropology was to study all the races, from the Chinese and the English 'down to the black slaves and the dwarf slaves', an age-old derogatory term for the Japanese.

Doubts about the biological foundations of the race led to the flourishing of eugenics, the pseudo-science of race improvement. The pressure of the superiority-inferiority complex felt by many educated Chinese was relieved by dichotomization: intellectuals were designated as the superior elements of the race, whereas the lower classes were branded inferior. By transferring the myth of superiority from race to class, the intellectuals set themselves up as a privileged social group, holder of racial purity. The task of the eugenists was to eliminate the inferior classes or to raise them up to the level of the superior class: in both cases, the nation's purity would be recovered and its superiority regained. The popularity of eugenics among the educated classes thus reflected both their concern with national revival and their sense of racial identity.

Conclusion

It was only after 1949 that the concepts of race and class would merge, giving the country a new sense of identity. Racial discrimination was expressly forbidden by the Chinese Communist Party after 1949. Widespread propaganda under the supervision of reformed anthropologists attempted to rectify racial thinking; it also fostered the idea that only Westerners could indulge in 'racism', as the Chinese were now the leaders of the victimized coloured people in the historical struggle against white 'imperialism'.

The idea of racial exclusiveness became taboo, but the underlying ideas that had led to its expression failed to disappear. The messianic idea of a universal mission of unification (the *datong*, or 'One World' ideal) was now expressed in a phraseology based on the concept of class struggle, whereas the artificial dichotomization between Chinese and Westerners in biological terms of 'race' was merely reformulated in social terms of 'class'. Moreover, racial prejudice in China has tended to reappear during periods of internal and external tension. During the Sino-Soviet rift, race made an official reappearance when the Communist party increasingly harped on the theme of biological differences between Soviets and Chinese. With the gradual rapprochement of the two superpowers nowadays, the idea of racial identity could prove to be dangerously tempting in an isolated China.

[From 'Group Definition and the Idea of "Race" in Modern China (1793–1949)', *Ethnic and Racial Studies*, 13/3 (1990), 420–31.]

ROBERT C. SMITH

22 Racism in the Post-Civil Rights Era

The Behavioral Dimension

Given that there is no necessary relationship between racist attitudes and racist behavior, we know next to nothing about the trend lines of racist actions by individuals in the post-civil rights era. There is no systematic data on individual racism—when individual whites take race into consideration in order to inflict injury, harm, or in other ways take actions calculated to subordinate blacks. Such data simply are not systematically collected. In 1969 the Department of Health, Education, and Welfare recognized this problem in *Toward a Social Report*, in which it stated, 'The nation has no comprehensive set of statistics reflecting social progress or retrogression. There is no government procedure for periodic stocktaking of the social health of the nation.' The report recommended the development by the federal government of a comprehensive social report with emphasis on the development of social indicators that would measure social change and facilitate the establishment of national social policy goals. Although some progress has been made since the 1960s in the development of social indicators in the areas of health, the environment, educational attainment, and income poverty, little has been done in the area of measuring racism. The 1969 report alluded to the problem of racism and racial conflict, however, the distinguished group of social scientists (headed by Daniel Bell and Alice Rivlin) who prepared the report failed to call for the development of indicators of racism. As a result while we can speak with some confidence about the nation's progress in health, education, and the environment since the 1960s, in the area of racism, arguably the nation's most pressing domestic problem, we are left to rely on sporadic data collected by private individuals or groups or, more frequently, simply anecdotal material reported in the press.

In recent years some attention has been given to the systematic collection of data on individual racism as it is manifested in acts of violence or harassment by whites against blacks and other minorities. This interest was sparked by certain well-publicized incidents of individual racism, such as the murder of young black men in the boroughs of Queens and Brooklyn, which gave rise to a sense that racism was on the increase in the 1980s. In a 1987 paper Howard University Professor Ronald Walters pulled together the scattered data on individual acts of racial violence and harassment in the post-civil rights era. Reports of human relations commissions in California, New York City, Montgomery County, Maryland, and from the Justice Department's Community Relations Service show a steady increase in incidents of racially motivated harassment and violence since the late 1970s. During this same period, there have been reports of increased incidents of individual racist harassment and violence on the nation's college and university campuses. Many observers see the rise of individual racist violence in the 1980s as an aberration—an interruption of a previous pattern of decline in such acts in the post-civil rights era as a result of a climate of intolerance or resurgent 'white nationalism' fostered by the Reagan administration. Others suggest that the figures may reflect not an increase in such incidents but rather an increase in the reporting of such incidents or simply better data collection efforts. In conclusion, we are back to where we started, we simply do not know the extent to which individual acts of racially motivated violence have increased, decreased, or simply stayed the same in the post-civil rights era. All we may properly infer from the available information is that racism of this type has not been completely eliminated in the post-civil rights era, which suggests once again the need for more systematic data collection.

Other forms of individual racism are just as difficult to make sense of empirically. For example, in the area of employment blacks have a widespread perception of racism on the part of individual employers. But we are hard-pressed to know the extent to which this perception is correct except for when the occasional case reaches the courts or is otherwise reported in the press. This is so in part because more than half the persons who perceive employment discrimination do not report it. Second, as Brooks points out:

discrimination does not exist, at least not in a legal sense, until a court (and, really the Supreme Court) says so. A judicial finding of discrimination, however, has an uncertain quality about it. The finding is empirical (a question of fact), analytical (a question of law applied to the facts), and policy driven (a question of who bears the burden of proof). In addition, a lower court's finding of discrimination is subject to reversal on direct appeal or years later when and if the issue comes before the court again in another case. Thus, a careful review of judicial determinations (the 'best' evidence available) is inconclusive evidence of the existence of even a legally controlled concept of discrimination.[1]

Given these difficulties in judicial determination of racism, Brooks and his colleagues relied in their research not on judicial proof of racism but the filing of claims of job discrimination in court or with government agencies, whether proved or not, as well as personal perceptions of discrimination.[2] Brooks concludes that these sources 'offer compelling evidence that complex racial discrimination faced by middle class African Americans [who are more likely that the lower class to report their perceptions of discrimination] is more than an intermittent phenomenon. They provide at least prima facia proof that such discrimination is regular and systemic in places of middle class employment'[3]. Brooks's 'juri-statistical' research on racism in employment is further substantiated by the occasional egregious 'case study' reported in the press. The two cases discussed below were widely reported in both the national print and electronic media. They are useful to discuss because they illustrate not only cases of individual racism but also how these individual acts become so embedded in systemic practices that it becomes all but impossible to disentangle the individual from the institutional type of racism.

The first is the seven-year ordeal of Donald Rachon, an African-American FBI agent. Since the FBI is the government's principal agency for the investigation of racism, especially the manifestly unlawful individual type, the Rachon case is a quite compelling example of the persistence of racism in the post-civil rights era. While assigned to the FBI's Chicago and Omaha offices in the early 1980s, Rachon reported a consistent pattern of racial harassment by his white colleagues, and after the incidents were reported, a systematic effort by Bureau supervisors' to cover them up. In charges that were upheld in administrative inquiries by the Justice Department and the Equal Employment Opportunity Commission, Rachon indicated, among other things, that his wife (who was white) received obscene, threatening telephone calls that often included lurid references to interracial sex; photographs were placed on his desk with an ape pasted over his son's head and in his mailbox with the image of a badly bruised black man. Another incident included a forged death and dismemberment policy taken out in his name by one of his colleagues. As a result of incidents of this sort, Rachon reports that he became physically ill and the emotional toll eventually broke up his marriage. In an out-of-court settlement, the FBI agreed to pay Rachon $1 million, his wife $150,000, and his lawyers a half million dollars, although the Bureau refused to concede any wrongdoing. Rachon, who as part of the settlement agreed to resign from the Bureau, claims his case was not, as the director said, an isolated case, but represented a systematic pattern of internal discrimination, harassment, and intimidation of black agents by their white colleagues. As with most instances of individual racism that come to light in court or the press, the analyst has little basis for making a judgment but the *perception* of systematically sanctioned racism by individuals in the nation's principal law enforcement agency is, on the basis of the Rachon case, not unwarranted.

The second case of individual racism involves four New York City employment agencies where employees under the direction of their managers systematically discriminated against blacks seeking jobs as low-level white-collar receptionists and secretaries in corporate offices. The case, reported on the CBS news program '60 Minutes' and in the *New York Times*, showed that the agencies routinely asked their corporate clients their racial preferences for employees and then used code words like 'All American,' 'front office appearance,' and 'corporate image' to alert would-be employers to the fact that the prospective employee was white. Once this situation came to light and suit was filed by the New York attorney general, the agencies responded with the now expected post-civil rights rejoinder that this was 'an aberration' that did not reflect institutional policies or practices. The analyst has no way of knowing but, again, if this kind of discrimination can be documented for such low-level white-collar jobs as receptionist, then this reinforces Brooks's argument that perceptions matter and that discrimination in white-collar employment may be widespread.[4] This perception is supported by one systematic study of entry-level white- and blue-collar jobs. In a study for the Urban Institute, Turner, Fix, and Stryck conducted a 'hiring audit' to determine the degree of racial discrimination in entry-level employment in Washington and Chicago. The research involved selecting black and white 'job testers' carefully matched in terms of age, physical size, education (all were college educated), and experience, as well as such intangible factors as poise, openness, articulateness, and sending them to apply for entry-level jobs identified in newspaper ads. The results found what the authors call 'entrenched and widespread' discrimination at every step in the process, with whites three times as likely as blacks to advance in the hiring process to the point of being offered a job. Again, the data here are limited, but the cases discussed should at least caution those who facilely dismiss racism in the post-civil rights era as a causal factor in black unemployment and the associated problems of the so-called black underclass.

On the day I was compiling material for this chapter in preparation for writing the first draft, the videotape of the brutal beating of Rodney King, a young black man, by officers of the Los Angeles Police Department was first broadcast. I watched the tape with ambivalence, revolted by the atrocity and feeling pain for the young man, yet clearly pleased that the tape provided unambiguous 'data' for my planned discussion of racist violence by the police in the post-civil rights era. I was neither surprised nor shocked by the tape (as I was by the jury's subsequent verdict of not guilty) because, having resided in Los Angeles during the late 1960s and early 1970s, I lived in constant fear of the police and as a frequent visitor to the city since then, I knew that black residents, especially young men, still lived in fear of being stopped and harassed, if not beaten by the police. Los Angeles, in this sense, is somewhat unique. In the 1950s and 1960s charges of harassment and brutality were frequently made against the police. The 1969 *Report of the National Advisory Commission on Civil Disorders* (the Kerner Report) found that police misconduct was one of the leading grievances of urban blacks against the local authorities and frequently a precipitant cause of the ghetto riots. Yet students of big city politics in the post-civil rights era have reported a decline in police misconduct in the last twenty-five years, in part as a result of the election of black mayors, the appointment of black police chiefs, and the racial integration and reform of many departments. In all cases except Los Angeles, that is, where, in spite of the election of a black mayor and some degree of racial integration, the perception remained that its police department was effectively out of control. This is certainly my perception as an individual who has lived for the last two decades in big cities—New York City, Washington, D.C., Houston, San Francisco, and Oakland, as well as Los Angeles—the latter is the only city where I approached the police with a palpable sense of fear and dread. The Rodney King videotape thus came as an unexpected piece of 'data' in the analysis of individual racism by the nation's police in the post-civil rights era.

Although anecdotal and scattered systematic data (systematic data are not routinely collected on a national basis on incidents of police conduct, although after the Rodney King incident Congress considered legislation to require the FBI to include such statistics in its Uniform Crime Reports) suggest a decline in police brutality since the 1960s, there are still ample anecdotes and statistical data to suggest that this form of individual racism is by no means a thing of the past. Indeed, in the post-civil rights era police violence has probably replaced the Ku Klux Klan and other white terrorist groups as the most pervasive racist threat to the individual security of blacks. In every major American city, every year or two an incident occurs to convince the black community, official findings notwithstanding, that the police murdered a black woman, child, or man. Richard Pryor's humor provides some perspective on this problem, a perspective that resonates well throughout black America. On the album 'That Nigger Is Crazy' Pryor tells the following story:

Cops put a hurting on niggers, white folks don't believe it; they say, 'I am tired of all of this talk about police brutality, those people were resisting arrest.' That's because the police live in your neighborhood and when an officer pulls you over you say 'Oh officer, glad to be of help' . . . a black doesn't say that. When he is pulled over he says, 'I am reaching in my pocket for my license because I don't want to be no mother-fucking accident.'

The official statistics seem to bear out Pryor's observation in that when the police kill blacks it is often ruled 'accidental'; because the officers claim they thought the victim had a gun, although when one looks at the data for any given year, in three out of four cases, the person killed was unarmed.

Blacks, who are about 12 percent of the population, usually constitute more than half the persons killed by police, and in some years the figures are even higher. For example, Walters cites figures from the Police Foundation that show that 78 percent of those killed and 80 percent of those nonfatally shot were minorities. Apparently, the police use of deadly force increased in the early 1980s, up 43 percent in 1983 from 1980, according to the Police Foundation data.[5] Walters notes that the police shootings were rarely prosecuted and that 'The only factors which appeared to restrain the growth of such official, racially motivated violence was not the criminal justice system itself, but the election of sensitive Black mayors who initiated new policies for the use of deadly force.'[6]

In the aftermath of the King verdict, a study of reports of police brutality in fifteen major daily newspapers between January 1990 and May 1992 found that the majority of the civilian victims of police brutality were black. Of 131 such cases reported, during this period 87 percent were black, 10 percent Hispanic, and 3 percent white. By contrast 93 percent of the officers involved were white, suggesting a national pattern of misconduct by white police officers toward black citizens. This form of individual racism under the cloak of authority must, however, be placed in the context of the extraordinarily high rate of violent crime in inner-city black communities. Just as in any given year half the persons killed by the police are black so in any given year half the murders committed in the United States are by blacks, usually blacks killing blacks. This form of communal violence has increased in the post-civil rights era in part as a result of changes in the structure of the urban economy. Other reasons include the violence associated with intensification of the drug wars, the turf disputes among gangs, and the increased availability of more lethal weapons. Thus, in a real sense many police officers view inner-city black communities as war zones, where, like in Vietnam, everyone is a potential enemy and one shoots first and ask questions later because to do otherwise might put their own lives at risk. Consequently, some unknown number of the shootings and killings of blacks by white police officers are surely justified. Yet in other cases when the police kill blacks it is simply murder, as in [. . .] the widely publicized Miami case in the 1980s when several police officers wantonly beat a young black man to death, precipitating several days of rebellion in the Liberty City ghetto after the clearly guilty officers were found innocent.

This is the significance of the infamous Los Angeles videotape 'data' because it unambiguously demonstrates individual racism by the police. The videotape not only clearly shows the persistence of this form of racist behavior by the individuals involved but it also suggests it was systematically or institutionally sanctioned. First, the two-minute beating occurred in full view of passing motorists and witnesses in nearby apartments, who shouted, 'Don't kill him. Stop, don't kill him.' One must infer here that the officers believed they could get away with it; the witnesses and the evidence of King's mangled body notwithstanding. Second, the fact that some twenty officers witnessed the incident but did not intervene suggests that this kind of individual racism had some peer sanction. Third, that this was more than an individual aberration is suggested by the fact that the officers casually joked over their radios about the beating with colleagues, leaving a record of racial slurs and intimations that this was not an unheard-of-occurrence. As one officer said, 'I haven't beaten anyone that bad in a long time'; another replied, 'I thought you agreed to chill out for a while.'

As I have reiterated throughout this chapter, any effort to chart the course of racism in the last twenty-five years is fraught with many difficulties in terms of data and methods. Facts and figures are hard to come by, and when they are available they may be ambiguously interpreted; seen as isolated incidents or aberrations. The Los Angeles videotape and the transcripts of the officers' conversations in the immediate aftermath of the incident are useful precisely because their meanings are beyond doubt. (I wrote this initially before the verdict was delivered in the case, on the assumption that no one, especially not a duly sworn jury—even if all white—could see the videotape and conclude that the police had not used excessive force. Thus, the jury verdict becomes an additional bit of data on the nature of individual racism in the post-civil rights era.)

White people—including social scientists—have better access to data on individual racism than do blacks. That is, in the course of their daily lives—personal and professional—whites have the opportunity to observe racist thinking and behavior that would probably be hidden given the presence of a black person. Perhaps, some white journalist or scholar ought to make a project of keeping a journal for several years on observed or reported racist behavior of white friends and colleagues. It might make a remarkable document. Skin color notwithstanding however, I conclude this chapter by discussing some personal encounters with individual racism in the post-civil rights era. While this may be unusual in an academic treatise, it may also be useful, first, because in some sense it is the 'data' I know best and, second, because all knowledge, even academic work, is in some sense personal. One's personal history exercises some influence, whether conscious or not, on even the most objective, quantitative analysis. I focus here not on minor irritants and slights that are a constant of an African-American's predicament in the United States but rather anecdotes that had or might have a significant effect on the life chances of me and my family.

My initial encounters with racism were in the rigidly segregated rural Louisiana of my youth; however, my encounters in the post-civil rights era have occurred in the urban north. On several occasions I have been arrested simply for being a black man in the wrong place at the wrong time. In 1971 I drove my wife to an appointment for a receptionist position at a Beverly Hills law firm (she didn't get the job). Dressed as usual in t-shirt and jeans, I casually window-shopped while waiting for her. When we returned to our car we were briefly followed by the police and then stopped. The car was illegally searched (apparently for drugs) and, as I told the officer he had no authority under the Fourth Amendment to search the car, he replied to his partner, 'I am not searching Joe, do you see me searching?' I was then arrested and held for several hours on the spurious charge that there was an outstanding warrant for my arrest on murder charges. On another occasion, in White Plains, New York, while shopping with my five-year-old daughter at a local supermarket I was arrested on the complaint of an elderly white woman that I had snatched her purse a week before. The charges were taken seriously, and if I had not had the good fortune to be on the faculty at the local university I might have been tried and imprisoned.

As it turned out, the president of the university called the police chief and in effect told him, 'you got the wrong nigger; he is a professor.' I was immediately released with profuse apologies to 'Dr' Smith.

Suburban Westchester County, like many other places, is segregated along race and class lines, which gave rise to two encounters with racism, one individual and one institutional. The individual incident involved my search for housing. A friend and colleague, Dale Nelson, a professor at Fordham University, informed me that there would soon be a vacancy in his apartment building and he would keep me informed so that I might make early application. Sure enough, a vacancy occurred, and my wife and I immediately applied, only to be told by the superintendent that there were no vacancies and none were anticipated. Knowing that he was lying, we informed the Nelsons, and when another vacancy occurred Dale offered to put a deposit to hold the apartment until we arrived within the hour. The superintendent angrily told him 'never to send a nigger to him for an apartment again.' Although we sought the assistance of the local Urban League office in filing a complaint, nothing came of this until a year or so later when we heard on the radio that the U.S. attorney's office had filed suit against the rental agency, and we and the Nelsons subsequently became principal witnesses for the government in the lawsuit. After much delay, the rental agency entered a consent decree in which it agreed to a rigorous affirmative action program of rentals to minorities and to pay modest damages to my wife and me and the Nelsons. This was a case of individual racism buttressed, according to the government's suit, by an institutional pattern of racism.

The second case involves a variant of institutional racism. As I indicated, Westchester County consists of many towns and villages segregated along race and class lines. I lived in White Plains, a relatively large city with segregation by race and class but also racially integrated neighborhoods. The nearby town of Harrison is an upper-class community, possibly all white, with homes selling for more than half a million dollars. The town operated a beautiful park that was nominally open only to residents but was used by residents of White Plains, at least white residents. My next-door neighbors (whites) frequented the park without any difficulties, and my wife, daughter, and I once accompanied them. Immediately, we were approached by a park official asking for our residency cards. Our neighbors had never been asked to prove residency, yet immediately when a black family is involved residency immediately becomes an issue—skin color serving as an indirect indicator that I was not a resident of Harrison, either because no blacks lived there or because the park attendant was able to recognize all two or three of them. Thus, I was deprived of the right to use a public park on the basis of race as surely as I was in rural Louisiana during the days of official segregation, yet it was, of course, all perfectly legal.

Let me conclude this discussion of personal encounters with racism in the post-civil rights era with a discussion of racism in the academy. I have been around academic institutions all my life and, except for minor racial slights and slurs, I have rarely encountered individual, overt racism, although at the white universities where I have taught I have frequently heard students remark, 'He is black, but he is good,' as if being black and a good teacher somehow don't go together. But professionally my encounters with racism have been institutional, not individual, revolving largely around my interest in black studies, black politics, and black colleges. As Hanes Walton writes:

Negro politics (as it was called as late as the mid 1960s) was long considered an 'off beat field of political science,' an academic graveyard for young scholars who sought academic respectability and an opportunity to rise to the forefront of the discipline. At best, it was viewed as an occasionally interesting subject—an intellectual toy that one might tinker with from time to time. But since it, like black people, was looked down upon by society and, therefore academia, one could not afford to devote extensive time, effort and attention to the subject in any sustained and consistent fashion.[7]

This institutional hostility to black politics in the discipline of political science and in the academy as a whole has been a part of my career from graduate school to the present, although in 1990 the American Political Science Association recognized black politics as one of its valid twenty or so subfields. This notion that the study of the politics of race—the nation's most enduring and pervasive cleavage—is somehow a 'backwater' not in the 'larger world' is a myopic feature of the post-civil rights era academy that operates as a continuing institutional barrier to the society's capacity to understand and deal with racism and its consequences effectively.

[From *Racism in the Post-Civil Rights Era: Now you see it, now you don't* (Albany, NY: State University of New York Press, 1995), 42–51.]

BARRY TROYNA AND RICHARD HATCHER

23   Racism in Children's Lives

The schools that we studied are similar to many hundreds of primary schools in urban areas, located in streets of Victorian terraces or new estates on the outskirts. They are similar, too, in containing a minority of black children, perhaps two or three, or half a dozen, in each class. A visitor in the classroom and playground will observe children working together and playing together, black and white, with no sign that 'race' is a significant feature of their lives as children. It is unlikely that such a visitor would overhear a racist remark or witness any other form of racist behaviour. It would be easy to conclude that racism among children is not an issue that such schools need to devote much attention to. These schools seem to confirm the validity of the 'contact hypothesis' that racial prejudice and discriminatory practices are dispelled by the positive experience of white and black children being together in school.

Our evidence does not support this view. On the contrary, it reveals that 'race', and racism, are significant features of the cultures of children in pre-dominantly white primary schools. By far the most common expression of racism is through racist name-calling. There is a wide variation in black children's experiences of racist name-calling. For some it may be almost an every-day happening. For others it is less frequent, with occurrences remembered as significant events whose recurrence remains a possibility in every new social sit-uation. For all, it is in general the most hurtful form of verbal aggression from other children.

The variation in the experiences of black children are not explicable in terms of differences of ethnic group, or of gender. Differences between schools seem to be mainly the consequence of the effectiveness of the stance that teachers, non-teaching staff, and in particular the headteacher, take towards racist inci-dents. But there is also a wide variation in the experiences of black children in the same school, which is mainly a function of differences in the characteristic patterns of social interaction that black children are involved in, and in particu-lar the level of conflict within them.

Many black children also have experiences of racism outside school. In some cases these are of harassment by other, perhaps older, children. School policies on racist behaviour may suppress it within the school but have no effect on the behaviour of some of the white pupils once they leave the school premises. In addition, many black children have experiences of racism in the adult world: disputes with neighbours, arguments in shops, conflict in the community. These experiences, and the roles taken up by black adults within them, provide a context for their experiences in school, their understanding of them and their responses to them, that other children, and school staff, may be unaware of.

A central objective of this book has been to explore the antecedents, nature and range of race-related incidents in primary schools where there are relatively few black children. Our theoretical starting point was that racist ideologies are not passively received but are used in ways which help children make sense of their material and cultural circumstances. It does not automatically follow, then, that the expression of racism in the parental or school culture, in the media or friendship group, will result in individual children articulating similar convictions. Racism has conditional status in people's lives; conditional, that is, on the extent to which it can be used to make sense of their world. On this view, racism does not exist in isolation, it is relational. It articulates in complex, some-times contradictory ways with other elements of children's common-sense un-derstandings of their lives. The intricate web of social relations in which children live their lives and the particular set of material and cultural circum-stances in which this is embedded have the potential to heighten the salience of racism as an appealing and plausible explanation for the 'way things are'.

The experience for white children of being in everyday contact with black youngsters generates contradictory dynamics, towards racial equality and the de-racialisation of relationships, but also towards the racialisation of existing social processes within children's cultures. In particular, racist name-calling is an important strategy within many children's interaction repertoires (though not in others'), and consequently one that all children have to take up a position in relation to. The meaning of this and other forms of racist behaviour can only be understood in the context of children's cultures, relationships and processes of social interaction.

Children's cultures can be analysed in terms of the interplay of processes of domination and equality. Elements of elaborated and common-sense ideologies, both racist and anti-racist, deriving from family, television and community, enter into and circulate within children's cultures. Here they interact with common-sense understandings generated by everyday social interaction among children. Social processes of dominance and conflict may become racialised in various ways to legitimise forms of racist behaviour. But interaction among children also gives rise to a strong egalitarian dynamic, which may be generalised to issues of 'race' and link up with anti-racist ideologies. Relationships of friendship between white and black children reinforce this egalitarian dynamic, but do not necessarily lead to its generalisation to all black children.

There is a wide variation among white children in their knowledge, attitudes and beliefs about 'race', both within children's culture and in the wider society. Some children are largely ignorant of processes of racial discrimination in society, but the majority of white children have quite an extensive knowledge base and set of interpretive frameworks through which they make sense of issues such as immigration, racial violence, South Africa, and relations between black and white people in their own community. The principal sources outside the school are parents and other adult relatives, television, and their direct experiences in the community. These make available a range of contradictory messages about 'race', and in any case children do not passively receive them but actively select and reinterpret.

The attitudes and beliefs of white children range from those who make use of racist frameworks of interpretation to those who are committed to well-developed notions of racial equality. Many children display inconsistent and contradictory repertoires of attitudes, containing both elements of racially egalitarian ideologies and elements of racist ideologies. The relationship between what we have called children's 'thematic' and 'interactional' ideologies of 'race' is not necessarily one of simple and direct correspondence. On the contrary, interactional ideologies have their own logic, which may be more, or less, congruent with children's 'thematic' attitudes and beliefs. In other words, a number of combinations of attitudes and behaviour is possible, ranging from children who hold racist beliefs but do not express them in behaviour, to children who hold racially egalitarian beliefs but use racist name-calling in certain situations. It follows that racist incidents have a variety of social meanings, and the meaning of any specific instance can only be determined by an analysis of the underlying social processes that produced it.

Within children's cultures, it is primarily interactional ideologies that animate racist ideologies and translate them into social practice. This is clearly the case with interactional ideologies of dominance, which can harness elements of racist ideologies in order to exert power over black children. But racist ideologies can also colonise interactional ideologies of equality. We have described many examples of this: white children using racist name-calling in self-defence; opposing the use of Asian languages on the grounds that it gives an unfair advantage; critical of school policies that seem to privilege the interests of black children. Concepts of equality may serve to justify forms of racial discrimination.

However, our findings also reveal strong dynamics of racial egalitarianism within children's cultures. We would account for them in terms of the combination of two factors. One is a growing awareness of the significance of racial discrimination in society, and its injustice. The other is the development of relationships among children on a basis of equality of treatment and an ability to take and value the viewpoints of others. The growing salience of these two factors during the junior school years may account for the relative decline of racist name-calling during this period that many children referred to. These processes can, however, be overridden and reversed during this period of adolescence by the emergence of powerful peer sub-cultures based on racist interpretive frameworks and interactional repertoires.

What Schools Can Do

The first step is to recognise that racism is an important issue for predominantly white primary schools. It has implications for their pastoral and disciplinary procedures and for the curriculum.

The evidence from our three schools is that a clear stance by the school against racist name-calling can be effective in reducing its incidence. Such a policy is welcomed by black children and approved of by almost all white children. The policy at Greenshire school in particular illustrated a number of features which contributed to a reduction in racist behaviour. The policy was well-known to all the children, as a result of statements by the headteacher in assembly and the firm action that she took in dealing with incidents that occurred. There was a clear system of escalating responses by the school, progressing from warnings to the threat of exclusion from the school. Parents were involved if there were repeated breaches of the school policy. In addition, the style adopted by the headteacher in dealing with incidents, combining firmness with a willingness to listen, was appreciated by the children.

There were, however, problems with the stances that all three schools took. For black children, the main problem was that such policies were not implemented effectively by many of the teachers, and also by classroom assistants and lunchtime supervisors. In all three schools the implementation of the policy relied very largely on the headteacher. Many black children saw this as evidence that other staff did not share the headteacher's commitment to the policy. This was reinforced by their experiences of having complained about racist incidents and finding that staff would not listen to them, and that sometimes they themselves got into trouble as a result, either for the original incident, or for complaining. Some black children interpreted this as evidence of racial prejudice on the part of some staff.

Black children face a dilemma if they feel that they cannot rely on staff to deal with problems of racist harassment. If the children try to ignore it it may encourage the offender to continue, but if they retaliate they may get into trouble themselves. The dilemma is particularly acute if their parents advise them to retaliate by hitting the offender. (White children also face this dilemma in other contexts, of course.)

The problem posed in relation to white children is this: a school policy may be effective in reducing racist behaviour within the school, but on its own it may do nothing to challenge the roots of racist behaviour in what we have called children's thematic and interactional ideologies. Racist behaviour may be partially suppressed inside the school but only driven outside the school gates. Furthermore, as long as the underlying roots of racist behaviour remain unchallenged, the existence of a school policy against racist behaviour may be seen as unfairly privileging black children and actually serve to reinforce racist ideas. It is clear therefore that a policy to deal with racist incidents has to be accompanied by a policy for dealing with issues of 'race' within the curriculum.

We have already voiced our scepticism about the efficacy of multicultural education as a strategy through which racism and racist incidents in schools might be tackled. Yet it remains a popular interventionist approach. Lord Elton, for instance, in his inquiry into bullying in schools insisted that the specific case of racist harassment might be obviated through the development of a cultural pluralist curriculum:

We believe that using the curriculum to emphasise the importance of tolerance and respect for other cultures is a . . . productive approach. A variety of subjects can be used to point out the achievements of different cultures. Where possible these achievements should be linked to cultures represented in the school . . . (Elton, 1989, p. 100)

The teachers' union, AMMA, agrees; however, it recommended intervention at a later stage in children's schooling. In its statement on multicultural and anti-racist education it advised members to ensure that 'pupils learn about the nature and mechanisms of group prejudice . . . in the formal curriculum, probably at secondary level when children are more likely to benefit from the approach of "knowing the enemy" ' (AMMA, 1987, p. 103). Whilst we support the demand for intervention we reject both the implied deference to the idealised conception of primary school children's understanding of race-related matters and the means advocated. Our objections revolve around two concerns. First, both black and white children have reservations about the promotion of ethnic life styles and cultures in the curriculum. Black children feel embarrassed, even stigmatised, in such lessons, and other research studies have highlighted their resentment towards the fossilised, sometimes racist presentations of their cultures in school curricula. White children, on the other hand, resent the school's apparent privileging of ethnic minority cultures and, as a corollary, the devaluation of their own. As we saw earlier, this resentment figured strongly in the Macdonald inquiry into the build-up to the murder of Ahmed Iqbal Ullah at Burnage High School. Multicultural education, according to Gus John, a member of the inquiry, implies that white working-class children 'have to pay due deference to the culture of others even before anybody checked out with them what their perception of their own culture actually was' (John, 1990, p. 70). The children in our schools also seemed to be left high and dry on such matters.

Our second reservation focuses on what we see as the illogical use of 'racial' and cultural categories to combat racism. This is both reductionist and is in danger of legitimating 'race' as an organising and differentiating category. Racist incidents in whatever form arise because 'racial' categories are used as a way of understanding and dealing with particular situations. In short, 'racial' categories have certain functional properties. If racist incidents are to be tackled effectively these categories must be replaced with others which offer young people superior and more plausible explanations for the way things are. Educationists who continue to organise children's experiences around 'racial' conceptions of reality are simply tempting fate.

Our study has a number of implications for a more effective approach to dealing with issues of 'race' in the curriculum. The first is the centrality of the personal experience of the child. We have seen how racist name-calling and other forms of racist behaviour are embedded in and mobilised by the typical social processes of children's cultures. We have also seen how children's ideas about 'race' in society are rooted in and confirmed by their own experiences— of going abroad on holiday, of events in the neighbourhood, and so on. In order to respond to the real meanings of 'race' in children's lives, the curriculum needs to open itself up to and engage with the full range of children's experiences. This point needs stressing in the context of a national curriculum the thrust of which is in the opposite direction. The consultative document on the national curriculum (DES, 1988) states that it will ensure:

that all pupils, regardless of sex, ethnic origin and geographical location, have access to broadly the same good and relevant curriculum and programmes of study, which include the key content, skills and processes which they need to learn and which ensure that the content and teaching of the various elements of the national curriculum bring out their relevance to and links with pupils' own experiences . . .

We share the concerns that Ken Jones expresses about the implications of this passage which are signalled by the conjunction of 'regardless' with 'relevant'.

The curriculum, apparently, will be relevant to everyone, even though it will have no re-gard to where they live, what sex they are, and what their racial background is: it will be the same for all, and yet relevant to all! There is a striking confidence that the learning programme devised by the curriculum planners will be fully congruent with the expe-rience of students, alongside an equally striking lack of interest in what that experience might be. That students differ in what their society has made of them; that the sexual, class or racial prisms through which they view the world affect their attitudes to learn-ing and their conceptions of relevance are not important matters. Because their lives are seen as empty and cultureless, the national curriculum seems all the more unproblem-atic. (Jones, 1989, pp. 96–7)

The children's experiences that we have drawn on in this book are of three types. There are the experiences of relationships and social interaction with other children. We have identified some of the typical social processes at work: domination and equality, hierarchies of age, gender relations, making and breaking friends, group inclusion and exclusion, acting tough, being jealous, and so on, as well as 'race'. It is rare that children have the opportunity to discuss these issues in the educational context. Yet there are ways in which teachers can, both directly and indirectly, through stories, drama, photographs and video, help children to develop their understanding of these issues which are so central to their lives.

The second area of children's direct experience is of 'the adult world': the family, the street, the neighbourhood. Of course, these are commonly reflected in the curriculum. But there is a danger that teachers' representations of these areas of experience may selectively filter out what is of concern to the child. We refer to just two examples from our discussions. 'The shop' is a staple item in the primary curriculum. But is it conceptualised in ways which engage with what the local Asian shop means to Simon, Ben and Richard, or is it divested of the so-cial relationships of 'race'? A number of the children talked about issues of crime and violence in the neighbourhood. Adam, for instance, was construct-ing racist notions of violence and black people out of a combination of his ex-periences with black children and the attack on his neighbourhood. Will the curriculum help Adam to make a different sense of issues like these?

The other most important source of children's experiences, including those of 'race', is television. Our point here is simple: what does school do to help chil-dren develop their understanding of television—in other words their skills in 'reading' visual media, whether it is the news or *Grange Hill* or *The Bill* or a Schwarzenegger film?

The curriculum needs to not only address the real experience that children bring with them to the classroom, it needs to offer them the conceptual tools to interpret it. There are two related elements in how the children in our study thought about 'race' that are pertinent here.

The first is their limited understanding of notions of social structure. Many had little or no understanding of how 'race' was socially structured by, for example, the economy and the state. This is a symptom of a general absence of political education in the primary curriculum. Yet it is clear from the evidence of children like Charlotte that children of 10 and 11 years are capable of understanding such ideas, even with little help from the curriculum. The consequence of the lack of 'sociological' concepts was that children tended to use concepts derived from their own experiences of interpersonal interaction to explain phenomena at the level of society. So, for example, lacking concepts of ideology based on material interests, many children explained racist behaviour in society in terms of personal motivations of 'jealousy', transferring a concept that was central to experiences of conflict in their own relationships.

The second conceptual limitation concerned the notion of equality that children used. For many children, white and black, this was a powerful principle capable of organising a consistent anti-racist perspective. But for others, it stumbled at the idea that to achieve equality for the unequal may require unequal treatment, particularly if the inequality is not just at the level of interpersonal relations but is socially structured in ways that the child is not aware of. The curriculum can make an important contribution towards helping children to develop the principle of equality that is so important in their personal lives into a more complex and encompassing concept of social justice.

Finally, we want to stress the two strands that run through the culture of children. We have demonstrated how significant racism is in the lives of white children. We have also been made aware of the strength of anti-racist attitudes and behaviour. The frequent presence of racially egalitarian elements in the thinking even of children who engage in racist behaviour is a crucial factor on which teachers can build. In doing so, the existence in every class of children who have a clear anti-racist commitment is potentially the most powerful resource, if they can be helped to gain the confidence, the skills and the knowledge to express it, both in the curriculum and in interpersonal interaction.

In conclusion, we believe that a school policy needs to have three mutually dependent elements:

1   A clear and firm policy to deal with racist incidents when they occur, which is implemented by all staff not just left to the head. This entails listening to and taking seriously the complaints of black children. The policy must combine both firm disciplinary measures, up to and including exclusion, with a willingness to listen to white children and understand the social meanings of racist behaviour within children's cultures.

2   Similar and related policies to deal with other forms of oppressive behaviour. These may be integrated into a more broadly conceived policy and set of practices which convey the school's stance on and commitment to tackling behaviour aimed at the oppression of discernible groups of pupils: black children, girls, children with disabilities, and younger children, in particular.

3 A curriculum, defined in formal and informal terms, that addresses issues of 'race' in association with related forms of inequality and injustice, both within children's cultures and in the wider society. As we have argued before in our analysis of the murder at Burnage High School, anti-racist teaching needs to be about more than 'race' (Troyna and Hatcher, 1991) Anti-racist education, when defined and put into operation in this inclusive way, should facilitate children's recognition that racist behaviour trades on and helps to reinforce much broader patterns of discrimination. On this view, anti-racist education will help to strengthen (and legitimise) the position of anti-racist children, black and white.

Quite simply, whilst the premise of the 'contact hypothesis' continues to attract support as a justification for not adopting an interventionist anti-racist policy stance, our evidence demonstrates that racism in mainly white primary schools is more prevalent, more complex and more entrenched than many educationists care to admit.

[From *Racism in Children's Lives: A Study of Mainly-White Primary Schools* (London: Routledge, 1992), 195–204.]

Section IV

Racist Movements

INTRODUCTION

It should be clear from the previous parts of this Reader that one of the most important features of racism throughout the past century and more has been the impact of racist ideas on political ideologies and movements. Social and political movements that articulate racial ideas and values have had an important impact on the history of a wide range of societies, often with deadly consequences when such ideas have been interlinked with state power. Racist movements are by no means uniform, and it is clear from the experience of the twentieth century that they can take a wide range of ideological forms. But it seems to be the case that such movements typically combine mystical ideas about race and myths of origin with the appropriation of scientific discourses about racial classification. It is precisely this combination of the mystical and the scientific that lies at the heart of the attempts by contemporary racist movements to reinvent their ideas around the language of 'national identity' and patriotism.

In this section we want to take the analysis of this aspect of racism a stage further by exploring through a number of key extracts the changing role of racist movements and ideas in shaping important features of contemporary social and political relations. The first extracts by William Tuttle and David Wellman can be seen as providing an insight into the changing morphology of attitudes and values about race in American society during the past eighty years. Tuttle covers a period in the history of America, namely the post-First World War years, when urban racial violence and race riots became a pervasive feature of racial relations. Tuttle seeks to show that the violence and riots which broke out in urban centres such as Chicago in the aftermath of the First World War were the product of broader trends in the development of racial and ethnic conflict in the USA. David Wellman extends the analysis of racism further by looking in some detail at the attitudes of white Americans to questions of race and racism. Wellman uses in-depth interviews with white Americans in order to unravel the types of reasoning and everyday values that make up what he defines as 'white racism'. Wellman's focus is very much on the contemporary United States and the changing forms in which racism is expressed and justified in everyday discourses. In this sense his account can be seen as a comment on the current dilemmas that dominate public debates about race relations as well as an analysis of the changing mechanisms through which racial inequalities are understood and legitimated.

The following extract from Michel Wieviorka provides a more conceptual overview of racism as a 'social anti-movement'. Drawing on the conceptual framework of studies of social movements in contemporary industrial societies Wieviorka seeks to locate racism firmly as the product of social and economic transformations that have helped to reshape societies and to produce conditions that are conducive to the emergence of movements that articulate in one way or another racist projects. In doing so he also suggests that there is a need to see racism as dynamic and constantly changing, rather than fixed by analytic categories more appropriate to previous historical periods. Influenced by recent debates about racism in France as well as other societies Wieviorka's account is a sharp reminder of the importance of locating the changing patterns of racist mobilization within a wider analytical framework.

The following three extracts provide in-depth accounts of some important elements of contemporary racist movements in America and Europe. Raphael Ezekiel's is a particularly innovative attempt to look at the everyday workings of what he calls the 'racist mind'. Based on his in-depth observation of extreme right-wing and racist movements in the USA this particular extract focuses on the ideas articulated by activists in these organizations about race, and specifically about Jews. Ezekiel's account provides a poignant reminder of the pure hatred that is an everyday element of the language used by activists in organizations of the extreme right and of the solidarities that such hatred helps to forge. Pierre-André Taguieff's account focuses on a rather different aspect of contemporary racist movements, namely the emergence of what he calls 'cultural racism'. Drawing on his wide-ranging analysis of the political discourses of racism and anti-racism in France Taguieff seeks to show that within the public discourses of the new right there has been an important shift in contemporary debates towards the positive evaluation of ideas such as 'cultural difference' and 'national culture', and a consequent move away from biological constructions of racial superiority. For Taguieff such a move poses important dilemmas for any rounded analysis of both contemporary racist movements and of anti-racism, and for the ways in which movements to counter racism articulate their oppositional discourses.

The final extract in this part, by Abby Ferber, moves the analysis further by seeking in a more self-conscious manner to explore the interplay between race and gender in the discourses of white supremacist movements in the United States. Ferber's account provides an interesting overview of some of the most recent trends in white supremacist movements and their ideological underpinnings. It is also a contribution to the growing body of work that has emerged in recent years on both sides of the Atlantic on the construction of 'whiteness'. Based on a careful analysis of the language and imagery to be found in white supremacist publications Ferber's analysis helps to highlight the complex meanings attached to 'whiteness' as a form of social identity and a mechanism for mapping racial boundaries about who belongs and does not belong within the national collectivity. In addition her account helps to illuminate the need for an analysis of racist movements that fully accounts for the ways in which gender is a key component of how racialized boundaries of the nation are drawn.

These extracts highlight the importance of understanding the dynamic nature of racism and the power of racial ideas to mobilize mass movements. They help to show forcefully that racism is not simply a set of abstract ideas and doctrines that function at the level of ideology. It is also a means of mobilizing and engendering social action and political identities. As we enter the next millennium it is perhaps this aspect of racism that is if anything becoming a more pervasive feature of political and cultural identities in a wide range of national and regional contexts.

24 Racial Violence in Chicago and the Nation

Thirty-eight dead, 537 wounded, hundreds homeless—this was the toll, and an awesome one it was. Walter Lippmann, writing in 1919, deplored the Chicago race riot as 'an event infinitely more disgraceful than that . . . Red Terror about which we are all so virtuously indignant. . . .' Black and white Chicagoans also deplored the city's racial bloodshed. Some white people expressed astonishment at the news of the violence. Why Chicago? the incredulous asked. Chicago was a dynamic city, they said, a little rough perhaps, but at least its diverse ethnic, religious, and racial groups had been able to coexist for years without resorting to such rioting. Amazement and disbelief did not strike the black community, just sadness and a reaffirmation of self-defense. The riot, a black man recalled many years later, brought Chicago's black people 'closer together than they had ever been before,' and it accelerated the trend toward arming for future danger.

The riot in Chicago should have surprised few people, black or white, for it was well within the context of two modern historical phenomena: twentieth-century urban racial violence in America, and the frenzy of the year 1919. Added to these, of course, were the many peculiarities of Chicago's troubled history of race relations. In fact, the surprising thing to a historian studying the riot is not that it happened, but that it did not happen time and time again, especially in the tense and potentially explosive months after July 1919. For if the historian, working as a social scientist, were to have fed the facts of Chicago's post-riot racial unrest into a computer, that machine, having digested the pre-riot history of Chicago's race relations, would in all likelihood have predicted renewed eruptions of racial bloodshed.

Not surprisingly, the Chicago race riot of 1919 marked no surcease to that period of transition between war and peace; it was just the midpoint in a year of unrest and violence that had several months yet to run. Not only was the nation still in the throes of the Red Scare, but in the succeeding months it became even more haunted by the specter of radicalism, Bolshevism and revolution. Worse yet in terms of deaths, racial warfare continued to erupt in America.

After Chicago, the next major riot of the Red Summer erupted in Omaha, Nebraska. A meat-packing center like Chicago, Omaha had also attracted thousands of Southern black men and women to its stockyards during the war, and by 1919 its black population had doubled to well over 10,000. As in Chicago, too, racial tensions in Omaha had mounted with its rising black population. And when the fires of racial hatred had flared out of control in Chicago in July and August, their ugly glare had made Omaha's black people uncomfortable and fearful for their lives. Black workers in South Omaha's packing plants had congregated in small groups on July 29 to discuss arming themselves; and before the chief of police could issue an order the next day banning the sale of firearms, black people had purchased scores of weapons and ammunition. Also at the time of the Chicago bloodshed, Mayor Edward P. Smith, realizing the precarious state of race relations in the city, had ordered a local movie house to cease showing *The Birth of a Nation* or to remain closed until aroused racial feelings had subsided. Unlike Chicago, however, white Omaha believed it was suffering from an epidemic of black criminality and especially of sex crimes. And when on September 28 police arrested William Brown, a black man accused of molesting a young white girl, a mob of whites began to assemble at the courthouse, angrily demanding that the authorities release the alleged rapist to them for the execution of quick justice. When Mayor Smith mounted the courthouse steps in an effort to persuade the whites to disperse peacefully, he was taunted and heckled as a 'nigger lover'; for to these people, the mayor, whose law firm was then in the employ of the NACCP to defend two black men accused of assaulting white women, represented the enemy. His appeal for calm unheeded and abused, Smith was then seized by the mob, which placed a rope around his neck, and had nearly succeeded in hanging him from a trolley pole when police cut the rope and rescued him. Still undeterred, and indeed even angrier, the mob lit a fire in the courthouse. Beginning on the first floor, the flames quickly lept up to the higher floors, but when the fire department arrived to extinguish the fire, the men in the mob cut the hoses. Still the flames rose, and, fleeing from them, the prisoners climbed to the roof, and there, to escape death themselves, several of them tried to throw Brown down to the mob. Finally, several men pushed past policemen and entered the building to capture Brown. Once the mob had him, Brown was shot, hanged from a lamppost, and his body burned, riddled with hundreds of bullets, and mutilated beyond recognition. Dreading another Chicago race riot, the state of Nebraska wired for federal assistance, and the War Department responded by dispatching troops from various forts in the region. Yet it was not just the Nebraska authorities who were apprehensive. In Springfield, Illinois, Mrs Frank O. Lowden recorded in her diary that the governor had read the 'sensational [newspaper] accounts of a mob in Omaha yesterday and of mob violence done. . . . Such actions,' she noted, 'stir up more trouble or are liable to elsewhere and Frank feels uneasy and so has decided to go to Chicago this evening.' No race riot erupted in Chicago; and in Omaha, assisted by a downpour so torrential that the city's streetcars had to stop operations for a half hour, the soldiers were able to restore order. But by then four people were dead and fifty injured.

On October 1, while federal troops were patrolling the streets of Omaha, news came from east central Arkansas of an armed insurrection of blacks against whites. In Phillips County, Arkansas, as in many cotton producing regions of the South, black farmers were not landowners but tenants or sharecroppers, working for a percentage of the cotton crops they cultivated. Much injustice plagued these black farmers. They could purchase provisions only at the 'plantation' or other specified stores; and being continually in debt, they purchased goods on credit and in anticipation of a percentage of the sale price of their crops. They not only paid more than the average retail prices, but they were unable to obtain from the stores itemized statements of their indebtedness. Nor was this all. When the landowner sold the cotton, he customarily would not show the bill of sale to his tenants and sharecroppers, so they, of course, could not know the dollar value of the portion to which they were entitled. But an incident in mid-June 1919 warned the local black citizens of the futility and danger of protesting against such a system. A black farmer in Star City, Arkansas, who objected by refusing to work, was lynched and 'a sign reading "this is how we treat lazy niggers" was tacked to his head.'

Yet black farmers in Phillips County, singing 'Organize, oh organize!' established a union, the Progressive Farmers and Household Union of America, through which they intended to protest to the landowners. Sixty-eight sharecroppers at a plantation near Ratio commissioned a white law firm in Little Rock to plead a test case. If the landowner would not produce an itemized statement of account, they would prosecute; failing that, they would refuse to pick cotton then in the field or to sell cotton belonging to them for less than the market price. Realizing the potential impact of this demand for their rights, black farmers in the county armed themselves. Then, on October 1, a special agent of the Missouri Pacific Railroad was shot to death outside a black church in Hoop Spur, and a deputy sheriff with him was wounded. There were two versions of the shootings, one stating that the white detective fired 'promiscuously' into the church, where a chapter of the Progressive Union was in session, and that the blacks returned the gunfire. The Little Rock *Arkansas Gazette* reported the other version, which was that the white men had parked near the church at Hoop Spur 'to repair a puncture, and while working on the car the party was fired upon by unidentified persons,' presumably black.

News of the clash at Hoop Spur spread rapidly throughout the county and to towns across the Mississippi River. Armed white men sped to Helena, Arkansas, from Clarendon, Marianna, and Marvell on the Arkansas side of the river, and from Lula, Tunica, Friars Point, and Clarksdale on the Mississippi side. Emergency posses, totaling 500 men and including a detachment from the American Legion post at Helena, inundated Elaine, Arkansas. Frightened for their lives, black men fled into the woods and canebrakes; and white men, motivated in part by reports that the Progressive Union was advocating 'social equality' and by rumors that the blacks had scheduled 'a general slaughter of white people in the locality' for October 7, pursued them and massacred them. Martial law was declared on October 2, and the violence abated as soldiers of the regular Army were ordered from Camp Pike to Phillips County at the request of Governor Charles Brough.

'The white citizens of the county,' Governor Brough declared on October 3, '. . . deserve unstinted praise for their action in preventing mob violence.' It is scarcely possible to conceive of a statement so hideously ludicrous. For at least twenty-five black people, and probably many, many more, had been hunted down by white mobs and slaughtered like animals, and at least five white men had been killed as well.

Other factors also make it difficult to explain why there was not a recurrence of race rioting in Chicago. In addition to the continuing presence of the year of transition, 1919, with its Red Scare and Red Summer, the fact of migration to Chicago was still abundantly evident. Not only did Southern blacks and demobilized soldiers continue to settle in Chicago, but efforts by recruiters to entice black people to the South after the riot were almost totally unsuccessful. Advertisements appeared in Chicago's newspapers, both black and white, after the riot. 'TO COLORED LABOR SEEKING HOMES,' read the statement in the *Broad Ax* of the Coahoma, Mississippi, Chambers of Commerce. Its purpose was to inform Chicago's black people that Coahoma 'offers a home and great opportunities to those who care to come. . . .' Kentucky advertised for coal miners and loaders, with its inducements being modern buildings, 'commissary the best,' steady work, and, perhaps above all, 'NO LABOR TROUBLES.' Recruiters also came to the city from Louisiana, Tennessee, and other parts of Mississippi, and they all seemed to be agreed on one thing. 'I want the southern Negro, who is familiar with the South's general attitude on the race question,' said a Mississippian who was looking for cotton pickers. A Louisianian added that he wanted 1,000 families, but not 'colored people who have always lived in the north. . . .' They wanted the migrants to come back, but the recruiters found few takers. 'The colored people in Chicago feel this is their last ditch,' explained banker Jesse Binga. 'Here is something to look forward to, [while] in the South they know there are Jim Crow cars, segregation, humiliation and degradation.' 'The colored people see that if they can't make it in Chicago,' noted A. L. Jackson of the Wabash Avenue YMCA, 'then it's no use to try somewhere else. Of all places they don't want to go back South.'

In addition, as the residents of Chicago's black community well knew, the hostility of the surrounding white ethnic groups had not diminished since the riot. Chicago's racial bloodshed had been the 'ideal-type' or 'type-case' of Northern urban violence, with the riot involving direct 'ecological warfare' between the residents of white and black neighborhoods. After the riot, the stereotypes and generalized beliefs, which the nearby Irish- and Polish-Americans and various other ethnic groups held about black people, continued to be invariably deprecating and hostile. The black skin not only served as a symbol arousing distinctly unfavorable feelings toward black people, it also helped to redefine ambiguous and anxiety-producing situations; how easy it was to identify and condemn the despised black people as the source of one's anxiety and as the threat to one's economic security and social status. Moreover, Chicago's press did not cease reporting the news of black people in a disparaging manner, frequently indulging in minority baiting. And, finally, white people continued to disdain black men and women as undesirable competitors—in the labor market, in politics, in contested neighborhoods, and in public accommodations.

[From *Race Riot: Chicago in the Red Summer of 1919* (New York: Atheneum, 1978; 1st pub. 1970), 242–50.]

DAVID T. WELLMAN

25 Toward a Sociology of White Racism

Introduction: The Contradiction

'The American society is faced not just with the necessity of actualizing those Negro aspirations to which it is officially committed,' writes Earl Raab, 'but of substantially reconciling the contrary and frustrated aspirations of the white community' (1962: 16). White Americans confront quite a problem when they try to reconcile their aspirations with the ones held by black Americans. In crucial respects there is a conflict of interest involved; gains for black people can mean losses for whites. Somehow white Americans must simultaneously attend to black demands and avoid the institutional reorganization that might cause them to lose ground. The problem is not easily solved.

To complicate matters considerably, white people have relatively few publicly acceptable ways to defend their interests. Defenses that vulgarly refer to biological differences are currently unacceptable in public arenas. Arguments that explain the situation in terms of racial subordination, on the other hand, are also unacceptable to many white Americans. Reasoning of this sort implies that blacks are not responsible for racial subordination; it directly implicates white people in the system of racial injustice. Most people are unwilling to accept this harsh judgment of themselves.

This, then, is the contradiction confronting white Americans. The racial advantages they have traditionally enjoyed are threatened and they have few acceptable or legitimate options for defending them. What are people in this situation to do; how are they to respond? The people in this study reflect five different ways in which white Americans come to grips with the contradiction. They justify Gus Tyler's claim that:

To ask people to be fearless when they have every reason to be afraid is to ask normal folk to act abnormally. They couldn't do it even if they wanted to. They will seek safety—no matter what political ribbon is wrapped around the prized package of survival. Castigating these people as stupid (some are) or racist (others are) does not solve the problem. They will in the end simply conclude that the lofty lecturer who thus looks down on them is himself either stupid or racist, or both [quoted in Lipset and Raab, 1970: 512].

The ways these people cope with racial issues also suggests that William Ryan was correct when he observed that: 'In order to persuade a good and moral man to *do* evil it is not necessary first to persuade him to *become* evil. It is only necessary to teach him that he is doing good. No one . . . thinks of himself as a son of a bitch' (1971: 19).

How, then, do white Americans deal with the racial situation—the troubles and aspirations of black people—without putting themselves at a disadvantage and thinking of themselves as sons of bitches? That is the issue facing all the people in this study.

Getting off the Hook

Stated simply, the answer is that they resolve the contradiction by minimizing racism. They neutralize it. The specific ways in which people defuse racial issues are numerous. Dick Wilson blames the victim for his or her own victimization: Racial inequality exists because black people lack motivation. Darlene Kurier and Roberta attribute the problem to ignorance: If black people weren't 'into a brawn scene' (Roberta), if they had more education (Darlene), there would be no racial problems. Gene Danich formulates the issue in personal terms: He is in favor of anything that does not affect him personally. Dick Wilson and John Harper affirm the viability of America: Dick feels that if he could be successful anyone can; John insists that decisions in America are based on qualifications, not skin color. Both Dick and John appeal to American ideals: America proclaims that all people are equal and there is no reason to believe otherwise. Roberta denies the injuries of racism: Blacks are groovy and soulful; they have more fun than whites. Harper denies responsibility for racial injustice. Agitators cause racial problems; white America does not.

Reduced to the basics, each formulation removes the speaker from complicity in the system of racial organization. Each of these people is, as Ryan describes it, '. . . most crucially, rejecting the possibility of blaming, not the victims, but themselves. They are all unconsciously passing judgments on themselves and bringing in a unanimous verdict of Not Guilty' (1971: 28). The functions served by these expressions, however, extend considerably beyond self exoneration: They legitimate America as well. None of them questions the basis of a racial hierarchy; its continuation is taken for granted. The privileges each of these people have, because they are white, are consequently maintained.

If the people in this study are any indication, white Americans use many variations and combinations of the above themes to resolve the contradiction that black subordination presents for them. Taken together, organized into a relatively consistent theme, the expressions add up to a formulation that rationalizes, and thereby defends, an individual's racial situation. In this study I have presented five formulations that I think are fairly typical of the ways that white Americans do this. Each position represents a relatively successful accommodation to the problem of how to cope with the existence of racial inequality without thinking of oneself as a 'son of a bitch.' Each formulation manages nicely to navigate the difficult waters between biological defenses of interests and those explanations of the situation that imply either self-blame or social change that might result in a loss of privilege. Each position is formulated in very acceptable, almost liberal, American terms. With some minor exceptions, there is not a prejudiced-sounding formulation among them.

At first glance there appear to be an amazing number of 'integrationists' or 'liberals' in the sample. No one insists that blacks be doomed to a subordinate position. No one opposes black demands for racial reasons. In varying degrees they are all open to changing the situation facing black people. Everyone would like to see a world in which skin color makes no difference. On the surface, at any rate, this seems strange. Only a few short years earlier, a civil rights movement based on similar color-blind principles was vigorously opposed by people who quite frequently looked very much like these. Nevertheless, there is little doubt that most of the people we spoke to, regardless of their class position, felt the ultimate solution to racial inequality was some sort of color-blind world in which all people are treated equally.

The finding is intriguing. It runs counter to many studies of racial attitudes that conclude that 'liberalism' or 'open-ness' is mainly found among young people and the middle class. Yet we find it among all groups. Could it be that the sample is unique? In part. But that does not explain the sentiments. Could it be the people lied to us about what they really felt? That is doubtful.

The 'intrigue' diminishes when the *solutions* these people found acceptable are subjected to closer scrutiny. The following were acceptable solutions to the problems faced by black people: change has to occur within the law; blacks have to conform to and/or be integrated into white society; blacks have to be educated and/or given equal job opportunities and/or become motivated; people have to become color-blind and/or whites have to cease being prejudiced. There is a common thrust to each of these solutions: None of them involves a basic change in the lifestyle of white people. Were any of them to be implemented, the racial status quo would prevail. [. . .]

The proposals most whites suggest for dealing with racial inequality are not, in any basic sense, 'solutions' for black people. About the only thing they 'solve' is the contradiction that racial inequality represents for white people and American ideology. That, they do well. The solutions allow white people to recognize the need for change without having that change affect them in important ways. They can have their cake and eat it too. They need not be reactionaries and they need not give up anything.

In addition, the solutions these people entertain allow them to be conscious of inequality and injustice without condemning themselves, to recognize a societal problem without implicating the society, and to defend their interests without referring to genes or race. This is possible because they recognize racial inequality either abstractly or as blocked access; they explain it in terms of the problems of its victims; and they 'solve' the problem with solutions that do not affect white people. This allows them to put distance between themselves and the problem, explain the situation without implicating themselves, justify their position in nonracist or unprejudiced terms, and avoid the imperative for social change. In short, they get off the hook and defend their racial privilege as well.

This raises a critical question. These are not 'prejudiced' people. The distinctive feature of their racial sentiments is neither hostility toward nor faulty generalizations about racial groups. As far as I can tell, their attitudes are not characteristically based on prejudgment or misjudgment. They do not categorically or systematically misinterpret facts. Nevertheless, they do not want social change that will significantly alter their relationship to the racial ordering of American society. If they are neither prejudiced nor amenable to change, what is the problem?

In part, the answer is that racism extends considerably beyond prejudiced beliefs. The essential feature of racism is not hostility or misperception, but rather the defense of a system from which advantage is derived on the basis of race. The manner in which the defense is articulated—either with hostility or subtlety—is not nearly as important as the fact that it insures the continuation of a privileged relationship. Thus it is necessary to broaden the definition of racism beyond prejudice to include sentiments that in their consequence, if not their intent, support the racial status quo.

Legitimacy of Grievance and Receptivity to Change: Some Differences

Extending the definition of racism is useful. However, it does not explain why the people in this study recognize certain problems and are unaware of others; why they support some demands and reject others; or why they are amenable to only certain proposals. More importantly, it does not explain the differences that exist *between* these people in terms of their understanding of the issues involved and their openness to changes in the racial order—the conditions under which they would be receptive to new arrangements.

The differences are important ones. For example: Gene Danich and Darlene Kurier recognize that some black grievances are legitimate and the problem is 'real.' Gene feels that, relative to whites, blacks lack good jobs and money. Mrs Kurier says 'power has always been on the white side.' Both of these people register genuine concern that something tangible happen: Blacks should be given more educational or occupational opportunities. Dick Wilson also recognizes the discrepant ways in which blacks and whites have been treated. While he admits that blacks 'have been denied opportunities,' he is less sympathetic than Danich or Kurier: The majority of blacks are 'bums.' John Harper and Roberta, at the other extreme, are barely conscious of the problems that blacks experience. The only problem Roberta can see is that blacks are 'ignorant,' 'hung-up,' on a 'brawn scene.' Harper says that he does not understand what people mean when they refer to 'white racism.'

There are other differences as well. Neither Gene Danich nor Darlene Kurier rejects the concept of black power out of hand. In fact, Gene is receptive to the idea; it speaks to the need to achieve equality. Mrs Kurier is more ambivalent. If it means bringing blacks into their own she has no objection; if it means power over whites she is opposed to it. Neither Gene nor Darlene is opposed on principle to school busing, although both of them would prefer that integration be achieved by other means. In the event that no other way was possible and if something positive came of busing, both would reluctantly go along with the strategy. When it comes to individuals, black militants like Stokely Carmichael are personally offensive to Danich and Kurier; but both recognize that he serves a legitimate function for the black community. Mrs Kurier says she 'understands why he is in such a hurry.' Gene admits that were he black, he would probably be a Carmichael follower. While neither Danich nor Kurier feel comfortable about social change that affects them directly, both feel that something must be done to change the lives of black people. Gene favors the impossible: anything from riots to better jobs, just as long as it does not touch him. Darlene is more traditional: Her solution is education.

Unlike Gene Danich and Darlene Kurier, Dick Wilson is hostile to the idea of black power. As far as he is concerned it is a 'grandstanding play,' of no use to the black community. It rationalizes irresponsible behavior and covers up incompetence. The idea burns him up. Dick is equally unsympathetic to black militants: They serve no legitimate purpose. They also burn him up. However, like Gene and Darlene, Dick would like to see things get better in the black community. While the solution he suggests does not directly involve him, it is a sincere one and would alter the situation of blacks. He proposes a 'GI Bill for the ghetto.'

Like Dick Wilson, John Harper and Roberta have little use for such notions as black power. In fact Harper never even refers to it explicitly. Since he does not know what white racism is, he obviously does not think much about black power. Roberta is not much interested or impressed with the idea either. She considers it a 'drag . . . trying to get your race equal.' Both Roberta and Harper discount militant black leaders; nothing they do seems justified. For Roberta, militants are 'intelligent spades' on an 'individual trip' for personal aggrandizement. To Harper, they are agitators; their aim is not to end injustice, but to destroy 'our way of life.' Roberta and John Harper express the least concern for what happens to blacks in the future. Unlike the other three, neither of them seems very open to serious proposals for concretely changing the situation. As far as Roberta is concerned, blacks should not get too upset about what others think of them; they should be above all that. Harper does not give the idea much thought. He is concerned with agitators, not inequality.

Ranking these five people on some sort of prejudice 'scale' would not be a very fruitful undertaking. The scale would be unable to distinguish clearly between them. Yet there are obvious differences between these people. (1) Danich,

Kurier, and Wilson are the most aware of the different ways in which blacks and whites are treated in the United States. Roberta and Harper are the least aware. (2) Danich and Kurier are the most receptive to group strategies like black power and the most willing to recognize that militant black leaders raise legitimate issues. Harper, Roberta, and Wilson, on the other hand, do not take kindly to militant strategies and barely tolerate militant leaders. (3) Danich, Kurier, and Wilson feel most strongly that something must be done to change the situation of blacks; all have their own private, concrete solution. Roberta and Harper seem indifferent—if not hostile—to the idea of concrete changes.

The picture is a curious one. In terms of these three dimensions, Danich and Kurier are the most open to changes in the racial order, Harper and Roberta the least receptive, and Wilson fluctuates somewhere in between. That seems strange. We expect people like Gene Danich to be the least agreeable to the idea of change and people like John Harper to be the most approving of it. How might this be explained? [. . .]

Conclusion

This is the situation within which racial sentiments are defined, the context within which racial attitudes exist. White people's sentiments toward blacks are not only forged in this context; they reflect it as well. If they oppose black demands for increased equality, it is not because of their personal predispositions or 'prejudices.' Their refusal is based primarily on their acceptance of American cultural standards. The people with whom we spoke are concerned about the consequences that racial changes will have for American norms and social institutions. They do not oppose demands raised by blacks in racial terms. Their opposition is based on an *acceptance* of and stake in standards and institutional priorities rather than a *rejection* of black people. If anything, they are more concerned about the things black people *lack*—money, education, middle-class values and aspirations—than about black people per se. In some instances, they seem more concerned about what is happening to them than they are about blacks. William Simon and John Gagnon put it the following way:

Change itself becomes the enemy. Much of the current racism may derive not so much from the factors we once associated with prejudice but with the increasing complications that the image of the Negro community now represents the most powerful symbol of 'disruptive' changes in their lives [sic] [1970: 49].

Lipset and Raab found this feeling among Wallace voters in 1968: '. . . it can best be seen as a backlash against change in which there is an almost absolute congruence between the backlash against dreaded change and the backlash targetry, that is, the change bearers' (1970: 341). The conclude that 'the nativist bigotry of such whites finds its genesis not so much in hatred of Negroes, but in the felt diminution of their own status' (1970: 510).

The distinctive feature of racist thinking, then, is not hatred. What sets it off from other thinking is that it justifies policies and institutional priorities that perpetuate racial inequality, and it does so in distinctively American terms. It is not race to which people refer, instead they speak of 'larger' societal interests and values, or the inability of blacks—for reasons for which they assume little responsibility—to compete with whites on equal terms.

I do not question the motives of the people expressing these sentiments. In fact, I am willing to grant that in some instances their intentions may be quite noble: They might actually want to see blacks achieve equality. Their motives, however, are irrelevant. Their thinking is based upon assumptions, and their competing priorities are judged within a framework, that usually insure that they will respond to issues raised by blacks in ways that continue their position of social advantage and therefore maintain their privileges. Their assumptions largely determine their solutions. Given the racial and class organization of American society, there is only so much people can 'see.' The positions they occupy in these structures limit the range of their thinking. The situation places barriers on their imaginations and restricts the possibilities of their vision.

The racist nature of their thinking is not minimized by the fact that white people are often unaware of the extent to which their advantaged position is based on race. The consequences is the same as if they were conscious of it. The subordinate position of black people is justified and the advantaged situation of whites is maintained even though nonracial terms are invoked in the reasoning. Racism, then, need not be distinct, in its content or emotional loading, from the more routine forms of competitive behavior white people engage in with other whites. A distinctive content or kind of emotional loading is not what makes certain sentiments 'racist.' A position is racist when it defends, protects, or enhances social organization based on racial advantage. Racism is determined by the *consequences* of a sentiment, not its surface qualities. Sometimes it is expressed in crude terms but, as this study shows, often it is not. White racism is what white people do to protect the special benefits they gain by virtue of their skin color.

[From *Portraits of White Racism* (Cambridge: Cambridge University Press, 1993, 1st edn. 1977), 206–13, 220–2.]

MICHEL WIEVIORKA

26 Two Patterns of Racism

Insofar as it arises out of the weakness or breakdown of a social movement, racism is not merely a consequence of that process, totally divorced from the movement in its content. The significations it expresses maintain a connection with the meaning which is being lost; they are not wholly dissociated from the relations of which the social movement is itself one of the terms. But they denature that connection, invent new, mythical relations, distort or invert the meaning which provides the social movement with its reference points: thus, in their opposition to the blacks, the white American trade unionists spoke of the betrayal of the working class; the anti-semitism which welled up within Solidarity was directed against the ascendancy or domination of the Jews, presented as the cause of the movement's setbacks and failures, as enemies of the cause. The themes on which racism plays move away from the themes of the social movement, but these latter are not so much forgotten as disfigured. This is why racism can be conceived as a negation of the social movement, and why we are led, as a result, to the notion of a social anti-movement.

1. The Notion of Social Anti-Movement

A social anti-movement is not exactly the reverse image of a social movement. It is made up of the same key elements, but these are considerably shunted around and transformed and the anti-movement is incapable of integrating them into action—a fact which finds expression in either the dissociation or fusional totalization of these elements.

This notion, which we take from the work of Alain Touraine, is an analytic construct which takes account, on the one hand, of the three principles constitutive of social actors, and, on the other, of the modes in which these principles are combined.

(a) In the social anti-movement the social identity of the actor is replaced by a reference to a being, an essence, a nature, by an identification with a cultural, moral or religious category—the forces of good, or justice—or, alternatively, with a mythical social figure, such as the working class, when this latter either does not exist or does not in any way recognize itself in the discourse of the actor. In the case of racism, the actor does not act in the name of the workers, of parents or any other specific social category; that actor speaks on behalf of a race which itself regards the other races as inferior or as not belonging to humanity;

(b) In the social anti-movement the image of a social adversary, which constitutes the principle of opposition in a social movement, dissolves and gives way to a double representation. Here, in effect, the actor may be ranged either against an enemy with whom it is implacably at war, or against an abstract, relatively indeterminate system which is more or less mythical in nature. The Other is no longer a real actor; he is either naturalized and objectivized or identified with a meta-social principle—for example: evil, the devil or decadence. Apart from the fact that he is supposed to be hatching plots, secretly manipulating power, undermining the actor in malevolent and mysterious ways, he becomes extremely distant and elusive, or, by contrast, may seem very close and concrete, but in this latter case he is reduced to a non-human or infra-human category—which enables him to be kept at a distance or identified with animality or makes it permissible for lethal violence to be used against him. It is in this way that racism arrives at the idea that the Other constitutes a threat, that he is evil and that a ruthless battle has to be waged against him.

(c) Lastly, with the social anti-movement, there is no longer conflict around stakes common to both the social actor and its adversary; there is no longer a shared conception of historicity, recourse to the same language as the adversary in doing battle with him, or a consciousness of acting to control or direct the same set of resources. There is no longer, for example, the idea, shared by the labour movement and the employers, that progress and industry go together and that the point is to manage them, each party acting towards that end. The actor retreats to its own ground and takes the view that there is no positive historicity outside its own; it defines itself by rupture, distance and the retreat into its own conceptions, not by belonging to the same field as its opponents. It becomes sectarian or warlike; it denies the idea of a structural conflict or a social relation; it constitutes a force for historical change or closes itself off from all communication with the outside; its plans are not targeted at the society in which it lives, but directed towards creating an homogeneous, purified unity. From this point of view, racism calls, with varying degrees of emphasis, for the setting apart or elimination of those who are not part of a historicity defined in terms of racial properties—properties which are themselves perceived as indissociable from a culture and a history.

It is the specific property of a social anti-movement that it is incapable of articulating the three principles we have just presented or of integrating them into a single action: it cannot speak in the name of a particular social category and a general, liberatory conception of society; it ceases to recognize stakes that are common to an adversary and to itself; and it quite simply cannot accept internal tensions and debates. As we shall see with regard to racism, it either withdraws into partial and perverted figurations of a social movement, or constitutes itself as a totalizing entity which constructs a system of imaginary action—an unreal and potentially lethal substitute for lost, rejected or impossible social relations.

2. Partial Racism, Total Racism

Between the complete breakdown of a social movement, or even a deep crisis of that movement, and the high point of its development, there are intermediate situations which favour the development of a racism which represents the dark side of that movement and may be described, in more precise terms, as a partial anti-movement.

This scenario involves the coexistence of two logics which give expression to the break-up of the system of action. On the one hand, the actor remains, in effect, engaged in social relations in a conflict which pits it against a clearly defined adversary; on the other hand, it is mobilized in racist practices and discourses which suggest a situation of competition rather than of conflict. This coexistence of two logics may last for as long as the social movement continues to enjoy a certain capacity for action, without, however, attaining a high level of projective content and integration. The effect is that the two logics are mutually limiting. This coexistence of two logics can be seen all the more clearly if we examine the principle structuring the actor's identity.

If the actor is incapable of acting—or powerless to act—in the name of all who are suffering comparable or complementary forms of domination, and if it decides only to defend and promote particular interests, then that means recognizing or introducing a split within the ranks of the population it is seeking to represent. It does, admittedly, continue to call for action and make social demands, but its struggle stops, on non-social criteria, at the point where that struggle might possibly relate to the racialized fraction of the group to which it belongs. It then singles out on racial lines people who can hardly be distinguished from the actor socially by their position within the prevailing relations of domination or, at least, people whom the actor should or could bring together in a single struggle; and it not only ignores these people, but rejects them and fights them.

The identity of the actor is here fragmented and transformed. It breaks up, on the one hand, into sub-identities covering a whole range of particular interests which, though still social, are not universal or general in their scope, and, on the other, into a definition which can no longer be social and becomes racial and racist. This explains how, in the labour movement in particular, racism can arise at the point of conjunction between sectional or corporatist demands and an effort to exclude certain racialized groups—blacks, for example—from the system in which these demands can be formulated.

More broadly, we can say of the partial anti-movement that it emerges in a process of duplication in which, on the one hand, the actor maintains, in a weakened form, an image of an identity and of a social adversary and a consciousness of involvement in a relation of domination, and, on the other hand, engages, in the name of race, in competitive practices on *markets*—particularly the housing and labour markets—where individual strategies and collective pressures, which may possibly be violent and are susceptible of translation to the political level, stand in for action. Whilst it combines these two characteristics, the racism involved here is more inegalitarian than differentialist, especially if those promoting it are able to maintain a social, economic or organizational superiority—for example, by retaining a monopoly on skilled labour and leaving the monotonous, dirty or unpleasant work to the racialized group. It does not necessarily involve an intermediate reference to a community—of nationality or religion, for example, which the Other may very well share. Such racism gives expression to a partial destructuring of the actor, and a state of duplication which permits many a conjunctural oscillation—between movement and anti-movement, social conflict and racial hatred or rejection.

But when the social movement goes into unstoppable decline or undergoes such a crisis that it loses all meaning for some of its protagonists, this phenomenon of duplication gives way to the social void. Here the actor is, as it were, cut free of all moorings in a social relationship; it is not—or not any longer—able to find the behavioural markers by which it was previously able to orient its action. It is no longer in a half-way house, as in the case just discussed where it was torn between two systems of action, simultaneously involved in a social conflict and a market; it is no longer located within a conflictual social field, or this no longer has any meaning for it. And, among the various possibilities—apathy or consumerist individualism, for example—there opens up the scenario of the formation of a racism which reconstructs, in imaginary mode, a fictive system of action which substitutes itself for the faltering social system. This impressive construction first of all entails the redefinition of the adversary, who now becomes an enemy identified with evil; and it involves the actor not, now, in a conflict, but in discourses of separation and rupture, if not indeed of violence, and is based on a reformulation of the actor's identity which can no longer be fragmented or duplicated, as in the previous case, but which, divested of all social reference, takes on a distinctly communal coloration, even before—or at the same time as—it assumes a racial one. The racism, here, is unlimited. It does not place the actor on a market or in competitive relations with those who share the actor's social condition or are not far removed from it; it takes itself out of this type of reality to establish a new space, dominated by the hate-filled pursuit of a scapegoat. This racism is much more differentialist than inegalitarian. In this sense, too, it is total, as indeed is the anti-movement from which it issues, whereas in the previous case it was merely partial.

3. Racism, Social Movements and Social Structure

The reader should not conclude from the preceding discussion that the only source of the growth of racism lies in the destructuring of social movements. This phenomenon, though not exceptional, is not—by a long way—directly responsible for the principal manifestations of racism, and it is not the sad or impotent figures of a movement which has become a social anti-movement that make up the big battalions of racist thinking or action. We must, none the less, continue to explore the idea of a connection between social movements, anti-movements and racism.

When it is powerful and has a high projective content—as was the case with the labour movement in Western societies up to the 1960s—a social movement does not merely have a considerable capacity to mobilize those who, because they have intense experience of the domination it has arisen to combat, immediately recognize themselves in it. Apart from the actions of its most immediate protagonists, it also structures—and confers meaning on—a wide range of behaviours extending far beyond its strict field of action. Thus, in all the places where it was a central reality, the labour movement constituted a reference point for all kinds of actors mobilized in neighbourhood politics, in universities, in cultural or sporting movements, or in action in the name of women, consumers or user-groups, or reformist or revolutionary political projects and also of grand principles such as justice and democracy, without those actors (and the above list is not an exhaustive one) necessarily having to regard themselves as sharing in a working-class social identity. And when such a central figure declines, when the reference point it represented becomes increasingly artificial or ideological, the actors to whom it offered a meaningful place are orphaned and weakened; they lose their capacity to see their specific practice as part of a more general struggle and also lose a political lever which enabled them to feel part of the relation structuring the whole of social life.

Hence the weakness, breakdown or absence of social movements exerts substantial, though indirect, effects on racism, particularly in a working-class milieu.

1. Racism and social exclusion

A first illustration of this phenomenon concerns the world of social outcasts and is provided by the experience of the 'underclass' formed by the blacks in the American 'hyperghettos'. These people are not in a position to mobilize the resources required for collective action; even action of a 'Black-Power' type, with a potentially high exemplary or violent content, seems precluded in their case.

When, responding to the attraction of the urban, industrial world, American blacks moved up from the South, particularly after 1910 or 1915, they could see themselves as a proletariat, as part of the working class—even when the white labour unions rejected them. They could exert social pressure, gain a hearing from some trade unionists, appeal to the idea of a labour movement and insist their plight not be dissociated from that of the other workers. Even if they were poverty-striken, they were not marginalized and could give a social meaning to their demands. Those who live in the hyperghetto today belong to a world which has become detached from the rest of society, including, as Wilson points out, from the black lower-middle class.[1] They can, if they so wish, kill one another, destroy themselves either with drugs or in a world of petty crime largely bounded by their own social space, and sink into poverty; they have hardly anything like the symbolic—or the political, organized—way-stations which the labour movement brought them, however inadequate these may have been, nor do they have even the aspiration to participate in such a movement. The breakdown of that movement, which certainly reached its peak somewhere between the 1930s and the 1950s or 1960s, makes the combination of racism and socio-economic exclusion more acute than ever. It enables the white working classes to get by better, as a result of the tremendous dualization which now separates them from the poverty-stricken black masses, who are pushed aside and left to their own devices—at best, to social welfare—and for whom social exclusion and economic difficulties are now so much of a concern that, paradoxically, racism has become a secondary issue. To put it another way, as long as a labour movement existed, the conditions for the expansion of anti-black racism were limited by a project of collective action in which all workers were united without distinction of race. From the point where this began to break up, millions of blacks—and not only blacks—found themselves defined by poverty, under-employment and unemployment and by their confinement in the vast expanses of the hyperghetto, where they are totally segregated and excluded and, as the victims of industrial and urban change in which an undeniably racist sorting process has taken place, take no part in the country's social debates and conflicts. For some decades, the social movement was able to keep alive the hope—and also, to some extent, the reality—of a socio-economic integration that was stronger than racism; with the historic decline of that movement, the project of social integration has given way, for many, to a total—racial and social—segregation.

2. The drift within the middle classes

A second illustration of the phenomenon we are concerned with here relates to the middle classes in the broad sense; contemporary French experience provides us with a particularly significant example.

As in the case throughout the Western world, the middle classes in France form a vast and thoroughly heterogeneous ensemble and exert considerable political and cultural influence. Up until the 1970s, when political and social life was organized around the central conflict which ranged the labour movement against the employers, the middle classes were, so to speak, polarized, having no option but to take up positions by reference to the two social adversaries who, through their struggle, gave society its structure. A copious literature, generally Marxist in inspiration, sought at the time to account for this phenomenon of polarization. There is nothing to suggest that the middle classes were, at that stage, fundamentally any more or less racist than they are today. But the debates which they took a hand in constructing were dominated by a sense that society was structured by a central divide and their commitments were largely determined by that divide. These classes, which were politically and culturally active, participated in the public action Albert Hirschman writes of,[2] and the presence of immigrants was certainly not a question which concerned them obsessively—immigration, though already a mass phenomenon, being defined at that time in terms not of population, but of labour.

The crisis of industrial society and, most especially, the decline of the labour movement have also demobilized these classes, to the point that many writers, their attention fixed on this vast range of social categories—and on them alone—have felt able to speak of a social void, of narcissism and a generalized individualism. Within a few years, in fact, the middle classes have seemed to lose all interest in any wide-ranging collective commitment and to go over solely to the pursuit of private happiness. The breakdown of the conflict which structured society propelled them, as it were, into a new universe, where their problem could no longer be one of situating themselves with regard to this general principle of organization but of finding their place on the ladder of social stratification. Being as far away from power as they are from the world of the social outcasts, they seem to belong to a society which is, for the moment, defined more by participation in consumption, by mobility, and by opportunities for going up in the world and the danger of going down. The transition from a class society to a society of stratification and exclusion, and also the waning of the new social movements—in which they played a considerable part in the 1970s— have found expression, where they are concerned, in many kinds of effects which are all, more or less, linked to their relative position on the social ladder. And, among these effects, the one which concerns us most is the opening up of a wider space for attitudes and behaviours which tend towards racism or border upon it. On the one hand, the middle classes—and even the least deprived of the lower classes—have attempted to mark themselves off not so much from the poor or the manual workers [le monde ouvrier] as from the immigrant population, which has increasingly come to be perceived as an ethnic and religious threat. They have deserted certain areas and moved to homogeneous suburbs; they have resorted to private education or to special dispensations, often based on personal favours, to take their children out of schools with a high level of immigrants, thus creating the beginnings of a social and ethnic segregation which is itself imbued with a certain racism. And, on the other hand, in the political crisis opened up by the decline of industrial society and the political forces which were its representatives, they have contributed indirectly to the rise of a populism which has found its chief expression in the Front National, a party in which racism, including anti-semitism, has its place.

Those sustaining this populism are not necessarily the same people who have managed to develop the individual strategies which are leading to a de facto segregation. Indeed, it is found much more among those who do not have the resources to permit them to adopt such strategies—who see their neighbourhood deteriorating, for example, or who end up in a run-down urban environment; it is the expression of an incapacity to offset the loss of the reference points once provided by classic industrial society in any other way than by reconstituting new ones on a xenophobic and racializing basis.

Here again, there is not one single logic at work, but two. The first of these— a segregative logic—keeps a racialized population at bay, avoids living in the same places as they do and marks its distance from people who signify both social decline and a different racial identity. The second builds up the racialized group—primarily, in the French case, the populations originating from the Maghreb—into a threat and a scapegoat. There is a constant interplay between these two logics and they are difficult to disentangle in practice. But they are distinct, and the way they differ is of the same order as the way partial racism differs from total.

4. The Two Modes of the Social Production of Racism

The notions of social movement and anti-movement thus allow us to elucidate the possible expansion of racism in a way which goes far beyond the actors most directly concerned. They also allow us to bring out clearly two fundamentally different modes of the social production of racism [. . .]

On the one hand, racism appears as a perversion of social relations, a degraded form of social behaviour, the space for which grows larger when the society in question is not highly structured by the existence of a social movement. For racism to appear, certain conditions must be fulfilled in both the racializing and the racialized groups. The racializing group must possess resources which remain social and a capacity for—individual or collective—action which is linked to economic or political means, to a status—even a threatened one—or, alternatively, to degrees of freedom in the recourse to violence or to a certain tolerance or permissiveness within the political system and the institutions. Racist behaviours find a favourable terrain in the existence of markets in which these resources are often sufficient to ensure discrimination, to force an inferior status on the Other in the spheres of job-seeking or employment or, alternatively, to bring about urban or educational segregation.

Such behaviours are also encouraged by the victim group bearing certain characteristics which are, to use John Dollard's terms, 'visible'—that is, the existence of physical or cultural markers which make any individual who belongs to the racialized population easily identifiable.[3]

On the other hand, racism appears as the totally imaginary construction of a system of action, the delusional invention of relations between races, the radical shift from a concrete, real stage to a fictive one, to a natural or cosmic order in which it is directed against a scapegoat.

This shift again implies resources, but these are not so much social as symbolic, historical and cultural in character; it involves a definition of the actor in terms of community—most often in terms of nation—by the activation or reactivation of myths rooted in what may be a history of substantial density—as is the case with anti-Jewish racism.

Here again, the choice of scapegoat is not accidental or conjunctural, at least in the case of those experiences which are to some degree stable over time (hatred of Jews and Gypsies in particular). If we follow Gordon W. Allport, we have to say that it owes much to historical and cultural factors specific to the victim group; it is based, as Yves Chevalier writes, with specific reference to the case of anti-semitism, on the fact that the Jews are 'a minority group with an identity of its own, and one that is geographically dispersed and which generally occupies partially—and, indeed, increasingly—distinct economic positions, and which has long maintained not unambiguous relations with the authorities'.[4]

These two modes of social production of racism bring us back to the opposition we have already established between differentialist and inegalitarian racism, though the two sets of terms do not overlap exactly. They are, however, sufficiently close for us to link partial racism with the predominantly inegalitarian variant, on the one hand, and total racism with the predominantly differentialist form, on the other. In some instances, these occur in succession, as though it were the case, in particular, that the exhaustion or impossibility of partial racism culminated in transition to a total racism. For example, the 'skinheads' first made their appearance as a manifestation of the British labour movement in its decomposition, as a form without social content, disconnected from any class conflict, still bearing the stamp of a certain working-class culture and carrying a charge of anger which soon went beyond partial anti-black or, more commonly anti-Asian racism—so frequently encountered among white workers—to develop, in a space which had extended to Europe, into a total neo-Nazi-inspired racism unconnected with any form of working-class action or with strategies on the labour or housing markets. In other cases, it would be more exact to speak of an intermediate zone, where the attempt to maintain a social order in which partial racism has its place combines with tendencies to move towards a total racism. This is, more or less, the territory of the 'poor white', whether we are speaking of the barbaric violence of popular lynchings in the USA, which went on into the 1920s, or, to take contemporary France, of that infra-racist populism in which the actor oscillates between a desire to keep the immigrants in a state of subordination and inferiority and a hate-filled call for their deportation.

This brings us to one final comment: the two modes of social production of racism just presented, which correspond to analytic categories, should not be confused with historical phenomena. Taken overall, such phenomena may very well involve one or other of these categories to a greater or lesser extent, but they may also involve both, and considerable degrees of variation over time and space may also occur. Though anti-black racism has most often been associated historically with practices of domination and with an inegalitarian or partial logic—as we have just seen with the example of the 'poor whites'—it also comprises a differentialist dimension which is not far removed from a total racism. By the same token, anti-semitism should not be seen as always—obeying the logic of total racism. Thus, in a robustly argued piece, Jacob Katz takes to task three types of explanation—the 'socio-political', the 'psychoanalytic' and the 'ideological'—which have in common a neglect of the real conflicts between Jews and non-Jews.[5] There are, explains Katz, three ways of detaching anti-semitism from its connection with real, concrete Jews: the first consists in seeing it as a displacement of social protests onto a group which provided an easier target than the real culprits; the second, exemplified by Saül Friedländer's book on Nazi anti-semitism, reduces the phenomenon to a collective psychosis;[6] the third puts the emphasis on the strength of racial ideology, leaving out of account the actual existence of Jews. It is true that anti-semitism, fictive as it may seem, generally develops in situations where there is a certain genuine Jewish presence, where Jews form more or less visible communities, and where some of them occupy economic, social, political or cultural positions. It is also true than anti-semitism without Jews is an extreme case and one which is historically exceptional, being met hardly anywhere but in Communist or post-Communist central Europe or, on a much smaller scale, in contemporary Japan. It is certainly true that, in some cases, anti-semitism falls under the heading of what, keeping to our terminology, we must call partial racism, as is very well illustrated by Victor Karady and Istvan Kémény in the case of inter-war Hungary, where the rise of anti-semitism occurred against a backdrop of competition with Jews on the labour and education markets.[7] But in very many cases, one would be missing the essential point if one were not sensitive to the imaginary and symbolic function performed by the Jews and the differentialist logic which rejects all conflict, and even all market competition with them, and calls for them to be set apart and destroyed. In its historical forms, anti-semitism frequently combines the two basic logics of racism; but if it occupies a central place in history, this assuredly has more to do with the expulsions and frenzied massacres which have been associated with it than with the inegalitarian relations it has very often been seen to accompany or used to rationalize.

[From *The Arena of Racism* (London: Sage, 1995; 1st pub. 1991), 92–101.]

RAPHAEL EZEKIEL

27 Klan Rally at Stone Mountain, Georgia

Three years after I had begun interviewing members of a neo-Nazi group in Detroit, I began the work with national leaders through conversations with the late Robert Miles at his farm in Cahoctah, Michigan. Miles had once headed the Klan in Michigan and now held unity meetings for far-flung racist groups at his farm twice a year, as well as publishing a monthly newsletter. His phone rang incessantly when we talked. The calls came from across the country; he was one of the main figures holding the white racist movement together and supplying it with ideas.

As we were talking one afternoon in July, he suggested that I go down to the Labor Day rally at Stone Mountain, Georgia, if I really wanted to know what the Klan was about. He gave me the names of several leaders who lived in Atlanta so that I could make arrangements. Late in August I decided this was a good idea. Other than Miles, I had never known anyone who openly discussed any connection to the Klan. I could observe a large group of Klansmen; it would be a good way to start this leg of the work. I called several people whom Miles had suggested; they were noncommittal but said to call them if I came down.

I flew down with misgivings. It was a long, long time since my boyhood in Texas. I had spent two years as a draftee in Georgia during the Korean War; in the 1970s I had once driven through North Carolina to the ocean. Other than that, I had not been in the South since 1944. But I had ideas: The South was where they killed people.

At the airport terminal in Detroit, I heard Southern accents. *This is nuts*, an inner voice said. But I did need to meet the South again, and, more, I needed to walk as a human among some Klanspeople and gain a sense of them as humans. A friend had suggested that for my safety I should let the FBI know what I was planning and where I was going to be. I had turned the suggestion down. My work has always depended on building an atmosphere of trust; I want respondents to be open with me, and I have to earn that openness by treating the respondents with honesty. I also thought it would be dangerous to have a police contact that I was trying to hide, and I have avoided contact with police agencies throughout this work. It looked like a very lonely three days coming up, and I had managed to contact an old student of mine who lived in Atlanta, and we hoped to see each other while I was down there.

The Atlanta terminal was a shock. The gleaming metals and sophisticated lighting in the hallways screamed the distance that this cosmopolitan center of the New South had moved since the mid-fifties. Much more impressive, and significant, were the self-confident faces, the brisk walls, the expensive, lustrous shoes, the crisp suit jackets, the narrow ties of the small army of African-American professionals and businessmen who marched through the terminal, with equally well-dressed and confident black women at their sides. Memories welled up: the misery of black life in my hometown, the rags and the dust. Obviously Atlanta must include the same poverty-filled stretches that Detroit did and the towns of my youth, but I was excited to see evidence of a healthy black middle class that was not minuscule. I looked with awe.

I phoned several of the people I had previously talked to long-distance; the first was evasive, but the second, an elderly leader named James Venable, told me to come on over. I bought maps and went looking for him. The village of Stone Mountain showed up okay, some ten miles east of Atlanta and at the foot of a massive block of granite rising abruptly from the plain—Stone Mountain itself. Finding Venable's house took a great deal longer; his directions didn't correspond to landmarks I could find, but after exploration I found the street and the right number. An old gray wooden farmhouse stood far in the back of a huge lot. No one answered the door; no one seemed to be about. I waited an hour in the silent, empty yard beneath the huge pecan trees, the quiet afternoon sky.

Then, morose and lonely, I drove to the little motel at the edge of Atlanta. I called Judy, my old student, and we arranged to have breakfast in the morning.

After a depressed supper, I drove back to Venable's house. I was getting nowhere; it was probably a waste of time to drive back out, but what else was there to do? The miles of ticky-tack did not cheer me up, nor the deepening dusk.

Venable was in. He led me from the door into a kitchen filled with steam. Four great cauldrons were bubbling on the stove. He was preparing soup for the rally, he told me.

Venable and the house were both old. The house recalled those of my home town: an aging country home, with stacks of old newspapers, old paper bags, scraps of this and that against the ancient wood. Cats wandered about.

Venable talked at length. He didn't especially understand who I was, but he wanted to teach me Klan lore. He gave me old newspapers from his branch of the Klan; he had been its national leader for many years. He went upstairs and got me a copy of the handbook with rules for initiation to the first degree— there seemed to be successive degrees, as in Freemasonry. The handbook was known as the *Kloran*. The *Kloran* listed the Klan's labels: The local cell is called a Klavern; its head is the Exalted Cyclops; officers below the Cyclops included the Klaliff, the Klokard, the Kludd, the Kligrapp, the Kladd, the Kliabee, the Klexter, and the Klarogo. The national head of a Klan, Venable told me, is known as an Imperial Wizard; a state director is a Grand Dragon.

Venable talked about how things had been in the olden days. Great crowds used to come to rallies, he said, great numbers to parades—there used to be ten thousand at the Labor Day rally, he said. There was much secret lore and special ways. You could always find another Klansman: When you pulled up to a gas station in a strange town, you would ask the attendant, 'Do you know Mr *Ayak*?' *Ayak* stood for *Are You A K*lansman? The attendant would answer, 'Well, I know Mr *Akia*.' And *Akia* stood for *A K*lansman *I A*m.

Venable's stories went on and on. He talked about huge cavalcades of Klan cars roaring through the black sections ('niggertown') to keep the black people ('niggers') in line. He talked about internal Klan politics; he talked about cere-monies, rituals, and fellowships—the Klan as a fraternal order. He seemed close to senility.

It was getting dark, and I wondered how I was going to find the rally ground the next day. Where should I park? Venable said we should drive down right then, so he could show me the way.

We drove through town toward the mountain, to a huge meadow at its foot. I saw little knots of men by small fires. We walked to a fire and met Dave Hol-land, a young leader who was organizing the rally, and two of his lieutenants. I walked across to four young men who leaned on a truck. They were hesitant and careful, but soon got interested in talking. I talked at length with two of them. They were friends, trying to keep a North Carolina Klan alive after the ar-rest of its leader, worried about how to do that work without seeming to try to take over the group. Both were twenty-two years old; both came from blue-collar families. They believed in the Aryan Jesus, the Aryan Israelites.

Men were setting up their sleeping bags around the fires. People had driven in from a distance. It felt like a camping trip, a kids' gang.

Later I talked more with Venable at the house, wrote some field notes in my motel room, and slept.

Saturday morning was cold with light rain. I had breakfasted with my former student, who wanted to join me in a brief morning reconnaissance. Raised in Chicago, Jewish, very thoughtful and very bright, Judy has lived in the South for some time, and I value her reactions. Back at the rally field we saw flags snapping in the wind: Masses of Reb flags lined the great stage that had been erected at the far edge of the meadow; flags flew from many of the dozens of vans and trucks that had by now accumulated—there were rattlesnake DON'T TREAD ON ME flags, Nazi battle flags with swastikas, and many more Reb flags.

We walked through the meadow. Additional vehicles arrived steadily. At four or five places, wooden booths set up beneath tents held books, buttons, and stickers for sale—WHITE BY BIRTH, SOUTHERN BY THE GRACE OF GOD, PRAISE GOD FOR AIDS. Judy chatted with an older women who talked of her own childhood in Michigan's Upper Peninsula. I listened to the conversations; I looked at the mass of Confederate flags up at the speaker stand—the racists had taken over the handsome symbol. I listened to the lively country-western music coming over the loudspeaker. I started to be able to understand the words in the lyrics: Again and again the lyrics used the word 'nigger.' They had their own music, their own songs, and they were getting joy by being able to say 'nigger' out loud.

I drove Judy back to the city. She talked about her work in nearby towns with country people. They are independent, she said; they are warm when they have accepted you; they are cautious, defensive, and secretive, afraid of being patronized by city people. This crowd at the rally ground had seemed familiar to her. My own mood was dark. I was getting a headache and feeling the strain: It is important for my goal to let a real sense of the stranger come into me, not to block it or distort it. At the same time I need to keep my own sense of myself. It would be less effort just to reject the stranger. But I would gain no understanding.

I thanked Judy and ate lunch. Wool socks made my feet warmer and I was happier. I returned to the rally field. The rain was lightening. Knots of men spread across the meadow; I walked past conversations:

'. . . What I can't understand—any white woman, I can look at any white woman, no matter how ugly-looking she is, and I can find something to admire. But what I can't understand, how anyone can take some bush monkey, some ape, and crown her Miss Mississippi.' (The man talking was a squat creature from Galveston.)

'. . . What is the worst, to see a couple—to see some white woman and some black man—ugh! It just turns my stomach!'

'. . . They don't tell you about the sixty-six million white Christians the Russians killed. The Bolshevik Jews created the Russian Revolution.'

'. . . They don't tell you, Trotsky, his real name was Bernstein, he was a New York Jew. They don't tell you, the three men who made the Russian Revolution, they were in New York, they were trained in sabotage and revolution by a team of Rabbis.'

'. . . The Jew is the seed of Cain. The Canaanite Jews are the children of the serpent.'

'. . . Talmud is their holy book. And I don't even have to tell you about the Kol Nidre. As I understand it, a man could go out and lie and cheat all the rest of the year.'

So the comments went, so the conversations flowed. The good folk took comfort, as they do at these meetings, passing tidbits on to one another, having their wisdom confirmed.

I soon found myself alongside a cluster engaged in picture taking, another favored pastime—souvenir photos of oneself in uniform or robe at the gathering. A tall fellow aimed his camera at two of the security guards, young men posed side by side in black T-shirts and black boots, Klan logo on the T-shirts, arms raised in Hitler salute.

The guard nearest me, a young man with short hair and blue eyes, asked me to be in the picture with him. I thought useful conversation might result and went to stand next to him.

He leaned close to me and said, 'Hey, are you kosherish?'

I was surprised. 'What?' I asked. 'Excuse me?'

'You wouldn't happen to be Jewish, would you?' he asked.

'Well, yes,' I said, 'I do happen to be Jewish.'

'*Out!*' he cried. 'Out the gate! Let's go!'

'Are you serious?' I asked.

The older, lean, taller man who had been taking the pictures said to him, 'Wait, Arthur, I know that. That's why I said you would want the picture to throw darts at. It's all right, Venable brought him in last night.'

'We'll *see*,' Arthur Prone said grimly, and stalked off to see Dave Holland.

The lean white man, Lennie, and I waited, side by side. It was a longish wait.

The young man returned, very put out. Lennie said, 'It's all right.' Young Arthur yelled back towards Holland, 'You're asking for some mighty hard decisions.'

Arthur stared at me. He ground his jaw. He looked hard into my face and said, 'I don't give a damn for kikes.' He said, 'Keep the dream alive. Kill a Jew. Keep Hitler's dream alive.'

Hatred hardened his voice. His eyes blazed. There was no way to communicate. I turned and walked off; I was not going to get into a macho contest.

I paced around, much agitated. He followed me with his eyes constantly. My stomach was rolling. I walked over to one of the guys from North Carolina, who stood by his truck, and spoke of what had just happened. That fellow said, 'He doesn't mean anything personal.'

'Well,' I said, 'I am here to learn. I don't like upsetting the man. I thought it was obvious I was a Jew.'

'You're not an Orthodox Jew, are you?' the North Carolinian youth asked. When I said no, he went on: 'Well, then. I take it you're here in a professional capacity, not as representing Jews. If you were here *that* way, I might have problems.'

I walked about for ten to twenty minutes. The incident raised problems for me. As a thin and nervous child, I had learned with great difficulty the necessity of standing up to intimidation. At the same time, I truly hate rudeness, and I felt that Arthur had a right to be startled that an agent of the arch-fiend had wandered into his gathering. I needed, for my dignity, to confront him; I felt that I needed, at the same time, to acknowledge his right to his own responses. These things had to be done, and perhaps good would come of it.

I walked back up to Arthur, who had been eyeing me steadily. I stood in front of him. I told him that, speaking as one man to another, it had not been my intention to upset him. I looked squarely at him.

'I told you what I mean,' he said. 'I don't like a kike.'

He stared at me. 'I have no use for a Jew. Keep Hitler's dream alive: Kill a Jew.'

He was still trying to provoke me.

He said again that he had no use for a Jew.

I said, 'Well, that's you.'

I had already told him I was studying the movement; I now said, truthfully, that I would like to hear more about what he was saying—that this wasn't the time or place, but if it were, I would want to hear more about this.

He said, 'If it were the time and the place, I would *show* you.'

'That's you,' I said in a level voice. I walked off.

I realize now, some years later and after much more interaction, that I must have been conspicuous since my first appearance. I had felt rather casual, strolling among the folk, nodding and saying 'howdy' now and then. I was dressed in no particular manner. I had supposed I seemed out of place, but not especially noteworthy. I much misunderstood, I now can see, the amount of fear in which these people live, and their belief that a Jewish power base was out to endanger them. There had undoubtedly been bits of gossip following me all morning and afternoon as I walked about. The incident with Arthur ignited that tinder; a strange few hours, harmless, deeply frightening, and deeply educational, followed.

As I experienced it, tentacles of hostility seemed to snake out from the encounter, seemed to spread through the meadow the rest of the afternoon. I was talking first with the North Carolina men, and someone called across from an enclosure, 'He's a Jew!' Soon, as I was asking one of the attendees where the afternoon's street parade was to be held, another called across, 'Don't tell the fucking Jew!' As I walked about the meadow, I picked up pieces of conversation: 'Jew,' 'Jewboy.' There were periodic catcalls. As I passed near a row of parked vehicles, one of the Klansmen hidden in a van called over a speaker system in a metallic, loud, and nasty voice, '*Yeah*, just move your niggerized self along, Jewboy! Just *move along.*' More catcalls; more frozen stares as I passed; more hard, hostile faces.

I talked then a long time with the men from North Carolina about Jews: What was the deal? I heard deep enmity. The Klan was profoundly anti-Semitic. I left that little group and continued to walk about; the catcalls followed, the nasty stares.

I talked after a while with a blond, bearded young fellow over by some cars. He talked to me about the Federal Reserve, about the conspiracies, about the Jews. The Jews are children of the Serpent.

'Look,' I said, thinking to myself that I must not answer in the terms of his delusion but as a real person, must see the effect, 'in real life, I get my ideas about people by what really happens, day by day what really happens with them. Now you, you're from a little town in North Carolina, I reckon.'

'No,' he answered. 'Tennessee.'

'Okay,' I said. 'But the point is, how many Jews were in your town?'

'None,' he said. 'None. But all I need to know about Jews—' He was shouting by now; he had grabbed his Bible and sprung it open, he thumped it, he lifted it into the air above his head, he slashed the air with it. 'All I need to know about Jews, I get it *right here!*' He slammed his hand onto the Good Word. 'All I need to know, *the Book* tells me!'

I stood near a tent, quietly. I was not willing to be driven away. More catcalls came. I understood: I would not be safe here if it were dark: If someone moved to hurt me, no one would stop him.

I had been defined. I was not 'Rafe,' not Raphael Ezekiel; I was not the individual my friends knew, my students knew, I knew. I was Alien, stripped of my particular history.

I was Jew.

It was incredibly lonesome.

[From *The Racist Mind* (London: Penguin, 1996), 5–13.]

PIERRE-ANDRÉ TAGUIEFF

28 The New Cultural Racism in France

The New Right's counter-offensive of anti-racism began also in 1983–1984. Launched by the *Front National* and its national Catholic auxiliary (the Comités Chrétienté Solidarité, the daily *Présent*, the weekly *Minute*), the reversal concerning racism was accepted by a portion of the conservative wing, which saw itself as part of 'national liberalism' as defined by the Club de l'Horloge. The first move was to stigmatize anti-racist Leftists as anti-French, anti-European, anti-Western, or anti-White 'racists' for siding with the enemies of all the aforementioned. The second was the substitution of one definition of 'racists' for another.

The most ideologically effective ploy, which has eluded Left criticism, is the differentialist argument. The praise of difference, after being emphasized by the ethnic doctrine of GRECE (Groupement de Reserches et d'Etudes pour la Civilisation Européene), was rapidly accepted within the neo-chauvinist camp and became fundamental to the nascent heterophobic ideology. This praise of difference was reduced to the claim that true racism is the attempt to impose a unique and general model as the best, which implies the elimination of differences. Consequently, true anti-racism is founded on the absolute respect of differences between ethnically and culturally heterogeneous collectives. The New Right's 'anti-racism' thus uses ideas of collective identities hypostatized as inalienable categories.

A third argument completes the first two—the disjunction between Right nationalists and Europeanists, on the one hand, and the 'racist' phenomenon reduced to the desire to erase differences, on the other. Differentialism is opposed to universalism, as authentic anti-racism is to true racism. Together, these three arguments reverse classical anti-racist discourse.

Anti-totalitarianism is the latest reversal, which draws on all the political consequences of three generations of liberal (or neo-liberal) critiques of totalitarianism—understood as a tendency toward state management and centralization. After the economic critique of the 1930s (Von Mises, Hayek), the political critique of the 1950s (Arendt, Aron), and finally the conjunction of the sociological (Baechler, Boudon, Bénéton), historical (Besançon, Furet) and philosophical (Lefort, Castoriadis) critiques, the absolute rejection of the totalitarian model and of all paths supposedly leading thereto became a precondition for the democratic ideal. The welfare state thus became the agency of totalitarianism *par excellence*. To be 'anti-totalitarian' means to refuse unconditionally all socialisms, above all the fatal first step of state control on the road leading to totalitarianism.

The purpose of these first three ideological appropriations was to make possible a *positive self-re-evaluation* of the Right which, starting with liberal conservatism, could be extended to various nationalist families who—except for the Gaullist faction—had been discredited after 1945. These appropriations were carried out by means of the rhetorical model of *reversal*, i.e., by borrowing the adversary's own arguments and turning them against him. Fascism, racism, and totalitarianism become at once key political words and demonized representations constituting the object of a consensual rejection. They function as criteria for distinguishing enemies, adversaries/competitors and even absolute enemies from friends.

Positive Values

Two strategies emerge in the struggle for legitimate appropriation. The first is a matter of presenting oneself as *sharing* with one's designated adversary, but with even more authenticity, the latter's declared values. The objective is to appropriate exclusive use of the adversary's arguments and thereby both to prevent those very same adversaries from using their own arguments and to lock the adversary into a defensive position with an indefensible future. However, there is another series of ideological appropriation of values regarded as positive. First, there is the celebration of a cultural *modernity* and the call for social *modernization*, where the modern is reduced to economics and technological innovation and linked to individualist, productivist and managerial values. Second, there is the appeal to the 'real' as opposed to the utopian, messianic, and ideological. This is a recent French recycling of the thesis of 'the end of ideology.' While the tendency toward 'deideologization' has never been confirmed, the theme remains ingrained in the social imagination, where propaganda can always rediscover it and exploit it. Third, there is *the praise of established roots*, which applies to property and all forms of inheritance, no less than to identities based on origins. Here, the 'right to be different' changes from a Left slogan (in the 1970s) to one of the Right (in the 1980s)—a displacement radicalized in neo-racist uses of the differentialist principle. But this 'right to be different' is a symptom of the aspiration to continuity and a longing for community that the modern destruction of traditional forms necessarily generates. Nostalgia for a close-knit community, for emotional ties inexorably neutralized by democratic contractualism and the atomization fostered by industrialization, are the affective substrata of the ideology of established roots. Ethnicity and neo-nationalism substitute for the meaning once provided by traditional societies.

Fourth in this series of ideological appropriations is the defense of *liberty* in an explicitly *anti-statist* perspective. Liberal-capitalist ideology defines its horizon by opposing the initiative and the responsibility of citizen-entrepreneurs to the social hell of the interventionist state bureaucracy. This generates the dream of a liberated civil society brought about by the marketplace freed of the state. This is the utopia of spontaneous social organizations. However, it contradicts the longing for security which demands order—something which can be guaranteed only by a strong state. Fifth, then, is *the demand for security*, and this demand for the security of people and property is a demand for order which translates into greater state authority. Yet, since the state is often negatively perceived as cut off from the people and suspected of inefficiency, this demand is bound to be frustrated.

The sixth appropriation is the ideal of the *national body* as a categorical imperative of political action. The decline of the internationalist project, whose goal was the abolition of national boundaries, and a world-wide renewal of national ideologies has meant the relegitimation of nationalism. This ideal has become 'a *common stake* in all movements and all parties that, directly or indirectly, portray themselves as the defenders of national interests.'[1] Beyond the fact that nationalism 'has everything it needs to please,'[2] and heads the list of leading ideologies (socialism, fascism and liberalism), it is the most natural ideology of the modern state and its most effective spontaneous mode of legitimation. In terms of total particularism, one consequence of a progressive discrediting of universalism begun with WWı has been that nationalism today has no serious ideological competitor and is thus an essential component of any concrete political project. The seventh and last appropriation is the exclusivist anchoring in the *republican tradition*. This is a polemical reappropriation meant to deprive the Socialist Left of a century-old heritage. [. . .]

From the 'Right to be Different' to a New Cultural Racism

Racism's new modes of legitimation derive from two fundamental operations: the production of new projects concerning the 'defense of cultural identities' and the refinement of new, acceptable arguments predicated on the privileging of difference. New commonplaces concerning cultural identity and difference have crystallized around the question of immigration. They are meant to conceal fears of racial intermingling, perceived as indirect genocide and ethnocide. Consider the following statements from texts published by radical right-wing groups in France: 'The truth is that the people must preserve and cultivate their differences. . . . Immigration merits condemnation because it strikes a blow at the identity of the host culture as well as at the immigrants' identity.'[3] 'It is because we respect ourselves and others, that we refuse to see our country transformed into a multiracial society in which each one loses one's specificity.'[4] 'Peoples cannot be summarily qualified as superior or inferior, they are different, and one must keep in mind these physical or cultural differences.'[5] 'In our mind, the immigration question can no longer be resolved except by the radical expulsion or organized repatriation of all foreigners. This does not apply to residents who are assimilable, i.e., those from the European Community.'[6]

The thesis of inassimilability of non-European immigrants and the racialist overlapping of biological and cultural arguments are used to promote respect for differences. The power of this new position comes from the fact that it is based on primary evidence and manipulates truisms by slightly altering them. Anthropological reality is reduced to what is most visible: everyone can see the differences in skin color or hear differences in accents. This immediate differential reality constitutes the grounding of neo-racism, portrayed as the defense of cultural identities and the champion of genuine anti-racism.

Paradoxically, racism can be articulated in terms of race or of culture, mindsets, traditions and religions, i.e., in the vocabulary of 'specificities' or of 'collective identities.' Racism does not just biologize the cultural, it acculturates the biological. Racist thought may be developed in terms of either of these registers or may even be presented as a syncretism of genetic reductionism and absolute cultural relativism. Its most radical forms are not always the most visible, or the most easily refuted.

There are two types of racism. A general type postulates the existence of a universal scale of values concerning races or civilizations, which are pinpointed as being suitable, less suitable or unsuitable, according to various criteria. A communitarian type establishes difference or group identity as an absolute. In this case, it is less a question of inequality than of incommunicability, incommensurability, and incomparability. The human species is broken down into self-contained, closed totalities. The differentialist imperative is the need to preserve the community as is, or to purify it. If the central obsession of discriminatory racism is the loss of rank, the debasement of superior peoples, the *idée fixe* of differentialist racism is the loss of what is characteristic, the erasure of the group's identity.

Discriminatory racism can be understood in terms of the classical theory of racial prejudice. It presupposes an imperial and/or colonial type of domination legitimated by the ideology of inequality of human types. The universalism of discriminatory racism derives from the positing of one model of hierarchical classification of races or civilizations. This formal universalism has nothing to do with the fundamental demand for universality of any ethics concerned with respect for individuals. There is no consistent anti-racism that does not postulate the dignity of every human being, whatever one's origins. This core of ethical anti-racism escapes all possible ideological instrumentalizations.

Differentialist racism cannot be reduced to a theory of inequality authorizing domination. Rather, it is predicated on the imperative of preserving the group's identity, whose 'purity' it sanctifies. It stigmatizes the mixing of cultures as the supreme mistake, and it vacillates between a system of exclusion (separate development/rejection) and a system of extermination (apartheid and genocide). Of course, history provides 'impure' examples or syncretic illustrations of these ideal types of racism. But to confuse the two is a theoretical error with serious consequences both for the anti-racist struggle and for an understanding of racist phenomena.

The latest New Right doctrine (since 1979–1980) places the utmost importance on *difference*. What Benoist terms anti-racism is a radical reinterpretation of 'the right to be different.' With racism defined by disrespect of differences, the New Right rejects the very idea of a 'differentialist racism.' Racism can only be an avatar of biblical universalism, an ideological heir of the monotheism that 'reduces' human diversity, the structure that eradicates differences. The New Right's anti-racism is a pseudo-universalism, whereas consistent anti-racism privileges universality over particularity. The right to be different is a *second implication* of a well-founded anti-racism: to grant this right pre-eminent status is to accept racism's premises. Respect for people involves the respect of their 'cultural' choices. Universalism is not universalist enough and thus, in its shadow, thrives a racism which is reductionist, homogenizing, and hostile to biological and cultural diversities.

Anti-racism today must be subjected to a rigorous critique concerning its political instrumentalization, its contradictions and inconsistencies, and its lack of theoretical foundations. All too often the anti-racist struggle draws its concepts of racism from a worn-out, accusatory, anti-fascist rhetoric. The anti-racists difficulty during the last ten years in identifying what they are fighting is a result of a problem of definition. They persist in seeing racism only as the rejection of what is different (*heterophobia*), which blinds them to unprecedented, gentle and euphemized forms of racism—forms which praise difference (*heterophilia*) and substitute 'cultures' for 'races.' The norm concerning respect for differences, far from embodying a fundamental human right (the right to otherness), has helped to make the obsession of contact and the phobia of mixing, which is at the heart of racism, respectable, even honorable. To maintain cultural differences means avoiding intermingling, the ultimate threat and the alleged beginning of irreversible decline. Racism can exist either as the blame or the praise of difference, in terms of races or cultures/mentalities/traditions/beliefs.

Racism and Nationalism

Exclusionary racism has been respectably introduced in the register of the generalized right to be different. Thus, on September 19, 1982, Le Pen declared: 'We have not only the right but also the duty to defend our national personality and also our right to be different.' In April 1985, Brigneau wrote: 'It is better to avoid crossings and intermingling. Not so as to preserve the superiority of the race to which I belong, but its difference, its originality.' In September 1987, Le Pen wrote: 'I love North Africans, but their place is in the Maghreb. . . . I am not racist, but a national. . . . For a nation to be harmonious, it must have a certain ethnic and spiritual homogeneity.' It is therefore necessary 'to resolve, to France's benefit, the immigration problem, by the peaceful, organized return of immigrants.'

When the nationalist rhetoric unfolds without relying on euphemisms, the chauvinism describes the 'task' of a 'nationalist revolution' in the following way: 'We consider that a nation rests, above all, on the ancestral values of blood and soil. We indicated—as a prerequisite to any detailed notion of a nationalist doctrine—that inassimilable foreign immigration threatened the very substance of our people, and that it was necessary to resolve this serious problem. We think, however, that this situation is a result of a general decadence of values of blood and soil—a situation threatened by the corruption of capitalist gold and the law of numbers.'[7]

The inassimilability thesis, even when translated as the praise of irreducible cultural identities, or phrased in terms of 'the respect of all peoples,' can hardly avoid the fundamental postulate to which it refers. 'One must respect the specificity of all the peoples of the world, that is to say, their traditions, their outlook on things, which are only the result of their genetic heritage.'[8] The *Revue Nationaliste Populaire d'Action Européenne*, regrouping the first dissidents of the *Front National* (1981), postulated the differential biological determination of cultural identities. The 'defense of the French' is reformulated either in the broad language of cultural pluralism, or in the identity language of an ethnic nationalism predicated on the imperative to 'remain oneself,' whose other side is the exclusion of those-who-are-not-the-same. 'Let the Algerians remain Algerian and the Senegalese, Senegalese: that seems legitimate and desirable, and that implies essentially that they stay at home or that they return there. What also seems legitimate and desirable is that we the French people remain French as well.... One never recovers from the mixing of bloods or cross-breeding which, itself, is an irreversible fact.... We want to remain ourselves.'[9]

This national-racist discourse joins two obsessions: the erasure of identity and interracial mixing. Xenophobia derives from mixophobia. The foreigner is detestable only in that he is postulated as being inassimilable without provoking a destruction of community identity. That is why nationalists claim that with immigration 'it is quite simply a question of the life or death of our nation.'[10]

Since 1980, the New Right has reformulated its arguments for the rejection of 'inassimilable' foreigners, individuals of non-European origin. Because of tolerant differentialism, the New Right has had to insist on the immigrants' own interests in *returning to their own homeland*. The undesirable must themselves be convinced of their undesirability outside of their nation of origin. In the name of an 'other Third-Worldism' that would be confused with a 'genuine differentialism' (inauthenticity being attributed to the defenders of the pluricultural society), Guillaume Faye declared with the serenity of the cynic or the naivete of the indoctrinated that 'in order to pursue the right to be different to its logical end, it would be necessary to refuse the multiracial society and envision the return of the immigrants to their country.'[11] If, for national populism, the Arabo-Islamic immigrant is inassimilable to the body of a France forged by centuries of Catholic monarchy, for the New Right the immigrant is inassimilable because his cultural traditions are radically foreign to those of the pre-Christian European civilization that survives beneath the mental colonization carried out by 20 centuries of biblical monotheism. It is not with respect to the same substantial identity that immigrants of non-European origin are declared to be foreigners by nature. In both cases, the raising of alterity to the status of an absolute barrier between 'us' and 'them' is the beginning of a prescription for exclusion / expulsion. 'We' are the descendants and heirs of the crusaders, 'we' are the last legitimate sons of the Indo-European horsemen. To safeguard the integrity of this 'we' implies the total rejection of any element of ethno-cultural heterogeneity. Pluralism must regulate only relations between ethnic groups, races and nations. It is not a question of practicing pluralism or differentialism in internal affairs of groups, whatever they may be. The praise of difference translates into the most ideologically respectable form of the will to keep everyone in their place. Behind the rejection of the multiracial or multicultural society there is a hidden postulate: the inevitability of racial struggle, as if there is a threat of conflict when different populations come in contact with one another.

From a defense of oppressed minorities and their 'cultural rights,' the 'right to be different' has been transformed into an instrument of legitimation for exacerbated calls to defend a 'threatened' national (and/or European) identity. The real question of ethnocide has been degraded, after a formative period of extreme Left anti-Western rhetoric, to the level of an instrumental myth of nationalist propaganda with a certain French xenophobic (the *Front National*) or a Europeanist (the New Right) tendency. To the demands for exclusion in terms of differentialist justification, a master ideologue like Benoist adds many nuances, restrictions and disclaimers to seemingly innocent themes such as the 'dialogue between cultures.' The New Right appropriates this theme with the proviso that 'cultures,' in order to 'discuss,' must have 'roots.' In order to be open, a cultural system must be closed.

During the last ten years, emphasis on difference has shifted from the far Left to the far Right. But in doing so, the issue has returned to its true intellectual origins. 'The racist recognizes difference and wants difference,' wrote someone who knew the question well in 1941, Julius Evola.[12] If the differentialist argument has once again found a welcoming structure within xenophobic nationalism, that is because nationalism and differentialism are coextensive and participate in a dialectic of chauvinism. Right-wing nationalism implies, first of all, 'the duty of peoples to remain themselves' (Ploncard d'Assac). That is why, in returning to its origins, right-wing nationalism is so often converted into a *national racism*.

[From 'The New Cultural Racism in France', *Telos*, 83 (1990), 111–14, 116–22; trans. Russell Moore.]

ABBY L. FERBER

29 Constructing Whiteness

Scholars of race have too long neglected the study of 'whiteness'. Over the past decade, however, sociologists and historians have begun to explore more systematically the construction of white racial identity.

This article contributes to this growing body of research. I explore the project of constructing white racial identity which is central to the contemporary white supremacist movement. This research contributes not only to our understanding of the white supremacist movement, but to the process of the construction of racialized identities, as well as to the interconnections between the construction of race and gender.

The white supremacist movement has largely been studied as an issue of race relations, and most research has failed to address issues of gender within the movement. The work of Kathleen Blee (1991a; 1991b) represents the only attempt to document the role and activities of women in the US white supremacist movement, focusing on women's involvement in the Ku Klux Klan in the 1920s. Blee also provides an analysis of gender in the ideology of the Klan at that time. The recent work of Suzanne Harper (1993) further contributes to a feminist analysis of the movement, exploring the intersections of race and gender in depictions of white men and women, black men and women, and Jewish men and women in contemporary white supremacist discourse.

Rather than reading white supremacist discourse as one which is *descriptive* of race, I am reading it as the *construction* of race. Research on the white supremacist movement traditionally defines the movement as one which attempts to represent white interests while espousing hatred towards blacks, Jews, and other non-white racialized groups, taking the given reality of race for granted. Instead, I read this movement as actively producing racialized and gendered subjects.

Contemporary racial theory, moving beyond earlier biological and assimilationist conceptualizations of race, refuses to take racial categorizations for granted, exploring instead the social construction of race. While it is popular today in academia to study racial 'diversity', this approach often ends up reifying racial categorizations. Alternatively, a social constructionist approach emphasizes the critical need for researchers to 'read the processes of differentiation, not look for differences' (Crosby 1992, p. 140). As Omi and Winant suggest, the meaning of race and racialized meanings are politically contested, and it is this contested terrain which needs to be explored. [. . .]

Because race and gender are social constructs, they are not constructed in isolation, but often intertwine with other categories of identity. Feminists of colour have criticized single-axis theories which try to separate race and gender, and emphasize the need for theories which account for both race and gender to explain adequately the lives of women of colour. Single-axis theories have assumed that the experiences of white women show us the meanings of gender, distinct from race. This approach, however, has reinforced the notion that race only shapes the lives of victims of racial oppression. My research, however, argues that we must also explore the interaction of race and gender in the construction of white identity and privilege.

This analysis provides a deconstructive textual analysis, revealing the discursive production of race and gender. Deconstructing rigid categories of race and gender in white supremacist discourse can contribute to our understanding of the construction of race and gender more generally, as well as the intersection between race and gender. [. . .]

While there are significant differences between the various white supremacist organizations, there are also sustained efforts to forge shared objectives. As Raphael S. Ezekiel found in his study of members of the movement, 'the agreement on basic ideas is the glue that holds the movement together, . . . the ideas are important to the members. The white racist movement is about an idea' (Ezekiel 1995, p. xxix). Most white supremacist organizations share a number of unquestioned beliefs. They believe that races are essentially and eternally different, not only in terms of visible characteristics, but also behaviourally and culturally, and that races are ranked hierarchically based on these innate differences. They believe that the white race is superior and responsible for all the advances of Western civilization. While these are the core beliefs of the movement, they also mobilize against a common threat: they believe that the white race faces the threat of genocide, orchestrated by Jews, and carried out by blacks and other non-whites. White supremacist discourse asserts that this genocidal plan is being carried out through forced race-mixing, which will result in the mongrelization and therefore the annihilation of the white race. Interracial sexuality is defined as the 'ultimate abomination' and images of white women stolen away by black men are the ever present symbol of that threat. The protection of white womanhood comes to symbolize the protection of the race, thus gender relations occupy a central place in the discourse.

Because of the similarities and shared concerns of these organizations, there is a great deal of overlap among their membership. As Harper observes, divisions within the white supremacist movement often have more to do with personality differences and clashes than with divergences in belief and ideology (Harper 1993, p. 56).

The contemporary US white supremacist movement is part of a broader backlash against the perceived gains of equality-based social movements. As Michael Omi explains, the Civil Rights movement and the subsequent shift in racial politics

ushered in a period of desegregation efforts, 'equal opportunity' mandates, and other state reforms. By the early seventies, however, a 'backlash' could be discerned to the institutionalization of these reforms and to the political realignments set in motion in the 1960s (Omi 1991, p. 78).

The contemporary white supremacist movement depicts these shifts as an attack on whites and has been able to attract a large number of disillusioned white people, primarily male, who now believe that their interests are not being represented. As Ezekiel suggests, 'white rule in America has ended, members feel. A new world they do not like has pushed aside the traditional one they think they remember' (Ezekiel 1995, p. xxv). As an article in *White Patriot* asserts, 'the White people of America have become an oppressed majority. Our people suffer from discrimination in the awarding of employment, promotions, scholarships, and college entrances' (*White Patriot* no. 56, p. 6).

While the contemporary white supremacist movement is concerned with re-articulating a white identity in response to the challenges of racial and ethnic social movements, this white identity is most certainly a gendered identity. The contemporary white supremacist movement is also a response to the second wave of the feminist movement and the challenges it has presented to traditional gender identities. Responding to what is perceived as a threat to both racial and gendered certainties, the contemporary white supremacist movement is primarily concerned with re-articulating white, male identity and privilege. In stark contrast to the images of active, sexually independent women put forth by the women's movement, white supremacist discourse depicts white women as passive victims at the hands of Jews and blacks, and in dire need of white men's protection.

Despite commonly held assumptions that white supremacists are uneducated, or especially hard hit victims of economic upheaval, research confirms that, like earlier incarnations of the Klan, contemporary white supremacist group members are similar to the US population in general, in terms of education, income and occupation. Additionally, there are white supremacist periodicals which target highly educated audiences (including *Instauration*, reviewed here).

Since the early 1970s a wide range of radical white supremacist organizations have been founded. In 1994 Klanwatch identified 329 white supremacist groups in existence throughout the US. It is difficult to estimate the membership of these groups, which is often concealed. Harper suggests that the general membership in white supremacist organizations is conservatively estimated to be around 40,000, while Ezekiel reports that hard-core members number 23,000 to 25,000, another 150,000 purchase movement literature and take part in activities, and an additional 450,000 actually read the movement literature, even though they do not purchase it themselves (Harper 1993, p. 43; Ezekiel 1995). The Anti-Defamation League [ADL] estimates that fifty white supremacist periodicals continue to publish (Anti-Defamation League 1988, p. 1).

Since the early 1980s the movement has become increasingly violent. Numerous organizations have established camps for paramilitary training, preparing members for the coming 'race war'. Tracking organizations like the ADL have provided documentation of many murders and attempted murders committed by white supremacists, culminating in the 1995 bombing of the Murrah Federal Building in Oklahoma City (Anti-Defamation League 1988, pp. 11–15). While certain arms of movement have become increasingly violent, other white supremacists, including the well-publicized case of David Duke have moved further into the mainstream, entering traditional American politics.

White men make up the bulk of the membership of the movement, and serve as the writers, publishers, and editors of white supremacist discourse. Ezekiel notes that the organizations he observed remain almost exclusively male, and tasks within the organizations are strictly segregated by gender. He notes, 'a few women are around, never as speakers or leaders; usually they are wives, who cook and listen. Highly traditional ideas of sex roles, and fears of losing male dominance, fill the conversation and speeches' (Ezekiel 1995, p. xxvii). Kathleen Blee's recent work on the contemporary movement, however, documents the efforts of many organizations to recruit women into their ranks. 'As a result,' Blee suggests, 'women now play a highly visible and significant role in the racist movement, constituting about 25% of the membership (and nearly

50% of the new recruits) in some Klan and neo-Nazi groups' (Blee 1995, p. 1). I suspect that these divergent accounts suggest that women's movement into the movement is uneven, and largely dependent upon the recruitment efforts of specific organizations. Women have been targeted for recruitment by various organizations as a strategy to increase membership and help stabilize the membership by bringing entire families into the fold. The discourse of the white supremacist movement remains highly gendered and patriarchal, and it will be important and interesting for future analyses to explore if and how the discourse changes in response to the growing numbers of women in these organizations. [...]

While white supremacist discourse adamantly supports the notion that race is a biological and/or god-given essence, a review of the discourse reveals the *social construction* of that essence. As Diana Fuss points out, 'there is no essence to essentialism ... essence as irreducible has been constructed to be irreducible' (Fuss 1989, p. 4). Exploring contemporary white supremacist discourse reveals the construction of race and gender as an inner essence rooted in nature and immutable.

Throughout white supremacist discourse, whiteness is constructed in terms of visible, physical differences in appearance. According to one article, true whites are Nordics, 'the thin, fair and symmetric race originating in Northern Europe' (*Instauration*, February 1980, p. 13). In another article, Nordics are described as:

the only cleanly chiselled faces around. And there are other ways they stand out. The world's finest hair and finest skin texture are in Scandinavia. Some of the world's tallest statures, largest body size and most massive heads are also found in Northern European regions (*Instauration*, January 1980, p. 15).

Jews are also constructed as a race in this discourse, made identifiable by physical markers such as 'long kinky curls and typical hooked nose, thick fleshy lips, slant eyes and other typical Jew features' (*Thunderbolt*, no. 301, p. 6).

A great deal of effort is put into physically distinguishing races from one another. Both the book and film entitled *Blood in the Face* take their name from some white supremacists' supposition that Jews cannot blush, and only true whites show 'blood in the face' (Ridgeway 1990). Rather than revealing race as a biological essence, this discourse reveals the continued effort required to construct racial differences. Judith Butler suggests that identities are constructed through 'the reiterative and citational practice by which discourse produces the effects that it names' (Butler 1993, p. 2). The construction of identity is not a singular act or gesture but, rather, a process or performance as Butler calls it, which must be continually repeated. The construction of racial and gender difference must '*repeat itself*' in order to establish the illusion of its own uniformity and identity' (Butler 1991, p. 24).

The process of repetition and reiteration which constructs race and gender also reveals the construction of these identities, thereby putting this identity permanently at risk . . . That there is a need for repetition at all is a sign that identity is not self-identical. It requires to be instituted again and again, which is to say that it runs the risk of becoming *de*-instituted at every interval (Butler 1991, p. 24).

As we find in white supremacist discourse, even though racial identity is posited as a biological or god-given fact of nature, the definition of whiteness is in constant flux, and there is disagreement among groups and individuals over who is or is not white, and what characteristics define whiteness.

As Harper observes, 'What it means to be white and who qualifies as white, is forged within the discourse of the publications' (Harper 1993, p. 69). In some of the discourse white skin and European heritage are the only requirements to be included in the category white (Harper 1993), while elsewhere Aryans are defined as strictly *Northern* Europeans, and there is much debate on where exactly to draw the line in Europe. As one white supremacist claims in the film *Blood in the Face*, 'We're more Nazi than the Nazis were!'

Because the visible characteristics constructed as markers of race are not always evident, discerning the race of individuals is of the utmost importance. Articles such as 'Racial Tagging' in *Instauration* reveal surprises in the racial identity of public figures. As this article explains:

Racial identification is a tricky game. As we keep our eyes open, we stumble across the most surprising information. Recently we have been looking into the Portuguese origins of public figures considered to have been solidly Northern European in racial makeup (*Instauration*, October 1976, p. 10).

As these periodicals construct racialized subjects, they construct race as existing in nature prior to their discourse. Racial identity is constructed as an essence within each person which merely needs to be discovered. The discovery of race, however, is the *production* of the racialized subject.

White supremacist discourse gains the authority to construct race as an origin and essence partly through citational practices which invoke the authority of science. Steven Seidman suggests that the power of discourse to create normative conceptions of race derives from the extent to which it can invoke 'the intellectual and social authority of science. A discourse that bears the stamp of scientific knowledge gives its normative concepts of identity and order an authority' (Seidman 1991, p. 135). Just as eugenic policies in the early twentieth century drew upon the supposedly scientific racial studies of anthropologists and ethnologists, contemporary white supremacist discourse invokes the authority of science to support its political ends. Discussion of racial difference almost always includes references to named scientists and doctors. For example, a typical article reports that

Dr. Audrey Shuey of Northern Illinois University states that the average negro has an I.Q. 15 to 20 points lower than that of an average White individual . . . Dr. Robert Gayre had conducted many studies which show that the negro brain is on the average 100 milligrams lighter than the White brain . . . Dr. Carlton Putnam . . . says that the convolutions and thickness of the suprannual layer of the negro brain cortex is 14% thinner than the Whites ... Professor Donald Swan of Hattiesburg University states that the difference between the races is up to 75% caused by heredity (*The Thunderbolt*, August 1979, p. 8).

Exploring white supremacist discourse raises difficult questions regarding just where to draw the line between white supremacist extremism and the 'mainstream'. Scientific studies of racial and sexual difference, including the work of contemporary sociobiologists, are often cited as justification for white supremacist goals within the discourse.

While a great amount of effort and written space is devoted to delineating physical racial differences, these physical differences are always interpreted as signifiers of deeper, underlying differences. In this discourse, physical characteristics and culture are linked, both determined by race and unchanging. For example, *The Thunderbolt* proclaims that

The White Race has created and developed most of the world's present and past civilizations ... responsible for almost all of the scientific, engineering and productive know-how that has raised the world's standard of living ... the only race which has been able to maintain a free democratic government. Liberty, justice and freedom only exist in White nations ... culture, art, humanities ... The charity and goodness of the White Race have time and again saved the non-White peoples of the world from famine and plague. The White Race in the past has established moral codes, rules and laws, and educational systems for the advancement of society that have been unsurpassed by any other race in the world (*The Thunderbolt*, 30 May 1975, p. 8).

Additionally,this racial essence is represented as immutable. As an *NSV Report* article about Jews claims.

We fight for things that they cannot understand because of their nature; and because of their nature, they can never understand because the are aliens. Even if they changed their religion, they will not be a part of our Folk. They can never be part of our Folk for they are aliens. They might as well be from another planet because they are not of our world (*NSV Report*, October/December 1987, p. 1).

Because racial differences are posited as inherent, immutable essences, attempts to question, modify or change these differences are ridiculed and depicted as fruitless. For example, a *New Order* article explains,

Negroes are best suited for and succeed best in the roles of servants and entertainers. Remove the White liberal from his traditional position, that is kissing the negro's posterior, and what happens to the negro? [He] clumsily shuffles off, scratching his wooley head, to search for shoebrush and mop. In the final debate, an ape will always be an ape (*New Order*, September 1979, p. 14).

Similarly, a *White Power* article admonishes:

Perhaps the cruelest hoax is the liberal lie of telling the Negro he's the equal of the White man and expecting to make an instant White man out of him by sending him to college, giving him a federal handout ... Let's have the honesty and decency to recognize the Negro for what he is, and not make impossible demands of him . . . This has nothing to do with 'hate' or 'bigotry'. I love my dog, for example, but I'm not about to recognize her as my equal (*White Power*, March 1973, pp. 3–6).

The recognition of difference, here, is depicted as merely common sense.

Within the equality versus difference framework, equality necessarily entails the denial of difference. The *National Vanguard* refers to equality as 'Man's Most Dangerous Myth' because it denies 'the essence of the inner nature' (*National Vanguard*, no. 68, p. 3). An *Instauration* article entitled 'The Hoax of all the Centuries' warns that 'the real hoax is the equalitarian hoax, the hoax of hoaxes, the universal lie that there are no differences in racial intelligence'. In order to counter this hoax, further documentation of racial differences are then provided. Within the equality versus difference framework, it is impossible to have equality while also acknowledging differences. Meaning here is constrained so that difference assumes inequality, and any attempt to increase racial equality is recast as a threat to difference.

Like racial difference, gender difference is posited as rooted in nature and biology. Throughout this discourse, great effort is made to constantly reiterate, and thereby produce the 'reality' of, sexual difference. It is common for many of the periodicals to invent new words in order to distinguish symbolically between males and females and naturalize difference. For example, there are frequent references to Jewesses, Negresses, Mulatresses, WASPesses, Shebrews, etc. (*New Order*, March 1979, p. 2; *Instauration*, December 1979, p. 13; *Instauration*, February 1981). Throughout the periodicals, female versions of words are created, exemplified by one article's reference to 'proditors and proditresses' (*Instauration*, December 1979, p. 13). As Cynthia Fuchs Epstein suggests, inventing female versions of words serves as a form of symbolic segregation, reifying gender difference (1988).

Like racial difference, gender difference is posited as not merely differences in physical and biological characteristics, but differences in character and personality as well. For example, a *White Power* article explains that 'our ancestors wisely realized that women were different from men not just biologically, but psychologically and emotionally as well. They recognized that the sexes had distinct but complementary roles to play in society . . . ordained by natural law' (*White Power* no. 105, p. 4).

The concept of gender equality, like racial equality, is ridiculed as a denial of innate differences. For example, a typical article entitled 'The One-Hemisphere Sex' wails:

They never stop beating the nurture drum! A Purdue professor recently came up with the silly notion . . . that one reason for the superior mathematical ability of boys is they 'are encouraged from an early age to do activities which develop spatial performance' . . . So to eliminate the different learning capabilities that separate the boys from the girls Dr. Wheatley tells us the latter must learn to do more cogitating with their right hemispheres. That they don't do this and have never done this has nothing to do with genetics, of course. It has been the fault of their teachers—or a residue of Paleolithic prejudice—or male chauvinism (*Instauration*, September 1979, p. 19).

This article ridicules those who refuse to accept what is posited as the simple fact that males and females are biologically different, and suggests that all other reasons for gender differences are simply excuses.

Both race and gender are constructed as immutable essences in this discourse, and they are often interdependent. Gender difference is posited as a key component of racial difference. Drawing upon the unfounded claims of nineteenth-century evolutionary theories, a number of articles point out that: 'Sexual dimorphism [the difference between the sexes] is greatest in the Caucasoids' (*Instauration*, January 1980, pp. 14–15; *Instauration*, March 1981, p. 7). Differentiation is posited as the key to advancement, and the more pronounced degree of differentiation between white men and women is read as a sign of white superiority. Similarly, males are posited as more differentiated than females, establishing white males, then, as superior to white women and to non-white men and women. As one article explains, 'Sexual dimorphism is greatest in the Caucasoids. We know further that women are less varied (smaller standard deviations) on most physical components, such as height, weight, and intelligence (relative brain size)' (*Instauration*, March 1981, p. 7). This matrix of differentiation perches white males firmly on top.

In addition to the degree of gender difference within each race, the differences between white and non-white females is also emphasized as a feature distinguishing the white race and signalling its superiority. The belief that white women represent the ideal of female beauty is widespread and considered common-sense knowledge in this discourse. An *Instauration* article credits '25,000 years of tough natural selection on the edge of glaciers' with producing 'these beauteous products of a very special kind of evolution . . . these magnificent-looking women' (*Instauration*, May 1981, p. 36). Further reflecting this sentiment, another article claims

the White woman stands at the apex of beauty . . . But what about the Black woman? Alas, she is truly a pitiable creature. White have never found her attractive, and Blacks began to scorn her after they caught a glimpse of a White woman (*National Vanguard*, May 1979, p. 11).

Attempting to establish the permanence and immutability of these differences, another article claims

Chinese archaeologists unearthed an ancient tomb containing a mummy of a female. They describe her as follows: 'The shape of her body was extremely beautiful and she was tall. She had blond, long hair that flowed to her shoulders. On her comely face was a pair of big eyes. You could still count her long eyelashes. Beneath her high nose were her tiny, thin lips.' The date of the remains indicated that gentlemen preferred blondes as early as 4480 B.C. (*Instauration*, May 1981, p. 23).

Gender is central to white supremacist discourse because the fate of the race is posited as hinging on the sexual behaviour of white women. Harper suggests that images of white women in this discourse depict them either as breeders of the race, or as traitors. They are defined solely in terms of their reproductive and sexual availability. Throughout this discourse, all discussions of interracial sexuality revolve around images of white women and black men, so interracial sexuality also represents a threat to white male authority, usurping his control over both white women and black men.

Interracial sexuality serves as the ultimate threat to racial and gender difference. Eliminating all racial differences and leading to 'mulatto zombies', interracial sexuality threatens the existence of the white race. Additionally, however, interracial sexuality is posited as a threat to gender differences. For example, an *Instauration* article depicts a fictional white survival demonstration where protestors chant:

'Sweden is going brown.' 'No more Ingrid Bergman.' 'America is going brown.' 'No more Cheryl Tiegs.' 'France is going brown.' 'No more Catherine Deneuve.' . . . 'What is the solution?' 'White separatism!' (*Instauration*, 'White survival', 1980, p. 18).

If beauty is what makes white women unique, it is threatened by race-mixing. As another article asserts, 'As the race goes, so goes beauty' (*Instauration*, 'Black Infusions', 1980, p. 19). Interracial sexuality comes to symbolize the ultimate threat to racial and gender identity in this discourse. [. . .]

The production of racial and gender difference is central to the project of white supremacy and the construction of race and gender are intertwined. Every white supremacist publication spends a great deal of space and effort producing and reiterating racial and gender difference. The difference versus equality framework links difference to hierarchy, so that any threats to difference or hierarchy are posited as leading to sameness. Interracial sexuality serves as the central metaphor of this threat. Any movements for equality are therefore recast as threats to difference. The civil rights movement, the women's movement, and all policies designed to redress inequality are ridiculed for ignoring the 'natural fact' of difference and simultaneously perceived as a threat to white identity.

Exploring and construction of race and gender within the framework of the difference versus equality opposition reveals how meaning works in this discourse. The construction of difference within this binary framework makes certain meanings possible, while rendering other ideas incomprehensible. Within this system of meaning, equality becomes impossible to imagine, because it signifies the denial of difference. The construction of race and gender and the maintenance of inequality are necessarily linked for white supremacists, and it is therefore increasingly important that researchers explore the construction of race and gender, rather than taking these identities for granted as prediscursive realities to be studied. This analysis suggests that we cannot comprehend white supremacist racism without exploring the construction of white identity. White identity defines itself in opposition to inferior others; racism, then, becomes the maintenance of white identity. The construction of whiteness is maintained through racist and misogynist discourse.

In order to delegitimize and resist white supremacy, we must explore the construction of race and gender within the white supremacist movement as well as within our own disciplines. When researchers fail to explore the construction of race, they contribute to the reproduction of race as a naturally existing category. In representing race as a given foundation, we obscure the relations of power which constitute race as a foundation. Rather than taking race for granted, we need to begin to explore the social construction of race, and the centrality of racism and misogyny to this construction.

[From 'Constructing Whiteness: The Intersections of Race and Gender in US White Supremacist Discourse', *Ethnic and Racial Studies*, 21/1 (1998), 48–60.]

Section V

Anti-Racism

INTRODUCTION

What is the role of anti-racist ideas and movements in contemporary societies? How can the influence of racial ideas and images be countered effectively? These are some of the underlying questions that are at the heart of many of the debates about racism in the social sciences as well as in everyday life. Whether one looks at debates at the level of policy or at a more conceptual level this remains a vexed and at times confusing area of debate. It has also become evident that under the general label of anti-racism there are in practice a wide range of ideological and political positions, with little agreement about either the conceptual meaning of the term or about the practical policy initiatives that may be necessary to tackle institutional forms of racial inequality and discrimination. Indeed, in some ways the question of anti-racism has come to occupy as central a role in current debates and controversies as the question of racism itself. The various extracts in this section address in one way or another important facets of this question, and of the political dilemmas that it gives rise to.

The first three extracts in this part are concerned with the attempts by activists and scholars from the Caribbean and the United States of America to develop counter-discourses to the dominant conceptualization of race in the first half of the twentieth century. The first extract is by Marcus Garvey, who remains perhaps one of the most influential black political activists of this century. Garvey's writings and activism were focused particularly on the need for black people to develop a sense of pride and identity of themselves as a 'race'. The extract from his work included here exemplifies this recurrent theme in his work, as does the second extract, by the African American writer Tony Martin. Martin is a leading contemporary advocate of the kinds of politics and ideas associated with Garvey, and in this extract he explores the ways in which the advocacy of 'race first' by Garvey and his followers was premised on a politics of 'converting the disabilities of race into a positive tool of liberation'. What is interesting about both extracts is the way they help to elucidate the often contradictory starting points of ideas of black politics premised on the need for 'self-reliance' and the 'primacy of race'. In this sense such ideas fit into the rhetoric and politics of anti-racism only in a very loose sense, in that far from being premised on the idea of moving beyond race they assert the positive value of the racial identity of being black. In this they are part of the wider trend towards a politics of separatism and nationalism that has played a significant role in black American political culture throughout much of the twentieth century.

'Black Power: Its Need and Substance', by Kwame Ture and Charles Hamilton, reflects an influential trend in theorizing about race relations in the United States of America since the 1960s. Ture and Hamilton's text, which represents an important benchmark in the development of the 'black power' movement in the United States during the 1960s, shares at least some common rhetorical language with the work of Garvey, in that it is premissed on the need for black people in the United States to redefine their identity against the depredations of economic, social, and cultural exclusion that has shaped much of black history during and after slavery. It is a self-conscious attempt to redraw the boundaries of black political identity, and under the banner of 'black power' the ideas articulated by Ture and Hamilton represented a symbolic turn in thinking about race in American society, whose consequences are still being worked through today.

Paul Gilroy's analysis of 'The End of Anti-Racism' symbolizes a shift in thinking about the question of anti-racism that has become more influential on both sides of the Atlantic in recent times. Gilroy's starting point is markedly different from the arguments exemplified by an earlier generation of black writers on these issues, since he carefully eschews any simple notion of a uniform black political or cultural identity. Rather he seeks to show, in a masterful overview of trends within the British political scene, how thinking on anti-racism has become heavily influenced by essentialist forms of political and cultural discourse that in effect naturalize and dehistoricize racial and ethnic difference. Gilroy's premiss is rather that we have to recognize and valorize the diverse social experiences and cultural identities which compose the everyday experiences of ethnic and racial groupings in contemporary societies. What this brings into play is the recognition of the immense diversity and differentiation of the historical and cultural experiences of minority communities in societies such as our own. This inevitably entails a weakening or fading of the notion that race or some composite notion of race around the term 'black' will either guarantee the effectivity of any cultural practice or determine in any final sense its aesthetic value. In exploring these issues Gilroy provides an interesting insight into the contradictory ways in which the political rhetoric of anti-racism overlaps with the language and symbols that are used by racist movements (a point also touched upon in the previous part by Taguieff).

The next extract by Heribert Adam and Kogila Moodley focuses on the ideas and values espoused by the Black Consciousness Movement in South Africa in the period since the late 1960s. Drawing on the specificities of the racialized boundaries and identities constructed under the apartheid state Adam and Moodley helpfully bring together key elements in the thinking of this movement in order to pinpoint how it attempted to utilize political identities based on black consciousness as a way of bringing together diverse racial groups under one banner in the struggle against the apartheid state. In doing this they usefully remind us in a very practical sense that identities based on race and ethnicity are not simply imposed, since they are also often the outcome of resistance and political struggle in which racialized minorities play a central and active role in defining themselves in relation to the 'other'. They also help to shed some light on the tenuous and limited impact of identities constructed on the basis of resistance, particularly in the environment of post-apartheid South Africa. The key arguments developed by Adam and Moodley are clearly a product of the experience of apartheid and the ideological constructions it helped to shape. But it is also worth noting that their analysis is of relevance in analysing trends and developments in other situations, as evidenced by the complex ways in which racialized minorities construct and reconstruct their identities.

The final two extracts in this part, by Cathie Lloyd and Phil Cohen, seek to explore in some detail the conceptual and political contradictions, to be found in contemporary forms of anti-racist politics and ideologies. Lloyd's account is structured around a comparison of the politics of anti-racism in the United Kingdom and France. She situates her account around an analysis of the political language and symbols used by the anti-racist organizations in each country, and highlights the role they have played in tackling specific aspects of racism in each country. What is particularly interesting in her analysis is the way she attempts to link the question of anti-racism to the wider issue of political culture and models of racial and ethnic incorporation. In doing so she is able both to show the limits of anti-racism as a model of political mobilization and outline the ways in which more effective mobilizations against racism can be fashioned in the future. Phil Cohen's account of what he calls the 'hidden narratives in theories of racism' is also centrally concerned with the question of the limits of anti-racist political discourses. He starts his analysis with an attempt to outline what he sees as the main shortcomings of how anti-racist discourses explain racism, and develops from this a critical analysis of what kind of future agendas need to be addressed by anti-racists. His suggestive untangling of the theoretical underpinnings of anti-racist discourses suggests that there is a need to develop a new agenda for tackling racism that goes beyond the simple dichotomies of contemporary anti-racist politics.

The extracts in this section include a diverse range of issues and programmatic arguments. They also highlight the often tenuous and contradictory meanings that are attached to political identities constructed in the struggles against racism in different national contexts. But they also help to show that this whole area remains an important one to address if we are to provide a basis for understanding how to overcome racism in all its forms.

30 Living for Something

No Negro should be objectless or purposeless in life. Always have a purpose. To waste time in non-essentials is to be purposeless. Playing bone dice is purposeless. There is nothing achieved in the time wasted in doing it. No great fortune is guaranteed, no great art is accomplished, no structure is built because it is a game of chance. Playing pool is waste, because like playing the dice it is a game of chance. Sitting around and going from place to place without an occupation is waste, valuable time is going and nothing is being registered by way of achievement; but when one settles down upon a given and worthy idea or occupation, such as an architect, an engineer, a builder, a farmer, a poet, a teacher, he or she is working on something that may become tangible in results. It is from such tangible assets that we build fortunes. Find something tangible to do, then, and use your time in doing it well. It is better that you be dead than having no purpose in life.

Ella Wheeler Wilcox says:—

> Have a purpose, and that purpose keep in view,
> Have a purpose, and that purpose keep in view,
> For drifting like a helmless vessel,
> Thou can'st ne'er to self be true.

The ship without a helm must flounder on the rock. Why be such a ship? Why not sail through life like the barque whose helm is perfect? Be a captain with chart in hand seeing his port as he sails steadily on. See your port, visualise it, and as the time comes, anchor in it.

The Dignity and Price [Pride?] of Race

God made man as a complete and finished being. [No] flaws in him but his sin. The race of man, therefore, must be perfect in its physical origin. Hence there is nothing to be ashamed of as far as [the] species is concerned.

The black man's origin is as true as the sun. He needs not therefore, to apologise for his existence. His place in the world is fixed as a star and as such it is incumbent on him to maintain the dignity and pride of his own manhood.

There is nothing unusual about the Negro other than he is himself as man. He is beautiful in himself and why not so? The Anglo-Saxon sees beauty through himself, the Teuton sees beauty through himself, and [the] Mongol sees beauty through himself and so naturally and logically the Negro ought to see beauty through himself. When the Negro attempts to see beauty through aquiline features of an Anglo-Saxon then he images the homeliness and ugliness of his own features because his features are [d]ifferent to those of the Anglo-Saxon.

Beauty must be reflected out of your own eyes. A Negro must be beautiful to a Negro, as an Anglo-Saxon is to an Anglo-Saxon. The highest standard of beauty, therefore, for a Negro, is the Negro. Never allow any race to say that your race is not beautiful. If there is ugliness in race, it is in the other race, not in yours, because the other race looks different to you. To the Anglo-Saxon the Mongol is ugly; to the Mongol the Anglo-Saxon is ugly. Compare the Anglo-Saxon and the Negro, it is the Anglo-Saxon who is ugly, not the Negro. The long sharp nose of the European cannot be considered beautiful against a strong, healthy, air-free nasal passage of the black man who is free from those nasal defects that make health difficult. The thin lip of the European could not be beautiful compared with the strong, healthy and developed lips of the African. These are the ways self-respecting people see themselves. The round healthy face of the African is much more beautiful than the straight, sickly looking face of the European. Then why surrender all that is good in you and discount it for that which doesn't reach a standard comparable to yours and others.

Always think yourself a perfect being, and be satisfied with yourself except you are a jelly fish.

Never allow anyone to convince you of your inferiority as a man. Rise in your dignity to justify all that is noble in your manhood as a race.

> My race is mine and I belong to it.
> It climbs with me and I shall climb with it,
> My pride is mine and I shall surely honour it,
> It is the height on which I daily sit.

The Social Confusion

Man at his best in his society is always quarrelling. He is never satisfied. Don't ex[pec]t that you will find in your lifetime the solution for all his problems and ills, attend only to those that concern you and your group. If you can solve your own group problems in your community you have done well. Let others solve theirs. The time you waste running around with others and helping them in their problems, you are robbing your group of that much time to help them solve their problems.

Whether a man is sober or drunk, he is a disagreeable beast—you will find it so in every community. So search out for your man, and tame the beast; he is never of the same mood all the time—at one time you think you can like him, at another time you think you could kill him. Tame him toward the end of your own social satisfaction for dabbling in the confusion of others will only make you more confused and your divided energy will only tend to defeat the special purpose which you should have in solving the problems of your race.

Never forget that all other groups in the society of your community are looking after their own individual group interest, and your interest except from the community point of view, is never theirs. Therefore, theirs should never be yours as far as the particular group interest is concerned. Don't be disappointed if other people shock you by their behaviour, because man is made that way, and he acts that way chiefly because he is racially different.

The White man may compliment you today and abuse you tomorrow, simply because of your race. Don't trust the whole community then if it is made up of different groups, because it is apt to disappoint you by being selfish at any moment, as far as the division of particular interest is concerned.

Always pick out your interest in the community and conserve it because others are doing the same. It is only when you tread on the heels of others eve[n] by accident, that you find out that there are differences between you and others, but your mistake doesn't prove a fact—the fact was there before your mistake, and it is always a fact that each group have their own individual and collected racial problems.

The white man never can be the Negro, and the Negro can never be the white man, except after eternity and you do not live so long.

You may be the same in soul but you cannot see soul, so that similarity is beyond you. What you see is yourself, physically, and there is no doubt that there is physical difference between you and the other man, so watch your step in the social confusion of life.

Always remember that another person is not you, for that other person knows too well that you are different to him, and is always on guard to divide the line of interest. This applies everywhere all around—in your home, in your office, in your workshop, in the street, in the community. Your wife will grab the article and say 'This is mine['] and will refuse to give it up, although you thought you were one and what was yours was hers and hers yours[.] She always has a time to claim her own either in peace or confusion.

So always have your own in the social confusion of life, because even you and your partner may have to run in different directions to save your skins, and if one person is gone with what is yours in another direction, you may lose your life following what you should have been carrying with you. Never forget this, it is of great importance to you for your own safety, you should always have your own fare to pay the conductor. You may have to walk whilst the other person rides, because you can never tell where a confusion springs up. It may be in the street near the neighbourhood, it may be 100 miles from town, and that will be a long walk if the car moves off, because of the confusion between you and the driver.

Always expect confusion in the dividing line in the social contact of life.

[From *Life and Lessons* (Berkeley and Los Angeles: University of California Press, 1987), 314–18.]

31   Race First and Self-Reliance

Marcus Garvey, unlike his major rivals in the United States, built a mass organization that went beyond mere civil-rights agitation and protest and based itself upon a definite, well-thought-out program that he believed would lead to the total emancipation of the race from white dominion.

Central to the ideological basis underpinning Garvey's program was the question of race. For Garvey, the black man was universally oppressed on racial grounds, and any program of emancipation would have to be built around the question of race first. The race became a 'political entity' which would have to be redeemed. Against the rival suggestion that humanity, and not the black race, should be the objects of his zeal, he argued that it was not 'humanity' that was lynched, burned, jimcrowed and segregated, but black people. The primacy of race characterized the UNIA from its beginnings in Jamaica and by 1919 United States government officials were drawing attention to what they considered this subversive doctrine.

Garvey went about the task of converting the disabilities of race into a positive tool of liberation with a thorough aggressiveness. 'No man can convince me contrary to my belief,' he declared, 'because my belief is founded upon a hard and horrible experience, not a personal experience, but a racial experience. The world has made being black a crime, and I have felt it in common with men who suffer like me, and instead of making it a crime I hope to make it a virtue.' Accordingly, the consciousness of Garvey's followers was saturated with the new doctrine. Black dolls were manufactured for black children; Garvey's newspaper proclaimed itself the *Negro World*; he encouraged his followers to support their black businessmen and professionals; the race catechism used by his followers disabused the minds of black folk concerning the claims of the Hamitic myth by explaining that contrary to this myth, black people were 'certainly not' the recipients of any biblical curse; he frowned upon advertisements of a racially demeaning nature, the *Negro World* sponsored beauty contests and published photographs of beautiful black women, a subject on which Garvey waxed poetic—'Black queen of beauty, thou hast given color to the world.' Indeed, practically every aspect of the organization was designed to bolster the black man's self-esteem and to foster pride in self.

The primacy of race in Garvey's thought was coupled with a deep pessimism concerning the future of the black man in America. He believed that the black man, with increasingly ample educational opportunities, would aspire to positions of influence, which would bring him into direct competition with the white power structure. Within fifty to a hundred years, he predicted, such confrontation would lead to a racial clash which would end disastrously for the black race.

This analysis led Garvey inevitably in the direction of racial separation. His economic ventures in the United States amounted to an attempt toward a nucleus of a self-sustaining (and therefore self-employing) black race in America. But his gaze looked more longingly toward Africa as the salvation of the African abroad. Even in Africa, though, he found the European overlords attempting to increase the seeds of future racial discord, as in 1938 when he protested British consideration of a proposal to resettle European Jews in Tanganyika, Kenya or British Guiana.

Garvey's concern over the salvation of the race led him to harsh criticism of any weaknesses he perceived among black people, and there was nothing that displeased him more than the black man who did not think in racial terms. Such criticism brought out the finest of his invective—'Yes, this an "Uncle Tom Negro." Yes, a "yes boss Negro"—a "howdi massa Negro"—a "yes Mass Charlie Negro." A Negro who will be satisfied to blacken a white man's shoes all the days of his life and lick the white man's spittle if he orders him to do so.'

Garvey's race-first doctrine found excellent expression in his acute awareness of the role of culture as a tool for liberation. He himself was a prolific poet of liberation. Indeed, his poems are as good a source of his ideology as any. They were replete with such themes as the beauty of the black woman, the need for self-reliance, the glories of African history, the necessity for an end to black participation in white wars, and protests at the Italian invasion of Ethiopia. This experimentation with the arts for purposes of politicizing the UNIA membership was also indulged in by one of Garvey's closest associates, John Edward Bruce. One Bruce play, *Preaching vs. Practice*, expressed Garvey's hostility toward unscrupulous black preachers. Another, *Which One*, provided an excellent example of the use of this medium for political education. The main characters were a Sennebundo Ajai, an African UNIA diplomat, and three young ladies, one each from Martinique, the British West Indies, and Afro-America, all of whom were in love with the hero, who was leaving for Nigeria on UNIA organizational business. In between the romantic escapades the audience was treated to monologues extolling the virtues of the UNIA. The set was liberally decorated with the red, black and green of the UNIA, and the hero and the lady of his choice eventually announced their intention to be married in a Liberty Hall in Africa. [. . .]

Garvey's doctrine of race first was severely tested by the presence within the race of large numbers of persons of mixed African and Caucasian origin. He took the position that 'there is more bitterness among us Negroes because of the caste of color than there is between any other peoples, not excluding the people of India.' He even asserted that prejudice within the race probably exceeded that directed against the race by alien races. This position brought Garvey into serious ideological conflict with middle-class leaders in the United States and the West Indies, many of whom were themselves of lighter hue. Such opposition was particularly hostile in the United States, where integrationist leaders such as

W. E. B. Du Bois argued that this problem either did not exist or was relatively minor in the United States and that Garvey, because of his West Indian background, was erroneously importing this feature of island society into an Afro-American scene that he did not understand.

Garvey had indeed come out of a West Indian society stultified by an exaggerated three-tiered system of white-brown-black social stratification, and he himself regularly discussed the problem from at least as early as 1913. His Jamaican daily, the Blackman editorialized in 1929: Some people are afraid, some annoyed and others disgusted that we, as they say,

Raise the Colour Question

The question has long ago been raised and put into vindictive operation. The colour question is the one and only reason that we cannot find a black girl or boy in store or office in this city when to our certain knowledge intelligent ones among them . . . have been refused at places filled with half illiterate brown and mulatto girls and boys affecting the attitude of superiors in behavior . . .

There is going to be fairplay in this country yet. 'The Blackman' is on the job and soon will blacken some of these stores and offices beyond recognition.

As the editorial suggests, even in Jamaica, where the color-caste distinctions were acute, the tendency of the brown class was to deny its existence, much as Du Bois and the Afro-American integrationists did. But Garvey was relentless in his attempts to bring the issue to the surface. 'This hypocritical cry of "Peace, Peace," when there is no Peace is ruinous to the peace and harmony of society,' he declared.

We deny the existence of a condition that is woven into the warp and woof of the fabric of our social and public life. We refuse to admit the presence of a feature in our national life, the inescapable results of whose insidious workings cause delay, irritation and annoyance. We rave against, we forbid, we threaten those [who] dare to refer to the evident, the patent facts and their glaring results. While the whole land is leavened and permeated with the evils of colour distinction and we cry out for harmony and peace. We are, to use a vulgar phrase, a bunch of cheats. We are dishonest, immoral, liars, hypocrites.

This type of assault on entrenched privilege brought Garvey a death threat from a self-styled 'Jamaican Secret Society of Colored Men,' which considered him a 'black swine.'

In Afro-America, too, Garvey observed a preference among employers for light-skinned people as clerks, waitresses, etc., and newspapers full of advertisements for skin whiteners, often couched in the crudest possible language. Added to this, he discovered in New York, Boston, Washington and Detroit the Blue Vein Society and the Colonial Club. 'The West Indian "lights" formed the "Colonial Club" and the American "lights" the "Blue Vein" Society.' These attitudes extended into the churches. It would appear then, that Garvey, as one of his supporters pointed out, did not 'appeal' to intrarace color prejudice in the United States but rather 'revealed' it.

Despite the similarities, of course, the situation in America, where the majority did not need the support of the buffer mulatto element to the same extent as the white minority in the islands, was not as serious as in the West Indies. Garvey was fully aware of this. The situation in America was serious enough to warrant exposure and attack, but in the West Indies it more nearly approximated a rigid caste structure. Garvey himself pinpointed this difference better than any of his critics:

In the term 'Negro' we include all those persons whom the American white man includes in this appelation of his contempt and hate. . . .The contents of the term are much reduced in Jamaica and the West Indies, but it carries no less of reprobation against the persons. . . .

The great curse of our Jamaica communal life is the failure of the hybrid population to realize their natural and correct identification. . . .

So whereas the UNIA in the United States numbered among its ranks people of all colors, excluding whites, and business and professional people in addition to the great mass of workers and peasants, in Jamaica it was largely confined to the 'humbler sections' of humanity. This led Garvey to surmise that 'God seems to save from the bottom upwards.'

Garvey's experience with the light-skinned element, both in the West Indies and America, led him to be hostile toward those who seemed to portray the supercilious attitudes he abhorred. It led him, too, to consider miscegenation to be an evil which should not be perpetuated—'We are conscious of the fact that slavery brought upon us the curse of many colors within our Race, but that is no reason why we of ourselves should perpetuate the evil. . . .'

The doctrine of race first had various implications for Garvey's attitude toward white people. It meant first of all the exclusion of white people from membership in the UNIA and affiliated organizations. Whites were also prevented from holding shares in Garvey's economic undertakings. His desire to build racial self-reliance led logically to the rejection of white financial philanthropy. In reply to a suggestion by a white reporter in 1921 that 'certain negrophiles in Massachusetts' might be prevailed upon to contribute to the UNIA, Garvey replied, 'We do not want their money; this is a black man's movement.'

Race first meant, however, not only race first for black people but for other races as well. As far as Garvey was concerned, white people of whatever political pursuasion put race before all other considerations. Accordingly he often preferred an honest expression of racism to the possibly transparent smiles of the philanthropist. He looked at the honest expression of racism as a blessing in disguise because it forced the black man into a heightened racial consciousness whereas the camouflaged variety could lull him into a sense of false security. Commenting in 1917 on the great strides Afro-Americans had made in independent racial endeavor, he wrote: 'The honest prejudice of the South was sufficiently evident to give the Negro of America the real start—the start with a race consciousness, which I am convinced is responsible for the state of development already reached by the race.' Thus he could say, 'We have to admire the white man who fixed the Bible to suit himself, and who even fixed tradition itself, telling us that everything worthwhile and beautiful was made by the white man; that God is a great white man, that Jesus was a white man, and that the angels, etc., whatever they are, are as beautiful as peaches in Georgia.'

By the same token, however, he saw white self-interest as largely detrimental to black self-interest. And within the confines of a country such as the United States, where whites formed a large ruling majority, white racial self-interest would tend inexorably toward the extermination of the black minority. These considerations strengthened Garvey's commitment to racial separation.

Despite the fact that Garvey would not accept white philanthropy or allow whites to join his organization, it did not follow that he could not work to a limited extent with white people. In fact, by maintaining an independent black power base, he had more freedom to work with or support widely differing types of white persons and organizations on specific projects or for limited objectives than some of his contemporaries who were straitjacketed in interracial organizations.

The first category of white people with whom Garvey could cooperate were certain types of radicals, usually those engaged in anticolonial, anti-imperialist or antiracist struggles. Often they were leaders of mass movements like his own and he could identify them as kindred spirits. Among persons in this category were Eamon De Valera, the Irish leader, who on one occasion was listed as a featured speaker at Garvey's Harlem Liberty Hall, and the Russian revolutionaries Lenin and Trotsky. He often had a good word for historical figures such as John Brown, Elijah Lovejoy, and others of abolitionist inclination. He also had great admiration for Captain A. A. Cipriani, white leader of the Trinidad Workingmen's Association (TWA), whose public career largely coincided with Garvey's in time and political outlook. Cipriani had become head of the TWA in 1919 at the invitation of the members, who were black. By this time the association had already become a Garveyite stronghold in Trinidad, and its struggles were being reported in the *Negro World*. Many of its meetings were held in Port-of-Spain's Liberty Hall and its second-in-command, W. Howard Bishop, as well as other members of its hierarchy were prominent Garveyites. Garvey corresponded with Cipriani, who made representations to the British government in 1937 to change their intention of barring Garvey from entry into the island. Another well-known white radical for whom Garvey seems to have had some respect was Nancy Cunard, renegade member of a wealthy shipping family who became involved in a variety of black causes. In 1932 Cunard visited Jamaica to gather material for her *Negro Anthology* and was the guest at a reception arranged by Garvey.

If Garvey could associate with some radical whites of the left in deference to their anti-imperialist stance or reputation as leaders of the masses, he could also associate, for different reasons, with segregationists on the far right. These latter shared one very crucial ideological tenet with Garvey: they, too, believed in race first and therefore in the separation of the races.

Despite Garvey's limited agreements with some white persons, however, the insistent black nationalist thrust of the UNIA ensured the hostility of the majority of whites. One white lady witnessing a UNIA parade on 125 Street in Manhattan in 1920 is said to have tearfully exclaimed, 'And to think, the Negroes will get their liberty before the Irish.'

Garvey's race-first doctrine was essentially a stratagem to ensure self-reliance and equality for the downtrodden African race. Unlike the white preachers of this doctrine with whom he collaborated, he did not go a step further and preach racial superiority. He more than once stressed that 'all beauty, virtue and goodness are the exclusive attributes of no one race. All humanity have their shortcomings; hence no statement of mine, at any time, must be interpreted as a wholesale praise of, or attack upon any race, people or creed.'

Self-reliance was a necessary corollary to race first. In his earliest extant pamphlet Garvey explained, in terms showing the probable influence of Booker T. Washington, that 'the Negro is ignored to-day simply because he has kept himself backward; but if he were to try to raise himself to a higher state in the civilized cosmos, all the other races would be glad to meet him on the plane of equality and comradeship.' He went on to express an idea which would later cause him much enmity from Afro-American integrationists: 'It is indeed unfair to demand equality when one of himself has done nothing to establish the right to equality.' Garvey never abandoned this dual tendency to score the white race for its injustice while simultaneously utilizing the language of condemnation to spur the black race on to greater self-reliance.

Garvey's belief in the necessity for self-reliance led him occasionally to speak in the language of Social Darwinism. He attacked the pseudo-scientific racists who tried to justify genocide against black people in terms of the Darwinian 'survival of the fittest' and turned their arguments to the cause of racial self-reliance. 'White philosophers,' he argued, 'Darwin, Locke, Newton and the rest . . . forgot that the monkey would change to a man, his tail would drop off and he would demand his share.' And not only had these philosophers been mistaken, but black heroism in World War I had finally given the lie to such false assumptions. He reminded his black audiences that 'that theory has been exploded in the world war. It was you, the superman, that brought back victory at the Marne.'

The urgency Garvey felt for racial independence and self-reliance led him to argue that in independent endeavor lay the only hope of eventual solution to the problem of race prejudice. The white race would cease its aggressiveness toward the black when it was met by independent black power of a magnitude equal to its own. White prejudice was manifested 'not because there is a difference between us in religion or in colour, but because there is a difference between us in power.' [. . .]

The insistent UNIA thrust for self-reliance can best be summarized in Garvey's own words:

The Universal Negro Improvement Association teaches to our race self-help and self-reliance, not only in one essential, but in all those things that contribute to human happiness and well being. The disposition of the many to depend upon the other races for a kindly and sympathetic consideration of their needs, without making the effort to do for themselves, has been the race's standing disgrace by which we have been judged and through which we have created the strongest prejudice against ourselves. . . .

The race needs workers at this time, not plagiarists, copyists and mere imitators; but men and women who are able to create, to originate and improve, and thus make an independent racial contribution to the world and civilization.

[From *Race First: The Ideological and Organizational Struggles of Marcus Garvey and the Universal Negro Improvement Association* (Dover, Mass.: Majority Press, 1976), 23–5, 27–33, 37.]

KWAME TURE AND CHARLES V. HAMILTON

32 **Black Power: Its Need and Substance**

Black people in the United States must raise hard questions, questions which challenge the very nature of the society itself: its long-standing values, beliefs and institutions.

To do this, we must first redefine ourselves. Our basic need is to reclaim our history and our identity from what must be called cultural terrorism, from the depredation of self-justifying white guilt. We shall have to struggle for the right to create our own terms through which to define ourselves and our relationship to the society, and to have these terms recognized. This is the first necessity of a free people, and the first right that any oppressor must suspend. [. . .]

Black people must redefine themselves, and only *they* can do that. Throughout this country, vast segments of the black communities are beginning to recognize the need to assert their own definitions, to reclaim their history, their culture; to create their own sense of community and togetherness. There is a growing resentment of the word 'Negro,' for example, because this term is the invention of our oppressor; it is *his* image of us that he describes. Many blacks are now calling themselves African-Americans, Afro-Americans or black people because that is *our* image of ourselves. When we begin to define our own image, the stereotypes—that is, lies—that our oppressor has developed will begin in the white community and end there. The black community will have a positive image of itself that it has created. This means we will no longer call ourselves lazy, apathetic, dumb, good-timers, shiftless, etc. Those are words used by white America to define us. If we accept these adjectives, as some of us have in the past, then we see ourselves only in a negative way, precisely the way white America wants us to see ourselves. Our incentive is broken and our will to fight is surrendered. From now on we shall view ourselves as African-Americans and as black people who are in fact energetic, determined, intelligent, beautiful and peace-loving.

There is a terminology and ethos peculiar to the black community of which black people are beginning to be no longer ashamed. Black communities are the only large segments of this society where people refer to each other as brother—soul-brother, soul-sister. Some people may look upon this as *ersatz*, as make-believe, but it is not that. It is real. It is a growing sense of community. It is a growing realization that black Americans have a common bond not only among themselves, but with their African brothers. In *Black Man's Burden*, John O. Killens described his trip to ten African countries as follows:

Everywhere I went people called me brother. . . . 'Welcome, American brother.' It was a good feeling for me, to be in Africa. To walk in a land for the first time in your entire life knowing within yourself that your color would not be held against you. No black man ever knows this in America [p. 160].

More and more black Americans are developing this feeling. They are becoming aware that they have a history which pre-dates their forced introduction to this country. African-American history means a long history beginning on the continent of Africa, a history not taught in the standard textbooks of this country. It is absolutely essential that black people know this history, that they know their roots, that they develop an awareness of their cultural heritage. Too long have they been kept in submission by being told that they had no culture, no manifest heritage, before they landed on the slave auction blocks in this country. If black people are to know themselves as a vibrant, valiant people, they must know their roots. And they will soon learn that the Hollywood image of man-eating cannibals waiting for, and waiting on, the Great White Hunter is a lie.

With redefinition will come a clearer notion of the role black Americans can play in this world. This role will emerge clearly out of the unique, common experiences of Afro-Asians. Killens concludes:

I believe furthermore that the American Negro can be the bridge between the West and Africa-Asia. We black Americans can serve as a bridge to mutual understanding. The one thing we black Americans have in common with the other colored peoples of the world is that we have all felt the cruel and ruthless heel of white supremacy. We have all been 'niggerized' on one level or another. And all of us are determined to 'deniggerize' the earth. To rid the world of 'niggers' is the Black Man's Burden, human reconstruction is the grand objective [p. 176].

Only when black people fully develop this sense of community, of themselves, can they begin to deal effectively with the problems of racism in *this* country. This is what we mean by a new consciousness; this is the vital first step. [. . .]

The adoption of the concept of Black Power is one of the most legitimate and healthy developments in American politics and race relations in our time.

The concept of Black Power speaks to all the needs mentioned in this chapter. It is a call for black people in this country to unite, to recognize their heritage, to build a sense of community. It is a call for black people to begin to define their own goals, to lead their own organizations and to support those organizations. It is a call to reject the racist institutions and values of this society.

The concept of Black Power rests on a fundamental premise: *Before a group can enter the open society, it must first close ranks.* By this we mean that group solidarity is necessary before a group can operate effectively from a bargaining position of strength in a pluralistic society. Traditionally, each new ethnic group in this society has found the route to social and political viability through the organization of its own institutions with which to represent its needs within the larger society. Studies in voting behavior specifically, and political behavior generally, have made it clear that politically the American pot has not melted. Italians vote for Rubino over O'Brien; Irish for Murphy over Goldberg, etc. This phenomenon may seem distasteful to some, but it has been and remains today a central fact of the American political system. There are other examples of ways in which groups in the society have remembered their roots and used this effectively in the political arena. Theodore Sorensen describes the politics of foreign aid during the Kennedy Administration in his book *Kennedy*:

No powerful constituencies or interest groups backed foreign aid. The Marshall Plan at least had appealed to Americans who traced their roots to the Western European nations aided. But there were few voters who identified with India, Colombia or Tanganyika [p. 351].

The extent to which black Americans can and do 'trace their roots' to Africa, to that extent will they be able to be more effective on the political scene.

A white reporter set forth this point in other terms when he made the following observation about white Mississippi's manipulation of the anti-poverty program:

The war on poverty has been predicated on the notion that there is such a thing as a community which can be defined geographically and mobilized for a collective effort to help the poor. This theory has no relationship to reality in the deep South. In every Mississippi country there are two communities. Despite all the pious platitudes of the moderates on both sides, these two communities habitually see their interests in terms of conflict rather than cooperation. Only when the Negro community can muster enough political, economic and professional strength to compete on somewhat equal terms, will Negroes believe in the possibility of true cooperation and whites accept its necessity. En route to integration, the Negro community needs to develop a greater independence—a chance to run its own affairs and not cave in whenever 'the man' barks—or so it seems to me, and to most of the knowledgeable people with whom I talked in Mississippi. To OEO, this judgment may sound like black nationalism. . . .[1]

The point is obvious: black people must lead and run their own organizations. Only black people can convey the revolutionary idea—and it is a revolutionary idea—that black people are able to do things themselves. Only they can help create in the community an aroused and continuing black consciousness that will provide the basis for political strength. In the past, white allies have often furthered white supremacy without the whites involved realizing it, or even wanting to do so. Black people must come together and do things for themselves. They must achieve self-identity and self-determination in order to have their daily needs met.

Black Power means, for example, that in Lowndes County, Alabama, a black sheriff can end police brutality. A black tax assessor and tax collector and county board of revenue can lay, collect, and channel tax monies for the building of better roads and schools serving black people. In such areas as Lowndes, where black people have a majority, they will attempt to use power to exercise control. This is what they seek: control. When black people lack a majority, Black Power means proper representation and sharing of control. It means the creation of power bases, of strength, from which black people can press to change local or nation-wide patterns of oppression—instead of from weakness.

It does not mean *merely* putting black faces into office. Black visibility is not Black Power. Most of the black politicians around the country today are not examples of Black Power. The power must be that of a community, and emanate from there. The black politicians must start from there. The black politicians must stop being representatives of 'downtown' machines, whatever the cost might be in terms of lost patronage and holiday handouts.

Black Power recognizes—it must recognize—the ethnic basis of American politics as well as the power-oriented nature of American politics. Black Power therefore calls for black people to consolidate behind their own, so that they can bargain from a position of strength. But while we endorse the *procedure* of group solidarity and identity for the purpose of attaining certain goals in the body politic, this does not mean that black people should strive for the same kind of rewards (i.e., end results) obtained by the white society. The ultimate values and goals are not domination of exploitation of other groups, but rather an effective share in the total power of the society.

Nevertheless, some observers have labeled those who advocate Black Power as racists; they have said that the call for self-identification and self-determination is 'racism in reverse' or 'black supremacy.' This is a deliberate and absurd lie. There is no analogy—by any stretch of definition or imagination—between the advocates of Black Power and white racists. Racism is not merely exclusion on the basis of race but exclusion for the purpose of subjugating or maintaining subjugation. The goal of the racists is to keep black people on the bottom, arbitrarily and dictatorially, as they have done in this country for over three hundred years. The goal of black self-determination and black self-identity—Black Power—is full participation in the decision-making processes affecting the lives of black people, and recognition of the virtues in themselves as black people. The black people of this country have not lynched whites, bombed their churches, murdered their children and manipulated laws and institutions to maintain oppression. White racists have. Congressional laws, one after the other, have not been necessary to stop black people from oppressing others and denying others the full enjoyment of their rights. White racists have made such laws necessary. The goal of Black Power is positive and functional to a free and viable society. No white racist can make this claim. [. . .]

It is a commentary on the fundamentally racist nature of this society that the concept of group strength for black people must be articulated—not to mention defended. No other group would submit to being led by others. Italians do not run the Anti-Defamation League of B'nai B'rith. Irish do not chair Christopher Columbus Societies. Yet when black people call for black-run and all-black organizations, they are immediately classed in a category with the Ku Klux Klan. This is interesting and ironic, but by no means surprising: the society does not expect black people to be able to take care of their business, and there are many who prefer it precisely that way.

In the end, we cannot and shall not offer any guarantees that Black power, if achieved, would be non-racist. No one can predict human behavior. Social change always has unanticipated consequences. If black racism is what the larger society fears, we cannot help them. We can only state what we hope will be the result, given the fact that the present situation is unacceptable and that we have no real alternative but to work for Black Power. The final truth is that the white society is not entitled to reassurances, even if it were possible to offer them.

We have outlined the meaning and goals of Black Power; we have also discussed one major thing which it is not. There are others of greater importance. The advocates of Black Power reject the old slogans and meaningless rhetoric of previous years in the civil rights struggle. The language of yesterday is indeed irrelevant: progress, non-violence, integration, fear of 'white backlash,' coalition. Let us look at the rhetoric and see why these terms must be set aside or redefined.

One of the tragedies of the struggle against racism is that up to this point there has been no national organization which could speak to the growing militancy of young black people in the urban ghettos and the black-belt South. There has been only a 'civil rights' movement, whose tone of voice was adapted to an audience of middle-class whites. It served as a sort of buffer zone between that audience and angry young blacks. It claimed to speak for the needs of a community, but it did not speak in the tone of that community. None of its so-called leaders could go into a rioting community and be listened to. In a sense, the blame must be shared—along with the mass media—by those leaders for what happened in Watts, Harlem, Chicago, Cleveland and other places. Each time the black people in those cities saw Dr Martin Luther King get slapped they became angry. When they saw little black girls bombed to death *in a church* and civil rights workers ambushed and murdered, they were angrier; and when nothing happened, they were steaming mad. We had nothing to offer that they could see, except to go out and be beaten again. We helped to build their frustration.

We had only the old language of love and suffering. And in most places—that is, from the liberals and middle class—we got back the old language of patience and progress. The civil rights leaders were saying to the country: 'Look, you guys are supposed to be nice guys, and we are only going to do what we are supposed to do. Why do you beat us up? Why don't you give us what we ask? Why don't you straighten yourselves out?' For the masses of black people, this language resulted in virtually nothing. In fact, their objective day-to-day condition worsened. The unemployment rate among black people increased while that among whites declined. Housing conditions in the black communities deteriorated. Schools in the black ghettos continued to plod along on outmoded techniques, inadequate curricula, and with all too many tired and indifferent teachers. Meanwhile, the President picked up the refrain of 'We Shall Overcome' while the Congress passed civil rights law after civil rights law, only to have them effectively nullified by deliberately weak enforcement. 'Progress is being made,' we were told.

Such language, along with admonitions to remain non-violent and fear the white backlash, convinced some that that course was the *only* course to follow. It misled some into believing that a black minority could bow its head and get whipped into a meaningful position of power. The very notion is absurd. The white society devised the language, adopted the rules and had the black community narcotized into believing that that language and those rules were, in fact, relevant. The black community was told time and again how *other* immigrants finally won *acceptance*: that is, by following the Protestant Ethic of Work and Achievement. They worked hard; therefore, they achieved. We were not told that it was by building Irish Power, Italian Power, Polish Power or Jewish Power that these groups got themselves together and operated from positions of strength. We were not told that 'the American dream' wasn't designed for black people. That while today, to whites, the dream may *seem* to include black people, it cannot do so by the very nature of this nation's political and economic system, which imposes institutional racism on the black masses if not upon every individual black. [. . .]

The racial and cultural personality of the black community must be preserved and that community must win its freedom while preserving its cultural integrity. Integrity includes a pride—in the sense of self-acceptance, not chauvinism—in being black, in the historical attainments and contributions of black people. No person can be healthy, complete and mature if he must deny a part of himself; this is what 'integration' has required thus far. This is the essential difference between integration as it is currently practiced and the concept of Black Power.

The idea of cultural integrity is so obvious that it seems almost simpleminded to spell things out at this length. Yet millions of Americans resist such truths when they are applied to black people. Again, that resistance is a comment on the fundamental racism in the society. Irish Catholics took care of their own first without a lot of apology for doing so, without any dubious language from timid leadership about guarding against 'backlash.' Everyone understood it to be a perfectly legitimate procedure. Of course, there would be 'backlash.' Organization begets counterorganization, but this was no reason to defer.

The so-called white backlash against black people is something else: the embedded traditions of institutional racism being brought into the open and calling forth overt manifestations of individual racism. In the summer of 1966, when the protest marches into Cicero, Illinois, began, the black people knew they were not allowed to live in Cicero and the white people knew it. When blacks began to demand the right to live in homes in that town, the whites simply reminded them of the status quo. Some people called this 'backlash.' It was, in fact, racism defending itself. In the black community, this is called 'White folks showing their color.' It is ludicrous to blame black people for what is simply an overt manifestation of white racism. Dr Martin Luther King stated clearly that the protest marches were not the cause of the racism but merely exposed a long-term cancerous condition in the society.

[From *Black Power and the Politics of Liberation* (New York: Vintage Books, 1992; 1st edn..
1967), 34–5, 37–9, 44–51, 55–6.]

PAUL GILROY
....

33 **The End of Anti-Racism**

Introduction

[. . .] For all its antipathy to the new racism of the New Right, the common sense ideology of anti-racism has also drifted towards a belief in the absolute nature of ethnic categories and a strong sense of the insurmountable cultural and experiential divisions which, it is argued, are a feature of racial difference. I have argued elsewhere that these ideological failures have been compounded firstly by a reductive conception of culture and secondly by a culturalist conception of race and ethnic identity. This has led to a position where politically opposed groups are united by their view of race exclusively in terms of culture and identity rather than politics and history. Culture and identity are part of the story of racial sensibility but they do not exhaust that story. At a theoretical level 'race' needs to be viewed much more contingently, as a precarious discursive construction. To note this does not, of course, imply that it any less real or effective politically.

It is possible then, that the idea of anti-racism has been so discredited that it is no longer useful. It is certain that we have to devise ways to move beyond anti-racism as it is presently constituted. I must emphasise that I am thinking not of anti-racism as a political objective, or a goal which emerges alongside other issues from the daily struggles of black people, from the practice of community organisations and voluntary groups, even from the war of position which must be waged inside the institutions of the state. I am not talking about the ongoing struggle towards black liberation, for there is much more to the emancipation of blacks than opposition to racism. I am thinking instead of anti-racism as a much more limited project defined simply, even simplistically, by the desire to do away with racism.

The anti-racism I am criticising trivialises the struggle against racism and isolates it from other political antagonisms—from the contradiction between capital and labour, from the battle between men and women. It suggests that racism can be eliminated on its own because it is readily extricable from everything else. Yet in Britain, 'race' cannot be understood if it is falsely divorced from other political processes or grasped if it is reduced to the effect of these other relations. Anti-racism in this sense is a phenomenon which grew out of the political openings created by the 1981 riots. In the years since then, anti-racists have become a discrete and self-contained political formation. Their activism is now able to sustain itself independently of the lives, dreams and aspirations of the majority of blacks from whose experience they derive their authority to speak.

To criticise anti-racism necessitates understanding racism and being able to locate the politics of 'race' from which it springs. Analysing what racism does in our society means, first of all, claiming 'race' and racism back from the margins of British politics. Racism isn't epiphenomenal. Yet just as racism itself views black settlers as an external, alien visitation, anti-racism can itself appear to be tangential to the main business of the political system as a whole.

The apparent marginality of race politics is often an effect of a fundamental tension inherent in anti-racist organising. A tension between those strands in anti-racism which are primarily anti-fascist and those which work with a more extensive and complex sense of what racism is in contemporary Britain. This simplistic anti-fascist emphasis attempts to mobilise the memory of earlier encounters with the fascism of Hitler and Mussolini. The racists are a problem because they are descended from the brown- and black-shirted enemies of earlier days. To oppose them is a patriotic act; their own use of national flags and symbols is nothing more than a sham masking their terroristic inclinations.

The price of over-identifying the struggle against racism with the activities of these extremist groups and grouplets is that however much of a problem they may be in a particular area (and I am not denying the need to combat their organising) they *are* exceptional. They exist on the fringes of political culture and for the foreseeable future are destined to have only tenuous and intermittent relationships with respectability. They are a threat but not the only threat. There is more to contemporary racism than the violence they perpetrate. We shall see in a moment that there are problems with the nationalism which goes hand in hand with this outlook.

A more productive starting point is provided by focusing on racism in the mainstream and seeing 'race' and racism not as fringe questions but as a volatile presence at the very centre of British politics actively shaping and determining the history not simply of blacks, but of this country as a whole at a crucial stage in its development.

The importance of racism in contemporary politics betrays something about the nature of the painful transition this country, and the overdeveloped world as a whole, is undergoing. The almost mystical power of race and nation on the political stage conveys something about the changing nature of class relations, the growth of state authoritarianism, the eclipse of industrial production, the need to maintain popular support for militarism and exterminism and the end of the nation state as a political form.

The highly charged politics of national identity that has been occasioned by these developments has been transposed into a higher, shriller key by current concern over the appeal of a wide pan-European disposition tailored to the new range of possibilities that flow from tighter political and economic integration of the European Economic Community. This potentially post-national European consciousness has racial referents of its own. It is however, felt by elements of both left and right to pose a threat to the sovereignty and cultural integrity of the United Kingdom. Whether it is possible to generate a political discourse capable of articulating the distinctive needs and historical experiences of black Europeans remains to be seen. Though the rich legacy of an extensive black presence on this continent suggests that it may be possible, for many commentators, the terms 'black' and 'European' remain categories which mutually exclude each other.

Racism and the Ideology of Anti-Racism

The first question I want to ask of contemporary anti-racism is whether it doesn't collude in accepting that the problems of 'race' and racism are somehow peripheral to the substance of political life. My view, which locates race in the core of politics, contrasts sharply with what can be called the coat of paint theory of racism. This is not in fact, a single theory but an approach which sees racism on the outside of social and political life—sometimes the unwanted blemish is the neo-fascists, sometimes it is immigration laws, other times it is the absence of equal opportunities—yet racism is always located on the surface of other things. It is an unfortunate excrescence on a democratic polity which is essentially sound, and it follows from this that with the right ideological tools and political elbow grease, racism can be dealt with once and for all leaving the basic structures and relations of British economy and society essentially unchanged.

Though not always stated openly, the different permutations of this view underpin much of contemporary anti-racism. I think there are particular problems posed by the fact that this type of theory is intrinsic to equal opportunities initiatives. The coat of paint approach is doubly mistaken because it suggests that fundamental issues of social justice, democracy and political and economic power are not raised by the struggle against racial subordination.

Seeing racism as determining rather than determinate, at the centre rather than in the margins, also means accepting that Britain's crisis is centrally and emphatically concerned with notions of race and national identity. It has been held together, punctuated and periodised by racial politics—immigration, the myriad problems of the riotous 'inner city' and by the loony left. These terms are carefully coded and they are significant because they enable people to speak about race without mentioning the word. The frequent absence of any overt reference to 'race' or hierarchy is an important characteristic of the new types of racism with which we have to deal. This kind of coded language has created further strategic problems for anti-racism. It is easy to call Mr Honeyford a racist and to organise against him on that basis but less easy to show precisely how and why this is the case.

We must be prepared to focus unsentimentally on anti-racism's inability to respond to other distinctive aspects of these new forms of racism. Apart from the way that racial meanings are inferred rather than stated openly, these new forms are distinguished by the extent to which they identify race with the terms culture and identity, terms which have their own resonance in anti-racist orthodoxy. The new racism has a third important feature which enables it to slip through the rationalist approach of those who, with the best will in the world, reduce the problem of racism to the sum of power and prejudice. This is the closeness it suggests between the idea of race and the ideas of nation, nationality and national belonging.

We increasingly face a racism which avoids being recognised as such because it is able to link 'race' with nationhood, patriotism and nationalism. A racism which has taken a necessary distance from crude ideas of biological inferiority and superiority and now seeks to present an imaginary definition of the nation as a unified *cultural* community. It constructs and defends an image of national culture—homogeneous in its whiteness yet precarious and perpetually vulnerable to attack from enemies within and without. The analogy of war and invasion is increasingly used to make sense of events.

This is a racism that answers the social and political turbulence of crisis and crisis management by the recovery of national greatness *in the imagination*. Its dreamlike construction of our sceptred isle as an ethnically purified one provides a special comfort against the ravages of decline. It has been a key component in the ideological and political processes which have put the great back in Britain. The symbolic restoration of greatness has been achieved in part through the actual expulsion of blacks and the fragmentation of their households which is never far from page three in the tabloids. [. . .]

Racial Justice and Civil Society

I think it is important to concede that what we can loosely call the anti anti-racist position associated with sections of the New Right and with populist politics has fed on crucial ambiguities in anti-racist and multi-cultural initiatives.

The definition of racism in the sum of prejudice and power can be used to illustrate these problems. Power is a relation between social groups not a possession to be worn like a garment or flaunted like an anti-racist badge. Prejudice suggests conscious action if not actual choice. Is this an appropriate formula? The most elementary lessons involved in studying ideas and consciousness seem to have been forgotten. Racism, like capitalism as a whole, rests on the mystification of social relations—the necessary illusions that secure the order of public authority.

There are other aspects of what has become a multi-culturalist or anti-racist orthodoxy which can be shown to replicate in many ways the volkish New Right sense of the relationship between race, nation and culture—kin blood and ethnic identity. I have already mentioned how the left and right distinction has begun to evaporate as formally opposed groups have come to share a sense of what race is. These problems are even more severe when elements of the black community have themselves endorsed this understanding. Here I am thinking of the definition of race exclusively in terms of culture and identity which ties certain strands in anti-racism to the position of some of the New Right ideologues.

By emphasising this convergence I am not saying that culture and identity are unimportant but challenging the routine reduction of race to them alone which obscures the inherently political character of the term. The way in which culture is itself understood provides the key to grasping the extraordinary convergence between left and right, anti-racist and avowedly racist over precisely what race and racism add up to.

At the end of the day, an absolute commitment to cultural insiderism is as bad as an absolute commitment to biological insiderism. I think we need to be theoretically and politically clear that no single culture is hermetically sealed off from others. There can be no neat and tidy pluralistic separation of racial groups in this country. It is time to dispute with those positions which, when taken to their conclusions, say 'there is no possibility of shared history and no human empathy'. We must beware of the use of ethnicity to wrap a spurious cloak of legitimacy around the speaker who invokes it. Culture, even the culture which defines the groups we know as races, is never fixed, finished or final. It is fluid, it is actively and continually made and re-made. In our multi-cultural schools the sound of the steel pan may evoke Caribbean ethnicity, tradition and authenticity yet they originate in the oil drums of the Standard Oil Company rather than the mysterious knowledge of ancient African griots.

These theoretical problems are most visible and at their most intractable, in the area of fostering and adoption policy. Here, the inflated rhetoric and culturalist orthodoxies of anti-racism have borne some peculiar fruit. The critique of the pathological views of black family life that were so prevalent in Social Services during the late 1970s and early 1980s has led directly to an extraordinary idealisation of black family forms. Anti-racist orthodoxy now sees them as the only effective repositories of authentic black culture and as a guaranteed means to transmit all the essential skills that black children will need if they are to 'survive' in a racist society without psychological damage. 'Same-race' adoption and fostering for 'minority ethnics' is presented as an unchallenged and seemingly unchallengeable benefit for all concerned. It is hotly defended with the same fervour that denounces white demands for 'same race' schooling as a repellent manifestation of racism. What is most alarming about this is not its inappropriate survivalist tone, the crudity with which racial identity is conceived nor even the sad inability to see beyond the conservation of racial identities to the possibility of their transcendence. It is the extraordinary manner in which the pathological imagery has simply been inverted so that it forms the basis of a pastoral view which asserts the strength and durability of black family life and, in present circumstances, retreats from confronting the difficult issues which result in black children arriving in care in the first place. The contents of the racist pathology and the material circumstances to which it can be made to correspond are thus left untouched. The tentacles of racism are everywhere, except in the safe haven which a nurturing black family provides for delicate, fledgeling racial identities.

The Forces of Anti-Racism

I want to turn now to the forces which have grouped around the anti-racist project and to the question of class. There is a problem here in that much of the certainty and confidence with which the term has been used have collapsed along with the secure life-time employment which characterised industrial capitalism. Today for example, I think it means next to nothing to simply state that blacks are working class when we are likely to be unemployed and may not recognise our experience and history in those areas of political life where an appeal to class is most prominent. Class politics does not, in any case, enjoy a monopoly of political radicalism. Obviously people still belong to classes but belief in the decisive universal agency of the dwindling proletariat is something which must be dismissed as an idealist fantasy. Class is an indispensable instrument in analysing capitalism but it contains no ready-made plan for its overcoming. We must learn to live without a theological faith in the working class as either a revolutionary or an anti-racist agent.

There is a major issue here but I want to note it and move on to consider a different aspect of how race and class intersect. A more significant task for class analysis is comprehending the emergence of a proto-middle class grouping narrowly constituted around the toeholds which some blacks have been able to acquire in the professions, mostly those related directly to the welfare state itself—social work, teaching, and now anti-racist bureaucracies. A Marxist writer would probably identify this group as the first stirrings of a black petit bourgeoisie. I don't think this grouping or grouplet is yet a class either in itself or for itself and it may never become one. For one thing it is too small, for another it is too directly dependent on the state institutions which pay its wages. But it is with this group that anti-racism can be most readily identified and we need to examine it on its own terms and in its relationship to other more easily identifiable class groupings. It is obviously in an uncomfortably contradictory position—squeezed between the expectations of the bureaucracies on which it relies and its political affiliation to the struggles of the mass of blacks which it is called upon to mediate, translate and sometimes police. It is caught between the demands of bureaucratic professionalism and the emotive pull of ethnic identification.

This not-yet-class plays a key role in organising the political forces of anti-racism centred on local authorities. It involves three opposed tendencies which have evolved an uneasy symbiosis. They are not wholly discrete. The black sections campaign for example, involves elements of each of them.

1. The equal opportunities strand, which has its roots in the social democratic 'race' interventions of the 1960s. It has also borrowed heavily from the experience of Afro-America's shift into electoral politics—the black mayors' movement and so on. This tendency is proud and secure in its bureaucratic status and it identifies equality (anti-racism) with efficiency and good management practice. Policy questions dominate political ones and anti-racism emerges from the production of general blueprints which can be universally applied. Of course, equal opportunities afford an important interface between struggles around race and gender and they can be a locus of possible alliances. However, in the context of local authorities these initiatives can also host a competition between different political forces over which of them is going to take immediate priority. We should therefore be wary of collapsing anti-racism let alone black emancipation into equal opportunities.

2. The second tendency is what used to be called black nationalism but is now fragmented into multiple varieties each with its own claim to ethnic particularity. It is now emphatically culturalist rather than political, each ethnic or national group arguing for cultural relativism in the strongest form. Very often, these mutually unintelligible and exclusive ethnic cultures just happen to be the same as the groups which common sense tells us are 'races'. Perversely and ironically, this tendency has happily co-existed with old style Labourism for which ethnic absolutism and cultural relativism have provided an obvious means to rationalise and balance its funding practices.

3. The third tendency is the most complex. It unendingly reiterates the idea that class is race, race is class and is both black and white. Its spokespeople have sought refuge from inter-ethnic conflict in some of the more anachronistic formulae of socialist class politics. For them class is the thing which will unify the diverse and end the polyphonic ethno-babble in the new municipal tower of babel. Class remains synonymous with organised

labour regardless of the fact that in the context of local authorities organised labour isn't always very radical. This tendency overlooks the role which the bureaucratic hierarchy plays in coercing the actually existing working class into anti-race line. So far its class-based line has been almost exclusively animated by a critique of race awareness training—a practical strategy which has been thrown up in the grating between the first two tendencies. This is an important issue but it is nonetheless the most gestural and superficial aspect of deeper problems namely, culturalism and ethnic absolutism. This tendency has mistaken the particular for the general—racism awareness training is a symptom, not a course in its own right.

Apart from their conceit, these diverse yet inter-dependent groupings share a statist conception of anti-racism. In making the local state the main vehicle for advancing anti-racist politics they have actively confused and confounded the black community's capacity for autonomous self-organisation. Here, we must make an assessment of the politics of funding community organisations and the dependency which that creates.

There is every likelihood that the versions of anti-racism I have criticised will wither away as the local state structures on which they have relied are destroyed by the conflict with central government. But anti-racist activities encapsulate one final problem which may outlive them. This is the disastrous way in which they have trivialised the rich complexity of black life by reducing it to nothing more than a response to racism. More than any other issue this operation reveals the extent of the anti-racists' conceptual trading with the racists and the results of embracing their culturalist assumptions. Seeing in black life nothing more than an answer to racism means moving on to the ideological circuit which makes us visible in two complementary roles—the problem and the victim.

Anti-racism seems very comfortable with this idea of blacks as victims. I remember one simplistic piece of GLC propaganda which said 'We are all either the victims or the perpetrators of racism'. Why should this be so? Suffering confers no virtue on the victim, yesterday's victims are tomorrow's executioners. I propose that we reject the central image of ourselves as victims and install instead an alternative conception which sees us as an active force working in many different ways for our freedom from racial subordination. The plural is important here for there can be no single or homogeneous strategy against racism because racism itself is never homogeneous. It varies, it changes and it is always uneven. The recent history of our struggles has shown how people can shrink the world to the size of their communities and act politically on that basis, expressing their dissent in the symbolism of disorderly protest while demanding control over their immediate conditions. However you feel about the useless violence of these eruptions, it was the riotous protests of 1981 which created the space in which political anti-racism became an option.

We must accept that for the years immediately ahead, these struggles will be essentially defensive and probably unable to make the transition to more stable, totalising forms of politics. But the challenge we face is the task of linking these immediate local concerns together across the international division of labour, transcending national boundaries, turning our back on the state and using all the means at our disposal to build a radical, democratic movement of civil society. This kind of activity could be called the micro-politics of race though in practice, as where we align ourselves with the struggles of our brothers and sisters in South Africa, it is more likely to prove the micro-politics of race's overcoming. [. . .]

[From 'The End of Anti-Racism', in Wendy Ball and John Solomos (eds.), *Race and Local Politics* (London: Macmillan, 1990), 192–7, 204–9.]

HERIBERT ADAM AND KOGILA MOODLEY

34   **Psychological Liberation**

Internalized Colonialism and the Psychology of Liberation
In the late 1960s the idea of Black Consciousness heralded an era of alternative political awareness in South Africa. A self-empowering, vibrant, reconstructionist world view emphasized the potential role of black initiative and responsibility in articulating the power of the powerless. Between 1968 and 1976 the Black Consciousness Movement (BCM) was one of the most significant developments in South Africa, not only because of the self-confident protest and rebellion that it unleashed but also 'because of the questions it posed about the nature of oppositional politics in South Africa and its relation to the nature of South African society.'[1]

Indeed, blacks in South Africa in the 1960s were ready for an ideology of liberation. The oppression of apartheid society was overt and blatant; all opposition had been silenced, and institutionalized racism flourished triumphant. Centuries of exclusionary practices led to what might be described as the 'inferiorization' of blacks: Blacks were portrayed as innately inferior, accustomed to dehumanized living, sexually promiscuous, intellectually limited, and prone to violence; blackness symbolized evil, demise, chaos, corruption, and uncleanliness, in contrast to whiteness, which equaled order, wealth, purity, goodness, cleanliness, and the epitome of beauty.

Inevitably, these racist stereotypes were at least partially internalized by South African blacks, although their self-doubt never matched that prevalent among blacks in the United States, where the official proclamations of equality misled many blacks into blaming themselves, rather than discrimination, for any miseries they experienced.

But undoubtedly, apartheid society also produced self-hatred. The limited range of opportunities open to blacks gave rise to rationalizations in favor of the status quo, and self-doubts and self-accusations led some blacks to accept their oppression as legitimate. In short, blacks blamed themselves. In addition, the fragmentation of the three black groups through differential privileges and incorporation led to a reinforcement of an intrablack hierarchy.

Thus, Black Consciousness emanated from the differential material and political circumstances in which blacks were situated. Its prime movers in the early phase were relatively privileged medical students, not workers, who served as educated articulators of the plight of the underprivileged and politically excluded. Yet, unlike most medical students elsewhere, many of them came from working-class backgrounds and were not insulated from the harsh conditions of apartheid society. They were joined by other students on the newly created segregated black campuses, where they operated under severe restrictions, and had to depend on the white-dominated National Union of South African Students (NUSAS) to speak and act on their behalf—though blacks were prohibited from joining this organization.

Yet even as some blacks at the open universities worked with NUSAS, they experienced the bifurcating effects of academic integration coupled with social separation. Much of their alienation was due to the vast gap between the life circumstances of black and white students. At the University Christian Movement, too, the initial promise of a liberal alternative soon evaporated when black students once more saw themselves reduced to the role of followers. The banning of the ANC in 1960 and the arrests of its leaders meant that blacks had to rely on liberal whites to articulate the case for black rights. Steve Biko, the best-known proponent of Black Consciousness, described how such enforced passivity dulled one's originality and imagination: 'it takes a supreme effort to act logically even in order to follow one's beliefs and convictions.'[2]

In the editorial introduction to the 1972 annual *Black Viewpoint*, Biko referred to the absence of black writers in the media: 'So many things are said so often to us, about us and for us but very seldom by us.'[3] He deplored the images of dependency created for blacks by the white press and expressed the need to deconstruct the implicit interpretive connotations, underlying values, attitudes, and interests of both the financial supporters and the readership of those newspapers. Biko articulated a general insight into conquest: that defeat for the losers has always meant more than physical subjugation. It means, as two historians of the Soviet Union have described in other circumstances, 'that the conquerors write the history of the wars; the victors take possession of the past, establish their control over the collective memory.'[4] In short, the victors' definition of reality becomes the dominant explanation.

The difficulty of working bilaterally with even the most sincere whites posed a moral dilemma for black students, who were the last to want themselves labeled racist. Yet for Biko and others the need for exclusive black organizations was very clear, something Ben Khoapa referred to as the need for 'regroupment.'[5] Blacks were considered to be an interest group, like workers in a trade union or teachers fighting their own battles. The collective segregation and oppression based on skin color therefore provided an eminently logical basis for self-assertion and independent organization. No longer would blacks allow themselves to be objectified in the negative image of 'nonwhites'—instead they would reconstruct themselves as blacks, as self-defining initiators. Gone were the days when they appealed to whites by seeking to convince them that blacks too had civilized standards. Black Consciousness was about pressuring whites through contesting the self-definitions of their opponents.[6] Accusations that this was a racist act were dismissed on the grounds that 'one cannot be a racist unless he has the power to subjugate.'[7]

Later, when Black Consciousness developed a socialist tinge, cooperation with white liberals was rejected not because of race or privilege, but because these would-be compatriots were seen as representing a bourgeois class enemy. Collaboration with representatives of racial capitalism would amount to betrayal. 'Black Consciousness,' writes George Frederickson, an American historian, 'had evolved from an effort to overcome a black sense of inferiority through independent, nonviolent action into an explosive combination of race and class revolutionism.'[8] Whatever the meaning of the latter phrase, Black Consciousness remained above all an awareness-raising movement, rather than an organization that practiced revolutionary violence.

The origins of blacks' disillusionment with nonracial opposition organizations go back to the adoption of the Freedom Charter in 1955 by the Congress of the People, which gave rise to a split between the Charterists (ANC) and those who formed the PAC. The latter's racial definition of *African* later evolved into a broadly inclusive subjective one, in that it included people of any group who considered themselves African and who identified with Africa and its people (as opposed to the exploiting settlers). By contrast, Black Consciousness utilized an objective definition of *black* to describe all those denied privileges by whites, as well as a subjective definition of those who consciously rejected white domination in all its forms. Even Bantustan leaders fell into the former category and were recognized as such for a while by the South African Students' Organisation (SASO).

What was distinctive about the BCM was 'its originality in elaborating an ideology of hope rooted in a theology of liberation which emphasized the solidarity of the oppressed regardless of race.'[9] Unlike the PAC, which, despite its stated goal of including all 'Africans,' is perceived as narrowly Africanist, Black Consciousness as an ideology was genuinely inclusive. From its inception the new movement sought to incorporate Indians and Coloureds. However, while it had its appeal for this 'middle group' in expressing political identification, as G. J. Gerwel points out, it failed to provide the psychological identity they needed.[10] In general, the BCM enjoyed greater support from activist Coloureds than Indians, not least because some students and clergy identified with its rejection of the label 'coloured' in favor of an inclusive black category that focused on political oppression. Many Indians, on the other hand, while prominent in the early leadership of SASO, came to feel rejected as insufficiently black enough, and they felt pressured to replace their cultural heritage with African symbols. Indeed, a few gave their children African names as a way of identifying with the movement. However, they were the exceptions—often alienated community members— rather than the precursors of a groundswell of Indian sentiments toward identification as blacks.

The fragile unity among the oppressed groups was frequently exposed. The ease with which Indians could be condemned for not identifying sufficiently with the black cause, and even for considering themselves a minority, is evident in a not untypical SASO newsletter article published in 1972, 'Ugandan Asians and the Lesson for Us.' In addition to exonerating Idi Amin for his treatment of Asian Ugandans, the latter were portrayed stereotypically as 'refusing to see themselves as part of the soil of Africa'; 'middlemen who continually saw themselves as a minority and by their practice of exploitation of the Africans through money lending at inflated interest rates, through the practice of bargaining . . . they contributed to the growth of animosity between themselves and the Africans who saw them as a hostile exploitative minority.'[11] Here the East African model was uncritically transposed to the South African situation, with no attention to the crucial fact that most Indians in South Africa were descendants of the indentured laborers. Unlike the trading minorities and the colonial civil servants in East Africa, the majority of Indian South Africans are members of the working class. But class analysis was not a tool of the movement at this initial stage.

The categorization of Indians as exploiting traders also ignored the fact that even the minority shopkeepers had to compete with white-owned monopolies in order to corner some of the increasing African consumer market. But because the owners of family stores came into direct contact with African shoppers, unlike the white owners of larger supermarkets and department stores, Indians' and Africans' perceptions of each other frequently focused on unequal exchange relationships. The mutual ambivalence was reinforced by the widespread practice in Natal industries for African workers to be supervised by Indians who, in turn, had to justify to their white employers their preferential treatment. Here, then, the message of black solidarity came up against a formidable institutionalized racial hierarchy in employment.

BCM transformed negative attitudes about subordinate 'non-whites' into a positive discourse of resistance. It offered psychological support to oppressed groups by providing a model for positive identification, and sought to alleviate the self-contempt often felt by the oppressed. Despite their efforts to provide an alternative to past descriptions, however, movements such as Black Consciousness have been criticized for implicitly accepting the legitimacy of color as a marker. In doing so, it is argued, they also reinforce the accuracy of the dominant discourse of race, by which they have been signified and exteriorized as the other.[12] In rebuttal, Sam Nolutshungu argues that 'the character of the state conditions not only the terms of domination and submission but also the ideologies and political behaviour that challenge and reject it.' The very role that the state gives to national and racial oppression, Nolutshungu explains, calls forth 'alignments among the subject population that are focussed primarily on the terms of political domination rather than those of exploitation.'[13]

Notably lacking in the initial stages of the formulation of Black Consciousness was an economic perspective on the nature of exploitation. Conceptualizations of South Africa in class terms remained peripheral and there was no systematic analysis of what was later termed racial capitalism. In part, this disinterest represented the rejection of Marxism as a white ideology and as the tool of the South African Communist Party. However, this indifference also reflected the censorship of Marxist literature at the tribal universities, as well as the students' exposure to existentialism, phenomenology, and philosophical psychology—subjects that were popular among some of the European-oriented faculty. Hence the movement's focus on values and essences, while its rejection of capitalism was couched in terms of dehumanization and materialism, not commodity fetishism.[14]

Although there was little of the 'black is beautiful' sloganeering that characterized American black protest, the BCM was influenced by trends in the United States. The movement worked to raise consciousness about the extent to which blacks, at great costs, were trying to copy white images of beauty, and the BCM helped to restore blacks' sense of self-appreciation and self-acceptance. Indeed, in the early stages of the movement in Natal, there were reports that some African men had beaten African women who had straightened their hair or lightened the color of their skin. One indicator of the success of Black Consciousness on this issue was the vastly reduced advertising and sale of bleaching creams in South Africa.

Barney Pityana describes the inspiration for the BCM as originating in African religious movements and prophets, in attempts by Africans to regain their land, in the history of the Industrial and Commercial Workers Union of Africa (ICU). Pityana also stresses the significance of both the Africanist and nationalist strands within the traditions of struggle. Philosophically, Black Consciousness was broadly influenced by the writings of Léopold Sédar Senghor, Aimé Césaire, Albert Memmi, Frantz Fanon, Eldridge Cleaver, Stokely Carmichael, and Paulo Freire—each of whom expressed the humiliation as well as the dignity of the colonized and also the power of the powerless. Though the BCM turned to these works on the psychology of oppression and the exorcizing of colonial humiliation, there is little evidence in the Black Consciousness literature that, for example, Fanon's central notion of the cleansing power of anticolonial violence found resonance among South African activists. At the early stage Black Consciousness also maintained a rather skeptical silence about the ANC's 'armed struggle.'

Unlike Black Power groups in the United States, the BCM had no need to become a revivalist movement, reconstructing a distant past and golden heritage, since African linguistic and cultural traditions had persisted despite apartheid. In the absence of the American trauma of slavery, young black Africans felt no need to search for putative roots. Leaders made a clear distinction between Black Consciousness and Black Power in the United States, where already enfranchised blacks wished to constitute themselves as a pressure group in a white majority society. In South Africa, the BCM was seen as a way of preparing people for equal participation in a transformed society that would reflect the outlook of the black majority.[15] Psychological liberation was sought through a return to African values of communalism, shared decision making, and more personal communication styles, in contrast to the individualism of white consumer society.

Despite the BCM's designation of the black community as communalistic, the division of labor within the BCM followed traditional sexist lines. All five officeholders in the 1972 executive were men. Women for the most part were relegated to taking responsibility for child care, moral education, and socialization in black cultural heritage, for health, nutrition, and the making of clothing. This view permeated the women's own self-definition, as is evident in the preamble to the constitution of the allied Black Women's Federation:

1. Black women are basically responsible for the survival and maintenance of their families and largely the socialisation of the youth for the transmission of the Black cultural heritage.
2. They need to present a united front and to redirect the status of motherhood towards the fulfillment of the Black people's social, cultural, economic and political aspirations.[16]

In contrast, the Institute of Black Studies, formed in 1975, was 'to provide a forum where the Black *man* can express himself. . . . a platform where issues facing the country can be analysed and interpreted.'[17]

The repetition of masculine pronouns, which prevailed in the SASO Policy Manifesto of 1971, may well have reflected and reproduced standard English usage of 'he' and 'man' in what was viewed as their generic sense. But despite the black cultural ideal of an inclusive communalism, the male is constructed as the empowered speaker, and women—even when included as 'sisters'—are presented as the other, powerless and voiceless.[18] The ancillary role of women in the leadership of SASO further corroborates this gender-based disparity. Few women were prominent in student representative councils or in campus activities. But structural factors may also have kept women from participating on a more equal basis—one cannot automatically attribute their underrepresentation in the movement solely to exclusionary practices.

Forms of Protest

In its earlier phases, the BCM was characterized by spontaneity and an easy evolution, without any rigid plan or agenda. The style was informal, free of organizational trappings, as exemplified by Biko's 'I Write What I Like.' Politics were consensually based, until the rude awakening caused by Temba Sono's public criticism of the BCM's directions in July 1972. After that, the membership was more carefully screened and the style of speeches became more prescribed.

Consciousness-raising often took the form of light-hearted, satirical, humorous utterances. College campuses during the late 1960s were the base for frequently staged political theater. For a while, it amused even Nationalist-oriented staff members, who seemed to rejoice at the way in which 'the natives' entertained themselves, in images derived from 'their own lingo.' The style of acting and diction was a refreshing change from the previous stilted, imitative, colonial models of the speech and drama genre. Afrikaner faculty at the tribal colleges loved this rejection of the British yoke, and there was a self-congratulatory air about how well these colleges allowed students to express themselves. The National government, however, was not amused at these developments on campuses it had established in order to ethnicize, depoliticize, fragment, and control the opposition. The theatrical performances were among the subversive activities charged by the state at trials of BCM leaders in the 1970s.

From the late 1960s until the arrest of its most articulate proponents in 1977, Black Consciousness filled the political and cultural vacuum created by the silencing of the ANC and PAC leadership. The main tenets of the BCM permeated the thinking of a generation of students, regardless of political persuasion. The movement's initial analytical focus on culture, identity, and value systems gradually shifted, and the struggle was defined in terms of racism and capitalism. In 1971 the preferred focus was to radicalize the population through direct political criticism of the regime; through infiltration of ruling organizations, including collaborating institutions, and conversion from within; and through 'orientation politics' that addressed a range of educational, cultural, religious, and economic needs. Under the influence of Julius Nyerere's ideas about self-reliance, various community projects explored ways in which blacks could become more self-supporting.

Black Review 1972 cited black community projects—literacy campaigns, health projects, and home education programs—throughout the country, mainly in rural and semirural areas in the Transvaal, Natal, and Eastern Cape.[19] Popular short-term notions of an imminent revolution were replaced by patient, disciplined preparation. The editor of *Black Review*, B. A. Khoapa, proposed that the philosophy of liberation required a frank appraisal of white institutions and policies and 'an advanced programme of economic democracy' in order to expand black interests to universal interests.[20] He called for a broadening of the movement beyond sheltered student politics toward a mobilization of the work force. If Black Consciousness was to effect a major transformation in society, the intellectuals would have to reach workers.

This goal implied not only a modification of language, but also a fundamental shift of concerns: establishing positive self-images seemed peripheral, at best, to people whose lives were heavily burdened by the daily drudgery of earning a living. The new projects, however, were severely hampered by the constraints of student life. Distances between campuses and townships, inadequate financial resources for travel and free time, and the need to work with Bantustan authorities inhibited outreach efforts. So, too, did the marginal status of young students, who could hardly hold themselves out as leaders to the workers. All these factors served to identify the need for an adult branch of the growing student movement.[21]

What was distinctive about the BCM at this time was its pragmatic willingness to forgo the rhetoric-laden, sterile, noncompromise party lines adopted by other opposition organizations. For a while the BCM even had contacts with adversaries like Gatsha Buthelezi. Indeed, Steve Biko and Buthelezi shared a platform when the BCM brought together an alliance of diverse black groups. Another sign of the BCM's openness was its effort to establish a socialist dispensation, while striving for nationalist liberation.

This unconventional mix of tendencies hampered fundraising. Prospective financial supporters were few, and those willing to fund the nationalist cause balked at supporting a movement marked by socialist sympathies. On the other hand, those who might have supported radical political initiatives would not back an organization that emphasized the significance of color. Faced with the choice between comprising its principles in order to attract funds or being independent, principled, locally based, and underfinanced, the BCM characteristically settled for the latter.[22]

Up through the early 1970s the BCM's relatively modest means and low-key profile provoked little reaction from Pretoria. During this period of tolerance the regime even praised BCM students for their 'apartheid-like' thinking, their enthusiasm for the state's program of separatist black education. On the surface the BCM appeared to be using the same symbols as the state, even as it refashioned black identity into a more inclusive category by raising awareness about the structure of oppression. SASO emphasized black content in education and attempted to subvert the authority structure by divulging the relations of power and Eurocentric bias in institutional life. At the SASO banquet of June 1973, for example, Ernest Baartman gave an eloquent address, 'Education as an Instrument for Liberation,' that demystified the relationship between knowledge, control, and hegemony.[23] Such analyses only highlighted the dialectic of apartheid education for the colonized, as had been predicted.[24] The ruling regime now came to understand that the BCM was appropriating the state's idioms in order to challenge its motives and subvert its power.

After a series of industrial strikes throughout Durban during 1973, for which the BCM was blamed but neither claimed nor disclaimed responsibility, the government retaliated by arresting eight SASO organizers, although there was little connection between SASO and the strikes. The last straw, from the government's point of view, was a Durban rally that SASO organized in 1974 to celebrate Mozambique's independence. The 'Viva Frelimo' cries of the crowd at the banned meeting were only intended to express black solidarity and strengthen the BCM, but the police violently overreacted. A series of arrests and bannings followed, culminating in a number of deaths in detention.

In response to massive arrests and police intimidation, some students saw armed struggle as the only alternative. In 1976 the rebellion of Soweto students was primarily headed by members of the South African Students' Movement (SASM), infused with the spirit of Black Consciousness in their rejection of Afrikaans-language instruction as a tool of their subjugation. Large numbers of these students subsequently escaped the country. Many were absorbed into ANC camps, although a Black Consciousness Movement in exile was also set up as a third South African liberation group.

The BCM's platform of education *for* liberation was in danger of devolving into what some viewed as calls from abroad for liberation *before* education. The deteriorating conditions in black schools and the unbridgeable rift between children and school authorities under the Department of Education and Training led a group of concerned parents to found the National Education Crisis Committee (NECC). Hoping to get the children to return to schools, the NECC promoted the idea of people's education as an alternative. The detention of most of NECC's active members prevented this initiative from gaining any momentum. Meanwhile, individuals and institutions sympathetic to Black Consciousness continued to conduct research and develop curriculum materials and policy perspectives for an alternative South Africa.

In the 1970s the BCM was said to have been cocooned as an intellectual crusade with little grass-roots support, lacking a solid base in organized labor. Some critics said the movement was heavy on moral purity and faced the danger of stagnating at the level of black solidarity, unable to translate its ideas into the 'politically possible' for 'political action.'[25] Others expressed concern about whether the movement was forward-looking enough to prepare itself for a post-apartheid society.[26]

While Black Consciousness has always been weak at best among organized workers, it did spawn its own union during the 1970s. The Black and Allied Workers' Union (Bawu) criticized its stronger Fosatu rival for employing white intellectuals. This practical nonracialism in a fledgling independent union movement contrasted with BCM's 'antiracism' under 'black leadership.' Successor organizations like the Council of Unions of South Africa (CUSA) and the Azanian Confederation of Trade Unions (Azactu) later formed the National Council of Trade Unions (Nactu), which has kept its organizational and ideological distance from Cosatu to this day, although both federations increasingly cooperate on tactical issues.

In 1978, after the banning of all constituent components of the BCM the previous year, the Azanian People's Organisation (Azapo) was formed. Its leaders incorporated a class analysis into their policy and directed attention toward the political involvement of the black working class. A focus on psychological liberation and blackness gradually gave way to more talk of socialist, anticapitalist alternatives. Those speaking on behalf of Azapo refuted charges that theirs was merely an intellectual movement, and they insisted that Azapo enjoyed wide support.

While initially favoring the Black Consciousness tendency, the state as well as liberal institutions in the 1980s began to look more favorably at the ANC supporters' nonracial promise. In 1991 Azapo students at Witwatersrand University, for example, complained about the university's nonrecognition of the BCM on the grounds that the organization was exclusively black and, therefore, violated the university's nonracial charter. The students argued that exclusively Jewish or Islamic student societies were always recognized, and that student fees were used to subsidize Charterist organizations through the local student representative councils. The vice-president of Azapo, Gomolemo Mokae, listed a series of incidents to argue that '"liberal" universities like Wits and Natal are guilty of complicity in Stalinistic censorship against non-Charterists' (*Frontline*, May 1991). His grievance reflects Azapo's practice of not distinguishing between legitimate ethnicity (cultural and religious groups) and illegitimate racial categories. In black and white nationalist thinking, ethnicity and race are identical.

Black Consciousness continues to rely on the development of a fictive kinship between all three 'nonwhite groups' who have experienced the shared indignity of oppression and material deprivation. The psychological appeal of this kinship arouses many in all groups, and the effectiveness of Black Consciousness relies on the moral feelings it evokes. But can these feelings be channeled into a sustained movement? One of the major obstacles to a broad coalition is to be found in the differential experience of apartheid. Material rewards co-opt and 'whiten,' as does feared loss of cultural terrain. [. . .]

[From *The Opening of the Apartheid Mind: Options for the New South Africa* (Berkeley and Los Angeles: University of California Press, 1993), 104–16.]

CATHIE LLOYD

35   Universalism and Difference

Introduction: The Crisis in Anti-Racism?

It has been widely argued that the anti-racist movement in France is suffering a crisis. I suggest here that something similar has been happening in the UK, but that it has been less openly acknowledged. The crisis in anti-racism has taken different forms in the UK and in France, but there are interesting parallels. The crisis is in part an aspect of the general crisis of the left, and associated values, particularly of modernity and universalism. In both countries, the 'left' has traditionally been identified with anti-racism (although this is a complex relationship). Thus the fragmentation of the left in recent years, particularly through the loss of confidence in the Enlightenment values of progress, and the dissolution of many left structures have sapped the vitality of anti-racist movements. In a weakened state, these movements are less able to confront the massive rise in racism and fascism, shown by recent events in Germany, but also in ex-Yugoslavia with 'ethnic cleansing', and in Holland, Belgium and France with the rise of new extreme-right parties. In the UK, racial violence is extremely widespread despite vigorous campaigning and policy making over many years.

This paper focuses on the basis of anti-racist beliefs and discourses: for instance, the ideas of human equality, universalism, and faith in the inevitability of progress and the possibility of the improvement of humanity. These ideas are particularly relevant to France, where much anti-racist discourse still resounds to the great names of the Enlightenment, and where it is claimed that the first anti-racists were some of the *philosophes* and revolutionaries of the eighteenth century (in particular the Abbé Gregoire).

In the UK, the problems of the anti-racist movements revolve around the weaknesses of the left, especially its exclusion from power, which has increased defensiveness, narrow labourism, lack of will and divisions in the left and encouraged a long-standing split between black and white approaches to organization.

In both countries there has been a contestation of ideas, particularly since the 1970s, involving a challenge to 'left universalism' based on the assertion of the importance of authentic experience (France) and the politics of identity (the UK). The argument here is that there can be fundamental (or significant) differences between individual experiences or cultures, and that minority cultures should be safeguarded. One problem that becomes evident, I would argue, is that the roots of Enlightenment universalism are full of contradictions and limitations, which suggest that universalism was (paradoxically) particular and Eurocentric (end even perhaps narrower than this). The ideas of the Enlightenment (especially in France) have been sites of considerable struggle, so that today they are appropriated in a number of different and complex ways. [...]

The UK and France: Different Traditions of Anti-Racism

There are some important common themes in discussions in the UK and France, such as the nature of the changes in contemporary society and the way to understand them, and the relationship between a traditionally universalist left anti-racism (in a crisis of self-doubt), particularism and difference. However, these issues are born out of quite different traditions of political debate and anti-racist organization.

It is to the question of different traditions of anti-racism that I will now turn. These traditions reflect to some extent the positions of the populations and social actors concerned in anti-racist work, and the growth of state structures and interventions in this area which, especially in the UK, has had an effect on the activity and organization of voluntary structures. In the UK, I will argue, the theme is increasingly related to racialized relations, while in France issues are related to new conceptions of citizens' rights.

In the UK, through the implementation of the Race Relations Acts, especially the 1976 Act, the state has played a leading role in developing anti-discrimination, multi-ethnic and 'anti-racist' policies. The 'race relations project' has been affected as a result of its being implemented during a period of growing social inequality and as part of a wider state policy of 'integration and control' (Lloyd, 1993). The Race Relations Acts in the UK came into effect at a time when there were efforts to form a national anti-racist, umbrella-style civil rights movement. The failure of the Campaign Against Racial Discrimination (CARD) in the 1960s illustrates the general difficulties of establishing a broad anti-racist movement in the UK. There were problems of a fundamental clash between reformists and radicals; the paternalism of white social democrats; and divisions between 'immigrant' groupings, in an attempt to establish an overambitious campaign with ill-defined goals.

The influence of developments in the USA led to attempts to transplant experiments which were continuously being outdated by transatlantic experiences. The efforts of other anti-racists to mediate between these antagonistic groupings were neutralized. These conflicts seem regularly to resurface in anti-racist organizations in the UK.

Divisions within the anti-racist/anti-fascist movement again began to emerge in the 1970s, despite massive mobilizations in opposition to National Front campaigning activity. Many questions which exercised French anti-racists in the 1980s, particularly over the limits of popular campaigning and their relationship with the media, and the development of 'Rock against Police' into the mega-concerts of SOS-Racisme, were rehearsed ten years earlier in British experience of 'Rock against Racism'. Gilroy's analysis of *Temporary Hoarding*, the punk-oriented journal of Rock Against Racism, which tapped into a popular culture similar to the early issues of *CARF*, suggests (Gilroy 1987, p. 129) that the anti-racist project was beginning to address 'universalist' questions, if only by a rearticulation of consumerist impulses through pop culture for radical ends:

it makes racism central to radical or revolutionary sentiment not because it was the most important dimension to life in the declining UK but because it was a moment in the process of social and political struggle where the system as a whole was vulnerable, where its irrationality, bias and brutality could be demonstrated to exist. It was the proof that everything that the left had said about capitalism in general and Britain in particular was true.

Fundamental disagreements about tactics quickly surfaced between those who wished to privilege defeating the National Front electorally and those with longer-term aims involving grass-roots organization against racism, which might have given rise to a structure similar to the MRAP's today. Sectarianism and unwillingness to listen to the experiences of black anti-racists within the white left exacerbated tensions, which ultimately blew organizations apart. Contemporary debates between the Anti-Racist Alliance, Anti-Nazi League and Anti-Fascist Alliance are reproducing those of the 1970s without apparently trying to draw lessons from them, but also within the new dynamic of a much stronger challenge from black leadership.

The 1980s was the decade of 'municipal anti-racism' led by the Greater London Council (GLC). After 1981 most left-wing (Labour) local authorities adopted policies to encourage the employment and promotion of 'ethnic minorities' and to take their special needs into account. Major debates took place about the way to tackle 'institutional racism', with strongly held positions about the respective merits of multiculturalism versus anti-racism.

However, the enactment of 'correct' policies at local level was fraught with difficulties. For instance, in the field of education there has been a complex reaction on the part of white parents (sometimes but not always fuelled by the organized extreme right) against anti-racist curricula. Following the killing of Ahmed Ullah in a Manchester school playground, the Burnage Report concluded that the anti-racist strategy adopted by the school was seen as concerning black but not white pupils and parents, and assumed that white people could not be anti-racist.

John LaRose (1992, p. 41), in discussing the intolerance of what he calls 'symbolic anti-racists' (i.e. those based in local authority race units) in preventing the views of white anti-racists from being expressed, writes:

I have been to meetings, numerous meetings in this country over the years, where a white worker gets up and begins to speak, and he says something about blacks and this and that, and immediately the whole meeting prevents him from continuing to speak; so you don't ever hear what his real grievances are . . . The middle classes tend with their liberalism to believe that they are being antiracist by preventing white workers from explaining their grievances and discussing their grievances openly, as they should, in meetings with black people, with Asian people, white people, with anybody, for example, who is interested in bringing about serious antiracism, racial equality and social justice.

The growth of a 'race relations industry' armed with a carefully tuned set of policies for different ethnic groups has in the UK eclipsed the role of association, many of which have in any case been sucked into competing for local authority grants a process (like in France) which has necessitated accommodation and, conformity with certain norms. The incorporation of independent community-based groups reduces the number of voices which can be heard, and tends to shape policies in a certain mould. Much theoretical literature about anti-racism does not address movements, but rather different levels of state policy.

The bitterness of the debate in the UK dividing people according to ethnic origin has deepened in the 1990s. I would argue here that the experience of 'race relations' policies in the 1980s has reinforced the racialization of social relations in contemporary Britain. I would add that this has been exacerbated by the neglect and gross insensitivity of the white 'left'. Tendencies which Heineman in 1972 described as tearing apart the CARD, particularly the gulf between the patronizing 'ownership' of white left-liberals and black radicals, have been strengthened. Thus, we have seen different parts of the anti-racist movement at bitter loggerheads about the legitimacy of their respective organizations or affiliations, sectarianism, specific attitudes to black leadership, the nature of the 'main enemy', and the relationship between anti-racism and community. [. . .]

The 'crisis of anti-racism' in France is taking place in a rather different structure. The 1972 Law Against Racism did not create an enforcement body like the CRE, but was rather the product of concerted campaigning and lobbying by established anti-racist organizations, notably the MRAP but also other organizations such as the Ligue des Droits de l'Homme. Since 1981, when Mitterrand made it easier for foreigners to form associations, there has been a massive expansion of associations particularly linked to the younger generation born in France, the most well known of which is SOS-Racisme. Some of these have now been established long enough to be able to take on cases under the 1972 law.

As in the UK, associations have been incorporated into the state mechanisms through competition for grants, which has had a distorting effect to their activities. In some instances, it was felt that anti-racists were being used in party political manipulations, as during the March 1992 regional elections when anti-racists mobilized across France to oppose Front National election meetings, but were 'warned off' when they began to succeed. The role of SOS-Racisme and France Plus as vectors of Socialist government policy have been hotly debated, and there is considerable evidence for this. In the past few years there has been a greater involvement of the state in the assessment of 'integration' policies, with annual reports from the Haut Conseil à l'Integration and the Commission Consultative de Droits de l'Homme.

In France, the crisis on the left, the decline of the French Communist Party (PCF), wide-spread unemployment, industrial restructuring and the crisis in education have created massive social deprivation and alienation. Anti-racists have also had to confront their failure to prevent the rise of the Front National, a mass movement which has used new right discourse increasingly, in recent years to deny its racist and fascist core.

The Crisis of Strategy: Which Racism?

If we can talk about different traditions in the UK and France, it is also clear that there are similar problems. In both countries, a central question is the nature of the racism to be confronted, and therefore the appropriate combative strategy. The success of the right has also highlighted the inadequacy of what the French see as the 'failure' of their traditional models of integration, which are linked in the debate to the decay of key social institutions such as the family, the education system, employment, trade unions and political parties (especially the PCF). Debate in France has to a large extent engaged outwards, perhaps partly as a result of the relationship between the anti-racists and intellectuals/researchers in France and the role of intellectuals in public life. Anti-racism is also seen as occupying a central place in political debate, to be linked with questions of national identity and citizenship.

I think that this is an important difference with the UK, where the debate focuses largely on problems with the anti-racist policies adopted by public authorities, and debates within and between anti-racist organizations, rather than an analysis of how to explain the continued existence of racism. Miles expresses this as 'labelling' rather than 'explaining' racism.

The British debate about multiculturalism has highlighted the way in which state policies fail to differentiate between different aspects of cultures, which may have unacceptable consequences for parts of a group. This was well illustrated during the debates around the Rushdie Affair, and continues to be manifest in attitudes to 'minority religions'. If 'minorities' are viewed in the UK as homogeneous groups defined solely by their religion, this enables religious leaders to 'edge themselves into positions of political as well as spiritual leadership, defining the community's agenda and power structure, and negotiating with the state for resources' (Bard, 1992). This development has a particularly pernicious effect on women, whose social marginalization is often not challenged by traditionalist multi-culturalism. Anti-racists, it is argued, have disenfranchised themselves from adopting a position on these issues, by privileging the struggle against 'racism' over the support for oppressed groups, by failing to understand the implications of religious fundamentalisms and by their distance from the 'minority groups' on whose behalf they mobilize.

Multicultural policies have been criticized as tending to encourage the development of simplistic models of 'minority' cultures and the formation of 'instant experts'. There are reasons for this inward approach—particularly the way in which governmental power has been exercised since 1979—but it is a weakness of which we need to be aware, rather than allowing it to continue to immobilize debate. This is one of the reasons why discussion about the French experience is useful and illuminating.

The French 'model of integration', which until recently operated through a fairly liberal access to nationality and citizenship (particularly the *jus solis* principle), is seen to be failing at a time when many French-born young people whose parents were immigrants are demanding their rights and a proper recognition of their position within French society. This is evident in the different grass-roots organizations from which sprang the 'marches for equality' of the early 1980s. The older anti-racist movements faced not only the problem of how to respond to the challenge of the new forms which young people created, but also the problem of how to act when the social framework which in the past formed the base of their activity had gone. One crucial debate which is just starting in the French anti-racist movement is what precisely are the limits and boundaries of anti-racism.

There is a perceived danger that the broad anti-racist movements will try to fill the vacuum left by the decayed primary and local institutions (the family, education and community-based organizations, even political parties), particularly through the activities of their local committees. There is concern that the specific struggle against racism will be absorbed by the wider social issues which desperately need an answer, and that the anti-racism movement will be under pressure to turn itself into a sort of substitute political party, and lose its specific role. This could be very damaging to a national organization like the MRAP, which includes members from different political parties, positions and religious perspectives. The situation is rendered more complicated because there is considerable evidence that the Front National has itself stepped into the vacuum, providing day-to-day support for people in marginal positions (those suffering unemployment, bad housing, insecurity, etc.) who have been abandoned by the main political parties.

In attempting to mobilize against the Front National, anti-racists in France have gone perhaps further than in the UK in discussing the implications of the new right. In the early 1980s, as we have seen, organizations were continuously referring back to traditional anti-racist ideas of the 1930s, 1940s and 1950s to explain what and why they should mobilize. This needs to be understood in the context of the violence used by extreme-right groups particularly in the late 1970s and early 1980s.

However, in the 1980s the anti-racists had to take account of two important factors. First, the main everyday target for racial violence and Front National propaganda were 'immigrants' from North Africa and the reference point was *Algerie française* and France's imperial greatness rather than 'Hitlerian Nazism', although of course there were links between the two in France. Second, the discourse of the extreme right was changing, partly to accommodate to the postwar period in which biological racism was less acceptable and scientifically disproved. A culturally based racism mirrored the discourse of the anti-racists (particularly the post-1968 'Third Worldists') in claiming the 'right to difference'. Thus the Front National could claim that it was against racism, but particularly racism against the French. Le Pen's famous comment illustrates this well: 'I prefer my daughters to my nieces and my nieces to my neighbours like everyone else . . . all men are the same'.

To anti-racists, part of the problem with the Front National's new discourse is that it is no longer possible simply to label the party because of its leader's fascist past, however important this may be. To many Front National voters, the sort of discourse I have just cited is common sense and reassuring. When this discourse is deployed, anti-racist 'demonizing' of the Front National seems to be counterproductive, although the current levels of racial violence in France point to an extremely serious situation. While there are many other, more convincing explanations for the rise of populist racism, there is a genuine problem: the failure to address the issues being currently raised by the Front National. Clearly, the nature of the 'racist' being opposed needs to be looked at again more carefully.

There is one powerful strand in critique of the anti-racists which suggests that their mistaken strategy in drawing attention and overreacting to racists is responsible for the rise of the Front National. A partial explanation is suggested by Taguieff (1991), who indicates the way in which anti-racist activity has become routinized, dominated by a teleological conception of 'racial prejudice' which traces a continuous link between a negative attitude towards 'Others' and racism as a system of extermination. This is well portrayed by an MRAP poster of the early 1980s, which was headed 'Attention! Racism Leads to Fascism!' It portrayed a male figure (probably of North African origin) fleeing from an aggressor who was wearing a military helmet and wielding a club, across a vast urban space reminiscent of the Nuremberg rallies and with swastikas festooned on a monolith. How were people to relate this dramatic representation to the racism which they would encounter in their everyday lives and which has sustained the Front National?

Taguieff (1991) argues that the crisis of anti-racism lies in the lack of a clear understanding of the racism(s) which has (have) to be fought. He distinguishes three types of anti-racism:

1 The economic reductionist view of racism, which reduced racism to a mode of legitimation of capitalist exploitation, and the linked belief that racism will disappear with imperialism.
2 A demonological anti-racism, in which racism incarnates absolute evil.
3 A rationalist pedagogical anti-racism, based on the idea that racism was a biological reductionism that could be 'disproved' and therefore eliminated by science or education.

As a result of these views it was thought that, if the notion of racial hierarchy had no scientific or economic basis, it could be expected to go away. What happened in anti-racist discourse was a sort of 'demonizing disqualification' (Taguieff, 1991, p. 31) which attempted to dispel racism by repeating rational arguments and disqualifying racists as 'bad' (or ignorant) scientists. The influence of cultural relativism meant that to reject racism was to reject all forms of ethnocentrism; the 'real' anti-racism became a sort of cultural relativism. Ideas of identity and differentialism were acceptable because they were consonant with individualist values (crucial, as we have seen, to social integration in France), a 'return to roots' and the abandonment of ideas of universality. Taguieff argues strongly that the fundamental mistake of the anti-racists was to fail to understand the way in which their project was being undermined by the new right, whose new racism was also based on the principle of the radical difference (here on the incommensurability) or different cultural forms.

In a recent essay, Stuart Hall (1992) debates this same issue but in a British context and argues:

The fact that this grounding of ethnicity in difference was deployed, in the discourse of racism, as a means of disavowing the realities of racism and repression does not mean that we can permit the term to be permanently colonized. That appropriation will have to be contested, the term disarticulated from its position in the discourse of 'multiculturalism' and transcoded, just as we previously had to recuperate the term 'black', from its place in a system of negative equivalences. (p. 257)

It seems to me that there are several initial problems with this brave project. First, in neither the French nor the British context have anti-racists fully grappled with the implications of the broader constituency made available to organizations like the Front National through their new-found discourse claiming respectability. Until this is further advanced, it will be difficult to change the terms of the debate. And to attempt to do so may be dangerous without taking up a strong position against the new right. Furthermore, the example given of a renegotiated term, 'black', was successful only for a limited period and space. New challenges are now present for anti-racists in Europe (Miles, 1992).

[From 'Universalism and Difference: The Crisis of Anti-Racism in the UK and France', in Ali Rattansi and Sallie Westwood (eds.), *Racism, Modernity and Identity: On the Western Front* (Cambridge: Polity Press, 1994), 222–3, 228–36.]

36   'It's Racism What Dunnit'

One of the things I want to argue is that in order to construct certain exemplary models of antiracist policy and practice it has been necessary to operate in terms of a reductive representation of racism, one which not only scales down its reality, but ignores its more complex features. It is this 'reductionism', this disavowal of complexity for the sake of pursuing moral certainties or political ideals, which has led to the present crisis of antiracist education. In taking this line of thought for a walk I have had to develop a model of antiracism itself, and this in the more properly social scientific sense of the word—the model as a typology of instances. I have tried to identify the pattern of presuppositions which underlay common-sense arguments about the meaning of my two study texts; I look both at their theoretical adequacy as explanatory models of racism, and at their rhetorical power as a means of winning consent for certain 'exemplary' or 'ideologically correct' formulations of how antiracist work should be done.

Although I do not develop this aspect of the analysis here, I also suggest that the images or metaphors which are applied to define racism by analogy hold the key to understanding people's emotional investment in antiracist positions. It is just as necessary to be aware of the role which desire, displacement and fantasy play in our own practices, as it is in relation to the perverse ideo-logic of racism itself. In the light of this discussion I offer some indications as to how a strategy of reading might be applied to the study of racist discourses, and invite readers to try out this approach on the two study texts, not in order to produce 'the right answer' but to compare what is gained and what lost in detail and depth of understanding by applying this kind of model compared to the others. At times this may seem a difficult and roundabout journey. But it will prove to be a necessary and worthwhile one if it leads us in the direction of a less doctrinaire and therefore more properly educational form of antiracism. [. . .]

Teleologies produce stable narratives in which the meaning of any conjuncture can be read off from the 'stage' it is supposed to represent in the dynamic unfolding of some ultimate and pre-defined goal. This is the *diachronic*, or *historicist* version. Alternatively the nature of any institution is read off from its underlying role in reproducing the social structure of which it is a part. This is the *functionalist* or *synchronic* version. Either form of explanation acts as an insurance policy taken out against the contingency of actions and events. Their outcome is guaranteed always and already to be inscribed in the process of their unfolding, according to certain overarching principles of causality.

How does this work in the case of theories of racism? Perhaps the dominant account still belongs to the Whig interpretation of history. This is a story of continuing progress, from the barbarity of slavery to the enlightenment of the contemporary race relations industry. The onward march of reason and tolerance is led by their 'natural' standard bearers, the European intelligentsia, and its various allies, who wage an unremitting battle against the irrational prejudices of both masses and traditional elites. The emancipation of the poor and oppressed is thus made part of a civilizing process, which is often seen to be conditional on assimilating their demands to the discourses of humanism and rationalism.

This is a fairy story version of race relations and it may reflect the hubris or wishful thinking of an intelligentsia which sets up its own preferred cultural practices as a referential model for everyone else. Increasingly it has been challenged by a rival account which might be called a 'teleology of the oppressed'. Here things do not get better and better, they go from bad to worse. The onward march of racism is traced through historical time and institutional space, from some presumed point of origination which defines its essential character, to a present conjuncture which is the summation of its effects. This narrative is often linked to another in which the victims of racism trace their own onward march, as an epic journey of emancipation from bondage, in which they alone carry the banner of human progress. These narratives can be read as two sides of the same story. The identity of Jews, blacks and others is made to depend on its inscription within an unfolding logic of racial oppression, which in turn is specified in terms of its formative effects upon their experience.

At one level, then, racism tends to be read as a kind of horrific soap opera in which the surface incidents are ever changing, but the underlying plot remains constant, generating one episode of discrimination after another, punctuated by atrocities which have no end even though paradoxically the final, cataclysmic outcome is never in doubt: for it will be the fire next time, the Armageddon which puts an end to chronic injustice, once and for all. Past and present struggles are transformed into 'epiphanies', special moments in which the conditions of oppression are transcended and which prefigure the ultimate goal of Liberation.

Such triumphalist narratives can be empowering in the symbolic sense that they invest ethnic minorities with special powers of knowledge and action. They break the signifying chains which have so often bound the project of emancipation to a strategy of cultural assimilation. Yet this radical autonomy of means and ends is itself dependent upon a circumscribed and self-confirming discourse of origins and destinies. It is like turning to the end of the story before you begin reading it, to find out if the baddies got their just deserts, or the good guys won. Or, as one of my students once put it to me, ironically, when I was still preaching this gospel, 'I know, Sir, it was racism what dunnit.'

Why are 'teleological tales' so central to the common sense of antiracism? I suspect that part at least of the explanation lies in the pressures which structures of racism exert on the forms of resistance to it. I am thinking here of two distinct but linked operations which constitute racism as a discursive practice. The first is a totalizing strategy which dissolves every distinction into the all-inclusive distinction of race: for example you are always and already defined as Jewish irrespective of age, class, gender, culture, or any other feature which might place you in a category with non-Jews. The other is a strategy of discrimination which magnifies and exploits every kind of social distinction (of wealth, culture status, etc.) to be found within a designated subject population and gives it a racist connotation as signifying certain 'exclusive traits'.

Used together these two strategies comprise that peculiar language game known as a double bind. Thus if you are Jewish and working class, your Jewishness is used to disqualify you from membership of labour organizations; but equally if you are Jewish and poor, your poverty is made to signify the essentially parasitic nature of your 'race' on the host community. How has the power of this system of classification been dealt with by those who have been victims of its perverse games of inclusion and exclusion?

Perhaps the main defence has been to construct an imagined community of resistance which cuts across all internal divisions by emphasizing the levelling effects of racist oppression. In this way diaspora communities are able to subsume all their disparate histories within a single meta-narrative which irons out all the 'wrinkles'. This may take the form of a genealogy which enables the present generation to see its own experience prefigured in the struggles of its ancestors, or to trace an unbroken line of descent to certain common codes and practices which define its 'roots'. Alternatively, it may provide a means of translating atrocity stories from simple acts of individual testimony into public iconographies, monuments in the living museum of collective memory. In either case, another chapter is added to a 'founding text', a text which both authorizes its own dissemination, and gives everything which is recounted in it the imprimatur of a special truth: this is the word of a chosen people.

Here we can see the influence of religious ideologies in furnishing commonsense explanations of racial intolerance and persecution. What often begins with a vision of racism as a global force of evil often becomes focused down into a conspiracy directed against a chosen people in a way which invests their suffering and sacrifices with a special redemptive meaning. The principle of salvation may be theological, as in the case of religious fundamentalism; or it may be purely secular, as with ethnic nationalism; or it may involve some combination of the two. But in every case the populist element is reinforced by a particular practice of reading and writing the founding text which stresses the prescriptive or predictive value of an elective destiny. This religious dimension is conserved as a subtext in many political ideologies, where it furnishes particular articles of faith in the self-emancipation of ethnic minorities, or in their special role as makers of their own history. In this context Marxism furnishes its own distinctive teleology of the oppressed, which can easily be transposed from class to nation or 'race'. Here the myth of the founding text is most clearly articulated to that of the founding fathers, whose word lays down the laws of a history in which women and children do not count.

These narratives do not work only to unite across space and time. They play a vital role in glossing over discontinuities in the here and now. Where a minority within an ethnic minority successfully pursues a strategy of contest mobility, and rises to positions of relative power and affluence, the teleologies of roots radicalism can reassert the organic links binding those who are moving onwards and upwards to those still in the ghetto. The racial success story turns those who have made it into narrative role models for the next generation, who are pledged to follow in their footsteps 'one day'. The elision between the onward march of the struggle against racism and the upward mobility of those who lead it, with its easy equation between individual success and collective emancipation has proved one of the more effective seductions offered by western democracies. It enables those who enter the professional middle class to avoid the worst traps of assimilation while disavowing the material advantages which now separate them from their erstwhile peers.

In such ways teleological tales of race and racism reinforce the imagined community of resistance at those points where divisions of class, gender or ethnicity threaten to break through. They ease the pain of lived contradictions, furnishing missing links between origins and destinies, stitching together scattered histories into a singular totalizing consciousness of what it means to be black or Muslim, Palestinian or Jew. The story lines which are woven together in this way are often spellbinding. Their telling and retelling relay important principles of hope rooted in political and moral certainties about the outcome of struggle. But do they really cauterize the wounds of historical separation and loss? Or do they merely invite us to count and compare our scars? Do these theoretical ideologies provide a strategic grasp of racism, or do they raise expectations which they cannot fulfil? [. . .]

Equally, some radical versions of multiculturalism make use of holistic arguments about power and ideology to legitimate ethnic minority cultures as an educational resource. Where multiculturalists and antiracists share common ground is in their general reliance on problematics which make the detailed reading and analysis of racist discourses seem irrelevant. This, I have argued, is evident both at the level of theoretical explanations and in the common-sense models of understanding which are deployed in the five statements I have quoted.

What all these approaches have in common is their *essentialism*. By this I mean their tendency to explain racism in terms of an 'ideal type' or model, which makes certain a priori assumptions about its origins, causes, meaning and effect. These assumptions correspond to particular forms or experiences of racism, which are translated into universal criteria defining its 'essence'. Types of racism which do not conform to this model are either ignored, marginalized, or 'redescribed' in ways which deny their independent significance. Racism becomes defined in terms of features which are specific to the black (or Afro-Caribbean) experience, for example, or to the peculiarities of English history, so that anti-semitism, or the specific articulations of racism which have developed in, say, the Irish or Scottish contexts, or in other European countries, are treated as 'special cases', because their inclusion would 'deconstruct' the ideal type. At the same time, at a micro level an assumption is made about who is racist and who is not in terms of a set of essential defining properties or predispositions.

This is not to suggest that each of the sample antiracist statements does not have something pertinent to say about the particular instance of racism which it privileges as paradigmatic. But putting these accounts together does not unfortunately add up to a multi-dimensional model which could provide the basis for a general theory; it only amplifies their essentialism. Indeed it is when these statements strive to go beyond themselves to grasp the complexities of the phenomena to which they refer that they are most likely to resort to rhetorical devices. These often take the form of images and metaphors which are used to define racism by analogy. [. . .]

The force of such metaphors is all the greater because of the unconscious effect which racist discourse itself exerts. For this is above all a discourse which ties a congenital link between origins and destinies, and which draws on images of birth and blood, the functions of the body and sexual reproduction, kinship and filiation, to do so. It is not surprising that such symbolism should unconsciously echo or evoke those infantile structures of representation through which identities and differences are first negotiated and invested with a sense of mastery, or that these models should be reproduced in the way racism is itself conceptualized. Of course these constructions are never just phantasies. The conspiracy theory of racism makes sense of a particular social reality: it is because the police force, which is supposed to uphold justice and protect ethnic minorities from racist attacks, is itself responsible for so much of the violence and injustice suffered by black communities that it is experienced as being part of the same oppressive system as the gang of white unemployed youth who are beating up people on the street. It is this kind of objective correspondence which makes it possible for the experience of racism to become connected to paranoid structures of feeling and phantasy which originate at a quite different and more unconscious level of representation.

In general, the more persecutory and overpowering the reality principles of racism, the more likely it is that they will be 'totalized' in this way. Logically such constructions should make ethnic minorities feel even more powerless than they actually are. But paradoxically, or rather, paralogically, they have the opposite effect. This is because they are embedded in what I have called a teleology of the oppressed. These metaphors are important rhetoric devices in narratives of empowerment and emancipation, where they are used to 'naturalize' particular victimologies, and even, sometimes, to justify the enterprise of revenge.

The issue is whether making the protean forms of racism seem more omnipotent, cohesive and enduring than they are does after all serve to strengthen and unify the antiracist movement, or whether it reinforces the more sectarian elements within it. On the positive side, I would argue that these devices may make it easier to withstand setbacks, to hold on to a belief in ultimate victory when times are hard, because they all underline the continuities of racial oppression. Indirectly this may also help legitimate an autonomous space of representation for ethnic minorities who have been otherwise silenced or marginalized, a place where they can find their own political voice, in their own mother tongue. But, on the other hand, this perspective produces global strategies which have little purchase on concrete instances, and tend to assume instead the burden of a messianic project in which the enemy is supposedly being smashed, crushed, or stamped out for ever. Pushed to the limit it leads to splitting the world into a racialized opposition between goodies and baddies. And once this kind of polarization is set in motion, it becomes a self-fulfilling prophecy in which everyone who is not with us is against us. If you're white, you're not part of the solution you're part of the problem . . .

It must be the matter of personal judgement, as well as political debate, as to whether the gains outweigh the losses when it comes to sustaining such a manichean, 'black and white' view of the world. In my view, in the longer term, and in the context of the more complicated state of contemporary race relations in Britain, the 'fix' or 'hold' or 'take' which this standpoint offers seems likely to prove disappointing. Even if the catechisms of 'correct thought' are updated and find new roots, and old upbeat endings are set to more popular and contemporary tunes, they will not be able to generate the more intricate models or maps which are required to confront successfully the types of racism which are evidenced by our two transcripts. But what kind of resources or strategies could be committed, both theoretically and practically to this task?

[. . .]

[From ' "It's Racism What Dunnit": Hidden Narratives in Theories of Racism', in James Donald and Ali Rattansi (eds.), 'Race', Culture and Difference (London: Sage, 1992), 63–4, 71–4, 83–6.]

Section VI

Racism and the State

INTRODUCTION

Approaches to racism in terms of individual attitudes and prejudices tend to suggest that collective racism is an aggregate of individual attitudes, a kind of atomistic view of the phenomenon. In this section, the role of the state in the maintenance of racism is briefly examined. The first case, a most extreme one, is the racial policies of the Nazi Reich between 1933 and 1945, which elevated the purification of the Aryan race into a first objective of official policy, and led to the annihilation of the Jews of Nazi-occupied Europe. Michael Burleigh and Wolfgang Wippermann document the progress of Nazi racial policy, which embraced other minority groups such as Roma and Sinti, mental patients, and mentally handicapped persons. A systematic policy of exclusion, arrest, and imprisonment and ultimately their murder was pursued through the agencies of the state. During the invasion of Russia in 1941–2, special military detachments called *Einsatzgruppen* advanced in the wake of the conquering army, charged with seizing and putting to death certain categories of people in the Soviet and Russian populations, particularly Jews. The state and its arms were used to implement a policy of mass destruction more savage than anything since the slave trade. The American historian Stanley Elkins indeed made a famous comparison between the treatment of slaves and conditions in Nazi concentration camps which involved the depersonalization and degradation of the inmates. The institution of slavery, however, was mediated through individual commercial enterprise, whereas the destruction of European Jewry was a matter of deliberate state policy.

Such major historical events have often led scholars to doubt any propositions about the improvement of mankind over time. The most atrocious event of recent times, the murder of six million Jews, occurred within the last sixty years, and as a deliberate act of state policy. There is prima-facie evidence therefore that the state may be a major actor in the creation and maintenance of racism.

In the next selection, Michael Omi and Howard Winant examine the relationship between the state and racial order in the United States. They observe that the major institutions and social relationships of the state in America have been structured by the racial order. From its inception, the US state's main objective was repression and exclusion of racial minorities. At the same time, even under slavery and to a greater extent since, it has been possible for members of repressed or disadvantaged minorities who are the object of racism to create oppositional cultures, and to maintain values more in keeping with the interests of downtrodden minorities. Omi and Winant characterize the relationship between state policy and social movements seeking to change the racial order as a situation of unstable equilibrium. Racial change is the product of the interaction between racially based social movements and the racial state. Such movements may seek change in the racial order in the direction of reform, but they may also include movements with a more conservative agenda such as those of the New Right.

Desmond King, in the piece which follows, suggests that the US federal government, in a whole range of areas, colluded in the maintenance of segregated race relations in the half-century before the Civil Rights Act of 1964. If one asks, for example, why the United States has such a high degree of residential segregation and why public housing (i.e. housing provided by the state for needy families who cannot otherwise find housing) is still predominantly segregated along racial lines, the answer has to be that the system was maintained and supported by the federal government at least until the 1960s. Until that period, public housing projects would not obtain federal approval, for example, unless it was shown that they conformed to local practices and laws in relation to racial segregation.

The South African situation again makes an instructive comparison. The apartheid system was formed and strengthened in the post-1948 period through specific acts of legislation, though custom and practice in the previous half-century meant that it was pushing further a racial order which was already in existence in outline. But the state was the agency by means of which the Afrikaner Nationalists imposed a system of racial separation upon the country, including a legal definition of the four racial groups (white, coloured, Indian, and African) which were the basis of the racial system created. Moreover the later dismantling of apartheid since the late 1980s, although still a comparatively recent event, was itself a matter of state action, initially to soften the sharper features of the system, then to bring about its collapse and replacement by a new system of multi-racial politics led by the African National Congress, the principal opponent of the apartheid regime. The post-1994 South African government, moreover, has used the state to try to implement a multi-racial order in which the different racial groups coexist and collaborate in a society still marked by profound racial divisions, and extremes of income and social provision. It provides a laboratory for the study of the limits of state action in securing social change in the racial order.

Australia, like the United States, is a country with an original indigenous population and a substantial immigrant minority, originally from parts of Europe but in recent times also from Asian countries. Castles and Vasta's analysis seeks answers to the questions of whether Australian society is still racist, and the part played in this by the state. Like the South African case, this is an instructive case study in the scope for state action to reverse policies which were until compara-tively recently based upon racial exclusion (the 'white Australia' policy) and white dominance.

The final selection, by Antonio Guimaraes, considers racism and anti-racism in Brazil, already discussed in relation to differences in the institution of slavery between North and South America. In contrast to the United States or South Africa, Brazil may be seen as having fuzzy boundaries between racial groups, and 'colour' was a substitute for race in a more fluid social order. 'Brazil is an amalgam of Creoles from different ethnic and racial backgrounds whose race and ethnicity were lost to gain Brazilian nationhood. Brazil generously offered a comfortable penumbra to hang over everyone's ancestry. Color remained the only trace of race, or better, became its coded name. Colonial racism, founded upon the idea of the ethnic purity of White settlers or conquerors, gave way after independence to the idea of mixed-blooded, mestizo nations.'

37 The Racial State

Racial Legislation

'Above all, I charge the leadership of the nation, as well as its followers, to a rigorous adherence to our racial laws and to a merciless resistance against the poisoner of all peoples—international Jewry.' This was one of the last sentences Hitler committed to paper. It is from his 'Political Testament', dictated in a bunker beneath the ashes and collapsing masonry of Berlin. Which racial laws did he have in mind, shortly before the end? Certainly, those which were directed against the Jews, described here as 'the poisoner of all peoples'. The first anti-Jewish laws were promulgated in April 1933, in the wake of the unsuccessful boycott action earlier that month. Legislation was designed to fulfil the twofold objective of assuaging rabid grass-roots Party activists, while not alienating either Hindenburg, or the Nazis' conservative coalition partners, by appearing to license disorder. Legislation commenced with the Law for the Restoration of the Professional Civil Service of 7 April 1933, followed by measures against Jewish physicians, teachers, and students, on the 22nd and 25th of the same month. The former sanctioned the dismissal of both the politically undesirable and 'non-Aryans' from the public service; the latter attempted either to remove Jews from, or to restrict their access too, the professions, while encouraging 'Aryans' to dispense with the services of Jews. All of these measures were hastily cobbled together, with a number of concessions to Hindenburg regarding categories of exemption, notably war veterans. The Nazis seem to have been taken by surprise by the number of Jews who could claim exemption on these grounds. Between 1933 and 1939 these measures were then extended to cover the 'dejewification' of other occupational groups.

The next wave of anti-Semitic legislation, in 1935, was designed to achieve legal discrimination, segregation, and precision in the question of who was a Jew. Discrimination began with the Military Service Law of May 1935 which made 'Aryan' ancestry mandatory for service in the armed forces. The Nuremberg Laws, promulgated after hasty consultations during the Party Rally that September, were the product of several circumstances: firstly, Hitler's desire to announce something more substantial to the Party faithful than a law forbidding Jews to hoist the national flag; secondly, the desire of the legal profession and registry officials for greater clarity concerning how to define a Jew. As a commentator in the journal of the League of German Jurists crisply observed:

While logic and consistency have traditionally been a special province of jurists and lawyers, it appears that since the seizure of power these faculties have eluded them. In looking through our racial laws it becomes apparent that we are lacking a certain conceptual clarity in using such terms as 'race', 'racial hygiene', 'eugenics', and others which fall into the same category. They are frequently used with different and contradictory meanings.[1]

Finally, the Party leadership was under pressure from both grass-roots activists and committed anti-Semites like Streicher, or the Reich Physicians Leader, Gerhard Wagner, to regulate marital and sexual relations between 'Aryans' and Jews. Under the ensuing Law for the Protection of German Blood and Honour, Jews were forbidden to marry or have extra-marital sexual relations with 'Aryan' partners. Under the Reich Citizenship Law, Jews were redefined as 'subjects', while 'political rights', which by this time were notional, were restricted to 'citizens of the Reich'. Although the official spokesmen of German Jewry were relieved that years of insecurity and uncertainty were apparently over, the Nuremberg Laws had officially rendered the Jews second-class citizens. These laws were accompanied by intensive discussions upon who was to be considered a Jew. The result was the First Supplementary Decree of the Reich Citizenship Law of 14 November 1935, which specified the criteria for determining who was a full or part Jew. Ironically enough, these criteria were based upon a religious, rather than a scientific, definition of race.

These anti-Semitic laws, and the subsequent decrees on their implementation, continue to preoccupy historians. This interest is warranted, for in addition to shedding light on the *ad hoc* way in which the regime legislated, these measures ultimately created a pseudo-legal basis for later policies, including mass murder. However, while Hitler may have regarded these laws as being the most significant creation of his regime, they were not unique. Anti-Semitic legislation was accompanied by other laws and decrees, whose object was the 'racial-hygienic improvement' of the 'body of the German nation'. Both 'alien' races and 'racially less valuable' members of the German population were excluded from their positive provisions. 'Elements' of 'lesser racial value' in the German population were subject to a series of 'negative' measures, ranging from compulsory abortion, castration, and sterilisation, via commitment to asylums, and on to murder. These racial-hygienic laws and measures were part of a continuum ranging from the progressively more covert measures taken against the Jews to initiatives in social policy and welfare which the regime publicised at every opportunity. The connections were both immanent, and central to the thinking of the politicians and experts in racial hygiene who were responsible for these measures. Consequently, it is impossible to study either anti-Semitic or racial-hygienic measures in isolation; the two were indivisible parts of the whole. Hence the following account of initiatives in 'social policy' is designed to bring out the underlying racial objectives.

One of the earliest, and most popular, initiatives in this field was the Law for the Reduction of Unemployment of 1 June 1933. This introduced marriage loans which couples could then pay off by having children. However, the loans were conditional upon the woman giving up paid employment. This had been the goal of a campaign against so-called 'double-earners' waged by both the Nazis and the Catholic Centre Party during the Weimar Republic. However, the desire to disburden the labour market of married women workers, in the interests of reducing the number of unemployed men, was no longer the primary object of policy-makers. The Law was also designed to force women back into their 'original' role as wives and mothers, in line with Nazi and conservative thinking about the 'natural' role of women. However, the Law also had a racial objective. According to the first decree on its implementation of 20 June 1933, loans could be refused 'if one of the prospective marriage partners is suffering from a hereditary or mental or physical illness which renders their marriage undesirable to the whole national community.' A second supplementary decree, issued a month later, stipulated that all applicants for a marriage loan would have to undergo medical examination. This opened a way for the racial registering of the population. Further philogenerative welfare measures, such as travel concessions and tax benefits for large families introduced in October 1934 and September 1935, were explicitly denied to persons deemed to be of 'lesser racial value'. A general decree dated 26 September 1935 stipulated that only 'citizens of the Reich according to the Reich Citizenship Law of 15 September 1935 and their children, in so far as they are free from hereditary mental or physical illnesses' should be allowed to take advantage of these welfare measures. From this time onwards, social policy was indivisible from the 'selection' of 'alien' races and those of 'lesser racial value'.

Initially, members of 'alien' races were 'only' subject to discrimination, loss of civic rights, and progressive economic ruination. By contrast, those sick and socially disadvantaged persons who were classified as being of 'lesser racial value' immediately suffered physical and psychological terror. The legal basis for this was supplied by the Law for the Prevention of Hereditarily Diseased Progeny of 14 July 1933, which came into force on 1 January 1934. This permitted the compulsory sterilisation of persons suffering from a series of allegedly hereditary illnesses as well as chronic alcoholics. Applications for sterilisation could be made by the persons themselves, but also by their legal guardians, physicians, and asylum or public health authorities. The decision to sterilise a person was taken by the newly-established Hereditary Health Courts, whose verdicts could only be challenged in a Higher Hereditary Health Court. If the appeal failed, then the sterilisation operation was carried out, regardless of the wishes of the person concerned or of those who raised objections on their behalf. In reality, persons were sterilised who were neither ill nor 'hereditarily ill', in the senses specified by the law. Their 'illness' consisted in being classified as 'asocial' or 'community aliens'. The law contained no provision for this last practice. Plans to include the 'asocial' within its provisions had been explicitly shelved, because of the imminence of separate legislation concerning these categories of person. The drafting of a law on the 'asocial' was under way when the law on compulsory sterilisation was promulgated.

The Law against Dangerous Habitual Criminals, which was promulgated on 24 November 1933, was a first step in this direction. This permitted the detention and compulsory castration of certain types of criminal as defined by 'racial-biological' investigation. Similar measures were then incorporated into the Law on the Punishment of Juvenile Offenders of 22 January 1937. A 'racial-biological' examination determined the duration and conditions of the sentence, a practice which was then applied to adult offenders too. To this end, a number of 'criminal-biological research centres' were established in various cities. Along with the illegal misapplication of compulsory sterilisation, measures like these were to be incorporated into the projected law on the 'asocial'. However, like its analogue—a law on 'Gypsies'—no comprehensive law on the 'asocial' was ever promulgated. This was due not to the collapse of the Third Reich, but rather, as was the case with the Jews, to the fact that the regime preferred to solve the 'question' without resorting to formal legislation or decrees.

The transition from the pseudo-legal to the totally illegal persecution of both 'alien' races and those of 'lesser racial value' occurred from approximately 1935 onwards. In that year the regime introduced two important racial-hygienic laws. The Law for the Alteration of the Law for the Prevention of Hereditarily Diseased Progeny of 26 June 1935 sanctioned compulsory abortion, up to and including the sixth month of pregnancy, for women who had been categorised as 'hereditarily ill' by the health courts. This law represented a qualitative radicalisation of existing racial-hygienic measures. The Law for the Protection of the Hereditary Health of the German People, issued on 18 October 1935, was designed to register, and hence more effectively exclude, 'alien' races and the 'racially less valuable' from the 'national community'. The law made possession of a 'certificate of fitness to marry' mandatory for all prospective marriage partners. The certificate was issued by public health authorities. They could refuse a certificate to those who were allegedly suffering from either 'hereditary illness' or contagious diseases, notably those which were sexually transmitted. This practice gradually made it possible to register and hence 'select' the whole German population. It also enabled health and registry offices to encompass statistically members of 'alien' races not covered by the Nuremberg Laws. Therefore this so-called Marriage Health Law represented an important link between the racial-anthropological and racial-hygienic measures of the regime. This connection requires some elaboration.

The first supplementary decree on the Law for the Protection of German Blood and Honour of 14 November 1935 stipulated that not only Jews were forbidden to marry or have sexual relations with 'persons of German blood'. More generally, marriages could not be contracted if 'offspring likely to be prejudicial to the purity of German blood' were anticipated. A circular issued by the Reich and Prussian Minister of the Interior on 26 November 1935 on the implementation of the law specified which marriages the regime had in mind, namely those between persons of German or related blood, and 'Gypsies, negroes or their bastards'. This point was taken up by Stuckart and Globke in their official commentary on the Nuremberg Laws.[2] According to them, 'in Europe', 'Gypsies, negroes, or their bastards' were normally counted alongside Jews as 'carriers of non-German or related blood'.

In the following period, further social legislation was promulgated, all of which contained racial-anthropological and racial-hygienic provisions, i.e., the exclusion of both 'alien' races and of 'lesser racial value' in the German population. These measures included decrees on child benefits, the Income Tax Law of 27 February 1939, and the decrees 'for the protection of marriage, the family, and motherhood' issued in 1942 and 1943 which increased maternity benefits. By contrast, no further racial legislation was promulgated. There were various reasons for this. Firstly, existing decrees and legislation were formulated so elastically that they could simply be applied to further groups of people without having to introduce new laws. Secondly, the Nazis did not regard it as either necessary or opportune to advertise their persecution of 'alien' races or the 'racially less valuable' through formal legislation. Finally, to legislate would have involved introducing order into the struggle over competences taking place between the rival agencies involved in racial policy, an issue which will occupy us below.

Racial Research

From the beginning, many academics and scientists were involved in the formulation and implementation of Nazi racial policy. Racial anthropologists, biologists and hygienicists, economists, geographers, historians, and sociologists created the conceptual framework and scientific legitimisation for the implementation of Nazi racial policy. Having imposed a logical structure on various forms of hatred and irrationality, the same academics and scientists voluntarily and enthusiastically put their skills at the service of the regime. For many disciplines, the advent of the Nazi regime was coterminous with the onset of 'boom' conditions. No one asked or compelled these academics and scientists actively to work on the regime's behalf. Most of them could have said no. In fact, the files of the regime's many agencies bulge with their unsolicited recommendations. They, and the card indexes, charts, diagrams, maps, books, articles, and statistics which they produced, were partly responsible for the clinically comprehensive and devastatingly effective manner in which Nazi racial policies were carried out. The application of skill and technical expertise extended from such details as the design of the electrified fencing and watchtowers at Auschwitz to the employment of modern data-gathering and demoscopic techniques to encompass and control the whole population, thus facilitating the 'eradication' of the 'alien' and 'less valuable'. Unlike many of the mindless sadists who worked in concentration camps, most of these 'desk-bound criminals' simply passed back into academic, professional, and public life after 1945, unless their profile was so high as to make Allied retribution unavoidable. [. . .]

Agencies, Institutions, and Racial Policy

From the beginning of the Nazi regime, a number of State and Party agencies and institutions were keen to concretise and implement a racial political programme which Hitler had merely outlined. This resulted in conflicts over areas of competence. Although Hitler reserved all fundamental decisions for himself, he rarely intervened in the details of policy-making, and then only when planning had reached an advanced stage. It was therefore important that the plans of a host of interested agencies be co-ordinated at an early stage. [. . .]

Ad hoc groups were formed for particular aspects of Nazi racial policy; in the last case, for the systematic mass murder of the mentally and physically handicapped. Intra-bureaucratic chaos served further to brutalise and radicalise Nazi racial policy. In every area of Nazi racial policy, State institutions—ranging from the ministerial to the communal level—frequently worked against, rather than alongside, a parallel hierarchy of Party agencies, whose relative influence waxed (Ley's German Labour Front or Himmler's SS-Police complex) or waned (the Racial Political Office of the NSDAP or the complex of agencies under Rosenberg). As the evolution of policy towards the Jews makes abundantly clear, this intra-bureaucratic chaos invariably radicalised, rather than tempered, the effects of the policies adopted.

However, in the course of time one man, Heinrich Himmler, seemed to gain power and influence in all areas of racial policy. He eventually succeeded in either gaining control of or co-ordinating virtually every institution involved in both racial policy and organised terror. In the beginning, Himmler was a relatively uninfluential Nazi functionary. From 1929 he commanded the SS, which by January 1933 consisted of some 52,000 men. It was technically subordinate to the SA leader Röhm. Himmler came away empty-handed from the earliest division of the political spoils. He received his first State appointment in March 1933, when he became Commissary President of the Munich police. However, by the close of 1933 he controlled not only the Bavarian political police but those of every German state, with the significant exception of Prussia. There, Göring had transformed Department 1a of the Berlin Police Praesidium, under Rudolf Diels, into a separate state agency, although one still subordinate to Frick's Ministry of the Interior. The new agency was called the Secret State Police, or Gestapo. In the autumn of 1933 this agency was directly subordinated to Göring. One by-product of Göring's rivalry with Frick was Diels' replacement by Himmler, on 20 April 1934, as Inspector of the Gestapo. Within a few months, Himmler had succeeded in shaking off Göring's tutelage and in merging the Gestapo with the political police in the other states of Germany. Disposing of a ramified local and regional apparatus, Himmler embarked upon the struggle against the regime's political opponents.

The same function was performed by the Security Service of the SS, the SD. The SD was established in 1931 as an internal Party intelligence service. Like the

Gestapo, the SD disposed of local and regional departments, the so-called Upper and Lower Sectors, but in contrast to the Gestapo it remained an organisation of the Party. It was commanded by Reinhard Heydrich, who also exercised executive authority over the Gestapo on Himmler's behalf. Both the SD and the Gestapo performed similar functions, namely the combating of political opposition to the regime. Since this resulted in an unnecessary duplication of activities, from 1934–5 the two organisations were allocated separate, though related, spheres of activity. This partially reflected the different backgrounds of the members of both services. While the Gestapo consisted of men who were professional policemen, the SD contained a large number of graduates and technocrats, for example Reinhard Hohn, Otto Ohlendorf, and Walter Schellenberg, whose ideological commitment and keenness to instrumentalise their learning compensated for their amateurishness as policemen. The Gestapo retained responsibility for executive actions against political opponents. Their methods ranged from interrogation to consigning persons to concentration camps. Neither practice was based upon judicial decisions or subject to judicial review. By contrast, the SD became primarily responsible for intelligence concerning the regime's ideological opponents. The latter included proscribed organisations of the labour movement, both churches, freemasons, and Jews. The SD's surveillance activity gradually assumed routine forms, resulting in the schematised 'Reports from the Reich', which were circulated to a restricted group of State and Party leaders. Reflecting the instrumentalisation of certain trends in sociology, these demoscopic reports—which were extrapolated from the reports of spies and informers—were a seismograph of changing public moods, and hence a means whereby decision-makers could take note of public opinion in a climate which denied it all formal expression.

Following the murder of Röhm and other SA leaders on 30 June 1934, the SS was removed from the aegis of the SA, becoming an independent agency of the NSDAP, directly subordinate to Hitler. The SS consisted of the so-called 'general SS', in other words part-timers, who combined a regular job with evening and weekend voluntary service in the organisation. By contrast, members of the SD and of the SS militarised formations (*Verfügungstruppe*) were fully paid employees of the Reichsführer-SS. Initially, the militarised units consisted of Hitler's SS bodyguards, who from 9 March 1933 were organised as the Adolf Hitler Bodyguard (Leibstandarte Adolf Hitler). Further armed units were formed in the following years. From 1938 these enjoyed a separate constitutional identity, and they took part in the Second World War as separate military formations. From 1940 onwards these military units were called the Waffen-SS. A further group permanently on the SS payroll after 30 June 1934 were the guards of concentration camps. From 1936 onwards these units were called the Death's Head Formation. In 1939 the Totenkopf Division became the nucleus of the field units of the Waffen-SS. The Death's Head Formations were commanded by Theodor Eicke, who on 1 July 1934 became Inspector of

Concentration Camps. Their training was designed to destroy any feelings of humanity they might have had towards their prisoners. It was obviously highly effective.

Existing official and 'wild' concentration camps were reorganised in line with the model pioneered by Eicke at Dachau. His regime included a graduated system of punishments, up to and including execution by firing squad, and the use of prisoners as forced labour. In order to maximise their labour potential the SS established stone quarries and brickworks in the immediate vicinity of concentration camps. A company was established, the German Excavation and Quarrying Company Ltd., to control production, distribution, and profits. The company's workforce consisted of persons who had been arrested by the Gestapo and sent to concentration camps. Initially these were mainly political prisoners, i.e. Communists and Social Democrats, but from 1934 they included ever-larger numbers of the 'asocial' who had been abducted from the streets, shelters, and doss-houses. This practice became the rule following Himmler's appointment as Chief of the German Police on 17 June 1936. Henceforth, not only the Gestapo could detain people in 'protective custody', but also the regular and criminal police, who could now keep the 'asocial' in 'police preventive custody'. This practice was retrospectively legalised on 14 December 1937 when Himmler issued a 'decree for the preventive fight against crime'.

In the ensuing period, the State police—i.e. the Gestapo, criminal, and regular police forces—drew ever closer to the various formations of the SS. On 27 September 1939 Himmler fused their upper echelons into one Reich Main Security Office. This was in turn sub-divided into a series of main offices, including the Gestapo and the domestic and foreign intelligence services of the SD. Apart from Heydrich's RSHA complex, other important SS departments were the Economic and Administrative Department under Oswald Pohl, which encompassed concentration camps, brickworks, mineral water marketing, military supplies, and of course the 560,000 soldiers who in 1944 comprised the Waffen-SS.

Acknowledging the hegemonial aspirations of the SS-Police complex in the field of racial policy, Göring commissioned Heydrich on 31 July 1941 with the preparation of 'an overall plan covering the organisational, technical, and material measures necessary for the accomplishment of the final solution of the Jewish question which we desire'. Representatives of the SS and various ministries then gathered to discuss Heydrich's proposals at a conference in the Berlin suburb of Wannsee on 20 January 1942. The representatives of the ministries agreed with Heydrich's overall suggestions, although the precise course and tone of the ninety-minute discussion were not reflected in the resulting minutes, notwithstanding a recent attempt to 'reconstruct' the discussion on film. Although the meeting was not the starting point of the Final Solution, it was the moment at which the SS gained formal control of the measures they had already embarked upon. This was probably one of the principal objects of the conference, and hence why secure telephone lines were installed in the villa to relay the successful outcome to the Reichsführer-SS.

The same SS ascendancy can be seen at work in other areas of Nazi racial policy. Persecution of the Sinti and Roma became the province of the Criminal Police. Special departments for 'Gypsy questions' were established in every local and regional Criminal Police Office. Building upon existing police records on 'Gypsies', the Criminal Police played a key role in the registering, 'criminal-biological investigation', arrest, and deportation of Germany's Sinti and Roma. Their activities were co-ordinated by a Reich Central Office for the Combating of the Gypsy Nuisance, which in turn drew upon the expertise of the Criminal-Biological Institute of the Security Police under Robert Ritter. The Reich Criminal Police Office was also host to a Reich Central Office for the Combating of Homosexuality and Abortion, whose object was to persecute those members of the 'national community' who failed in their duty to increase and improve the 'stock' of the German 'race'. Two further agencies, directly subordinate to Himmler, were 'Ancestral Heritage' ('Ahnenerbe') and the 'Well of Life' ('Lebensborn'). The former, founded in 1935, provided a pseudo-scholarly forum for the substantiation of Himmler's aberrant, ahistorical, holistic cultural-political vision, while satisfying the SD's more pragmatic desire to extend its control into the nation's intellectual life. In addition to archaeological digs and research on early German history, 'Ancestral Heritage' also sponsored expeditions to Tibet, homeopathic cures, and attempts to scientifically validate 'world ice teaching' or the belief that the 'Aryans' had arrived fully-formed from 'heaven', being preserved in 'eternal ice' before stalking the earth armed with superhuman 'electrical powers'. During the war, scientists working under the aegis of the 'Ahnenerbe's' Institute for Applied Military Research carried out lethal research on concentration camp inmates to evaluate human tolerance of high altitudes and prolonged immersion in freezing temperatures. [. . .]

Did the Third Reich pursue modern rather than profoundly reactionary policies? This question is among the most important posed by recent research. If the Third Reich was a modern and modernising regime, then it can hardly be said to have been the culmination of a German separate road of historical development, but rather is to be compared to other modern regimes, whether Communist, Fascist, or democratic. Questions concerning whether Hitler or other agencies and individuals were responsible for particular policies pale into insignificance beside the implications of this thesis. If the modernising theory is correct, then not only do the crimes of Nazi Germany cease to be singular, but they become comparable with the crimes of other regimes, or indeed part of the 'pathology' of advanced societies in general. Just as the highly dubious Milgram psychological tests apparently 'prove' that we are all capable of torture, so the modernisation theorists would like us to believe that all our societies are latently like Nazi Germany. Of course this is not so. Vacuous notions like 'body fascism' and the indiscriminately inflationary use of the term 'fascist' to describe anyone who happens to disagree with a particular point of view compound this (discomforting) delusion.

Although in our opinion the question of the modern or anti-modern character of the Nazi regime is of central importance, it has received relatively little attention in the existing secondary literature, firstly because there has been no comprehensive treatment of Nazi racial and social policy, and secondly because the inner relationships between the different areas of policy have been neglected. Finally, it is often overlooked that social policy was designed to achieve a global remodelling of society in accordance with racial criteria.

The essential elements of the resulting barbaric utopia had been considered long before Hitler achieved political power. Racial ideologies were not solely concerned with a return to some imagined past social order. They also reflected the desire to create a future society based upon the alleged verities of race. Hitler took over existing ideas and converted them into a comprehensive programme for a racial new order. Without doubt, racial anti-Semitism was the key element in a programme designed to achieve the 'recovery' of the 'Aryan Germanic race'. Various racial-hygienic measures were designed to achieve this goal. These ranged from compulsory sterilisation to murdering the sick, the 'asocial', and those designated as being of 'alien race'. The extermination of the Jews was crucial to these policies. In Hitler's mind they were not only 'racial aliens', but also a threat to his plans for the 'racial recovery' of the German people. They were both a 'lesser race' and one bent upon destroying the 'racial properties' of Hitler's 'Aryans'.

Under the Third Reich, this racial-ideological programme became the official dogma and policy of the State. Racism replaced the Weimar Republic's imperfect experiment in political pluralism. Along with the political parties and trade unions, the Nazis also endeavoured to destroy the existing social structure. Although there were undoubtedly social classes in Nazi Germany, it was a society organised increasingly upon racial rather than class lines. The regime's racial policies struck at people whether they were rich or poor, bourgeois, peasants, or workers.

This racial new order was based upon the 'purification of the body of the nation' of all those categorised as being 'alien', 'hereditarily ill', or 'asocial'. That meant Jews, Sinti and Roma, the mentally and physically handicapped, 'community aliens', and homosexuals. Obviously there were major quantitative and qualitative differences in the degree of persecution to which these groups were subjected. Jews, as the racial group whom the Nazis regarded as the greatest threat, undoubtedly constituted the largest single group of victims and were persecuted in the most intensive and brutal manner. Persecution undoubtedly had different specificities. This should not result in attempts either to relativise or to overlook the sufferings of others. Let alone a ghoulish and profoundly inhuman competition to claim the right to having been most persecuted. All of these people were persecuted for the same reasons, although the degree of persecution was bound up with how threatening the regime perceived them to be.

The regime's 'national community' was based upon the exclusion and extermination of all those deemed to be 'alien', 'hereditarily ill', or 'asocial'. These 'elements' were subject to constant and escalating forms of selection. The 'national community' itself was categorised in accordance with racial criteria. The criteria included not merely 'racial purity' but also biological health and socio-economic performance. Members of the 'national community' were also compelled to reproduce through a series of measures ranging from financial inducements to criminal sanctions. The inducements contained in the regime's social legislation were also conditional upon an individual's racial 'value', health, and performance.

For biological reasons, women were particularly affected by the regime's attempts at racial selective breeding. Women's worth was assessed in terms of their ability to produce as many Aryan, healthy, and capable children as possible. Women were therefore reduced to the status of mere 'reproductive machines'. Racially-motivated anti-feminism represented a significant departure from traditional Christian-Conservative anti-feminism. The Nazis' hierarchically organised, racist society, with healthy, 'Aryan' German man at the apex, began to rival the existing social order. However, it failed to supersede it for a variety of reasons. The first is that changes on this scale required longer than twelve years to be realised, a fact which makes any generalisations concerning the impact of the regime on German society difficult. Secondly, there were disagreements within the ruling cartel about the forms, radicalism, and tempo with which a consensually approved racial programme should be implemented. Finally, political and military considerations forced the regime to establish priorities and to postpone some of its plans until the post-war period. In other words, social policy was heavily influenced by military, economic, and domestic-political considerations, not least by the desire to integrate and pacify the population in a wartime crisis.

The main object of social policy remained the creation of a hierarchical racial new order. Everything else was subordinate to this goal, including the regime's conduct of foreign affairs and the war. In the eyes of the regime's racial politicians, the Second World War was above all a racial war, to be pursued with immense brutality until the end, that is until the concentration camps were liberated by invading Allied armies. All of these points draw attention to the specific and singular character of the Third Reich. It was not a form of regression to past times, although the regime frequently instrumentalised various ahistorical myths to convey the idea of historical normalcy. Its object were novel and *sui generis* to realise an ideal future world, without 'lesser races', without the sick, and without those who they decreed had no place in the 'national community'. The Third Reich was intended to be a racial rather than a class society. This fact in itself makes existing theories, whether based upon modernisation, totalitarianism, or global theories of Fascism, poor heuristic devices for a greater understanding of what was a singular regime without precedent or parallel.

[From *The Racial State: Germany, 1933—1945* (Cambridge: Cambridge University Press, 1991), 44–6, 48–52, 57–60, 62–5, 304–7.]

MICHAEL OMI AND HOWARD WINANT

38   Racial Formation in the United States

Introduction: The Trajectory of Racial Politics

Two recent incidents reveal some of the ironies and incongruities of contemporary racial politics:

- In 1989, the Republican National Committee established a tax-exempt foundation called Fairness for the 90s. The group's mission was to provide money and technical assistance to black and Latino organizations seeking to create minority-dominated legislative and congressional districts. In anticipation of the legislative redistricting that would follow the 1990 census, the Republicans offered black and Latino leaders and organizers the prospect of creating 'safe seats' for minority legislators. The Republicans went so far as to ally themselves with black and Latino plaintiffs in redistricting suits brought under the Voting Rights Act. What accounted for the strange bedfellows of redistricting politics? The answer was simple: Republicans sought to segregate racial minority voters into separate districts, to divide white from nonwhite Democrats, and so to increase their opportunities to win legislative seats in adjoining white districts.
- In the late 1980s, Asian American academic leaders, civil rights organizations, and university students began to suspect that informal quotas for Asian American admissions had been put in place in the leading U.S. universities in violation of civil rights laws. As they mobilized to confront this situation and initiated negotiations with university administrators on various campuses, they suddenly received support from an unsolicited, and unexpected, quarter. In November, 1988, Ronald Reagan's neoconservative Deputy Attorney General for Civil Rights, William Bradford Reynolds, not only agreed that such quotas had been established, but blamed these restrictive practices on the existence of affirmative action admissions policies. 'The phenomenon of a "ceiling" on Asian American admissions is the inevitable result of the "floor" that has been built for a variety of other favored racial groups,' Reynolds said. Asian Americans were alarmed that the issue of 'quotas' would be used as part of a broader attack on preferential policies for under-represented minorities.

As these examples illustrate, advocacy groups and movement organizations which seek to represent racially defined minority interests, mobilize minority group members politically, and articulate minority viewpoints, are frequently faced with bitterly ironic political choices. No sooner did egalitarian and antidiscrimination policies emerge from the political tempests of the 1960s than they began to 'decay.' From the early 1970s of Richard Nixon to the early 1990s of Bill Clinton, the state has sought to absorb, to marginalize, and to transform (or 'rearticulate') the meaning of the reforms won in the earlier decade.

How have these transformations occurred? What are the dynamics of the relationships between the state and racial minorities? Why does a pattern of alternating activism and quiescence characterize both state racial activities and movement ebbs and flows? In this chapter we consider these questions in an effort to understand the *trajectory* which contemporary racial politics—and thus racial formation processes—follow in the contemporary U.S.

By 'trajectory' we mean the pattern of conflict and accommodation which takes shape over time between racially based social movements and the policies and programs of the state. We consider the central elements of this trajectory to be the state and social movements, linked in a single historical framework of racial formation.

Social movements and the state are interrelated in a complex way. Racial movements arise, and race becomes a political issue, when state institutions are thought to structure and enforce a racially unjust social order. State institutions acquire their racial orientations from the processes of conflict with and accommodation to racially based movements. Thus 'reform,' 'reaction,' 'radical change,' or 'backlash'–indeed every transformation of the racial order–is constructed through a process of clash and compromise between racial movements and the state.

These are the dynamics of present-day racial politics in the U.S. Yet there is nothing permanent or sacred about this pattern. Indeed, the existence of political channels for the expression of racial conflict is a relatively recent phenomenon. The broad sweep of U.S. history is characterized not by racial democracy, but by racial despotism, not by trajectories of reform, but by implacable denial of political rights, dehumanization, extreme exploitation, and policies of minority extirpation. Democracy has never been in abundant supply where race is concerned. The very emergence of political channels through which reform can at times be achieved is an immense political victory for minorities, and for democracy itself.

In order to understand the interaction of today's racial state and minority movements, we must examine the origins of racial politics in the U.S. In the next two sections of this chapter, we survey the historical context from which modern racial politics emerged, and the role of the state in the process of racial formation. We then proceed to a theoretical sketch of the contemporary political dynamics of race.

Historical Change in the U.S. Racial Order

Since the earliest days of colonialism in North America, an identifiable racial order has linked the system of political rule to the racial classification of individuals and groups. The major institutions and social relationships of U.S. society–law, political organization, economic relationships, religion, cultural life, residential patterns, etc.–have been structured from the beginning by the racial order.

Clearly the system of racial subjection has been more monolithic, more absolute, at some historical periods than others. Where political opposition was banned or useless, as it was for slaves in the South and for Native Americans during much of the course of U.S. history, transformation of the racial order, or resistance to it, was perforce military (or perhaps took such economic forms as sabotage). An oppositional racial ideology requires some political space, a certain minimal conceptual flexibility about race, upon which to fasten in order to recast racial meanings and constitute alternative racial institutions. During much of U.S. history, this political and ideological space was extremely limited.

But even at its most oppressive, the racial order was unable to arrogate to itself the entire capacity for the production of racial meanings, of racial subjects. Racial minorities were always able to counterpose their own cultural traditions, their own forms of organization and identity, to the dehumanizing and enforced 'invisibility' imposed by the majority society.

As the voluminous literature on black culture under slavery shows, black slaves developed cultures of resistance based on music, religion, African traditions, and family ties through which they sustained their own ideological project: the development of a 'free' black identity and a collectivity dedicated to emancipation. The examples of Geronimo, Sitting Bull, and other Native American leaders were passed down from generation to generation as examples of resistance, and the Ghost Dance and Native American Church were employed by particular generations of Indians to maintain a resistance culture. Rodolfo Acuña has pointed out how the same 'bandits' against whom Anglo vigilantes mounted expeditions after the Treaty of Guadalupe-Hidalgo–Tibúrcio Vasquez, Joaquín Murieta—became heroes in the Mexicano communities of the Southwest, remembered in folktales and celebrated in *corridos*.[1] We do not offer these examples to romanticize brutal repression or to give the air of revolutionary struggle to what were often grim defeats; we simply seek to affirm that even in the most uncontested periods of American racism, oppositional cultures were able, often at very great cost, to maintain themselves.

Without reviewing the vast history of racial conflict, it is still possible to make some general comments about the manner in which the racial order was historically consolidated. Gramsci's distinction between 'war of maneuver' and 'war of position' will prove useful here.

For much of American history, no political legitimacy was conceded to alternative or oppositional racial ideologies, to competing racially defined political projects. The absence of democratic rights, of property, of political and ideological terrain upon which to challenge the monolithic character of the racial order, forced racially defined opposition both *outward*, to the margins of society, and *inward*, to the relative safety of homogeneous minority communities.

Slaves who escaped, forming communities in woods and swamps; Indians who made war on the U.S. in defense of their peoples and lands; Chinese and Filipinos who drew together in Chinatowns and Manilatowns in order to gain some measure of collective control over their existence—these are some examples of the movement of racial opposition *outward*, away from political engagement with the hegemonic racial state.

These same slaves, Indians, and Asians, as well as many others, banned from the political system and relegated to what was supposed to be a permanently inferior sociocultural status, were forced *inward* upon themselves as individuals, families, and communities. Tremendous cultural resources were nurtured among such communities; enormous labors were required to survive and to develop elements of an autonomy and opposition under such conditions. These circumstances can best be understood as combining with the violent clashes and the necessity of resistance (to white-led race riots, military assaults, etc.) which characterized these periods, to constitute a racial *war of maneuver*.

However democratic the U.S. may have been in other respects (and it is clear that democracy has always been in relatively short supply), in its treatment of racial minorities it has been to varying degrees *despotic* for much of its history. 'War of maneuver' describes a situation in which subordinate groups seek to preserve and extend a definite territory, to ward off violent assault, and to develop an internal society as an alternative to the repressive social system they confront.

More recent history suggests that war of maneuver is being replaced by *war of position* as racially defined minorities achieve political gains. A strategy of *war of position* can only be predicated on political struggle—on the existence of diverse institutional and cultural terrains upon which oppositional political projects can be mounted, and upon which the racial state can be confronted. Prepared in large measure by the practices undertaken under conditions of war of maneuver, minorities were able to make sustained strategic incursions into the mainstream political process beginning with World War II. 'Opening up' the state was a process of democratization which had effects both on state structures and on racial meanings. The postwar black movement, later joined by other racially based minority movements, sought to transform dominant racial ideology in the U.S., to locate its elements in a more egalitarian and democratic framework, and thereby to reconstruct the social meaning of race. The state was the logical target for this effort.

Historical Development of the Racial State

The state from its very inception has been concerned with the politics of race. For most of U.S. history, the state's main objective in its racial policy was repression and exclusion. Congress' first attempt to define American citizenship, the Naturalization Law of 1790, declared that only free 'white' immigrants could qualify. The extension of eligibility to all racial groups has been slow indeed. Japanese, for example, could become naturalized citizens only after the passage of the McCarran-Walter Act of 1952.

Historically, a variety of previously racially undefined groups have required categorization to situate them within the prevailing racial order. Throughout the 19th century, many state and federal legal arrangements recognized only three racial categories: 'white,' 'Negro,' and 'Indian.' In California, the influx of Chinese and the debates surrounding the legal status of Mexicans provoked a brief juridical crisis of racial definition. California attempted to resolve this dilemma by assigning Mexicans and Chinese to categories within the already existing framework of 'legally defined' racial groups. In the wake of the Treaty of Guadalupe Hidalgo (1848), Mexicans were defined as a 'white' population and accorded the political-legal status of 'free white persons.' By contrast, the California Supreme Court ruled in *People v. Hall* (1854) that Chinese should be considered 'Indian' [!] and denied the political rights accorded to whites.

The state's shifting racial perspective is also revealed by the census. Latinos surfaced as an ethnic category, 'Persons of Spanish Mother Tongue,' in 1950 and 1960. In 1970 they appeared as 'Persons of Both Spanish Surname and Spanish Mother Tongue,' and in 1980 the 'Hispanic' category was created. Such changes suggest the state's inability to 'racialize' a particular group—to institutionalize it in a politically organized racial system. They also reflect the struggles through which racial minorities press their demands for recognition and equality, and dramatize the state's uncertain efforts to manage and manipulate those demands.

The state is the focus of collective demands both for egalitarian and democratic reforms and for the enforcement of existing privileges. The state 'intervenes' in racial conflicts, but it does not do so in a coherent or unified manner. Distinct state institutions often act in a contradictory fashion.

Does the state, however clumsily, actually capture, steer, or organize the realities of racial identity and racial conflict? There is some validity to the idea of a racially 'interventionist' state. With this theoretical concept, it is possible to investigate certain racial dimensions of state policy. The 1960s civil rights reforms, for example, can be interpreted as federal intervention in the area of racial discrimination.

Yet this approach does not reveal how the state itself is racially structured; it depicts the state as intervening, but not *intervened*, structuring, but not *structured*. Such a state is not basically shaped by race since it intervenes in race relations from *outside* them. The treatment afforded to racial politics is thus confined to 'normal' political arenas.

In contrast to this, we suggest that the state *is* inherently racial. Far from *intervening* in racial conflicts, the state is itself increasingly the pre-eminent site of racial conflict. In the following sections of this chapter, we examine this expanding involvement of the state in the racial formation process. We first present a model of the racial state, and then consider contemporary patterns of change in the racial order, focusing on the interaction between state and social movements.

A Model of the Racial State

The state is composed of *institutions*, the *policies* they carry out, the *conditions and rules* which support and justify them, and the *social relations* in which they are imbedded.

Every state *institution* is a racial institution, but not every institution operates in the same way. In fact, the various state institutions do not serve one coordinated racial objective; they may work at cross-purposes. Therefore, race must be understood as occupying varying degrees of centrality in different state institutions and at different historical moments.

To illustrate this point, let us contrast two agencies of the federal state, the Department of Housing and Urban Development (HUD) and the National Science Foundation (NSF). HUD must deal directly with questions of residential segregation, urban development pressures, housing subsidization programs, and the like; it is staffed by numerous minority-group members, and is subject to constant pressures from lobbies, community groups, and local and state governments (many of which address racial issues or are organized along racial lines). Thus it can be expected to be more racially oriented than the National Science Foundation, where staffing along professional/academic lines, a technical mandate, and a politically more limited range of constituents limit the racial agenda. Nevertheless, in certain areas (e.g., hiring policies, funding priorities, positions taken in respect to racially oriented scientific disputes—does Shockley get a grant?) the NSF too is a racial institution.

Through *policies* which are explicitly or implicitly racial, state institutions organize and enforce the racial politics of everyday life. For example, they enforce racial (non)discrimination policies, which they administer, arbitrate, and encode in law. They organize racial identities by means of education, family law, and the procedures for punishment, treatment, and surveillance of the criminal, deviant and ill.

State institutions and their policies take shape under a series of *conditions and rules*. These 'rules of the game' integrate the disparate racial policies of different state agencies, define the scope of state activity, establish 'normal' procedures for influencing policy, and set the limits of political legitimacy in general. To speak, for example, of an agency's 'mandate,' of a policy's 'constituency,' or of an epochal political 'project' (the 'Keynesian welfare state,' the 'conservative opportunity society') is to accept a set of political rules about who is a political actor, what is a political interest, and how the broad state/society relationship is to be organized.

The specific *social relations* through which state activity is structured constitute the materiality of politics. Examples include the complex linkages of agencies and constituencies, the dynamics of coalitions and governing or oppositional blocs, and the varieties of administrative control exercised by state agencies throughout civil society. Racial politics are not exceptional in this respect. For example, civil rights organizations, lobbying groups, and 'social programs' with significant constituency bases, legal mandates, etc., may engage the state in the 'normal' politics of interest-group liberalism, adopt movement tactics of direct action and confrontation 'from without,' or—as is most likely— combine these tactics.

The state is also imbedded in another kind of social relations: the cultural and technical norms which characterize society overall. These affect the organizational capacities of state agencies, their coordination, both with 'external' social actors and with each other, and the practices of their own personnel. In racial terms, these relationships are structured by 'difference' in certain ways: for example, minority officials may establish caucuses or maintain informal networks with which to combat the isolation frequently encountered in bureaucratic settings.

Despite all the forces working at cross-purposes within the state—disparate demands of constituents, distinct agency mandates and prerogatives, unintended and cross-cutting consequences of policy, etc.—the state still preserves an overall unity. This is maintained in two ways: first, strategic unity is sought at the apex of the apparatus by key policy makers, and in legislative and judicial agencies by established decision rules. Second, unity is imposed on the state by its thorough interpenetration with society. In advanced capitalist societies *hegemony* is secured by a complex system of compromises, legitimating ideologies (e.g., 'the rule of law'(, by adherence to established political rules and bureaucratic regularities, etc. Under all but the most severe conditions (economic collapse, war), this severely limits the range and legitimacy of both dominant and oppositional political initiatives, no matter how heavy the conflicts among contemporary U.S. political institutions and their constituents may appear to be.

The Trajectory of Racial Politics

It is useful to think of the U.S. racial order as an 'unstable equilibrium.' The idea of politics as 'the continuous process of formation and superseding of unstable equilibria' has particular resonance, we think, in describing the operation of the racial state.[2] The racial order is equilibrated by the state—encoded in law, organized through policy-making, and enforced by a repressive apparatus. But the equilibrium thus achieved is unstable, for the great variety of conflicting interests encapsulated in racial meanings and identities can be no more than pacified—at best—by the state. Racial conflict persists at every level of society, varying over time and in respect to different groups, but ubiquitous. Indeed, the state is itself penetrated and structured by the very interests whose conflicts it seeks to stabilize and control.

This unstable equilibrium has at times in U.S. history gone undisturbed for decades and even centuries, but in our epoch its degree of 'stability' has lessened.

Under 'normal' conditions, state institutions have effectively routinized the enforcement and organization of the prevailing racial order. Constituency relationships and established political organizations are at least implicitly and frequently explicitly racial. Challenges to the racial order are limited to legal and political marginality. The system of racial meanings, of racial identities and ideology, seems 'natural.' Such conditions seemed generally to prevail from the end of Reconstruction to the end of World War I, for example.

Now let us imagine a situation in which this unstable equilibrium is disrupted. There can be many reasons for this, and the disruption may take many shapes, for example the emergence of a mass-based racial movement such as took place in the 1960s, or of a powerful counter-egalitarian thrust such as appeared in the 1870s (with the beginnings of Asian exclusion and Jim Crow), or in the 1980s (with the institutionalization of new right and neoconservative interpretations of race). We shall be concerned with movement phenomena presently. Here we are interested chiefly in the effects on the state of racial disequilibrium.

Under conditions of disrupted equilibrium inter-institutional competition and conflict within the state is augmented, as some agencies move toward accommodation of challenging forces while others 'dig in their heels.' Recomposition of constituencies and political alliances takes place. Opposition groups may resort to 'direct action,' and explicitly seek to politicize racial identities further; challenge will also take the route of 'normal politics' (legislation, legal action, electoral activity, etc.), assuming this possibility is open to racially identified minorities. Strategic unity will therefore become more necessary for the governing forces or bloc.

The establishment or restoration of conditions of unstable equilibrium—let us say by means of reform policies—suggests an opposite cyclical phase. Such a situation guarantees the relative unity of the racial state by reducing the stakes of intra-state, or inter-institutional, conflict. It poses formidable obstacles to the fomenting of oppositional political projects. It minimizes the government's need to strategize and promises the automatic reproduction of the prevailing order, obviously an optimum situation from the standpoint of the dominant racial groups.

Disruption and restoration of the racial order suggests the type of cyclical movement or pattern we designate by the term *trajectory*. Both racial movements and the racial state experience such transformations, passing through periods of rapid change and virtual stasis, through moments of massive mobilization and others of relative passivity. While the movement and state versions of the overall trajectory are independently observable, they could not exist independently of each other. Racially based political movements as we know them are inconceivable without the racial state, which provides a focus for political demands and structures the racial order. The racial state, in its turn, has been historically constructed by racial movements; it consists of agencies and programs which are the institutionalized responses to racial movements of the past.

The point at which we begin to examine the trajectory of racial politics, then, is arbitrary. Let us assume, therefore, a beginning point of *unstable equilibrium*. At this historical point, the racial order is (relatively) undisturbed by conflict and mobilization. The racial state is able to function (again relatively) automatically in its organization and enforcement of the racial order. We first address the racial movement version of the trajectory, and then that of the racial state.

Racial movements come into being as the result of political projects, political interventions led by 'intellectuals.' These projects seek to transform (or rearticulate) the dominant racial ideology. They thereby summarize and explain problems—economic inequality, absence of political rights, cultural repression, etc.—in racial terms. The result of this ideological challenge is a disparity, a conflict, between the pre-existing racial order, organized and enforced by the state, and an oppositional ideology whose subjects are the real and potential adherents of a racially defined movement. When this conflict reaches a certain level of intensity, a phase of *crisis* is initiated.

During a period of crisis, racial movements experiment with different strategies and tactics (electoral politics, 'spontaneity,' cultural revitalization efforts and alternative institution-building, lobbying, direct action, etc.). We assume that at least some of these are successful in mobilizing political pressure, either through 'normal' political channels or through disruption of those channels. Indeed the success of a racial movement probably depends on its ability to generate a wide and flexible variety of strategies, ideological themes, and political tactics, as both the minority movements of the 1960s and the new right/neoconservative movements of the present have demonstrated.

In response to political pressure, state institutions adopt policies of absorption and insulation. *Absorption* reflects the realization that many demands are greater threats to the racial order before they are accepted than after they have been adopted in suitably moderate form. *Insulation* is a related process in which the state confines demands to terrains that are, if not entirely symbolic, at least not crucial to the operation of the racial order. These policies then become ideological elements which are employed both by movements and state institutions. State agencies might argue, for example, that they have already met reasonable movement demands, while movement groups might claim that reforms don't address the problem, don't go far enough, etc.

Once the general contours of state reformism are clear, movements undergo internal divisions. A certain segment of the movement is absorbed ('coopted,' in 1960s parlance) along with its demands, into the state, and there constitutes the core staff and agenda of the new state programs or agencies with which reform policies are to be implemented. The remaining active segment of the movement is 'radicalized,' while its more passive membership drops away to take up the roles and practices defined by a rearticulated racial ideology in the newly restabilized racial order (*unstable equilibrium*).

Considering the trajectory of racial politics from the standpoint of the state, *unstable equilibrium*$_1$ at first coexists with a series of effectively marginalized political projects located outside the 'normal' terrain of state activity. In racial terms the state's trajectory of reform is initiated when movements challenge the pre-existent racial order. Crisis ensues when this opposition upsets the pre-existing *unstable equilibrium*$_1$. The terms of challenge can vary enormously, depending on the movement involved. Opposition can be democratic or authoritarian, primarily based in 'normal' politics or in disruption; opposition can even reject explicit political definition, as in the case of cultural movements.

Crisis generates a series of conflicts within and among state agencies as particular demands are confronted and the terms of the state response (repression, concessions, symbolic responses, etc.) are debated. Agency and constituent groups, confronted by racial opposition, explore the range of potential accommodations, the possibilities for reconsolidating the racial order, and their possible roles in a racial ideology 'rearticulated' in light of oppositional themes. 'Hard-liners' and 'moderates' appear, and compromises are sought both with the opposition and within the state itself.

Ultimately a series of reforms is enacted which partially meets oppositional demands. Reform policies are initiated and deemed potentially effective in establishing a new *unstable equilibrium*$_2$. These policies are then regularized in the form of agencies and programs whose constituency bases, like those of other state apparatuses, will consist of former adherents and sympathizers of the movement (as well as 'free riders,' of course). A new racial ideology is articulated, often employing themes initially framed by the oppositional movements.

The concept of the trajectory of racial politics links the two central actors in the drama of contemporary racial politics—the racial state and racially based social movements, and suggests a general pattern of interaction between them. Change in the racial order, in the social meaning and political role played by race, is achieved only when the state has initiated reforms, when it has generated new programs and agencies in response to movement demands. Movements capable of achieving such reforms only arise when there is significant 'decay' in the capacities of pre-existing state programs and institutions to organize and enforce racial ideology. Contemporary patterns of change in the racial order illustrate this point clearly.

Contemporary Change in the U.S. Racial Order

In the period with which we are concerned, the 'rules of the game' by which racial politics are organized have become tremendously complex. In the pre-World War II period change in the racial order was epochal in scope, shaped by the conditions of 'war of maneuver' in which minorities had very little access to the political system, and understood in a context of assumed racial inequalities (i.e., comprehensive and generally unexamined racism). Today all of this has been swept away.

In the present day, racial change is the product of the interaction of racially based social movements and the racial state. In the postwar period, minority movements, led by the black movement, radically challenged the dominant racial ideology. As a result of this challenge, the racial order anchored by the state was itself destabilized, and a comprehensive process of reform was initiated. Later still, the reformed racial state became the target for further challenge, this time from the right. Racial politics now take place under conditions of 'war of position,' in which minorities have achieved significant (though by no means equal) representation in the political system, and in an ideological climate in which the *meaning* of racial equality can be debated, but the desirability of some form of equality is assumed. The new 'rules of the game' thus contain *both* the legacy of movement efforts to rearticulate the meaning of race and to mobilize minorities politically on the basis of the new racial ideologies thus achieved, and the heritage of deep-seated racism and inequality.

As we have argued, social movements create collective identity, collective subjectivity, by offering their adherents a different view of themselves and their world; different, that is, from the characteristic worldviews and self-concepts of the social order which the movements are challenging. Based upon that newly forged collective identity, they address the state politically, demanding change. This is particularly true of contemporary racial movements. In fact these movements largely established the parameters within which popular and radical democratic movements (so-called 'new social movements') operate in the U.S.

Racial movement mobilization and 'normal' politics (the state, electoral activity, constituency formation, administrative and judicial systems, etc.) are now linked in a reciprocal process. Demands for state reform—for the transformation of racial society as a whole—are the consequences of transformations in collective identity, indeed in the meaning of race itself, 'translated' from the cultural/ideological terrain of everyday life into the terms of political discourse. Such 'translations' may come from movements themselves, or they may originate in 'normal' political processes as electoral bases are sought, judicial decisions handed down, administrative procedures contested, etc. Our conception of the 'trajectory' of racial movements and state reform policies suggests that the transformation of the racial order occurs by means of an alternately equilibrated and disrupted relationship between the formation of racial ideology and the elaboration of state policy.

Today racial movements not only pose new demands originating outside state institutions, but may also frame their 'common identity' in response to state-based racial initiatives. The concept of 'Asian American', for example, arose as a political label in the 1960s. This reflected the similarity of treatment that various groups such as Chinese Americans, Japanese Americans, Korean Americans, etc. (groups which had not previously considered themselves as having a common political agenda) received at the hands of state institutions. The census, the legislatures, the courts, the educational system, the military, the welfare state apparatus—each in its own way a racial institution—are all sources of such racial change.

At the same time racial movements (both radical and conservative) continue to present the state with political demands. We understand this process as the *rearticulation* of racial ideology. Racially based movements begin as political projects which both build upon and break away from their cultural and political predecessors. Movement projects take shape in the interaction of civil society and the racial state. Movements set out to question the meaning of race and the nature of racial identity (e.g., 'blackness,' 'Chicanismo,' 'minority' status; or for that matter, 'majority' status, 'whiteness'), while state initiatives seek to reinforce or transform the 'unstable equilibrium' of racial politics in response to movement demands. Such 'projects' challenge pre-existing racial ideology. They are efforts to *rearticulate* the meaning of race, and responses to such efforts.

The rearticulation of pre-existing racial ideology is a dual process of *disorganization* of the dominant ideology and of *construction* of an alternative, oppositional framework.

The dominant ideology can be disorganized in various ways. An insurgent movement may question whether the dominant racial ideology properly applies to the collective experience of its members. Examples of this interrogation of the pre-existing system of racial categories and beliefs may be found, not only in militant movement rhetoric,[3] but also in popular and intellectual discourse. During the 1960s, for instance, minority economists, political scientists, sociologists and psychologists rejected dominant social science perspectives on racial grounds:

For years, traditional (white) social science research—especially on political life and organizations—told us how politically workable and healthy the society was, how all the groups in society were getting pretty much their fair share, or moving certainly in that direction. There was a social scientific myth of consensus and progress developed.[4]

Similarly, during the 1970s, conservative, whites-oriented racial movements, such as those of the 'new right' or the 'unmeltable' ethnics, developed counteregalitarian challenges to the reforms which minority movements had achieved in the previous decade. In this way the overarching racial ideology—in which racial minorities and the white majority alike recognize themselves—is called into question.

Insurgent racial movements also try to redefine the essential aspects of group identity. Demands for 'self-determination' (which of course are linked to important democratic traditions in the U.S.) attain currency, while past organizational efforts are criticized. For example, militants of the 1960s attacked the political accommodations and compromises into which pre-existing community organizations and leaderships had entered. The NAACP and Urban League, the G.I. Forum and LULAC were criticized as 'Uncle Toms' and 'Tio Tacos' who had succumbed to 'cooptation'. Militants also denounced various cultural practices in minority communities which were judged to reinforce submission and dependence. Malcolm X, for instance, excoriated the black practice of 'conking' (i.e., straightening) the hair with lye.

The construction of an oppositional movement employs a wide variety of ideological themes. Racially based movements have as their most fundamental task the creation of new identities, new racial meanings, and a new collective subjectivity. Not only does the articulation of a new racial ideology involve the recombination of pre-existent meanings and identities, but it also draws on quite heterodox and unexpected sources.

The disorganization of the dominant racial ideology, the construction of a new set of racial meanings and identities, the transition from political project to oppositional movement, is a complex, uneven process, marked by considerable instability and tension. Change is being demanded, but any change in the system of racial meanings will affect all groups, all identities. Challenging the dominant racial ideology inherently involves not only reconceptualizing one's own racial identity, but a reformulation of the meaning of race in general. To challenge the position of blacks in society is to challenge the position of whites.

Racial movements, built on the terrain of civil society, necessarily confront the state as they begin to upset the unstable equilibrium of the racial order. Once an oppositional racial ideology has been articulated, once the dominant racial ideology has been confronted, it becomes possible to demand reform of state racial policies and institutions. There has been a change in the 'rules of the game.' A new political terrain has been opened up.

By the same token, once such challenges have been posed and become part of the established political discourse, they in turn become subject to rearticulation. The state reforms won by minority movements in the 1960s, and the racial definitions and meanings embodied in these reforms, provided a formidable range of targets for 'counter-reformers' in the 1970s and 1980s. 'New right' and neoconservative currents, armed with the still-dominant social-scientific paradigm of ethnicity theory, were able to carry on their own political 'project.' They were able to rearticulate racial ideology and restructure racial politics once again.

[From *Racial Formation in the United States: From the 1960s to the 1990s* (New York: Routledge, 1994), 77–91.]

39 Separate and Unequal

What I hope to have demonstrated is how the Federal government, in a range of areas, colluded in the maintenance of segregated race relations in the half-century before the Civil Rights Act of 1964. Federal authority was used either to impose or to accommodate segregated race relations in government departments and public policies. The transformation of the US Civil Service Commission from an agent of meritocratic appointment at its establishment in 1883, to a discriminating barrier from 1914, was explained and the consequences for Black Americans investigated. Black Americans working in the Federal government between 1914 and the 1960s rarely achieved positions in the professional or senior administrative classes, and were disproportionately confined to clerical, janitorial, or custodial positions. The restriction of Black employees to such grades was aided immensely by the decision in 1914 to require applicants for government positions to attach photographs to their application forms. This practice quickly undermined the impartiality of the 'rule of three' appointment criterion proudly extolled by the US Civil Service Commission. The abolition of the photograph requirement in 1940 coincided with the expansion of the Federal government necessitated by wartime. After 1945 the Civil Service Commission's enforcement of the 'rule of three' system continued to evoke protest from Black American interest groups as Black applicants continued to encounter discrimination in the 1950s. One consequence of these trends was to stunt and trammel the potential for equality of treatment by race in the Federal government. If Black American citizens could not look to the national government to act impartially on their behalf, but rather witnessed it reproducing narrow racist interests from society, then their prospects were indeed circumspect.

The pervasiveness of the Federal government's support of segregated race relations demonstrated the extent to which segregation was not merely a system of separation but in reality a mechanism for the domination of Black Americans by Whites. The 'separate but equal' framework did not preclude the daily interaction of Black Americans and Whites—whether in a government department, branch of the Armed Forces, prison, or job centre—but segregation did dictate the terms on which these interactions occurred. Injustices and discriminatory behaviour had to be protested by Black Americans. It was Whites who could object to working with Blacks. Thus, segregated race relations were inherently unequal, and sat with a national politics which between the 1890s and 1960s denied equality to Black Americans: in the South this denial was often sufficiently explicit to include disenfranchisement; in the North the right to vote did not remove discrimination and prejudice in a range of areas such as employment and housing. The discriminations and inequalities coexisted with segregation race relations in the Armed Forces and Federal penitentiaries, illustrating how Federal authority of segregation extended into all areas of the government. Federal support of segregated race relations permeated into a segregated society. The US Employment Service (USES) did little to challenge or supplant discrimination in the labour-market. Its employment offices were segregated and many administrators were reluctant (if not willing) to register Black job-seekers for any positions other than menial or domestic ones. Remarkably, this reluctance—and the related one of accepting 'Whites only' vacancy notices—extended to the USES's supply of candidates for Federal government department posts. In Federal housing programmes, the government's own criteria for evaluating the value of different properties and neighbourhoods incorporated explicit racial assumptions mirroring those effected in society through racial covenants and prejudice. Government policy reinforced, and on occasion engendered, segregated residential housing.

Black Americans' employment experience of the Federal government has altered dramatically since the middle of the 1960s and passage of the Civil Rights Act. The Civil Rights Act of 1964 was the most important legislation in the field since Reconstruction and empowered the US Department of Justice extensively to investigate and prosecute discrimination and other abuses of citizens' rights. Section 717 of the Act referred to 'nondiscrimination in federal government employment'. It declared that 'all personnel actions affecting employees' throughout the Federal government and military should be 'free from any discrimination based on race, color, religion, sex or national origin'. The US Civil Service Commission was charged with monitoring and enforcing this directive, by investigating complaints and issuing judgements. The 1964 Act created the EEOC to regulate discrimination in employment but gave it modest enforcement powers. Consequently, to pursue recalcitrant employers, Congress was compelled to strengthen the powers of the EEOC in the Equal Employment Opportunities Enforcement Act in 1972. The EEOC was empowered to sue employers in the Federal district courts who failed to respond to orders. In 1978, this responsibility was transferred from the EEOC. Each department and agency was directed to formulate and implement an 'equal employment opportunity plan' which included affirmative employment action for Federal employees. This arrangement was not uncriticized and in October 1992 the EEOC issued new regulations to improve the system under which Federal employees (including applicants for positions) charging discrimination could seek redress.

[...] [D]ata documenting the improvement in the employment position of Black Americans in the Federal government. [There have been] significant increases between 1961 and 1965 in the number of Black Americans working in general schedule categories; by the end of the 1980s Black American employees constituted over 16 per cent of total government employees. The trend in general schedule positions is particularly important since this category covers many professional positions. Between 1963 and 1974 the percentage of Black American employees in these grades rose from 9.2 to 12.7 per cent. However, Black American employment in the general schedule by grade level, when examined shows that while Blacks had made significant advances in the middle and lower grades, their presence in the senior grades by 1980 was less impressive. This issue concerned a congressional committee in 1978 which, in its report, noted that 'government wide statistics show a concentration of minorities in the lower salary grade ranges (GS 1–4 and WG 1–4) in 1975 with only a very slight improvement in 1977. Individual Agencies also show this same disproportionate concentration in the lower salary grade levels.' But in aggregate terms, the number of Black American employees in the Federal government had undoubtedly increased significantly by the 1980s compared with the half-century preceding the Civil Rights Acts. Black American employees had also made substantial inroads into the middle ranks of the civil service grades, though less so at the senior levels. Discrimination and equality of opportunity are pursued vigorously.

Of the multiple legacies of the Federal government's collusion in maintaining segregated race relations for contemporary American politics three are notable.

First, major areas of American public policy have a fundamental racial dimension which springs directly from the way in which Federal government programmes were formulated. Residential housing is massively segregated in the United States and this has profound consequences for labour-market participation and equality. In Federal welfare and training programmes, the continuing effect of discrimination and segregation derived from their initial administration is apparent. The marginalization of Black Americans from the Social Security Act of 1935, and the stigmatization associated with welfare benefits—initially through the ADC and later AFDC programmes—is a fundamental aspect of modern citizenship in the United States. The new emphasis upon training and apprenticeship programmes by the Clinton administration (an enthusiasm shared with many other advanced industrial democracies) is constrained and diluted by the historically discriminatory stance of Federal agencies and labour unions toward Black Americans. However, as Sniderman and Piazza rightly stress, the place of and attitudes about race in such a range of policies differs: 'a distinguishing mark of the contemporary politics of race is the number of fundamentally different arguments being conducted over race at the same time. The clash over affirmative action is not the same as the conflict over more conventional forms of government assistance, and differences of opinion over an issue like fair housing have their own dynamic.'[1] Sniderman and Piazza, in the same major study, stress how political attitudes about policy areas—or what they term agendas—structure preferences: 'the contemporary politics of race has as much to do with politics as with race.'[2] This view needs also to be complemented by an appreciation of how racial biases were built into many important Federal programmes. Federal government programmes which assumed or privileged segregation race relations have, by institutionalizing inequality and second-class citizenship, contributed to the terms of these contemporary debates. Instead of squashing such distinctions by race the Federal government gave a basis for their persistence. The NAACP, and other groups working in behalf of Black Americans, repeatedly and patiently explained to the Federal administrators, with whom they tirelessly corresponded, that citing Black Americans' acceptance of segregation was an inappropriate defence of this practice: it was not the role of the Federal government to foster and sustain such distinctions between its citizens, since this would emulate practices in society. Thus, the NAACP Special Counsel, Thurgood Marshall, protested to the US Bureau of Prisons in 1942 about the latter's uncritical acceptance of the notion of 'self-segregation' amongst Black inmates:

you mention in your letter that it is impossible to allow the prisoners to choose with whom they may associate. It is interesting to note that several other officials of state institutions have made the statement that they separate the races 'because Negroes like to be by themselves.' Both of these reasons, to my mind, are without bearing on the particular protest. It is not a question of whether or not a Negro wants to be associated with a particular white individual. The only problem is whether or not the Federal Government is justified in segregating Negro Americans as a group and as a race.

Segregation meant inequality and this is the legacy which Federal programmes confront.

Second, to what extent affirmative action programmes should be instituted to compensate for the pernicious and inegalitarian effects of a half-century of segregated race relations is a question of profound importance. The problems now faced were presciently anticipated in the 1960s by the Executive Secretary of the President's Committee on Government Employment Policy, as he entered the minefield of discrimination created by segregation. He wondered: how should the incidence of discrimination be established? 'A mere head count showing the absence of negro personnel simply is not enough information upon which to make a judgment, for the reason may be, and in many situations is, the absence of Negroes on certificates which the agency is using.' Consequently, any blame for discrimination should be directed at the Civil Service Commission and not individual departments: 'the Committee has not charged agencies with discriminatory practices even when such information has been at hand.' He understood the mounting pressure for affirmative action:

Our critics would then say that the hiring practices of the agencies should be reviewed. But to do this either we or the agencies must be able to identify, through a review of certificates, those Negroes who have been considered and determine whether or not they have been passed over. With the absence of any identifying racial information on the certificates, it becomes impossible to review past practices. The only possibility lies in a current review on a day-to-day basis, based almost entirely on identifying those

Negroes who appear for personal interviews. Even if such identifications are made (and it may be possible to do so) there remains the further problem of determining the relative qualifications of those Negroes passed over as compared with the whites who were hired before any finding of discrimination can be made. On any large scale this would be a very involved process.

To rectify such a pattern required a different course: 'the only alternative to this difficult process that I can see at present is simply to take the position that where there are no Negroes there ought to be some, and direct the agencies to find and employ them.' But this strategy was also problematic: 'this comes close to the "quota" idea, and in any event would put the program in the position of deliberate preference for Negroes. There are, of course, many who believe that the situation now demands such preference if Negro employment in the South is to increase.' This analysis accurately foresaw many of the problems in ensuring equal opportunity for Black Americans in the Federal government. Unfortunately, the record of inequality arising from segregation gave the nebulously specified critics not inconsiderable grounds for their views. Sniderman and Piazza's careful research also confirms how fissural an issue affirmative action remains.

Finally, there is considerable irony, and indeed paradox, in the now quotidian claim that government policy to address issues such as poverty and inequality is inherently flawed and doomed to fail, a view commonly expressed on the political right in the United States. As the material in this book has demonstrated, for over half a century the Federal government played a significant role in shaping and reinforcing the system of race relations which disadvantaged Black American citizens. Furthermore, it was resources deployed by the same Federal government which brought democracy to the South in the 1960s and which tackled discrimination in hiring both in government and outside. Contrary to the common view that the US Federal state is a weak one, at both of these stages the Federal government proved powerful and effective. It is unclear why the conviction that the Federal government cannot be harnessed through its public programmes to the pursuit of equality of opportunity and treatment, for example in the housing- and labour-markets and in training schemes, has become so commonplace in the final decade of the twentieth century. Such a view certainly imputes an inconsequentiality to the Federal government belied by the historical record of its role in upholding the fiction of 'separate but equal' segregated race relations.

Earlier, I drew attention to the partisan and judicial sources of segregated race relations. The Federal government tolerated these relations within their own agencies and permitted their extension into society, in large part, because of the dominant partisan interests in Congress and the executive. One good example of this partisan grip was the consistently weak anti-discrimination measures established by the executive and the hostility of many members of the Congress to such initiatives. Thus, Franklin Roosevelt's agreement to found the

FEPC in 1941 did not include many of the other measures sought by A. Philip Randolph and the March on Washington Movement, such as Executive Orders to abolish discrimination in government defence training programmes, impose substantial sanctions with which to penalize discriminators in receipt of government contracts or in government departments, and abrogate segregated race relations in Federal government departments. Congress would have thrown out proposals which moved toward these reforms. The executive bodies created after the demise of the FEPC faced comparable limits. This political and partisan context dictated the Federal government's role in maintaining segregated race relations in the state and in society. Since this constellation of political and electoral forces was able to use the Federal government to protect and accommodate segregated race relations, it is far from self-evident that a different configuration or coalition of political interests could not deploy Federal authority to address the enduring inequalities and disadvantages which remain for Black Americans.

[From *Separate and Unequal: Black Americans and the US Federal Government* (Oxford: Clarendon Press, 1995), 205–10.

STEPHEN CASTLES AND ELLIE VASTA

 40 Multicultural or Multi-racist Australia?

Australia advanced proudly into nationhood and the twentieth century as an openly racist society. Will we enter the twenty-first century with a genuine commitment to anti-racism? That is the central theme of this book.

The racist world view dominant among Australians in the early part of the century had two central components: racism against Aboriginal and Torres Strait Island peoples, and racism against immigrants. For the first group, a set of popular, religious and scientific beliefs in the inferiority of indigenous peoples was matched by a set of practices of exclusion, control and discrimination tantamount to physical and cultural genocide. With regard to immigrants, exclusion of non-Europeans was the purpose of one of the earliest laws passed by the new Federal Parliament: the Immigration Restriction Act of 1901. This was the legal expression of the White Australia policy which was supported by most Australians irrespective of class or political persuasion. Non-British Europeans (such as Italians and Germans) were not excluded, since their pioneering skills and labour were needed, but they were kept in positions of inferiority through discriminatory practices, including restrictions on land ownership, exclusion from certain occupations, and prohibition of foreign-language schools and newspapers.

We have come a long way since then. Most Australians now see themselves as tolerant and unprejudiced, willing to give everyone a fair go, whatever their

colour, culture or origins. Overtly racist laws and policies towards both indigenous people and immigrants were abolished in the 1960s and 1970s. Multiculturalism—introduced in the 1970s and continually reaffirmed and refined in the
1980s and 1990s—seeks to provide a new inclusionary definition of Australian
national identity. Cultural diversity is seen as crucial to our future, both in terms
of interethnic relations and in terms of the need to find a new place in the Asia-
Pacific region. Racism should have no place in this new Australian world-view.

Moreover, government policies explicitly recognise the existence of barriers
to equal participation in economic, social and political life, based on race, ethnicity, gender, religion and culture. The *National Agenda for a Multicultural Australia* (OMA 1989) declared that it was the duty of the state to overcome such
barriers. A wide range of laws, policies and agencies exist for this purpose. The
Native Title Act of 1993 (which was a response to the *Mabo* decision of the High
Court) appears particularly symbolic as a measure of atonement for past
wrongs against indigenous people, and as part of a strategy of national recon-
ciliation. The *Mabo* decision raises such issues as the importance of an economic base for indigenous Australians , the protection of Aboriginal heritage,
the relationship between indigenous and non-indigenous law, and the position
of indigenous rights in the Australian Constitution. *Mabo* has an anti-racist
potential. In the light of such developments it might appear that multicultural
Australia is not only a non-racist country, but even an anti-racist one.

But is this really the case? The actual experience of members of minorities,
especially those who are visibly different, does not fit in with this comfortable
image. They report frequent instances of verbal abuse, discrimination and even
violence, as was documented a few years ago by the Human Rights and Equal
Opportunities Commission in its *Report of the National Inquiry into Racist Violence* (HREOC 1991). Aboriginal people have the most frequent experience of
racism, often at the hands of the police and other government officials, but
people of Asian appearance also report many instances of abuse or violence,
while discrimination and prejudice of various kinds still affects immigrants of
non-English-speaking background (NESB) in general. The heated debate surrounding the Racial Vilification Bill of 1994 was indicative of widespread unwillingness to confront racism.

While it is widely believed that Australian racism has declined since the 1960s,
we have no accurate way of knowing whether matters have got better or worse
in recent years. There is no systematic monitoring of incidents of racist violence or discrimination—unlike the USA, where special legislation in the late
1980s introduced monitoring of 'hate crimes', or Britain, where the police and
Home Office collect systematic data on racially motivated crimes. The various
bodies set up under federal and state laws to combat racial discrimination and
vilification do not provide any comprehensive information on the incidence of
such practices—they merely respond to complaints. For instance, HREOC received 458 complaints under the Federal Racial Discrimination Act in 1993–94,

while the New South Wales Anti-Discrimination Bureau received 329 complaints on grounds of racial discrimination and 86 on grounds of racial vilification (ACTU 1995, p. 5). But there is strong evidence that only a small percentage of such cases is actually reported (ACTU 1995, pp. 10, 15). This is partly because of lack of information on the part of victims of racism, partly because of the complex and lengthy procedures faced by those who do complain, and partly because existing laws are weak and rarely provide effective remedies. For example, the NSW Anti-Discrimination Board received 448 complaints on grounds of vilification over a five-year period; of these, three cases were eventually recommended for prosecution, but not in fact proceeded with (ACTU 1995, p. 10). In the light of this, people may feel that complaints are a waste of time.

But even if we have no way of quantifying racism, there is ample evidence that it is a widespread and serious problem. Here are just a few examples taken from the Australian Council of Trade Union's overview of racism for the year 1994 (ACTU 1995):

- Jewish organisations reported increasing numbers of anti-Semitic incidents.
- A survey of engineers showed that employment prospects were significantly affected by race, with a clear bias in favour of Europeans.
- 1994 was the last year that Federal government departments were required to report publicly on their equal opportunity programs. This requirement has been abolished, although only 9 per cent of recent appointments to the Public Service were NESB people.
- Attorney General's Department had 519 members in its statutory and non-statutory bodies, of whom only two were NESB people.
- The NSW Ombudsman released a discussion paper which suggested that 'the behaviour of some police officers was often racist and negative stereotyping was part of a learnt police culture'.
- Mr Downer, then leader of the Federal Opposition, admitted appearing on the platform of a meeting organised by the racist League of Rights.
- The National Committee for Discrimination and Employment has 'fallen in a heap' according to the ACTU, and there is no coordinated strategy by federal and state authorities to combat discrimination in employment.
- Federal and state bodies concerned with implementing multicultural policies and combating discrimination were demoralised and marginalised, and had their resources cut.

Thus, despite multiculturalism, the official response to racism and marginalisation of minorities is ineffective and evasive. All available social indicators show that Aborigines and Torres Strait Islanders are still highly disadvantaged with regard to health, housing, education, employment, life expectancy and social conditions. They suffer exclusion, discrimination and racist violence. Immigrants too experience discrimination of various kinds. However, the experience of various groups differs, and they cannot be dealt with as a single category.

White immigrants from highly developed countries often have incomes and conditions at or above the national average, and suffer little or no discrimination. The experience of the pre-1970s Eastern and South European settlers was frequently marked by discrimination and socio-economic disadvantage. This group—now often nearing or past retiring age—still faces serious problems of exclusion and poverty. Their children—'the second generation'—may have achieved upward mobility, but still find themselves treated as 'wogs' in certain contexts. Their bicultural identity is often conditioned by experiences of racism.

More recent immigrants from Asia, Latin America and the Pacific Islands vary greatly in characteristics like education, qualifications and language skills. Immigrants and refugees without recognised skills may experience a double exclusion: they have high rates of unemployment or are forced into low-paid informal sector jobs, while at the same time suffering racial discrimination, harassment or even violence. Highly skilled non-European immigrants often do very well in the labour market (though not always, for barriers to skill recognition and employment still exist). But they may still suffer various forms of personal racism on account of being visibly different.

So racism *is* still a problem in multicultural Australia. We should not forget that the name Australia was until recently synonymous with racial exclusion and white dominance, to the point that many people in Asia and Europe are still surprised when told that Asian immigration is now common. The two centuries in which racism was an almost universal tenet have left their mark on institutions, social practices, intellectual discourse, popular ideas and national culture. The anti-racism of official policies and public rhetoric is often only skin-deep: it masks the continuing reality of differentiation and discrimination based on biological and cultural markers which are linked to discourses of race and ethnicity. There is no single racism in Australia, no simple black-white divide. Rather, there is a whole range of intersecting sets of ideas and practices among different groups, which in turn interact with ideas and practices concerning class and gender. Thus, in our title we echo the notion of a 'multi-racist' society coined for Britain by Cohen and Bains (1988): Australia is in the contradictory position of being both a multicultural and a multiracist society. This is another way of saying that multiculturalism is incomplete and unstable, as long as it co-exists with various forms of racism.

Discourses of tolerance and diversity are not unimportant—indeed they are a great step forward compared with our racist past—but they can only be seen as genuine anti-racism if they are matched by a commitment to fundamental change in institutions, attitudes and practices. In principle and (in the long run) in practice, multiculturalism and racism in any form are incompatible. Yet, as the contributions to this book show, a commitment to fundamental change is still missing in many areas of Australian life. Contemporary Australia has shown a capability for change and innovation, but much remains to be done if we are to enter the twenty-first century as a non-racist society.

Social Science and Racism

Australian anti-racists still have a major task ahead of them. Achieving change is above all an issue of political practice, but social scientific analysis is a vital pre-condition for such practice. A central problem of anti-racist movements throughout the world has been their frequent failure to keep up with changes in racist ideologies and practices. We hope that this book will help contribute to an awareness and understanding of contemporary Australian racisms, especially those which seem able to coexist with the ostensibly anti-racist tenets of multi-culturalism.

We have already indicated that there is no single *racism* in Australia, but rather a range of *racisms*, which affect different groups in different contexts. However, at the same time it is important to be aware of the *unity of racism* as a process of social differentiation which has played a central role in Western society since the beginnings of modernity and colonialism. In the Australian context this means understanding that both indigenous people and immigrants have been subjected to processes of racialisation, as a means of controlling them and subordinating them to the interests of the dominant group. The forms and effects of racialisation have been very different. Above all, racism against indigenous people has been much more brutal and destructive than against immigrants. Yet the ideologies, practices and interests on which they have been based are essentially the same.

In Australia, there has always been a dichotomy between studies of the situations of Aboriginal people, and studies of immigrants and their descendants. This dichotomy has reflected the administrative division between Aboriginal affairs on the one hand and immigration and ethnic affairs policy on the other. Frequently a division has been made between the study of race relations (concerning indigenous people) and the study of ethnic relations (concerning immigrants). There is no theoretical or analytical basis for this division, and it tends to undermine understanding of the process of racialisation as well as making it harder to develop anti-racist perspectives.

It is in this context that we can see one of the central dilemmas of Australian social scientific work on racism or race relations. Social scientists have played a major role in shaping attitudes and policies on racial and ethnic difference. But on the whole there has been little effort to understand the common roots of practices of discrimination and exclusion towards both indigenous people and immigrants. To do so would mean admitting that racism arises out of the structure and culture of our own society, rather than out of the specific characteristics of the racialised groups. Thus social scientists have not only ignored the unity of racism, but have often denied the existence of racism altogether.

In the nineteenth century, Australia with its great wealth of cultural groups became an El Dorado for anthropologists. These helped create myths of separate and 'authentic' indigenous cultures, and somehow missed the reality of how colonialism was destroying Aboriginal society. Anthropology became both an instrument of control and a way of asserting the superiority of the dominant group. Immigration studies were carried out by sociologists, demographers, economists and others, who addressed issues like: How many more people does Australia need? What types of people (based on ethnic origins) can Australia assimilate? How can immigrants be absorbed without changing the existing society and culture? What policies are most conducive to assimilation? In other words, the perspective of social science on difference until recently has been that of the dominant group in society: first the British colonial power, then the emerging Anglo-Australian ruling class. Indigenous people and immigrants were represented and objectified in academic and policy debates, and had little or no opportunity to represent themselves.

However, since the 1960s another, more critical, approach has developed. Australian social scientists began to support calls for Aboriginal rights and the abandonment of the White Australia policy. The work of people like Rivett (1962) and Yarwood (1964) was influential in debates on immigration policy. Writers like Rowley (1970), Lippmann (1973) and Stevens (1970) showed some of the brutal realities behind Australia's frontier myths. Social scientists began to take on a critical function as agents for change in official racist policies. This was possible for three reasons. The first was the world-wide movement against racism connected with decolonisation and the revulsion against Nazism. The second was the fact that oppressed groups in Australia were finding a voice and putting difficult questions to the people who had hitherto claimed to represent them .When Aboriginal people began to question the European scientific notions of truth against their own 'dreaming' versions of truth, and began voicing their own experiences of repression, then intellectuals were forced to re-examine their own role. At the same time, people of immigrant background began to take a part in immigration policy debates and immigration research and began to question the racist effects of assimilationism and the White Australia policy.

The third reason for the growth of critical analysis was, of course, that official policies were failing. The White Australia policy and the denial of rights to Aboriginal people had become international embarrassments, while the doctrine of assimilation was rapidly collapsing in the face of community formation and ethnic mobilisation. Critical knowledge was needed, because large sections of Australia's political class were beginning to understand the need for change. Social scientists were to play a major role in the development of the new discourses for dealing with diversity: Aboriginal self-management and multiculturalism.

To say this is to point to one of the fundamental problems of critical social science in a modern democratic country: people who are trying to work for change, emancipation and equality are at the same time contributing to new strategies of control and conflict management within a system based on economic and political inequality. This dilemma of social scientists mirrors that of both Aboriginal and immigrant political activists in Australia, who have to walk a narrow line between pressing for real change and becoming coopted into the consultative structures of a multicultural welfare state.

There is no space for a detailed review of the great volume of recent work relevant to the study of racism in Australia, but a few observations can be made. To start with, most research still follows the administrative division between Aboriginal affairs and policies towards immigrants. There are some exceptions, however, such as Yarwood and Knowling (1982), Pettman (1992) and Markus (1994), who try to examine racism as a whole, and to link it to other central issues in Australian society. Many social scientists see themselves as agents of change. Some anthropologists have been involved with Aborigines in their struggle against the vestiges of racism and colonialism, for instance by giving expert evidence to support land rights claims. Scholars like Reynolds (1981, 1987), Cowlishaw (1988), Bennett (1989) and Eades (1993, 1994) have changed our understanding of the various dimensions of unequal power relations between indigenous and non-indigenous Australians.

In immigration studies, sociologists such as Jeannie Martin (1978) and Jerzy Zubrzycki (1977) played a major role in the 1970s in exposing the failure of assimilationist policies, and showing the extent of immigrant social disadvantage. Zubrzycki was highly influential in the development of the Fraser Government's model of multiculturalism. Zubrzycki's approach rested on a conservative culturalist perspective in which ethnic group difference was to be promoted and respected. In turn, this concentration on a static and traditionalist concept of culture was criticised by social scientists who focused on the political economy of racism.

Recent work sets out to link issues of ethnicity, class and gender with the role of the state and with the politics of identity and community. Such analyses have played a role in the redefinition of multiculturalism by the Australian Labor Party (ALP) Government of the 1980s and 1990s, with its dual focus on principles of cultural diversity and of social justice.

It should be noted that most work in this area is not explicitly on racism, but on various aspects of the situation of Aboriginal people or of immigrants. An implicit critique of racism is frequently present, but coherent and systematic analyses are rare. Even where racism is dealt with as a central theme, there is generally a failure to adequately analyse its causes and its changing forms. As Cowlishaw (1988, p. 267) points out, such important works as Stevens (1970) and Yarwood and Knowling (1982) reduce racism to biological difference, especially that based on skin colour. Social and cultural dimensions of racism are ignored. In a recent work, Markus (1994) provides a comprehensive history of race relations in Australia up to the early 1990s, yet his chapter on 'the idea of race in western culture' barely goes beyond the nineteenth century. This lack of up-to-date theorisation of racism is a serious problem, especially at at time when racist ideologies are everywhere shifting from biological to cultural principles.

In any case, the tradition of social science based on the gaze of the dominant group is still strong. It exists above all in the administratively orientated research commissioned by government departments and special agencies like the Bureau of Immigration, Multicultural and Population Research. Such work reproduces willy-nilly the bureaucratic division of labour and the policy concerns of those who hold political power. This is not to question the soundness of such work, nor the integrity of those who carry it out. Indeed, highly critical approaches are sometimes to be found in official reports. But it is important to realise that the funding structures which determine most research in the field almost inevitably lead to short-term approaches, compartmentalised choice of themes, lack of theoretical reflection, and a top-down perspective.

The issue of representation of difference in the social sciences is a significant one, particularly for indigenous Australians. As they have become more publicly politicised, social scientists have come under attack not only for their representation of blacks as Other, but also for positioning themselves as the purveyors of knowledge about Aborigines in a way that created 'truth-effects' which ultimately reproduced the power of whites over blacks. Over the past few years two significant debates have emerged within Aboriginal studies and anthropology. The first concerns a discussion about representation which took place in *Oceania* in 1992 (see Hollinsworth 1992; Mudrooroo et al. 1992). Its starting point was the concern expressed by white scholars that Aboriginal stress on blood lines and biological continuity was damaging to the Aboriginal cause for social justice. The argument was that biological essentialism could lead only to racial hierarchies and new forms of racism. According to this view, racial hierarchies should not be accepted from any person or group.

The other closely related debate refers to recent work which not only describes the power relations between Aborigines and whites but also examines Aboriginal resistance. In her research in a rural area of New South Wales, Cowlishaw (1988) illustrates how drinking, swearing and general 'unruly' behaviour operates as an oppositional culture to white authority. The critics of this position argue that such resistance is self-destructive and ultimately does not change racist structures and practices. Lattas (1993, pp. 245–6) has argued that such critiques are indicative of a 'new paternalism' in Aboriginal studies. White scholars now have to share the task of representation with the voices of indigenous peoples, yet still try to preserve their role as 'experts' who can help decide on how to constitute the identity of the Other. Thus:

when Aborigines seek to give a mythological content to, or to reclaim, a primordial past for themselves then they are accused of essentialism and of participating in their own domination. This is identity without content and without a primordial past; it is identity stripped to the bare logic of being simply a relation. The demand that Aborigines produce their popular consciousness along the lines of a social theory of identity is a request that they become conscious of themselves as purely relational identities; they are to be resisters without producing an essence for themselves (Lattas 1993, pp. 245–6).

Or, to put it in more directly political terms: 'myths of the "Other" permeate relations between indigenous and non-indigenous people . . . As objects of this history, indigenous Australians have created their own myths in order to survive an oppressive system' (see Chapter 6). Ultimately, as Lattas (1993, p. 254) asks, should we treat Aboriginal essentialism as something which is dangerous and false, or do we accept it as a process which provides a sense of continuity and groundedness? Cowlishaw gets to the core of the matter when she suggests that some academics believe that if they get their theoretical frameworks correct, then they can rest free of political anxieties. However, she continues: 'No theory can guarantee political correctness, as it is in the *uses* of theory that its effects are manifested' (1993, p. 183).

Social scientists do have to share responsibility for the attitudes, practices and policies which arise from their work. The economic and social constraints of scholarly work in a period of erosion of academic independence are issues which have to be negotiated, but they are not a justification for reproducing ideas of domination and hierarchy. No researcher today can work outside official structures of funding and control. Yet the very complexity of issues of cultural difference and the growing ambiguity of the interests of state and capital in this area provide a space in which critical knowledge is needed and even encouraged. This makes it possible to develop alternative ideas on issues of difference, equality and participation. The dilemma of the social scientist is to avoid cooption into mechanisms of domination over minorities. There is no easy way to achieve this, but the key must lie in cooperation and negotiation with members of minority groups, and participation in the development of anti-racist strategies.

[From *The Teeth are Smiling: The persistence of racism in multicultural Australia* (St. Leonards, NSW: Allen and Unwin, 1996), 1–11]

ANTONIO GUIMARÃES

41 Racism and Anti-Racism in Brazil

Any study of racism in Brazil must begin by reflecting on the very fact that racism is a taboo subject in Brazil. Brazilians imagine themselves as inhabiting an anti-racist nation, a 'racial democracy.' This is one of the sources of their pride and, at the same time, conclusive proof of their status as a civilized nation.

This anti-racist claim has deep roots in both factual and literary history. Since the abolition of slavery in 1888, Brazil has not experienced legal segregation or overt racial conflicts. In literature, since the pioneering studies of Freyre in the early 1930s and Pierson in the 1940s, and as late as the 1970s, the professional research of sociologists and anthropologists has reassured both Brazilians and the rest of the world that the Brazilian pattern of race relations is relatively harmonious. In the latest edition of Cashmore's *Dictionary of Race and Ethnic Relations* (1994), the summarization of the entry on Brazil reads:

> In short, Brazil may be described as a society where class distinctions are marked and profound, where class and color overlap but do not coincide, where class often takes precedence over color, and where 'race' is a matter of individual description and personal attractiveness rather than of group membership. (p. 9)

In this chapter, I argue that this interpretation of race and racism in Brazil is due to a certain political and social Western *problématique*, largely supplanted from the 1970s onward, but still present in Brazil. This *problématique* includes the meaning of race and racism. My main concerns are twofold: first, I argue that the language of color and class has always been used in Brazil in a racialized way. Color variations 'naturalized' harsh categorical racial inequalities that could disrupt the self-image of a racial democracy. Second, I show the historical, native, and political issues of racism and anti-racism in Brazil. Although my primary sources are social scientific literary discourses, I refer to the popular, grassroots usage of these discourses as well. Before these issues are addressed, I must briefly reconstitute the idea of 'race as a floating signifier' and the changing agenda of anti-racism in the West.

The Changing Agenda of Western Anti-Racism

The field of scientific inquiry broadly known as 'race relations' is of North American inspiration. Social scientists frequently took the U.S. pattern of race relations as a standard for comparison and contrast in their understanding of race in other societies, especially Brazil. Elevated as an archetype, the U.S. pattern molded the formation of race relations studies in Brazil. The U.S. type exhibited a segregationist, conflictive, violent pattern of relations commonly known as *Jim Crow*, which had precise rules of group affiliation based on biological reasoning that defined race. The Brazilian type, in contrast, paraded a sophisticated etiquette of distancing, sharp status, economic differentiation, egalitarian laws, and an ambiguous but very complex system of identification based mainly upon color nuances.

Why were these two systems put in sharp contrast? Why were their functional similarities unnoticed during the dominance of structural-functionalism in sociology? Three main reasons account for this dualism. First, the political agenda of anti-racism itself stressed the legal and formal status of citizenship instead of its actual organization in Brazilian society. This agenda reflected mainly the liberal interests prevailing in the United States, South Africa, and the

European colonies. In Brazil, this agenda was advanced by White, middle-class intellectuals who overlooked the popular, Black anti-racism of their time, which clashed against the barriers raised by color prejudice. By differentiating prejudice from discrimination and putting the former into the realm of individual privacy, erudite anti-racism operated, functionally, as an ideological effort to obscure real existing racism.

Second, the definition of *race* as a biological concept concealed both the actual character of color distinctions and its constructed, social, cultural dynamic in Brazilian society. If race was about concrete biological differences, so went the reasoning, then color was not a race-related notion, but a subjective and preferential notion.

Third, the search for objective realism in the social sciences that looked for definite essences and causal explanations neglected the web of slippery discursive images that concealed racism under class or status metaphors. The symmetry of the language of race and class in Brazil, although noticed, was largely misinterpreted as a proof of the insignificance of race.

The focus on formal structure and the search for objectivity were world trends. In fact, during the aftermath of World War II, anti-racism was too simple and clear-cut in its aims: to show the unscientific, mythological character of races and the barbaric, inhuman consequences of racism. Both goals operated in a field of obvious realism and vivid experience in Europe: the holocaust and the demise of *race* as a scientific concept.

The postwar agenda of intellectual anti-racism had two obvious targets: segregation in the United States and apartheid in South Africa, the two remaining systems of formal state racism. This agenda could be measured concretely by objective change in formal social organization—the dismantling of formal legal segregation. This was a convenient logic for White Brazilians that obscured the historical assimilationist racism of Brazil.

But Anglo-American elite anti-racism was a no less active participant in the mystification and idealization of Brazil as a racial paradise. In a recent book edited by Hellwig (1992), one cannot find a single observation of racial discrimination in Brazil by African American travellers or social scientists from 1910 to 1940, and from 1940 to 1960, the registered evidence is usually explained by class reasoning.

Perceptions began to change only when civil rights laws were enacted in the United States. Only then could unequal racial opportunities be seen clearly operating and reproducing themselves through social mechanisms—schooling, unemployment, historic poverty, and urban de facto segregation. The changing perceptions of racial discrimination in the United States influenced both the Anglo-American perception of Brazil and the agenda of Western anti-racism. Thereafter, the identification of structural racial inequalities disguised in class or status terms became an important issue. Brazilian and North American racism had become much more alike.

North American Black nationalism and the feminist revolution of the 1970s shed another light on the structuring of anti-racist perceptions; the universalist and assimilationist view of postwar intellectual anti-racists was called racist because it favored the cultural annihilation of African origins and did not see the relation between cultural genocide and Black subordinate status. The women's movement stressed the way sexual differences had been historically 'racialized' to naturalize and justify social and cultural hierarchies.

The historical framework of changing perceptions was completed more recently by the massive immigration of Third World people (East Indians, Caribbeans, Latin Americans, Africans, Chinese, Koreans) toward European and North American democracies. Now these immigrants are viewed as 'unassimilables': colored strangers presenting sharp religious (Islam), linguistic (Arabic or Spanish speakers), or cultural (Rastafarian) threats to the native White populations. These were the ingredients for awareness of a 'new racism' and a new look at race in Brazil. What is now obvious is that when it comes to race,

culture is conceived along ethnically absolute lines, not as something intrinsically fluid, changing, unstable and dynamic, but as a fixed property of social groups rather than a relational field in which they encounter one another and live out social, historical relationships. When culture is brought in contact with race it is transformed into a pseudo-biological property of communal life. (Gilroy, 1993, p. 24)

Theorizing Racism

The changing anti-racist agenda reverberated in the social thinking about racism. In the 1970s, from the point of view of its structures, functions, and mechanisms, race was defined as 'a group of people who in a given society are socially defined as different from other groups by virtue of certain real or putative physical differences' (Van den Berghe, 1970, p. 10). With this definition, race could no longer be distinguished from gender, ethnicity, or class.

In fact, if one examines any list of characteristics said to define and specify race, one sees that the structural and functional characteristics presented are shared by many other social hierarchies. The theorists of the 1970s, however, could not live with this ambiguity. Most of the time, even when defining race and race relations in a flexible manner, they were not conscious that their definitions encompassed other forms of hierarchy. One exception to this pattern was Van den Berghe (1970), who, reflecting on this ambiguity, wrote:

It became increasingly clear to me over the years that the subject had no claim to a special place in a general theory of society. In other words, race and ethnic relations are not sufficiently different from other types of social relations—nor, conversely, do various types of race and ethnic relations have enough that is exclusively common—to justify special theoretical treatment. (p. 9)

In the 1980s, the tide of poststructuralism that came from France brought self-consciousness to the ambiguous definition of *race*. Deconstructionism in the social sciences favored the widespread use of *race* as a metaphor. The analysis of the discursive field of racism, both old (biological images) and new (cultural differentialism) was based on the same underlying reality disguised as different empirical phenomena.

Again, social scientists remained unable to distinguish racism from discriminations arising from other social hierarchies (gender, class, ethnicity, sexuality). To call racism any kind of discrimination based on 'essentialist' or objective constructions transforms racism into a political metaphor.

Delacampagne (1990) provides a good example of this broad reconceptualization of racism and its metaphorical use:

Racism, in the modern sense of the term, does not necessarily begin as soon as one speaks of the physiological superiority, or cultural superiority, of one race or another; it begins when one makes (alleged) cultural superiority directly and mechanically dependent on (alleged) physiological superiority, that is, when one group *derives* the cultural characteristics of a given group from its biological characteristics. Racism is the reduction of the cultural to the biological, the attempt to make the first dependent on the second. Racism exists wherever it is claimed that a given social status is explained by a given natural characteristic. (pp. 85–86)

The definition is imprecise partially because it reduces the idea of 'nature' to a biological notion. But there are many ways to connect social hierarchies to biological differences. In the general sense, 'natural' signifies an ahistoric or transhistoric order, devoid of related and particular interests, thus representing only one general attribute of the human species or the divinities. This presumed natural order may rest upon different bases: a theological justification (divine origin), a scientific justification (endo-determined), or a cultural justification (historical necessity).

Consequently, all social hierarchies appeal to natural order, yet they may be justified and rationalized in different ways. The economic order can be justified as a product of individual virtue (the poor are poor because they lack noble sentiments, virtues, and values); by the same token women are said to occupy subordinate positions due to the characteristics of the female gender, and Africans or African descendants were enslaved or kept in an inferior position because their race was thought to be intellectually and morally incapable of civilization. In each case, when a natural order limits social formations, systems of rigid and inescapable hierarchies emerge. But note that in the three cases outlined, a 'scientific' theory of nature (biology and genetics) was used only in the latter two cases.

This process of naturalization seems to be a necessary trait of all social hierarchies. As Guillaumin (1992) observes,

the ideological implication of the idea of nature (and natural groups) cannot be abolished from social relations in which they occupy a central place. Ideologically hidden (since ideology lurks under 'evidence'), the 'natural' form, whether it is common sense or institutionalized practice, is one of the main technical means used by the dominant groups in their relations with subordinate groups. (p. 192)

Certainly, one can use racism as a metaphor for any type of naturalization resulting from systematic discriminatory practices. This, however, is a loose usage of the term, because race could be empirically absent but lending its figurative meaning to the discriminatory discourse. My presumption is that if one speaks of some discriminatory practices as sexism, class discrimination, or ethnism, that is because race is subsumed under other differences or is only a trope of irreducible differences. With this new thinking about race, the more complicated and subtle imbedding of race in class and cultural differences in Brazil comes under new attention. To use Gates' (1985) word:

Race has become a trope of ultimate, irreducible difference between cultures, linguistic groups, or adherents of specific belief systems which—more often than not—also have fundamentally opposed economic interests. Race is the ultimate trope of difference because it is so very arbitrary in its application. (p. 5)

Race and Color

In the literature relating to race relations in Brazil, as Wade (1994) points out, 'the distinction between appearance and ancestry is often left unclarified and made to parallel a distinction between the insignificance and the significance of "race" ' (p. 28). In contrast to the United States, races in Brazil are not defined by the rule that there is no clear rule of biological descendance for belonging to a racial group, but rather, classifications of physical appearance and an 'interplay between a variety of achieved and ascribed statuses' (Harris, 1974). This would mean that there are no racial groups in Brazil, only 'groups of color' (Degler, 1991, p. 103).

Sociologists widely accepted the idea that, in Brazil and in Latin America in general, there was no racial prejudice, just 'color prejudice.' Azevedo (1955) writes, 'Since color and somatic traits function, to a great degree, as symbols of status, resistance to inter-marriage suggests both class and race prejudice' (p. 90). Wright (1990) is even more explicit in his discussion of Venezuela: 'But Venezuelans consider only those individuals with black skin as black. Color rather than race—appearance rather than origin—play far more important roles in influencing the Venezuelans' perceptions of individuals' (p. 3).

As Fernandes (1965) points out, the idea of color prejudice is better used as a native's notion, first conceptualized by the Frente Negra Brasileira (Black Brazilian Front) in 1940. The group referred to the peculiar type of racial discrimination that oppresses Brazilian Blacks, one wherein color—viewed as a spontaneous, natural fact—and not race— viewed as an artificial, abstract, scientific concept—is decisive.

The conception of color as natural phenomenon rests on the pretense that physical appearance and phenotypical traits are neutral, objective, biological facts. But that is just the way in which in Brazil, color is a figure for race. When scholars incorporate in their discourse color as the criterion for constituting 'objective' groups, they refuse to perceive Brazilian racism. Their conclusion is superficial and formalistic. With history and clear rules of descendance, there would be no races, just spontaneous groups of color.

But there is nothing spontaneously natural about phenotypical traits or color. Gates (1985) says,

It takes little reflection, however, to recognize that these pseudoscientific categories are themselves figures. Who has seen a black or red person, a white, yellow or brown [person]? These terms are arbitrary constructs, not reports of reality. But language is not only the medium of this often insidious tendency; it is the sign. Current language use signifies the difference between cultures and their possession of power, spelling out the distance between subordinate and superordinate, between bondsman and lord in terms of their 'race.' (p. 6)

This position is strengthened by the argument that nothing in skin color, hair type, width of nose, thickness of lips is more naturally visible or discriminating than other traits, such as foot size, height, eye color, or any other physical trait. Such traits have meaning merely within a preexisting ideology (an ideology that creates the facts it organizes), and only because of this do they function as meaningful classifications or criteria.

In sum, a person can only have a color and be classified in a color group if an ideology exists in which the color of people has meaning. That is, people do not have any color except within racial ideologies, *stricto sensu*.

Racism in a South American Way
What is the ideology that particularizes racism in Brazil? The distinctiveness of Brazilian racism, or Latin American racism in general, comes from the fact that the Brazilian nationhood was not formed, or 'imagined' to use Anderson's (1992) metaphor, as a community of ethnic dissimilar individuals coming from all parts of Europe, as was the United States. Brazil is an amalgam of Creoles from different ethnic and racial backgrounds whose race and ethnicity were lost to gain Brazilian nationhood. Brazil generously offered a comfortable penumbra to hang over everyone's ancestry. Color remained the only trace of race, or better, became its coded name. Colonial racism, founded upon the idea of the ethnic purity of White settlers or conquerors, gave way after independence to the idea of mixed-blooded, mestizo nations, or to a *nação morena* in the Brazilian case, whose citizenship was granted by place of birth, not by ancestry.

Of course the United States or South Africa, for example, presents a similar place-of-birth citizenship; however, they have developed an image of themselves more as a European transplantation (the ethnic melting pot) than a multirace mixture. Their extreme sense of racial community has corresponded with nationality based upon 'mixophobia'—the aversion toward racial mixture, to use Taguieff's (1987) term. To understand it further, one must comprehend how Whiteness is defined in Brazil.

The other main characteristic of race relations in Latin America is the existence of an oligarchical order in which race (color), status, and class are intimately linked. Oboler (1995) writes:

As a result of extensive miscegenation throughout the colonies, racial classifications, social status, and honor evolved into a hierarchical arrangement that Lipschütz has called a 'pigmentocracy.' As Ramón Gutiérrez has described, this was a racial system whereby whiter skin was directly related to higher social status and honor whereas darker skin was associated both with 'the physical labour of slaves and tributary indians' and, visually, with 'the infamy of the conquered.' The Spanish notion of *pureza de sangre*, or purity of blood, was thus imbedded in the New World aristocracy's understanding of the inter-related concepts of race, social status, and honor. (p. 28)

In Brazil, this system of hierarchy is layered with gradations of prestige, where social class (occupation and income), family origin, color, and formal education are buttressed by a dichotomy expressed as highborn/rabble and elite/masses. But the hierarchy and the dichotomies are founded on the racial dichotomy of White/Black, which has sustained the slavocratic order for three centuries.

Da Costa (1988) recognizes this origin of color prejudice in Brazil when she writes about the Second Empire: 'Racial prejudice served to maintain and legitimize the distance between a world of privileges and rights and one of deprivation and duties' (p. 137). The 19th-century liberal doctrine that held that the poor were poor because they were inferior found legitimacy in Brazil in the cultural destruction of Africans by European social customs and the conditions of poverty and cultural unpreparedness of free Blacks and mestiços. The servile condition of slaves, like the poverty and misery of free Blacks and mestiços, was taken as a sign of racial inferiority.

As Da Costa (1988), Fernandes (1965), and others have so well demonstrated, the entire Brazilian elite (including the Abolitionists) was prisoner to this logic, which justified social inequalities. For liberals, slavery was only an obstacle to their ideas. They did not have a critical reflection on race relations and did not care about the conditions of Blacks after Abolition. The admission of universal human equality was placed on the level of theory (dogma), beyond any contact with, or commitment to, the interests of real people. As today, this theory co-existed with a great social distance and a sense of superiority in relation to Blacks, mulattos, and the general populace.

In fact, the idea of color, despite being affected by class hierarchies (thus, 'money whitens,' as does education), is founded upon a peculiar notion of race. This notion revolves around the dichotomy of whiteness/blackness just as in the Anglo-Saxon world. This working definition is peculiar in terms of its definition of 'whiteness,' that is, the rule that defines group belonging. In Brazil, Whiteness was not formed through the exclusive ethnic melting pot of European people, as in the United States; on the contrary, 'Whiteness' absorbed mixed-race, light mulattos who could exhibit the dominant symbols of Europeans: a Christian upbringing and Portuguese literacy. By extension, the rules of belonging minimized the Black pole of this dichotomy, thereby separating mestiços from Blacks. The meaning of the word *Black*, therefore, crystallized the absolutely different, the non-European. By this meaning, a real Black could not be a complete Christian (should exhibit some syncretic animist beliefs) or a cultivated man (Black women were not even considered in the identification reasoning). Therefore, in Brazil, only those with very dark skin suffer the same degree of prejudice and discrimination as Black Africans. Those with varying degrees of mestiçagem may enjoy, according to their degree of Whiteness (both chromatic and cultural, as white is a feature of Europeanness), some of the privileges reserved for Whites.

Dzidzienyo (1979) was perhaps the first to note this peculiarity of race relations in Brazil. Defining the 'hallmark of the much-vaunted Brazilian "racial democracy,"' was,

the bias that white is best and black is worst and therefore the nearer one is to white, the better. The hold which this view has on Brazilian society is all-evasive and embraces a whole range of stereotypes, role-playing, job opportunities, life-styles, and, what is even more important, it serves as the corner-stone of the closely-observed 'etiquette' of race relations in Brazil. (p. 3)

Corroborating Dzidzienyo's thesis, Cleveland Donald, Jr., a Black American journalist visiting Brazil in 1972, noted, 'In fact, it does not matter that the Brazilian mulatto is not a "Negro"; far more important is the fact that he is never White' (cited in Hellwig, 1992, p. 212).

Changing Patterns of Racism in Brazil

Any analysis of Brazilian racism must consider at least three major historical processes: the process of nation formation; the intermingling of race in the discursive, ideological field with the other major social hierarchies of class, status, and gender; and the transformations of the socioeconomic order and its regional effects.

A discussion of nationhood is of foremost importance because in Brazil, as suggested before, the rules of nation-belonging were intended to subsume and suppress ethnic, racial, and community feelings. The Brazilian nation was first thought of as culturally uniform in terms of religion, race, ethnicity, and language. In this idea of nation, Brazilian racism could only be characterized by a fear of others, making it necessary to negate others' differences, however they may be defined (Taguieff, 1987, p. 29).

But negation of differences does not mean that universal, enlightened racism is necessarily a hidden racism, one that is ashamed to say its name. On the contrary, in the beginning of the 20th century, Brazilian fear of others was still explicit. The fundamental grounding of Brazilian racialism at this time rested upon a peculiar adaptation of scientific racism. If every racism has a particular history, whitening is what specifies Brazil's. According to Skidmore (1993), this doctrine was based, on the assumption of white superiority—sometimes muted by leaving open the question of how 'innate' inferiority might be, and using the euphemisms 'more advanced' and 'less advanced' races. But to this assumption were added two more. First, the black population was becoming progressively less numerous than the white for reasons which included a supposedly lower birth rate, higher incidence of disease, and social disorganization. Second, miscegenation was 'naturally' producing a lighter population, in part because whiter genes were stronger and in part because people chose partners lighter than themselves. (pp. 64–65)

In summary, the particularity of Brazilian racialism resided in the importation of racist theories from Europe, excluding two important conceptions— 'the innateness of racial differences and the degeneracy of mixed bloods—in order to formulate their own solution to the "Negro problem"' (Skidmore, 1993, p. 77). White blood was thought to purify, dilute, and exterminate Black blood, thus opening the possibility for mestiços to elevate themselves to a civilized state. Whitening was the response of a wounded national pride assaulted by doubts and qualms about its industrial and economic genius. It was a way to rationalize the feelings of racial and cultural inferiority suggested by scientific racism and the geographical determinism of the 19th century.

Freyre, Pierson, and the whole project of social anthropology represented a blow against this shameless racism. Although I do not intend to discuss the academic merits or pitfalls of these works, I do examine some of their ideas in the perspective of a changing nationhood.

When Pierson (1942), Azevedo (1955), and others conducted their research, the second Brazilian-born generations of Italian, Spanish, German, and Japanese immigrants were climbing the social and economic ladder of the southern states. São Paulo would become the major industrial city in Latin America. The old stock of Brazilians, mainly from the sertão, were emigrating in large numbers to São Paulo and entering subordinate positions in the labor market. The traditionally imagined Brazilian nationality was, as a result, under profound stress. This stress came from the fact that the 'new Creoles' (the native-born children of recent immigrants) did not present the same cultural uniformities as the older ones and maintained some sense of community and ethnic belonging. This novelty was far more important because these new Brazilians were situated in the consolidated, dynamic industrial and agricultural areas of southern and southeastern Brazil, toward which the cultural national axis of the country was turning—toward Rio de Janeiro, São Paulo, and Rio Grande do Sul.

The historic cultural areas of Bahia, Pernambuco, and Minas Gerais remained almost untouched in their racial composition by the new wave of immigration (Merrick & Graham, 1979; Skidmore, 1993). Freyre's work and the social anthropology of the 1940s and 1950s were done in Pernambuco and Bahia, as part of the reaction of established Brazilianhood to the cultural challenge represented by the new economic axis of São Paulo. In this sense, racial democracy as reinterpreted by the cultural anthropology of Freyre (1938) can be said to be a founding myth of a rapidly transformed nation.

It would be an error, however, to think that the culturalist thought of the mid-20th century—after Freyre and Pierson—changed the racist assumptions of whitening. Actually, the whitening thesis was adapted to the basic tenets of social anthropology and came to signify the mobility of mestiços within the social hierarchy. On the one side, whitening was an empirical statement of fact, an upward mobility track followed by Blacks; on the other side, it presupposed a racist view of blackness to which the theory remained silent and acritical.

The Eurocentric perspective of the culturalist version of whitening can be found in Freyre (1938), Pierson (1942), Azevedo (1955), and all the most prominent and progressive Brazilian anthropologists of the 1950s:

Through mixing and other socio-biological factors, the darker group, of black phenotype, is slowly being absorbed in the ethnic caldron; the white group is growing faster and the mestiços increase in numbers, registered in statistics as *pardos* (brown), to be ultimately submerged, through mixing, by the group predominantly of European heritage. (Azevedo, 1955, p. 51)

Whitening hereafter signified the capacity of Brazil (defined either as an extension of Europe or as a country wherein a new race was born) to absorb and integrate mestiços and Blacks. This capacity implicitly requires a willingness of people of color to repudiate their African or indigenous ancestry. Thus, whitening and racial democracy are, in fact, concepts of a new racialist discourse. The racist substance to these concepts resides in the idea, at times implicit, that there are three founding races of Brazilian nationality that have made different contributions and have qualitatively different cultural potential. The color of people, like their customs, are indexes of the positive or negative value of these races. At the core of this thought is the supposition that the mark of color is indelible not only because it signals inferior ancestry, but also because it symbolizes the presumed inferiority of this race.

It also means, implicitly, a very definitive notion of Brazilianness. Writing about the colored elites in Bahia, a city where 80% of the population has a census-declared African ancestry, Azevedo (1955) successively says:

Because of its architecture and its urban style, its antiquity, and its moderate rhythm of life, Bahia is considered today Brazil's most European city. (p. 25)

Bahia considers itself one of the most Brazilian communities in the whole country by virtue of its reduced number of foreigners and by virtue of being constituted by the original elements who settled in Brazil. (p. 38)

No other Brazilian state which has a large black population shows such a high degree of racial mixture (mestiçagem) as Bahia. This demonstrates that Bahia is probably the most important Euro-African ethnic melting pot in Brazil. (p. 48)

In these passages, the discursive slippage between Europeanness, Brazilianness, and mestiçagem clearly reveals the 'European' character of this imagined nationhood, operating through the Creolization of Europeanness by the whitening of mestiçagem.

These same passages, which uncover a racialized nationhood—typical of the northeastern elites of Brazil—also unravel the strains to this nationhood brought by the European immigrant wave of 1890 to 1920, when thousands of Italians, Spaniards, Portuguese, Germans, and Japanese settlers entered the southern states in a partially official policy of whitening.

The Whiteness produced by the southern melting pot is very different from the consolidated, colonial melting pot Azevedo (1955) refers to. The main difference lies in the fact that those Whites did in truth mix in the Brazilian middle class and, to a much lesser degree, the working classes. The *paulista* (from São Paulo) working class was racially transformed through the absorption of northeastern immigrants, mainly Blacks and mestiços (Andrews, 1991). Indeed, the rapid upward mobility of European immigrants is testimony to the relative lenience of Brazilian society toward Europeans, in contrast to the subordinate assimilation of Africans.

Japanese descendants offer, in this respect, an extremely interesting case. Although placed outside the imagery of Brazilianness (they are still called *nisei*), they were not assimilated into the White–Black status gradient inherited from slavery but entered directly into the class gradient of the competitive order. As a result, they found enough leeway and arranged sufficient cultural and economic capital to make a better journey through the Brazilian society than those of African descent.

The new ethnic communities of immigrant descendants who, at first, saw and were seen by Brazilians (the traditional) as foreigners were absorbed into the Brazilian mainstream. They were also incorporated into the southern Brazilian elites and ended up redefining the racialized others, mainly working-class or underclass 'traditional Brazilians,' as *baianos* (Bahians) and *nordestinos* (northeasterners). Baianos and nordestinos are Black or mixed-race Brazilians from the working class; they have become the special targets of Brazil's new racism.

Theorizing about Racism and Anti-Racism in Brazil

There is something very special in this racism that comes also from the peculiar way Brazilianness is imaged. As Anderson (1992) argues, the nation in Latin America was mainly defined by 'substantial landowners, allied with somewhat smaller number of merchants, and various types of professionals (lawyers, military men, local and provincial functionaries)' (p. 48). Despite the fact that all Brazilians did not gain economically, the potential for conflict was averted by elite actions. This was done by incorporating mixed-race Blacks and Native Americans more 'as potential recruits to mixedness' (Wade, 1993, p. 3) than as full citizens. In fact, mixed-race Blacks and Native Americans were excluded from the beginning through the very process of their emancipation, as an underclass.

Brazilian racism has a prerepublican origin. Reis (1993) shows how Africans in the mid-19th century, manumitted or not, were discriminated against in Bahia and forced back to rural areas or to Africa. Africans were the first 'other,' the absolute different, and when there were not Africans left but Creoles, black became a figures for Africanness.

This holds true for the upper classes and the lower classes alike. In the popular usages of Brazilianness, mainly in the soccer subculture, Creoles who do not fit the ideal mixed-race pattern of *morenidade* are called *negão* if Black or *alemão* (German) or *galego* (Galician) if White. This apparent chromatic symmetry of black and white applied by and for poor people is reversed in the chromatology of status, whereby they distinguish between a *branco fino* (those of pure European lineage) and a *branco de terra*, the mixed-Creole White, thereby stressing the importance of being European.

To mark the origins of this racism, Fernandes (1965) calls it the 'slave metamorphosis,' to mean how black, the skin color, was used from Abolition onward as a signifier for subordinate, underclass Brazilians.

Actually, racism in Brazil has been played mainly through the contradictory game of a broadly defined citizenship, guaranteed by formal juridical rights, on the one side, but largely ignored, not enforced, and structurally limited by poverty and everyday state violence, on the other side. Racism is perpetrated through the curtailment of citizenship and the social distance created by huge economic, cultural, and social inequalities separating Blacks from Whites, poor from well-to-do, north from south.

Elites in Brazil, encompassing landowners, capitalists, intellectuals, and middle classes, represent a factual, broad compromise between wild exploitation and *bonne conscience*. On one side, elites can boast a radical, modern legislation; on the other side, it can be sure the sophisticated laws are highly inoperative. Universal franchise, for example, until recently (1988) was limited to literate people, which represented disenfranchisement for the Black illiterate mass. Still another example: Racism was first considered a misdemeanor by a Congressional Act of 1951 (Lei Afonso Arinos, no. 1390); in 1988, as a result of lobbying by the Black movement, the new democratic constitution made racism a felony. To this date, however, nobody has been sentenced on a racist charge. On the contrary, victims' attorneys opt for charges that stand a better chance for winning the case (Guimarães, 1994). This is the current Brazilian pattern of racism, which does not show its face and hides behind enlightened universalism, masking itself as anti-racism, and denying the full presence of the other, the African Brazilian or the Native Brazilian.

How does anti-racism unmask a racism that does not recognize itself as racism, that naturalizes the other through chromatic metaphors, regionalism, and class etiquette?

Marxist thought, which strongly influenced the doctrines and actions of the emerging Brazilian middle class in the 1960s, 1970s, and 1980s, did nothing to reverse this status quo. On the contrary, Marxist insistence that races are nonexistent and color is an epiphenomenon merely gave racial democracy a socialist bent. Or rather transformed it into an ideal to be achieved only through class struggle. Marxist thought adapted very well to the idea of capitalism (here a trope for Europeanness) as a civilizing force, to which the people of the entire world would naturally have to submit before reaching the socialist stage. Even when the inherent racism of these cultural theories and refined color classifications (which substitute bipolar classification) is recognized, the counter-argument remains that in Brazil racism is 'milder.' Its mildness is suggested by the relative conformity of the Black population and the absence of legal mechanisms to thwart inequality and discrimination.

In a certain sense, the ideal of racial democracy is really a founding myth of Brazilian nationality and can only be denounced as myth, as broken promises. In fact, the studies by Andrews (1992), Castro and Guimarães (1994), Hasenbalg (1979), Lovell (1989), N. Silva (1980), P.C. Silva (1993), Telles (1992), and others unmask the mildness of Brazilian racial democracy. They show the profound inequalities that separate Blacks from other groups. They reveal a de facto job, residential, and educational segregation between White and non-White.

A critical challenge for those who struggle against racism in Brazil is to show not only inequalities, but their daily reproduction by institutions of production (public and private enterprises), institutions of public order (the police, the judicial and correctional systems), and educational and health care institutions. This is an important way through which one can hope to displace the centenarian, invisible veil that wraps the dichotomies of elite/masses and White/Black in Brazilian society.

For the African Brazilian population, those who call themselves *negros* (Blacks), anti-racism must mean first the admission of race; that is, a perception of themselves—the racialized others—as the racialized 'we.' It means the reconstruction of the self, drawing upon African heritage—the Afro-Brazilian culture of *candomblé*, *capoeira*, and *afoxés*, but also upon the cultural and political reservoir of the 'Black Atlantic' legacy—the Civil Rights Movement in the United States, the Caribbean cultural renaissance, and the fight against apartheid in South Africa.

The new cultural forms of the Black movement in Latin America and Brazil (Agier, 1993; Agier & Caravalho, 1992; Wade, 1993) have stressed the process of Black reidentification in ethnic terms. It seems that only a racialized discourse can sustain a sense of pride, dignity, and self-reliance, largely destroyed by a century of invisible, universalist, enlightened racism. This ethnic resurgence is constructed upon a land to be retrieved, such as the former Maroon territories, or the transformation, largely symbolic, of poor urban areas into Black neighborhoods or new Maroons—*quilombos*. Second, there is need for the culture to redeem and repurify in contact with an imaginary Africa, the Africa brought and maintained as memory.

This concrete, popular agenda of anti-racism is still fiercely combated by Brazilian nationalists, all over the political spectrum, who believe in the official, mythological anti-racism of Brazil. They are very susceptible to what they call the reverse racism of Black organizations, or the importation of foreign categories and feelings. In truth, nothing harms the Brazilian ideal of assimilation more than the cultivation of differences. Even within the Black movement, one can hear dissident views, dissenting against a narrow definition of blackness or the essentialism involved in any ethnic formation.

Trapped at the crossroads of different types of racism, Latin American intellectuals, mainly those who view themselves through European lenses, must begin to realize that racism does not exist outside a particular history. There is no absolute, metahistorical concept of race or racism. By exploring the linkages between racism and anti-racism in the Brazilian context and situating them in the broader world system, one can hope to contribute to rescuing Brazilian race relations from its myths. That is the only way Latin American anti-racists can fight not others' but their own racism.

['Racism and Anti-Racism in Brazil: A Postmodern Perspective', in B. P. Bower (ed.), *Racism and Anti-Racism in World Perspective* (Thousand Oaks, Calif.: Sage, 1995), 208–26.]

Section VII

Theories of Racism

INTRODUCTION

What do we mean by the notion of racism? What are the main analytical models used to explain the nature of racism in contemporary societies? How do we understand the changing forms of racialized social relations and the political structures that underpin them? These are questions that have attracted much attention among scholars and researchers in a variety of social science and humanities disciplines. The outcome of this interest is reflected in the growing body of theorizing about race and racism and in the heated nature of theoretical disputes and controversies. The extracts we have included in this section are intended as an overview of the key arenas of theoretical debate and link up with many of the questions that were touched upon in previous sections from a historical perspective.

The extracts presented here have been selected with two main concerns in mind. First, we have sought to include some extracts that give an overview of theoretical debates and concerns over time. This is partly because we felt it important to contextualize more recent debates against a broader historical canvas, against the tendency to conceptualize contemporary debates in isolation from previous scholarship and research. Second, we have sought to reflect the diversity of theoretical perspectives evident in this field rather than focus on one particular paradigm. This is because one of the most important aspects of theorizing in this field over the past decade or so has been the evident breakdown of orthodoxies of one kind or another. A plethora of studies have sought to broaden the boundaries of how we study race and ethnicity in various national or global settings.

The first extracts take us back to the attempts by Robert Park and John Rex to define the study of race and ethnicity as a discrete area of scholarship. As two of the scholars who have helped to define the boundaries and analytical tools of race and ethnic studies both Park and Rex can be seen as attempting to link sociological theorizing to the analysis of actual situations in which racial and ethnic categorizations play an important role in shaping what they call race relations. Park's work was heavily influenced by the experience of race in the United States, but he was also interested in the broader question of the conditions that lead to the development of 'race relations' situations in different societies. Park assumes that race relations have to do with interactions between cultural groups, drawing on a concept of culture stretched to include a corresponding social psychological theory that the development of racial categories was also related to individual needs, such as the need for recognition, esteem, identity, and the needs of social groups for cohesion and morale.

The extract from John Rex's classic attempt to locate the concept of race in relation to sociological theory symbolizes another important strand in theorizing in this field, namely the attempt to link the analysis of race relations to other sets of social relations such as class. Within the terms of Rex's analytic model the definition of social relations between persons as race relations is encouraged by the existence of certain structural conditions: frontier situations of conflict over scarce resources, the existence of unfree, indentured, or slave labour, unusually harsh class exploitation, strict legal intergroup distinctions and occupational segregation, differential access to power and prestige, cultural diversity and limited group interaction, and migrant labour as an underclass fulfilling stigmatized roles in a metropolitan setting. Although Rex's work also draws to some extent on the earlier tradition of sociological theorizing linked to the work of Park his own model is consciously located within a framework that is based on notions of class rather than culture.

The next three extracts feature the work of scholars who have sought to move the analysis of race and racism in new directions. Although each extract is characterized by its own mode of analysis they can be seen as linked to a broader trend in theorizing in this field that has become evident since the 1970s, namely an attempt to draw on a neo-Marxist perspective to analyse the interrelationship of class relations and forms of social differentiation based on racial and ethnic categories. The extract from Robert Miles exemplifies the most consistent attempt to outline a specifically Marxist approach to the study of racial categories. Miles's work is concerned with the analytical and objective status of race as a basis of action, and he has consistently argued against what he sees as the reification of race in much of the social science literature in this field. He has forcefully argued that the very notion of 'race' should be rejected as an analytic category in the social sciences, insisting on the need to always place it in scare quotes in his own work. More importantly, however, Miles's work points to the need to focus analysis on the processes of racialization that produce the conditions for 'race' to become an important means of social categorization. In this sense his work touches on some of the key themes to be found in the work of other recent theorists of race and racism, who have also been keenly concerned to deconstruct and go beyond the very notion of race and to highlight the ways in which it is essentially contested.

The extracts from Colette Guillaumin and David Theo Goldberg can be seen as examples of this broader intellectual and political trend. Guillaumin's work draws on both historical controversies about the notion of race as well as on more recent debates in France about the issue of racism. On the basis of her account one of the ironies of the current situation is that although it is widely acknowledged that 'race does not exist' racism has become, particularly in the twentieth century, one of the most important categories used to justify ideological domination, subordination, and privilege. Dominant representations of race operate in such a way as to construct symbolic boundaries between racialized groups and ethnic groups, leading to a situation where despite agreement that 'races' do not exist as such it is in the name of race that differences are accorded social significance and are named and explained. More importantly the usage of race carries with it brutal material consequences for those who are included within, or excluded from, the boundaries of who belongs and who does not.

Goldberg's work, which has been influential in recent years, shares some common ground with the work of both Miles and Guillaumin, but it seeks to locate the analysis of race within a more dynamic political framework. The central emphasis in his work is on the complex ways in which different kinds of racism, or what he calls racist expressions, are produced through racialized discourses. For him discourses about race are by no means fixed and have to be seen as firmly located in specific times and contexts. From this starting point he produces a nuanced account of the variety of forms and meanings that are attached to the notion of race, emphasizing in particular the need to situate meanings attached to race in specific political, ideological, and cultural contexts.

The final extract by Patricia Hill Collins engages with a question that has preoccupied many scholars in this field, on both sides of the Atlantic, in recent years. She attempts to bring the question of gender, and its complex interrelationship with racial and class categorization, to the fore of her analysis of black feminism. Collins's work is emblematic of a trend during the past decade or so to question the relative neglect of questions about gender within the mainstream of race relations research. Her account focuses particularly on the need to include in any rounded discussion of race the insights of black feminism, particularly in relation to the importance of the interface of racism, sexism, and gender differences in shaping everyday social processes.

We hope that when read together these extracts help to situate a number of the important trends in theorizations of race and racism. We are aware that given the recent proliferation of debate in this field there are a number of aspects of contemporary theoretical contributions that we have not been able to include in this section, though we have provided an overview of some of these in the General Introduction. But we hope that we have included enough even in this context to make readers think about some of the larger conceptual questions that need to be tackled if we are to come closer to an understanding of both the past and the future of racism.

42 The Nature of Race Relations

Race relations, as that term is defined in use and wont in the United States, are the relations existing between peoples distinguished by marks of racial descent, particularly when these racial differences enter into the consciousness of the individuals and groups so distinguished, and by so doing determine in each case the individual's conception of himself as well as his status in the community. Thus anything that intensifies race consciousness; anything, particularly if it is a permanent physical trait, that increases an individual's visibility and by so doing makes more obvious his identity with a particular ethnic unit or genetic group, tends to create and maintain the conditions under which race relations, as here defined, may be said to exist. Race consciousness, therefore, is to be regarded as a phenomenon, like class or caste consciousness, that enforces social distances. Race relations, in this sense, are not so much the relations that exist between individuals of different races as between individuals conscious of these differences.

Thus one may say, without doing injustice to the sense in which the term is ordinarily used, that there are, to be sure, races in Brazil—there are, for example, Europeans and Africans—but not race relations because there is in that country no race consciousness, or almost none. One speaks of race relations when there is a race problem, and there is no race problem in Brazil, or if there is, it is very little if at all concerned with the peoples of African and European origin.

On the other hand, when one speaks of race relations and the race problem in South Africa one does not think of the African and the European. The African does, to be sure, constitute a problem, but in South Africa, it is described as the 'native problem.' South Africa has, also, the problem of the Cape Coloured, a hybrid people of mixed Hottentot and European origin. The native, as the term is there used, is a Bantu, and of a quite different racial origin than the 'native.' South Africa has, likewise, the problem of the East Indian. Hindus were first imported into Natal about 1860 in the interest of the sugar industry in that province. However, when one speaks or writes in common parlance of the race problem in South Africa, it is to the relations existing between the English and the native Dutch or Africaners that this expression refers.

In this context and in this sense the expression race relations seems to describe merely the sentiments and attitudes which racial contacts invariably provoke and for which there is, apparently, no more substantial basis than an existing state of the public mind. For the purpose of this chapter, however, the term has been employed in a somewhat wider universe of discourse, in which it includes all the relations that ordinarily exist between members of different ethnic and genetic groups which are capable of provoking race conflict and race consciousness or of determining the relative status of the racial groups of which a community is composed.

Race relations, in this more inclusive sense, might comprise, therefore, all those situations in which some relatively stable equilibrium between competing races has been achieved and in which the resulting social order has become fixed in custom and tradition.

Under such circumstances the intensity of the race consciousness which a struggle for status inevitably arouses, where it did not altogether disappear, would be greatly diminished. The biracial organizations of certain social institutions that have come into existence in Southern states since emancipation exhibit the form which such racial accommodations sometimes take. Some of these, as in the case of the churches and the labor organizations, seem to have grown up quite spontaneously and have been accepted by both races as offering a satisfactory *modus vivendi*. In other instances, as in the case of the public school, the segregation which such dual or biracial organizations necessitate, in spite of certain advantages they offer, has been bitterly opposed even when they have later been reluctantly accepted by the colored people. They were opposed (1) because of the discrimination they inevitably involve and (2) because the separation of the races in the schools as elsewhere has seemed to imply the acceptance of an inferior civic and social status.

All this suggests that the term *race relations*, as here conceived, includes relations which are not now conscious or personal, though they have been; relations which are fixed in and enforced by the custom, convention, and the routine of an expected social order of which there may be at the moment no very lively consciousness.

Historically, the races of mankind at different times and places have lived together in a wide variety of ways. They have lived over long periods of time in a relationship not unlike that existing between the plant and animal species occupying the same territory, that is to say, a relationship of biotic interdependence, without interbreeding. Under these conditions the different races, like the different species, have been able to maintain their integrity as distinct races while living in a form of association that might be described as symbiotic rather than social. Examples of this sort of symbiosis among human creatures are the gypsies of Western Europe or the Wild Tribes of India, particularly the so-called 'Criminal Tribes.'

On the other hand, other racial stocks, notably those that have fused to create the existing peoples of Europe, have lived together in an intimacy so complete that the original racial differences that once distinguished them have almost wholly disappeared, or at best can now only be clearly determined by the formal investigations of anthropologists. This is the case, for example, of the Germanic and Slavic tribes which, politically united by the conquests of the Markgraf of Brandenburg and the Teutonic Knights, in the thirteenth century, eventually fused to produce the Prussian people.

Evidence of this modern instance of racial amalgamation are the occasional 'racial islands,' particularly in East Prussia, where, because the process of fusion has not been completed, some remnants of the Slavic peoples and their cultures still persist. Perhaps the most notable example of this incomplete amalgamation and assimilation is the existence, a short distance from Berlin, of an ancient Wendish folk, which still preserves its language and culture, and still cherishes a kind of tribal identity. They are called the *Spree-wälder*, i.e., the people of the Spree Forest, where they exist in the midst of a German population, as a kind of racial and cultural enclave.

There are, however, numerous examples of such isolated racial islands nearer home. There are, for example, the interesting little communities of Negro, Indian, and white mixed bloods, of which there are a great number scattered about in out-of-the-way corners of the Southern and Eastern states. Perhaps the most notable of these is the community of white and Negro half-castes, living near Natchitoches, Louisiana, described by Lyle Saxon in his recently published novel, *Children of Strangers*.

All these various and divergent types of isolated, and more or less outcast racial and cultural groups, have recently been classed, for the purposes of comparison and study, as minority groups, although the term as originally used acquired its meaning in a European rather than American context. Among these such sectarian and religious groups as the Amish of Eastern Pennsylvania, or the Mormons of Utah, have sometimes been included.

The classic examples of such racial minorities, however, are the Jewish communities in Europe and the Near East, where Jews have maintained, in spite of their very intimate association with other peoples, their racial identity and their ancient tribal religion.

All these relations of cultural or racial minorities with a dominant people may be described, for our purposes, as types of race relationship, even though no evidences exist either of active race conflict, on the one hand, or of obvious racial diversity on the other. [. . .]

Looking at race relations in the long historical perspective, this modern world which seems destined to bring presently all the diverse and distant peoples of the earth together within the limits of a common culture and a common social order, strikes one as something not merely unique but millennial! Nevertheless, this new civilization is the product of essentially the same historical processes as those that preceded it. The same forces which brought about the diversity of races will inevitably bring about, in the long run, a diversity in the peoples in the modern world corresponding to that which we have seen in the old. It is likely, however, that these diversities will be based in the future less on inheritance and race and rather more on culture and occupation. That means that race conflicts in the modern world, which is already or presently will be a single great society, will be more and more in the future confused with, and eventually superseded by, the conflicts of classes.

[From *Race and Culture* (New York: Free Press, 1950), 81–4, 116.]

43 The Concept of Race in Sociological Theory

The Political Importance of a Theoretical Problem

The problem of race relations challenges the consciences of sociologists in a way that probably no other problem does. Just as physicists have been reminded of their social and political responsibilities as the full meaning of nuclear warfare became apparent, so sociologists, who are expected to understand the relationships that exist between groups, have been confronted in our own time with problems of racial conflict and racial persecution of a quite unprecedented kind. Before and during the Second World War millions of Jews were exterminated, allegedly because of their race, and with the support of a phoney kind of biological and sociological theory. In our own day discrimination against, or exploitation of, men distinguished by their skin colour prevents millions of human beings from enjoying basic human rights. And in the pattern of international history that is being woven for our future, the one overriding theme seems to be that of race war.

In the world of 1945, still reeling from the experience of Nazism, it was the biologists who were asked by the United Nations to analyse the phenomenon of racism, and their work led to the formulation of expert statements in 1941, 1951, and 1964. But, while the biologists were able to answer the question, 'In what sense does biological science distinguish races and other genetically based groups?'—a question that itself requires a highly technical answer—they were not able to answer the separate question, 'Why are groups of men between whom political differences exist sometimes called races?' All they could say was that such groups bore no relation to 'races' in the biological sense. The problem therefore was handed over to the sociologists.

The problem with which we are faced is not, however, simply an empirical one. It is not a question, for example, of discovering what correlations there are between prejudice towards coloured persons, on the one hand, and a variety of other sociological indices, on the other. There have probably been more than enough studies of this kind already. The real problem is to distinguish among the various studies made by sociologists those which are distinguishable as race-relations studies. This is a complex *theoretical* question. It is one that must be answered, however, before any really systematic approach to the full range of situations leading to the growth of racism can be analysed. The fact that so little attention has been directed towards it can only be regarded as something of a professional scandal. [. . .]

Stratification and Other Structural Aspects of Race-Relations Situations

We said above that the notion that race-relations situations were explicable in terms of the theory of stratification had some validity, if the term stratification was used in an inclusive sense. I now wish to suggest that there are at least six kinds of situation that would have to be included. They are:

1 Frontier situations, in which a politically organized group, with an advanced technology and education, encounters another such group whose levels of technology are lower.

2 The particular form of the social relations of production, which is to be found on slave plantations, and in the societies that come into existence immediately after the abolition of slavery.

3 Situations of class conflict in the Marxist, and in the rather wider Weberian, sense, where there is a confrontation of groups possessing differing degrees of market power.

4 Estate and caste systems, in which groups enjoying differing degrees of prestige and of legal rights take on a corporate character and may become occupationally specialized.

5 Situations in which esteem and prestige are not accorded to corporate groups, as such, but are thought of as providing a basis for a continuum, so that any one individual may be thought of as having more or less prestige.

6 Situations of cultural pluralism, such that a number of distinguishable groups interact for limited (e.g. economic) purposes but continue to lead separate communal lives.

Arising from these there appear to be a number of particular problems of metropolitan societies that are recurrently regarded as racial problems:

(a) Urban situations in which a complex system of 'stratification' based upon several of the factors mentioned above exists.

(b) Situations in which a particular group of outsiders is called upon to perform a role, which, although essential to the social and economic life of a society, is in conflict with its value system, or is thought to be beneath the dignity of the society's own members.

(c) Situations in which, in times of crisis, a group that is culturally or physically distinguishable is blamed for the existence of a threat to the society's wellbeing, i.e. scapegoat situations. This process is often connected with the structural situation under (b) above.

The first kind of situation listed is that which Toynbee refers to as characterized by the presence of an external proletariat. It existed when the 'barbarians' were at the gates of Rome, and it has existed on nearly every frontier during the expansion of European nations overseas. It may lead to the extermination of the external proletariat, to their slow subordination and incorporation into the more advanced society, or to a more complex process in which the external proletariat is, militarily speaking, victorious but, culturally speaking, absorbed. Whatever the outcome, however, the encounter between the groups is marked by tension and by the emergence of stereotypes and belief systems that govern the interaction of members of one group with those of another. These may range from those based upon simple moral derogation, as in the case of Jan Van Riebeck's description of the Hottentots as 'dull', stupid, stinking people', through Aristotle's claim that the barbarian is less than a man, to modern theories that different moral characteristics derive from differing genetic inheritance.

Such frontier situations are one of the basic starting-points from which colonial societies emerge. Another alternative, however, is that in which the colonialist, as a part of his economic enterprise, introduces an alien labour force of varying degrees of freedom or unfreedom. Here the central institution is the slave plantation. Slave plantations are characterized by labour-intensive agricultural work and by the fact that the workers are owned by their employer. That is to say they are essentially productive enterprises. Racist belief systems are not necessary to their existence. Slave plantations existed in antiquity without being justified in racist terms, and it is clear that they have existed without masters and slaves being physically distinguishable. None the less, the capacity to regard other human beings as slaves does impose strains on the belief system of any society and bridging beliefs of some kind will nearly always be found. Racist beliefs are to be found in modern plantation situations as well as in the aftermath of abolition, and would seem to be meaningfully related to the legal and economic institution of slavery.

Turning from these colonial situations to what are more commonly thought of as problems of class and stratification, we find that the dominant theory, based upon experience of the race problem in the United States, was for a long time that of Lloyd Warner (1936), that the race-relations situation was best understood as caste in its incipient phase.

The distinguished Negro Marxist sociologist, Oliver Cromwell Cox (1959), has performed a useful service in reminding us, in opposition to this view, that a great many of the situations classified as racial in modern industrial societies are nothing more or less than class situations in the classic Marxist sense. Thus, for example, the black proletariat of South Africa is clearly distinguishable, both from the white owning class and from white organized labour, by the fact that it has a distinct relationship to the means of production. Equally, the almost permanently unemployed Negro youth of America's urban ghettos look more and more like a class in revolt.

One feature of this class-conflict aspect of race relations that is of the very first importance is the development of a militant or revolutionary Black Power movement on an international scale. The situation here appears to be analogous to that which Marx was suggesting when he wrote of the transition from a local trade-union consciousness to a world-wide revolutionary consciousness. In that case, as in this, we are not necessarily dealing with an actual organized revolutionary class, but the sort of quasi-group that arises from a belief in the existence of a common political destiny. In any case the study of this blackpower revolution is central to the study of race relations.

Cox is perhaps wrong, however, in suggesting that class conflict has always been the determining factor in black–white relations. Underdeveloped societies and those undergoing one-sided development through agriculture and mining might well produce some of the main features of the social and political systems to which he attaches the terms caste and estate. The existence of legal inequality and inequality of esteem, together with the maintenance of the authority of a land-owning ruling class, has been a feature of some Latin American societies and it is this which leads some students to the view that a caste-like situation often underlies a problem that comes to be thought of as racial.

It is not sufficient to characterize such societies as paternalist. Indeed it is gravely misleading, for the actual relations between upper and lower 'classes' are often brutally exploitative. If they are distinguishable from what some sociologists call competitive situations, it is not because the lower orders regard their masters as fathers but because, as in medieval Europe, their social situation, and sometimes their legal status, makes any challenge to the authority of their superiors impossible. It is this which leads us to the view that some race-relations situations are in fact based on caste and estate systems.

An objection might be made here by either Warner or Cox that in the case of true caste systems an exploitative element such as we have described is not present. We concede that this may be so in the Indian case. But no other society has attained a fully developed caste system, even by Warner's reckoning. The main point in our using the term is that estate systems mentioned above could develop in the direction of considerable occupational specialization. Where this occurs we may say that an estate system is developing in a caste-like direction.

Another feature of the Caribbean and Latin American situations, however, is the sheer fact of cultural pluralism brought about through the coming together of Negro, Asiatic, and European labour. It is not surprising, therefore, that the concept of the plural society first pioneered by J. S. Furnivall in Indonesia has been applied there. According to Furnivall's ideal type, a situation might be expected in which ethnically distinct groups meet only in the market-place. And while relations there are based upon exploitation of the harshest sort, each group can and does withdraw to its own independent quarter, where it is not subject to the authority of the others.

In fact, most sociologists found that in applying this concept a measure of inequality of power and status extending beyond the market-place had to be accounted for, but this is not to say that the simple differentiated and pluralist society described by Furnivall is not useful, at least as an extreme ideal type against which degrees of inequality can be measured.

Again, while it is useful in order to grasp the flux and variety of historical experience, to see some Latin American and African situations as approximating to a feudal estate system, it is none the less clear that such a system nowhere exists in a pure form. What does seem to be the case, however, is that as a system of this kind or, for that matter, a plantation system becomes less and, less perfect, it breaks down into a status system. Everyone is therefore allocated a certain standing in the society along a quantitatively varying status scale. Thus the position accorded to a man may be high or low according to the lightness or darkness of his skin.

Nearly all of the problems so far discussed are problems that have been encountered at one time or another by British people in their colonial dealings. What is new, however, is the fact of the emergence of a 'racial problem' in the cities of the metropolitan country itself. The more complex subcategories I have listed are intended to provide a framework for the analysis of this problem.

The first fact to notice about colonial immigrants in British society is that not only are they distinguishable on the basis of their skin colour, language, religion, and domestic culture but also they are known through these indicators to have come from fulfilling colonial roles to adopting the role of worker in the metropolitan society. Thus there is at the moment of encounter with the native metropolitan population a double-banked criterion for role ascription. With this said, however, it has still to be noted that relations between such a differentiated group and their hosts are further shaped by the nature and structure of the metropolitan society itself.

One feature of that metropolitan society that increasingly comes to notice, and has been even more clearly brought to notice by the arrival of immigrants, is the existence of a number of unwanted and low-status industrial roles. The more technological advance and educational levels make other kinds of work less arduous or more satisfying, the greater the relative deprivation of those who fulfil these roles. They are therefore shunned by native workers and an alien group can easily be assimilated into them.

Thus far in the British post-war experience, however, it has not been on the industrial front that the immigrant has faced the most acute conflict. Rather it has been with his neighbours in the city. Elsewhere it has been argued that the city can at least in part be analysed as a system of housing class conflict, modified by the emergence of a status-stratified neighbourhood system. I suggest that it is within a system of this kind that immigrants already identified as colonials, and already marked by their past colonial roles, have to take up positions and to encounter their fellow citizens and workers. Of course, the problem comes to be defined as primarily a racial problem, but it should also be clear from what has been said that the pattern of interaction and conflict with which we are dealing here derives partly from the structure of colonialism and partly from the urban class system; neither of which is simply and solely a racial situation.

Taking together the two facts of the emergence of relatively deprived industrial roles and of deprived neighbourhoods, one can see that the immigrant worker is likely to be categorized as belonging to a pariah group, and, in times of crisis, made a scapegoat. Immigrants form pariah groups both in doing unwanted jobs and in providing a kind of housing and neighbourhood that the city needs but that its value system cannot allow it to tolerate. Along with other clearly visible minority groups (e.g. students), they can easily act as scapegoat to be blamed for any hardship suffered by majority groups.

Scapegoating is too often discussed as though it were a purely psychological phenomenon. True, the punishment of the scapegoat is a means of restoring mental equilibrium to those whose personality systems are disturbed. But scapegoating is also a means of restoring *social* equilibrium. Thus certain groups or individuals are threatened because of the hostility their actions or incompetence have engendered. The indication of a scapegoat is a social mechanism whereby resentment may be expressed and the existing power structure maintained. It is the social process *par excellence* that literally fulfils Parson's description of one of his functional subsystems as pattern maintenance and tension management.

Pariah groups may exist without becoming scapegoat groups. Pariah status simply refers to the fact that the group's social function, though necessary, is held to be undesirable. The group may be hated and may even be punished. It does not, however, become a scapegoat unless or until it is blamed for acts it has not committed.

In most cases, of course, a pariah role does go with scapegoating. Jewish moneylenders in European history, the Asian trader in Colonial Africa, the immigrant landlord in European cities, have all performed this double function. One part of it, the pariah part, lies in actually carrying out or even being forced to carry out certain duties and being punished for so doing. The other, or scapegoat part, consists in being held generally to blame for failures of the system. [. . .]

The Nature and Role of Racist Belief Systems

The presence of these two factors (i.e. in the broadest sense of the term, a 'stratification' factor and the possibility of ready classification of those who perform different social roles in terms of some simple ascriptive criterion) is, according to the view adopted here, a necessary condition for the emergence of a race-relations problem. That is to say, we are arguing that any attempt to explain the structure and dynamics of race-relations situations in terms of the strangeness of the newcomer, of culture shock, or in terms of immigrant and host, is inadequate if taken by itself. We would insist that without the power or stratification element there would be no race-relations problem.

On the other hand, it must be pointed out that neither 'stratification' taken by itself, nor even stratification coupled with role allocation in terms of ascriptive criteria, is by itself sufficient reason for describing a problem as a race-relations problem. The other necessary condition is that the belief systems in terms of which roles are explained, described, and justified should have a particular character. In other words, it is not possible to give an adequate and complete account of a race-relations situation without reference to the fact of racism. Even if it could not be argued that racist beliefs played an independent causal role within the total structure, it would still be the case that a complete description and analysis of that structure required a consideration of racism and its relation to structural factors. As we see it, however, racism has a double importance as a part of the total situation and as having an independent causal role in the dynamics of stratification and race-relations structures.

All social situations depend for their character upon the definitions we give to them in our culture. We cannot see society or social institutions or social relations. We simply learn to accept that the occurrence of certain sorts of behaviour may be read as indicating the operation of a social institution or that the presence of a person with certain characteristics implies the existence of a certain pattern of rights. We do not, however, rest content with labelling the various sorts of social interaction in which we engage any more than we rest content with a world of discreet physical things. We grope after anchoring and validating principles that explain why things are as they are and why they should be so. Myth and theology, philosophy and science, all provide us with systematic ways of meeting this need.

There are, however, two quite distinct kinds of belief system that, for lack of a better word, we may call deterministic and undeterministic. When the former are applied to the justification of a social structure the social structure comes to be seen as inevitable and unalterable, and transition from one kind of role to another may be held to be impossible.

The clearest example of such a deterministic theory is the one to which the term racist is most often confined. What happens in this case is that the fact that a particular group suffers discrimination is attributed to an incapacity to perform a role or a special capacity to behave in particular ways that is determined by genetic inheritance. This is the most completely deterministic theory in that it is argued that nothing any individual can do can alter the situation and the pattern of rights in the society.

The specific problem of racism as it was posed to the United Nations in 1945 was concerned with a consideration of a belief system of this kind. It therefore seemed sufficient to gather together expert opinion to show that role performance in modern social systems did not depend upon man's genetic inheritance. This, however, left open a number of other possibilities and the disrepute into which racist theories in the narrow sense have fallen has simply meant that those who profited from them have sought other means of ideological support.

Long before justifications for inequality and exploitation were drawn from biological science they were drawn from theology. Indeed, it could be argued that it was only because the ideological extremism of nineteenth-century positivism demanded the justification of everything in terms of natural science, that biological theories assumed the predominance they did and that the decline of scientism would inevitably lead to the recurrence of other forms of theory. Theology, it is true, might play only a small part but *sociological* doctrines about the superiority of particular cultures and social systems might come to play their part. Thus we should not take the disappearance of the specifically biologically oriented theories of race that were so important in the thirties to mean that the class of sociological problems to which they referred has disappeared. Other deterministic theories would still be used and the essential distinguishing feature of this class of situations, namely inequality between men being justified in a deterministic way, would still be present.

Thus we seem to have arrived at a clearer understanding of the specific field of study with which the sociology of race relations should be concerned. It is concerned with a broad range of stratification situations (using this term in a wide sense to include any situation in which power and privilege are unequally distributed between groups or individual role-players in a social structure), but only in so far as roles or group-memberships are ascribed in terms of observable physical or cultural characteristics such as those which distinguish groups of colonial conquerors and conquered and only if the system as a whole is justified by deterministic beliefs.

It should perhaps be pointed out here that the distinction between deterministic and undeterministic belief systems is not absolute and that deterministic assumptions might well be found hidden in a theory of an undeterministic kind. Thus it may be said that a group of people are not yet ready in terms of education or economic advancement to assume equal rights, but if it is also held that the group concerned cannot be expected to advance economically or educationally during 25, 50, or 100 years, the belief operates deterministically. Furthermore, it might well be that, while the implicit belief of a governing group might be that the governed are inferior from a biological or theological point of view, their explicit statements might all refer to non-ascriptive criteria of role allocation. In this case the sociologists' task would not merely lie in describing the structure and the explicit belief system in terms of which it was justified (a process that itself has the character of unmasking or demystification); it would first involve the discovery or unmasking of the implicit theory that itself had to be unmasked by reference to the actual social structure. [. . .]

Conclusion: The Central Role of Theory and Comparative Studies in Race-Relations Research

The programme and definition of the field that we have suggested for race-relations research is in no way remarkable. Indeed, it would appear to conform to the sociological procedure outlined by Durkheim when he suggests that in the study of any social phenomenon we should,

'indicate first of all by what characteristic one might recognize the thing so designated, then classify its varieties, investigate by methodical inductions what the causes of its variation are, and, finally, compare these results in order to abstract a general formula' (Durkheim 1950: 25).

The really surprising thing is that so little of the sociology of race relations in Britain has conformed to this plan of attack.

The principal obstacle to the development of this programme has probably been quite simply and quite discreditably a disinclination on the part of some sociologists to look at race-relations problems in ways that might be disturbing to the liberal political establishment. Clearly, though, if the assumptions outlined here are correct, the study of race relations is, among other things a part of political sociology. This must mean that when we consider race relations problems in Britain, the behaviour of governments and the policies advocated by all political parties must be up for description and analysis along with other phenomena. We cannot simply assume that there is a basic situation of good will in Westminster or Whitehall and that what we have to do is merely to test particular hypotheses as part of a programme of piecemeal social engineering. All too often this is precisely what sociologists have been asked or encouraged or have undertaken to do.

This response has necessarily led to trivialization of sociological concepts in the race-relations field. But sometimes trivialization seems to have been chosen for its own sake. Thus, although I believe that there is a great deal of scope within an overall framework such as I have outlined for micro-sociological studies, too often the cart has been put before the horse and potentially useful concepts referring to immigrant-host relations, to the stranger and colour-class hypotheses, to role theory and to status-crystallization, have been used as though they by themselves provide a sufficient theoretical foundation for the study of race relations. I find it difficult, myself, to regard work such as this as professionally serious.

I believe that in the field of race relations what we are faced with today is a test of our professional integrity, of our capacity to pursue an objective and systematic programme of sociological study. The area of race-relations research is and will continue to be politically sensitive and those who work in it will be under continual pressure to confine themselves to undertaking only those studies or producing only those conclusions which are least disturbing to government. Work of an alternative kind has only just begun. The object of this paper is to urge that we agree on our theoretical programme and then set out to produce the research workers and to create the necessary institutions to carry it out.

[From 'The Concept of Race in Sociological Theory', in Sami Zubaida (ed.), *Race and Racialism* (London: Tavistock, 1970), 35–6, 39–46, 48–51, 53–5.]

44 Racism as a Concept

In using racism as a concept to describe and explain aspects of the structure and processes of concrete social formations, it is necessary first to know what the word refers to, what particularity it identifies. That this is considered to be problematic may appear surprising in the first instance, given the generally common understanding of, for example, Nazi discourse about the Jews, the justifications for the establishment of apartheid in South Africa, and official legitimations of British colonial settlement and rule. Nevertheless, the concept of racism is contested. In essence, the debate concerns the scope of the concept, and in two senses.

First, for those who define the concept as referring to a particular instance of *ideology*, there is disagreement about the form and content that ideology must possess to warrant categorisation as racism. Second, some writers have claimed that the concept should be used to refer to not only ideology but also intentional practices and/or unintended processes or consequences. There has been, therefore, a process of conceptual inflation whereby the concept has been redefined to refer to a wider range of phenomena. [. . .]

Racism as Ideology

Although the word 'racism' is now widely used in common-sense, political, and academic discourse, it is of very recent origin. There is no reference to the word in the *Oxford English Dictionary* (OED) of 1910 (although there are entries for race and racial). The *OED Supplement* of 1982 defines racism as 'the theory that distinctive human characteristics and abilities are determined by race' and records its first appearance in the English language in the 1930s. Critics of scientific theories of 'race' prior to this decade did not use a concept of racism to identify their ideological object. For example, in a wide-ranging critique published in the late 1920s, Friedrich Hertz referred to 'race hatred' (1928: 1–19). The term racism was used as a title for a book written by Magnus Hirschfeld in 1933–4 in German and subsequently translated into English and published in Britain in 1938. In *Racism*, Hirschfeld set out to refute those arguments of the nineteenth century which, as I have shown in the previous chapter, claimed the mantle of science to sustain the notion of the existence of discrete 'races', hierarchically ordered. But he does so without offering any formal definition of racism and without clarifying how racism is to be distinguished from the concept of xenophobia, which he also employs in his argument (1938: 227).

The original definition and use of the word arose from the coincidence of two processes. The first was the growing body of scientific evidence which undermined the idea of 'races' as natural, discrete and fixed subdivisions of the human species, each with its distinct and variable cultural characteristics and capacity for 'civilisation'. The second was the reaction to the rise of Fascism in Germany and the use of the 'race' idea, legitimated partly by reference to science, by Hitler and the German Nazi party in their identification of Jews as an alien and inferior 'race' in Germany. As the Nazi campaign against the Jews in Germany unfolded, there developed elsewhere in Europe and North America an increasing awareness of the way in which the discourse of 'race' was being used to legitimate the exclusion and genocide of the Jews and other sections of the German population. It became an imperative for some academics and scientists, as well as political activists, to formulate a coherent rejection of the way in which the 'race' idea was utilised in Nazi Germany.

These two developments reinforced each other. There was an intensification of the debate about the scientific status of the discourse of 'race', evident in the publication during the 1930s and 1940s of a number of books which were explicitly critical of either a certain usage of the idea or, in certain instances, the idea itself. Although there was no unanimity amongst these critics, the fact that a critical appraisal of the claim that 'race' was a biological fact was taking place was indicative of a paradigm change within the academic, scientific world. The object of that critical appraisal came to be defined as racism (for example, Hirschfeld 1938).

The absence of unanimity can be demonstrated by a brief review of the key literature of the period. In We Europeans: A Survey of 'Racial' Problems, Huxley and Haddon (1935) argued that there was no scientific evidence to sustain the idea of distinct and discrete 'races' and that 'racial biology' was a pseudoscience. Much of the book consisted of a scientific refutation of classifications based on somatic characteristics and an evaluation of contribution of genetics to an understanding of human variation, from which Huxley and Haddon concluded that the word 'race' should be dropped from scientific vocabulary, to be replaced by 'ethnic group' (1935: 108, 164, 268). Their justification for this recommendation was, at least in part, political.

They argued that the term 'race', like many other pseudo-scientific terms, could be used to 'rationalise emotion' (1935: 262) and that science had a responsibility to identify the truth value of ideas employed in political life (Huxley and Haddon 1935: 287). They made reference to the then contemporary situation in Germany, specifically denying that Nordic or Jewish 'races' existed and identified Nazi theories of 'race' as a 'creed of passionate racialism' (1935: 277). They continued, 'Racialism is a myth, and a dangerous myth at that. It is a cloak for selfish economic aims which in their uncloaked nakedness would look ugly enough' (1935: 287). This myth of racialism was explained as an attempt to justify nationalism.

While Haddon and Huxley rejected any scientific use of the idea of 'race' and, almost as an afterthought, employed the concept of racialism to refer to Nazi ideologies of 'race', their text demonstrates a contradiction over the significance of biological classification. Although they argued that 'any biological arrangement of the types of European man [sic] is still largely a subjective process' (1935: 166), they proceeded to construct one using 'those characters which are the most convenient and readily observed' (1935: 169), specifically skin colour, and hair and nose type. They concluded

We can thus distinguish three major groupings of mankind:
(1) Black woolly hair, dark brown or black skin, and a broad nose.
(2) Wavy or curly hair of any colour from black to flaxen, dark brown to white skin, and a typically medium or narrow nose with usually a high bridge.
(3) Straight lank dark hair, yellowish skin, nose with a tendency to be broad and low-bridged. (1935: 169–70)

Despite their mastery of the scientific evidence, from which they concluded that biological classifications were subjective, they nevertheless reproduced a taxonomy that differed only from nineteenth century classifications in that it did not label these groups as 'Negroid', 'Caucasian' and 'Mongoloid' and described them as 'ethnic groups' rather than 'races'.

Jacques Barzun was more consistent in his pursuit of an objective similar to that of Huxley and Haddon. In *Race, A Study in Modern Superstition* (1938) Barzun offered a critical history of the discourse of 'race' in order to demonstrate that 'race-thinking is . . . a form of erroneous thinking that can be charged with a dozen ulterior motives' (1938: 26) but he did not devise any form of biological taxonomy of the human species. He too made specific reference to Nazi Germany, identifying the Third Reich as 'the most blatant apostle of racialism' (1938: 6), but focusing more broadly on 'racialism as a European phenomenon' (1938: 10). Although Barzun was not explicit, he (like Huxley and Haddon) seemed to use the concept of racialism rather than racism to identify what he referred to as 'race thinking'.

A rather different argument was offered in a book first published in 1942. In *Race and Racism*, Ruth Benedict rejected Barzun's claim that race is a modern superstition, asserting that 'race is a classification based on traits which are hereditary' (1983: 6) and that race constitutes a 'scientific field of enquiry' (1983: 96). Benedict legitimated much of the nineteenth century anthropological and biological classification when she asserted that three main races can be identified, the Caucasian, Mongoloid, and Negroid (1983: 31–2). But she distinguished what she defined as the scientific study of race from racism which she identified as, 'the dogma that one ethnic group is condemned by nature to congenital inferiority and another group is destined to congenital superiority' (1983: 97). Therefore, the concept of racism refers to a set of claims which are contrary to the scientific evidence and which therefore constitute a denial of science. Additionally, she claimed that racism is a temporally and geographically specific phenomenon when she argued that 'racism is a creation of our own time', of 'high European civilisation'.

In the same year that *Race and Racism* was first published, Ashley Montagu's text *Man's [sic] Most Dangerous Myth: The Fallacy of Race* appeared. In it, Montagu defined racism as an ideology which alleged that something called 'race' is the prime determiner of all the important traits of body and soul, of character and personality, of human beings and nations. And it is further alleged that this something called 'race' is a fixed and unchangeable part of the germ plasm, which, transmitted from generation to generation, unfolds in each people as a typical expression of personality and culture. (Montagu 1974: 14)

Despite an agreement on the definition of the concept of racism, Montagu's use of quotation marks signals his disagreement with Benedict's claim that 'race' is a biological reality which can be studied scientifically. He argued (1974: 62), 'Based as it is on unexamined facts and unjustifiable generalisations, it were better that the term "race", being so weighed down with false meaning, be dropped altogether from the vocabulary.'

Two analytical points arise from this literature. First, the original concept of racism presupposed the existence of a discourse of 'race' because it was defined to refer to the nineteenth century beliefs that the human species consisted of a number of different 'races', identified phenotypically, and that these 'races' were ranked in a hierarchy of superiority and inferiority. This interlock was evident in the very title of Benedict's book, *Race and Racism* (1983). Second, the act of labelling the 'race-thinking' of the nineteenth century as racism was simultaneously to label it as a scientific error. Within the scientific arena, this challenge to the nineteenth century idea of 'race' led in two directions, one of which retained this interlock while the other broke it. Thus, respectively, the critique led to either a retention of the discourse of 'race' accompanied by a redefinition of the referent or a rejection of both the discourse of 'race' and the reality to which it supposedly referred.

Benedict's argument was therefore rather different from those advanced by Huxley and Haddon, Barzun, and Montagu. While the latter sought to reject the discourse of 'race', Benedict wished to retain it as a scientific concept and she sought to do so by defining as racism that particular usage of the discourse of 'race' as biological hierarchy which could not be justified by science. In this way, Benedict's definition of racism served to sustain and legitimate the discourse of 'race'. Nevertheless, all these writers were agreed on using a concept of racism or racialism to refer to a very specific ideology, that is, to the product of late eighteenth and nineteenth century scientific thought. So if we consider the long history of European representations of the Other, only those advanced from the late eighteenth century which embodied an explicit discourse of 'race' in order to refer to a discrete biological group can be identified as racism. All earlier representations of the Other are excluded from this definition of racism and therefore qualify as instances of some other ideology or ideologies. It has been common to define these earlier representations as 'ethnocentrism'.

The experience of the Second World War and the knowledge of the consequences of Hitler's 'final solution' to the 'Jewish question' led to new initiatives after 1945 to try to prevent the discourse of 'race' from being used for similar political purposes in the future. The most significant was undertaken by UNESCO,

and claimed the status of science, and of international collaboration and unanimity, to legitimate its objectives. During the 1950s and 1960s, UNESCO as-
sembled, on four separate occasions, a group of scientists of international
reputation who were asked to summarise the scientific evidence concerning the
nature of 'race'. The objective was to demonstrate that the barbarism of the
'final solution' rested on 'a scientifically untenable premise' (Montagu 1972: x).
Of the four UNESCO statements on 'race', only the fourth explicitly addressed
the issue of a definition of racism. The first two statements did not employ the
term at all while the third noted that the biological evidence contradicted the
'tenets of racism' (Montagu 1972: 154) without defining what they were. These
three statements were intended primarily to demolish 'the myth that race determines mental aptitude, temperament, or social habits' (Montagu 1972: x) and
only the fourth broadened its scope in order to address directly the nature of
racism.

This fourth UNESCO statement repeats (but, as we shall see shortly, also inflates) the definition offered by Benedict and other writers of the 1930s and
1940s. Thus it defines racism as a falsification of the scientific knowledge about
human biology: 'Racism falsely claims that there is a scientific basis for arrang-
ing groups hierarchically in terms of psychological and cultural characteristics
that are immutable and innate' (Montagu 1972: 158). In common with Benedict,
this definition includes those arguments which mistakenly identify a hierarchy
of human groups, each of which is in some way naturally and inevitably distinct
from all others.

The essence of Benedict's definition was repeated in the 1960s and 1970s by
writers such as Van den Berghe (1978: 11) and Banton (1970). The latter defined
racism in the late 1960s as 'the doctrine that a man's [sic] behaviour is determined by stable inherited characters deriving from separate racial stocks having
distinctive attributes and usually considered to stand to one another in relations
of superiority and inferiority' (Banton 1970: 18). He too was referring exclusively to the nineteenth century scientific arguments about 'race', as a result of
which, given that those ideas had been discredited by science, he concluded that
racism was dead (1970: 28). Banton subsequently defined this nineteenth century scientific doctrine as 'racial typology' rather than racism (1977: 27–8, 47,
1980: 28) and so, at least to his satisfaction, abolished racism as a concept in sociological analysis (Banton 1987: ix).

Banton's rejection of the concept of racism is indicative of four problems
that arose from the fact that this original concept of racism was shaped by the
particular historical context, and political strategies, of the 1930s and 1940s.
First, the concept of racism was forged largely in the course of a conscious attempt to withdraw the sanction of science from a particular meaning of the
idea of 'race'. This required a rejection of the product of nineteenth century science which thereby underwent a transformation from the status of an assumed
fact to that of ideology. But in the process of effecting this transformation,

racism was defined narrowly to refer exclusively to this specific ideological object, with the result that when it was applied to other social contexts or when the social context changed, the concept proved vacuous. Simply, in the absence of this nineteenth century discourse of 'race', with all of its correlate assertions, the analyst could only conclude that racism did not exist or had evaporated.

This was recognised by those who drafted the fourth UNESCO statement on 'race'. The statement notes that the widespread exposure of the falsity of assertions that the human species is composed of a hierarchy of biologically distinct groups has transformed the content of racism.

Whenever it [racism] fails in its attempts to prove that the source of group differences lies in the biological field, it falls back upon justifications in terms of divine purpose, cultural differences, disparity of educational standards or some other doctrine which would serve to mask its continued racist beliefs. (Montagu 1972: 159)

In other words, the exposure of nineteenth century racism as a false and politically dangerous doctrine has changed the social context, with the result that explicit assertions that 'race' determines culture either cannot be sustained or are not articulated in the public domain because they are beyond the boundaries of acceptable argument (although they continue to be articulated in the informal domain and have certainly not disappeared). One therefore has the choice of concluding either that racism has disappeared, as Banton and others have done, or that the definition of racism should be revised in order to express the claim that racism is an ideology that takes a number of different forms.

I shall argue later in favour of this second option (but also against the specific formulation outlined in the UNESCO statement) but for the present purposes I presuppose this argument in order to sustain my case that Benedict's definition of racism, because it is a historically specific product, must have limited applicability outside of that context. Once this is recognised, there is an alternative to Banton's rejection of the concept of racism; this is to refer to this ideological product of nineteenth century science as 'scientific racism'. Comas has used this terminology and I, along with others, have followed and elaborated upon this conceptual strategy. This presumes a generic definition of racism, of which this scientific form is but one instance.

Second, this early definition of racism, by focusing on the product of nineteenth century scientific theorising, tended to presume that racism was always, and therefore was only, a structured and relatively coherent set of assertions, usually sustained by reference to formally organised empirical evidence. This is demonstrated in Banton's early definition of racism as a doctrine. Such a definition excludes less formally structured assertions, stereotypical ascriptions and symbolic representations which draw much of their meaning from unstated assertions or assumptions of causal determination and which in themselves do not meet the criterion of constituting an explicitly 'logical' structure.

Third, this original definition of the concept of racism tended to remain inextricably entangled with, and consequently to legitimate, the idea of 'race'. Because the definition of racism was confined to the nineteenth century discourse of 'race', in a context where either the idea of 'race' was given scientific legitimacy (as Benedict did) or was not explicitly rejected on the grounds of having no real referent, the concept of racism, while rejecting as unscientific the formulation that 'race' determines culture, left the idea of 'race' unquestioned and unchallenged. Thus, racism was exposed as a false doctrine, but it was conceded, certainly by default, and sometimes explicitly, that nevertheless the human species was divided into 'races'. In Barzun's terms, 'race-thinking' remained, sanctioning some form of biological classification as meaningful and useful.

Fourth, because racism became a label attached to a set of beliefs about 'race' that were used to justify exclusionary actions and, ultimately, genocide, the historical context ensured that the concept of racism carried with it a prominent moral and political content. To refer to a set of assertions as racism, and to the person who articulated them as a racist, consequently associated those ideas and those persons with Hitler and Fascism. Hence, viewed from within a liberal and humanitarian tradition, the ideas and arguments that the concept of racism came to refer to were morally reprehensible and politically unacceptable to those writers who coined and employed the term. Thus, it was a concept that claimed scientific justification for its rejection of the claims of nineteenth century scientific investigation but which also embodied a clear value judgement about what were acceptable beliefs.

My argument to this point is that the historical context in which racism was identified initially as an ideology shaped its definition in such a way that it had little or no meaning outside of that context. As we have seen, the UNESCO statement of 1967 sought to revise this definition on the basis of the reasoning that an ideology need not have a biological referent but may utilise 'justifications in terms of divine purpose, cultural differences, disparity of educational standards or some other doctrine which would serve to mask its continued racist beliefs' (Montagu 1972: 159). In other words, racism cannot be identified exclusively as an ideology with a specific biological content or reference.

One of the members of the UNESCO group of scientific experts who met in 1967 was John Rex who subsequently advanced a very similar argument in the course of critically evaluating Banton's early analysis of the nature of racism. Suggesting that biological arguments which identify and justify group differentiation have functional substitutes derived from quite different discourses, Rex argued that

the common element in all these theories is that they see the connection between membership of a particular group and of the genetically related sub-groups (i.e. families and lineages) of which that group is compounded and the possession of evaluated qualities as completely deterministic. (Rex 1970: 159)

In other words, the concept of racism refers to any argument which suggests that the human species is composed of discrete groups in order to legitimate inequality between those groups of people.

According to this definition, the concept of racism should refer to the function rather than the content of discourses: the focus of the definition is no longer upon a particular ideological content but the intention and/or consequence of any deterministic assertion about group differences. Using such a definition to analyse the historical material presented in chapter 1 leads to a generally inclusive conclusion. Most, if not all, of the representations of the Other discussed there identified the Other as a member of a distinct group by virtue of possessing a variety of biological and/or cultural characteristics, and most also justified either potentially or actually unequal treatment. For example, European representations of Muslims asserted that they were naturally violent and lascivious, an assertion that qualifies as an instance of racism according to Rex's definition. [. . .]

Institutional Racism

The 1967 UNESCO statement inflated the concept when it offered a further definition of racism as 'antisocial beliefs and acts which are based on the fallacy that discriminatory intergroup relations are justifiable on biological grounds' (Montagu 1972: 158). While the UNESCO statement neglected to justify and failed to explore the implications of this inflation of the scope of the concept to include practices as well as discourse, other writers have pursued the logic of this inflation in two, interrelated, directions since the late 1960s. The first has been to define as racism all processes which, intentionally or not, result in the continued exclusion of a subordinate group. This is commonly captured by the concept of institutional racism. The second has been to define as racism all those activities and practices which are intended to protect the advantages of a dominant group and/or to maintain or widen the unequal position of a subordinate group. In both instances, the dominant and subordinate groups are usually designated by reference to skin colour, that is, as 'whites' and 'blacks' respectively, the corollary being that racism is, by definition, a process effected, intentionally or otherwise, by 'white' people to the disadvantage of 'black' people.

Above, I have argued that a key historical determinant of the early definition of racism was the rise of Fascism and the Nazi practice of genocide in Europe. These new definitions were shaped by a quite different historical context, the political struggle of Afro-Americans against their position of inequality in the United States. The experience of material deprivation and exclusionary practice in the southern rural areas and in the northern cities of the United States gave rise to political resistance which increased in scope and intensity during the twentieth century. In the context of the resistance and riots of the 1960s, Carmichael and Hamilton published *Black Power* (1968) which presented what became an influential political analysis and strategy. They defined racism as 'the prediction of decisions and policies on considerations of race for the purpose of *subordinating* a racial group and maintaining control over that group' (1968: 3). They distinguished between overt and individual racism on the one hand and covert and institutional racism (which they also described as colonialism) on the other. The former was defined as explicit actions by individuals and the latter as those actions and inactions which maintain 'black' people in a disadvantaged situation and which rely on 'the active and pervasive operation of anti-black attitudes and practices' (1968: 5). Thus, the concept of racism was expanded in meaning to include not only beliefs but, more important, all actions, individual and institutional, which had the consequence of sustaining or increasing the subordination of 'black' people.

A number of American academics took up this idea of institutional racism and attempted to give it more coherence and a greater analytical power in an academic context where the dominant concept was prejudice and the dominant paradigm was social psychological in nature, a concept and paradigm that located the origin of the problem in the cognitive errors of individuals. Not all of these attempts achieved these objectives. Knowles and Prewitt (1969), for example, fail to offer a formal definition of institutional racism but seem to use it to mean practices within institutions which ensure that 'black citizens . . . are consistently penalised for reasons of color' but which may be neither intentional nor motivated by 'conscious bigotry' (1969: 4-7). Blauner is more careful to define his concepts explicitly. He argues that the definition of the concept of racism should be extended so as to refer not only to individual prejudiced attitudes but also to processes that sustain 'white' domination:

The processes that maintain domination—control of whites over non-whites—are built into the major social institutions . . . Thus there is little need for prejudice as a motivating force. Because this is true, the distinction between racism as an objective phenomenon, located in the actual existence of domination and hierarchy, and racism's subjective concomitants of prejudice and other motivations and feelings is a basic one. (Blauner 1972: 9–10)

Thus, Blauner expanded the concept of racism so as to refer to two different phenomena which are very similar to Carmichael and Hamilton's distinction between individual racism and institutional racism. Significantly, Blauner fails to define the criteria by which one might identify either 'prejudice' or those processes which ensure the 'control of whites over non-whites'.

The second direction I have identified is represented by Wellman who also explicitly extends the definition of racism to refer to more than 'prejudiced beliefs'. While Wellman uses the concept to refer to personal prejudice, he argues that 'the essential feature of racism is . . . the defense of a system from which advantage is derived on the basis of race' (1977: 221–2) and hence he claims that 'racism is a structural relationship based on the subordination of one racial group by another' (1977: 35). Wellman's inflated definition refers therefore to beliefs or sentiments and practices which he considers to constitute racism, not on the basis of their content, but on the basis of their effects:

> A position is racist when it defends, protects, or enhances social organisation based on racial disadvantage. Racism is determined by the consequences of a sentiment, not its surface qualities ... White racism is what white people do to protect the special benefits they gain by virtue of their skin colour. (Wellman 1977: 76)

What is common to the arguments of Blauner and Wellman is an inflation of the definition of the concept to include not only (or not so much) discourses (whether formal or disaggregated), but also (and more important) all actions and processes (whatever their origin or motivation) which result in one group being placed or retained in a subordinate position by another. The concept of racism is used therefore to refer to a range of phenomena (beliefs as well as intended and unintended actions and processes) but with a specific emphasis upon their consequences for the domination of one group over another. These groups are defined, respectively, as 'black' and 'white', and consequently racism is conceived as something that 'white' people think about and do to 'black' people.

This inflation of the meaning of racism is accompanied by a complimentary narrowing which defines racism as an exclusively 'white' phenomenon. For Wellman, it is a matter of definition that only 'white' people express sentiments and act in ways which are defined as racism. This argument has been endorsed and developed by Katz, who argues not only that 'racism is a White problem in that its development and perpetuation rest with White people' (1978: 10) but that racism is a psychological disorder which is 'deeply embedded in White people from a very early age on both a conscious and an unconscious level' and which has 'deluded Whites into a false state of superiority that has left them in a pathological and schizophrenic state' (1978: 14–15). Thus the concept of racism refers not only to all actions or inactions, all sentiments and silences, which sustain 'black' subordination, but also to a form of schizophrenia, which all 'white' people 'have' in the sense that it structures the totality of their experience and being in the world. In sum, all 'white' people are universally and inevitably sick with racism. [. . .]

Conclusion

Considered historically, the concept of racism has had a relatively short career during which its analytical definition has been expanded in two directions. On the one hand, a number of writers have continued to confine the use of the term to refer to specific discourses, but have inflated its meaning to include ideas and arguments which would not be included by those who initially formulated and used it. Thus, there is a logical connection between the British debate about the definition of racism in the late 1960s and the debate about the new racism in the 1980s. Both debates reflect the fact that, at least within the formal political domain, claims about the existence of biologically inferior and superior 'races' have largely disappeared, but a discourse of the Other continues with a new ideological content. On the other hand, other writers have inflated the analytical meaning of the concept so as to refer largely to individual and institutionalised practices which have as their outcome the determination and/or reproduction of 'black' disadvantage, regardless of intention and legitimating ideology. Hence, discourses of the Other are either largely irrelevant or secondary to this analytical position.

Why has this analytical inflation occurred? Or, to put it another way, why have so many writers resisted Banton's rejection of the concept on the grounds that the ideology that the concept originally referred to is 'dead'? There are two (interrelated) reasons, one analytical and one political. The first is that, seen from a particular theoretical perspective, the long history of the interdependence of capitalist development and 'black' subordination began a new chapter with the migration of 'black' people from the peripheries of capitalism (whether they be overseas colonies, as in the case of Britain and other European nation states, or the southern agricultural plantations in the case of the United States) to the metropolitan centres. Within the peripheries of capitalism in the eighteenth and nineteenth centuries, the exploitation of 'black' labour power in unfree relations of production placed 'black' people in a subordinate position to the emergent proletariat at the centre and was legitimated by representations of the Other which identified those so exploited as belonging to biologically inferior 'races'.

Consequently, an analytical interdependence of capitalism and racism was established. Hence, following migration, when it became apparent that the commodification of 'black' labour power was accompanied by subordination 'below' the position occupied by the majority of 'white' labour power (evident in the concentration of 'black' wage labourers in the poorest quality housing and in semi- and unskilled manual labour, for example), it was concluded that the essential structure of 'black' subordination had not changed, even if the ideological justification had. The point of emphasis became the continuity of 'black' structural subordination rather than ideological transformation, and consequently the meaning of the concept of racism was inflated in order to take account of this.

And this brings us to the second factor, for the decision to inflate the definition of racism must have an explanation. From a radical, and certainly from a Marxist, point of view this transformation sustained the argument that linked racism and capitalism in some sort of causal dependency. Thus, the political critique of capitalism could be broadened and capitalism could be damned for yet another reason. Morally, this critique was sustained by the horror and outrage concerning the holocaust, which ensured that the word racism took on a new sense of disapproval after 1945. There were therefore good political and moral reasons to continue to employ the concept because it carried with it a strong negative evaluation. To label someone or something as an instance of racism was to place the person or event outside the boundaries of civilisation.

However, this theoretical and political perspective is not sacrosanct. Indeed, it is problematic for two reasons. First, the essential continuity perceived is open to question. The migration from periphery to centre was not only a spatial migration but also often a movement from one (non-capitalist) mode of production to another (capitalist) mode of production and hence from one set of class relations to another. And, within the capitalist mode of production, the complex interdependence of capital accumulation, bourgeois individualism, commodification, and relative freedom from relations of personal dependence (the equation between female gender and domestic labour is a central exception) creates opportunities for at least some of those people previously directly subordinated by colonisation and unfree relations of production to move into a number of different class locations.

Second, much of the British and North American theorising about capitalism and racism since the 1960s, while drawing upon the immoral status of racism which derives to a significant degree from the final solution, utilises a colonial model which has little scope to explain much of the European racism of the nineteenth and twentieth centuries, and certainly not that form of racism which others label anti-semitism; it does, however, have a relevance to the controversial debate about whether or not Zionism can be defined as an instance of racism. Consequently, we are offered definitions and theories of racism which are so specific to the history of overseas colonisation (that is, specific to the domination of 'white' over 'black' as so many writers express it) that they are of little value in explaining any other (non-colonial) context.

[From *Racism* (London: Routledge, 1989), 41–53, 66–8.]

COLETTE GUILLAUMIN

45   The Changing Face of 'Race'

The idea of race is one of the most contradictory and violent in our world today. Having been for so many years, probably more than a century, a sort of first truth, something so obvious that no one ever thought to call it into question (in much the same way as sex today), it has become over the last few decades an explosive topic. As something which was part of, and exploited by, a world becoming increasingly efficient technologically, and more and more centralized, race became transformed in the middle of the present century into a means for states to achieve their goals of domination, exploitation and extermination. This is a matter of simple fact.

Race is not a Neutral Idea
No, the term 'race' is not just one banal, harmless designator among others. Nor is it a 'given', a word which in itself is neutral and can be used socially in a

way which is either 'good' or 'bad', indifferent or pernicious, according to the circumstances. The notion of categorizing humankind into closed, anatomical and physiological entities is a strange one, and it seems astonishing that as it grew and became more complex it was not greeted with greater suspicion. At a time when the whole idea of 'race' was becoming socially accepted (essentially around the beginning of the nineteenth century), de Tocqueville was virtually alone in sensing that there was something shameful underlying its use. No doubt the same thing was seen by other, less famous people whose voices were not so widely heard, but among the notable intellectuals and politicians of the day, precious few showed any reticence.

At the very time when the idea of race was acquiring such social importance, during the first half of the nineteenth century, the anthropologist Franz Boas was already aware of the unreliability of anatomical measurements, which varied from one generation to the next according to living conditions, so that the shape of the bones in our skull was influenced by that most vulgar of commodities, the food we ate . . . Today we know perfectly well (as we probably always did, but what we know and what we are prepared to acknowledge are not always the same thing . . .) that any physical characteristic whatsoever can be made into a 'discriminator' in some socially or politically motivated system of classification (by opposition to a disinterested, scientific one). The choice of somatic criteria is symbolic of the intentions of the classifiers, and nothing more. The Nazis deciding who was (and was not) a Jew, as they put it more than once (when offering Fritz Lang an important role in the cinema industry of the Third Reich, for instance), or the government of the Republic of South Africa classifying Chinese people as belonging to one race and Japanese to another, are sufficient illustration that these things are a matter of politics rather than objective reality, and that the users of such distinctions are well aware of the fact.

'Race does not Exist'

What is the position today? For about the last ten years we have clearly been at a crucial stage in the development of the notion of race. A number of voices have been raised claiming that 'race' does not exist. They are not very numerous, but their importance is considerable. While the meaning of the term has been constantly changing since its emergence, this is the first time any attempt has been made to destroy the very concept itself, which is extremely important. It is certainly crucial in that it marks a break with one of the most untouchable sacred cows of our time, but it becomes even more so when we look at the real significance of this attempted rejection. A number of researchers are currently working to ensure that 'race' is shelved away among other notions which, in the history of science (and natural science in particular), belong firmly to the past. This tendency developed progressively through the period 1965–75, beginning with the questioning of the idea on theoretical and conceptual grounds. The physical anthropologist Jean Hiernaux remarked at the time: 'Race is not a fact, but a concept'.[1] This apparently simple observation in fact represents a turning-point. It acts as a logical introduction to the statement made by the haemo-typologist Jacques Ruffié in his inaugural lecture at the Collège de France in December 1972:

In our part of the world, in most Latin countries, physical anthropology has gradually become separated from the sociology of culture . . . Now, in man, there is no such thing as race. That is why, despite numerous and rigorous studies, nobody has ever been able to agree on how humanity should be divided up into races.

This position and its variants underlie the critique of race advanced by population geneticists as well as by physical anthropologists in the strict sense of the term.

How is it that the scientific community should have arrived at a position so startlingly opposed to the common-sense view of our age?

What we today call a race was not, contrary to widespread opinion, something self-evident to people of earlier centuries. While there may be arguments among historians, sociologists and researchers in all the other disciplines that are concerned with the role of race in society about the precise historical moment when the notion emerged in the form in which we know it today, when both the term and the idea were born, there is no debate about the thing itself.

The word 'race' (which came into French only relatively recently, in the sixteenth century) originally had a very precise sense: it meant 'family' or, more accurately, 'family relationship'. Moreover, it was only ever applied to important dynasties (the race of the Bourbons, the race of David, etc.). In no way was it applied at that time to large groups of people with no legal link of kinship between them. From referring to legally circumscribed, noble families, it shifted to being applied to much wider groups, the attribution to whom of some common physical trait served as a pretext for designating them as a single entity, now called a 'race'. This shift from surname to skin colour is a considerable one: from narrow legal link binding family groups together, to complete geographical dispersion, the term underwent a semantic journey of extraordinary proportions. However, it took a long time, and a major change in our ways of thinking, before 'race' became applied to groups of people lumped together according to some common physical characteristic, rather than just a shared surname.

The evolution of the term then went through another important stage. During the first half of the nineteenth century, other, quite different characteristics began to be slipped in alongside the physical (or supposedly physical) common denominators of human groups: these were social, or cultural, traits. Philological research had identified specific groupings (Indo-European languages, Semitic languages, etc.) among the language-forms then known, and these were quickly absorbed into the systems of somatic classification which were then sweeping all before them. It was a short step from there to suggesting the existence of Indo-European and Semitic races. We all know what that led to a century later.

But What Actually is 'Race'?

The concept 'race' was formed at a historically determined (or determinable) period, as the result of an oscillation between meanings generated from diverse sources, and the combining of several different types of classification (legal, anatomical, linguistic . . .). Heterogeneous lines of thought came to be fused in the single claim that human groups were differential by nature, and that there was a natural line of separation between them. This has now become the *de facto* everyday meaning of the term 'race'. But, however irritating it might be to go on repeating it, we should never forget that 'race' is not a spontaneously given product of perception and experience. It is an idea built up (and slowly, at that) from elements which might equally well be physical traits as social customs, linguistic peculiarities as legal institutions, lumped together and homogenized according to the precept that they must ultimately all be biological phenomena. This idea carries a great deal of weight in a society obsessed with the sanctity of 'Science', which has been invested with the power not only to unveil and understand natural phenomena, but to establish what actually constitutes those phenomena themselves.

Jacques Ruffié's assertion that no such physical category exists within humanity certainly marked a turning-point. At the same time, though, it fell within a critical tradition which was not new, but had been expressed quite differently in the middle of the present century.

This was the period when race, which had originally been a purely descriptive notion, became transformed into a legal one. From being an 'idea' it was turned into a concrete social fact. The scientific community in the 1930s, particularly people working in the social sciences, made strenuous efforts to oppose this and to defuse the legalization of the notion of race which the Nazi regime was bringing about. They proclaimed the complete inadequacy of such a 'purely physical' notion to account for, describe and influence those aspects of human life which were dependent on society and culture, although they did not challenge its relevance to the physical domain. Many different stands were taken at that time. In December 1938, for instance, the American Psychological Association declared that:

> In the experiments which psychologists have made upon different peoples, no characteristic, inherent psychological differences which fundamentally distinguish so-called 'races' have been disclosed. [. . .] There is no evidence for the existence of an inborn Jewish or German or Italian mentality. [. . .] The Nazi theory that people must be related by blood in order to participate in the same cultural or intellectual heritage has absolutely no support from scientific findings.

But these warnings could never be more than symbolic, since the legal and political systems which exploited the notion of race were already in place.

So a critical attempt was made to break the syncretic link between physical and socio-cultural traits which had been forged and developed over the preceding centuries. But it did not call the notion itself into question. It was a statement of principle as well as a moral protest. Both are necessary, but not sufficient. The idea of race was left very solidly in place, and in the end went absolutely unquestioned as such. There had been an attempt to limit the damage, it had failed, and in 1945 the state of South Africa in its turn adopted legal categories of race.

These stands were to influence various declarations of the international organizations throughout the 1950s. Their concern was still the same: to demonstrate that the material, physical fact of 'race' (which still went unchallenged except by the occasional isolated researcher) was quite separate from social or psychological characteristics. The intention was to show that race, still assumed to exist in itself, had no connection with or influence over the way in which human beings behaved.

The UNESCO 'Statement on the Nature of Race and Race Differences' of 1951 provides a good illustration of this position:

Since race, as a word, has become coloured by its misuse in connexion with national, linguistic and religious differences, and by its deliberate abuse by racialists, we tried to find a new word to express the same meaning of a biologically differentiated group. On this we did not succeed, but agreed to reserve race as the word to be used for anthropological classification of groups showing definite combinations of physical (including physiological) traits in characteristic proportions. [. . .] National, religious, geographical, linguistic and cultural groups do not necessarily coincide with racial groups; and the cultural traits of such groups have no demonstrated connexion with racial traits. Americans are not a race, nor are Frenchmen, nor Germans; no ipso facto is any other national group. Moslems and Jews are no more races than are Roman Catholics and Protestants; nor are people who live in Iceland or Britain or India, or who speak English or any other language, or who are culturally Turkish or Chinese and the like, thereby describable as races. The use of the term 'race' in speaking of such groups may be a serious error, but it is one which is habitually committed.[2]

Talking about 'Difference'

Looking back on this from our position today, we are struck by the pathetic aspect of a protest so resolute and yet so far removed from a reality of repression and violence. It is also striking to see that we are forgetting here—and when I say 'we', I mean all of us who work in the human sciences and are reduced to exasperation and despair by this notion so difficult to tie down—that the idea of race did not belong exclusively to the natural sciences, either historically, or socially, or ideologically. Despite that, however, the idea was challenged as if it did. Moreover, as if that were the only way in which race could, and should, be envisaged.

And yet, while it had become a geographical classification in the work of Linné, and was extrapolated into linguistics in the first half of the nineteenth century during the triumph of philology, race was also a subject for debate in the streets, in political quarters, in the salons, where it came to represent what was 'peculiar' about each human group. It was the equivalent of our 'difference', and that is certainly how it was understood. A case in point was Balzac, the first major novelist to make extensive use of the idea. The current vogue notion of difference is so ambiguous that it is often defended just as much by traditional racists as by anti-racists, whilst even the victims of racism themselves invoke it as something they wish to cultivate. This is because difference has come to inherit all the connotations relating to the specificity of human groups which in the old days were carried by the notion of race. It is true that the idea of difference is an attempt to get away from the imperative of physical naturality imposed by race, and in that sense its aim is certainly to break down the rigidity of the racist system of thought. But at the same time it attracts those who persist in thinking in racist terms, but no longer dare use the word 'race'. When, for reasons of censorship, political prudence or simply cynicism, these people choose 'difference' instead of 'race', they know that they will still be understood as saying something about the 'natural' specificity of human groups. For it is impossible to destroy the deeper strata of a system of thought simply by taking away a particular element; its configuration needs to be modified by adding some new trait.

So, the social sciences forgot the circumstances in which the idea of race came into existence and developed, and failed to take account of the fact that the great theorists of race were from their own camp, rather than from the natural sciences. Gobineau was not a scientist, nor were Vacher de Lapouge and, later, Chamberlain and Rosenberg, and so on.

Today, a few people in the human-related sciences are awakening from this lethargy and trying to reject a notion whose origin is clearly to be sought in socio-intellectual modes of thought which have nothing to do with experimental scientific practice. But this awakening has come as a surprise for the social sciences, which thought that they had discreetly disposed of a category for which they were largely responsible by pushing it off into the domain of the natural sciences. If the responsibility is indeed theirs, it is less because they had a part in the invention of 'race' than because they are the very disciplines on which the study of the phenomenon depends: as a social trait, it falls within their sphere of understanding and analysis. Sociologists, historians and epistemologists were perhaps unwilling to see that this hot potato was their problem, but that is certainly the case. And the natural sciences keep reminding them of it by denying that race has anything to do with them.

What is the Position of 'Race' Today?

We now find ourselves at a stage where the pertinence of the notion of race in the natural sciences of man is being refuted on grounds of scientific reason and intellectual honesty (not to mention logic and common sense). This is quite an event, something new in these fields of research. As we have seen, however, it is not an isolated move, for race has been analysed and challenged by other disciplines for some decades now. But this stand is unlikely to achieve its desired aim of eliminating the idea that human beings are 'naturally' different, and that the great divides in society (national, religious, political, etc.) reflect 'natural' differences. For negations are not recognized as such by our unconscious mental processes. From this point of view, a fact affirmed and a fact denied exist to exactly the same degree, and remain equally present in our affective and intellectual associative networks. Just talking about race means that it will always be there in residue. 'Race' is about the least conceptional, cold and abstract of notions, so it appeals from the start to the unconscious side of the mechanisms we have for acquiring knowledge and relating to other human beings. The ideologues of racism have always been well aware of this, which is why they are still peddling their views today.

In other words, simply showing that a category of this type has no scientific basis is insufficient to remove it from the mental universe not simply of the majority of people, but even of those who are intellectually convinced that it does not exist as a 'natural' reality. It is a necessary operation, but not a sufficient one.

The human sciences began by saying: 'race' is a matter for the natural sciences, it is none of our business, it has no influence on cultural and social phenomena, and so on. Today, the natural sciences are replying: 'race' does not exist, it is not a pertinent criterion of classification. Each of these two propositions is partially true, but they hide a third which comes much closer to fitting the real facts. And if ever one revolution or one proposition could conceal another, this is certainly a case in point. Whether race is or is not 'a fact of nature', whether it is or is not a 'mental reality', it is today, in the twentieth century, a legal, political and historical reality which plays a real and constraining role in a number of societies.

(a) That is why any appeal to race (even under the pretext of a love of different cultures, or the search for 'roots', etc.) is a political move which can never be neutral, given the facts. For it is a question of facts, and not one of intentions or opinions, as some people would once again have us believe.

(b) That is why simply rejecting the notion of race is not enough. Denying its existence as an empirically valid category, as the human, social and, ultimately, natural sciences are trying to do, can never, however correct the intention, take away that category's reality within society or the state, or change the fact that while it may not be valid empirically, it certainly exerts an empirical effect. To claim that a notion which is present in a society's vocabulary, i.e. in both its way of organizing the world and in its political and human history, can be negated in this way is a paradoxical position, because that which is negated has *de facto* existence. It is perhaps also an attempt to take away the horror of that reality, its unbearable brutality: it is impossible that something of that kind should exist. Precisely because its existence is unbearable.

However, while the reality of 'race' is indeed neither natural and biological, nor psychological (some innate tendency of the human mind to designate the other as a natural entity), it does nevertheless exist. It is not possible to argue that a category which organizes whole states (the Third Reich, the Republic of South Africa, etc.), and which is incorporated into the law, does not exist. It is not possible to claim that the category which is the direct cause, the primary means, of the murder of millions of human beings does not exist.

But the slow path to intellectual understanding traced by successive and cumulative attempts to elucidate the concept shows that race is a social category of exclusion and murder. Its real nature has gradually been unmasked. The process has not been a simple one, for it is hard not to believe that 'race does not exist' when the idea that it is a 'natural' category has been proved false (as indeed it is), while at the same time that idea was all that was left after the patient critique undertaken by the social sciences. And when, above all, that celebrated 'natural' definition was the very same one which 'legitimized' the legal inscription of 'race' in racist regimes.

Yet the legal inscription of race and the practices that accompany it certainly do exist. And they are precisely the reality of race. Race does not exist. But it does kill people. It also continues to provide the backbone of some ferocious systems of domination. And in France today it is rearing its ugly head once again. Not in the shameful margins of our society, but behind the honourable mask of 'opinion' and 'ideas'. Let us be clear about this. The idea, the notion of race is a technical means, a machine, for committing murder. And its effectiveness is not in doubt. It is a way of rationalizing and organizing by murderous violence the domination of powerful social groups over other groups reduced to powerlessness. Unless anyone is prepared to claim that, since race does not exist, nobody is or can ever have been repressed or killed because of their race. And nobody can make that claim, because millions of human beings have died as a result of their race, and millions of others are now dominated, excluded and repressed for the same reason.

No, race does not exist. And yet it does. Not in the way that people think; but it remains the most tangible, real and brutal of realities.

[From *Racism, Sexism, Power and Ideology* (London: Routledge, 1995), 99–107.]

DAVID THEO GOLDBERG

46 **The Semantics of Race**

Of all the expressions that make up racialized discourse, some are more centrally constitutive of the discursive formation than others, and by extension more primary to the forms of its reproduction and diachronic transformations. It may be predicted, roughly, that the more directly related a concept is to these central constituents of racialized discourse the more likely it is to structure reproductive or transformative expressions in a racialized social order, and by extension to effect their articulation of racist exclusions.

This account may seem to suggest that there is no racism without or at least before some allusion to the *concept* of race, that the concept necessarily precedes, both conceptually and as a matter of historical fact, the phenomenon of racism. I want to resist this set of implications, and not only because there is no single transhistorical phenomenon that we can identify as racism *per se*. My point, rather, is that the emergence of racialized discourse, and hence as a matter of necessity the concept of race, sets the social conditions for racist expression in some or other manifestation to take place. Racisms (which I prefer to call racist expressions) began to emerge with the appearance of the concept of race, that is, with the set of interests the concept expressed at the time of its emergence. It should be obvious, then, that there is in my view no racism without some reference, however veiled, to racialized discourse. It is, of course, possible to think of the set of social conditions that we call racism as historically presupposing the concept of race. We should, however, be clear about this: it is conceptually feasible, not empirically sound. It makes little sense to ask which came first, the concept or the disposition to distance and exclude that inheres at least historically in *this* constitution of otherness. The transformation of one racism into another is closely entwined—as cause, as effect, sometimes only as affect—with the sets of interests that 'race' in its varied and altering forms increasingly expressed from the sixteenth century on as dominant social conditions changed.

This way of looking at things suggests that we proceed not by defining 'race' conceptually—in terms, that is, of necessary and sufficient conditions. We should focus, rather, on a different set of concerns: how has the term been used at different times, what has it signified, and how has it served to articulate a conception for its users of self- and group-identity, of self and other?

To proceed in this way flies in the face of the prevailing methodology applied to the study of race in the social sciences. There are two basic ways to get at the meanings of socially significant terms. The first is purely conceptual: to stipulate definitions largely *a priori* on the basis of what the terms *ought* to signify, at least in relation to the conceptual scheme in which they are taken most convincingly to make sense; and then to look for empirical instantiations of the phenomena thus defined. The second way is historical: to lay out how the terms have predominantly been used, the sorts of implications and effects they have had, and how these have all and interrelatedly transformed over time.

Prevailing conceptions of race in the social sciences have largely proceeded in the former way. By contrast, definitions of racism since the 1940s have mostly mirrored perceptions of the term's popular usage, namely, as an irrational group prejudice that assumes racial others to be inferior purely in terms of their racial membership biologically conceived. I wish to invert this definitional process, and doubly so. I will proceed in the case of race by looking at the way the concept has been used historically, and how these usages have changed over time. Thus, my concern is to see whether any transhistorical features common to these uses emerge, features which might be said to direct any further use of the concept, to set the limits to its transformative applicability and adaptability. In the case of racism, however, I think it necessary to *stipulate* a definition. This definition must be sensitive not only to the way in which the term has been variously used this past half-century. More importantly, it must enable identification of those features constitutive of various social formations that have been expressed this past half millennium in racist fashions. The arguments underlying the latter claims are not my focus here. Suffice to say that I take any racist expression minimally to consist in the promotion or the actual exclusion of people in virtue of their being deemed to be members of different racial groups, however racial groups are taken to be constituted. My concern in this article will be with the constitution of races.

Race as Natural Kind

Banton (1988) has usefully identified the changes in prevailing theories about the nature of race since the emergence of the concept in European languages in the late-fourteenth and early-fifteenth centuries. Historical shifts in theorizing about the nature of race have resulted in shifts in the very meaning of the concept of *race*. Given the early racial emphasis on descent in terms of origin, breed, or stock, the general commitment to race as *lineage* was overriding (Banton 1988, pp. ix; 11). In the name of monogenism, this sense dominated the pre-eighteenth century 'philosophical' explanation of human origins. Monogenism considered all human beings traceable to common godly origins. Racial distinctions were ascribed to group correlated geographic, climatic, and social differences.

Emerging in the eighteenth century as a theoretical challenge to monogenism, polygenism came to assume in the first half of the nineteenth century the status of *the* prevailing paradigm of natural history and anthropological science. Though polygenism continued to read 'race' in terms of origins, it differed from monogenism in emphasizing biological inheritance and hierarchy over pedigree. The shift from thinking of people predominantly in terms of their pedigree to conceiving them foremostly in terms of their group identity is reflected in the growing emphasis on the concept of *population*. To be a member of a given population was to be identifiable on the basis of invariant, heritable characteristics. On the monogenic view of race, the genesis of all human beings was taken to lie in the line of descent from Adam and Eve, and racial distinction was ascribable to environmental difference. Yet no account was forthcoming for the mechanisms by which races were environmentally determined. Polygenism resolved this difficulty by supposing racial difference to inhere originally in population groupings: contemporary difference in type was a matter simply of inheritance. What raised grave doubts about polygenism in the second half of the nineteenth century, however, was a radically new way of thinking: the emerging evidence of evolution imparted new meaning to the notion of race (Banton 1988, pp. xi-xii; 167–9). Mere populations gave way to 'breeding populations', varieties or types to subspecies.

It was Darwin who reconceived species as breeding populations, and who imparted a fluidity to the taxonomic categories missing altogether from polygenism. Races for the polygenist were tantamount to species, fixed more or less since their separate inception and incapable of interbreeding. On Darwin's view, species are breeding populations and races are simply subspecies. Both are capable of evolving; indeed, a subspecies may eventually evolve into a separate species. In due course the conceptual relations at the heart of Darwinism came to be expressed genetically. Races, on the latter view, are simply populations that diverge from each other in their relative gene frequencies or, in other words, in the relative degree of possessing certain inherited features. Racial differences are merely agglomerations of individual hereditary characteristics (alleles or strings of genes) which even within a single population tend not to converge.

So, the theory of evolution serves as a warning, though often ignored, to those who would proceed in rigidly classifying the human species into races on genetic grounds, and perhaps to those who would proceed in such classifications at all. Darwin issued the challenge to any theory investing explanatory power in the conception of race, and it did this at the very moment that race had assumed discursive hegemony in colonizing social space. Race had set the parameters to what could be rational and reasonable, credible and utterable. It had drawn the bounds around common sense. Nevertheless, prompted by Darwin's influence and at first tentatively, race began to occupy the position not of *explanans* but of *explanandum*, of the social object requiring rather than furnishing scientific explanation.

Racial Semantics and Social Reduction

Prompted by nineteenth-century positivism, the primary methodological form assumed by explanations of social groups and their relations this century is reductionistic. The concern has been with ways to reduce relatively complex levels of group structure and relations to simpler explanatory levels taken to lie at their foundation; to explain entities deemed to be less real in terms of those thought to be more real. The less complex levels or more real entities may be held variously to determine, or to order, or simply to set, the boundaries of the more complex structures and behaviour, or of those entities considered less real.

Explanations of race and racialized phenomena in the past hundred years have tended to reflect two general forms. The first accepts the standard biological sense of race as subspecies genetically interpreted, of race as natural kind. It attempts to explain relations between real racial groups so interpreted, or their social appeal, or at least the social significance of such appeal, by reducing the racialized phenomena to underlying social (or, in some cases, biological) terms or relations. These underlying terms are deemed more primary, more universal, more constitutive or basically motivating, and more fundamentally determining of social structure. Where these underlying levels are seen as irreducibly social, they are cast as either class or culture; where biological, they are read as biological kinship or common gene pool.[1] By contrast, the other explanatory paradigm gives no independent content to the notion of race. It takes race as a social kind, and interprets appeals to 'race' as nothing other than recourse to social considerations and relations, again, like class or culture. If the first paradigm reifies race as an unquestioned biological given, the second conceives race and racial characterization of social relations as ghost-like. Lacking a determining or motivational force of its own, any appeal to 'race' is seen as a mystification, a form of (self-deceived) false consciousness or misleading ideology.

Race as class

Leaving biological interpretations aside for the moment, the primary contemporary uses of *race* accordingly assume significance in terms of class or culture. *Qua* class, race can be understood to mean either socio-economic status (under some interpretations) or relation to the mode of production. As status, race is simply an index of social standing or rank reflected in terms of criteria like wealth, education, style of life, linguistic capacity, residential location, consumptive capacity, having or lacking respect, and so on. Status has to do with one's ranking in a social system relative to the position of others, where the ranking involves a criterial complex of self-conception and (de)valuations by others. Those who 'act white' in these terms will be considered so. There is an almost natural tendency here to equate race with class. Class position defines social distinction. It involves classification into groups occupying distinct social positions, and on the view at hand this is just what race does. It requires a further step to identify the given class position with racial configuration, but until recently this was—and in some countries remains—a relatively straightforward feature of social formation. This may be thought true also of class defined in the second and narrower sense: as fundamental economic or structural relationships, in terms of relations to the mode of production and their corresponding interests. Here, race is conceived as masking these relationships and interests. So, for those rejecting the biological connotation of 'race', races are identified with socially formed and materially determined class position. In either case race is considered empty in itself, and it assumes the sense of that conception of class which is taken to determine it.

Now class analysis, whether in terms of status or modal relation, has made us more fully aware that social position is constructed and imposed rather than natural and necessarily inherited. There are clearly ways in which social position is socially inherited, and here the history of racial ascription has played a central part. Illuminating race in terms of class, then, reflects just this feature of race. Yet it must be insisted that there are finite limitations to any identification of race with class. Conceiving race in terms of class is tendentious, for we are thus encouraged to identify race misleadingly as class, as class under another name. This either leaves unexplained those *cultural* relations that race is so often taken to express or it wrongly reduces them to more or less veiled instantiations of class formation.

Cultural race

Cast in these terms, another conception of race emerges: race as culture. As the biological conception (or, more accurately, set of conceptions) has been increasingly attacked, the cultural is a sense (or set of senses) that has come to enjoy considerable commitment, though not without controversy. Generally, the cultural conception includes identifying race with language group, religion, group habits, mores or customs, a dominant style of behaviour, dress, cuisine, music, literature and art. Primarily at issue in such cultural differentiations are group-circumscribed values.

Such identifications in the name of race are not new. Strictly linguistic differentiations of racial groupings were popular in the nineteenth century and can be traced back a century before that. Turning on the dictum that it is 'language that makes man' (Müller 1895, p. 45), European linguists at the time looked not to physical markers by which to classify races, but to affinities and differences in the system of linguistic representations of the various language groups. In 1808 Friedrich Schlegel argued that German, Greek, and Latin—and therefore French and English derivitively—were commonly rooted in Sanskrit. The ancient superiority of Aryan sagacity was to be inherited linguistically rather than biologically, by way of the classical grammar of the Greeks and Romans. The virtues represented by these classical grammars (independence, self-reliance, etc.) were supposed by Müller and others to be relayed through linguistic acquisition to the bearers of modern civilization. 'Inferior' civilizations, derivative from Chinese or Semitic rather than from Aryan origins, were supposedly marked by linguistic incapacity and inability to assimilate. It was thought, for instance, that the wandering Jew was culturally incapable of speaking German properly.

What is new here is that since World War II, and especially in the past fifteen years or so, the cultural conception of race has tended to eclipse all others. It has become paradigmatic. It has also suppressed, however, hierarchical judgements of inferiority and superiority as the basis of exclusions, coding the exclusions that it promotes in terms merely of racial difference. This raises a fundamental question about the cultural conception. Many insist that racial differentiation inevitably appeals, if only implicitly, to underlying *biological* claims (see, for example, Miles 1989, pp. 70–1; 74–6). Even where the surface expression is cultural, commitment to racial groupings is thought necessarily to be commitment to biological distinction. Thus the only difference, if any, between nineteenth- and twentieth-century forms of racial differentiation seems to be at the level of surface expression.

Appiah is the most articulate representative of this biologically based view. He insists that what differentiates ideas about race from earlier ideas about group difference, and from claims about ethnicity, is this: that necessary to the former, but missing from both of the latter, is commitment to the view that common racial membership entails shared 'biologically heritable, moral and intellectual characteristics' not shared with members of other races. This, in turn, has entailed the widespread claim, not necessarily but as a matter of historical fact, that 'some races were superior to others'. That racial differentiation necessarily presupposes a biological claim means that though Appiah's admission about the centrality of hierarchical judgements to the development of race thinking rests on historical grounds, the more basic idea is meant to be transhistorical. The latter is a transcendental claim about the nature of racial differentiation. Yet it is a transcendental claim with distinct historical implications, for it necessarily implies that Appiah, like others committed to the biological claim, narrows the occurrence of race thinking primarily to its nineteenth-century apogee (Appiah 1990b, pp. 276–7; 280).

I do not wish to challenge Appiah's historical contention that ideas about race developed with a commitment to judgements of superiority and inferiority. He is right about the historical point, though race-based discourse is less committed to hierarchical judgements than it once was. The underlying reason why Appiah admits that claims of superiority are contingent to race thinking is that he wants to hold on to the undeniable point that cultural expression by the racially oppressed has sometimes also assumed a racialized form, that the racially oppressed may assume racial self-identification not as a form of self-degradation but as a mode of self-advancement. Appiah wants to suggest that what separates such expression, which he benignly identifies as a form of 'racialism', from the extremities of racist expression is not the mistaken idea about biological inheritance but insidious judgements of superiority and inferiority (Appiah 1990a, pp. 3–17). What I find questionable is the wider claim that ideas about race are inherently committed to claims about biological inheritance, whether of physical or intellectual and moral characteristics.

To see the narrowness of Appiah's conception of race, and by extension of any view committed to limiting claims concerning race necessarily to presuppositions of biological heritability, consider the transcendental argument that he offers. The appeal in differentiating races to historical criteria, Appiah argues, must of necessity presuppose a belief in biologically distinct races as the only way of identifying the subjects whose distinct histories these are taken to be. To claim that I am white in virtue of sharing a history with Thomas Jefferson, Calvin Coolidge, Enoch Powell, Margaret Thatcher, and P. W. Botha (to take any number of names not quite randomly) is only logically feasible, on Appiah's argument, if there is first some independent way to identify members of the racial group who are taken to share their history. If I share a history with them in virtue of group membership, I cannot consistently claim membership in virtue of sharing this history. (Actually, I doubt whether I share much of anything non-biologically with the names cited here.) There must be an independent way of picking out group members who can then be said to share their history. And the only contestant for the criterion of racial membership, according to Appiah, is the false belief in biological heritability (Appiah 1986, p. 27).

In criticizing a transcendental argument, all one need show is either that it is *conceptually* possible to think otherwise about the phenomenon at hand or that there is at least a single *empirical* counter-example. Appiah's argument, I would suggest, is wanting on both counts. Conceptually, consider the case of two pairs of people: Baldwin and Baker, and Buber and Benjamin. The parties of each pair consider themselves members of the same racial group, and the others as members of another racial group upon discovering (through reading the writings of each respectively) that they have suffered a pairwise similar form of oppression at the hands of some third, racially defined group of oppressors. Each pair agrees internally to use some relatively obvious but rough-and ready visible marker, phenotypical or cultural, as an identifying *sign* of their pairwise common oppression (and of others who have a similar set of experiences), in contrast to different markers picking out both the other pair (and those like them) and their oppressors. In accounting for the origins of their oppression and for the cultures of their resistance to it, Baldwin and Baker, in the one case, Buber and Benjamin, in the other, are similarly willing to historicize the considerations they take to have motivated the commonability of their respective group statuses. Thus, in the contingent construction of racial identities no appeal need be made to, or assumed about, some biological factor. That the criteria of identification in each case may only be rough-and-ready entails nothing more than what Appiah generally insists on for matters of race definition, namely, that it is at best a loose mode of group constitution.

Empirically, what is required is a single historical instance of race thinking that feasibly does not rely upon biological presupposition. Jews, for example, sometimes refer to themselves as a race fully cognizant of the fact that it can be no more than shared traditions and culture that binds them together, or at most a culturally defined law of maternal descent. Appiah might deny that this is a proper use of the term. He can do so, however, only at the empirical cost of denying the fact of such use. Nor can he insist that to characterize Jews as such is to turn them falsely into a racial group (implying that there is some other objective form of racial reference). As there are no real races on Appiah's view, all such references imply falsity, and so it cannot be this that differentiates the reference at hand from others.

Additional examples are not hard to find. In addressing the issue of immigration in the context of British politics in 1978, the then prime minister, Margaret

Thatcher, identified the fear of native Britons being 'swamped by people (from the New Commonwealth and Pakistan] with a different culture'. Here race is coded as culture, what has been called 'the new racism' (Barker 1981), making no reference to claims of biology or superiority. By contrast, in attempting more appealingly to uncover the possibility and existence of new forms of cultural identity, Stuart Hall emphasizes a style of cultural self-construction that is not just nostalgic but future-oriented, not simply static but transformative, concerned not only with similarity and continuity but also with difference and rupture (Hall 1990, pp. 235–7). That it is *cultural* identity here distances it from biological presupposition or implication. That such identities could be called races (though Hall is careful not to do so) is not a testament to the biological grounds of such identification (they have, *ex hypothesi*, been denied), but to the fluidity of race as a concept. In its non-biological interpretation, then, race stands for historically specific forms of cultural connectedness and solidarity, for what Appiah elsewhere acknowledges as 'feelings of community . . . the feeling of people with whom we are connected' (Appiah 1989, p. 48). Appiah might want to insist that wherever race assumes cultural reference it simply disguises claims of biological difference. Nevertheless, the fact of the examples cited here, together with my conceptual counter-argument, suggest that the burden of proof now lies with Appiah.

He is clearly correct in holding that to talk of Blacks or Jews (or anyone, for that matter) as a race is to take as homogeneous large numbers of people with otherwise very different sets of experience and ideas, and that this could form the rationale for a dangerous exclusivist turn. This is a problem facing group thinking in general, and it is no doubt part of the reason that Hall places such emphasis upon *self*-constructed identities. However, it is not the point under contention here. What is at issue is the claim that ascriptions of race are inevitably reducible to a single, essential claim about biological heritability. I have argued, by contrast, that this is a misleading way of characterizing race thinking, conceptually and historically. It wrongly turns on a singular, unchanged, and transhistorical reading of the significance of race.

There is a wider point at issue concerning the liberal interpretation of 'race' as a morally irrelevant category, an interpretation to which Appiah gives a sophisticated reading. Where race, or supposed racial characteristics are invoked to distinguish people for distributive purposes, say, they serve not just simply but as signs, forms of shorthand, for some further considerations. When a film director properly insists on casting a black actor to play the lead in a portrayal of Martin Luther King's life, 'race' stands for the commonality of experience, understanding, and empathy that would inform authenticity in the role. Any auditioning black actor who failed to exhibit these qualities would be as undeserving as a white one. Those supporting the liberal interpretation may object that racial consideration may improperly exclude the best available actor—a white member of the Royal Shakespeare Company, say. The wonders of modern make-up skills may render some semblance of plausibility to this view, though only in terms of a broadly defined sense of fine acting. Nevertheless, it strikes me as highly dubious that a white Shakespearean actor, excellent though he may be, could impart authenticity—in look, manner, speech, and so on—to a black public figure like Martin Luther King. In social structures whose social relations show a semblance of being racialized, even subtly or implicitly, it may turn out that the criteria for fine acting are likewise racialized. It was after all, only seventy years ago that Vasco da Gama, the famous Brazilian soccer team then consisting entirely of black players, was expelled from the Brazilian league for refusing 'to whiten' themselves for games by being doused with talcum powder. Moreover, the first black person to play 'America's game' at the highest professional level broke into national baseball less than fifty years ago. It is not beyond comprehension that, against such a background, a fine actor like Richard Harris, say, may be chosen, preposterously, over Paul Winfield to play the part of King. It is possible, of course, that a white actor may be able 'to pass' for a black character. The likelihood of 'successful passing' will generally be greater the more an actor is able to assume, or has assumed the cultural habits identified with 'blackness' as his or her own rather than merely emulating them in acting.

So, the consideration warranting desert is not the supposedly natural property itself but its place-marker for or development into the relevant skills. Even in picking out a person in a crowd in terms of skin colour, we can only rarely be employing merely skin colour as the sole mark of identification. For 'black' and 'white' are never single shades of skin hue, indeed, are rarely properly black or white in colour at all, and are often confused with one another (as in the case of 'passing' and sun tans). What pigmentation often stands for in such cases of ostensive reference, as Wittgenstein (1968, paras 28–38, especially para. 35) may be read to suggest, is a range of encultured characteristics that include (but need not be limited to) a model of dress, bearing, gait, hairstyle, speech, and so forth.

Ethnorace

The way of looking at race that I have suggested—as a fluid, transforming, historically specific concept parasitic on theoretic and social discourses for the meaning it assumes at given historical moments—seems to imply that race is simply a form of ethnicity. If this is so, how can one insist, as I want to, that racism and pre-modern forms of ethnocentrism differ?

In one sense, invoking the concept of race is inevitably ethnocentric. Ethnicity is the mode of cultural identification and distinction. Consider now the interpretation of race seemingly most antithetical to this construal, namely, the biological reading at issue in Appiah's contention. As Brown (1986, pp. 177–8) suggests, assigning significance to biological or physical attributes, in the way required by the conception of race, is a cultural choice. The biological in a sense becomes one amongst the possible cultural criteria for determining ethnicity.

The influential distinction drawn by Van den Berghe between an ethnic group as 'socially defined on the basis of cultural criteria' and a race as 'socially defined but on the basis of physical criteria' (Van den Berghe 1967, p. 9) collapses in favour of the former. It is not so much that natural and social kinds are conflated, though they may often be. Rather, the choice of natural kind as the criterion of group construction and difference is inevitably a social one.

There may be theoretical resistance to acknowledging as a form of race what for the sake of convenience I shall call *ethnorace*. This is because the (self-)ascriptions of specific groups thus engendered as races turn out in their contours to be quite like those which are supposed to be biologically determined. That this is so is largely the result of interpreting cultural connectedness in terms of some form of what Sollors has named descent relations (Sollors 1986). It is this claim of common descent that gives to ascriptions of race their affectation of natural and heritable qualities. It should be clear from the examples I have cited above, however, that ethnoraces can also be established by consent. Here membership turns more or less straightforwardly on choice and self-affirmation. [...]

By insisting that race and ethnicity may at times be used synonymously, I am not suggesting that race be *explained* in ethnic terms. There are convincing reasons to avoid the lure of ethnic reduction, to resist the pervasiveness of what Omi and Winant identify as the 'ethnic paradigm' (Omi and Winant 1987, pp. 14–24). Popularized by Myrdal (1944), Park (1950), Glazer and Moynihan (1963), this model has pervaded the social science explanation of race. It reduces racial formations to ethnicity and analogizes the future trajectory of the racial condition to the melting-pot experience of immigrant assimilation. Nevertheless, the paradigm ignores the specific experiences of racially defined groups, and differences within the groups so defined. Because it takes the formative experience of ethnic groups as generally similar, it overlooks experience in the social constitution of groups of oppressive conditions like colonialism, slavery, exclusion, and in some cases virtual extirpation. Perceived failures of some racially defined groups to advance or integrate are then taken to be a function not of dominant boundary construction, restriction, and exclusion but of the absence of certain kinds of values on the part of the group itself. This paradigmatic disposition to blame the victim implicitly reifies as given the very racial definition of otherness that it is claiming to erode, much as it takes for granted the assumption of ethnic identification that it valorizes. The racial other is necessarily different, but essentially alike within this categorial difference. This, by the way, is central to the logic of apartheid: circumscribe racial others as undifferentially Other in order to set them apart. But once in the majority, disaggregate the other along ethnically defined lines so as to divide and rule.

In insisting that race sometimes assumes or is made to assume ethnic connotation, I am not so much submitting an explanation of race in terms of the ethnic paradigm as suggesting one possible contemporary *meaning* for race.

Thus, race sometimes takes on significance in terms of ethnicity, both (and relatedly) through ordinary folk usage and in virtue of the prevailing paradigm of social science reduction. [. . .]

The Significance of Race

I have argued that race is not a static concept with a single given meaning. Its power has consisted in its adaptive capacity to define population groups, and by extension social agents, as self and other at various historical moments. It has thus facilitated the fixing of characterizations of inclusion and exclusion, giving an apparent specificity otherwise lacking to social relations. To be capable of this, race itself must be almost but not quite empty in its own connotative capacity, able to signify not so much in itself as by adopting and giving naturalized form to prevailing conceptions of social group formation at different times. The historically specific connotations of the concept have been fixed by the insinuation of race into the paradigmatic views of group formation of the day. Initially, race meant root or pedigree. With the emergence of the formalized study of population groupings, race was used synonymously with variety, family, or type of population. In terms of the Darwinian revolution, it signified subspecies or breeding population or common gene pool. It is possible to identify general correlations between the historically specific connotations of 'race' and the broad forms of racist expression. Very roughly, we may say that lineage can be identified with the 'discovery', physical or conceptual, of the racial other, of the initial 'empirical' observation of significant differences in the drive to empire and domination. The specification of race as population is more or less coterminous with the maturing of the colonial condition; as breeding population is with separation and extended subjugation of those racialized as other; and gene pools may be found at the heart of more formalized and often legally sanctioned segregation. These are simply rough-and-ready correlations, or signposts, and I do not mean to imply that the concepts originated on functional imperatives. With the shift in emphasis from explanatory principle to object of explanation, by contrast, race first identified class or status, and then more emphatically culture, ethnicity, or nation.

It follows that the prevailing meaning of race at a given historical conjuncture is embedded in and influenced by prevailing conditions within the social milieu at that time. What is little noticed (though Banton for one is not guilty of this omission) is that foremost amongst these conceptually significant conditions is the history internal to racial thinking. This history sets the limits on the thinkable at that moment, on the evidence available, and on the range of acceptability of argument and explanation. In fixing a historically specific meaning for race, what is as important as knowledge of social conditions at the time is the socio-logic of racialized knowledge. Banton divides the study of race into three periods. The first established knowledge of races; the second elaborated expertise concerning management of intra- and interracial relations; and the third explained race sociologically rather than biologically (Banton 1988, pp. xi; 63). This account rests upon assuming a realist account of race, and so conceiving of race as a singular and given phenomenon. What alters historically on Banton's view is not the conception of race as such, but the way in which the existence of the phenomenon of race is explained, the theories of and about race. Race is a given; racial theories transform with time. Nevertheless, if we see race as a fluid, fragile, and more or less vacuous concept capable of alternative senses, then we shall not take the various notions identified above first and foremost as theories about race. We shall take them alternatively as transformed and historically transforming *conceptions* of race, subjective identity, and social identification.

Race, on this formulation, is ironically a *hybrid* concept. It assumes significance, in both senses, in terms of prevailing social and epistemological conditions at the time, yet simultaneously bearing with it sedimentary traces of past significations. Since 1500, race has been the subject of intense political and epistemological contestation in and through which it has assumed the symbolic power to colonize the given terms of social interpretation, habit, and expression; to dominate, without quite silencing competing social discourses.

That race, conceptually, is not completely vacuous is crucial, for its traces colour all social and scientific theorizing into which it is insinuated. The minimal significance that race bears in itself is not of biological but of naturalized group relations. Race serves to naturalize the groupings that it identifies in its own name. In articulating *as* natural ways of being in the world and the institutional structures in and through such ways of being are expressed, race both establishes and rationalizes the order of difference as a law of nature. This law may be of human and not merely of biological nature. Thus, race gives to social relations the veneer of fixedness, of long duration, and invokes, even silently, the tendency to characterize assent relations in the language of descent. As such, group formation seems destined as eternal, fated as unchanging and unchangeable.

In this way race has been able, along with other forms of group identity, to cover over the increasing anonymity of mass social relations in modernity. Race brings together in self-conception individuals who otherwise have literally nothing to do with each other. In this, race pushes to its extreme the logic of national identification; hence the gratuitous ease with which racism and patriotism seem to intersect. This anonymity also facilitates, through the modes of distantiation inherent in it, the faceless forms of exclusion, exploitation, oppression, and annihilation so much accompanying the history of racial creation.

The question now arises whether, emerging from this analysis, any generally abstract characterization approaching definition can be extended to the concept of race. It should be obvious by now that race cannot be a static, fixed entity, indeed, is not an entity at all in any objective sense. I am tempted to say that race is whatever anyone *in* using that term or its cognates conceives of collective social relations. It is, in this sense, any group designation one ascribes to oneself as such (that is, as race, or under the sign), or which is so ascribed by others. Its meanings, like its forces, therefore, are always illocutionary. In using 'race' and the terms bearing racial significance, social subjects racialize the people and population groups whom they characterize and to whom they refer. In order to get at the specific connotations of the term in this process by which peoples and populations are transformed into races, one has to determine, in a sense both empirically and archaeologically, how the term is being used. That the range of reference has largely turned on characteristics such as skin colour, physiognomy, blood or genes, descent or claimed kinship, historical origin or original geographical location, language, and culture is a fact of the historical condition; it could have extended, and could extend beyond these. Thus, it could be or could have been that 'exclusion of women' was defined as racism, if women were or were to be defined as a race.[2] Race, accordingly, is a form of imagined grouping of broad plant, animal, or human populations, the given form of which assumes content influenced by social factors and relations at a given time but is not reducible to them.

Conceived in this way, the concept that has assumed wide currency in characterizing the process by which human groups are constituted as races is *racial formation* (or, more awkwardly, *racialization*). Racial formation involves the structural composition and determination of groups into racialized form, the imparting of racial significance and connotation at given socio-structural sites to relationships previously lacking them. The particular conception of race that follows is taken by Omi and Winant to be a function of struggles around competing political and ideological projects with differing pre-existing and equally constructed racial dimensions.[3] While I am in some agreement with Omi and Winant's general formulation, I want to substitute for their notion of *racial formation* a designation that signifies a greater subjective dimension. In Omi and Winant's view, racial formation is *structural* in determination, and so retains a form of the abstract social scientific reductionism it is trying to evade. Racial formation is to emerge seemingly magically out of political struggles, and somehow—we are never told exactly how—a different struggle involving a different set of contesting relations will produce a new set of racial categories. No place is cited/sited for (self-)constitution of the (racialized) subject. Hence I will speak of *race creation* (an act of anthropic gods) and of *racial constitution*. [. . .]

The indissolubly political dimension to race is revealed most deeply and directly in the contestation between the imposition of racial definition and racial self-ascription. The forced imposition of racial definition is reflected not only in acts of overt domination, but also in more subtle formulations such as: 'He acts like a Jew', or 'You're being Irish', or 'If you behave like a Black you'll be taken or treated as one'. Indeed, this indissolubly contested nature of race definition sets very finite limits to the just application of race-based preferential treatment programmes. This political character is also reflected in what Appiah warns against, namely, that race is assumed as a category of political contestation, of resistance, a rallying point of the racially oppressed and marginalized. Here, the criterion of membership is not self-declaration but a history of actual subjugation, a point that rubs up against racial self-ascription. Non-Blacks and non-Jews can side *with* Blacks or Jews, but this does not make them black or Jewish. This way of formulating the issue may tend to reify the very racial categories being contested; but the counterpoint is Fanon's crucial one that standing inside or assuming the categories of oppression has proved liberating, at least in part, both in itself and as a means to material emancipation.

In resisting racially defined oppression Fanon (1970), for example, uses those metaphors of animality employed historically to rationalize subjugation of 'his kind'.[4] Fanon's point that racialized categories may be assumed, indeed, invaded as a challenge to racist exclusion and exploitation, reveals—actually demands—that races have no ontological status. In the case of *race*, then, there is literally no object referred to, no given phenomena to be saved. That racialized objects are manufactured in the simulacrum of reference suggests that the issue is not the fact but the terms of asserted reference, its mode, styles, affects, and effects. The fabrication and manipulation of racial construction acquire significance purely instrumentally. It follows that the elaboration of 'racial knowledge' need not serve, or be seen to serve, generically political ends: those concerned to create this knowledge might sincerely claim to be motivated solely by an epistemological drive. So, Omi and Winant go too far in insisting that all racial categories and every racial distinction necessarily discriminate.[5]

Nevertheless, this knowledge and its uses fit into a historical order of racialized power. Any such use accordingly tends to reify and extend the conceptually necessary conditions of racially discriminatory power relations. Consequently, although the expression of 'There's a *black* woman standing over there' seems innocuous enough in a narrow sense, it reproduces on a structural level the set discursive conditions for racist expression to be perpetuated. At the same time, it must be acknowledged that given contemporary socio-discursive conditions, this expression may be an emphatic affirmation in the most positive, nonvalorizing sense of the person's identity as both black and woman. Yet a racialized category like 'black' bears with any use the history of its significations, the irrepressible traces of its repressive modes. This is all the more obviously so in the continuing employment of categories like 'Caucasian' on US government affirmative action and census reports, or 'minority' in everyday discourse and political reportage. It is this return of the repressed, then, that metaphorically poses the dilemma for those wanting to invest resistant power in the assumption of these categories. There clearly seem to be ways to acknowledge the virtues of Jewish culture, say, without presupposing racial character. The question is whether we can affirm the obvious values in the culture taken as black, say, without invoking the presumption of race. More generally, can we speak in either way at this historical moment without reifying race?

To give greater force to this latter point, to be in a better position to set the range of racist expressions, to specify their influences, determinations, natures, and consequences, a more precise picture of what is ment by racisms would have to be painted. That must wait for another occasion.

[From 'The Semantics of Race', *Ethnic and Racial Studies*, 15/4 (1992), 543–4, 556–61, 564–5.]

 PATRICIA HILL COLLINS

47 Defining Black Feminist Thought

Widely used yet rarely defined, Black feminist thought encompasses diverse and contradictory meanings. Two interrelated tensions highlight issues in defining Black feminist thought. The first concerns the thorny question of who can be a Black feminist. One current response, explicit in Patricia Bell Scott's (1982) 'Selected Bibliography on Black Feminism,' classifies all African-American women, regardless of the content of our ideas, as Black feminists. From this perspective, living as Black women provides experiences to stimulate a Black feminist consciousness. Yet indiscriminately labeling all Black women in this way simultaneously conflates the terms *woman* and *feminist* and identifies being of African descent—a questionable biological category—as being the sole determinant of a Black feminist consciousness. As Cheryl Clarke points out, 'I criticized Scott. Some of the women she cited as 'black feminists' were clearly not feminist at the time they wrote their books and still are not to this day' (1983, 94).

The term *Black feminist* has also been used to apply to selected African-Americans—primarily women—who possess some version of a feminist consciousness. Beverly Guy-Sheftall (1986) contends that both men and women can be 'Black feminists' and names Frederick Douglass and William E. B. DuBois as prominent examples of Black male feminists. Guy-Sheftall also identifies some distinguishing features of Black feminist ideas: namely, that Black women's experiences with both racial and gender oppression that result in needs and problems distinct from white women and Black men, and that Black women must struggle for equality both as women and as African-Americans. Guy-Sheftall's definition is helpful in that its use of ideological criteria fosters a definition of Black feminist thought that encompasses both experiences and ideas. In other words, she suggests that experiences gained from living as African-American women stimulate a Black feminist sensibility. But her definition is simultaneously troublesome because it makes the biological category of Blackness the prerequisite for possessing such thought. Furthermore, it does not explain why these particular ideological criteria and not others are the distinguishing ones.

The term Black feminist has also been used to describe selected African-American women who possess some version of a feminist consciousness. This usage of the term yields the most restrictive notion of who can be a Black feminist. The ground-breaking Combahee River Collective (1982) document, 'A Black Feminist Statement,' implicitly relies on this definition. The Collective claims that 'as Black women we find any type of biological determinism a particularly dangerous and reactionary basis upon which to build a politic' (p. 17). But in spite of this statement, by implying that only African-American women can be Black feminists, they require a biological prerequisite for race and gender consciousness. The Collective also offers its own ideological criteria for identifying Black feminist ideas. In contrast to Beverly Guy-Sheftall, the Collective places a stronger emphasis on capitalism as a source of Black women's oppression and on political activism as a distinguishing feature of Black feminism.

Biologically deterministic criteria for the term *black* and the accompanying assumption that being of African descent somehow produces a certain consciousness or perspective are inherent in these definitions. By presenting race as being fixed and immutable—something rooted in nature—these approaches mask the historical construction of racial categories, the shifting meaning of race, and the crucial role of politics and ideology in shaping conceptions of race. In contrast, much greater variation is afforded the term feminist. Feminists are seen as ranging from biologically determined—as is the case in radical feminist thought, which argues that only women can be feminists—to notions of feminists as individuals who have undergone some type of political transformation theoretically achievable by anyone.

Though the term Black feminist could also be used to describe any individual who embraces Black feminist ideas, the separation of biology from ideology required for this usage is rarely seen in the works of Black women intellectuals. Sometimes the contradictions among these competing definitions can be so great that Black women writers use all simultaneously. Consider the following passage from Deborah McDowell's essay 'New Directions for Black Feminist Criticism':

I use the term here simply to refer to Black female critics who analyze the works of Black female writers from a feminist political perspective. But the term can also apply to any criticism written by a Black woman regardless of her subject or perspective—a book written by a male from a feminist or political perspective, a book written by a Black woman or about Black women authors in general, or any writings by women. (1985, 191)

While McDowell implies that elite white men could be 'black feminists,' she is clearly unwilling to state so categorically. From McDowell's perspective, whites and Black men who embrace a specific political perspective, and Black women regardless of political perspective, could all potentially be deemed Black feminist critics.

The ambiguity surrounding current perspectives on who can be a Black feminist is directly tied to a second definitional tension in Black feminist thought:

the question of what constitutes Black feminism. The range of assumptions concerning the relationship between ideas and their advocates as illustrated in the works of Patricia Bell Scott, Beverly Guy-Sheftall, the Combahee River Collective, and Deborah McDowell leads to problems in defining Black feminist theory itself. Once a person is labeled a 'Black feminist,' then ideas forwarded by that individual often become defined as Black feminist thought. This practice accounts for neither changes in the thinking of an individual nor differences among Black feminist theorists.

A definition of Black feminist thought is needed that avoids the materialist position that being Black and/or female generates certain experiences that automatically determine variants of a Black and/or feminist consciousness. Claims that Black feminist thought is the exclusive province of African-American women, regardless of the experiences and worldview of such women, typify this position. But a definition of Black feminist thought must also avoid the idealist position that ideas can be evaluated in isolation from the groups that create them. Definitions claiming that anyone can produce and develop Black feminist thought risk obscuring the special angle of vision that Black women bring to the knowledge production process.

The Dimensions of a Black Women's Standpoint

Developing adequate definitions of Black feminist thought involves facing this complex nexus of relationships among biological classification, the social construction of race and gender as categories of analysis, the material conditions accompanying these changing social constructions, and Black women's consciousness about these themes. One way of addressing the definitional tensions in Black feminist thought is to specify the relationship between a Black women's standpoint—those experiences and ideas shared by African-American women that provide a unique angle of vision on self, community, and society—and theories that interpret these experiences. I suggest that Black feminist thought consists of specialized knowledge created by African-American women which clarifies a standpoint of and for Black women. In other words, Black feminist thought encompasses theoretical interpretations of Black women's reality by those who live it.

This definition does not mean that all African-American women generate such thought or that other groups do not play a critical role in its production. Before exploring the contours and implications of this working definition, understanding five key dimensions of a Black women's standpoint is essential.

All African-American women share the common experience of being Black women in a society that denigrates women of African descent. This commonality of experience suggests that certain characteristic themes will be prominent in a Black women's standpoint. For example, one core theme is a legacy of struggle. Katie Cannon observes, 'throughout the history of the United States, the interrelationship of white supremacy and male superiority has characterized the Black woman's reality as a situation of struggle—a struggle to survive in two contradictory worlds simultaneously, one white, privileged, and oppressive, the other black, exploited, and oppressed' (1985, 30). Black women's vulnerability to assaults in the workplace, on the street, and at home has stimulated Black women's independence and self-reliance.

In spite of differences created by historical era, age, social class, sexual orientation, or ethnicity, the legacy of struggle against racism and sexism is a common thread binding African-American women. Anna Julia Cooper, a nineteenth-century Black woman intellectual, describes Black women's vulnerability to sexual violence:

I would beg . . . to add my plea for the *Colored Girls* of the South:—that large, bright, promising fatally beautiful class . . . so full of promise and possibilities, yet so sure of destruction; often without a father to whom they dare apply the loving term, often without a stronger brother to espouse their cause and defend their honor with his life's blood; in the midst of pitfalls and snares, waylaid by the lower classes of white men, with no shelter, no protection. (Cooper 1892, 240)

Yet during this period Black women struggled and built a powerful club movement and numerous community organizations.

Age offers little protection from this legacy of struggle. Far too many young Black girls inhabit hazardous and hostile environments. In 1975 I received an essay entitled 'My World' from Sandra, a sixth-grade student who was a resident of one of the most dangerous public housing projects in Boston. Sandra wrote, 'My world is full of people getting rape. People shooting on another. Kids and grownups fighting over girlfriends. And people without jobs who can't afford to get a education so they can get a job . . . winos on the streets raping and killing little girls.' Her words poignantly express a growing Black feminist sensibility that she may be victimized by racism and poverty. They also reveal her awareness that she is vulnerable to rape as a gender-specific form of sexual violence. In spite of her feelings about her community, Sandra not only walked the streets daily but managed safely to deliver three younger siblings to school. In doing so she participated in a Black women's legacy of struggle.

This legacy of struggle constitutes one of several core themes of a Black women's standpoint. Efforts to reclaim the Black feminist intellectual tradition are revealing Black women's longstanding attention to a series of core themes first recorded by Maria W. Stewart. Stewart's treatment of the interlocking nature of race, gender, and class oppression, her call for replacing denigrated images of Black womanhood with self-defined images, her belief in Black women's activism as mothers, teachers, and Black community leaders, and her sensitivity to sexual politics are all core themes advanced by a variety of Black feminist intellectuals.

The existence of core themes does not mean that African-American women respond to these themes in the same way. Diversity among Black women produces different concrete experiences that in turn shape various reactions to the core themes. For example, when faced with stereotypical, controlling images of Black women, some women—such as Sojourner Truth—demand, 'ain't I a woman?' By deconstructing the conceptual apparatus of the dominant group, they invoke Black women's legacy of struggle. In contrast, other women internalize the controlling images and come to believe that they are the stereotypes.

A variety of factors explain the diversity of responses. For example, although all African-American women encounter racism, social class differences among African-American women influence how racism is experienced. A young manager who graduated with honors from the University of Maryland describes the specific form racism can take for middle-class Blacks. Before flying to Cleveland to explain a marketing plan for her company, her manager made her go over it three or four times in front of him so that she would not forget *her* marketing plan. Then he explained how to check luggage at an airport and how to reclaim it. 'I just sat at lunch listening to this man talking to me like I was a monkey who could remember but couldn't think,' the Black female manager recalled. When she had had enough, she responded, 'I asked him if he wanted to tie my money up in a handkerchief and put a note on me saying that I was an employee of this company. In case I got lost I would be picked up by Traveler's Aid, and Traveler's Aid would send me back' (Davis and Watson 1985, 86). Most middle-class Black women do not encounter such blatant incidents, but many working-class Blacks do. For both groups the racist belief that African-Americans are less intelligent than whites remains strong.

Sexual orientation provides another key factor. Black lesbians have identified homophobia in general and the issues they face living as Black lesbians in homophobic communities as being a major influence on their angle of vision on everyday events. Beverly Smith describes how being a lesbian affected her perceptions of the wedding of one of her closest friends: 'God, I wish I had one friend here. Someone who knew me and would understand how I feel. I am masquerading as a nice, straight, middle-class Black "girl"' (1983, 172). While the majority of those attending the wedding saw only a festive event, Beverly Smith felt that her friend was being sent into a form of bondage.

Other factors such as ethnicity, region of the country, urbanization, and age combine to produce a web of experiences shaping diversity among African-American women. As a result, it is more accurate to discuss a Black *women's* standpoint than a Black *woman's* standpoint. [. . .]

Contemporary Black women intellectuals continue to draw on this tradition of using everyday actions and experiences in our theoretical work. bell hooks describes the impact working as an operator at the telephone company had on her efforts to write *Ain't I a Woman: Black Women and Feminism* (1981). The women she worked with wanted her to 'write a book that would make our lives better, one that would make other people understand the hardships of being black and female' (1989, 152). To hooks, 'it was different to be writing in a context where my ideas were not seen as separate from real people and real lives' (p. 152). Similarly, Black feminist historian Elsa Barkley Brown describes the importance her mother's ideas played in the scholarship she eventually produced on African-American washerwomen. Initially Brown used the lens provided by her training as a historian and assessed her sample group as devalued service workers. But over time she came to understand washerwomen as entrepreneurs. By taking the laundry to whoever had the largest kitchen, they created a community and a culture among themselves. In explaining the shift of vision that enabled her to reassess this portion of Black women's history, Brown notes, 'it was my mother who taught me how to ask the right questions—and all of us who try to do this thing called scholarship on a regular basis are fully aware that asking the right questions is the most important part of the process' (1986, 14).

Rearticulating a Black Women's Standpoint

The existence of a Black women's standpoint does not mean that African-American women appreciate its content, see its significance, or recognize the potential that a fully articulated Afrocentric feminist standpoint has as a catalyst for social change. One key role for Black women intellectuals is to ask the right questions and investigate all dimensions of a Black women's standpoint with and for African-American women. Black women intellectuals thus stand in a special relationship to the community of African-American women of which we are a part, and this special relationship frames the contours of Black feminist thought.

This special relationship of Black women intellectuals to the community of African-American women parallels the existence of two interrelated levels of knowledge. The commonplace, taken-for-granted knowledge shared by African-American women growing from our everyday thoughts and actions constitutes a first and most fundamental level of knowledge. The ideas that Black women share with one another on an informal, daily basis about topics such as how to style our hair, characteristics of 'good' Black men, strategies for dealing with white folks, and skills of how to 'get over' provide the foundations for this taken-for-granted knowledge.

Experts or specialists who participate in and emerge from a group produce a second, more specialized type of knowledge. The range of Black women intellectuals discussed in Chapter 1 are these specialists, and their theories clarifying a Black women's standpoint form the specialized knowledge of Black feminist thought. The two types of knowledge are interdependent. While Black feminist thought articulates the taken-for-granted knowledge shared by African-American women as a group, the consciousness of Black women may be transformed by such thought. The actions of educated Black women within the Black women's club movement typify this special relationship between Black women intellectuals and the wider community of African-American women:

It is important to recognize that black women like Frances Harper, Anna Julia Cooper, and Ida B. Wells were not isolated figures of intellectual genius; they were shaped by and helped to shape a wider movement of Afro-American women. This is not to claim that they were representative of all black women; they and their counterparts formed an educated, intellectual elite, but an elite that tried to develop a cultural and historical perspective that was organic to the wider condition of black womanhood. (Carby 1987, 115).

The work of these women is important because it illustrates a tradition of joining scholarship and activism, and thus it taps the both/and conceptual orientation of a Black women's standpoint.

The suppression of Black feminist thought in mainstream scholarship and within its Afrocentric and feminist critiques has meant that Black women intellectuals have traditionally relied on alternative institutional locations to produce specialized knowledge about a Black women's standpoint. Many Black women scholars, writers, and artists have worked either alone, as was the case with Maria W. Stewart, or within African-American community organizations, the case for Black women in the club movement. The emergence of Black women's studies in colleges and universities during the 1980s, and the creation of a community of African-American women writers such as Toni Morrison, Alice Walker, and Gloria Naylor, have created new institutional locations where Black women intellectuals can produce specialized thought. Black women's history and Black feminist literary criticism constitute two focal points of this renaissance in Black women's intellectual work (Carby 1987). These are parallel movements: the former aimed at documenting social structural influences on Black women's consciousness; the latter, at exploring Black women's consciousness (self-definitions) through the freedom that art provides.

One danger facing African-American women intellectuals working in these new locations concerns the potential isolation from the types of experiences that stimulate an Afrocentric feminist consciousness—lack of access to other Black women and to a Black women's community. Another is the pressure to separate thought from action—particularly political activism—that typically accompanies training in standard academic disciplines. In spite of these hazards, contemporary Afrocentric feminist thought represents the creative energy flowing between these two focal points of history and literature, an unresolved tension that both emerges from and informs the experiences of African-American women.

The potential significance of Black feminist thought as specialized thought goes far beyond demonstrating that African-American women can be theorists. Like the Black women's activist tradition from which it grows and which it seems to foster, Black feminist thought can create collective identity among African-American women about the dimensions of a Black women's standpoint. Through the process of rearticulation, Black women intellectuals offer African-American women a different view of themselves and their world from that forwarded by the dominant group (Omi and Winant 1986, 93). By taking the core themes of a Black women's standpoint and infusing them with new meaning, Black women intellectuals can stimulate a new consciousness that utilizes Black women's everyday, taken-for-granted knowledge. Rather than raising consciousness, Black feminist thought affirms and rearticulates a consciousness that already exists. More important, this rearticulated consciousness empowers African-American women and stimulates resistance.

Sheila Radford-Hill stresses the importance of rearticulation as an essential ingredient of an empowering Black feminist theory in her essay 'Considering Feminism as a Model for Social Change.' In evaluating whether Black women should espouse feminist programs, Radford-Hill suggests, 'the essential issue that black women must confront when assessing a feminist position is as follows: If I, as a black woman, 'become a feminist,' what basic tools will I gain to resist my individual and group oppression' (1986, 160)? For Radford-Hill, the relevance of feminism as a vehicle for social change must be assessed in terms of its 'ability to factor black women and other women of color into alternative conceptions of power and the consequences of its use' (p. 160). Thus Black feminist thought aims to develop a theory that is emancipatory and reflective and which can aid African-American women's struggles against oppression.

The earlier definition of Black feminist thought can now be reformulated to encompass the expanded definition of standpoint, the relationship between everyday and specialized thought, and the importance of rearticulation as one key dimension of Black feminist thought. Restated, Black feminist thought consists of theories or specialized thought produced by African-American women intellectuals designed to express a Black women's standpoint. The dimensions of this standpoint include the presence of characteristic core themes, the diversity of Black women's experiences in encountering these core themes, the varying expressions of Black women's Afrocentric feminist consciousness regarding the core themes and their experiences with them, and the interdependence of Black women's experiences, consciousness, and actions. This specialized thought should aim to infuse Black women's experiences and everyday thought with new meaning by rearticulating the interdependence of Black women's experiences and consciousness. Black feminist thought is *of* African-American women in that it taps the multiple relationships among Black women needed to produce a self-defined Black women's standpoint. Black feminist thought is *for* Black women in that it empowers Black women for political activism.

At first glance, this expanded definition could be read to mean that only African-American women can participate in the production of Black feminist thought and that only Black women's experiences can form the content of that thought. But this model of Black feminism is undermined as a critical perspective by being dependent on those who are biologically Black and female. Given that I reject exclusionary definitions of Black feminism which confine 'black feminist criticism to black women critics of black women artists depicting black women' (Carby 1987, 9), how does the expanded definition of Black feminist thought address the two original definitional tensions? [. . .]

What Constitutes Black Feminism? The Recurring Humanist Vision
A wide range of African-American women intellectuals have advanced the view that Black women's struggles are part of a wider struggle for human dignity and empowerment. In an 1893 speech to women, Anna Julia Cooper cogently expressed this alternative worldview:

We take our stand on the solidarity of humanity, the oneness of life, and the unnaturalness and injustice of all special favoritisms, whether of sex, race, country or condition. . . . The colored woman feels that woman's cause is one and universal; and that . . . not till race, color, sex, and condition are seen as accidents, and not the substance of life; not till the universal title of humanity to life, liberty, and the pursuit of happiness is conceded to be inalienable to all; not till then is woman's lesson taught and woman's cause won—not the white woman's nor the black woman's, not the red woman's but the cause of every man and of every woman who has writhed silently under a mighty wrong. (Loewenberg and Bogin 1976, 330–31)

Like Cooper, many African-American women intellectuals embrace this perspective regardless of particular political solutions we propose, our fields of study, or our historical periods. Whether we advocate working through separate Black women's organizations, becoming part of women's organizations, working within existing political structures, or supporting Black community institutions, African-American women intellectuals repeatedly identify political actions such as these as a *means* for human empowerment rather than ends in and of themselves. Thus the primary guiding principle of Black feminism is a recurring humanist vision.

Alice Walker's preference for the term *womanist*, a term she describes as 'womanist is to feminist as purple is to lavender,' addresses this notion of the solidarity of humanity. To Walker, one is 'womanist' when one is 'committed to the survival and wholeness of entire people, male and female.' A womanist is 'not a separatist, except periodically for health' and is 'traditionally universalist, as is "Mama, why are we brown, pink, and yellow, and our cousins are white, beige, and black?" Ans.: "Well, you know the colored race is just like a flower garden, with every color flower represented"' (1983, xi). By redefining all people as 'people of color,' Walker universalizes what are typically seen as individual struggles while simultaneously allowing space for autonomous movements of self-determination.

In assessing the sexism of the Black nationalist movement of the 1960s, Black feminist lawyer Pauli Murray identifies the dangers inherent in separatism as opposed to autonomy, and also echoes Cooper's concern with the solidarity of humanity:

The lesson of history that all human rights are indivisible and that the failure to adhere to this principle jeopardizes the rights of all is particularly applicable here. A built-in hazard of an aggressive ethnocentric movement which disregards the interests of other disadvantaged groups is that it will become parochial and ultimately self-defeating in the face of hostile reactions, dwindling allies, and mounting frustrations. . . . Only a broad movement for human rights can prevent the Black Revolution from becoming isolated and can insure ultimate success. (Murray 1970, 102)

Without a commitment to human solidarity, suggests Murray, any political movement—whether nationalist, feminist or antielitist—may be doomed to ultimate failure.

bell hooks' analysis of feminism adds another critical dimension that must be considered: namely, the necessity of self-conscious struggle against a more generalized ideology of domination:

To me feminism is not simply a struggle to end male chauvinism or a movement to ensure that women will have equal rights with men; it is a commitment to eradicating the ideology of domination that permeates Western culture on various levels—sex, race, and class, to name a few—and a commitment to reorganizing U.S. society so that the self-development of people can take precedence over imperialism, economic expansion, and material desires. (Hooks 1981, 194)

Former assemblywoman Shirley Chisholm also points to the need for self-conscious struggle against the stereotypes buttressing ideologies of domination. In 'working toward our own freedom, we can help others work free from the traps of their stereotypes,' she notes. 'In the end, antiblack, antifemale, and all forms of discrimination are equivalent to the same thing—antihumanism. . . . We must reject not only the stereotypes that others have of us but also those we have of ourselves and others' (1970, 181).

This humanist vision is also reflected in the growing prominence of international issues and global concerns in the works of contemporary African-American women intellectuals (Lindsay 1980; Steady 1981, 1987). Economists Margaret Simms and Julianne Malveaux's 1986 edited volume, *Slipping through the Cracks: The Status of Black Women*, contains articles on Black women in Tanzania, Jamaica, and South Africa. Angela Davis devotes an entire section of her 1980 book, *Women, Culture, and Politics*, to international affairs and includes essays on Winnie Mandela and on women in Egypt. June Jordan's 1985 volume, *On Call*, includes essays on South Africa, Nicaragua, and the Bahamas. Alice Walker writes compellingly of the types of links these and other Black women intellectuals see between African-American women's issues and those of other groups: 'To me, Central America is one large plantation; and I see the people's struggle to be free as a slave revolt' (1988, 177).

The words and actions of Black women intellectuals from different historical times and addressing markedly different audiences resonate with a strikingly similar theme of the oneness of all human life. Perhaps the most succinct version of the humanist vision in Black feminist thought is offered by Fannie Lou

Hamer, the daughter of sharecroppers, and a Mississippi civil rights activist. While sitting on her porch, Ms. Hamer observed, 'Ain' no such thing as I can hate anybody and hope to see God's face' (Jordan 1981, xi).

Taken together, the ideas of Anna Julia Cooper, Pauli Murray, bell hooks, Alice Walker, Fannie Lou Hamer, and other Black women intellectuals too numerous to mention suggest a powerful answer to the question 'What is Black feminism?' Inherent in their words and deeds is a definition of Black feminism as a process of self-conscious struggle that empowers women and men to actualize a humanist vision of community.

[From *Black Feminist Thought* (London: Unwin Hyman, 1990), 19–24, 29–33, 37–9.]

Section VIII

The Future of Racism

INTRODUCTION

This book appears as the third millennium dawns. We have come far from the world of 1900 in which racial domination and difference was so much part of the social structure of industrial societies and of the colonial world. So much has occurred in the intervening century—Jim Crow has been overturned, the direct colonization of whites by non-whites has passed, the mass migration of black, Asian, and Hispanic peoples has taken place, the creation of a Jewish state has occurred—but the colour line of which Du Bois wrote in 1903 is still in existence, race still matters in the world today, and racism has not gone away. It has taken new forms, it is in some respects less blatant, but it continues to exercise sway. What then is the future of racism?

Patricia Williams, in her first Reith Lecture of 1997, reflects upon the possibilities of a colour-blind future, and the confusion which it created in her young son being told that colour was not important. She wants to believe that it is possible that the future will be colour blind, but recognizes the extent to which colour is still a signifier. Being coloured in a world of normative whiteness—the world evoked in Henry Louis Gates Jr's autobiography *Colored People*—recalls the observations of W. E. B. Du Bois in 1903 about the ubiquity of the colour line. As Williams observed, 'none of the little white children who taught me to see my blackness as a mark probably ever learned to see themselves as white. In our culture, whiteness is rarely marked in the indicative there! there! sense of my bracketed blackness. And the majoritarian privilege of never noticing oneself was the beginning of an imbalance from which so much, so much else flowed.'

The piece by Paul Sniderman and Edward Carmines draws upon their research into American public opinion on racial issues. They argue that the way forward for liberals who are enmeshed in the dilemma that reducing racial injustice may involve measures which they themselves object to, is to shift the emphasis from seeking to achieve *racial* justice to seeking *social* justice more generally, which would subsume racial justice within it. In particular, they argue that 'continuing to reduce the complexities of race to a morality play dividing the right thinking and racially tolerant on the one side from the intolerant and self-interested on the other will sink constructive efforts to relieve the real and persisting problems of race for another generation'. Racism has become more complex, and analyses of the subject must recognize this.

The following extract, by Joe Feagin and Melvin Sikes, argues that the voice of the people who are the objects of racism must be heard, and the location of the source of racism in *white* racism must be understood and acknowledged. This is congruent with the increasing theoretical emphasis on 'whiteness' in social theory. The gulf revealed in their study between black middle-class and white Americans is substantial. The black respondents do not interact with, and when they do they are not 'heard' by, their white coevals. 'Too often whites see no reason why they should "know" blacks, except perhaps in a special situation where a token black person will be called on to speak for all black Americans'. The legacy of slavery and Jim Crow racial segregation is a profound one—what Douglas Massey and Nancy Denton have called 'American apartheid'—which despite the social changes which have taken place, is a persisting one. What happens to race and racism in the United States is important not only because the USA is a superpower and migration magnet around the world, but because, as Gunnar Myrdal observed over half a century ago, it embodies such contrary tendencies between the idealistic aims of the American creed on the one hand, and the reality of substantial and continuing institutionalized and personal racism on the other.

Lest we spend too much time pondering the United States, the final extract considers racism and nationalism in Europe, and offers some analysis. Far from anticipating a harmonious, pacified, transparent society, Alberto Melucci urges recognition of the ambivalent character of social action: 'It sets us down squarely in the middle of the paradox of social action and it stresses the role of tensions and conflicts, the fact that the singular cannot be reduced to the plural, uniqueness to communication; at the same time it points out the radical need to co-exist.'

Let us end with some conceptual points about the phenomena embraced by the topic of racism. Classification by race, for example in population censuses and administrative records alike, is likely to remain a salient and controversial issue. A particular issue concerns how people of mixed racial origin will classify themselves. Although this may seem a technical point (which it is), classifications are likely to change as a result both of variability in people's self-perception, and increasing racial mixture. Growing numbers of members of societies of in-migration are themselves or have children who are of mixed racial origin. No longer are those of mixed origin assigned, as historically in the USA, to the black group. However one describes this, whether in terms of mixed descent, 'hybridity', or a person's racial identity, what are treated as socially defined racial groups are likely to become less sharply delineated in future, and an increasing number of people will identify with more than one racial group or some kind of mixed group.

Analytically, distinctions need to be made and maintained between personal, ideological, and societal racism. The first refers to the personal experience of racism in face-to-face interaction, the second and third to forms of institutional racism which manifest themselves somewhat differently. That there has been a marked diminution in the acceptability of the second type of racism, ideological racism, during the twentieth century, does not mean there has been a parallel decline in either personal or societal racism. Sometimes the manifestations of personal racism have become less apparent, sometimes the evidence for societal racism has become less obvious, but racism is still a phenomenon with which the social scientist and social commentator has to grapple.

Finally, there is the moral dimension. As Section V shows, a commitment to anti-racism does not guarantee agreement about how best to prevent or diminish racism. The arguments, for example, for and against multiculturalism suggest that such general objectives are capable of various interpretations, and need to be set in the context of particular national conceptions of citizenship, the public welfare, and the character of the state. The French Republican ideal, for example, with its antipathy to recognizing the legitimacy of certain kinds of difference, is at odds with the American tendency to recognize the reality of racial difference and seek overt means such as affirmative action to diminish its impact. The phenomenon is contested, the concept is contested, there is ample scope for argument, but there is a reality to racism which means that it will necessarily remain a major preoccupation.

48 The Emperor's New Clothes

My son attends a small nursery school. Over the past year, three different teachers in his school assured me that he was colour-blind. Resigned to this diagnosis, I took my son to an ophthalmologist who tested him and pronounced his vision perfect. I could not figure out what was going on until I began to listen carefully to what he was saying about colour.

As it turned out, my son did not misidentify colour. He resisted identifying colour at all. 'I don't know,' he would say when asked what colour the grass was; or, most peculiarly, 'It makes no difference'. This latter remark, this assertion of the greenness of grass making no difference, was such a precociously cynical retort, that I began to suspect some social complication in which he somehow was invested.

The long and the short of it is that the well-meaning teachers at his predominantly white school had valiantly and repeatedly assured their charges that colour makes no difference. 'It doesn't matter,' they told the children, 'whether you're black or white or red or green or blue,' Yet upon further investigation, the very reason that the teachers had felt it necessary to impart this lesson in the first place was that it *did* matter, and in predictably cruel ways: some of the children had been fighting about whether black people could play 'good guys'.

My son's anxious response was redefined by his teachers as physical deficiency. This anxiety redefined as deficiency suggests to me that it may be illustrative of the way in which the liberal ideal of colour-blindness is too often confounded. That is to say, the very notion of blindness about colour constitutes an ideological confusion at best, and denial at its very worst. I recognise, certainly, that the teachers were inspired by a desire to make whole a division in the ranks. But there is much overlooked in the move to undo that which clearly and unfortunately matters just by labelling it that which 'makes no difference'. The dismissive, however unintentional, leaves those in my son's position pulled between the clarity of their own experience and the often alienating terms in which they must seek social acceptance.

There's a lot of that in the world right now: someone has just announced in no uncertain terms that they hate you because you're dark, let's say, or Catholic or a woman or the wrong height, and the panicked authority figures try to patch things up by reassuring you that race or gender or stature or your heartfelt religion doesn't matter; means nothing in the calculation of your humanity; is the most insignificant little puddle of beans in the world.

While I do want to underscore that I do embrace colour-blindness as a legitimate hope for the future, I worry that we tend to enshrine the notion with a kind of utopianism whose naïvety will assure its elusiveness. In the material world ranging from playgrounds to politics, our ideals perhaps need more thoughtful, albeit more complicated, guardianship. By this I mean something more than the 'I think therefore it is' school of idealism. 'I don't think about colour, therefore your problems don't exit.' If only it were so easy.

But if indeed it's not that easy then the application of such quick fixes becomes not just a shortcut but a short-circuiting of the process of resolution. In the example of my son's experience at school, the collective aversion to confronting the social tensions he faced resulted in their being pathologised as his individual physical limitation. This is a phenomenon that happens all too frequently to children of colour in a variety of contexts. In both the United States and the United Kingdom, the disproportionate numbers of black children who end up in special education or who are written off as failures attest to the degree to which this is a profound source of social anxiety.

In addition, the failure to deal straightforwardly with the pervasive practices of exclusion that infect even the very young allowed my son's white schoolmates to indulge in the false luxury of a prematurely imagined community. By this I mean that we can all be lulled rather too easily into a self-congratulatory stance of preached universalism—'We are the world! We are the children!' was the evocative, full-throated harmony of a few years ago. Yet nowhere has that been evoked more passionately than in the face of tidal waves of dissension, and even as 'the' children learn that 'we' children are not like 'those', the benighted creatures on the other side of the pale.

This tension between material conditions and what one is cultured to see or not see—the dilemma of the emperor's new clothes, we might call it—is a tension faced by any society driven by bitter histories of imposed hierarchy. I don't mean to suggest that we need always go about feeling guilty or responsible or perpetually burdened by original sin or notions of political correctness. I do wish, however, to counsel against the facile innocence of those three notorious monkeys, Hear no evil, See no evil, and Speak no evil. Theirs is a purity achieved through ignorance. Ours must be a world in which we know each other better.

To put it another way, it is a dangerous if comprehensible temptation to imagine inclusiveness by imagining away any obstacles. It is in this way that the moral high ground of good intentions knows its limits. We must be careful not to allow our intentions to verge into outright projection by substituting a fantasy of global seamlessness that is blinding rather than just colour-blind.

This is a dilemma—being coloured, so to speak, in a world of normative whiteness—whiteness being defined as the absence of colour. The drive to conform our surroundings to whatever we know as 'normal' is a powerful force—convention in many ways is more powerful than reason, and customs in some instances are more powerful than law. While surely most customs and conventions encode the insights of ancient wisdom, the habits of racial thought in Western society just as surely encapsulate some of the greatest mistakes in human history. So how do we rethink this most troubled of divisions, the fault line in our body politic, the fault line in ourselves. The ability to remain true to *one* self seems to me to be not only an ultimate goal of our political and social aspirations but must begin with the ethical project of considering how we can align a sense of ourselves with a sense of the world. This is the essence of integrity, is it not, never having to split into a well-maintained 'front' and a closely-guarded 'inside'.

Creating community, in other words, involves this most difficult work of negotiating real divisions, of considering boundaries before we go crashing through, and of pondering our differences before we can ever agree on the terms of our sameness. For the discounted vision of the emperor's new clothes (or a little boy's colour) is already the description of corrupted community.

Perhaps one reason that conversations about race are so often doomed to frustration is that the notion of whiteness as 'race' is almost never implicated. One of the more difficult legacies of slavery and of colonialism is the degree to which racism's tenacious hold is manifested not merely in the divided demographics of neighbourhood or education or class but also in the process of what media expert John Fiske calls the 'exnomination' of whiteness as racial identity. Whiteness is unnamed, suppressed, beyond the realm of race. Exnomination permits whites to entertain the notion that race lives 'over there' on the other side of the tracks, in black bodies and inner-city neighbourhoods, in a dark netherworld where whites are not involved.

At this level, the creation of a sense of community is a lifelong negotiation of endless subtlety. One morning when my son was three, I took him to his preschool. My son ran straight to a pile of Lego and proceeded to work. I crossed the room and put his lunchbox in the refrigerator, where I encountered a little girl sitting at a table, beating a mound of clay into submission with a plastic rolling pin. 'I see a Mommy,' she said to me cheerfully. 'That must mean that your little boy is here somewhere too.'

'Yes, he's here,' I answered, thinking how sweetly precocious she was. 'There, he's over by the Lego.'

She strained to see around the bookcases. 'Oh yes,' she said. 'Now I see that black face of his.'

I walked away without responding, enraged—how can one be so enraged at an innocent child—yet not knowing what to say just then, rushing to get the jaggedly dangerous broken glass of my emotions out of the room.

I remember being three years old so well. Three was the age when I learned that I was black, the coloured kid, monkeychild, different. What made me so angry and wordless in this encounter forty years later was the realisation that none of the little white children who taught me to see my blackness as a mark probably ever learned to see themselves as white. In our culture, whiteness is rarely marked in the indicative there! there! sense of my bracketed blackness. And the majoritarian privilege of never noticing oneself was the beginning of an imbalance from which so much, so much else flowed.

But that is hard to talk about, even now, this insight acquired before I had the

words to sort it out. Yet it is imperative to think about this phenomenon of clos-
eting race, which I believe is a good deal more widespread than these small examples. In a sense, race matters are resented and repressed in much the same
way as matters of sex and scandal: the subject is considered a rude and trans-
gressive one in mixed company, a matter whose observation is sometimes inevitable, but about which, once seen, little should be heard none the less. Race
thus tends to be treated as though it were an especially delicate category of social infirmity—so-called—like extreme obesity or disfigurement.

Every parent knows a little of this dynamic, if in other contexts: 'Why
doesn't that lady have any teeth,' comes the child's piping voice. 'Why doesn't
that gentleman have any hair?' And 'Why is that little boy so black?' *Sssshhhh!*
comes the anxious parental remonstrance. The poor thing can't help it. We
must all pretend that nothing's wrong.

And thus we are coached upon pain of punishment not to see a thing.

Now to be sure, the parent faces an ethical dilemma in that moment of childish vision unrestrained by social nicety. On the one hand, we rush to place a
limit on what can be said to strangers and what must be withheld for fear of imposition or of hurting someone's feelings. As members of a broad society, we
respect one another by learning not to inflict every last intimate, prying curiosity we may harbour upon everyone we meet.

That said, there remains the problem of how or whether we ever answer the
question, and that is the dimension of this dynamic that is considerably more
troubling.

'Why is that man wearing no clothes, Mummy?' pipes the childish voice once
more. And the parent panics at the complication of trying to explain. The naked
man may be a nudist or psychotic or perhaps the emperor of the realm, but the
silencing that is passed from parent to child is not only about the teaching of restraint; it is calculated to circumnavigate the question as though it had never
been asked. *'Stop asking such silly questions.'*

A wall begins to grow around the forbidden gaze; for we all know, and children best of all, when someone wants to change the subject, forever. And so the
child is left to the monstrous creativity of ignorance and wild imagination.

Again, I do believe that this unfortunate negotiation of social difference has
much in common with discussions about race. Race is treated as though it were
some sort of genetic leprosy or a biological train wreck. Those who privilege
themselves as Un-raced—usually but not always those who are white—are always anxiously maintaining that it doesn't matter even as they are quite busy
feeling pity, no less, and thankful to God for their great good luck in having been
spared so intolerable an affliction.

Meanwhile, those marked as Having Race are ground down by the pendular
stresses of having to explain what it feels like to be You—why are you black, why
are you black, why are you black, over and over again; or alternatively, placed in
a kind of conversational quarantine of muteness in which any mention of racial

circumstance reduces all sides to tears, fears, fisticuffs and other paroxyms of unseemly anguish.

This sad, habitual paralysis in the face of the foreign and the anxiety-producing. It is as though we are all skating across a pond that is not quite thoroughly frozen. Two centuries ago, or perhaps only a few decades ago, the lake was solidly frozen, and if for those skating across the surface things seemed much more secure, it was a much more dismal lot for those whose fates were frozen at the bottom of the pond. Over time, the weather of race relations has warmed somewhat, and a few of those at the bottom have found their way to the surface; we no longer hold our breath, and we have even learned to skate. The noisy, racial chasm still yawns darkly beneath us all, but we few brave souls glide gingerly above, upon a skim of hope, our bodies made light with denial, the black pond so dangerously and thinly iced with the conviction that talking about it will only make things worse.

And so the racial divide is exacerbated further by a welter of little lies that propels us foolishly around the edges of our most demanding social stresses: black people are a happy people and if they would just stop complaining so much, they would see how happy they are. Black people who say they're unhappy are leftist agitators whose time would be better spent looking for a real job. White people are victims. Poor Bangladeshis are poor because they want to be. Poor white people are poor because rich Indians stole all the jobs under the ruse of affirmative action. There is no racism in the market-place, 'each according to his merit' goes the cant, even as the Commission for Racial Equality receives 1700 formal complaints of racial discrimination every month; even as top executives funnel the jobs to school chums and their next of kin, or chief executives at major corporations are captured on tape destroying subpoenaed records of ongoing discriminatory practices. Immigrants are taking over the whole world, but race makes no difference. If sixty per cent of young black men are unemployed in the industrialised world, well, let them watch Oprah. If some people are determined to be homeless, well then let them have it, if homelessness is what they like so much. . .

'Triage' is a word I hear bandied about a lot these days. I have heard it used by many of my friends who are economists; they used it to convey an urgency of limited resources. If there's not enough to go around, then those with the least should be written off first because it will take more to save them anyway. And we don't have more.

This word *triage* originally cropped up in the context of the medical profession. It is a term borrowed from overtaxed hospitals in theatres of war. On body-strewn battlefields, doctors would divide the survivors into three groups. The third in the worst condition might be left to die because bandages were better spent wrapped around those more likely to survive.

In the context of today's ghettos, inner cities and those places doomed to be called the Third World, I hear the word *triage*.

I worry about this image that casts aside so many so easily. It envisions poor and dying populations as separate, distant, severable. I worry that perhaps we have mis-chosen our metaphors.

I fear *triage*; I fear that one cannot cut off a third of the world without some awful, life-threatening bleeding in the rest of the body politic. The Malthusian nightmare has never been a simple matter, I think, of letting someone else go hungry, or of letting someone else die. It is a matter of amputation—that's the metaphor I'd rather use. And one can't cut off one's leg and pretend it never belonged.

It is as though we are employing, in our economic analysis of distributive justice, the images of the very earliest days of medical experimentation. *Oh, well, let's see now . . . The soul abides in the liver . . . therefore we can chop of that troublesome, heretical head and no one will be less holy for it . . .*

Maybe. But quite a few martyrs have been made that way.

Anthropologist Michael Taussig has written about the phenomenon of public secrets. He writes of a ritual in Tierra del Fuego in which the men come out of the men's hut wearing masks. The women hail them by singing 'Here come the spirits!' On some level, everyone must know that these are not spirits but husbands and brothers and fathers and sons, but so powerful is the ritual to the sense of community that it is upon pain of death that the women fail to greet them as spirits.

In our culture, I think that the power of race resembles just such a public secret. I understand the civic ritual that requires us to say in the face of all our differences, we are all one, we are the world. I understand the need for the publicly reiterated faith in public ideas as binding and sustaining community. Such beliefs are the very foundation of institutional legitimacy and no society can hold itself together without them. Yet such binding force comes from a citizenry willing to suspend disbelief for the sake of honouring the spiritual power of our appointed ideals. And where suspicion, cynicism and betrayal have eaten away at a community to the degree that the folk parading from the men's hut look like just a bunch of muggers wearing masks—or badges, as the case may be—then hailing the spirit will sound like a hollow incantation, empty theatre, the weary habit of the dispossessed.

There is a crisis of community in the United States no less than in the rest of the world, of specific and complicated origin perhaps, but in this moment of global upheaval, worth studying for possibilities both won and lost. Whites fear blacks, blacks fear whites. Each is the enemy against whom the authorities will not act.

If racial and ethnic experience constitute a divide that cannot be spoken, an even greater paradox is the degree to which a sense of commonality may be simultaneously created as well as threatened by notions of ethnicity and race. It is no wonder we end up deadlocked with so many of our most profound political problems. The 'O. J. divide' (as it's come to be known in America) is merely a convenient metaphor for everything else we disagree about. Are you one of 'us' or one of 'them'? When I say 'we' am I heard as referring only to other black people? When I employ the first person, will it only be heard as an exercise of what might be called the 'royal I'—me as representative stand-in for all those of my kind . . .

Certainly the great, philosophically-inspiring quandary of my life is that despite the multiculturalism of my heritage and the profundity of my commitment to the notion of the 'us'-ness of us all, I have little room but to negotiate most of my daily lived encounters as one of 'them'. How alien this sounds. This split without, the split within.

Yet in this way the public secret of human fallibility, whose silence we keep to honour our symbolic civic unity, is vastly complicated by the counter secret of palpitating civil discord. Hail the spirit of our infallibly peaceful coexistence. Hail our common fate (even as young white men are forming their own private militias complete with grenade launchers and one in three young black men are in jail or on probation. . . But shush, don't stare. . .

Such is the legacy of racism in the modern world. Perhaps it is less and less fashionable these days to consider too explicitly the kinds of costs that slavery and colonialism exacted, even as those historical disruptions have continued to scar contemporary social arrangements with the transcendent urgency of their hand-me-down grief.

I realise therefore that it might be considered impertinent to keep raising the ghost of slavery's triangle trade and waving it around; there is a pronounced preference in polite society for just letting bygones be bygones. And I concede that a more optimistic enterprise might be to begin any contemporary analysis of race with the Civil Rights Movement in the United States, or the Notting Hill riots in the United Kingdom. Beginning at those points is a way of focusing one's view and confining one's reference to the legitimately inspiring ideals that coalesced those movements: the aims of colour-blindness, equality of all people, and the possibility of peaceful coexistence.

Yet if that well-chosen temporal slice allows us to be optimistic about the possibility of progress, there are none the less limitations to such a frame. First, it is the conceptual pre-history of those movements that explains the toll of racism and its lingering effects. There can be no adequate explanation without reference to it. Secondly, the diasporic complexity of today's social problems requires an analysis that moves those ideals of the social movements of the 1960s and 1970s beyond themselves, into the present, into the future—to a more complex, practical grappling with such phenomena as the hybridising of racial stereotypes with the fundamentalisms of gender, class, ethnicity, religion. Thirdly, the problem of race is overlaid with crises in environmental and resource management that have triggered unparalleled migrations from rural to urban locations within national boundaries, and that have impassioned debates about immigration across national boundaries. Finally, not a few aspects of our new-age global economics, much like the commercial profiteering of colonialisms past, threaten to displace not just the very laws to which we persistently make such grand appeal but the nation state itself. I believe that a genuine, long-term optimism about the future of race relations depends on a thorough excavation of the same.

A memory slips into my mind. I was riding the train from New York to Washington DC some years ago. I was on my way to some lawyers' conference or other; I was accompanied by two black colleagues. An hour into the trip, the train stopped in the city of Philadelphia. A young white woman got on whom my colleagues knew. She was also a lawyer, headed to the same conference. She joined us, sitting among us in a double row of seats that faced each other. A little while later, the conductor came along. The new woman held up her ticket, but the conductor did not seem to see her. He saw four of us seated and only three ticket stubs.

'One of you hasn't paid,' he said, staring at me, then at each of my two black friends. I remember pointing to the white woman and someone else said, 'Over there.' But the conductor was resolute.

'Which one of you hasn't paid?' he asked again. Two of us kept saying, 'Our receipts, see?' and the white woman, speaking *very* clearly said, 'Here. I am trying to give you my ticket.'

The conductor was scowling. The conductor still did not hear. 'I am not moving 'til one of you pays up.'

It was the longest time before the conductor stopped staring in all the wrong directions. It was the longest time before he heard the new woman, pressing her ticket upon him, her voice reaching him finally as though from a great distance, passing through light years of understanding as though from another universe. The realisation that finally lit his face was like the dawning of a great surprise.

How precisely does the issue of colour remain so powerfully determinative of everything from life circumstance to manner of death, in a world that is, by and large, officially 'colour-blind'? What metaphors mask the hierarchies that make racial domination frequently seem so 'natural', so invisible, indeed so attractive? How does racism continue to evolve, post-slavery and post-equality legislation, across such geographic, temporal and political distance?

No, I am not saying that this is the worst of times. But neither will I concede that this is the best of all possible worlds. And what a *good* thing, is it not, to try to imagine how much better we could be. . .

'I had a dream,' said my son the other morning. Then he paused. 'No,' he said, 'it was more of a miracle. Do you know what a miracle is?'

'Tell me,' I said, thunderstruck, and breathless with maternal awe.

'A miracle is when you have a dream and you open your eyes in it. It's when you wake up and your dream is all around you.'

It was a pretty good definition, I thought. And even though my son's little miracle had something to do with pirates meeting dinosaurs, I do think that to a very great extent we dream our worlds into being. For better or worse, our customs and laws, our culture and society are sustained by the myths we embrace, the stories we recirculate to explain what we behold. I believe that racism's hardy persistence and immense adaptability are sustained by a habit of human imagination, deflective rhetoric and hidden license. I believe no less that an optimistic course might be charted, if only we could imagine it. What a world it would be if we could all wake up and see all of ourselves reflected in the world, not merely in a territorial sense, but with a kind of non-exclusive entitlement that grants not so much possession as investment. A peculiarly anachronistic notion of investment, I suppose, at once both ancient and futuristic. An investment that envisions each of us in each other.

[From *Seeing a Colour Blind Future: The Paradox of Race* (London: Virago, 1997), 1–14.]

PAUL SNIDERMAN AND EDWARD CARMINES

49 Tangled Politics

Race was once supposed to be an issue we would put behind us. Progress would be difficult, conflict protracted, short-term set-backs inevitable, struggles on many fronts necessary. Certainly a formal guarantee of equality under the law for black Americans was only a beginning. But America was steadily becoming a more open and open-minded society, as increasingly better-educated and more tolerant Americans took the place of ill-educated and intolerant ones. With time, it was said, the rancor and bitterness over race would abate.

But race has not receded into the background of American life. On the contrary, gaping cleavages are obvious, not just at the margins of American society but at its center, in its institutions of government and advanced education. As every person of prominence in American thought and politics recognizes, race remains as divisive as ever. Why, more than a quarter of a century after the landmark civil rights laws of the 1960s, does the issue of race still cut so deep?

Many believe that the continuing clash over race is rooted ultimately in the persistent reluctance of white Americans to accept black Americans as equals—that is, in prejudice. Granted, this idea has not always been given the careful exposition it deserves: it is easy to point to a parade of commentators and social scientists who have made extreme and crude assertions about the continuing power of racial prejudice in American life. But a truth should not be denied just because it has been overstated. Recognition of prejudice's pervasiveness in the American experience represents a hard-won accomplishment of the civil rights movement, and for a generation now educated and public-spirited Americans have found it next to impossible to understand the issue of race in other than moral terms. Furthermore, agreement that a historic wrong had been done to blacks, it was believed, would prove a decisive political force in itself, assuring that the public action required to achieve racial equality would in the end be taken.

But in a way that no one anticipated a generation ago, what ought to be done to achieve equality has proven politically controversial, even morally problematic. Meanwhile, the objective conditions of life of large numbers of blacks have gotten worse, also in a way that no one foresaw. Today, black Americans remain significantly more likely than whites to be poor, to be raised by a single parent, to be segregated residentially and educationally, and to die young. Although more blacks are better off than ever before, a frighteningly large number are immiserated: ill-educated, ill-housed, and underemployed or unemployed.

In consequence, in the minds of many Americans, both black and white, the issue of race is now defined by an ominous trinity: the worsening of inequality as a social fact; the deepening of whites' resistance to governmental action to overcome it; and the hypocrisy of their commitment to racial equality in principle but not in public policy. For many who are most sympathetic to the problems of blacks, the very meaning of the issue of race has been transformed. Instead of testifying to the moral power of the American values of fairness and equal opportunity, race has exposed the futility of the American Creed. In place of optimism and pride, there is now resentment and bitterness. The small steps toward racial equality that have been taken only underscore the great distance that remains.

Other Americans have come to see the issue of race from a very different perspective, however. As they view it, the intensity of the continuing clash over race owes less to the tenacity of racial prejudice and more to the very efforts undertaken to overcome it. In the name of achieving racial equality and tolerance, they contend, the ideas of equality and tolerance have themselves been upended. No shortage of self-serving acts have been defended as morally commendable, under the shield of civil rights. Especially egregious examples—say, the Tawana Brawley case or the defense of black anti-Semites—have provided a larger context in which more problematic ones—say, racially gerrymandering voting districts—are now set. In surveying the contemporary politics of race from this second perspective, it is, again, easy to focus on the failings of individual personalities engaged in the debate, but so narrow a view would miss the deeper concern: that in the effort to put right a terrible wrong, we have committed ourselves to policies that many find wrong in themselves.

A very large part of the contemporary argument over race seems to consist in a debate between these two views, the one emphasizing the tenacity of racial prejudice, the other stressing the polarizing effects of our efforts to overcome it. Although some conservatives are concerned about the persistence of prejudice, this worry is more common among those with a broadly liberal view; and although, increasingly, some liberals are expressing apprehension about the polarizing impact of government policies on race, this criticism is more common among those with a broadly conservative view.

Partly because of this convergence between ideological outlook and critical orientation, the currents that charge the contemporary debate over race are powerful and deep. Among those concerned about prejudice, many see the criticisms of public policies designed to move blacks forward as being themselves an added layer of racial prejudice, more subtle than old-fashioned bigotry but just as noxious. On the other hand, many of those who emphasize the polarizing consequences of racial policies see these claims of prejudice as a ploy to defend acts by both individuals and governments which are otherwise morally indefensible.

Obviously, one can simultaneously agree with both sides in the debate; the truth of the one does not establish the falsity of the other. But it is very far from clear how to put these two perspectives together coherently. They seem to point to two fundamentally opposed attitudes toward the American experience itself. The emphasis on the continuing power of prejudice is, and is meant to be, critical; the focus on the polarizing effects of racial policies is, and is meant to be, exculpatory.

We, the authors of this book, have thought about what is going on and why for some time, and we report here what we have discovered. Our findings rest on a fundamental claim: that the current clash over race must be interpreted in the context of a deeper debate on the proper role of government. In saying this, we are very far from suggesting that either racial prejudice or racial polarization are not genuine problems. But we are persuaded that it is not possible to understand either without understanding that the contemporary debate over racial policy is driven primarily by conflict over what government should try to do, and only secondarily over what it should try to do *for blacks*.

Liberalism has made an exceptional commitment in behalf of racial equality, transforming the politics of race, and it has made this commitment out of moral conviction. But in seeking to do the right thing, and perhaps especially in wishing to do it for the right reason, there are great risks as well as great rewards.

A call for a national undertaking to bring to an end the legal segregation of black Americans, and to work actively to overcome the legacy of slavery and discrimination, had a natural appeal to liberals. The values of liberalism—the commitment to equality, belief in the efficacy of government as an agent of social change, openness to change, and concern for the less well-off—combined to serve as a foundation for a collective effort to improve the conditions of life for blacks. This is not to say that conservatives were opposed, on principle, to a national struggle for racial equality: and, on an individual level, large numbers of conservatives did support the struggle for civil rights. But a deliberate and public effort at social change in behalf of the disadvantaged, through the medium of the national government, had an indisputably stronger appeal for liberals. Liberalism has, in consequence, been the dominating political force that has energized and directed the campaign for civil liberties and civil rights of black Americans.

Viewed from the perspective of traditional American liberalism, the politics of race has centered on the resistance of white Americans to public policies designed to achieve racial equality. The reasons for white resistance are variously conceived. Some believe that the root of opposition is racial prejudice pure and simple. Others believe that the obstacle is the American value of individualism, or perhaps the American vice of self-interestedness. Still others see the problem as group interest, that is, whites acting in the interest of whites whether it is in their individual interest or not. But whether they believe that opposition to policies designed to achieve racial equality is rooted in opposition to racial equality itself or in some other factor, traditional liberals agree that the resistance of whites is the principal barrier to achieving racial equality. The problem of race, now as ever, is defined by them as a problem in the hearts and minds of white Americans.

From this view of the racial problem a political strategy followed: in order to improve the conditions of life for blacks, it is first necessary to change the beliefs and sentiments of ordinary white Americans—above all, to beat back the racial prejudice and resentment that was preventing blacks from achieving equality. Over time, almost imperceptibly, seeing blacks better off became itself the animating objective of liberalism, the goal liberals sought even when it was at odds with liberal values, tolerance and the moral irrelevance of race among them. Liberals thus came to evaluate racial policies increasingly in the light of their fundamental desire to see blacks better off, and only secondarily in light of the constitutive values of liberalism itself. And precisely because of the sincerity of liberalism's moral commitment to overcoming racial inequality, politically engaged liberals found themselves, at least in the early years, disposed to make use of the coercive power of government to a degree they would ordinarily abhor. Many still see the benefits to be gained from the determined use of public power in programs like busing or affirmative action, and indeed some believe that if a mistake has been made it has been to underuse, not overuse, the authority of government to promote racial equality and oppose the resistance of whites. Many liberals are committed to staying the course.

But alongside these traditional liberals now are many other liberals who believe that liberalism itself has taken a wrong turn. Their objection is not to the cost of government in alleviating inequality, nor is it even to the use of government power to promote equality, at any rate not in the abstract. The difficulty instead is moral. The campaign for racial equality, which they support as liberals, has come to serve ends to which they object as *liberals*. Programs dedicated to equal opportunity, as a practical matter, have condoned unequal treatment under the law, in the form of race-conscious policies, just as the effort to promote racial tolerance on college campuses by imposing 'hate speech' codes has come to seem at odds with freedom of expression itself. The result is that, quite apart from having to wrestle with conservatism, liberalism is now engaged in a struggle with itself.

For many years, we intuitively believed, along with many traditional liberals, that racial prejudice, pure and simple, still shaped the political thinking of white Americans. At the start of our studies of public opinion, we, like everyone else, wanted to address the question: To what extent does racial prejudice persist? It is manifestly important to answer this question, and in the chapters that follow we shall present much in the way of new evidence bearing on it. For example, we will describe the surprising finding—surprising to us certainly—that although prejudice is more common on the political right, it is more powerful on the left, among liberals themselves. Still, judged by the objective evidence, the overall impact of racial prejudice on the political choices that white Americans make turns out to be surprisingly modest. We first discovered this when examining our own surveys of American racial attitudes; then we corroborated it, analyzing every other survey available. The conclusion to draw now is clear: racial prejudice is not the dominant reason for the resistance of white Americans to current policies intended to help black Americans.

But there is another question, equally important to answer. As the story of race has been told, it has focused on whether racial prejudice has declined. Some argue that a real change has taken place, others that the changes have been superficial. But with all the debate over whether the decline in prejudice has been large or small, another change has escaped attention. Not only has there been a decrease in the number of whites who harbor ill will toward blacks, but there has also been an increase in the number of whites who bear good will toward them—indeed, so much so that there are now two forces at work, not just one: a weakening strain of animosity *and* a strengthening desire that, at last, blacks be better of. To fail to see that, now, at least as large a number of whites genuinely wish blacks well as wish them ill is to fail to see the possibilities for positive political action.

Whether this new well-spring of good will is put to use, and, no less important, what use it is put to, depends upon the choices that political leaders offer to the public at large and the arguments they make in their behalf. The results we have uncovered and present in this book suggest a strategy for achieving racial equality that is quite different from the now conventional liberal approach. It is *not* necessary to change the hearts and minds of white Americans to win support for public policies that make things go better for blacks. It is instead necessary to change the terms on which political leaders appeal for support. Public support can be won, provided political leaders appeal directly to the moral principles that give the issue of race itself a moral claim upon us.

Our findings suggest that the very same policies meant to reach out and help those most in need of help will win markedly more public support if they are championed on the basis of universal principles that reach beyond race instead of being justified on racially specific grounds. The advantage of a color-blind politics is not that it wins the support of whites who would otherwise object to programs to help blacks, whether out of racial prejudice or self-interestedness. Reaching beyond race has a power to it, not because it evades the reach of prejudice but because it calls into play the principle of fairness—that all who need help should be helped, regardless of their race.

An appeal to fairness or compassion without a special focus on race is interpreted by some liberals as an effort to undercut special claims that blacks may make for government assistance. They argue that because blacks have been forced to bear unique burdens, they are entitled to make unique claims. The effect is to cast racial politics as a form of reparation. But this view of racial politics confuses two different questions: Who should be helped and why they should be helped? A policy may focus on helping blacks. But that does not mean it must be argued for on racial grounds. Indeed, the most effective way to argue on behalf of blacks, as we shall show, is to argue on grounds that do not apply exclusively to blacks.

If political leaders will move from arguments restricted to considerations of racial justice to arguments centered on broader considerations of social justice, they can build a biracial coalition in support of policies to assist those in need of assistance regardless of race. Political leaders are themselves constrained by public opinion, but the choices we make as citizens depend on the choices they make as leaders. They not only establish the alternatives but also fix the justifications for alternative courses of action. Political leaders thus define both the lines of government action that citizens may choose to support or oppose, and the reasons why they should do one rather than the other.

In saying this, we are not saying that public opinion can easily be swayed or that majorities can be conjured up out of minorities on issues of race simply by cunningly framing the issues in one way rather than another. Bringing about a change in the center of gravity of public opinion, on issues that are inescapably controversial, is inherently difficult. But it is doable. And what seems to us so unfortunate about the longstanding fixation with the malignant strain in American popular culture is the impression of fixity that it gives to the politics of race. It suggests that intolerance remains the primary factor shaping public reactions to matters of race and that, unless and until it is eliminated—an event which appears nowhere on the horizon—political leaders who engage problems of race face a huge risk of provoking resentment and a vanishingly small chance of winning public support.

If this view of the hegemony of racial prejudice and resentment is accurate, political leaders have little to gain from attempting to move the discussion of race forward: they will earn plaudits from a few; they will suffer censure from many. It is our deep belief that this view is wrong. The all-too-common tendency to cast the politics of race as a clash between two nations, one white, the other black, obscures what is most crucial to the politics of race—namely that whites do not form a singleminded nation. On the contrary, there is a real division among whites over race. Approximately as many support many policies to help blacks as oppose them, and still others can be won from one side to the other. Moreover, to change the minds of those whose minds are open to change does not require that their core ideas about race be altered. It does require that political leaders, both in public office and out of it, change the moral arguments they make to them as to what should be done about race and why.

But change their minds about what? A generation ago, in a fundamental sense there was only one question to decide. If you believed that it was wrong to forbid blacks from drinking from the same water fountain as whites, it followed that it was wrong to forbid them to attend the same schools as whites. If segregation was wrong in one situation, it was wrong in all situations. Now, there is more than one question to decide. If you believe that government should help blacks in some ways, it does not follow that it ought to help them in all ways.

More than one decision now needs to be made about racial policy. Our aim, accordingly, is to establish how ordinary Americans believe these different decisions, some involving race-conscious policies and some not, should be made. In the chapters that follow we map public opinion about an array of proposals for public action, among them to boost black employment, to improve public education, to provide job training programs, to combat discrimination in employment and housing, to reduce poverty. With the exception of affirmative action—understood as requiring preferential treatment or racial quotas—all are politically contestable. On each of these issues large numbers are wedded to their positions, but substantial numbers are not. They can be won from one side to the other—from opposing government assistance for blacks to supporting it, or from supporting it to opposing it, or indeed from sitting on the sidelines to taking a stand.

To sum up our view of the politics of race, we believe (1) that there is not one problem of race but a number of distinguishable problems calling for different courses of action; (2) that to talk of a solution to the issue of race is misleading, not only because there is more than one problem of race to deal with but also because no one has a credible plan for the complete solution of any of the fundamental problems; (3) that it is essential, as both a moral and practical matter, to establish priorities, and although middle-class blacks are not yet as well off as middle-class whites, they are now decisively better off than poor blacks and poor whites; it follows, in our view, that those who are badly off should be given priority over members of the middle-class, regardless of race; (4) that any effort to help those who are badly off will require increased public efforts to improve their opportunities for education and employment; (5) that winning public support for such efforts will require a coalition of blacks and whites, working together on the basis of values they believe in by virtue not of being black or white but of being American; and (6) that continuing to reduce the complexities of race to a morality play dividing the right thinking and racially tolerant on the one side from the intolerant and self-interested on the other will sink constructive efforts to relieve the real and persisting problems of race for another generation.

We shall assume the first four points and, in the chapters that follow, demonstrate the last two.

But is it possible to establish what white Americans really think about matters of race? A generation ago, it seemed self-evident that the way to find out what citizens thought on the issues of the day was to conduct a systematic survey of public opinion. Since then, cynicism has set in on the value of public opinion polls, perhaps especially on matters of race. Can we learn, by means of opinion surveys, not what white Americans think they should say but what they really think? Can we establish whether, if they say they wish blacks to be treated fairly, they mean what they say? One does not have to be a cynic to be skeptical about what people say in public opinion interviews. Race is still an emotionally charged issue, difficult to discuss with friends, harder still with strangers.

Given the manifest difficulty of determining whether people mean what they say when they talk about race, it is ironic that so many popular commentators are so sure that they really know what the ordinary white American thinks about blacks. Even when politically committed commentators are aware of the carefully compiled record of public opinion surveys since the 1940s showing a dramatic decline in levels of racial prejudice among whites, they nonetheless point out that some whites are not telling the truth about how they feel about blacks. But, from a valid premise—that one cannot be certain that everyone is telling the truth—they draw an invalid conclusion—that one can be confident that large numbers of them are not telling the truth. The result: some of the best-known commentators contend that racial prejudice, rather than being in decline, remains pervasive. Yet they do not themselves present reliable evidence of what even a small number of white Americans actually think. So skepticism, with the assistance of self-righteousness, passes into cynicism.

For more than a decade, we have been developing a new approach to public opinion interviews which allows us to illuminate aspects of Americans' thinking about race hitherto hidden. The key to this approach is to embed complex, genuinely randomized experiments in public opinion interviews and carry them out in a way that is invisible to the person being interviewed. The experiments we have developed, which rely on computer-assisted interviewing, take many different forms. Here we will briefly describe one, in order to illustrate the new light this approach can throw on American racial attitudes.

We call this group of experiments the Excuse Experiments, and the idea behind them is to create a situation in which a randomly selected set of white interviewees who say they think well of blacks are deliberately given a socially acceptable excuse to make a negative judgment of blacks, precisely in order to see if they take advantage of it. Suppose—for the moment setting aside the mechanics of how this is to be done—that a mother on welfare is characterized as a high school dropout one half of the time and as a high school graduate the other half. Suppose, moreover, that she is black one half of the time and white the other half. Then ask everyone whether they think the welfare mother they were asked about is likely to make an honest effort to get off welfare in the next year.

Imagine how whites who said they like blacks but really don't would answer when the mother was black and a high school dropout. Just so far as they think ill of blacks, even though they say they think well of them, they should be inclined to say that a black mother who is a high school dropout is unlikely to make an honest effort to get off welfare in the next year. That is what they are free to say, if that is what they think, because we have deliberately put them in a position to claim that the mother on welfare was unlikely to try to find a real job not because she is black but because she is a high school dropout. However, by seeing if their confidence is similarly undercut in the case of a white woman on welfare, we can tease out the proportion of whites who really are prejudiced without their being able to tell that we can tell. For it if turns out that being a high school dropout is more stigmatizing if the woman on welfare is black rather than white, then that difference is a proof of racial prejudice among whites who profess to think well of blacks.

The Excuse Experiments are only one group of many experiments that we will describe in this book. These new interviewing procedures make visible aspects of Americans' thinking about matters of race previously invisible. We are not suggesting that the truth about American racial attitudes now can be established completely and decisively, or that older procedures were without value. Every procedure, new or old, is imperfect, and all procedures, perhaps especially if they are new, can be improved. We do, however, believe that because of its novel approach, our study can address questions that thoughtful people have asked about the validity of public opinion polls on matters of race in a way that previous studies have not been able to do.

[From *Reaching beyond Race* (Cambridge, Mass.: Harvard University Press, 1997), 1–14.]

JOE FEAGIN AND MELVIN P. SIKES

50 Changing the Color Line: The Future of U.S. Racism

Today blatant, subtle, and covert discrimination against African Americans persists in virtually all aspects of their public lives. Racism is central to the lives of white Americans too, even though many whites deny its presence or effects. Racial discrimination is pervasive, and cumulative and costly in its impact. Is there any hope for significant change? Near the end of most interviews with our middle-class respondents we asked several questions about future U.S. racial relations: whether they saw things getting better or worse for black Americans in the next few years; what major changes they would most like to see in white society; and what they feel black Americans should be doing to fight discrimination. Their responses open up interesting windows into how they view this society's racial order now and in the future.

But their responses offer more than just another view of the racial order. Understanding their perspective is crucial to taking major steps to combat white racism. Why should white Americans listen to these black voices? When one considers the loss of prestige and honor for the United States when governments and the mass media overseas critique outbursts of U.S. racism; when one calculates the human costs and multibillion dollar property losses of racial riots in the last decade in cities from Miami to Los Angeles; when one reads numerous reports to escalating hate crimes against black and other minority Americans; when one becomes aware of the terrible loss of human energy, talent, and achievements that results from black struggles with everyday racism; and when one examines the disintegration of the social fabric of cities where many black youth have lost hope of attaining the American dream, a white person has excellent reasons to listen to the voices of those most affected by racism.

But these voices must not only be listened to, they must be *heard*. Sadly, black and white Americans mostly live in separate worlds and often do not speak the same language. Our respondents regularly show how they and other African Americans are often not 'seen' or 'heard' by white Americans in everyday settings. Too often whites see no reason why they should 'know' blacks, except perhaps in a special situation where a token black person will be called on to speak for all black Americans. Unless we find better ways to communicate, for whites to listen to black Americans, the 'two societies, one black, one white—separate and unequal' that the prophetic Kerner Commission envisioned will never change, and racial violence will become all but inevitable. The recent call of some Ku Klux Klan leaders and other white supremacists for a racial war against people of color comes doubtless because they feel the time is ripe to attack.

A first step toward change is for white Americans to admit the reality of current white racism, a point underscored by a university researcher:

I get sick and tired of seeing things on television, white people saying that 'people aren't racist any more.' That's a lie. They are racist. They don't want to recognize it, they refuse to recognize it. They say, 'Let's not think about the past.' Well, how do you go forward in the future if you don't think about the past? . . . You still have people in 1989 saying that same stuff. They do studies on the size of people's brains; they do studies on whether or not a black athlete is better than a white athlete, and this kind of stuff, which in itself says that this place is still racist. So, I would like for them to go ahead and, you know, it's almost like being an alcoholic. Admit that you're an alcoholic and go on to solve the problem.

Until whites recognize that they have been raised in a racist society and harbor its hidden influence even when they deny it, until whites recognize that they too must take action to deal with personal and societal racism, no matter how subtle, and to eradicate it, the racial situation in the United States will only worsen. Once most whites recognize that they and the system their ancestors created are deeply racist, then most black Americans will doubtless be willing to cooperate and be patient as real programs to eradicate racism are created. This task of educating white Americans will not be easy, but it is possible. Once the problem is admitted, the solutions can at least be envisioned and implemented. . . .

Writing in the 1940s in *An American Dilemma*, Gunnar Myrdal noted that most blacks, like most whites, were under the spell of the American creed, the 'ideals of the essential dignity of the individual human being, of the fundamental equality of all men, and of certain inalienable rights to freedom, justice, and a fair opportunity.' The basics of the American dream include not only liberty and justice but also the pursuit of happiness, which can be seen as including a decent-paying job, a good home, and a sense of personal dignity.

Can all Americans achieve this dream? The logic of equal rights and equal opportunity would dictate that a black person who has reached middle-income status should have no difficulty in realizing the promises of the American dream. Middle-class African Americans have paid their due and are asking to be accepted for their contributions and their ability to contribute, rather than to be viewed in terms of skin color. Yet the experiences of these African Americans with discrimination in traditionally white institutions are often destructive of their hopes and ambitions, of their ability to achieve true equality of opportunity and the multifaceted dream of being middle class. Recall the television broadcaster who argued forcefully that there is 'no black middle class, by the way. You know that's relevant. Every time I use "middle class," I know that. Because a black middle-class person is still not a middle-class person.'

In this book we have reported on concrete black *experience* with everyday racism. Racial discrimination is not an abstraction for these Americans, nor is it mainly a problem of the recent past. For most of these Americans racial discrimination is not a matter of isolated incidents, but instead a succession of negative experiences with whites from the early years of childhood to the last years of adulthood. Our interviews also put whites into the spotlight. We observe in the accounts that a large proportion of the discriminators are indeed middle class whites with power and resources.

Mainstream discussions emphasizing the benefits to black Americans of expanded employment in white-collar jobs often neglect the fact that as a group middle-class blacks are subordinate to middle-class whites in wages, salaries, and workplace power. Typically the white-collar workplace offers no shelter from white racism, for it is a site where white peers and supervisors may isolate black employees, sabotage their work, or restrict their access to better jobs and good promotions. Nor does the university or college provide reliable security and support. Black students in mostly white colleges face many hurdles and pitfalls, from epithets to social isolation, professorial indifference, and, often, a Eurocentric curriculum. Even one's home and neighborhood may not be a place of refuge from white hostility; white realtors and homeowners may try to keep blacks out of white neighborhoods, and white neighbors may be insensitive or hostile. In public accommodations African Americans still experience a range of discrimination, from poor treatment in restaurants and department stores to hostility in pools and parks. In street sites white hostility can be especially dangerous and threatening, for a black person never knows when a racist epithet signals violence to come.

As of this writing, what is missing in the mass media and the mainstream intellectual literature is a single in-depth article or book on the role of white racism in creating the foundation for current racial conflict. What is missing not only in the mass media but in the nation is white Americans, especially middle-class whites and powerful white leaders, taking responsibility for the widespread prejudice and discrimination that generate rage and protest among black Americans. It was white Americans who created slavery and the segregation of African Americans, and it is white Americans who today are responsible for most continuing discrimination against African Americans.

Even some white liberals see the racial relations dilemma as a problem of everyone's prejudices. In 1992 the liberal organization People for the American Way published the results of a survey they commissioned on young Americans. They concluded from their research that 'benign neglect' was no longer the answer for U.S. racial problems and that it was time to get young people in all racial and ethnic groups to reconsider their racial attitudes. They recommended that an 'assignment of blame' should be avoided and that it was time to 'find common ground.' They continued by underscoring a vicious cycle of mutual resentment: 'Minority citizens believe with more certainty that whites are responsible for the hostility between the races; whites believe the same thing about minorities with equal certitude. This is an exercise in bitterness that is bound to have no affirmative or beneficial end.'[1] This important survey of young Americans provided valuable information and some useful suggestions for change, but its conclusions were much too weak. The U.S. racial problem, now and in its origin, is fundamentally a white problem, for whites have the greatest power to perpetuate or alter it. The conditions of antiblack discrimination have specific creators, and the creators are mostly white Americans.

As a nation we have been misled by an influential group of mainstream liberal and neoconservative analysts, most of whom are white, who have told us that the primary cause of persisting racial tensions and problems in this country is not white racism, but rather the black underclass, or black families, or black dependency on welfare. These apologists have blamed the underclass for its immorality and the black middle class for not taking responsibility for the underclass. To deny white racism and blame the black victims of racism have become intellectually fashionable in recent years. Our respondents call for a new racial education for most white Americans. White Americans must be exposed to the real history of the united States, including a starkly realistic revelation of the ravages of slavery, of the delay and failure of civil rights laws, and of the lack of courage of white presidents and legislators to demand equity in education, employment, housing, and other sectors of this society. What being white in the United States means can only be understood by delving deeply into the white-on-black history too often left out of the public discussions of American racial relations. Our respondents do not ignore the responsibility of black Americans to attend to problems of discrimination, but they also stress that white Americans have to confront and fight against white racism.

In *Faces at the Bottom of the Well*, legal scholar Derrick Bell has argued very forcefully that 'Black people will never gain full equality in this country. Even those herculean efforts we hail as successful will produce no more than temporary "peaks of progress," short-lived victories that slide into irrelevance as racial patterns adapt in ways that maintain white dominance.' For Bell, an African American and former professor at Harvard Law School, the goals of racial equality and justice have been laudable, but in the final analysis they are usually sacrificed by whites to their own interests in day-to-day political struggles. This veteran of legal battles for civil rights is very pessimistic, and as a result he provides little in the way of concrete proposals and plans, beyond writing a better history of black struggles and a contemporary 'defiance' of whites, for continuing the black struggle. Our black middle-class respondents are also veteran grass-roots theorists of white oppression, and they too take a broad view of the past, present, and future of this society—its strengths and hopes, as well as its weaknesses and destructiveness. Although many seem to share, to some degree, Bell's despair over the permanence of white racism, for the most part they continue to believe in or work for practical solutions to some of the nation's major race-related problems: good jobs for all black Americans, decent housing for all black Americans, vigorously enforced antidiscrimination laws, the reeducation of whites away from racist attitudes, and the strengthening of solidarity in black communities. Against all odds, and in spite of the terrible obstacles, most somehow retain some hope for change in the future.

In our interviews, as well as in other accounts, African Americans have often hinted at or expressed openly the hope for future empowerment, not a wish for black domination of whites, but rather a humanist vision of shared development, one that stresses self-respect, self-determination, and self-actualization for all Americans. Indeed, expanding such an encompassing humanist and egalitarian vision *among whites* may be the only hope for a peaceful and prosperous future for the United States. Considering the discriminatory conditions black Americans face today, a majority of white Americans show little or no empathy; they seem to have lost the ability to 'walk in another person's shoes.'

Securing full human rights for African Americans will necessarily bring benefits for all Americans. Nearly a century ago Du Bois showed how the African slave trade not only dehumanized African Americans but also white Americans.[2] White racism has long been inseparable from white identity, white history, and white culture and has greatly demeaned and sabotaged the ideals of liberty and justice prized by all Americans. If a humanist and egalitarian vision is to be realized, whites must no longer deny the power inequality and the attitudinal imperialism at the heart of white racism. Giving up racism means not only giving up racist attitudes but also giving up substantial power and privilege. In a famous speech at an 1881 civil rights mass meeting in Washington, D. C., Frederick Douglass declared that 'No man can put a chain about the ankle of his fellow man without at last finding the other end fastened about his own neck.'[3]

[From *Living Racism: The Black Middle Class Experience* (Boston: Beacon Press, 1994), 319–21, 359–64.]

ALBERTO MELUCCI

51 Difference and Otherness in a Global Society

1. The Point of View

Contemporary debates on 'racism' and 'antiracism' are good examples as well as metaphors for the world situation today. Students and activists discussing these issues are themselves already experiencing and practicing their relationship to the 'other' (the stranger, the foreigner, the different). They are already transforming their deep attitudes towards the issue of difference into discursive practices. They come from different cultural and political backgrounds, different countries, different professional communities. It is therefore extremely important to realize that the way the discourse is constructed, the forms in which people communicate their ideas are already ways of experiencing the possibilities and the predicaments of dealing with difference. We should then be aware of the fact that we are always situated speakers, writers, observers. We are always located somewhere in a social and cultural field and that we should be able to account for our specific location in this field and for the partiality of our point of view. But since we speak or write, we are also interested in some form of communication.

In a text on 'racism' and 'antiracism' it is therefore necessary to take a self-reflexive attitude and to make clear my own point of view, the fact that I am writing from a specific personal and professional perspective. I am a sociologist and a clinical psychologist. For the last twenty years I have been working on collective action, trying to understand how people act together and in doing so construct a common 'we', their collective identity. But in a parallel way, as a psychotherapist I have been working with individual pain and suffering, with the fears and emotions that individuals face when they are confronted with the dramatic changes of our society in their everyday life: changes in time and space dimensions, in affective relationships, passages in the course of life, stress, psychosomatic illnesses. These are social phenomena which affect, on a great scale, individual life. Their roots are deeply found in our social situation and in the texture of people's everyday life practices. In fact, in my clinical work I currently deal with social problems as they are actually experienced by individuals, who not only think and calculate, but feel emotions, suffer, experience love and hate, are passioned or frightened, when confronted with global changes that reach them within their everyday activities and relationships. In my practice I deal with the answers and the failures in answering to the fundamental question that individuals today increasingly address to themselves and to society: 'Who am I?': a question that cannot be avoided when one's identity is exposed to so many challenges and so many risks.

The fact that I am located at the border of two scientific and professional territories provides me with both advantages and disadvantages. A border is simultaneously a frontier which separates, but also a line which sets the limits. Being at the border puts me sometimes in the uncomfortable position of not knowing exactly to which side I belong. But when you are the border you can sometimes see things that are invisible within one territory. When you walk at the border you become aware of the limits of a given territory, the shortcomings and the partiality of each language. I do not know which balance I can draw between the advantages and disadvantages, but I know that by trying to work at the border of two different fields I have been able to ask myself questions that I could not have addressed within a single perspective: in my scientific work I have tried to understand how macro-structural changes of our society affect individual lives and, conversely, how individual action and everyday experiences intervene in social processes, shape cultural change and influence public life. I will bring this perspective to the text here.

A self-reflexive attitude should also be applied from the beginning to the issue of 'racism' (and 'antiracism') itself: why has racism recently become such an important issue and why are scientists and ordinary people interested in it? There are many possible answers to such a question, but in terms of a sociology of knowledge we should try to connect the growing interest in this issue to the characteristics of a society constructed and shaped by information. First of all, we should realize that we do not know exactly how to name this society. We use a variety of different names, such as post-industrial, post-modern, complex, late-capitalist, and so on. This panoply of prefixes and adjectives is a very interesting symptom of our theoretical impasse. We are presently unable to conceptualize in a proper way the kind of society in which we live, but we know that the traditional frameworks inherited from modernity, that of industrial society and that of capitalism, do not any longer provide a satisfactory understanding of contemporary society. We need different names because the old ones are losing their conceptual strength and because we lack appropriate new concepts to substitute them. We are hiding this conceptual weakness behind an allusive language. To call this society complex, post-material, post-modern or post-industrial does not make much difference. To me it is more important to acknowledge the theoretical impasse and to stress the fact that we are using new names because we live in a society which is increasingly different from that which was conceptualized by the modernity theorists.

The issue of racism and antiracism is such a controversial one because, in fact, it is not a unified conceptual object but a field of cultural and political debates which reflects the deep changes which our society is undergoing on the world-scale. The discussion on racism, together with all the connected notions of nationalism, identity politics, multiculturalism etc., is in fact addressing critical issues of contemporary society and tries to make sense of the many differences that we are confronted with, in a world that has, at the same time, become a single arena for cultural and political debates. The conflicting definitions of these notions are all symptoms of the fact that we are living in a society which is increasingly shaped by information and defined by its cultural dimensions, so that the differences in cultures and the definition of cultures and identities themselves become critical social and political issues. The discourse on these notions (scientific discourse, everyday discourse, media discourse) becomes an arena in itself, and the control over its meaning is at stake in cultural and political debates: the issue of 'racism' can be a goal and a political objective for very innovative or very conservative social movements, it can be the banner for a new rhetoric manipulated by elites who seek to impose their ideology and their control over an increasingly differentiated social environment, and/or it can be the defensive shield for individuals and groups who feel deeply threatened by the increasing exposure to 'otherness' and difference.

With all these cautions in mind, I will address some distinctive features of contemporary societies and list what I consider are its main qualitative differences from previous societies and cultures, in order to deal more specifically with the topic of difference and otherness. As I said, the various allusive definitions we use are mostly interchangeable and what really matters today is the conceptual effort to acknowledge the legacy of modernity and to advance beyond it.

2. Information, Power, Autonomy

i) For the first time in human history society has acquired a capacity to intervene on itself and on its environment, which was never reached before. Nuclear power is the material and the symbolic sign of such a power. A society which can destroy itself, dramatically declares that it depends entirely on its capacity to manage its internal relations and its equilibrium with the environment. The power of intervening on biology through genetic engineering is transforming even human nature into a social product.

'Material' goods are produced by information systems and symbolic universes controlled by huge organizations. They incorporate information and become signs circulating through markets of worldwide proportions. Social conflicts move from the economic-industrial system to the cultural sphere. They focus on personal identity, the time and space of life, the motivation and codes of daily behaviour. Conflicts reveal the logic governing highly differentiated systems. These systems allocate increasing amounts of resources to individuals, who use them to become autonomous subjects of action; but the systems also exact increasing integration. In order to maintain themselves, they must extend their control by regulating the deep lying sources of action and by interfering with the construction of its meaning. Contemporary conflicts reveal the contradictions in this process and bring to the fore actors and forms of action which cannot be fitted into the conventional categories of industrial conflict or political competition among interest groups. The production and reappropriation of meaning seem to lie at the core of contemporary conflicts; and this entails a redefinition of collective actors and forms of action expressing social conflicts.

ii) The revolution in information and communication technologies has accentuated the reflexive, artificial and constructed character of social life. Life experiences take place in contexts which are produced by social action, broadcast by the media, interiorized and enacted in a sort of spiral which turns 'reality' into images and signs. Most of the trivial activities of daily life are increasingly marked by, and depend on, the impact of information. Ever new technologies incorporate an increasing quantity of information and contribute in turn to the massive expansion of information output. We live in an artificial environment because it is completely produced through our social relations; even nature becomes a product of society, because it is preserved or destroyed by our decisions and policies.

iii) Another feature which seems to indicate a qualitative leap is what is usually addressed as globalization, but what I prefer to call the planetarization of the world system. 'Planetarization' reminds us of the relation with the planet as the physical basis for social life and stresses the fact that we do not have another place to stay, for the moment at least.

The planetarization of the system means that the social and cultural environment produced by human action has reached its limits, both in space and time. There is no other space outside the social system because the entire space available is socialised through human action. There is no time outside the system, there is no future conceivable as a passage to a 'new world', to a final society freed from the chains and the constraints of the present one. There will not be 'another time', not because we cannot think of change, but because all the foreseeable changes will take place within the limits of this planet and this system.

The circulation of information ties the world system together and raises new trans-national problems over the control, circulation and exchange of information. At the same time it inflates the issues and arenas of conflict into worldwide proportions. The geographical localization of a problem becomes of secondary importance compared with its symbolic impact on the planetary system. The processes of globalization reactivate ethnic and local conflicts that seek to give a stable and recognizable basis to identity in a space that has lost its traditional boundaries.

iv) Information is a reflexive resource, that is to say that in order to be recognized and used as a resource, it implies a capacity for symbolization and decodification. Information is not a thing, but a good which to be produced and exchanged presupposes a high cultural capacity. It is, then, a resource which becomes such for the society as a whole only when other needs have been satisfied and when the capacity for symbolic production has been sufficiently freed from the constraints of reproduction. The notion of 'post-material society' captures, at least in part, these transformations in progress. That is to say, systems that increasingly rely on information resources presume the acquisition of a material base and the ability to build symbolic universes endowed with autonomy (which, in turn, become conditions for the reproduction or the broadening of the material base itself). An information society implies a high degree of autonomy of cultural life from material constraints.

v) Information does not exist independently of the human capacity to perceive it. Being able to use a reflexive resource of this kind depends on the biological and motivational structure of human beings, as transmitters and receivers of information. The massive investments that complex societies make in biological research, in research into the brain and the motivational and relational mechanisms of behaviour, demonstrate that information as a decisive resource entails greater human intervention in 'inner nature', an increased capacity of self-reflection, which reaches the point of the 'production of reproduction', the point where the deep biological structure of the species is interfered with. Information is then necessarily tied to what in the past was considered the 'subjective' dimensions of human life. This same dualistic notion of 'subjective' dimensions as opposed to 'objective' structures has to be rejected, when material resources increasingly depend on the human capacity to produce, process, and decode symbolic languages.

vi) In a society based on information, the possibility of exerting power shifts from the contents of communication and social exchanges to the formal structures, to the codes that organise the flow of information. If information is characterized by the speed of its circulation and its rapid obsolescence, it becomes of crucial importance to control the codes by which mutable information is organized and interpreted. Knowledge is therefore less a knowledge of contents and increasingly an ability to codify and to decode messages. Information is linear and cumulative; it constitutes the quantitative base of the cognitive process. Knowledge structures, it establishes relations, links and hierarchies. There is a widening gap between these levels of experience and what used to be called wisdom, which has to do with the perception of meaning and its integration into individual existence.

Control over the production, accumulation and circulation of information depends upon control over codes. However, this control is not equally distributed, and access to knowledge therefore becomes the terrain where new forms of power, discrimination and conflict come into being. Simultaneously, the meaning of individual experience—i.e. the ability to incorporate the increasing quantity of information transmitted and received into an interior principle of unity—becomes increasingly fragile. A split opens up between the realm of instrumental knowledge, which efficiently manipulates the symbolic codes that select, order and direct information, and wisdom as the integration of meaning into personal experience. Hence the quest for self that reaches down into the nethermost regions of human action: the body, the emotions, the spiritual dimensions of experience irreducible to instrumental rationality. This search may easily take the form of a return to organized religion or of a resurgence of sects and fundamentalisms, but it may also open the way for a 'desacralized' experience of the sacred and a renewal of spiritual values.

vii) Power is increasingly based on the control over the codes and languages that master the flow of information. This dramatic picture of a power hidden and incorporated in everyday relations and languages, has always another face. Power based on information is fragile because of the very fact of being diffused and communicated, information is a resource difficult to control. It spreads through many different channels: language or interpersonal communication, the objects that incorporate information, or a more elaborate corpus of a symbolic kind. Moreover, unlike other physical goods, information can be divided without losing its quality. It can be multiplied and divided among various actors without its specific content being affected. The simple acquisition of a code puts the actors in a communicative relation on the same level. If the world system tends towards the concentration of informational powers, these powers are also easily challenged because of their very nature.

viii) There is an increasing autonomy of individuals in their definition of themselves. This autonomy and the capacity to differentiate oneself as an individual will vary according to the resources distributed at the systemic level. Therefore the process of identity building is already an arena for new inequalities and a potential field for conflicts. The degree to which individuals are allowed to define themselves as autonomous individuals is not distributed equally and to this new capacity could be applied the traditional analysis of inequality, in terms of structural disadvantages and unequal distribution of power.

But a 'structural' analysis of the new inequalities should take into account that the embodiment of personal identity within the broad 'structural' processes has changed the status of individual experience. The individual level is over-socialized, but at the same time it becomes the locus of resistance and the potential arena of conflict. Individual identity is subjected to social pressures and to new forms of power, which require a 'structural', systemic level of analysis. But the embodiment of individual identity into the systemic processes needs also a new kind of analysis and a specific consideration of what used to be labeled as 'subjective' experience.

3. Dilemmas of Complexity and Social Conflicts

To be effective, power must then continuously shift its basis and take control of new codes. The codes on which the new forms of power build and develop themselves are invisible, and the possibility itself of the word is already organized within them. There is no discourse other than that which privileged areas and groups in the system control through their power of naming and the monopoly that they seek to impose on language through self-justifying, operational expertise. Thus information is not a resource circulating among all actors, which they can exchange and with which they can cumulatively build their potential for knowledge. It becomes instead a system of empty signs, the key to which has been hidden. Those consuming these signs need no longer concern themselves as to their meaning.

Simultaneously, however, the potentially limitless extension of information also increases the margins of uncertainty for the entire system. Uncertainty derives first of all from the difficulty of establishing links in the enormous mass of information transmitted and received. The disproportionate growth of information increases the options but also makes decision-making difficult. Hence the increasing requirement for complex systems to produce decisions in order to reduce uncertainty. An information system expands its decision-making capacity to keep pace with this requirement to cope with uncertainty, and increasingly assumes the features of a decisional, contractual system: decisional because reducing uncertainty means assuming the risk of the decision; contractual because, in order to decide, agreement must be reached over the rules of the game.

Uncertainty cannot be reduced except by making decisions and by agreeing on the framework within which these decisions are to be reached. The level of uncertainty constantly renews itself and expands (also because of decisions themselves, which resolve problems but also create new ones). The decisional and contractual dimensions become central to the social life of complex systems. In other words, contemporary societies must continually establish and renew the pacts that bind them together and guide their action.

In systems of this kind, can we still speak of a dominant logic? Certainly the spatial metaphors that characterized industrial culture (base vs. superstructure, centrality vs. marginality) are increasingly inadequate in describing the workings of centre-less, and by now head-less, complex societies. The decentralization of the loci of power and conflict makes it more and more difficult to identify 'central' processes and actors. Does this statement actually mean that we must renounce any attempt to identify a dominant logic? That in complexity everything becomes the same as everything else, in the interchangeable circularity so dear to theories of exchange?

A logic of dominance is not in contradiction with the idea of complexity. Contemporary societies have a dominant logic, but the site of this logic constantly changes. The areas and levels of a system which ensure its continuity may change in time, just as the loci of conflict vary. Power does not inhere once and for all in certain 'structures', and its concrete manifestations in the form of actors and relations are not definitive. Conflicts, too, may involve different actors and different sectors of the system. Although lying within a circumscribed area, they often bring to the surface the crucial dilemmas of complexity and the power forms that such complexity produces, and render them visible to society as a whole.

These dilemmas reveal the basic constraints of social life and cannot be overcome; they can only be managed in different ways through political decision-making, but they cannot be cancelled as such. We cannot choose between the two poles, we can only find some arrangement between them. There is a dilemma between autonomy and control, between the capacity of defining autonomously one's own identity and the fact of being defined by external powers, regulations, languages. Another dilemma is that between omnipotence and responsibility. We could apparently expand our power on society and the environment without limits thanks to the progress of science and technology. On the other hand, we have to assign some boundaries and recognize some limits.

We meet the same impossible choice with the fact that the knowledge we have reached cannot be erased (unless in the hypothesis of a final catastrophe). This irreversible knowledge which provides us with the power of self-destruction depends nevertheless on the reversibility of political choices and decisions. We cannot get rid of our power, we can only decide how to use it.

There is finally a dilemma between differentiation and integration. The more the system is differentiated, the more it expands the possibility of autonomous definition of identities (ethnic, group, gender, but also cultural self-defined identities). On the other hand, the problem of ensuring the integration of a highly differentiated system increases the pressures exerted at the world scale by apparatuses which operate mainly through the media, the market, the generalization of consumption patterns. The alternative, exclusion vs. assimilation, expresses in a dramatic way this dilemma: marginal cultures struggle for their survival against increasing homogenization and the trans-nationalization of business, science, media, and consumption.

Social conflicts make visible the dilemmas mentioned above. Conflicts tend to arise in those areas of the system most directly involved in the production of information and communicative resources but at the same time subjected to intense pressures for integration. The crucial dimensions of daily life (time and space, interpersonal relations, birth and death), the satisfying of individual needs within welfare systems, the shaping of personal and social identity in educational systems—these today are constructed through the production and processing of information. Individuals and groups are allocating increasing amounts of information resources with which to define themselves and to construct their life spaces. At the same time, however, these same processes are regulated by a diffuse social control which passes beyond the public sphere to invade the very domain where the sense of individual action takes shape. Dimensions that were traditionally regarded as 'private' (the body, sexuality, affective relations), or 'subjective' (cognitive and emotional processes, motives, desires), or even 'biological' (the structure of the brain, the genetic code, reproductive capacity) now undergo social control and manipulation. Over these domains the technico-scientific apparatus, the agencies of information and communication, the decision-marking centres which determine 'policies', wield their power. But these are precisely the areas where individuals and groups lay claim to their autonomy, where they conduct their search for identity by transforming them into a space where they reappropriate, self-realize and themselves construct the meaning of what they are and what they do.

Social conflicts are therefore carried forward by temporary actors who bring to light the crucial dilemmas mentioned above. The conflicts I describe here (which do not exhaust the range of social conflicts) concern the production and the appropriation of resources which are crucial for a global society based on information. These same processes generate both new forms of power and new forms of opposition: conflict only emerges insofar as actors fight for control over the allocation of socially produced potential for action. This potential is no longer exclusively based on material resources or on forms of social organization, but to an increasing extent on the ability to produce information.

The conflicts I am referring to, do not chiefly express themselves through action designed to achieve outcomes in the political system. Rather, they raise a challenge which recasts the language and cultural codes which organize information. The ceaseless flow of messages only acquires meaning through the codes that order the flux and allow its meanings to be read. The forms of power now emerging in contemporary societies are grounded in an ability to 'inform' (give form). The recent forms of collective action occupy the same terrain and are in themselves a message broadcast to society conveying symbolic forms and relational patterns which cast light on 'the dark side of the moon'—a system of meanings which runs counter to the sense that the apparatuses seek to impose on individual and collective events. This type of action affects institutions because it selects new elites, it modernizes organizational forms, it creates new goals and new languages. At the same time, however, it challenges the apparatuses that govern the production of information, and prevents the channels of representation and decision-making in pluralist societies from adopting instrumental rationality as the only logic with which to govern complexity. Such rationality applies solely to procedures, and imposes the criterion of efficiency and effectiveness as the only measure of sense. The recent forms of collective action reveal that the neutral rationality of means masks interests and forms of power; that it is impossible to confront the massive challenge of living together on a planet by now becoming a global society without openly discussing the 'ends' and 'values' that make such cohabitation possible. They highlight the insuperable dilemmas facing complex societies, and by doing so force them openly to assume responsibility for their choices, their conflicts and their limitations.

4. Ethnic and Cultural Conflicts

'Racism' and 'antiracism' as collective phenomena should be located within the framework outlined above and not taken as unified facts, but as pluri-dimensional phenomena. The defensive resistance to the 'other' is easily transformed into an aggressive attitude against the threat that the other represents. But also the claims to reciprocal understanding and communication are not entirely free from defensive attitudes. Analysis should always decompose the unity of the empirical phenomenon and tell us how the compound is formed.

In terms of *orientations* of action, the appeal to ethnicity or cultural difference can provide a criterion along which to organize the defense of material interests of a group against discrimination, marginalization, exploitation. Secondly, ethnicity can be a channel through which people express their demands for new rights and try to define a political space for excluded social groups. Besides material or political goals, ethnic and cultural identification can finally play the role of a symbolic and selective resource to answer the challenges of identity in a complex society. The legacy of ethnic and cultural traditions provides a ready answer to the critical question of identity. It offers, particularly to the younger generations, the opportunity to reinterpret in a selective way the cultural material of tradition, in order to answer new questions, or to resist to the pressures imposed by a global society.

Other analytical distinctions among different forms of ethnic and cultural conflicts concern their social and political *contexts*. At least four different dimensions should be separated. Ethnic problems are related to global migration processes, the interdependence and the imbalances within the world labor market and the reactions of the host societies. Secondly, ethnic problems can be related to the pluralism of groups of relatively equal size within the borders of a nation-state. A third dimension has to do with inter-state conflicts when the same ethnic or cultural group lives on the border. And finally, ethnic claims for autonomy or independence can be addressed by minority groups to a relatively homogeneous nation-state in order to achieve the political control over a given territory.

A third level of analysis concerns the *meaning* of ethnic and cultural action, which can vary from defence and resistance against modernization processes, to demands for political rights, to a challenge to the international system, which is in fact an interstate system: conflicts that mobilize ethnic and cultural identities make visible the crisis of the nation-state and bring to the fore the need for a new trans-national world system capable of recognizing and integrating differences. The nation-states are losing their authority as, towards the top of the system, planetary interdependence and the emergence of trans-national political and economic forces shift the locus of real decision-making elsewhere, while, towards the bottom, the proliferation of autonomous decision-making centres endows 'civil societies' with a specific power.

An articulated set of conceptual tools which have been just shortly outlined here, can help to differentiate the many levels of ethnic and cultural conflicts which too often are treated as homogeneous. Such an analysis makes it easier to understand that these conflicts, together with the old problems of economic discrimination and marginalization and with the claims to political autonomy and recognition, bring to the surface new problems. They address the redefinition of a world system based on international relations; a system formally organized on the relations among sovereign states, but in fact governed by the north-south imbalances, by central and regional powers, by the lack of a global responsibility. These conflicts make clear the necessity of a different global organization of political issues.

But they also raise another important challenge, the right to name the world in a specific way. Every ethnic or traditional culture speaks its own language and tries to have this right recognized. But besides the political aspect of recognition, there is a deeper importance of this issue. Culture is increasingly shaped by anonymous apparatuses imposing the names and the languages through which people understand and relate to reality. Naming the world in a different way challenges this homogenization and the imposition of standardized codes. In this respect ethnic and cultural conflicts join other recent forms of collective action challenging the new powers, which tell people how to name reality (personal and gender relations, relation to nature, health, sexuality, freedom).

5. A New Morality?

These critical issues call for a new moral attitude. A Greek word summarizes the ethical implications of the analysis presented here. 'Metamorphosis' literally means to change form or to overcome one's form. The expression of differences is intrinsically connected with the need for communication and solidarity when the survival of the species as such is at stake. But in order to meet otherness, one needs to change form. We cannot communicate or relate to differences by simply staying ourselves. In regard to coexistence, which implies some capacity and will to meet the 'other', there is a profound moral implication: the necessity to keep and to lose, to cope with fears and resistances, but also to transcend our given identities.

There is therefore a necessity to deal with ambivalence as no one is free from ambivalent feelings towards the 'other'. The possibility of meeting each other requires a deep leap in consciousness, which allows people to accept that they exist as separate individuals and social groups, but also that they can co-exist and communicate. To take responsibility for one's own identity means also an acceptance of one's limits, opening up to the other through a negotiated, ongoing partnership which, in turn, does not deny the shadow that every difference carries with itself.

Misunderstandings are part of the present situation in political, scientific and everyday exchanges. To take responsibility for our misunderstandings, the permanent sources of which are differences in languages, in frameworks, and in values, and to avoid transforming them into violent confrontations, means that we have to first acknowledge them and not just condemn them in order to communicate in regard to them. Trying to make our starting point as clear as possible and trying to listen to the other person or group as much as possible, are ways to overcome the simple expression of differences. I do not believe that difference in itself and difference alone could be a value. Difference is just one side of the coin of human relations. Community, solidarity, and communication are the other side. When difference alone becomes a banner, the results are, more often, violent. Unfortunately the extreme stress on differences is today seriously leading to dramatic forms of fundamentalism and violence. The problem is never just difference, but the parallel necessity to overcome it, to make a constant effort towards listening and understanding each other.

Far from prefiguring a harmonious, pacified, transparent society, the view I am proposing here is one in which the ambivalent quality of human action is accentuated, both on an individual and a collective scale. It sets us down squarely in the middle of the paradox of social action and it stresses the role of tensions and conflicts, the fact that the singular cannot be reduced to the plural, uniqueness to communication; at the same time, it points out our radical need to *co-exist*.

We need a new ethic which does not exempt us from the risk of choice and that will enable us to meta-communicate regarding the goals and criteria behind the choices themselves. Our salvation is no longer guaranteed by historical destiny. Western rationalism is questioned, together with its claims to absolute truth and its will to supremacy. But we still cling to a hope for meaningful human existence, reasonable in coexistence and in the experience of our limits. If values no longer bear the seal of the absolute, their only foundation lies in the human capacity for agreement. Social movements, which have emerged in the last decades, have been the first announcement of this enormous cultural change which is already taking place. To reduce them to their political outcomes is like believing that our shadow could exist without our person. The politics emerging from recent collective actions are eminently personal politics, rooted in a profound need to exist as autonomous subjects, capable of respect and communication.

Contemporary social movements remind us by their *forms* of action that we can work more on processes than on contents to face the challenges and the dilemmas of a complex world. They are important signs of the critical issues of our time because they point out, through their action, where the fundamental dilemmas of social life emerge and they allow society to openly address them through political action, social mobilization, and cultural change.

Behind the questions raised by ethnic and cultural conflicts, behind the legacy of unresolved tensions left-over in the aftermath of the development and decline of the nation-state of modernity, and even behind the resistance by minority cultures against modernization, which appear anachronistic and which often become violent, there emerges today an entirely new field for social action; the plea for society to be given the power to decide its own existence and to control its own development, framed by new relations among the components constituting planetary reality (individuals, groups, interests, cultures, 'nations'). A new model of intersocietal relations is one of our greatest contemporary aspirations. Humankind must make an enormous effort to give political shape to its co-living; a political arrangement able to govern the plurality, the autonomy and the richness of differences—however, one that also expresses humanity's shared responsibility for the fate of the species and the planet. There is no guarantee that this challenge will be met. But our hope and our will to try is already the beginning and a path towards facing this challenge.

In a society which is totally interdependent, the unintended consequences of human action can become extremely dangerous and even irreversible, and this is a qualitative difference from the past. For the first time we are able to produce irreversible consequences on ourselves and our environment, as well as on mankind as a whole. Our image of the future will shape the future itself, therefore it is not indifferent as to the kind of future we are able to imagine. I am not saying that we should naively live in the present, indifferent to constructing workable projects of society in which differences can coexist. On the contrary, being in the present today means to be able to imagine a different future for our world. Because of the role of information and knowledge, I think that the way we imagine the future will actually shape the future, and at best will reduce the unintended consequences of human action. This is the only thing we can do when facing a world of differences that cannot be totally integrated into a homogeneous unity. We can try to reduce the scope of unintended consequences and set the conditions for a coexistence with the minimum possible degree of violence. In this respect social sciences and social knowledge are an important part of this effort to shape our future from our present. Social movements are also crucial actors in this scenario because through their action they make the issues visible and allow political systems to take responsibility for workable so-lutions. The issue of racism and anti-racism opens an arena for a different defi-nition of democracy in complex societies—one in which the notion of rights, identity and citizenship has to be redefined beyond the legacy of modern liberal democracy.

But in order to translate the dilemma of difference into a new 'democratic' political order (whatever this notion could mean beyond the legacy of moder-nity) and in order to reduce the amount of violence implied by the threatening and 'reactionary' response of racism, we need to imagine and practice in the present a new way of relating to difference. Because what we think now, how we are able to imagine, not a new society for a distant future, but the fact that a different world is possible from now on, is already a way towards contributing to it. This is not just a dream or an illusion, but a new way of contributing to the future made possible by a complex, interdependent society based on informa-tion. Our knowledge, our feelings, and our imagination already shape the fu-ture because of the interconnectedness of our world, because of global interdependence, because of the enormous influence that each small part of the system can have on the whole. Social scientists have an enormous responsi-bility and even if sometimes they can consider themselves as marginal or, on the other side not concerned with political issues, they contribute greatly to the way people perceive the society in which they live. And today the way in which people perceive their society is already creating the future.

This is a significant change in reference to the past. People's imaginations have always contributed to the future, but today this is true for our society in a more immediate sense. What we think and practice in our everyday lives is al-ready creating the conditions for a possible future *or* is leading us towards disas-ter. The possibility to avoid this outcome and to contribute to a more sustainable and liveable world for human beings is increasingly contingent upon our present capacity for meaningful action. This does not prevent us from taking sides in crucial issues like opposing racism , but *the way* we do it matters as much as the 'good reasons' that support our choices.

['Difference and Otherness in a Global Society: Individual Experience and Collective Action', in Sandro Fridlizius and Abby Peterson (eds.), *Stranger or Guest? Racism and Nationalism in Contemporary Europe* (Stockholm: Almquist & Wicksell International, 1996), 39–56.].

Notes and References

General Introduction

Banton, M. (1977), *The Idea of Race* (London: Tavistock).

——(1980), 'The Idiom of Race: A Critique of Presentism', *Research in Race and Ethnic Relations*, 2: 21–42.

——(1987), Racial Theories (Cambridge: Cambridge University Press).

——and Harwood, J. (1975), *The Race Concept* (Newton Abbot: David & Charles).

Biddiss, M. (1979), *Images of Race* (Leicester: Leicester University Press).

Blackburn, R. (1988), *The Overthrow of Colonial Slavery 1776–1848* (London: Verso).

——(1997), *The Making of New World Slavery, 1492–1800* (London: Verso).

Bulmer, M. (1996), 'The Ethnic Group Question in the 1991 Census of Population', in D. Coleman and J. Salt (eds.), *Ethnicity in the 1991 Census, i: General Demographic Characteristics of the Ethnic Minority Populations* (London: HMSO).

——and Solomos, J. (eds.) (1999), *Ethnic and Racial Studies Today* (London: Routledge).

Colley, L. (1992), *Britons: Forging the Nation 1707–1837* (New Haven: Yale University Press).

Cornell, S., and Hartmann, D. (1998), *Ethnicity and Race: Making Identities in a Changing World* (Thousand Oaks, Calif.: Pine Forge Press).

Cox, O.C. (1970 [1948]), *Caste, Class and Race* (New York: Monthly Review Press).

Curtin, P. (1964), *Image of Africa: British Ideas and Action 1780–1850*, 2 vols. (Madison: University of Wisconsin Press).

Du Bois, W. E. B. (1989) [1903], *The Souls of Black Folk* (New York: Penguin Books).

Engerman, S. L., and Genovese, E. D. (1975), *Race and Slavery in the Western Hemisphere: Quantitative Studies* (Princeton: Princeton University Press).

Frederickson, G. M. (1981), *White Supremacy: A Comparative Study in American and South African History* (New York: Oxford University Press).

——(1988), *The Arrogance of Race* (Middletown: Wesleyan University Press).

Furnivall, J. S. (1948), *Colonial Policy and Practice* (Cambridge: Cambridge University Press).

Goldberg, D. T. (1993), *Racist Culture* (Oxford: Blackwell).

——(ed.) (1990), *Anatomy of Racism* (Minneapolis: University of Minnesota Press).

Gossett, T. F. (1997) [1963], *Race: The History of an Idea in America* (New York: Oxford University Press).

Hutchinson, J., and Smith, A. D. (eds.) (1996), *Ethnicity* (Oxford: Oxford University Press).

Jordan, W. (1968), *White over Black: American Attitudes towards the Negro 1550–1812* (New York: W. W. Norton).

Kiernan, V. G. (1969), *The Lords of Human Kind: European Attitudes to the Outside World in the Imperial Age* (London: Weidenfeld & Nicolson).

King, D. (1995), *Separate and Unequal: Black Americans and the US Federal Government* (Oxford: Clarendon Press).

Kohn, M. (1995), *The Race Gallery* (London: Jonathan Cape).

LOVEJOY, P. E. (1983), *Transformations in Slavery: A History of Slavery in Africa* (Cambridge, Mass.: Cambridge University Press).

MANNING, P. (1990), *Slavery and African Life* (Cambridge: Cambridge University Press).

MILES, R. (1989), *Racism* (London: Routledge).

MONTAGU, A. (1997) [1942], *Man's Most Dangerous Myth: The Fallacy of Race*, 6th edn. (Walnut Creek, Calif.: AltaMira Press).

MOSSE, G. (1985), *Toward the Final Solution: A History of European Racism* (Madison: University of Wisconsin Press).

PATTERSON, O. (1982), *Slavery and Social Death* (Cambridge, Mass.: Harvard University Press).

PETERSEN, W. (1997), *Ethnicity Counts* (New Brunswick, NJ: Transaction).

PETERSON, P. E. (ed.) (1995), *Classifying by Race* (Princeton, NJ: Princeton University Press).

POLIAKOV, L. (1982), 'Racism from the Enlightenment to the Age of Imperialism', in R. Ross (ed.) *Racism and Colonialism* (The Hague: Martinus Nijhoff).

POSEL, D. (1991), *The Making of Apartheid 1948–1961: Conflict and Compromise* (Oxford: Clarendon Press).

REX, J. (1970), *Race Relations in Sociological Theory* (London: Weidenfeld & Nicolson).

SAMUEL, R. (ed.) (1989), *Patriotism: The Making and Unmaking of British National Identity*, 3 vols. (London: Routledge).

SMITH, M. G. (1969), 'Some Developments in the Analytical Framework of Pluralism', in L. Kuper and M. G. Smith (eds.), *Pluralism in Africa* (Berkeley and Los Angeles: University of California Press).

SOLOMOS, J., and BACK, L. (1996), *Racism and Society* (Basingstoke: Macmillan).

SOLOW, B. L., and ENGERMAN, S. L. (eds.) (1987), *British Capitalism and Caribbean Slavery* (Cambridge: Cambridge University Press).

TINKER, H. (1974), *A New System of Slavery: The Export of Indian Labour Overseas, 1830–1920* (London: Oxford University Press for the Institute of Race Relations).

TODOROV, T. (1993), *On Human Diversity: Nationalism, Racism and Exoticism in French Thought* (Cambridge, Mass.: Harvard University Press).

WIEVIORKA, M. (1998), 'Is Multiculturalism the Solution?' *Ethnic and Racial Studies*, 21/5: 881–910.

WILLIAMS, E. (1944), *Capitalism and Slavery* (London: Andre Deutsch).

WILSON, W. J. (1973), *Power, Racism and Privilege* (New York: Macmillan).

WINANT, H. (1998), 'Racism Today: Continuity and Change in the Post Civil Rights Era', *Ethnic and Racial Studies*, 21/4: 755–66.

WOLF, E. (1982), *Europe and the People without History* (Berkeley and Los Angeles: University of California Press).

Extract 2

PHILIP CURTIN: *The Africans' 'Place in Nature'*

1. John Matthews, *Voyage to the River Sierra-Leone* (London, 1788), 158–9; Edward Long, *History of Jamaica*, 3 vols. (London, 1774), ii. 373–4.
2. T. Bendyshe, 'The History of Anthropology', *Memoirs Read before the Anthropological Society of London*, I, 335 (1863–4).
3. Charles White, *An Account of the Regular Graduations in Man ...* (London, 1799), 1. See also A. O. Lovejoy, *The Great Chain of Being* (Cambridge, Mass., 1936).

Extract 3

MICHAEL BANTON: *The Racializing of the World*

BLYDEN, EDWARD W. (1887), *Christianity, Islam and the Negro Race*. New edition (1967). Edinburgh: Edinburgh University Press.

EDWARDS, W. F. (1829), *Des caractères physiologiques des races humaines, considérés dans leur rapports avec l'histoire: lettre à M. Amédée Thierry*. Paris: Compère Jeune.

KNOX, ROBERT (1850), *The Races of Men: a fragment* (second edition 1860). London: Renshaw.

PRICHARD, JAMES COWLES (1826), *Researches into the Physical History of Mankind* (second edition). London: Arch.

THOMAS, J. J. (1889), *Froudacity: West Indian Fables by James Anthony Froude* (with new introduction, 1969). London and Port of Spain: New Beacon Books.

Extract 4

GEORGE MOSSE: *Eighteenth-Century Foundations*

1. J. F. Blumenbach, 'De generis humani varietate nativa', *The Anthropological Treatises of Johann Friedrich Blumenbach* (London, 1865), 305.

2. Gaspard Lavater, *L'Art de Connaître les Hommes par la Physionomie*, ed. M. Moreau (Paris, 1820), II, 168.

3. Edward Tyson, *Orang-Outang, Sive Homo Sylvestris Or, the Anatomy of a Pigmie Compared wtih that of a Monkey, an Ape, and a Man, etc.* (London, 1699), 9, 11, 12.

4. Meiners, *Grundriss der Geschichte des Menschheit* (Lengo, 1785), 35.

Extract 5

REGINALD HORSMAN: *Superior and Inferior Races*

1. George H. Calvert, ed., *Illustrations of Phrenology: Being a Selection of Articles from the Edinburgh Phrenological Journal, and the Transactions of the Edinburg Phrenological Society* (Baltimore, 1832), 29, 30, 32–6.

2. Amariah Brigham, M.D., *Observations on the Influence of Religion upon the Health and Physical Welfare of Mankind* (Boston, 1835), 300–2.

3. Richard H. Colfax, *Evidence against the Views of the Abolitionists, Consisting of Physical and Moral Proofs, of the National Inferiority of the Negroes* (New York, 1833), 29.

4. Bachman, *The Doctrine of the Unity of the Human Race Examined on the Principles of Science* (Charleston, S.C., 1850).

5. William Frederick Van Amringe, *An Investigation of the Theories of the Natural History of Man* (New York, 1848), 157, 205, 213, 217.

6. Lieut.-Col. Charles Hamilton Smith, *The Natural History of the Human Species*, intro. S. Kneeland (Boston, 1852), 15, 94–5.

7. John H. Van Evrie, *Negroes and Negro 'Slavery': The First an Inferior Race: The Latter Its Normal Condition*, 3rd edn. (1853; New York, 1863), 44, 47, 80.

Extract 6

MICHAEL BIDDISS: *Gobineau and the Origins of European Racism*

1. Arthur de Gobineau, *Essai sur l'inégalité des races humaines* (1st edn., 4 vols., Paris, Firmin Didot, 1853–5), i. 353.

Extract 8

DAVID BRION DAVIS: *The Expansion of Islam and the Symbolism of Race*

1. Bernard J. Siegel, 'Some Methodological Considerations for a Comparative Study of Slavery', *American Anthropologist*, vol 47, 1947, 390 n. 67; Dev Raj Chanana, *Slavery in Ancient India, as Depicted in Pali and Sanskrit Texts* (New Delhi, 1960), 19, 22, 94, 105–6, 108–9.

2. Leon Carl Brown, 'Color in Northern Africa', in John Hope Franklin, ed., *Color and Race* (Boston, 1968), 192–3; Bernard Lewis, *Race and Color in Islam* (New York, 1971), 64. Orlando Patterson argues that 'perceived racial differences between masters and slaves' have been common to a significant number of slaveholding societies throughout the world, as has the assumption that slaves belong to an innately inferior group. He also emphasizes that the 'sambo' stereotype has been universal, 'an ideological imperative of all systems of slavery' (*Slavery and Social Death*, 58, 96–7, 176–7).

3. Stephen Jay Gould, *The Mismeasure of Man* (New York, 1981).

4. Ephraim Isaac, 'Genesis, Judaism, and the "Sons of Ham"', *Slavery and Abolition*, 1 (1980), 7–9, 15–16; Song of Songs 1: 5; Psalms 68: 31; Jean Marie Courtès, 'The Theme of "Ethiopia" and "Ethiopians" in Patristic Literature,' in Jean Devisse, *The Image of the Black in Western Art*, vol. 2, *From the Early Christian Era to the 'Age of Discovery'*, pt. 1, *From the Demonic Threat to the Incarnation of Sainthood* (New York, 1979), 14–16. For Origen, as one might expect, the conversion and symbolic 'whitening' of Ethiopia also signified a repudiation of the 'black' synagogue.

5. Courtès and Devisse, *Image of the Black*, II, pt. 1, 19–20, 27–8, 46–80, 96; Rotter, *Die Stellung des Negers*, 156, 176–7.

Extract 10

GEORGE FREDRICKSON: *Social Origins of American Racism*

1. Michael Banton, *Race Relations* (London, 1967), 8.

2. See Earl Raab and Seymour Martin Lipset, 'The Prejudiced Society,' in Earl Raab, ed., *American Race Relations Today: Studies of the Problems Beyond Desegregation* (New York, 1962), 29–55.

3. Phillip Mason, *An Essay on Racial Tension* (New York and London, 1954), 80.

4. J. Jean Hecht, *Continental and Colonial Servants in Eighteenth Century England* (Northampton, Mass., 1954), 56. Quoted in Banton, *Race Relations*, 369.

5. Winthrop D. Jordan, *White Over Black: American Attitudes Toward the Negro, 1550–1812* (Chapel Hill, 1968), 80.

6. Marvin Harris, *Patterns of Race in the Americas* (New York, 1964), 70.

7. Jordan, *White Over Black*, 79.

8. James M. Wright, *The Free Negro in Maryland, 1634–1860*, Columbia University Studies in History, Economics, and Public Law, no. 97 (New York, 1921), 27.

9. Robert C. Twombly and Robert H. Moore, 'Black Puritans: The Negro in Seventeenth-Century Massachusetts,' *William and Mary Quarterly* 24 (April 1967): 224–42.

10. John H. Russell, *The Free Negro in Virginia, 1619–1865*, Johns Hopkins Studies in Historical and Political Science, no. 31 (Baltimore, 1913), 125.

11. Harris, *Patterns* of Race, chap. 7.

12. The Reverend William Perkins, quoted in Christopher Hill, *Society and Puritanism in Pre-Revolutionary England* (New York, 1964), 283.
13. William Yancey, quoted in *Liberator*, 26 October 1860.

Extract 11

EUGENE GENOVESE: *Class and Race*

1. Pierre L. van den Berghe, *Race and Racism: A Comparative Perspective* (New York, 1967), 6. This little book is an important contribution to the vast literature on race relations and has influenced this discussion. Among recent works mention should be made of three of special relevance: Harmannus Hoetink, *The Two Variants in Caribbean Race Relations: A Contribution to the Sociology of Segmented Societies*, trans. Eva M. Hooykaas (New York, 1967); Magnus Mörner, *Race Mixture in the History of Latin America* (Boston, 1967); and Winthrop D. Jordan, *White over Black: American Attitudes Toward the Negro, 1550–1812* (Chapel Hill, N.C., 1968).
2. Jordan, *White over Black*, 43, 72. Emphasis in original.
3. C. R. Boxer, *Race Relations in the Portuguese Colonial Empire, 1415–1825* (Oxford, 1963), 56.
4. C. Prado Jr., *The Colonial Background of Modern Brazil* (Berkeley, 1969), 319.
5. Hoetink, *Two Variants*, 88–9 and *passim*.
6. Marvin Harris, *Patterns of Race in the Americas* (New York, 1964).
7. Roger Bastide, 'Race Relations in Brazil', *International Social Science Bulletin*, IX, No. 4 (1957), 495–6.
8. On the recent racial situation see esp. Roger Bastide, 'The Development of Race Relations in Brazil,' Ch. 1 of Guy Hunter, ed., *Industrialisation and Race Relations: A Symposium* (London, 1965).
9. Hubert Aimes, *A History of Slavery in Cuba, 1511–1868* (New York, 1967), 216.
10. Alexis de Tocqueville, *Democracy in America* (2 vols.; New York, 1961), I, 427; Eugene H. Berwanger, *The Frontier Against Slavery: Western Anti-Negro Prejudice and the Slavery Extension Controversy* (Urbana, Ill., 1967).

Extract 12

ORLANDO PATTERSON: *Slavery as Human Parasitism*

1. Anatol Rapoport, *Flights, Games, and Debates* (Ann Arbor: University of Michigan Press, 1960), 62–71.
2. The relevance of this discussion to the recent debate on the economics of slavery should be obvious. See Paul A. David et al., *Reckoning with Slavery* (New York: Oxford University Press, 1976); Robert W. Fogel and Stanley L. Engerman, *Time on the Cross: The Economics of American Negro Slavery* (Boston: Little, Brown, 1974), chaps. 5 and 6; idem, 'Explaining the Relative Efficiency of Slave Agriculture in the Antebellum South: A Reply,' *American Economic Review* 67 (1977): 275–96; Thomas L. Haskel, 'Explaining the Relative Efficiency of Slave Labor in the Antebellum South: A Reply to Fogel and Engerman,' *American Economic Review* 69 (1979): 206–7; D. F. Schaefer and M. D. Schmitz, 'The Relative Efficiency of Slave Agriculture: A Comment', *American Economic Review* 69 (1979): 208–12; Paul A. David and Peter Temin, 'Explaining the Relative Efficiency of Slave Agriculture in the Antebellum South: Comment,' *Amer-*

ican Economic Review 69 (1979): 213–18; Gavin Wright, 'The Efficiency of Slavery: Another Interpretation', *American Economic Review 69* (1979): 219–26; Robert W. Fogel and Stanley L. Engerman, 'Explaining the Relative Efficiency of Slave Agriculture in the Antebellum South: Reply', *American Economic Review 70* (1980): 672–90.

3. The relationship between slavery, the exploitation of the free nonslaveholder, and economic development has not been explored with anything approaching the same depth in other areas of the Americas or Africa. For discussions of the issues with respect to the English-speaking Caribbean see George L. Beckford, *Persistent Poverty* (New York: Oxford University Press, 1972).

   For an examination of these relationships in the case of Puerto Rico, see Sidney W. Mintz, *Caribbean Transformation* (Chicago: Aldine, 1974), chaps. 3 and 4. And for an even stronger statement of the effects of the expanding slave system of nineteenth-century Puerto Rico on 'free' labor and Puerto Rican development in general, see Francisco Scarano, 'Slavery and Free Labor in the Puerto Rican Sugar Economy, 1815–1873,' in Vera Rubin and Arthur Tuden, eds., *Comparative Perspectives on Slavery in New World Plantation Societies* (New York: New York Academy of Sciences, 1977), 553–63.

   On Cuba see Manuel Moreno Fraginals, *The Sugarmill* (New York: Monthly Review Press, 1976), 17–30, 131–53. On Brazil see Florestan Fernandes, 'Slave-holding Society in Brazil,' in Rubin and Tuden, *Comparative Perspectives on Slavery*, 311–42; Robert Conrad, *The Destruction of Brazilian Slavery, 1850–1888* (Berkeley: University of California Press, 1972), esp. chap. 3.

4. Joseph E. Brown in the Jackson (Mississippi) *Daily Clarion*, June 20, 1867. Cited in Lawrence J. Friedman, *The White Savage: Racial Fantasies in the Post-bellum South* (Englewood Cliffs, N.J.: Prentice-Hall, 1970), 24.

5. *The White Savage*, 21–36.

6. Cited ibid. 25.

7. Ibid, 31.

8. Pliny the Elder, *Natural History*, 28, 14. Cited in Thomas Wiedemann, *Greek and Roman Slavery* (Baltimore: Johns Hopkins University Press, 1981), 73.

9. *Freedom* (New York: Basic Books, 1953), 19.

Extract 13

VICTOR KIERNAN: *Africa*

1. J. Newton, *Thoughts upon the African Slave Trade* (1788), 22–4, 31.

2. E. A. Raspe, *Baron Munchausen* (1785), Sequel, Chapter 21.

3. Ibid., Chapter 24.

4. A. Smith, *A Month at Constantinople* (1850), 128–30.

5. W. M. Thackeray, *Notes of a Journey from Cornhill to Grand Cairo* (1845), 126–7, 293–5 (1888 edn).

6. Ibid. 260–1.

7. R. F. Burton, *A Pilgrimage to Al-Madinah and Meccah* (1855), Vol. 2, p. 252 (Bohn Library edn).

8. J. Ruskin, *Modern Painters*, Part 2 (1846), Sec. 5, Chapter 3, paras. 39–40.

9. W .H. G. Kingston, *The Three Midshipmen* (2nd edn., 1873), Chapter 8ff.

10. B. Davidson, *The African Awakening* (1955), 38ff.

11. E. S. Grogan and A. H Sharp, *From the Cape to Cairo* (1900), 183 (Nelson edn, n.d.).

Extract 15

PHILIP MASON: *Patterns of Dominance*

1. Robert E. Park, *Race and Culture: Essays on the Sociology of Contemporary Man.*
2. Michael Banton, *Race Relations.*
3. P. L. van den Berghe, *Race and Racism.*
4. Julian Steward, *Contemporary Change in Traditional Societies*, vol. 1.

Extract 18

PAUL FOOT: *Politics and the Alien*

1. Royal Commission on Population, 1949.

Extract 20

STEPHEN CORNELL: *The Transformations of the Tribe*

1. 'Tribe' is a problematic term. Its complexities have troubled anthropologists and students of political development for years and there is little consensus on its meaning. Some eschew its usage altogether; others have tried in various ways to specify it; still others see it as politically pregnant but technically useless. In much of the Third World it is pejorative; among most Native Americans it is not only in everyday use but often carries substantial emotional or spiritual significance. On the latter point, see the remarks in Russel Lawrence Barsh and James Youngblood Henderson, *The Road: Indian Tribes and Political Liberty* (Berkeley: University of California Press, 1980), pp. vii–viii. On the term in general, see Morton H. Fried, *The Notion of Tribe* (Menlo Park: Cummings Publishing, 1975); and June Helm, ed., *Essays on the Problem of Tribe* (Seattle: University of Washington Press, 1968).

   Definitional and usage issues, however, are peripheral to the current enterprise. Indians traditionally have been divided, through either aboriginal history or contact and conflict with non-Indians, into groups referred to by non-Indians and, eventually, by Indians as 'tribes'. Whether or not these groups fit technical definitions of 'tribe', and whether or not the term is analytically advantageous, are not at issue here. What is of interest is the collectivities to which 'tribe' has come to refer and the ways they have changed in the historical course of Indian-White interaction.
2. Henry F. Dobyns, 'The Indian Reorganization Act and Federal Withdrawal', *Applied Anthropology* 7, no. 2 (Spring 1948): 37.
3. Nancy Oestreich Lurie, 'The Indian Claims Commission Act', *Annals of the American Academy of Political and Social Science* 311 (May 1957): 62.
4. Ronald L. Trosper, 'Native American Boundary Maintenance: The Flathead Indian Reservation, Montana, 1860–1970', *Ethnicity* 3, no. 3 (September 1976): 267.

Extract 22

ROBERT C. SMITH: *Racism in the Post-Civil Rights Era*

1. Roy Brooks, *Rethinking the American Race Problem* (Berkeley: University of California Press, 1990): 187. Brooks also writes (p. 187), 'Personal perceptions of discrimination

cannot be ignored. Even if they are "wrong" or exagerated they are real to the perceiver. More important, these perceptions affect an African American individual's behavior and chances for success.'

2. Ibid. 45.
3. Ibid..
4. Ibid. 187.
5. Ronald Walters, *White Racial Nationalism in the United States* (Washington: Eaford, 1987), 14.
6. Ibid.
7. Hanes Walton, Jr., 'Foreword', Jeffrey Elliot (ed.), *Black Voices in American Politics* (New York: Harcourt Brace 1986): xi.

Extract 23

BARRY TROYNA AND RICHARD HATCHER: *Racism in Children's Lives*

AMMA (1987), *Multi-Cultural and Anti-Racist Education Today*, London: AMMA.

DES (1988), *Education Reform Act 1988*, London: HMSO.

ELTON, LORD (1989), *Discipline in Schools: Report of the Committee of Enquiry*, London: HMSO.

JOHN, G. (1990), 'Taking Sides: Objectives and Strategies in the Development of Anti-Racist Work in Britain', pp. 68–71 in *London 2000*, London: Equal Opportunities Unit.

JONES, K. (1989), *Right Turn*, London: Hutchinson.

TROYNA, B. AND HATCHER, R. (1991), 'Racist Incidents in Schools: A Framework for Analysis', *Journal of Education Policy* 6 (1), 17–31.

Extract 25

DAVID T. WELLMAN: *Toward a Sociology of White Racism*

LIPSET, S. M. and EARL RABB (1970), *The Politics of Unreason*. New York: Harper & Row.

RAAB, E. (1962), 'Introduction', *American Race Relations*. New York: Anchor.

RYAN, WILLIAMS (1971), *Blaming the Victim*. New York: Pantheon.

SIMON, W. and J. GAGNON (1970), 'Working-Class Youth: Alienation without an Image', in L. Howe (ed.), *The White Majority*. New York: Vintage Books.

Extract 26

MICHEL WIEVIORKA: *Two Patterns of Racism*

1. See William J. Wilson, *The Declining Significance of Race* (University of Chicago Press, Chicago, 1978), and *The Truly Disadvantaged: The Inner City, the Underclass and Public Policy* (University of Chicago Press, Chicago, 1987).
2. Albert Hirschman, *Shifting Involvements: Private Interest and Public Action* (Martin Robertson, Oxford, 1982).
3. John Dollard, *Caste and Class in a Southern Town* (University of Wisconsin Press, Madison, 1988), 446.
4. Cf. Gordon W. Allport, *The Nature of Prejudice* (Addison-Wesley, Reading, MA, 1987), chapter XV, and Yves Chevalier, *L'Antisémitisme* (Editions du Cerf, Paris, 1988), 371.

5. Jacob Katz, 'Misreading of Anti-Semitism', *Commentary*, no. 76 (July 1983), 39–44.
6. Saül Friedländer, *L'Antisémitisme nazi. Histoire d'une psychose collective* (Éditions du Seuil, Paris, 1971).
7. Victor Karady and Istvan Kémény, 'Les Juifs dans la Structure des classes en Hongrie: essai sur les antécédents historiques des crises antisémites du XXᵉ siècle', *Actes de la recherche en sciences sociales*, no. 22 (June 1978), 25–9, and 'Antisémitisme universitaire et concurrence de classe: la loi du numerus clausus en Hongrie entre les deux guerres', *Actes de la recherche en sciences sociales*, no. 34 (September 1980), 67–96.

Extract 28

PIERRE-ANDRÉ TAGUIEFF: *The New Cultural Racism in France*

1. Pierre Ansart, *Idéologies, conflits et pouvoir* (Paris: Presses Universitaires de France, 1977), 258.
2. Jean Baechler, *Qu'est-ce que l'ideologie?* (Paris: Gallimard, 1976), 253, 346.
3. Robert de Herte [Alain de Benoist], 'Avec les imigrés contre le nouvel esclavage', *Éléments pour la civilisation européene*, no. 45 (Spring 1983), 2.
4. Pierre Pascal, 'Les vrais racistes', *Militant* [*Revue nationaliste populaire d'action européenne*], 16, no. 156 (January 1984), 15.
5. Jean-Marie Le Pen, 'Le Pen et l'Église' [interview], *National Hebdo*, no. 44, 19 (April 1985), 8.
6. 'Pourquoi nous combattons', *Jeune Nation Solidariste* [*organe de Troisième Voie*], no. 10 (July–August 1986), 6.
7. Ibid. 10.
8. *Militant*, 15th year, no. 144, 1982, *Dossier immigration*, 14.
9. Ibid. 14, 16.
10. 'Demain il sera trop tard', *Militant*, no. 153 (November 1983), 2.
11. *Éléments*, no. 48–9 (Winter 1983–4).
12. Julius Evola, *Indirizzi per una educazione razziale* (Naples: Conte, 1941); French trans. Gérard Boulanger, *Éléments pour une éducation raciale* (Puiseaux: Pardès, 1985), 29.

Extract 29

ABBY L. FERBER: *Constructing Whiteness*

THE ANTI-DEFAMATION LEAGUE OF B'NAI B'RITH 1988, *Hate Groups in America: A Record of Bigotry and Violence*, New York.

BLEE, KATHLEEN (1991a), Women in the 1920s' ku klux klan movement', *Feminist Studies*, vol. 1. Spring, pp. 57–77.

——(1991b), *Women of the Klan: Racism and Gender in the 1920s*, Berkeley, CA: University of California Press.

——(1995), 'Engendering conspiracy: women in rightest theories and movements', in Eric Ward (ed.). *Conspiracies: Real Grievances, Paranoia, and Mass Movements*, Seattle, WA: Peanut Butter Publishing.

BUTLER, JUDITH (1991), 'Imitation and gender insubordination', in Diana Fuss (ed.), *Inside/Out: Lesbian Theories, Gay Theories*, London: Routledge pp. 13–31.

——(1993), *Bodies That Matter: On the Discursive Limits of Sex*, New York: Routledge.

CROSBY, CHRISTINA (1992), 'Dealing with differences', in Judith Butler and Joan Scott (eds), *Feminists Theorize the Political*, New York: Routledge.

EZEKIEL, RAPHAEL S. (1995), *The Racist Mind: Portraits of American Neo-Nazis and Klansmen*, New York: Viking.

FUCHS EPSTEIN, CYNTHIA (1988) *Deceptive Distinctions: Sex, Gender, and the Social Order*, New York: The Russell Sage Foundation.

FUSS, DIANA (1989), *Essentially Speaking: Feminism, Nature & Difference*, New York: Routledge.

HARPER, SUZANNE (1993), 'The Brotherhood: Race and Gender Ideologies in the White Supremacist Movement', PhD dissertation, The University of Texas, Austin.

OMI, MICHAEL (1991), 'Shifting the blame: racial ideology and politics in the post-civil rights era', *Critical Sociology*, vol. 18, no. 3, pp. 77–98.

——and WINANT, HOWARD (1986), *Racial Formation in the United States: From the 1960s to the 1980s*, New York: Routledge.

RIDGEWAY, JAMES (1990), *Blood in the Face*, New York: Thunder's Mouth Press.

SEIDMAN, STEVEN (1991), 'The end of sociological theory: the postmodern hope', *Sociological Theory*, vol. 9, no. 2, pp. 134–6.

Extract 32

KWAME TURE AND CHARLES V. HAMILTON: *Black Power*

1. Christopher Jencks, 'Accommodating Whites: A New Look at Mississippi', *The New Republic* (April 16, 1966).

Extract 34

HERIBERT ADAM AND KOGILA MOODLEY: *Psychological Liberation*

1. Sam C. Nolutshungu, *Changing South Africa* (Manchester: Manchester University Press, 1982), 147–8.
2. Aelred Stubbs, ed., *Steve Biko: I Write What I Like* (London: Penguin, 1988), 32.
3. B. S. Biko, ed., *Black Viewpoint* (Durban: Black Community Programmes, 1972), 7.
4. Mikhail Heller and Aleksandr Nekrich, *Utopia in Power: The History of the Soviet Union from 1917 to the Present* (New York: Summit Books, 1988), 9.
5. B. A. Khoapa, ed., *Black Review* 1972 (Durban: Black Community Programmes, 1973), 64.
6. Heribert Adam, 'The Rise of Black Consciousness in South Africa', *Race* 15, no. 2 (October 1973): 155.
7. Stubbs, *Steve Biko*, 39.
8. George M. Fredrickson, 'The Making of Mandela', *New York Review of Books*, September 27, 1990, p. 27.
9. Robert Fatton, *Black Consciousness in South Africa* (New York: State University of New York, 1986), 66.
10. G. J. Gerwel, 'Coloured Nationalism' in T. Sundermeier, *Church and Nationalism in South Africa* (Braamfontein: Raven Press, 1975).
11. SASO, *Newsletters* [vols. 1 and 2, 1971–1977] (Durban: SASO), 7.
12. R. Miles, *Racism* (London: Routledge, 1989), 73–6.
13. Nolutshungu, *Changing South Africa*, 149.
14. Ibid. 155–7.

15. Mokgethi Motlhabi, *Black Resistance to Apartheid* (Johannesburg: Skotaville Publishers, 1985), 115.
16. Asha Rambally, ed., *Black Review 1975–6* (Durban: Black Community Programmes, 1977), 143.
17. Ibid. 135.
18. Dorothy Driver, 'Women, Black Consciousness and the Discovery of Self,' unpublished paper, 1990.
19. Khoapa, *Black Review 1972*, 25–6.
20. Ibid. 66.
21. Gail Gerhart, *Black Power in South Africa: The Evolution of an Ideology* (Berkeley: University of California Press, 1979), 291–2.
22. M. Seleoane, 'The Black Consciousness Movement', *South African Foundation Review*, December 1989.
23. E. Baartman, 'Education as an Instrument for Liberation' in H. W. van der Merwe, *African Perspectives on South Africa* (Cape Town: David Philip, 1978), 273–8.
24. Kogila Adam, 'Dialectic of Higher Education for the Colonized' in Heribert Adam, ed., *South Africa: Sociological Perspectives* (London: Oxford University Press, 1971).
25. Heribert Adam, 'The Rise of Black Consciousness', 154.
26. Richard Turner, *The Eye of the Needle: Toward a Participatory Democracy in South Africa* (Maryknoll, N.Y.: Orbis Books, 1978).

Extract 35

CATHIE LLOYD: *Universalism and Difference*

BARD, J. (1992), 'The priests have it', *New Statesman and Society*, 1 May.
GILROY, P. (1987), *There Ain't No Black in the Union Jack*, London: Hutchinson.
HALL, S. (1992), 'New ethnicities', in Donald, J., and Rattansi, A. (eds), '*Race', Culture and Difference*, London: Sage.
HEINEMAN (1972), *The Politics of the Powerless: A Study of the Campaign Against Racial Discrimination*, Oxford: Oxford University Press / IRR.
LAROSE, J. (ed.) (1992), *Racism, Nazism and Racial Attacks*, Paris: European Action for Racial Equality and Social Justice.
LLOYD, C., (1993) 'National approaches to immigration and minority policy', in Rex, J., and Drury, B. (eds), *The Mobilisation of Ethnic Minorities and Ethnic Social Movements in Europe*, Centre for Research in Ethnic Relations, University of Warwick.
MILES, R. (1992), 'Migration, racism and the nation state in contemporary Europe', in Satzewich, V. (ed.), *Deconstructing the Nation: Immigration, Multi-Culturalism and Racism in 90s Canada*, Toronto: Garamond Press.
TAGUIEFF, P.-A. (1991), 'Les metamorphoses idéologiques de racisme et la crise de l'anti-racisme', in Taguieff, P.-A. (ed.), *Face au Racisme*, Vol. 2: *Hypothèses, Perspectives*, Paris: La Découverte.

Extract 37

MICHAEL BURLEIGH AND WOLFGANG WIPPERMANN: *The Racial State*

1. Falk Ruttke, 'Erb- und Rassenpflege in Gesetzgebung und Rechtsprechung des

Dritten Reiches', in *Deutsches Recht*, 25 January 1933, pp. 25–7, cited by Karl A. Schleunes, *The Twisted Road to Auschwitz: Nazi Policy toward German Jews 1933–1939* (London, 1970), 120.

2. Wilhelm Stuckart, Hans Globke, *Kommentar zur deutschen Rassengesetzgebung* (Munich, 1936), Vol. 1, p. 55.

Extract 38

MICHAEL OMI AND HOWARD WINANT: *Racial Formation in the United States*

1. Rodolfo Acuña, *Occupied America: A History of Chicanos*, 2nd ed. (New York: Harper and Row, 1981); see also Leonard Pitt, *The Decline of the Californios* (Berkeley: University of California Press, 1966).

2. Antonio Gramsci, *Selections from the Prison Notebooks,* (New York: International, 1971), 182.

3. 'The Mexican Americans now view the political system as an Anglo system. They feel that only a Mexican American political system can serve their needs. ...' Jose Angel Gutierrez, 'La Raza and Revolution' [1968], in M. S. Meier and F. Rivera, eds., *Readings on La Raza* (New York: Hill and Wang, 1974), 231.

4. Charles V. Hamilton, 'Black Social Scientists: Contributions and Problems', in Joyce Ladner, ed., *The Death of White Sociology* (New York: Vintage, 1973), 472–3.

Extract 39

DESMOND KING: *Separate and Unequal*

1. P. M. Sniderman and T. Piazza, *The Scar of Race* (Cambridge, Mass.: Harvard University Press, 1993), 20.

2. Ibid. 30.

Extract 40

STEPHEN CASTLES AND ELLIE VASTA: *Multicultural or Multi-racist Australia?*

ACTU (Australian Council of Trade Unions) (1995), *Combating Racism: Discrimination and Racism During 1994—How far in fact have we come*, ACTU, Melbourne.

BENNETT, S. (1989), *Aborigines and Political Power*, Allen & Unwin, Sydney.

COHEN, P. and BAINS, H. S. eds. (1988), *Multi-Racist Britain*, Macmillan Education, Basingstoke and London.

COWLISHAW, G. (1993), Introduction: representing racial issues, *Oceania*, vol. 63, no. 3, pp. 183–94.

EADES, D. (1993), 'The Case for Condren: Aboriginal English, Pragmatics and the Law', *Journal of Pragmatics*, vol. 20, no. 2, pp. 141–62.

——(1994), 'A Case of Communicative Clash: Aboriginal English and the Legal System', *Language and the Law*, ed. J. Gibbons, Longman, London.

HOLLINSWORTH, D. (1992), 'Discourses on Aboriginality and the Politics of Identity in Urban Australia', *Oceania*, vol. 63, no. 2, December, pp. 137–55.

HREOC (Human Rights and Equal Opportunity Commission (1991), *Racist Violence: Report of the National Inquiry into Racist Violence in Australia*, AGPS, Canberra.

LATTAS, A. (1993), 'Essentialism, Memory and Resistance: Aboriginality and the Politics of Authenticity', *Oceania*, vol. 63, no. 3, March, pp. 240–67.

LIPPMANN, L. (1973), *Words or Blow. Racial Attitudes in Australia*, Penguin, Ringwood, Vic.

MARKUS, A. (1994), *Australian Race Relations*, Allen & Unwin, Sydney.

MUDROOROO, ATWOOD, B., LATTAS, A., AND BECKETT, J. (1992), 'Comments on Hollinsworth', *Oceania*, vol. 63, no. 2, pp. 156–7.

OMA (Office of Multicultural Affairs) (1989), *National Agenda for a Multicultural Australia*, AGPS, Canberra.

PETTMAN, J. (1992), *Living in the Margins: Racism: Sexism and Feminism in Australia*, Allen & Unwin, Sydney.

REYNOLDS, H. (1981), *The Other Side of the Frontier*, Penguin, Ringwood, Vic.

——(1987), *Frontier*, Allen & Unwin, Sydney.

RIVETT, K. ed. (1962), *Immigration: Control or Colour Bar?*, Melbourne University Press, Carlton, Vic.

ROWLEY, C. (1970), *The Destruction of Aboriginal Society*, Australian National University Press, Canberra.

STEVENS, F. S. ed. (1970), *Racism. The Australian Experience*, 3 vols, ANZ Book Co., Sydney.

YARWOOD, A. and KNOWLING, M. (1982), *Race Relations in Australia*, Methuen, Sydney.

YARWOOD, A. T. (1964), *Asian Migration to Australia. The Background to Exclusion*, Melbourne University Press, Carlton, Vic.

ZUBRZYCKI, J. (1977), 'Towards a Multicultural Society in Australia', *Australia 2000: The Ethnic Impact*, ed. M. Bowen, University of New England, Armidale, NSW.

Extract 41

ANTONIO GUIMARÃES: *Racism and Anti-Racism in Brazil*

AGIER, M. (1993), *Ilê Aiyê: A invenção do mundo negro*. Unpublished manuscript.

——& Carvalho, M. R. (1992, November 12–13), *Nation, race, culture: La trajectoire des mouvements noir et indigène dans la societé brésilienne*. Presented at the meeting 'Nation, État, Ethnicité,' Association des Chercheurs de Politique Africaine, Centre d'Études d'Afrique Noire, Bordeaux, France.

ANDERSON, B. (1992), *Imagined Communities*. London: Verso.

ANDREWS, G. (1991), *Blacks and Whites in São Paulo, Brazil, 1899–1988*. Madison: University of Wisconsin Press.

ANDREWS, G. R. (1992), Desigualdade racial no Brasil e nos Estados Unidos: Uma comparção estatística. *Estudos Afro-Asiáticos*, 22, 47–48.

AZEVEDO, T. (1955), *As elites de cor, um estudo de ascenso social*. São Paulo: Cia Editora Nacional.

CASHMORE, E. (1994), *Dictionary of Race and Ethnic Relations* (3rd ed.). London: Routledge.

CASTRO, N. G. & GUIMARÃES, J. A. (1993), Desigualdades raciais no mercado e nos locais de trabalho. *Estudos Afro-Asiáticos*, 24, 23–60.

DA COSTA, E. V. (1988), *The Brazilian Empire: Myths and Histories*. Belmont, CA: Wadsworth.

DEGLER, C. N. (1991), *Neither Black nor White*. Madison: University of Wisconsin Press.

DELACAMPAGNE. (1990), 'Racism and the West: From praxis to logos'. In D. T. Goldberg (ed.), *Anatomy of Racism* (pp. 85–6). Minneapolis: University of Minnesota Press.

DZIDZIENYO, A. (1979), *The Position of Blacks in Brazilian Society*. London: Minority Rights Group.

FERNANDES, F. (1965), *A integração de negro na sociedade de classes* (2 vols). São Paulo: Cia Editora Nacional.

FREYRE, G. (1938), *Casa grande & senzala: Formação da família brasileira sob o regime da economia patriarcal*. Rio de Janeiro: Schmidt.

GATES, H. L., Jr. (1985), Editor's introduction: 'Writing "race" and the difference it makes'. In H. L. Gates, Jr. (ed.), *Race, Writing, and Difference* (pp. 1–20). Chicago: University of Chicago Press.

GILROY, P. (1993), *Small Acts: Thoughts on the Politics of Black Cultures*. London: Serpent's Tail.

GUILLAUMIN, C. (1992), *'Race et nature,' sexe, race et pratique du pouvoir: L'idée de nature*. Paris: Côté-Femmes Éditions.

GUIMARÃES, J. A. (1994), *Racial Conflicts in Brazilian Law*. Providence, RI: Brown University, Afro-American Studies Program.

HARRIS, M. (1974), *Patterns of Races in the Americas*. New York: Norton.

HASENBALG, C. (1979), *Discriminação e desigualdades raciais no Brasil*. Rio de Janeiro: Gral.

HELLWIG, D. J. (ed.). (1992), *African American Reflections on Brazil's Racial Paradise*. Philadelphia: Temple University.

LOVELL, P. (1989), *Income and Racial Inequality in Brazil*. Unpublished doctoral dissertation, University of Florida.

MERRICK, T., & GRAHAM, D. (1979), *Population and Economic Development in Brazil*. Baltimore: Johns Hopkins University Press.

OBOLER, S. (1995), *Ethnic Labels, Latino Lives: Identity and the Politics of Re-presentation*. Minneapolis: University of Minnesota Press.

OMI, M., & WINANT, H. (1986), *Racial Formation in the United States, from the 1960's to the 1980's*. London: Routledge.

PIERSON, D. (1942), *Negroes in Brazil: A Study of Race Contact in Bahia*. Chicago: University of Chicago Press.

REIS, J. J. (1993), A greve negra de 1857 na Bahia. *Revista USP*, *18*, 8–29.

SILVA, N. (1980), O preço da cor: Diferenciais raciais na distribuição de renda no Brasil. *Pesquisa e Planejamento Econômica*, *10*(1), 21–44.

SILVA, P. C. (1993), *Negros à luz dos fornos: Representações do trabalho e da cor entre metalurgicos da moderna indústria baiana*. Master's thesis, Universidade Federal da Bahia, Salvador.

SKIDMORE, T. (1993), *White into Black*. Durham, NC: Duke University Press.

TAGUIEFF, P. A. (1987), *La force de préjugé: Essai sur le racisme et ses doubles*. Paris: Gallimard.

TELLES, E. (1992), 'Residential segregation by skin color in Brazil.' *American Sociological Review*, *57*, 186–97.

VAN DEN BERGHE, P. (1970), *Race and Ethnicity*. New York: Basic Books.

WADE, P. (1993), *Blackness and Race Mixture: The Dynamics of Racial Identity in Colombia*. Baltimore: Johns Hopkins University Press.

——(1994), 'Race, nature and, culture.' *Man (N.S.)*, *28*, 17–34.

WRIGHT, W. R. (1990), *Café con leche: Race, Class, and National Image in Venezuela*. Austin: University of Texas Press.

Extract 43

JOHN REX: *The Concept of Race in Sociological Theory*

COX, OLIVER CROMWELL (1959), *Caste, Class, and Race*. New York: Monthly Review Press.

DURKHEIM, E. (1950), *Rules of Sociological Method*. Glencoe, Ill.: Free Press.

WARNER, W. LLOYD (1936), 'American Class and Caste', *American Journal of Sociology*, 42: 234–7, Sept.

Extract 44

ROBERT MILES: *Racism as a Concept*

BANTON, M. (1970), 'The Concept of Racism', in S. Zubaida (ed.) *Race and Racialism*, London: Tavistock.

——(1977), *The Idea of Race*, London: Tavistock.

——(1987), *Racial Theories*, Cambridge: Cambridge University Press.

BARZUN, J. (1938), *Race: A Study in Modern Superstition*, London: Methuen.

BENEDICT, R. (1983), *Race and Racism*, London: Routledge & Kegan Paul.

BLAUNER, R. (1972), *Racial Oppression in America*, New York: Harper & Row.

CARMICHAEL, S. and HAMILTON, C. V. (1968), *Black Power: The Politics of Liberation in America*, London: Jonathan Cape.

HERTZ, F. (1928), *Race and Civilisation*, London: Kegan Paul, Trench, Trubner & Co.

HUXLEY, J. and HADDON, A. C. (1935), *We Europeans: A Survey of 'Racial' Problems*, London: Cape.

KATZ, J. H. (1978), *White Awareness: Handbook for Anti-Racism Training*, Norman: University of Oklahoma Press.

KNOWLES, L. L. and PREWITT, K. (1969), *Institutional Racism in America*, Englewood Cliffs: Prentice-Hall.

MONTAGU, A. (1972), *Statement on Race*, London: Oxford University Press.

——(1974), *Man's Most Dangerous Myth: The Fallacy of Race*, New York: Oxford University Press.

REX, J. (1970), *Race Relations in Sociological Theory*, London: Weidenfeld & Nicolson.

VAN DEN BERGHE, P. L. (1978), *Race and Racism: A Comparative Perspective*, New York: Wiley.

WELLMAN, D. (1977), *Portraits of White Racism*, Cambridge: Cambridge University Press.

Extract 45

COLETTE GUILLAUMIN: *The Changing Face of 'Race'*

1. See J. Hiernaux, 'De l'individu à la population: l'anthropobiologie', in *La Science face au racisme* (re-edition of the first issue of *Le Genre humain*), Brussels, Éditions Complexe, 1986.
2. In A. Montague (ed.), *Statement on Race* (Oxford, Oxford University Press, 1972, 3rd edition), 139–47 (p. 141, p. 143).

Extract 46

DAVID THEO GOLDBERG: *The Semantics of Race*

1. Sometimes explanations will conflate the social and biological, for example, in reducing racial phenomena to psycho-sexual drives (Stember 1976).
2. Contra Miles (1989, p. 61). While Miles may think this conceptual inflation, the historical analogizing of women and Blacks suggests otherwise. Miles tries to make the same point concerning the Jews and the Irish: namely, that to deem their exclusion racist is conceptual inflation. Here he is just historically mistaken. Elsewhere,

and more or less at the same time, Miles acknowledges that the 'Irish' have been characterized as a 'race'. One would think that exclusion in terms of this characterization would accordingly amount to a case of racism (Miles 1988, p. 246).

3. Race, on this view, is an 'unstable and *decentred* complex of social meanings constantly being transformed by political struggle' (Omi and Winant 1987, pp. 68, 64, 66–7).

4. 'The Negro is an animal . . . the little boy throws himself into his mother's arms: Mama, the nigger's going to eat me up.' To which Fanon responds, '. . . I had incisors to test. I was sure they were strong' (Fanon 1970, pp. 80–1).

5. This is a necessary implication of the definition Omi and Winant offer for 'racism'.

APPIAH, KWAME ANTHONY (1986), 'The uncompleted argument: Du Bois and the illusion of race', *Critical Inquiry*, vol. 12, no. 1 (Autumn), 21–37.

——(1989), 'The conservation of race', *Black American Literature Forum*, vol. 23, no. 1 (Spring), 37–60.

——(1990a), 'Racisms', in David Theo Goldberg (ed.), *Anatomy of Racism*, Minneapolis: University of Minnesota Press, 1990, pp. 3–17.

——(1990b), 'Race' in Frank Lentricchia and Thomas McLaughlin (eds), *Critical Terms for Literary Study*, Chicago: Chicago University Press, pp. 274–87.

BANTON, MICHAEL (1988), *Racial Theories*, Cambridge: Cambridge University Press.

BARKER, MARTIN (1981), *The New Racism*, London: Junction Books.

BROWN, KEVIN (1986), 'Keeping their distance: the cultural production and reproduction of racist non-racism', *Australian and New Zealand Journal of Sociology*, vol. 22, no. 3 (November), 394–5.

FANON, FRANTZ (1970), *Black Skin, White Masks* (trans. Charles Lam Markmann), London: Paladin.

GLAZER, NATHAN and MOYNIHAN, DANIEL PATRICK (1963), *Beyond the Melting Pot*, Cambridge MA: Harvard University Press.

HALL, STUART (1990), 'Cultural identity and diaspora' in Jonathan Rutherford (ed.), *Identity: Community, Culture, Difference*, London: Lawrence and Wishart, pp. 222–37.

MILES, ROBERT (1988), 'Racialization' in Ellis Cashmore (ed.), *Dictionary of Race and Ethnic Relations*, London: Routledge, pp. 246–7.

——(1989), *Racism*, London: Routledge.

MÜLLER, FRIEDRICH MAX (1895), *Three Lectures on the Science of Language*, Chicago: Regnery.

MYRDAL, GUNNAR (1944), *An American Dilemma: The Negro Problem and American Democracy*, New York: Harper and Row.

OMI, MICHAEL and WINANT, HOWARD (1987), *Racial Formation in the United States: From the Sixties to the Eighties*, London: Routledge.

PARK, ROBERT E. (1950), *Race and Culture* (ed. E.C. Hughes), London: Collier Macmillan.

SOLLORS, WERNER (1986), *Beyond Ethnicity. Consent and Descent in American Culture*, Oxford: Oxford University Press.

STEMBER, CHARLES HERBERT (1976), *Sexual Racism*, New York: Harper Colophon.

VAN DEN BERGHE, PIERRE (1967), *Race and Racism: A Comparative Perspective*, New York: John Wiley.

WITTGENSTEIN, LUDWIG (1968), *Philosophical Investigations*, trans. G. E. M. Anscombe, Oxford: Basil Blackwell.

Extract 47

PATRICIA HILL COLLINS: *Defining Black Feminist Thought*

BROWN, ELSA BARKLEY (1986), *Hearing Our Mothers' Lives*. Atlanta: Fifteenth Anniversary of African-American and African Studies, Emory University (unpublished).

CANNON, KATIE G. (1985), 'The Emergence of a Black Feminist Consciousness.' In *Feminist Interpretations of the Bible*, edited by Letty M. Russell, 30–40. Philadelphia: Westminster Press.

CARBY, HAZEL (1987), *Reconstructing Womanhood: The Emergence of the Afro-American Woman Novelist*. New York: Oxford.

CHISHOLM, SHIRLEY (1970), *Unbought and Unbossed*. New York: Avon.

CLARKE, CHERYL (1983), 'The Failure to Transform: Homophobia in the Black Community.' In *Home Girls: A Black Feminist Anthology*, edited by Barbara Smith, 197–208. New York: Kitchen Table Press.

The Combahee River Collective (1982), 'A Black Feminist Statement.' In *But Some of Us Are Brave*, edited by Gloria T. Hull, Patricia Bell Scott, and Barbara Smith, 13–22. Old Westbury, NY: Feminist Press.

COOPER, ANNA JULIA (1892), *A Voice from the South; By a Black Woman of the South*. Xenia, OH: Aldine Printing House.

DAVIS, GEORGE, and GLEGG WATSON (1985), *Black Life in Corporate America*. New York: Anchor.

GUY-SHEFTALL, BEVERLY (1986), 'Remembering Sojourner Truth: On Black Feminism.' *Catalyst* (Fall): 54–7.

HOOKS, BELL (1981), *Ain't I a Woman: Black Women and Feminism*. Boston: South End Press.

——(1989), *Talking Black: Thinking Feminist, Thinking Black*. Boston: South End Press.

JORDAN, JUNE (1981), *Civil Wars*. Boston: Beacon.

LINDSAY, BEVERLEY, ed. (1980), *Comparative Perspectives of Third World Women: The Impact of Race, Sex, and Class*. New York: Praeger.

LOWENBERG, BERT J., and RUTH BOGIN, eds. (1976), *Black Women in Nineteenth-Century American Life*. University Park: Pennsylvania State University Press.

MCDOWELL, DEBORAH E. (1985), 'New Directions for Black Feminist Criticism.' In *The New Feminist Criticism*, edited by Elaine Showalter, 186–99. New York: Pantheon.

MURRAY, PAULI (1970), 'The Liberation of Black Women.' In *Voices of the New Feminism*, edited by Mary Lou Thompson, 87–102. Boston: Beacon.

OMI, MICHAEL, and HOWARD WINANT (1986), *Racial Formation in the United States: From the 1960s to the 1980s*. New York: Routledge & Kegan Paul.

RADFORD-HILL, SHEILA (1986), 'Considering Feminism as a Model for Social Change.' In *Feminist Studies/Critical Studies*, edited by Teresa de Lauretis, 157–72. Bloomington: Indiana University Press.

SCOTT, PATRICIA BELL (1982), 'Selected Bibliography on Black Feminism.' In *But Some of Us are Brave*, edited by Gloria T. Hull, Patricia Bell Scott, and Barbara Smith, 23–36. Old Westbury, NY: Feminist Press.

SMITH, BEVERLY (1983), 'The Wedding.' In *Home Girls: A Black Feminist Anthology*, edited by Barbara Smith, 171–6. New York: Kitchen Table Press.

STEADY, FILOMINA CHIOMA (1981), 'The Black Woman Cross-Culturally: An Overview.' In *The Black Woman Cross-Culturally*, edited by Filomina Chioma Steady, 7–42. Cambridge, MA: Schenkman.

——(1987), 'African Feminism: A Worldwide Perspective.' In *Women in Africa and the*

African Diaspora, edited by Rosalyn Terborg-Penn, Sharon Harley, and Andrea Benton Rushing, 3–24. Washington, DC: Howard University Press.

WALKER, ALICE (1983), *In Search of Our Mothers' Gardens*. New York: Harcourt Brace Jovanovich.

——(1988), *Living by the Word*. New York: Harcourt Brace Jovanovich.

Extract 50

JOE FEAGIN and MELVIN P. SIKES: *Changing the Color Line: The Future of U.S. Racism*

1. People for the American Way, *Democracy's Next Generation II*, (Washington, D.C.: People for the American Way, 1992) 48–9.
2. William E. B. Du Bois, *The Suppression of the African Slave-Trade to the United States of America, 1638–1870* (1896; New York: Schocken Books, 1969), 93–199.
3. Quoted in Emily Morison Beck, ed., *John Bartlett's Familiar Quotations*, 15th ed. (Boston: Little, Brown, 1980), 556.

Further Reading

General

CORNELL, S., and HARTMANN, D (1998), *Ethnicity and Race: Making Identities in a Changing World* (Thousand Oaks, Calif.: Pine Forge Press).

COX, O. C. (1970) [1948], *Caste, Class and Race* (New York: Monthly Review Press).

MALIK, K. (1996), *The Meaning of Race: Race, History and Culture in Western Society* (Basingstoke: Macmillan).

MONTAGU, A. (ed.) (1964), *The Concept of Race* (New York: Free Press).

MOSSE, G. (1985), *Toward the Final Solution: A History of European Racism* (Madison: University of Wisconsin Press).

PATTERSON, O. (1977), *Ethnic Chauvinism: The Reactionary Impulse* (New York: Stein & Day).

POLIAKOV, L. (1974), *The Aryan Myth: A History of Racist and Nationalist Ideas in Europe* (London: Chatto & Heinemann for Sussex University Press).

SCHERMERHORN, R. A. (1978), *Comparative Ethnic Relations: A Framework for Theory and Research* (Chicago: University of Chicago Press).

SOLOMOS, J., and BACK, L. (1996), *Racism and Society* (Basingstoke: Macmillan).

STONE, J. (1985), *Racial Conflict in Contemporary Society* (London: Collins).

WILSON, W .J. (1973), *Power, Racism and Privilege* (New York: Macmillan).

I. Racist Ideas

BANTON, M. (1977) *The Idea of Race* (London: Tavistock).

COOMBES, A. (1994), *Reinventing Africa* (London: Yale University Press).

EZE, E. C. (ed.) (1997), *Race and the Enlightenment: A Reader* (Oxford: Blackwell).

FREDRICKSON, G. M. (1971), *The Black Image in the White Mind* (New York: Harper & Row).

MONTAGU, A. (1997), *Man's Most Dangerous Myth: The Fallacy of Race*, 6th edn., (Walnut Creek, Calif.: AltaMira Press).

PIETERSE, J. M. (1992), *White on Black: Images of Africa and Blacks in Western Popular Culture* (New Haven: Yale University Press).

STEPAN, N. (1982), *The Idea of Race in Science* (London: Macmillan).

STREET, B. (1975), *The Savage in Literature: Representations of Primitive Societies in English Fiction, 1858–1920* (London: Routledge).

TODOROV, T. (1993), *On Human Diversity: Nationalism, Racism and Exoticism in French Thought* (Cambridge, Mass.: Harvard University Press).

II. Institutional Forms of Racism: Slavery, Imperialism, and Colonialism

(A) Slavery

DAVIS, D. B. (1966), *The Problem of Slavery in Western Culture* (New York: Oxford University Press).

——(1984), *Slavery and Human Progress* (New York: Oxford University Press).

DRESCHER, S. (1987), *Capitalism and Antislavery: British Mobilisation in Comparative Perspective* (New York: Oxford University Press).

ELKINS, S. (1963), *Slavery: A Problem in American Institutional and Intellectual Life* (Chicago: University of Chicago Press).

ENGERMAN, S. L., and GENOVESE, E. D. (1975), *Race and Slavery in the Western Hemisphere: Quantitative Studies* (Princeton: Princeton University Press).

GENOVESE, E. (1970), *The World the Slave Holders Made: Two Essays in Interpretation* (London: Allen Lane).

MANNING, P. (1990), *Slavery and African Life* (Cambridge: Cambridge University Press).

THOMAS, H. (1997), *The Slave Trade: The History of the Atlantic Slave Trade 1440–1870* (New York: Simon & Schuster).

WILLIAMS, E. (1944), *Capitalism and Slavery* (London: Andre Deutsch).

(B) Imperialism and Colonialism

BALLHATCHET, K. (1980), *Race, Sex and Class under the Raj: Imperial Attitudes and Policies and their Critics, 1793-1905* (London: Weidenfeld & Nicolson).

FREDRICKSON, G. M. (1981), *White Supremacy: A Comparative Study in American and South African History* (New York: Oxford University Press).

FURNIVALL, J. S. (1948), *Colonial Policy and Practice: A Comparative Study of Burma and Netherlands India* (Cambridge: Cambridge University Press).

HOBSON, J. A. (1988) [1938], *Imperialism: A Study* (London: Unwin Hyman).

KIERNAN, V. G. (1969), *The Lords of Human Kind: European Attitudes to the Outside World in the Imperial Age* (London: Weidenfeld & Nicolson).

MANNONI, O. (1964), *Prospero and Caliban: The Psychology of Colonisation* (New York: Fredrick A. Praeger).

MASON, P. (1970), *Patterns of Dominance* (London: Oxford University Press for the Institute of Race Relations).

MEMMI, A. (1965), *The Colonizer and the Colonized* (New York: Orion Press).

TINKER, H. (1974), *A New System of Slavery: The Export of Indian Labour Overseas, 1830-1920* (London: Oxford University Press for the Institute of Race Relations).

TODOROV, T. (1984), *The Conquest of America: The Question of the Other* (New York: Harper & Row).

WOLF, E. (1982), *Europe and the People without History* (Berkeley and Los Angeles: University of California Press).

YOUNG, R. (1995), *Colonial Desire: Hybridity in Theory, Culture and Race* (London: Routledge).

III. Racism in the Twentieth Century

ADAM, H. (1984), 'Racist Capitalism v Capitalist Non-Racialism', *Ethnic and Racial Studies*, 7/2: 269–82.

AHMED, A. (1995), 'Ethnic Cleansing: A Metaphor for Our Times?', *Ethnic and Racial Studies*, 18/1: 1–25.

BARKAN, E. (1992), *The Retreat of Scientific Racism* (Cambridge: Cambridge University Press).

BARZUN, J. (1938), *Race: A Study in Modern Superstition* (London: Methuen).

BENEDICT, R. (1982) [1942], *Race and Racism* (London: Routledge & Kegan Paul).

CELL, J. W. (1982), *The Highest Stage of White Supremacy: The Origin of Segregation in South Africa and the American South* (Cambridge: Cambridge University Press).

COHEN, P., and BAINS, H. (eds.) (1988), *Multi-Racist Britain* (London: Macmillan).

GUILLAUMIN, C. (1995), *Racism, Sexism, Power and Ideology* (London: Routledge).

KUPER, L. (1981), *Genocide* (Harmondsworth: Penguin).

LEWIS, D. L.(1993), *W.E.B. Du Bois: Biography of a Race*, i: *1868–1919* (New York: Henry Holt).

IV. *Racist Movements*

EZEKIEL, R. (1995), *The Racist Mind: Portraits of American Neo-Nazis and Klansmen* (London: Viking).

GOLDFIELD, D. R. (1990), *Black, White and Southern: Race Relations and Southern Culture—1940 to the Present* (Baton Rouge, LA.: Louisiana State University Press).

GRIFFIN, R. (ed.) (1996), *Fascism* (Oxford: Oxford University Press).

HOWE, S. (1998), *Afrocentrism: Mythical Pasts and Imagined Homes* (London: Verso).

TAGUIEFF, P.-A. (1988) *La Force du préjugé: essai sur le racisme et ses doubles* (Paris: La Découverte).

WELLMAN, D. T. (1993), *Portraits of White Racism*, 2nd edn. (Cambridge: Cambridge University Press).

WIEVIORKA, M. (1995), *The Arena of Racism* (London: Sage).

V. *Anti-Racism*

ADAM, H., and MOODLEY, K. (1993), *The Opening of the Apartheid Mind* (Berkeley and Los Angeles: University of California Press).

BODY-GENDROT, S. (1998), 'Now You See, Now You Don't', *Ethnic and Racial Studies*, 21/5: 848–58.

CAMBRIDGE, A. X. and FEUCHTWANG, S. (eds.) (1990), *Antiracist Strategies* (Aldershot: Avebury).

GILROY, P. (1987), *There ain't No Black in the Union Jack* (London: Hutchinson).

LLOYD, C. (1998), *Discourses of Antiracism in France* (Aldershot: Ashgate).

MARTIN, T. (1976, *Race First: The Ideological and Organisational Struggles of Marcus Garvey and the Universal Negro Improvement Association* (Dover, Mass.: Majority Press).

PALMER, F. (ed.) (1986), *Anti-Racism: An Assault on Education and Value* (London: Sherwood Press).

TURE, K., and HAMILTON, C. V. (1967), *Black Power and the Politics of Liberation* (New York: Vintage Books).

WIEVIORKA, M. (1998), 'Is Multiculturalism the Solution?', *Ethnic and Racial Studies*, 21/5: 881–910.

VI. *Racism and the State*

ARENDT, H. (1973), *The Origins of Totalitarianism*, new edn. (San Diego: Harcourt Brace).

BAUMAN, Z. (1989), *Modernity and the Holocaust* (Oxford: Blackwell).

BURLEIGH, M., and WIPPERMANN, W. (1991), *The Racial State: Germany, 1933–1945* (Cambridge: Cambridge University Press).

GREENBERG, S. B. (1980), *Race & State in Capitalist Development* (New Haven: Yale University Press).

KING, D. (1995), *Separate and Unequal: Black Americans and the US Federal Government* (Oxford: Clarendon Press).

OMI, M., and WINANT, H. (1994), *Racial Formation in the United States: From the 1960s to the 1990s* (New York: Routledge).

VII. Theories of Racism

ANTHIAS, F., and YUVAL-DAVIS, N. (1992), *Racialized Boundaries* (London: Routledge).

BALIBAR, E., and WALLERSTEIN, I. (1991), *Race, Nation, Class: Ambiguous Identities* (London: Verso).

BANTON, M. (1987), *Racial Theories* (Cambridge: Cambridge University Press).

Centre for Contemporary Cultural Studies (1982), *The Empire Strikes Back: Race and Racism in 70s Britain* (London: Hutchinson).

COLLINS, P. H. (1990),*Black Feminist Thought* (London: Unwin Hyman).

GATES, H. L. Jr (ed.) (1986), *'Race', Writing and Difference* (Chicago: University of Chicago Press).

GILROY, P. (1993), *The Black Atlantic: Modernity and Double Consciousness* (London: Verso).

GOLDBERG, D. T. (1993), *Racist Culture* (Oxford: Blackwell).

HOOKS, B. (1981), *Ain't I a Woman: Black Women and Feminism* (Boston: South End Press).

LACAPRA, D. (ed.) (1991), *The Bounds of Race: Perspectives on Hegemony and Resistance* (Ithaca, NY: Cornell University Press).

MILES, R. (1989), *Racism* (London: Routledge).

PARK, R. (1950), *Race and Culture* (New York: Free Press).

RATTANSI, A., and WESTWOOD, S. (eds.) (1994), *Racism, Modernity and Identity: On the Western Front* (Cambridge: Polity Press).

REX, J., and MASON, D. (eds) (1986), *Theories of Race and Ethnic Relations* (Cambridge: Cambridge University Press).

STANFIELD II, J. H. (ed.) (1993), *A History of Race Relations Research: First Generation Recollections* (London: Sage).

VIII. The Future of Racism

BHATT, C. (1997), *Liberation and Purity: Race, New Religious Movements and the Ethics of Postmodernity* (London: UCL Press).

BRAH, A. (1996), *Cartographies of Diaspora* (London: Routledge).

ESSED, P. (1991), *Understanding Everyday Racism* (Beverley Hills, Calif.: Sage).

FANON, F. (1965), *The Wretched of the Earth* (London: McGibbon & Kee).

FEAGIN, J., and SIKES, M. P. (1994), *Living Racism: The Black Middle Class Experience* (Boston: Beacon Press).

FRANKENBERG, R. (1993), *White Women, Race Matters: The Social Construction of Whiteness* (London: Routledge).

GATES, H. L .Jr (1994), *Colored People: A Memoir* (New York: Knopf).

GOLDBERG, D. T. (ed.) (1994), *Multiculturalism: A Critical Reader* (Oxford: Blackwell).

HALL, S. (1991), 'Old and New Identities, Old and New Ethnicities', in A. D. King (ed.), *Culture, Globalisation and the World System* (London: Macmillan).

KYMLICKA, W. (1995), *Multicultural Citizenship* (Oxford: Oxford University Press).

MILLS, C. W. (1997), *The Racial Contract* (Ithaca, NY: Cornell University Press).

PAPASTERGIADIS, N. (1998), *Dialogues in the Diasporas: Essays and Conversations on Cultural Identity* (London: Rivers Oram Press).

ROEDIGER, D. (1994), *Towards the Abolition of Whiteness: Essays on Race, Politics, and Working Class History* (London: Verso).

WEST, C. (1993), *Race Matters* (Boston: Beacon Press).

WILLIAMS, P. (1997), *Seeing a Colour Blind Future: The Paradox of Race* (London: Virago).

Biographical Notes

HERIBERT ADAM is Professor of Sociology at Simon Fraser University, British Columbia. He also holds a visiting chair at the University of Cape Town Business School. His main areas of research interest are political sociology, Southern Africa, and nationalism and ethnic conflict. He is the author of a number of books, including *Modernising Racial Domination* (1971), *Ethnic Power Mobilised* (1979), and *South Africa without Apartheid* (with Kogila Moodley, 1986), and *Comrades in Business* (1997).

MICHAEL BANTON is Professor Emeritus of Sociology at the University of Bristol. He is a former President of the Royal Anthropological Institute of Great Britain. He has written widely on race and ethnicity, and he played a leading role in the development of the study of race relations. His books include *Racial and Ethnic Competition* (1983), *Promoting Racial Harmony* (1985), *Racial Theories* (1987), and *International Action against Racial Discrimination* (1996).

MICHAEL BIDDISS is Professor of History at the University of Reading. He previously taught at the University of Cambridge and the University of Leicester. His main research interests are in the areas of nineteenth- and twentieth-century European history and political and intellectual thought. He has published a number of books, including *Father of Racist Ideology: The Social and Political Thought of Count Gobineau* (1970) and *Images of Race* (1979).

MICHAEL BURLEIGH holds the Raoul Wallenberg Chair of Human Rights at Rutgers University, New Jersey. He is the author of *Germany Turns Eastwards* (1990), *Death and Deliverance: 'Euthanasia' in Germany 1900–1945* (1994), and *Confronting the Nazi Past* (ed., 1995), among other works. He writes regularly for the *Times Literary Supplement*.

EDWARD CARMINES is Professor of Political Science at Indiana University at Bloomington. His books include *Issue Evolution: Race and the Transformation of American Politics* (with J. A. Stimson, 1990) and *Measurement in the Social Sciences* (with R. A. Zeller, 1980).

STEPHEN CASTLES is Professor of Sociology, Institute for Social Change and Critical Inquiry at the University of Wollongong. He has studied migration, ethnicity, and racism in Europe and Australia, and he is the Director of the Secretariat of the Asia-Pacific Migration Research Network. His books include *Immigrant Workers and the Class Structure in Western Europe* (with Godula Kosack, 1973) and *The Age of Migration: International Population Movements in the Modern World* (with M. Miller, 2nd edition 1998).

PHIL COHEN is Reader in Cultural Studies and Director of the Centre for New Ethnicities Research at the University of East London. He has written and researched on contemporary youth cultures and on contemporary forms of racism. He has written *Rethinking the Youth Question* (1997).

PATRICIA HILL COLLINS is Charles Phelps Taft Professor of Sociology in the Department of African-American Studies at the University of Cincinnati. She has written widely on issues of gender, race, and social class, especially in relation to African-American women. She is the author of *Black Feminist Thought: Knowledge, Consciousness, and the Politics of Empowerment* (1990) and *Fighting Words: Black Women and the Search for Justice* (1998).

STEPHEN CORNELL is Director of the Udall Centre for Studies in Public Policy at the University of Arizona, and a leading scholar of Indian Americans. He has previously held posts at Harvard University and the University of California, San Diego. His most recent book is *Ethnicity and Race: Making Identities in a Changing World* (with D. Hartmann, 1998).

PHILIP CURTIN is Herbert Baxter Adams Professor of History Emeritus at the Johns Hopkins University. He has researched and written on the history of slavery, the history of Africa, and the development of trade routes. He is the author of many books including *Cross Cultural Trade in World History* (1984), *Death by Migration* (1989), *The Rise and Fall of the Plantation Complex* (1990), and *The Atlantic Slave Trade: A Census* (1969).

DAVID BRION DAVIS is Sterling Professor of History at Yale University. He has written and edited numerous books including his prize-winning *The Problem of Slavery in Western Culture* (1969) and *The Problem of Slavery in the Age of Revolution 1770–1823* (1975).

FRANK DIKÖTTER is Lecturer in Chinese History at the School of Oriental and African Studies, University of London. His works include *The Discourse of Race in Modern China* (1992) and *Sex, Culture and Society in Modern China* (1995). He has pioneered the study of race and gender in China.

W. E. B. DuBOIS (1868–1963) was the most prominent and incisive black intellectual in the United States in the first half of the twentieth century. He was a staff member of the National Association for the Advancement of Colored People (NAACP) and the editor of its journal *The Crisis* from 1910 to 1934. Prior to that he was the first African American to gain a Ph.D. from Harvard University and taught sociology at Atlanta University. His books include *The Philadelphia Negro* (1898), *The Souls of Black Folk* (1903), and other works. Toward the end of his life he became disillusioned with America, and he died in Ghana as a citizen of that country. See his biography by David Levering Lewis.

RAPHAEL EZEKIEL taught for over thirty years in the psychology faculty of the University of Michigan and is now based at the Harvard School of Public Health. He has carried out research on the lives of inner city African Americans in Detroit and on Peace Corps volunteers in Ghana.

FRANTZ FANON (1925–61) was a West Indian psychoanalyst and social philosopher from the island of Martinique in the French Antilles. He worked as a psychiatrist in Algeria under French rule, joined the Algerian liberation movement in 1954, and was their ambassador to Ghana 1960–1. His works include *Black Skin, White Masks* (1991), *Studies in a Dying Colonialism* (1989), and *The Wretched of the Earth* (1961).

JOE FEAGIN is Graduate Research Professor in Sociology at the University of Florida. He is President of the American Sociological Association for the year 2000. He is the author of twenty books and six dozen articles dealing with various aspects of racial relations in the United States and globally. Among his most recent books in this area are *Double Burden: Black Women and Everyday Racism* (1998; with Y. St Jean); *The Agony of Education: Black Students at White Colleges and Universities* (1996; with H. Vera and N. Imani); and *White Racism* (1995; with H. Vera).

ABBY L. FERBER is Assistant Professor of Sociology at the University of Colorado at Colorado Springs. Her main research interests are in the areas of theory and social thought, sex and gender, and race and ethnic relations. She is the author of *White Man Falling: Race, Gender and White Supremacy* (1998).

PAUL FOOT is a well-known British journalist who writes about current social issues. He is the author of *Ireland: Why Britain Must Get Out* (1989), *The Rise of Enoch Powell* (1969), and *Who Killed Hanratty?* (1988) among other works.

GEORGE FREDRICKSON is Professor of History at Stanford University, and a comparative historian. His books include *The Black Image in the White Mind* (1971), *White Supremacy: A Comparative Study of American and South African History* (1981), and *The Comparative Imagination* (1997).

MARCUS GARVEY (1887–1940) was born in Jamaica and travelled widely in the Caribbean and Central America before starting the Universal Negro Improvement Association in the United States. During the 1920s he became a leading figure in the development of mass organizations among blacks in the United States and an advocate of pride in Africa, its culture and history. He has influenced a wide range of political and cultural movements in the period after his death in London, following his deportation from the United States.

EUGENE GENOVESE is Professor of History at the University of Rochester, New York State. He is the author of many works on American slavery including *Slavery in the New World* (with L. Foner, 1972), *In Red and Black* (1984), *The Political Economy of Slavery* (1989), *Roll, Jordan, Roll: The World the Slaveholders Made* (1975), and *The Southern Tradition* (1992).

PAUL GILROY is Professor of African American Studies and Sociology at Yale University. He is one of the leading theorists on questions of race and culture in relation to the African diaspora and his major books include *There Ain't No Black in the Union Jack* (1987), *The Black Atlantic* (1993), and *Small Acts* (1993).

DAVID THEO GOLDBERG is Director and Professor in the School of Justice Studies at Arizona State University. He has researched and written on the history and contemporary expression of racism and is one of the founding editors of the journal *Social Identities*. Among his books are *Anatomy of Racism* (1990), *Racist Culture* (1993), *Jewish Identity* (1993), and *Multiculturalism* (1994).

JAMES R. GROSSMAN holds a Ph.D. in History from the University of Chicago, where he taught, and is on the staff of the Newberry Library on Chicago's Near North Side. His publications include *Land of Hope: Chicago, Black Southerners and the Great Migration* (1989) and *The Frontier in American Culture* (ed., 1994).

COLETTE GUILLAUMIN is Head of Research at the Centre Nationale de la Recherche Scientifique in Paris. Her book *L'Idéologie raciste* (1972) was one of the early contemporary studies of ideas about race and racism in France, and she has written extensively on questions about racism and gender.

ANTONIO GUIMARÃES is Adjunct Professor of Sociology at the Universidade Federal da Bahia in Salvador, Brazil. He has been a Research Fellow at the CNPq (Brazilian Research Foundation), is one of two editors of *Revista Apro-Asia*, and has held a visiting appointment at Brown University, Rhode Island.

CHARLES V. HAMILTON is Wallace S. Sayre Professor Emeritus of Political Science at Columbia University. He has researched and written widely on American politics, race, and public policy. His books include *American Government* (1981) and *Adam Clayton Powell Jr* (1991).

RICHARD HATCHER is Senior Lecturer in Educational Studies at the University of Central England at Birmingham. His books include *Racial Equality and the Local Management of Schools* (1996) and *Education after the Conservatives* (co-editor 1996).

REGINALD HORSMAN is Distinguished Professor of History at the University of Wisconsin, Milwaukee. His main areas of research interest are in American expansion, Indian policy, race, and medical history. He has written, among other books, *Dr Nott of Mobile: Southerner, Physician and Racial Theorist* (1987) and *Expansion and American Indian Policy* (1992).

WINTHROP D. JORDAN was Professor of History at the University of California at Berkeley for over twenty years, and is currently William F. Winter Professor of History and African-American Studies at the University of Mississippi. His many publications include *White Over Black: American Attitudes toward the Negro 1550-1812* (1968), *The Negro Versus Equality 1762-1826* (ed., 1969) and *Tumult and Silence at Second Creek: An Inquiry into a Civil War Slave Conspiracy* (1993).

V. G. KIERNAN is Professor Emeritus of History at the University of Edinburgh. His early career was spent in India. He has written on sixteenth-century Europe, modern Spain, Latin America, modern India and China, and his books include *Colonial Empires and Armies* (1998), *The Duel in European History* (1988), *Imperialism and its Contradictions* (1994), and *The Lords of Human Kind* (1969).

DESMOND KING is Professor of Politics in the University of Oxford and Fellow of St John's College. His publications include *Actively Seeking Work? The Politics of Unemployment and Welfare Policy in the United States and Great Britain* (1985), *Social Citizenship Rights in the Welfare State* (1987), and (with Ted Robert Gurr) *The State and the City* (1987).

CATHIE LLOYD is at the Centre for Cross-Cultural Research on Women at Queen Elizabeth House, University of Oxford. She previously worked at the Commission for Racial Equality and the Centre for Research and Ethnic Relations at the University of Warwick. She has researched and written widely on the history of anti-racism in Britain and France, and has written *Discourses of Antiracism in France* (1998).

TONY MARTIN is Professor of Africana Studies at Wellesley College, Massachusetts. He studied in England and the United States, and moved to Wellesley in 1973. He is a leading exponent of Afrocentric thought and has written widely on the history of Garveyism. He has lectured widely in the United States, the Caribbean, and Africa. Among his books are *Race First* (1976) and *African Fundamentalism* (1983).

PHILIP MASON (1906–99) began his career as an Indian administrator, latterly representing the Government of India in the Indian state of Hyderabad. After Independence in 1947 he returned to Britain and wrote a series of books on *The Men Who Ruled India*. He then became Director of the Institute of Race Relations in London, a research institute which pioneered the study of the subject and established the academic journal *Race*. He was the author of many works including *Race Relations* (1970), *Patterns of Dominance* (1970), *Man, Race and Darwin* (ed., 1960) and *Prospero's Magic: Some Thoughts on Class and Race* (1962).

ALBERTO MELUCCI is Professor of Sociology at the University of Trento in Trentino-Alto Adige, and a practising psychotherapist in Milan. His interests include the study of post-industrial society and the investigation of social and cultural networks. His books include *Corpi Estranei* (1988), *Nomads in the Present* (1989), and *Challenging Codes* (1996).

ROBERT MILES is Professor of Sociology at the University of Glasgow. He has written widely on various aspects of the history of 'race' and racism and has carried out extensive research on the history of processes of racialization in Britain. Among his books are *Racism and Migrant Labour* (1982), *Racism* (1989), and *Racism after 'Race Relations'* (1993).

KOGILA MOODLEY is Professor of Anthropology and Sociology of Education at the University of British Columbia. Her main research interests are in South Africa, comparative race and ethnic relations, and policy studies. She has written a number of books, including *Democratising South Africa* (with Heribert Adam, 1992).

GEORGE MOSSE (1918–1999) was Professor Emeritus of History at the University of Wisconsin, Madison. He has written and researched on a wide range of issues, including studies of modern German and European history. Among his books are *The Crisis of German Ideology* (1966), *The Nationalization of the Masses* (1975), and *Nationalism and Sexuality* (1985).

MICHAEL OMI is associate professor of Asian American Studies and Ethnic Studies at the University of California at Berkeley. With Howard Winant, he is the author of *Racial Formation in the United States* (1994) and numerous articles on racial theory and politics. He has also written about right-wing political movements, Asian Americans and race relations, and race and popular culture.

ROBERT PARK (1864–1944) was one of the leading figures in the Chicago School of Sociology. He, along with his students, made major contributions to the development of urban sociology, and to the study of race relations, collective behaviour and social control. He co-authored *An Introduction to the Science of Sociology* (1921, with E. Burgess) and *The City* (1925), and after his death a number of volumes of his collected papers were published, including *Race and Culture* (1950).

ORLANDO PATTERSON is a graduate of the University of the West Indies and of the London School of Economics, where he also taught sociology. He is Professor of Sociology at Harvard University. His books include *The Sociology of Slavery* (1969), *Ethnic Chauvinism: The Reactionary Impulse* (1977), and *Slavery and Social Death: A Comparative Study* (1982). He has also been a special adviser to the former Prime Minister of Jamaica, Michael Manley.

LEON POLIAKOV was Maître des Recherches at the Centre de Recherches Nationales Scientifiques in Paris. He was one of the leading authorities on anti-Semitism and the rise of nationalist and racist ideas in Europe. His publications included *Harvest of Hate* (1954), *The Aryan Myth* (1974), and the four-volume *The History of Anti-Semitism* (1957–75).

JOHN REX is Professor Emeritus of Sociology at the University of Warwick and former Director of the Centre for Research on Ethnic Relations (CRER). He has researched and written widely on theories of race relations and on race relations in Britain. Among his books are *Race Relations in Sociological Theory* (1970), *Race, Colonialism and the City* (1973), *Race and Ethnicity* (1986), and *Ethnic Minorities in the Modern Nation State* (1996).

MELVIN P. SIKES is a retired professor of educational psychology at the University of Texas at Austin. He has a long career of distinguished service in government agencies and as professor and administrator in US college and university settings. His research interests include racial relations, African-American studies, multicultural curricula, and issues of alcoholism. He has recently done consulting with major police agencies on racism and multiculturalism issues.

The late M.G. SMITH was Professor of Anthropology at Yale University, and also taught at the University of California, Los Angeles, University College London, and the University of the West Indies at Mona. He theorized the concept of the plural society and made influential studies of West African and West Indian societies. His publications include *Government at Zazzau* (1960), *Pluralism in Africa* (ed. with L. Kuper 1969) and *Corporations and Society* (1974).

ROBERT C. SMITH is Professor of Political Science at San Francisco State University. He is the author, with Richard Seltzer, of *Race, Class and Culture: A Study in Afro-American Mass Opinion* (1992).

PAUL SNIDERMAN is Professor of Political Science at Stanford University. His works on race in America include the prizewinning *Reaching beyond Race* (1998), *Race and Inequality* (1985), and *The Scar of Race* (1993).

FRANK SNOWDEN is Professor Emeritus of Classics at Howard University. His two major books on *Blacks in Antiquity (1970)* and *Before Color Prejudice* (1983) helped to shape the study of blacks in ancient societies.

PIERRE-ANDRÉ TAGUIEFF is based at the Centre Nationale de la Recherche Scientifique in Paris. He has written extensively on the role of racism and of anti-racism in France, including *La Force du préjugé* (1987) and *Face au racism* (1991).

The late BARRY TROYNA was Professor of Education at the University of Warwick, and the author of many books on race in English education, including *Racism, Education and the State* (1986), *The Educational Needs of a Multi-Racial Society* (1993), and *Anti-Racism, Culture and Social Justice* (1996). He was involved in anti-racist education for over thirty years as a teacher, campaigner, lecturer, and school governor.

KWAME TURE (originally known as Stokeley Carmichael) was one of the leaders of the Black Power movement in the United States during the 1960s. He then moved to Guinea and continued to play an active role in Pan-Africanist politics until his death in 1998.

WILLIAM M. TUTTLE JR. is Professor of History, University of Kansas. He has written and researched on aspects of American history and on race relations in America. Among his books are *Daddy's Gone to War* (1993) and *A People and a Nation* (1994).

ELLIE VASTA is Senior Lecturer in Sociology at the University of Wollongong. She is co-editor of *Australia's Italians* (1992) and has written on the relationship between multiculturalism, identity, culture, and difference.

DAVID T. WELLMAN is Professor of Community Studies at the University of California, Santa Cruz, and Research Sociologist at the Institute for the Study of Social Change at the University of California, Berkeley. He has researched and written widely on racism in the United States.

MICHEL WIEVIORKA is Professor at the École des Hautes Études en Sciences Sociales and Director of the Centre d'Analyse et d'Intervention Sociologiques (CADIS) in Paris. He has carried out extensive research on social movements and on theories of racism as well as racist movements in France. Among his books are *La France raciste* (1992) and *Racisme et modernité* (1993).

PATRICIA J. WILLIAMS is Professor of Law at Columbia University. She also writes a column for the *Nation*, and her books include *The Rooster's Egg* (1995) and *Seeing a Color-Blind Future* (1997).

HOWARD WINANT is Professor of Sociology at Temple University, Philadelphia. He is the author of *Racial Conditions: Politics, Theory, Comparisons* (1994) and of *Racial Formation in the United States: From the 1960s to the 1990s* (with M. Omi, 1994), and has research interests in Latin America.

WOLFGANG WIPPERMANN is Professor of Modern History at the Freie Universität, Berlin. His research interests include the history of fascism, racism and totalitarianism, minorities and German-Slav relations, and the historiography of Italian Fascism and of National Socialism. His books include *Faschismustheorien* 5th ed, (1989), *Der 'deutsche Drang nach Osten'* (1981), and *Der konsequente Wahn, Ideologie und Politik Adolf Hitlers* (1989).

Source Acknowledgements

HERIBERT ADAM AND KOGILA MOODLEY, Psychological Liberation, extract from *The Opening of the Apartheid Mind* by Heribert Adam and Kogila Moodley (Berkeley: University of California Press 1993). Reprinted by permission of University of California Press.

MICHAEL BANTON, The Racializing of the World, extract from *The Idea of Race* (London: Tavistock 1977). Reprinted by permission of Tavistock.

MICHAEL BIDDISS, Gobineau and the Origins of European Racism, extract from Gobineau and the Origins of European Racism *Race*, Volume 13, no. 1, July 1971. Reprinted by permission of the Institute of Race Relations.

MICHAEL BURLEIGH AND WOLFGANG WIPPERMANN, extract from *The Racial State: Germany, 1933–1945* (Cambridge: Cambridge University Press, 1991). Reprinted by permission of Cambridge University Press.

STEPHEN CASTLES AND ELLIE VASTA, Multicultural or Multi-racist Australia?, extract from *The Teeth are Smiling: the persistence of racism in multicultural Australia* (St Leonards, NSW, Allen and Unwin, 1996). Reprinted by permission of Allen and Unwin.

PHILIP COHEN, "It's Racism What Dunnit": Hidden narratives in theories of racism, in J. Donald and A. Rattansi (eds) *'Race', Culture & Difference* (London: Sage 1992). Reprinted by permission of Sage Publications Ltd.

PATRICIA HILL COLLINS, Defining Black Feminist Thought, extract from *Black Feminist Thought* by Patricia Hill Collins. Copyright © 1990. Reproduced by permission of Routledge, Inc.

STEPHEN CORNELL, The Transformations of the Tribe, from *The Return of the Native: American Indian Political Resurgence* by Stephen Cornell. Copyright © 1988 by Oxford University Press, Inc. Used by permission of Oxford University Press, Inc.

PHILIP CURTIN, The Africans' 'Place in Nature', extract from *The Image of Africa: British Ideas and Actions, 1780–1850* (London: Macmillan 1965). Reprinted by permission of Macmillan Press Ltd.

DAVID BRION DAVIS, The Expansion of Islam and the Symbolism of Race, extract from *Slavery and Human Progress*, copyright © 1984 by David Brion Davis. Used by permission of Oxford University Press, Inc.

FRANK DIKÖTTER, Group Definition and the Idea of 'Race' in Modern China 1793–1949, in *Ethnic and Racial Studies*, Vol 13, 3, July 1990, pp. 420–31. Reprinted by permission of Routledge.

W. E. B. DU BOIS, Of Our Spiritual Strivings, from *The Souls of Black Folk* (First published in the USA by AC McClurg and Co, New York, 1903).

RAPHAEL EZEKIEL, Klan Rally at Stone Mountain, Georgia, from *The Racist Mind*. Copyright © 1995 by Raphael S. Ezekiel, used by permission of Viking Penguin, a division of Penguin Putnam Inc.

FRANTZ FANON, The Wretched of the Earth, extract from *The Wretched of the Earth* (1963, Paris, Présence Africaine, London: McGibbon and Kee, 1965).

JOE FEAGIN AND MELVIN P. SIKES, Changing the Color Line: The Future of U.S. Racism, from *Living racism* by Joe Feagin and Melvin P. Sikes, © 1994 by Joe Feagin and Melvin P. Sikes. Reprinted by permission of Beacon Press, Boston.

ABBY L. FERBER, Constructing Whiteness, from *Ethnic and Racial Studies*, Vol 21 Part 1, 1998. Reprinted by permission of Routledge.

PAUL FOOT, Politics and the Alien, from *Immigration and Race in British Politics* by Paul Foot (London, Penguin Books, 1965), copyright © Paul Foot, 1965. Reprinted by permission of Penguin Books, Ltd.

GEORGE FREDRICKSON, Social Origins of American Racism, from *The Arrogance of Race: historical perspectives on slavery, racism and social inequality,* © 1988 by George M. Fredrickson, Wesleyan University Press, by permission of University Press of New England.

MARCUS GARVEY, Living for Something, from *Life and Lessons* edited by Robert A. Hill. Copyright © 1987 The Regents of the University of California. Reprinted by permission of the University of California Press.

EUGENE GENOVESE, Class and Race, extract from *The World the Slave Holders Made.* Copyright © 1969 by Eugene D. Genovese. Reprinted by permission of Pantheon Books, a division of Random House, Inc.

PAUL GILROY, The End of Anti-Racism, in W. Ball and J. Solomos (eds) *Race and Local Politics* (Macmillan 1990). Reprinted by permission of Macmillan Press Ltd.

DAVID THEO GOLDBERG, The Semantics of Race, from *Ethnic and Racial Studies*, Vol 15 Part 4 1992. Reprinted by permission of Routledge.

JAMES R. GROSSMAN, Don't Have to Look up to the White Man, from *Land of Hope: Chicago, Black Southerners and the Great Migration* (Chicago: University of Chicago Press, 1989). Reprinted by permission of University of Chicago Press.

COLETTE GUILLAUMIN, The Changing Face of 'Race', extract from *Racism, Sexism, Power and Ideology* (London: Routledge 1995). Reprinted by permission of Routledge.

ANTONIO GUIMARÃES, Racism and Anti-Racism in Brazil, from *Racism and Anti-Racism in World Perspective* by B. P. Bowser (ed) (Thousand Oaks, CA: Sage 1995). Reprinted by permission of Sage Publications.

REGINALD HORSMAN, Superior and Inferior Races, reprinted by permission of the publisher from *Race and Manifest Destiny* by Reginald Horsman, Cambridge, Mass.: Harvard University Press, Copyright © 1981 by the President and Fellows of Harvard College.

WINTHROP D. JORDAN, First Impressions: Initial English Confrontation with Africans, from *White over Black: American attitudes toward the negro, 1550–1812* by Winthrop D. Jordan. Copyright © 1968 by the University of North Carolina Press. Used by permission of the publisher.

VICTOR KIERNAN, Africa, extract from *The Lords of Human Kind: European Attitudes to the outside world in the imperial age* (Serif, 1995). Copyright © 1969 Victor Kiernan. Reprinted by permission of the publisher.

DESMOND KING, *Separate and Unequal: Black Americans and the US Federal Government* (Oxford: The Clarendon Press, 1995). Reprinted by permission of Oxford University Press.

CATHIE LLOYD, Universalism and Difference: the Crisis of anti-Racism in the UK and France, in A. Rattansi and S. Westwood (eds) *Racism, Modernity and Identity: On the Western Front* (Cambridge: Polity Press 1994). Reprinted by permission of Blackwell Publishers.

TONY MARTIN, Race First and Self-Reliance, extract from *Race First: The ideological and organizational struggles of Marcus Garvey and the Universal Negro Improvement Association* (Dover, Mass.: The Majority Press 1976). Reprinted by permission of Majority Press Inc.

PHILIP MASON, Patterns of Dominance, extract from *Patterns of Dominance* (Institute of Race Relations/Oxford University Press UK, 1970). Reprinted by permission of Oxford University Press.

ALBERTO MELUCCI, Difference and Otherness in a Global Society, in S. Frizlidius and A. Peterson (eds) *Stranger or Guest? racism and nationalism in contemporary Europe* (Stockholm: Almquist and Wicksell, 1996). Reprinted by permission of the publisher.

ROBERT MILES, Racism as a Concept, extract from *Racism* (Routledge 1989). Reprinted by permission of Routledge.

GEORGE MOSSE, Eighteenth-Century Foundations, extract from *Toward the Final Solution: A History of European Racism* (New York: Howard Fertig, 1985). Reprinted by permission of Howard Fertig Inc.

MICHAEL OMI AND HOWARD WINANT, from *Racial Formation in the United States* by Michael Omi and Howard Winant. Copyright © 1994. Reproduced by permission of Routledge, Inc.

ROBERT PARK, The Nature of Race Relations, reprinted with permission of The Free Press, a division of Simon & Schuster, Inc. from *Race and Culture*, Robert Park and Everett C. Hughes. Copyright © 1950 by The Free Press; © renewed 1978 by Everett C. Hughes.

ORLANDO PATTERSON, Slavery as Human Parasitism, reprinted by permission of the publisher from *Slavery and Social Death* by Orlando Patterson, Cambridge, Mass: Harvard University Press, Copyright © 1982 by the President and Fellows of Harvard College.

LEON POLIAKOV, Gobineau and His Contemporaries, extract from *The Aryan Myth: A History of Racist and Nationalist Ideas in Europe* (Sussex University Press, 1974).

JOHN REX, The Concept of Race in Sociological Theory, in S. Zubaida (ed.) *Race and Racialism* (Tavistock 1970). Reprinted by permission of Tavistock.

M. G. SMITH, Ethnic and Cultural Pluralism in the British Caribbean, from *The Plural Society in the British West Indies* (Berkeley, University of California Press, 1965). Reprinted by permission of Mrs M. F. Smith.

ROBERT C. SMITH, Racism in the Post-Civil Rights Era, reprinted by permission of the State University of New York Press © 1995, State University of New York Press. All rights reserved.

PAUL SNIDERMAN AND EDWARD CARMINES, Tangled Politics, reprinted by permission of the publisher from *Reaching Beyond Race* by Paul Sniderman and Edward Carmines (Cambridge, Mass: Harvard University Press). Copyright © 1997 by the President and Fellows of Harvard College.

FRANK SNOWDEN, Images and Attitudes, reprinted by permission of the publisher from *Before Color Prejudice* by Frank Snowden, Cambridge, Mass: Harvard University Press Copyright © 1983 by the President and Fellows of Harvard College.

PIERRE-ANDRÉ TAGUIEFF, The New Cultural Racism in France, *Telos*, Vol 83, 1990, reprinted by permission of Telos Press.

BARRY TROYNA AND RICHARD HATCHER, *Racism in Children's Lives*, (London, Routledge, 1992). Reprinted by permission of Routledge.

458 SOURCE ACKNOWLEDGEMENTS

KWAME TURE AND CHARLES V. HAMILTON, Black Power: Its Need and Substance, extract from *Black Power and the Politics of Liberation* by Stokely Carmichael and Charles V. Hamilton. Copyright © 1967 by Stokely Carmichael and Charles V. Hamilton. Reprinted by permission of Random House, Inc.

WILLIAM M. TUTTLE JR., Racial Violence in Chicago and the Nation, extract from *Race Riot: Chicago in the Red summer of 1919* (New York: Atheneum 1978). Reprinted by permission of WM Tuttle.

DAVID T. WELLMAN, Toward a Sociology of White Racism, extract from *Portraits of White Racism* 2nd edition (Cambridge: Cambridge University Press 1993). Reprinted by permission of Cambridge University Press.

MICHEL WIEVIORKA, Two Patterns of Racism, *The Arena of Racism* (London: Sage 1995). Reprinted by permission of Sage Publication Ltd.

PATRICIA WILLIAMS, The Emperor's New Clothes, from *Seeing a Colour Blind Future* by Patricia Williams. Copyright © 1997 by Patricia Williams. Reprinted by permission of Brandt & Brandt Literary Agents, Inc.

BEJAMIN ZEPHANIAH, 'White Comedy' in *Propaganda* (Bloodaxe Books Ltd, Newcastle on Tyne 1996). Reprinted by permission of the publishers.

Index